MW00800370

The Oxford Guide
for
Writing Tutors

The Oxford Guide
for
Writing Tutors

Practice and Research

MELISSA IANETTA
University of Delaware

LAUREN FITZGERALD
Yeshiva University

New York   Oxford
OXFORD UNIVERSITY PRESS

Oxford University Press is a department of the University of Oxford.
It furthers the University's objective of excellence in research,
scholarship, and education by publishing worldwide.

Oxford   New York
Auckland   Cape Town   Dar es Salaam   Hong Kong   Karachi
Kuala Lumpur   Madrid   Melbourne   Mexico City   Nairobi
New Delhi   Shanghai   Taipei   Toronto

With offices in
Argentina   Austria   Brazil   Chile   Czech Republic   France   Greece
Guatemala   Hungary   Italy   Japan   Poland   Portugal   Singapore
South Korea   Switzerland   Thailand   Turkey   Ukraine   Vietnam

Copyright © 2016 by Oxford University Press

For titles covered by Section 112 of the US Higher Education
Opportunity Act, please visit www.oup.com/us/he for the
latest information about pricing and alternate formats.

Published by Oxford University Press
198 Madison Avenue, New York, New York 10016
http://www.oup.com

Oxford is a registered trademark of Oxford University Press

All rights reserved. No part of this publication may be reproduced,
stored in a retrieval system, or transmitted, in any form or by any means,
electronic, mechanical, photocopying, recording, or otherwise,
without the prior permission of Oxford University Press.

Library of Congress Cataloging-in-Publication Data
Ianetta, Melissa.
   The Oxford guide for writing tutors: practice and research/Melissa Ianetta,
University of Delaware; Lauren Fitzgerald, Yeshiva University.
       pages cm
   Includes bibliographical references and index.
   ISBN 978-0-19-994184-1 (alk. paper)
   1. English language—Study and teaching 2. Tutors and tutoring—Training of.
I. Fitzgerald, Lauren. II. Title.
   PE1404.I16 2014
   808'.0420711—dc23

                                                                    2014028316

Printing number: 9 8 7 6 5

Printed in Canada on acid-free paper

BRIEF CONTENTS

CONTENTS

SECTION III   RESEARCH METHODS FOR WRITING TUTORS   187

PREFACE

WELCOME

If you're reading this book, you're probably a student who is learning about the writing process and one-to-one writing instruction, an individual preparing to tutor, or an instructor preparing for a semester as the teacher of tutors. To both students and teachers we say, welcome to *The Oxford Guide for Writing Tutors: Practice and Research*!

A WORD ABOUT PEOPLE, PLACES, AND WRITING INSTRUCTION

We have written this book with both teachers and students in mind. Of course, one could argue these are two very different audiences with very different needs and goals. Whenever we look at most educational spaces on campus, for example, the distinction between student-learners and teacher-educators is usually quite clear. In the classroom in particular, the differences between teacher and student are often readily evident and can appear vast—teachers are grading, students are getting graded: teachers assign the work, students (teachers hope!) do the work. When you walk into a classroom, it's often easy to see who the teacher is: he or she is often the only one with the "freedom" to walk around the room, and those participating as students will often defer to the teacher by allowing her to interrupt conversation, for example, or to insert herself during group work.

In individualized writing instruction, however, the lines between learner and teacher are less clear. Think about a **writing center**—which in this book refers to a fixed location where writers can receive assistance reaching their writing goals through one-to-one and/or small group assistance. Students come to the writing center for much the same reason they come to the writing classroom—with an expectation of receiving help with their writing. But in the writing center, it is often students who provide, as well as receive, that help. Indeed, a new visitor to a writing center may have trouble determining who are the "teachers" and who are the "learners." Unlike a classroom, where the environment is often designed to reinforce the instructor's role by the size of the desk, for example, or the elevation of her eye level above those of her students by the placement of her desk on a platform, the writing center space is often organized to foster one-to-one conversations—and so visually demonstrates the collegiality of its location. That is, in many writing centers, there are tables scattered through the room each with a few chairs, to encourage simultaneous small group or one-to-one conversations. Often, too, if one desk or table is differently configured or somehow otherwise set apart, it's not positioned as the place of authority, like a teacher's desk, but as a place of welcoming, where visitors are greeted and assisted with their needs.

Think too of **writing fellows programs**, which refers to discipline—and/or course-specific individualized writing instruction that may or may not be housed in a writing center. In such programs, tutors (a.k.a. "fellows") focus on helping writers in a single discipline or class. While writing fellows and writing tutors share a lot of the same responsibilities and tasks, there are also some differences, which we discuss in more detail later in this book. But for the purposes of comparison, writing fellows and writing tutors are similar in that they both work in spaces that are markedly different from traditional classroom settings. We can see these similarities if we compare the writing fellows program to the classroom. Like the writing center, the writing fellows program can often visually blur the lines established in the traditional classroom setting. When writing fellows are present in a class, for example—a model often called **course-based tutoring**—it can be impossible to determine visually which individuals are tutors and which are students in the class. During an in-class workshop, for example, tutors may lead small-group workshops alongside the instructor and so redistribute any notion of in-class authority. Finally, writing fellows who meet with students outside of class can engage in these kinds of teaching-and-learning activities anywhere, breaking down the classroom model entirely. Indeed, if you're reading this book in a library, campus coffee shop, or student union, there could be a tutorial going on nearby right now. In an **online writing center** (a.k.a. **OWL**), tutoring takes place online in virtual space, thus changing, complicating, and in some ways disposing of the notion of space altogether.

A WORD ABOUT THE WORK WE DO

The redistribution of authority is evident in other ways beyond the configurations of people. In writing centers, for example, the student writer decide what piece of writing to work on, and in this way she is like the classroom teachers who set the daily agenda and create the assignments upon which students in the classroom will work. In the writing center venue, writers and student tutors can share the ability to move around the room to gather resources or settle in to work more comfortably. And in many writing centers, if there is an instructor present, that person is often the only one *not* "instructing": while tutors and writers work together to advance their mutual understanding of the writing process, that instructor is often facilitating check-in, reviewing the schedule, or troubleshooting the administrative details that need attention if the writing center is going to thrive. Indeed, sometimes the instructors themselves come to the center for assistance, whether it's to find out how the writing center can support their teaching or to receive help with their own writing.

As these contrasts suggest, learning through writing tutoring programs can look quite different from the images popularly associated with school classrooms. As we acknowledge elsewhere in this book—and as is evident throughout the field of writing center studies—many people have made this argument: Kenneth Bruffee, Muriel Harris, Neal Lerner, Anne Geller, Michelle Eodice, Frankie Condon, Meg Carroll, and Elizabeth H. Boquet among others have celebrated and critiqued the distinctive learning modes of the writing center.

This book, however, takes that argument one step further to claim that individualized writing instruction is not just a place where teaching—the *transmission* of knowledge—is different; it's also a place in which the *creation* of knowledge can be—and, we think, should be—different, too. After all, whether they work in a center or in a fellows program, if tutors are the ones who help disseminate information about writing, aren't these same tutors, with their firsthand experience and their unique perspectives as students *and* tutors *and* writers, important scholarly voices to hear? We certainly think so!

We do not, of course, claim to be the first people to listen for the knowledge tutors create. In fact, over thirty years ago, Kenneth Bruffee was persuasively articulating the kinds of knowledge that peer tutoring can create, and *The Writing Lab Newsletter* has been running a tutor-authored column since 1984. Such articulations of the centrality of tutors' knowledge seem to have foreshadowed the more recent explosion of interest in undergraduate research in writing. There is an entire journal dedicated to the topic—*Young Scholars in Writing: Undergraduate Research in Writing and Rhetoric*—and increasing numbers of instructors are taking a "writing-about-writing" approach to teaching undergraduate writing. That is, such scholars as Elizabeth Wardle and Douglas Downs have argued that the most effective way to teach undergraduates to become better writers is to introduce them to the knowledge of our field as not only consumers but, ultimately, producers.

WRITING ABOUT TUTORING

In this book we work to add these two conversations—about the creation of new knowledge about writing and about tutor research—to the kinds of preparation writing tutors need. We believe that this approach to tutor training provides several benefits. First, it allows tutors to test their theories of *what* might work in a writing center session and helps them to move our professional conversation toward *why* such things happen. In other words, these inquiries help us bridge the theory/practice divide that often frustrates both novice and experienced tutors. Second, by conducting research to answer such questions, tutors can help themselves and the writers with whom they work, as well as their fellow tutors and the writers with whom *they* work. Finally, this approach gives the reader new methods for appreciating and critiquing scholarly arguments and so helps us to understand the best ways to help writers and to move our field forward. These are the reasons we wrote this book—and, we hope, are the reasons you will find it a helpful perspective on tutoring and on writing center studies.

A WORD ABOUT THE BOOK'S STRUCTURE

As writing tutoring programs take on a variety of forms and pursue a range of missions, we aimed to create a flexible text whose contents could be easily rearranged to support a broad spectrum of reader needs. Each chapter, accordingly, can be read independently; the text does not rely on a sequential reading to create meaning. Tutor education programs that emphasize research methods, for example, may want to focus on Section III, "Research Methods for Writing Tutors," while writing centers whose training takes place in the day(s) just prior to classes or during the first part of the semester or term may wish to start with Section II, "A Tutor's Handbook" and perhaps pair the methods chapters with the "Selected Readings" in Section IV as part of ongoing training.

Even as we've worked to design a text that will be responsive to a wide range of environments, we've also included intratextual and extratextual references for the reader who wants to inquire further. That is, throughout the book, we refer to material in other chapters that might be of interest to the reader intrigued by the topic at hand. The historical account in Chapter 2, for example, refers both to Chapter 10, on historical research, and an historical essay included in the readings in Section IV, Neal Lerner's "Searching for Robert Moore." All of these resources can serve in turn as springboards for the assignments that appear at the end of Chapter 4. So too, in each chapter we include references to and citations of the scholarship that supports much of the "common knowledge" of the field, including, in the Handbook, both previous tutor education textbooks and research from the field. Our aim is to aid the interested reader's inquiry into the scholarship of the field as well as to ground our advice about practice in research that testifies to the effectiveness of a range of tutoring strategies.

But probably the most important, and for us the most exciting, feature of the scholarship we cite throughout the book and include in Section IV is that much of it is authored by undergraduate tutor-researchers as well as several former tutors who were graduate students when they published their articles. This aspect of the book is central to our vision because we believe that such work best models the ways in which tutors themselves can bring together practice and research, in their day-to-day practice and in their informed thinking about this work. As a result, in the Handbook, you will notice repeated references to scholarship by former undergraduate tutors, such as Molly Wilder, Jennifer Nicklay, Frances Nan, and Jonathan Doucette, whose *Young Scholars in Writing* and *Writing Center Journal* articles we reprint in Section IV, as well as dozens of other tutor-authors whose work you can access either online or through your library. Including tutors' voices is an important tradition of the tutor education textbook, and we feel privileged to feature these voices to speak to the issues that concern tutors in a range of institutions and programs across the country and around the world.

Through these structural and citational means, then, we've tried to create a text that can be used in many writing centers, writing fellows programs, and other programs that offer individualized writing instruction. Within each chapter, we've worked to include materials that are similarly flexible. In the chapters that make up Sections I and II, you'll find an assortment of questions for reflection, discussion, writing, and research. We've categorized these questions into the following categories:

> **For Discussion:** These are questions to consider before reading particular chapters and sections of chapters. They are meant to help you better understand the reading, to facilitate discussion with others, and, above all, to reflect on the material's connections to your own and other tutors' and writers' experiences.
>
> **For Writing:** These questions are more formal than those in *For Discussion* but less elaborate than the *For Inquiry* prompts. They are designed to facilitate writing assignments, such as reading responses, tutor journal entries, and blog postings. These assignments will help you establish connections among the materials and with your own growing understanding of best tutoring practices.
>
> **For Inquiry:** These assignments emphasize original research to facilitate such projects as case studies, surveys, discourse analyses, historical research, and theoretical analyses that might in turn become class projects, conference presentations, and publications. They bridge the various sections of the book, helping you see the connections between practice, method, and research.

Such questions are not included in Sections III or IV. For the material contained in Section III is intended to function as a resource for exploring the reader's own tutoring practice, just as Section IV is meant to support the explorations of the reader's question via a selection of the published scholarship.

We hope you'll enjoy reading this book as much as we've enjoyed writing it. We'd also love to hear how you've used it and what you think of it.

ACKNOWLEDGMENTS

Like learning to be a writing tutor, learning to write this book was a deeply social process requiring the help of many people. We gratefully acknowledge Oxford University Press, particularly the support of Frederick Speers and Carrie Brandon—you have both been helpful colleagues and good friends. We thank, too, Rita Malenczyk and Kelly Ritter. You contributed more to this book than you know, but we'll tell you all about it next time we see you. We appreciate the feedback we received on drafts of Chapter 3 from Sipai Klein and members of his Response to Writing course and the Clayton State University Writers' Studio as well as Rita Malenczyk, Lauren Rosenberg, and several Eastern Connecticut State University Writing Center tutors. And we acknowledge Wilf Campus Writing Center tutors at Yeshiva University for cheerfully testing out a draft of Section II. Jane Greer and Laurie Grobman deserve our thanks for creating an important space for undergraduate research and for putting us in contact with a number of *Young Scholars in Writing* authors. We thank, as well, our friends in the writing center community: Beth Boquet, Harry Denny, Michele Eodice, Brian Fallon, Anne Geller, Paula Gillespie, Joyce Kinkead, Neal Lerner and Sue Mendelsohn. Without your contributions to build on, this book couldn't exist. We are indebted to our professional reviewers as well: Tabetha Adkins, Texas A&M University, Commerce; Linda S. Bergmann, Purdue University; Tom Deans, University of Connecticut; Violet Dutcher, Eastern Mennonite University; Clint Gardner, Salt Lake Community College; Kat Gonzo, Northeastern University; R. Mark Hall, University of Central Florida; Joyce Kinkead, Utah State University; Neal Lerner, Northeastern University; Sarah Liggett, Louisiana State University; Dan Melzer, California State University, Sacramento; P. Darin Payne, University of Hawai'I; Jason Schneiderman, Borough of Manhattan Community College; Trixie Smith, Michigan State University; Tisha Turk, University of Minnesota; and Jennifer Wells, New College of Florida.

Melissa would like to thank her husband, Iain Crawford. Without his emotional and editorial support, this book would not have happened. She is grateful, too, to her University of Delaware colleagues who have supported this work with their friendship and professional expertise: Stephen Bernhardt, Carolyn Clark, Christine Cucciarre, Barbra Lutz, Michael McCamley, and Kathleen Pusecker. She thanks, too, the University of Delaware for the year of sabbatical and ongoing support that made her work possible.

Lauren thanks Efrayim Clair, Arel Kirshstein, and Israel (Sruly) Heller, the Wilf Campus Writing Center tutors who served as research assistants on this book and whose work was supported by the Faculty Book Fund at Yeshiva College, sponsored by Dr. Kenneth Richard Chelst, Dr. Bertram M. Schreiber, and Dr. Fred Zwas. She is grateful to Yeshiva College colleagues who made it possible for her to take a research leave to work on this project, Dean Barry Eichler and former Associate Dean Raji Viswanathan, Lane Anderson, and Gillian Steinberg.

For their conversations, advice, and encouragement, she thanks Sarah Blazer, Andrea Efthymiou, Diane Gibson, Alfie Guy, Maria Jerskey, and Heather Masri. She owes a debt of gratitude to her partner Brian Culver for his love and patience as she worked on this project and all the projects that led up to it.

Finally, we thank those many tutors with whom we have worked over the years. This is your book as much as it is ours, and we are grateful for your commitment to writing and learning.

This book is dedicated to the memory of Linda Bergmann, whose kindness, wit, and generosity serve as a model to all of us who help writers and each other. Bergmann represents the very ideal of writing center ethos: generous, honest, clear-sighted, supportive, loyal, curious, committed, interdisciplinary, and flexible. Her legacy asks of us all, potentially, what kinds of scholar-mentors do we want to be, and how will that mentoring cause others to remember us?

SECTION I

Introduction to Tutoring Writing

1

CHAPTER 1

Introduction to Writing and Research

For Discussion

1. How did you learn to write?
2. What do you know about the writing habits of successful authors? What do they do? How do these practices differ from those of writers who identify as unsuccessful? From where did you get the information you drew upon to create these descriptions?

INTRODUCTION

A common complaint among writing teachers is that the writing activities seen on television and in films bear little resemblance to the work involved in real-life writing. A movie, such as *Eat, Pray, Love* or *The Help*, for example, makes writing look like the mere transcription of events—whether those events are the author's epiphany via pasta or an account of social injustice in 1960s Mississippi. Such works make writing look like something that happens after an idea is realized and casts the work of writing as recording, not creating. This is an idea whose accuracy and popularity we hope to help you investigate in this section of the book. In this chapter, then, we introduce questions and concepts from the larger world of writing research that inform and illustrate the work that takes place in the writing center. In the following chapter, we focus this investigation more specifically on the writing center context by turning to the scholarship of the field.

Common Misconceptions of Writing

Even in the real world beyond the small or big screen, there are conceptions of writing and how writing should be taught that run counter to both individual teachers' experiences and the sum of scholarly research. For example, the media periodically reports a student writing "crisis" in which some group or another tells us that student writing is worse than it ever has been. In recent years, for instance, there have been claims that texting, Tweeting, and Facebook-ing are making students worse writers—whatever "worse" means in this context. And yet, as people who study the history of writing instruction can tell you, and as we discuss in more depth in Chapter 2, there is a longstanding history of decrying the state of student writing. In the United States this tradition can be traced back to 1872 and Harvard's creation of both the first national standardized writing examination and the first course in composition meant to remedy those errors in writing deemed widespread after this exam, such as "utter ignorance of punctuation as to put commas at the end of complete sentences, or between words that no rational being would separate from one another . . . Many spelled as if starting a spelling reform, each for himself" (Brereton 49–51). This episode was but the first in a long line of literacy "crises." And since the inception of the writing center, tutors have been coping with the ramifications of these so-called crises.

Common Misconceptions of Writing Instruction

More contemporary than such origin stories—and more controversial in current civic debate—are ongoing public discussions about how writing instruction should be conducted. How can we best help students learn to write:

- By teaching them grammar?
- By letting them write about their personal experiences?
- By having them read literary texts and write about those works?
- By giving them standardized multiple-choice tests?
- By using plagiarism detection software?
- By teaching them the five-paragraph essay?
- Or none of these things?
- Or all of them?

When we listen for these conversations—at our schools, in our local communities, and in the press—we find that there are lots of conflicting ideas. We also find, however, that many people argue passionately about such issues with very little evidence for their claims. Instead politicians and pundits will often argue from supposed "common sense."

Such common sense, however, appeals to what the listener believes to be true, rather than what can be proven by using evidence-based arguments. For example, many parents, politicians, and school leaders believe that the best way to help students is to get "back to basics"—that is, to focus the writing classroom on grammar lessons in particular, giving students practice in identifying the parts of speech and on learning rules for correct usage. Such an approach to many seems intuitively right—that teachers should start with the identification of individual words before having students write grammatically correct sentences. And then, in turn, teachers should have students write grammatically correct sentences before allowing them to progress to grammatically correct paragraphs. Only then should students attempt to write grammatically correct multiple-paragraph essays.

The common sense to this approach is readily grasped: students will learn smaller units of meaning and master those before progressing to larger, more complex tasks. Moreover, there is something morally appealing about this idea— students must work hard, rid themselves of errors, and prove mastery of a smaller skill before they can move on to a larger one. This approach, then, aligns with both commonly held notions of learning—that you move from small simple tasks to larger ones—and commonly held values: that you should work hard and attempt to free yourself of error.

And yet, research has shown us that "common sense" approaches like this may not be sufficient.

For Writing

1. Ask a few of your friends to each describe how a "good student" writes. What's similar about their depictions? What's different? Ask them what they drew upon in their descriptions. What, if anything, does this suggest to you about where most people get their ideas about successful writers?

2. Consider a popular movie or television show that deals with writing. How is the creation of text depicted? What does it teach the viewer about how the writing process works?

WRITING RESEARCH

Several studies have shown that teaching students descriptive grammar (i.e., drilling them in identifying parts of speech) and in usage (learning rules of correctness) does nothing to improve their writing ability (see Hartwell; Braddock, Lloyd-Jones, and Schoer). Rather, like trying to learn the parts of an engine before driving a car, such instruction focuses students on classifying terms rather than writing persuasive texts. Researchers who study how writing works have known this fact for many years. Indeed, as long ago as 1963, a group of researchers definitively asserted that the "teaching of formal grammar has a negligible or, because it usually displaces some instruction and practice in actual composition, even a harmful effect on the improvement of writing" (Braddock, Lloyd-Jones, and Schoer 37–38). And in the almost fifty years since these studies were published, data-driven research that involves native speakers of English has demonstrated consistently that grammar instruction is not helpful to improving most students' ability to write in their native language (Hartwell). Nevertheless, many teachers still focus on grammar in the writing classroom and many schools still focus their curricula on such matters. There are numerous reasons for this situation, such as personal beliefs about effective teaching and the external curricular requirements of a program, school, or district. However, most people would agree that a big part of the reason that grammar is still emphasized is the reliance on one's own experience or the accounts of others' experiences in school: we do it this way because we have always done it this way.

Recognizing the Problems with Tradition-Bound Approaches

Of course, accepting knowledge for tradition's sake in this manner has drawbacks. It is often difficult, for example, to discern the accuracy of long-held beliefs without a consistent, evidence-based exploration. Also, a tradition-based approach discourages curious minds from asking why things are the way they are, or suggesting ways in which they might be better. The writing center community, which you are stepping into as you read this book, is inclined to be particularly suspicious of such tradition-bound approaches because of the central role of student-tutors in the writing center. These individuals provide directors and other tutors with an ongoing opportunity to look at our work through fresh eyes, envisioning and re-visioning our practice in new ways and helping us combat "common sense" with scholarly knowledge. Further, as tutors leave their positions and move into their professional lives, they become "writing ambassadors" whose expert knowledge can help us improve public understanding of the teaching of writing. So we hope this book, in particular the description of research methods in Section III and the essays that can serve as models in Section IV, will help you structure your practice and inquiry in productive and satisfying ways.

In addition to facilitating your contribution to the writing center community, we also believe the research-based model of this book will help the reader to become a better tutor, and so complement the work found in "Section II: A Tutors' Handbook." Even as we've assembled what we think are the best practices in tutoring writing, we are also aware that future research will prove some of these ideas wrong or will show tutors better strategies and approaches. We encourage you, then, to draw your own connections among the materials you find here, using the essays in the final section to complicate and critique the "Tutors' Handbook," for example, and using the discussion of research methods to appreciate and critique the research studies. Ultimately, we envision research, writing, teaching, and learning as inseparable facets of an ongoing process.

Understanding the Methods of a Research-Based Approach

So far, we've used the word *research* in a generalized way, one that you might associate with, for example, the kinds of research papers in which the author assembles sources to demonstrate careful reading on a particular topic. In a high-school English class many students will read *Julius Caesar* and then examine historical sources to understand the kind of commentary that the play makes on the world of its author, William Shakespeare. Even when presented as an argument—like *"Julius Caesar* reflects the political unrest of the Elizabethan period"—this kind of research is largely a compilation of scholarship in which the student writer's claims are proven by using someone else's arguments. While this kind of scholarship can certainly be useful to both writer and reader, it is not the kind of inquiry we talk about in later chapters of this book. Rather, we use the term **research** to mean method-based, systematic inquiry that generates new knowledge for both the researcher and the work's audience.

Understanding Research as an Ongoing Practice

Such research is not the only kind of scholarship there is, however. As Ernest Boyer argued in *Scholarship Reconsidered*, there are many types of scholarly activity. In addition to the kind of work we're calling research—which Boyer called "the scholarship of discovery," and which he described as "following in a disciplined fashion, an investigation, wherever it may lead," there are other influential kinds of scholarship (17). Among these, Boyer included:

- The scholarship of integration, which involves integrating extant knowledge in new ways (18–21)
- The scholarship of application, which involves applying extant knowledge in new ways (21–23)
- The scholarship of teaching, which involves the dissemination of knowledge (23–25).

You can find all of these types of scholarship at play in the field of writing center studies. You'll regularly see tutors integrate what they know from other disciplines into their practice as tutors, creating new approaches to help an individual writer or in a specific kind of writing situation. You'll practice the scholarship of application as you apply what you know about writing both in tutorials and in conversation with this text. And you'll practice the scholarship of teaching in these tutorials as well, sharing knowledge about writing processes. In the written scholarship of the field, too, all of these forms of scholarship have been important, and you'll find examples of them throughout this text. Increasingly, however, writing center scholars and researchers have called for methods-based research (see, for example, Babcock and Thonus; Driscoll and Purdue; Liggett, Jordan, and Price). This book is, in part, an attempt to answer that call.

Before introducing the kinds of research a tutor-researcher might encounter or produce, we should offer a word of warning: we are not trying to be exhaustive in our accounting of research methods. We mean this assertion in two senses. On the one hand, there are research methods we do not substantively engage in this text, such as longitudinal studies or reflective analyses. On the other hand, even for those methods we do address, you will need to engage materials beyond this text's chapters on method if you wish to become truly expert in any area under investigation. To aid you in this work, you'll find a bibliography at the end of each methods chapter. Rather than an all-authoritative, all-knowing tome, this work is meant to be an introduction to avenues for further exploration, a guide to understanding the scholarship in the field and the routes you might take in your own scholarly work. In other words, it's a bit like a writing tutor.

Later in this book, we explore some of the kinds of publications that are particularly useful for creating new knowledge in the writing center and reflect upon the kinds of answers they might provide to the questions you'll develop in your own tutoring work. To get you thinking about what kinds of work might excite you and what considerations you'll have to take into account with all research, however, we conclude this chapter with a brief introduction to some of the kinds of scholarship you may wish to pursue and some words on issues common to all research.

Lore

Perhaps the most common kind of writing center scholarship is based in what Stephen North has termed "lore." According to North, lore is "concerned with what has worked, is working, or might work in teaching, doing or learning writing" (*Making* 23). The purpose of lore is to produce more successful practice, and its primary source of evidence is firsthand experience. Thus, when you try a new-to-you approach in tutoring that a colleague has told you about—asking the writer to make a goal list at the start of the tutorial and then returning to that list at the end of the session, for example—you're engaging the body of lore. And your general impression about how well the session worked will serve as the evaluation of the effectiveness of your research. Finally, when you report the results of your efforts at a staff meeting, you are, in a sense, publishing your results.

Historical Research

In this context, historical research concerns itself with the past events of a writing center, writing fellows program, or other program devoted to extracurricular writing instruction. Such research can often be useful to counter claims of "We tried that before, and it didn't work." If your writing center has an archive of materials related to its past practices, you may find this a useful and interesting place to start. And if your center does not have such a collection of documents, interviews, and artifacts, as Chapter 10 describes, starting an archive can be an exciting and illuminating place to begin this research.

Theoretical Research

While lore is likely the most common form of writing center inquiry, theoretical research may be the second most popular form. Oft-cited disciplinary touchstones like Meg Woolbright's "Tutoring and the Patriarchy," Harry Denny's "Queering the Writing Center," or Nancy Welch's "Playing with Reality: Writing Centers After the Mirror Stage" apply lenses built from theories in writing center studies and/or other fields to offer new ways of viewing our work, defamiliarize the everyday, and argue for new approaches, actions, and understandings.

Empirical Research

Skimming through recent issues of *The Writing Center Journal,* the field's main forum for long-form scholarship and research, suggests that data-driven studies examine writing center practices through:

- Careful description of a group (ethnographic research) or an individual (case study),
- Study of conversation (discourse analysis), or
- A comparative numerical evaluation (quantitative research).

While of ever-increasing interest within the writing center community, some of these methods can be used to particularly powerful ends when mounting an argument to audiences external to the center, either on campus or in the world beyond the university.

Rhetorical Scholarship

Finally, a word on **rhetorical scholarship**, a term we use to describe a form for writing research common in the field's early years. Rather than basing its primary argument in clearly described data, firsthand experience, or another evidence set, rhetorical research often argues from a community's shared values in an attempt to motivate a change in attitude or action from the reader. Such work often employs appeals to the reader's emotions as well as identifying commonly held beliefs as part of the attempt to move the audience. If it accurately connects with its intended audience's perceptions and values, such work can be very effective at moving a field. Stephen North's "The Idea of a Writing Center," for instance, or Andrea Lunsford's "Collaboration, Control, and the Idea of a Writing Center" are both examples of rhetorical scholarship that became foundational to forming the discipline.

Of course, many studies combine approaches: it is entirely possible to have an empirical piece that uses a strong theoretical lens in an attempt to build a rhetorical argument intended to appeal to community values. Such methodological mixing is no better or worse than using only one method. Rather, your method(s) should be dictated by your goals. This is particularly true in writing center studies; because it draws from fields across the humanities and social sciences, writing center studies is a field marked by **methodological pluralism**, a commitment to a variety of methods. Instead of worrying about what method is "best" or sticking with one method, it's important to keep in mind the relationships among your methodological approach, the evidence you use, and the claims you make. We discuss this in more detail in Section III. For now, we ask you to notice these connections in the materials you encounter in this book.

For Writing

1. Look back at the list you made of the habits of good writers at the beginning of this chapter. Focusing on a single habit, pick two of the four kinds of research we've discussed—historical, theoretical, empirical, rhetorical—and describe the kinds of evidence that each might generate to support or challenge the accuracy of the writing habit you've identified. What answers would each kind of scholarship yield? To whom would such answers be useful or persuasive?

2. What kinds of research methods have you encountered in your classes or elsewhere? Which methods seem the most useful or the most interesting to your work in the writing center? Are there methods beyond the discussion here that you are familiar with and that would be useful in the writing center? What kinds of questions would such methods best answer?

THREE CONCERNS FOR ANY RESEARCHER

Even as each approach to inquiry offers its own distinct opportunities and challenges, you should always ask yourself three questions early in the research process:

- Is my research valid?
- Is my research reliable?
- Is my research ethical?

Is My Research Valid?

Validity and reliability are concepts borrowed from statistical analysis, but they are important when planning any research. Validity in this context refers to whether your research/argument proves what you claim it proves. Counting the number of users who come to the writing center, for example, could be a valid measure of the popularity of writing center services only if center visits are not a required element of your institution's curriculum. So too, a study that takes place in only one center is not proof for what all centers could—or must—do. There's more on this issue later in the text, but for now you'll want to be thinking about how evidence supports claims in the writing center research that you read and you produce.

Is My Research Reliable?

Reliability refers to the consistency of data. You might, for example, plan a study to determine the most common opportunities for improvement in those papers from a first-year writing course that are brought to the writing center, and you may decide that having tutors read the essays to determine these issues is the best method for research. If, however, your readers cannot agree to a high degree upon what issues are present in each essay, you have not achieved reliability.

We share some strategies to boost reliability in this situation later in the book, but for now, we ask you to be aware of the manner in which the evidence presented in the research you encounter was produced.

Is My Research Ethical?

A trend across colleges and universities in this country has been a dawning awareness of the need to make sure our research achieves the highest levels of ethical conduct. The most immediate implication of this increasing concern for planning research is to gain familiarity with your institution's **Institutional Review Board (IRB)**. The policies and procedures of IRBs vary drastically from campus to campus, but their unifying purpose is to oversee all research involving humans as subjects. At first, this may conjure up images of science labs and drug trials, but, as much of our inquiry involves those writers visiting the writing center, IRB approval is often required. We talk in later chapters about the ins and outs of writing center research ethics, but for now, we'd invite you to consider how the writers themselves are represented in the writing center scholarship you produce and read. Is there a chance of any negative impact on any of the human subjects involved?

PLACES TO SEARCH FOR RESEARCH IN THE FIELD

Now that we've discussed the kinds of research in writing center studies, you may be wondering where you can find this work. Because the contributors to writing center studies borrow from and contribute to an array of disciplines, including English Studies, Education, Linguistics, and Writing Studies—really, any discipline that pays attention to its own writing practices—it can be difficult, if not impossible, to identify a single search aid that will find all the sources related to a topic of concern. How you locate relevant information will, of course, depend upon your research question.

There are, however, several search engines and databases that might help you get started. CompPile (www.comppile.com) is a free, online bibliographic database of writing studies research. If you type in the term wcenter (CompPile's special term for writing centers) as a search term, you'll find thousands of entries that you can cross-search for material related to your particular topic. Your library may have other resources available to help you find citations of writing center research. The MLA International Bibliography and the ERIC database, too, each return hundreds of citations for the phrase *writing center*. If you wish to use them, you'll need to determine whether your library has a subscription to these services.

In addition to online databases, there are easily accessed online journals and databases. Currently, the archives of the *Writing Center Journal*, available at the Writing Center Research Project, and *The Writing Lab Newsletter* are also online and free. So too, *Praxis: A Journal of Writing Center Research* is open-access.

You may also find *PeerCentered, Young Scholars in Writing,* and *The Dangling Modifier* to be useful sources. They are all available online and are easily accessed via an Internet search.

In this chapter, we've worked to introduce quickly the relationship of research and practice, as well as some of the issues that concern all writing center scholars. In the next chapter, we start to explain in more detail individualized writing instruction and the contexts and concepts in which all this inquiring and practicing will take place.

For Inquiry

1. Find the three most recent stories on writing that have appeared in your school newspaper or in the local press. How is writing depicted? How does the writing process work according to these stories? How is good writing defined? How do these representations align with your own understanding of the writing process or that of your friends? How do they correspond with the discussion of "common sense" approaches to writing in this chapter?

2. Reading an essay through the lens of its methodological approach can often change your reading of the work. Select an essay from Section IV. First read the essay while focusing on its arguments—that is, look to its primary assertion and the statements that back the assertion. Now identify the method and read it again, looking for the evidence and analysis. Is the methodological approach consistent through the essay? Does the author's presentation of material make the argument seem reliable? Does it seem valid? Does focusing on method change at all your reading of this essay?

3. It can be illuminating to read rhetorical scholarship looking for the values it reflects. Select an essay that seems primarily rhetorical in its approach—Brian Fallon's in Section IV, for example. See if you can identify the values that are being appealed to as well as any emotional appeals. What does this tell you about writing center studies at the time the work was composed? About the shared values? The emotional reactions that this work seems planned to elicit?

4. Conduct a search for a specific research project in writing center studies in at least two databases. You might try, for example, the MLA Bibliography and CompPile. How many of the records from these two searches were the same? How many were different? Can you draw any comparisons between the two searches? Which search seems most promising for the project?

CHAPTER 2

Tutoring Writing
What, Why, Where, and When

For Discussion

1. Where do you do your best writing? That is, what's your ideal location for writing? How does your writing process work best? That is, what's your most effective method of writing?

2. How does your program or center define its goals? Where is it located? Do you think most students on your campus know where to find your center or program? Do they know what it does? Which do you think is more common knowledge—the location or the service? Is one kind of information—your site or your method—more useful to writers?

3. Compare this general student impression with the way your program or center describes itself in its own materials. Does the center as represented on your website or in your promotional materials match the impressions common among the student body? Do they match what you see day to day in the center?

4. Spend some time looking at how tutors in your center use their physical surroundings when working with writers. Does your center seem well constructed to support this work? Are tutors and writers comfortable? Do they have the right kind of space to work in? Can both groups—tutors and writers—see the projects they're working on? Can they hear one another? Do tutors find ways to adapt their environment to better suit their work, and if so what are these means?

5. Where does your writing tutoring program explain what it does and why it does so? What ideals does your program implicitly or explicitly endorse about writing? About learning to write? About writers?

INTRODUCTION

In Chapter 1, we discuss a range of environments in which one-to-one writing instruction takes place; the writing center, the writing fellows program, and in-class tutoring are all part of the discussion in this book. And yet, we also referred to the scholarly field involved in his work as "writing center studies," and many of the scholarly examples included in the final section focus specifically on the writing center. So the overlaps of all these terms can sometimes seem confusing.

To clarify how these terms are organized in this book and where we find the fundamental similarities between these various models of individualized writing instruction, we now turn to a dynamic marked by Elizabeth H. Boquet in "'Our Little Secret': A History of Writing Centers, Pre- to Post-Open Admissions." Here, Boquet asks, "Is the writing center primarily a *space* . . . ? Or a *temporality*, an interaction between people over time, in which the nature of the interaction is determined not by site, but by the method?" (464). In other words, is the defining essence of the writing center its physical location or the individualized learning about writing that takes place in that location? Boquet is interested in these queries as a means of looking into ways in which social power has been channeled, challenged, and replicated through writing instruction, but here we are interested in understanding questions of site versus method as a way of determining for ourselves what, if anything, is fundamental to writing centers and other forms of individualized writing instruction.

Writing Centers as Sites

When we consider the writing center or tutoring program as primarily a **site**, we might conjure up images of a particular place—a room or rooms with people, tables, books, computers, and other resources that support writers and tutors in their work. Or, if we consider an online writing center, we might imagine the digital space in which tutorials take place and where writers can find resources to help them plan, write, and revise their work. Thinking of a tutoring program as a site can help emphasize its connection to its campus and of the particularities of the way it has "grown" out of the campus environment. Thinking of a tutoring program as a site can also help us consider the qualities that define it as a community; in other words, reflecting on it in this manner focuses our attention on the groups of people who come into contact with one another in that locale.

Writing Centers as Method

If thinking of a tutoring program as a **method**—as a way of thinking, talking, and learning about writing—we may think of the one-to-one and small-group exchanges that take place, either in a location named the "writing center," a program called a "writing fellows program," or elsewhere on campus. In a sense, it's a "writing center" whenever two peers sit down to talk about writing—whether that's in a center, classroom, or coffee bar. Thinking of the defining quality of tutoring as its method in this way takes it beyond its physical walls (or firewalls) and focuses our attention on the goals, purposes, and strategies that define the work of a writing center, regardless of its location. It can also help us to think of our individual programs as part of a global community, for, as we hope to demonstrate in the next section, we can move beyond the peculiarities of our unique contexts to share our strategies for individualizing the learning of writing and so connect the writing center community across campuses.

These two terms—site and method—are not absolutely separate, of course. The activities (methods) of a writing center are, to some extent, determined by its space, for example. A center without computers is unlikely to be able to support online writing tutoring, while a center that is comprised entirely of single-seat computer stations will have difficulty comfortably housing one-to-one or small-group writing instruction. Thus method is shaped by site. So too a site can be shaped by a method—it is common to find tutors who "hack the center"—that is, modify an inhospitable or uncomfortable environment to better suit the method of their work. Tutors accomplish such "hacking" by, for example, pushing computers out of the way or pulling two-person tables together to support a whole-group discussion. Thus, the site and method of a writing center or other tutoring program are mutually shaping forces. Ultimately, however, this book locates the heart of any tutoring in its method—a method that connects one-to-one tutors to other writers, to one another in a center, as well as across writing centers, writing fellows programs, course-based tutoring, online writing centers—and even across countries.

WHAT IS A WRITING CENTER?
WHAT IS A WRITING TUTOR?

For Writing

1. Write a description of one location where your program tutors. What kinds of activity does this space encourage? Inhibit? What things are easy to do there? What is difficult? Do you or the other tutors in this space ever alter it to better suit the activity at hand?

2. Research another tutoring program on your campus. What kind of tutoring does it offer and how does its staff do so? In what ways are its methods similar to yours and in what ways are they different? In light of this comparison, would you consider these two programs as constituting a community? Why or why not?

Just as there are different sites of tutoring that are considered part of the writing center community, so there are different kinds of writing tutors. And these differences aren't just between tutors who work in writing centers that focus on generalized tutoring strategies and those course- and discipline-specific tutors who focus on a particular set of writing conventions. Writing center tutors can also be drawn from different parts of the university population: you'll find centers and programs staffed by high school students, undergraduates, graduate students, faculty, staff, and even volunteers. As we'd expect with all these different populations, there are differences in tutoring pedagogies that are, in part, attributable to the specifics of these tutors' positions, including disciplinary expertise, and the tutor's relative authority outside of the tutorial situation.

The Role of Tutor Disciplinary Expertise

While many writing centers and programs prepare their tutors to focus on generalizable writing strategies that can be applied in a wide variety of situations, others prepare their tutors for more highly defined writing occasions by focusing on the expectations of a specific audience. As Jean Kiedaisch and Sue Dinitz suggest, such expertise can significantly influence the scope of a tutorial ("Look Back"). Thus tutors working with writers in their own fields of study will have different challenges and opportunities than will, for example, generalist tutors helping writers from disciplines different from their own. Admittedly, a tutor with disciplinary expertise might have a deeper repository of relevant knowledge to draw from; at the same time, however, this expert tutor will have to attend carefully to where the writer's situation might diverge from the tutor's experience. The writer's audience, for example, may have a different understanding of disciplinary **rhetorical moves**, those qualities of style and genre that are defined by an audience's expectations and that differ from discipline to discipline. Moreover, writers may be producing, for pedagogical reasons, genres not specific to the subject matter's discipline, such as reflective writing, "think pieces," or process descriptions, that have more to do with learning *about* the discipline than about writing *in* the discipline. In these situations, the disciplinary authority of the tutor is less important than the writer's understanding of the assignment. Tutors with discipline-specific expertise may face a unique need to challenge their own assumptions, then.

The Tutor's Institutional Authority Outside the Tutorial Situation

While many tutors are undergraduate students who work primarily with undergraduate writers, there are also tutors who occupy other roles in the institution. There are:

- graduate students, who tutor as an apprenticeship to teaching, or in addition to teaching their own first-year writing classes;
- high-school students who work in their school's writing center;
- graduate students from disciplines beyond English and writing studies who work in the writing center as generalist tutors;
- instructors who hold appointments in the writing center as part of their teaching duties;

- staff and professional tutors whose exclusive roles on campus are as writing tutors;
- and directors and administrators who often tutor in addition to leading their center or program.

These positions can situate the tutor differently from the peer tutor, who often uses his or her student status as a means to see the writing situation from the writer's point of view, using peer-based conversation to help the writer to see the audience's needs and expectations from this shared viewpoint. Often, however, those tutors whose primary institutional role is beyond the writing center will have more practice viewing the writer's situation from that of another audience, such as a teacher or other community member, and may face particular challenges in respecting and encouraging the writer from the perspective of a collegial fellow writer.

What Tutors Have in Common

These are just a couple of the kinds of challenges faced by varying tutor populations. Given these differences, it might be easy to think that there is no "tutors' community" but a disparate smattering of groups, each with its own pedagogies, possibilities, and problems. And yet, we do think that the similarities among writing tutors greatly overshadow the differences. These similarities include:

A Commitment to "Friendly Talk"

Ultimately, tutoring is a friendly conversation. This single element packs together a lot of what unites writing tutors. First, tutors believe that important learning happens when people are comfortable with one another, when there's an environment of trust established. Tutors, in other words, understand the importance of interpersonal relationships. Second, tutors believe in talk—that high-impact learning involves a back-and-forth among the parties involved. Such conversation may not always happen face-to-face—there can be online conversations between tutors and the writers who consult them, for example. But it is the opportunity to work together to understand ideas and try out options that separates much individualized tutoring in writing from the mass-format instruction that might be found in other parts of the institution.

Understanding Writing—and Learning to Write—as Processes

Unlike those images from popular culture that equate "writing" with "moment of inspiration" or "innate God-given ability," most writing tutors understand writing as an ability (or set of abilities) that can be improved. As we discuss in Chapter 4, most tutoring pedagogies look at writing as a process—a series of stages that take the writer from initial idea to finished document. Most experienced writing tutors understand their job as helping writers move along this continuum. Further, tutors understand that writers do not smoothly progress through the writing process: a writer might come into the center today thinking she has almost finished her paper and is at the final editing stage. After reviewing her work and assignment sheet with a tutor, however, she may realize she has more to do than she originally planned and leaves the tutorial determined to return to the research process, to restructure the essay, or even start again. Rather than seeing this as a sign of imminent failure, most tutors believe all of this progression is part of the process.

Believing in Writing Relationships Outside the Teacher–Student Relationship

Writing tutors in their various program formulations are united by their understanding of the powerful roles that individuals outside the classroom can play in the learning process. In addition to facilitating a less-structured exploration by the writer than is afforded by the classroom, the tutorial is guided by the writer's own needs and goals, allowing for a high-impact learning experience. The tutorial is unlike the classroom setting in another important way: in the classroom, success is quite often equated to grades, and grades are achieved by understanding the material in a manner that is defined by the instructor and that is assessed by how well students meet the instructor's expectations. In contrast to this equivalence between the student's success and the instructor's priorities, in a writing tutorial success is determined by an agenda negotiated by the tutor and writer, and often its primary assessment of success is conducted by writer herself, either in an end-of-session feedback form or other reflective activity. Whether a tutor is a professional staff member working in a community college, an MBA student working part time in the university writing center, or an undergraduate tutoring writing in his major, then, it can be assumed that the tutorial's ends and means will be dictated by the goals and needs of the individual writer.

Ultimately, then, while we use the term "writing center" to describe the location of an individual writing program and "writing tutor" to describe the individual facilitating its work, we have tried to be mindful of the issues, strategies, and opportunities that constitute the work of writing tutors in various locales, who are inhabiting different institutional roles and working under differently configured and differently named positions. Moreover, we recognize that many of these programs have grown out of a common teaching approach and have a common history. In what follows, we describe a brief history of individualized writing instruction. As we move forward, remember to draw connections to your own experiences, where this generalized history that we describe corresponds with your own local history, and where it does not account for the evolution of your own writing center. Note too, that while we use the term "tutor" consistently throughout this book, such individuals are known by an array of terms, such as writing coach, writing consultant, peer advisor, or writing assistant. This variety of terms denotes the local cultures of the programs from which they have sprung.

For Writing

1. What are tutors called in your program? Compare that title with another, either from those named here or from your own experience. What images does each connote? Which do you prefer and why?

2. Search online for images of "tutor" or "tutoring." You might search on your institution's website or across the Web. Working from one or two images that you find, describe the ways in which tutoring is portrayed. What does the image suggest tutoring is? Who offers it? Who uses it? Does this depiction align with the tutoring offered in your program?

WHAT IS A WRITING CENTER? HISTORICAL VIEWS

In the previous section, we defined writing tutoring through the beliefs that members of this community share. There are other ways to understand the idea of a writing center, however, and in this section we look at writing center history as a way to understand the evolution of the field and to provide some historical context for the writing center or program in which you work.

The history of tutoring writing in Western civilization can be traced back to the very beginnings of the art of eloquence itself. Stephen North, for example, has traced it back to Classical Greece and "a tutor called Socrates" ("Idea" 446). A scholar of the history of rhetoric may wish to push the date back even further—at least to Aspasia, a woman who, according to Plato, Socrates called "his most excellent mistress in the art of rhetoric" (2). Even as tutoring writing is part of a 2,500-year history of rhetorical education, much of its contemporary formation springs from two sources: first, the invention and evolution of writing as a college course that long defined writing students as deficient, and second—and more recently—the evolution of college writing from merely a single course or set of courses to a knowledge-based discipline that offers theories of writing that value the writing process as well as the particularities of each writing occasion. As we see later in this chapter, such theories frame writing as inherently collaborative in that we as writers are participating in an ongoing conversation. When we compose we never really write alone; it's an activity that requires us to write to an audience.

Writing Instruction: A Brief History

Before moving to the contemporary theoretical rationale for individualized writing instruction, however, it's useful to understand the historical forces that shaped—and continue to shape—the teaching of writing. We don't have to look at the story of writing instruction very long before we see that many of the "problems" faced by tutors in the writing center and many of those issues decried in the media as "literacy crises" have been with us a long, long time—almost as long as the United States has been a country, in fact.

Writing instruction at the college level began in the United States. Prior to the eighteenth century, college entrance was predicated on the young man's knowledge of the classical languages, Latin and, particularly, Greek. The study of these languages was believed to instill a mental precision and level of self-discipline needed for success in college. Requiring fluency in the classical languages also served a gatekeeping function: it maintained the social order by ensuring that, by and large, only the sons of wealthy families could attend university (Miller). This tradition was primarily European in its roots, however, and the United States pushed toward a more democratic access to education. The American universities therefore began to follow the path set by those Scottish universities that did not require classical languages of their students. This change did, however, raise a question: how would institutions assure themselves that students were adequately prepared for college-level study? In 1872, Harvard's answer was to administer a national writing exam for all potential Harvard students. This exam required to students to write extemporaneously on previously announced literary works and so, the thinking went, would allow the examiners to evaluate both the students' writing skills and intellectual fitness for college. That is, this exam was designed to see whether students could write clear and elegant prose and to question their levels of taste: were their literary analyses reflective of a correct aesthetic judgment and moral values?

The answer to these questions was, apparently, "no"—or at least in the opinion of the Harvard examiners. Students who took the annual exam were found vastly lacking. In response to this perceived deficit, Harvard set up the first required writing course, English A, to remedy the weaknesses seen in the majority of students' writing. At this time in U.S. history, where Harvard went, other American colleges and universities were quick to follow. As John C. Brereton notes, "[m]ost colleges in 1860 had no course in composition or in English literature. By 1900 . . . every college had an array of English courses" (4). Unlike other disciplines, then, the study of both literature and composition in the United States originated in an attempt to remedy students' deficits rather than in an agenda of advanced research seen in other fields, such as the sciences. The more banal origins of English would drive the leaders of both its subfields, literary studies and writing studies, to find ways to assert the legitimacy of their disciplines, to prove that they were no less rigorous and valuable than other areas of study.

Writing Studies: A Brief History

Disciplinary legitimacy would come far later for writing than for literature. As Gerald Graff describes in *Professing Literature,* by connecting itself to research rather than teaching, professional literary study rose in popularity and prestige from its initial appearance in the last quarter of the nineteenth century to its entrance into the present century. On the other hand, while college classes in writing appeared alongside early literary studies in the nineteenth century, it wouldn't be until the last quarter of the twentieth century that writing studies would affix a similarly secure disciplinary place in the modern university.

In part, this delay in the development of writing studies as its own subdiscipline had to do with the remedial origins of the teaching of writing. From its inception, composition has struggled against the popular notion that college writing teachers were only instructing lazy or slow students in basic skills that they should have learned long before. The lack of prestige that attached itself to writing instruction also had a lot to do with its identification as a teaching subject. Unlike literary studies scholars, whose identity coalesced around the creation of original research, writing teachers focused on the dissemination of knowledge. And, in part, writing instructors' lack of institutional power had to do with the working conditions of the nineteenth-century writing teacher. As composition historian Robert Connors notes: "Composition courses of the latter half of the nineteenth century became hells of overwork which drove away all those teachers who were mobile and ground down those who were not" (*Composition-Rhetoric* 189). Connors reports that in 1892, Harvard professor Barrett Wendell read "daily and fortnightly themes from 170 students—over 24,000 papers each year" (191). Needless to say, their system was not based on the one-to-one teaching of writing; rather, this teaching model was based in the wholesale marking of error, encouraging the students to note the errors they had made, and urging them to be careful not to repeat these mistakes on future daily themes.

Teaching Writing, Past and Present

This early history of writing instruction may seem disconnected to work as a tutor, but it is nevertheless worth attention since many of the problems that beset early writing teachers still challenge many writing centers today. Some centers, for example, are seen as places that only work with students on literacy skills that should have been acquired prior to college. And like early composition programs, writing centers are sometimes tasked with the vast challenge of fixing all student writing—although, one hopes, not in a "hell of overwork" like Connors describes. Moreover, this early model of teaching—in which an instructor only reads a single draft of each student's paper, marks errors, awards a grade, and, perhaps, adds a brief terminal comment—may seem quite familiar to some of the readers of this book, for it is still in practice in many places today. This holdover is due to a combination of the weight of tradition—the very durability of the model argues for its continuation—and the conditions in which many teachers work, since it is still not uncommon for a writing teacher to have 100-plus writing students in a semester. Thus the notion of site shapes method applies in the writing classroom as well as in the center.

In these ways, our nineteenth-century origins are still with us. There is even an analogous writing center model, as Andrea Lunsford has described in

"Collaboration, Control, and the Idea of a Writing Center," namely "The Center as Storehouse":

> [T]he Center as Storehouse operates as [an] information station or storehouse, prescribing and handing out skills and strategies to individual learners. They often use "modules" or other kinds of individualized learning materials. They tend to view knowledge as individually derived and held, and they are not particularly amenable to collaboration . . . (3)

While it's easy to dismiss such a writing center as a site of so-called skill, drill, and kill, as Lunsford goes on to note, such centers "do a lot of good work" (4) and thrive on campuses where their approach aligns with campus notions of literacy. Therefore, even centers whose defining philosophies conflict with this model may well use frequently and to great effect some of the items and approaches associated with a Storehouse center: handouts, for example, or helping students to find the online resources that might help them independently improve their own work going forward. Even while noting that this model of the writing center seems to have lost much of its popularity, the writing center scholar—or tutor-researcher—must acknowledge the past impact as well as the ongoing influence of this writing center model.

The Evolution of Writing Centers

Even this Storehouse model of a writing center had to wait many years before it circulated widely in American education, for writing centers did not become a common campus fixture until the last quarter of the twentieth century. Indeed, Harvard itself may have been the progenitor of first-year writing, but it did not actually open a writing center until the end of the 1970s. There are, however, historical records of early writing center sites and methods. As early as 1895, for example, John Franklin Genung of Amherst College described teaching writing as "laboratory work" (174), and in 1904, high-school teacher Philo Buck described teaching writing using laboratory methods (Carino, "Early" 105). Writing center historian Neal Lerner has done much to further our understanding of the evolution of writing centers throughout the twentieth century, drawing our attention to the ways in which the insularity of individual writing centers long obscured our shared history. In the final section of this book, you'll find "Searching for Robert Moore," in which Lerner describes the influences of our assumptions about writing center history, and the ways in which evidencing—and correcting—these assumptions improves our understanding of our shared past.

But even while such historians are doing good work by identifying the early precursors to the current state of the art in writing centers, many individual writing centers identify origins that are far more recent. Indeed, 96 percent of respondents to a 2001 study reported writing centers that went back no further than the 1970s (Perkes 15). While we can trace our roots back, then, the popularity of writing centers is a fairly recent phenomenon. That same study noted that significant portions of respondents indicated that their centers opened in the 1970s (23 percent of respondents) and the 1980s (28 percent of respondents) (15). These "growth spurts" reflect important paradigm shifts that fostered the growth of writing centers. The 1970s, for example, was a time that saw an increase in concern with the individualities of student writers. Two causes are often cited for this shift in perspective; namely, change in student populations and changes in language pedagogy. That is, the open admissions movement of the 1960s and 1970s opened college doors to previously underrepresented groups who had traditionally been unable to access higher education. For example, a well-known researcher of underprepared writing students, Mina Shaughnessy, describes open admissions at the City University of New York (CUNY) in her book *Errors and Expectations*. According to Shaughnessy, legislation that guaranteed New York high-school graduates access to a college education opened the doors of CUNY to new ethnic and socioeconomic demographics. These students brought literacy needs that were unfamiliar to professors who were used to a student body that represented a far smaller—and more elite—segment of the population. Even as those new students were showing up in college and university classrooms, instructors like Shaughnessy were adapting methods to meet this new opportunity.

Writing Centers and the Wider Culture

It is important to note that education access did not come without cultural turbulence, and as writing center historian Peter Carino has described, these conflicts reflected the larger culture of social unrest being experienced by the rest of the country:

> It is an understatement to say that the approximately ten years of the late 1960s and the middle 1970s, when open admissions programs were initiated and developed, were one of the most volatile periods of social unrest in American history. With the unprecedentedly large generation of baby boomers approaching college age, the Civil Rights Act of 1964 affording African Americans increased societal participation, more women forsaking homemaking for careers, and large numbers of working-class males returning from Vietnam with education funding guaranteed by the GI bill, open admissions policies were designed to address the needs of the nation's most diverse group ever of rising adults. (Carino, "Open" 32)

Attendant to this new concern with educating the diversity of individuals who make up the U.S. population, there was an increase in attention to the ways in which education needed to be customized to meet learners' needs. In 1966, for example, the Dartmouth Seminar, a highly influential meeting on the best ways of teaching writing and language, "brought together some 50 leading teachers and scholars from America and Britain . . . [to] . . . define English as a school subject and to outline the best ways it might be taught" (J. Harris, "After" 631). Although, and as one might expect, these individuals did not arrive at a single approach to teaching English, many composition scholars nevertheless look upon it as a watershed moment in our understanding of how language, including writing, is learned. Broadly speaking, Dartmouth has come to be associated with a moment when the field of English study shifted from "[a]n old model of teaching centered on the transmission of skills (composition) and knowledge (literature)" to a "'growth model' focusing on the experiences of students and how these are shaped by the use of language" (J. Harris, "After" 631). Most influential on the development of peer tutoring, perhaps, was Kenneth Bruffee's convening of the Brooklyn College Summer Institute in Training Peer Writing Tutors in 1980. The Brooklyn Institute comprised an evolving membership of college professors from across the country who met for three summers, first to explore, and then to adapt and promote on their own campuses, a collaborative model of peer tutoring in writing. It is from the pedagogies and practices of such events as the Brooklyn Institutes and the Dartmouth conference that we developed the bulk of the tutoring strategies we still use today.

Circulating Writing Knowledge

The knowledge that was created during the creation and implementation of these new practices of peer tutoring was disseminated through the growth of research journals and other publication venues in the field. 1977 saw the first issue of *The Writing Lab Newsletter* (*WLN*), a periodical originally focused on the concerns of writing center administrators (although when you look at *WLN* today you'll certainly notice its scope has broadened to include both directors and tutors). In 1980, *The Writing Center Journal*, which specialized in longer, research-based essays, was founded, and 1981 saw a peer tutor's journal published by the Berkeley site of the National Writing Project, a professional development network for writing teachers from "K–16"—for individuals working with learners from preschool through college (Goldsby). Given the growth in publication venues, it might come as no surprise that some of the field's foundational essays were published during this time, including, in 1984, Kenneth Bruffee's "Peer Tutoring and the 'Conversation of Mankind,'" a highly influential essay and one that you will find in the final section of this book. We say more about it in the following chapters.

Perhaps more central to the purposes at hand, however, this era saw increasing opportunities for peer tutors to meet their counterparts at other schools and to share the knowledge they were creating in their writing centers. This represented an advancement in the understanding of tutoring *methods* as they were used across a range of tutoring *sites*, if you will. The first meeting of the National Conference on Peer Tutoring in Writing (NCPTW) took place at Brown University in 1984, for example, and *WLN* published its first "Tutor's Column" in that same year. Other conference venues brought together writing center administrators and tutors, such as the National Writing Centers Association, founded in 1982 (Kinkead 131), as well as the many regional writing center associations that sprung up across the country. In 1994, Pennsylvania State University published its first issue of *The Dangling Modifier*, a publication by and for peer tutors. Tutor research has figured prominently the undergraduate research journal *Young Scholars in Writing* since its first issue in 2003.

Even while tutors were connecting from across campuses through conference attendance and research publication, they were finding new ways to connect to their own campuses as well. In addition to serving as the host of the first National Conference on Peer Tutoring in Writing, for example, Brown University is also acknowledged as the site of the first writing fellows program. As founder Tori Haring-Smith describes, both the writing center and the writing program were started in the early 1980s as a response to perceived writing skill deficiencies among the elite university's undergraduates (123). While Brown is identified with the origins of this movement, Haring-Smith notes that by 1992 "there were more than 100 schools with some version of a writing fellows program. Even though it began at a research institution, the program works in many different settings. Neither the size of the institution nor the selectivity of its admission criteria seems to affect the success of the writing fellows program" (127). Like writing center-based tutoring, then, upon their inception, writing fellows programs quickly grew in and across campuses, thus indicating a clear need in the institution for individualized writing support.

Writing Center Studies Today

Thus far, we've painted a picture of writing center studies that is largely U.S.-centric and based on the one-to-one—and, implicitly, face-to-face—discussion of writing and rhetorical precepts. During the last two decades of the twentieth century, however, both of these elements of writing center history underwent tremendous development. Technology, in particular, seemed to spring up overnight in writing center discourse. As Peter Carino notes, for example, from 1979 to 1982, "no articles in *Writing Lab Newsletter* discuss computer tutorials" but:

> a spurt of discourse on computers in the writing center . . . bears out the cliché that technology moves fast. The 1984 *Writing Lab Directory* (compiled in 1983) lists 88 of 184 centers as having at least one computer, and center professionals began to make their voices heard [concerning technology], with three articles directly treating computers and two discussing them within broader topics in the *Proceedings of the Writing Centers Association Fifth Annual Conference* (1983) and at least one paper delivered at the First Midwest Writing Centers Association Conference that same year. (Carino, "Computers" 176)

Once new media took hold in the writing center community, discourses concerning its use and influence grew to become an integral part of our disciplinary conversations. In 1987, for example, Jeanette Harris and Joyce Kinkead edited "Computers, Computers, Computers," a special issue of *The Writing Center Journal* focused on the role of technology in the writing center. The information offered in this issue was welcomed by the writing center community, as demonstrated by the editors' receipt of the National Writing Centers Association Outstanding Scholarship Award in 1989.

Further support for technological issues—as well as any other writing center-related question a tutor or administrator could think to ask—was offered by WCENTER, the listserv for writing center professionals, which was launched by Lady Falls Brown of Texas Tech University in 1992. WCENTER is a lively list and the first stop for many writing center research projects for tutors and administrators, as well as the place where writing center professionals can engage their counterparts at other schools.

In addition to playing a key role in individualized writing instruction and in the administration of many writing centers, technology has facilitated another evolution of our field: the internationalization of writing centers. That is, while writing centers developed from the U.S. educational system, the transition from the last century to our present one saw their increasing popularity in other parts of the world. Spring 1998, for example, saw the founding of the European Writing Centers Association—the first regional writing center organization outside the United States. Reflecting the growing globalization of the writing center community, in 1999 the organization changed its name to the International Writing Centers Association and welcomed the Middle East-North Africa Writing Centers Alliance as an affiliate in 2007.

In general, and as Christiane Donahue has noted, writing centers have proven easier to export than other forms of U.S. postsecondary writing instruction, such as the first-year writing requirement:

> As writing centers have evolved in other countries, discussions across national boundaries have increased as well. It is interesting to note that the writing center conversation, one particularly supportive of both the challenges of writing in the disciplines and the challenges for students learning to do disciplinary work in English, has been the strongest development to date in terms of exchanges of teaching practice and pedagogical framing, always explored in context. This makes eminent sense, given the nature of the curriculum in many non-U.S. university systems, which tend toward disciplinary focus from year one . . . (222–23)

In the internationalization of writing centers, we can see the same elements that helped writing centers to thrive during their early years in the United States: a focus on connecting with individual learners rather than on connecting to (or disrupting) the curriculum by creating a specific class, a commitment to supporting writers across the disciplines and the range of rhetorical situations they encounter, and a pedagogical flexibility that allows writing centers to flourish in institutions with a wide range of missions and educational philosophies. It seems, then, as Andrea Lunsford said in the 2010 keynote of the International Writing Centers Association Conference, that "writing centers will continue to flourish" and, as she jokingly concluded, eventually "take over the world" (Lunsford and Ede 22–23).

For Writing

1. Working only from what is readily available in your program or online, write a brief history of your program. When did it start and why? How has it changed, if at all, since its founding? Can you find any correlation between these events and the larger history of the field described here?

2. Look online at two of the common venues of tutor-research described in this section, namely *The Dangling Modifier, Young Scholars in Writing,* or the "Tutor's Column" from *WLN.* Compare the kinds of work found in these two venues and the editorial mission of each publication. Are there differences in the kinds of undergraduate work they publish? Which publication do you find more interesting? More useful? Why?

3. Compare an early example of the "Tutor's Column" from *WLN* with a current one. Has it evolved over the years? How has the periodical itself? Can you make any connections between the sample publications you selected and the description of writing center history in this chapter?

WHAT IS A WRITING CENTER?
THEORETICAL VIEWS

The last section looks at writing centers as a historical development by focusing on the events that facilitated and defined, at in least part, their evolution. When looking broadly across the field, such work can be helpful when you're trying to contextualize your center to larger institutional, national, and international forces in education. Or, when looking at the history of a school that is similar to yours in meaningful ways, such historical work can act as a means of exploring the impact of specific programs or decisions in an environment similar to your own and so help decide the best course of action for your own center.

There are, however, other ways to analyze a writing center or tutoring program. In this section, for example, we're going to look at theorizing the writing center by surveying the ideas that have shaped the learning goals and strategic means of writing centers. Before launching into such a survey, though, it is important to note that this relatively brief survey is highly selective: there are many, many other ideas that have contributed to our ideas of what a writing center can and should be, including scholarship from outside writing center studies. Indeed, a hallmark of this field is the ongoing inclination of writing center researchers to incorporate ideas from a diverse range of disciplines. But in the interest of concision, we focus the discussion below on writing center scholarship itself and have paid far less attention to the theories from other fields. However, if you pursue the theories and works described below, they will lead you to other works, both in and out of writing center studies, that extend the conversations about theory that are described below. Further, Chapter 9 tells you more about how to create and apply theory.

Writing Centers and the Need for Theory

If such a theorizing of individualized writing instruction strikes you as a pointless, self-important, or impractical endeavor, you would not be alone. In earlier days of writing center scholarship, in particular, writing center specialists worried that engaging in such work was a futile attempt to win the respect of our colleagues who undertake such work in other disciplines (Hobson) or a meritless "selling out" to the academic hierarchy (Riley). And yet, without a theoretical framework to help us evaluate how—and if—our practices work, we are hard pressed to determine whether our strategies and goals for individualized writing instruction are, in fact, appropriate and successful. By looking at the writing center through different theoretical lenses, we enrich our understanding of what actually takes place in these locales. Writing center practice and theory are thus permanently fused—something you'll no doubt notice in the following "Tutor's Handbook" section of this book, which outlines practices that are inextricably informed by theory. As Lisa Ede described, for best effect, we need to see theory and practice as integrally connected, for "[t]heory without practice is likely to result in ungrounded, inapplicable speculation. Practice without theory, as we know, often leads to inconsistent, and sometimes even contradictory and wrongheaded, pedagogical methods" (4). Put another way, unless we know why we're doing what we're doing and where we expect to get by doing it—unless we *theorize* it—we won't be able to assess whether we are making the best choices for the writers who visit our centers.

Writing Centers: Practicing Theory

In the daily work of a tutor, then, theory helps us set our goals and define our vision. If we consider the model of "writing center as Storehouse" introduced earlier in this chapter, we can better understand how such abstruse theorizing might change our day-to-day practice. The Storehouse writing center described by Lunsford, with its handouts, grammar resources, and focus on students' errors, can be seen as the result of an internally consistent philosophy that integrates a specific notion of writing excellence with an understanding of how the individual learns to write. On the one hand, we have a concept of writing that privileges sentence-level correctness and, often, adherence to external forms such as the five-paragraph essay. In this center, the success of a piece of writing is less about the author's intent or purpose and more about demonstrating proficiency via avoiding errors and following the rules. The people and resources of this center, then, work toward communicating those rules to the writer, who is thought to be in the writing center because he or she does not know the rules of common genres, such as the compare/contrast essay, or how to construct grammatically correct sentences.

This focus on sentence-level correctness correlates strongly with the understanding of how students learn to write that such centers embrace. That is, Storehouse centers are often based on a notion that students must learn to write in an incremental and fragmented way—first learning to construct a simple sentence correctly, then moving on to more complicated sentences, then learning to write paragraphs of increasing complexity. Only when this work is accomplished can students progress to writing papers. Such an understanding of learning explains why such centers focus on sentence-level issues when helping underprepared writers.

Often, such **pedagogies** (a word for teaching philosophies) are called "**current-traditional**," a term that is used loosely in writing studies to describe approaches that work inductively in this manner and that prioritize the correction of local error. Such terminology, however, has to be used carefully. For one, current-traditionalism, or really any -ism, is a term used when attempting to find the similarities among a group of teachers and / or theorists. Categorizing an individual theorist in this way therefore obscures differences in approach. Were you told that you were just like all the other students in your major, for example, you would no doubt be able to list several ways in which you are a unique individual and would want people to consider you as such. Such intellectual caution has to be observed when labeling theorists who would similarly argue their particularity, and even more care should be used with a term such as "current-traditional" that is consistently used in a pejorative sense to criticize an approach to writing instruction. It's often framed as the "bad old days" from which we have, thankfully, progressed. Such black-and-white thinking can distort both our historical understanding of what has actually happened and our understanding of what theories have actually existed and had—or still have—influence.

Thinking About Theories in Writing Centers

When looking at more recent theories that circulate in writing studies and the writing center, it can be useful to consider them in terms of **centripetal theories** (those that emphasize community by focusing on the commonalities among writers and writing processes) and **centrifugal theories** (those that emphasize individualities among writers, either by focusing on the interaction of the writing center with the rhetorical practices of specific groups or by emphasizing the complete uniqueness of each writer and writing occasion). You can see that in the "Tutor's Handbook" section we emphasize this way of looking at writers, as unique individuals, although you can also see that it's sometimes necessary to look at commonalities (as we do in Chapters 4 and 5). Similarly, by lumping the theories below into these two categories, we are engaging in the same sort of labeling we just warned you about! But such a taxonomy is worth considering nonetheless because of the ways in which such a mapping allows us to see the continuities and disconnects among those theories that have influenced both individual writing centers as well as the larger field of writing center studies. We talk more about theory and method in Chapter 8.

Centripetal Theories: All Writers, Writing Situations, or Writing Centers Are Alike

Many of the centripetal theories of writing center studies can be understood as attempts to help us understand those commonalities among writing experiences that will allow us to engage in cross-situational discussions of teaching and to explore learning strategies that can be used in a variety of writing situations. In this section we look at those theories that are of mutual interest to those of us who tutor writing.

All Writing Is a Process

Writers and teachers such as Donald M. Murray, a well-known writing instructor and journalist, have long urged writing teachers to move their attention away from teaching writing as a product and toward writing as a process, arguing that students' failure to create vibrant prose is more attributable to our focus on teaching product—which Murray calls "conscientious, doggedly responsible, repetitive autopsying"—than to the students themselves:

> The product doesn't improve so, blaming the student—who else?—we pass him along to the next teacher, who is trained, too often in the same way we were. Year after year the student shudders under a barrage of criticism, much of it brilliant, some of it stupid and all of it irrelevant. No matter how careful our criticisms, they do not help the student since when we teach composition we are not teaching a product, we are teaching a process. (3)

When we move from Lunsford's Storehouse center, which focus on teaching students via correction of error and attention to a required form, to a writing center that embraces such a process-based approach, then, we turn from an emphasis on error avoidance to a focus on helping students to understand that writing has stages—prewriting, writing, revision, and editing. Also, contemporary process-based pedagogy assumes that these stages are **recursive**; to achieve the best effect, a writer does not move lockstep through these stages but will shuttle among them. We talk more about recursivity and the role of tutoring in writing as a process in Chapters 3 and 4, but for the purposes of this chapter, you'll want to understand process pedagogy as marking an important shift from an emphasis on what the writer should produce to a focus on how the writer will do so.

In this process, Murray notes, much of the learning about writing takes place through a conversation with the writer—a conversation in which it is the student, not the teacher, who is doing most of the talking:

> How do you motivate your student to pass through this process . . . ? First by shutting up. When you are talking he isn't writing. And you don't learn a process by talking about it, but by doing it. Next by placing the opportunity for discovery in his hands. When you give him an assignment you tell him what to say and how to say it, and thereby cheat your student of the opportunity to learn the process of discovery we call writing. [. . .] We have to be quiet, to listen, to respond. (5)

In addition to focusing on the writing processes, then, this approach means we focus on writers. And not what they've done well or wrong in the past via comments on previously written essays, but on what they are doing right now by facilitating their current writing activities. Such a strategy not only corresponds well to the tutorial setting—where students often bring unfinished work to discuss how to develop it—but to a second set of ideas that help define what we do in the writing center and why we do it: collaborative theories of learning.

All Texts Are Rhetorical

Even as many—if not most—tutoring programs will emphasize that their primary focus is on the writer and his or her writing process, such programs still acknowledge the importance of the texts that writers create. This importance is rooted in the power of these texts to instigate change—be that change in the world at large or more intimately in the mind of the individual reader or the writer. Rhetorical theory concerns itself with these changes, for such systems of ideas focus on how communication creates meaning and influences the world.

In Chapter 7, we use rhetorical theory to investigate the intersections of new media and tutoring practice. Such theories, broadly speaking, concern themselves with the impact of communication and so are useful in our consideration of both tutorial interactions and the impact of writers' texts. Further, rhetorical theory pays particular attention to the context of a particular speech or text. As rhetorician Lloyd Bitzer explains, "understanding a speech hinges upon understanding the context . . . in which the speech is located" (3). Such context-sensitive approaches lend themselves particularly well to individualized writing instruction, which places a premium on the particularities of the individual writer, tutor, tutorial, or tutoring program.

The application of rhetorical theory to tutoring is as varied as the history of rhetoric itself, from treatments of *kairos*, the ways in which a text responds to and (re)shapes a particular circumstance or occasion (Glover; Lebduska; M. Scott), to the role of improvisation in tutoring and tutor training (Boquet, *Noise*). Rhetorical theory scholarship in writing center studies also includes that work which takes rhetoric as an explicit part of its focus, such as aggression in the tutorial (Bokser) or plagiarism (Shamoon and Burns). Arguably, however, the contribution to rhetoric exceeds these boundaries. For any writing center scholarship that focuses on the crafting and creation of a message—be that "message" a writer's attempt to accomplish an assignment or a tutor's attempt to communicate effectively with a writer—could be considered rhetorical scholarship. Indeed, there are those in rhetorical studies who argue for **Big Rhetoric**, that idea that because all forms of inquiry take place in language and because rhetorical study concerns itself with the ways that language creates meaning, all study is, in fact, rhetorical study (Gaonkar; McCloskey; Schiappa). Whether or not the idea of rhetorical studies as the study of all things is compelling to you, however, its more localized application is a common approach to theoretical understandings of the writing center.

All Writers Learn from and with Knowledgeable Peers

For writing centers, arguably the most important collaborative theorist is Kenneth Bruffee, whose highly influential institutes on collaborative writing we discuss in the previous section. In works such as his "Peer Tutoring and the 'Conversation of Mankind,'" Bruffee describes collaborative learning in general and peer tutoring in particular as a greatly needed "alternative to the classroom" (325, this book) and focuses on explaining why such tutoring works. Two lines of argument help him to make this case. First, he asserts that thought, conversation, and writing are strongly interwoven. Thought, he claims, is "internalized conversation" (327, this book); it is basically a conversation with oneself, while conversation is, by extension, thought externalized by interaction with another. By engaging in *external* conversations that reflect the ways of thinking valued by a given community, we *internalize* the ways of thinking that community values. Central to the tutoring process, according to Bruffee, is that writing is also related to this talking and thinking, albeit in a more convoluted fashion. This idea is foundational to much of Bruffee's contribution to writing center studies and so worth quoting at length:

> Writing is at once both two steps away from conversation and a return to conversation. By writing, we re-immerse conversation in its social medium. Writing is two steps removed from conversation because, for example, my ability to write this essay depends on my ability to talk through with myself the issues I address here. And my ability to talk through an issue with myself derives largely from my ability to converse directly with other people in an immediate social situation.
>
> The point is not that every time I write, what I say must necessarily be something I have talked over with other people first, although I may well often do just that. What I say can originate in thought. But since thought is conversation as I have learned to internalize it, the point is that writing always has its roots deep in the acquired ability to carry on the social symbolic exchanges we call conversation. The inference writing tutors and teachers should make from this line of reasoning is that our task must involve engaging students in conversation at as many points in the writing process as possible and that we should contrive to ensure that that conversation is similar in as many ways as possible to the way we would like them eventually to write. (328, this book)

Through this conversation in its many forms—oral, written, thought—one learns the kind of discourse valued by the community in which one is engaged. Or, to put it another way, if you read books by engineers, talk with engineers, think about engineering, and write for engineers, you will learn to create and understand the kinds of discourse valued by the professional community of engineers. Such a set of talk and writing is called a **normal discourse**. Normal discourse is the communication forms of a "community of knowledgeable peers" and includes both the ways of thinking (for example, what counts as a valid argument) and the ways of expressing that thinking (Bruffee 332, this book). Since normal discourse can only take place among peers, Bruffee notes, the best way to initiate undergraduates into the normal discourses of academe is in peer-based conversations, whether that conversation takes place in writing or speech. In Chapter 6, we say more about how you as a tutor can work with writers' "normal discourses" in other disciplines.

The implications of Bruffee's theories for the development of writing center theory have been immense. For one, he positions individualized writing instruction as an alternative to the writing classroom—a possibility for all writers—rather than a place to garage writers while they develop the minimal adequacy required to join the writing classroom—a place for poor writers. Bruffee thus expands the writing center's inclusivity. Further, by explaining the ways that conversation both influences writing and leads to an understanding of normal discourse, Bruffee helps us understand how the one-to-one conversation that makes up the bulk of most tutorials helps students to learn writing skills that they can carry beyond the individual assignment. Such a writing center, Lunsford tells us, "would place control, power and authority not in the tutor or staff, not in the individual student, but in the negotiating group" (41), thereby exhibiting that holistic centripetal impulse that sees the writing center as a coherent community. It is worth noting that such collaborative theories of learning are often discussed, as Lunsford does here, in conjunction with theories of writing based in **social constructivist** ideas of knowledge.

A social constructivist approach to the writing center emphasizes the ways in which writing creates new meaning. In "Writing as a Social Process: A Theoretical Foundation for Writing Centers," Lisa Ede argues that it is not just learning to write that is a collaborative activity; writing itself creates meaning collaboratively. Such an assertion may seem counterintuitive; after all, as we say more about in Chapter 4, much of the Western literary tradition is based on the idea that meaning is created by the individual author whose work is entirely original. And yet, such an assertion can be readily disproven by multiple lines of argument. For one, authors are responding to the conversations that take place around them and in the works of others. For scientists, these conversations may be in the research upon which they build, for example, while for literary authors, such conversations may include the styles in which they choose to write or to rebel against or the subjects they consider worthy for attention. In other words, both scientific and literary traditions can be seen as collaborative conversations. So too can undergraduate research projects in which students are encouraged to put their ideas "in conversation" with the sources they cite. By collaborating with others in this fashion we improve the knowledge we create.

In like fashion, all authors collaborate to create meaning, in some sense, with audiences. Any writer must assume certain knowledge on the part of the audience and build from that shared agreement to create new knowledge. As authors of this book, for example, we assume that the reader agrees with us on certain "facts." Presumably, for example, our readers think that learning to write well is an important part of education. We assume too that our reader agrees that writing well is not strictly an innate skill—that one can and should learn to write more effectively. And as a final example, we presume that the reader agrees that writers can help one another improve their writing abilities. There are other groups who believe otherwise, that writing well is simply a matter of talent or that not everyone needs to write. But the writing center community has tested and accepted this knowledge; for this group, these facts are true. This book attempts to build from this previously created, currently accepted, knowledge to create a specific vision of the tutor and the role of research in the tutoring process. And we're hopeful that this vision may contribute to the conversation of our field and so help create new knowledge and enlarge our community's understanding of the role of the tutor. Thus, this book is socially constructed: it builds from the knowledge accepted by the community and strives to use this knowledge to create something new.

Writing process theories, rhetorical theory, collaborative learning ideals, and social constructivism give us ways to look at learning to write and the writing center itself as holistic entities that can be discussed in unified and intelligible terms. There are many benefits to examining the similarities among individual writers and writing centers, for doing so allows us to converse across contexts and articulate to those stakeholders who are not engaged in writing instruction, such as parents, administrators, and the public at large, what we do and why we do it in this fashion. In these ways, then, centripetal theories give coherence, definition, and continuity to the work we do. And yet, as writers we know that every writer is different in some way, as is every writing occasion. In the next section, then, we look at those centrifugal writing center theories that help us tease out the distinctions among writers and writing occasions.

Centrifugal Theories: All Writers Are Different

Even as there are shared values and beliefs that unite writing tutors across programs and institutions, there are other theories that prioritize the individuality of each writer and, by extension, of each tutorial situation. In this section we look at the theories that emphasize the differences among writers.

Expressivism: Each Writer Thinks Differently

To look at theories that emphasize individuation among writers, we can return to Donald Murray, for while he is known for articulating the concept of writing as a process described above, he is also associated with an intersecting pedagogical movement known as expressivism, which emphasizes the individuality of the writer's voice and "places knowledge inside the individual writer" (Kennedy 5). Like the notion of writing-as-a-process, expressivism, too, has been highly influential on writing centers. Broadly speaking, expressivists are more focused on writing as a means to discovering one's own individual truth and the expression of that truth in writing. And, as Linda Adler-Kassner has observed of the classroom, while such truth-writing may ultimately be meant to be shared with an audience, it was written for the writer. Expressivist writing instruction, then, is focused "generally not to help students become better citizens/participants in the democracy, but to help them fulfill their own needs and desires for self-understanding" (Adler-Kassner 218). Thus, expressivism takes as its goal self-knowledge and articulation of one's unique vision.

As Lunsford points out, writing centers based in this expressivist model, which she calls Garret Centers, see their "job as helping students get in touch with this knowledge, as a way to find their unique voice, their individual and unique powers" (5). Writing centers based on this model offer "conferences in which the tutor . . . listens, voices encouragement, and essentially serves as a validation for the students' I-search. . . . [Such centers] view knowledge as interiorized, solitary, individually derived, individually held" (5). While few writing centers would readily identify as wholly expressivist, we can nevertheless see the influence of these pedagogies in (1) an emphasis on an writer's individual needs; (2) those introspection-provoking questioning techniques that are at the heart of many tutoring strategies; and (3) approaches that promote the writer's sense of owner-ship over his or her texts. Or, as Don Bushman observes in "Theorizing a 'Social-Expressivist' Writing Center," "expressivism and social constructionism are the principal epistemologies for writing centers; we see them in the reflections of Murray-esque conferences and in Bruffee-esque collaborations" (6). While Bushman goes on to argue for a theorizing of writing centers that blends social constructivism with expressivism, his central tutorial image concretizes the heart of an expressivist view of tutoring:

> When we encounter writing that lacks adequate detail or that compresses the steps of a line of reasoning, our response, when working one-to-one, is to get students talking, to get them to articulate *in speech* the steps they failed to put in writing. And as most of us have experienced, students are generally able to provide these missing steps when we get them talking; it is as if this information is "within" them waiting to be released. (8)

Thus the job of the expressivist tutor is to help the writer articulate this inner, already existing, vision. Even those writing centers that do not actively embrace an expressivist ideal will often display elements of an expressivist orientation through, for example, a heavy reliance on questioning as the primary means of assistance and a belief that if a tutor asks sufficiently insightful questions, the writer will be able to create a plan for writing and/or revision from what she already knows.

If you think about the role of such questioning in tutorials (which we say more about in Chapter 3), it quickly becomes apparent that expressivism has had a strong impact. It has also, however, received a fair amount of critique both in writing center studies as well as in the larger discourses of writing studies. One of the most cogent critiques of expressivism in the writing classroom is made by Susan Jarratt, who notes that emphasis on the individual voice camouflages the "complexities of social differentiation and inequity" (109). That is, even as expres-sivism valorizes the individual, it also assumes "common human experiences and values" that elide important differences (107). Indeed, according to Jarratt, such homogeneity is not only tacitly assumed in this model, it is in fact actively and erroneously encouraged. And when looking at Elbow's description of the writing group in *Writing Without Teachers* as working best when participants are "people who have a lot in common" (Elbow 79), Jarratt notes the problematic nature of such homogeneity both for the writing classroom as well as for a society that values diversity:

> This vision of communication fails to acknowledge fundamental clashes in values that underlie issues of style, effect and meaning. How would those differences be negotiated in Elbow's writing group? They wouldn't, because the group is essentially value-free. [. . .] Elbow encourages, even demands, uncensored accounts of the experience of reading and self-evaluation of writing. But this view assumes the writers will be able to do whatever he or she wishes with the responses because of the equality of all group members. (110)

Thus, by celebrating the individuality of all voices, we arrive at a strangely featureless scene of writing, one in which issues of identity and social differences are elided.

To translate into writing center terms, tutors with heavily expressivist orientations might find themselves conflicted concerning the expression of the writers' individual and possibly idiosyncratic voices versus the demands of various writing situations. Or an expressivist tutor may struggle to respond to a piece of writing whose content is inappropriate or even offensive. Put another way, asserting that "everyone is unique" provides a specific challenge in both writing and tutoring situations. We say more about what this tension might look like in practice in Chapter 5.

Feminism

In its attention to individual experience, a valuing of personal voice, a flattening of the hierarchy, and an emphasis on writing as a journey of self-discovery, feminist theory brings to the writing center some concerns that are similar to those raised by expressivism. To these foci, however, feminist theories of the writing center pay particular attention to gender—that is, to notions of what is seen as "naturally" masculine or feminine and to how these constructs affect individual writers and tutors as well as our ideas about language and, indeed, the writing center itself.

These concerns are articulated in writing center research in a variety of ways. Sometimes, feminist theory grounds explorations of the ways in which tutoring itself is potentially feminist action. In "Feminine Discourse in the University: The Writing Center as a Site of Linguistic Resistance," for example, Janet Bean emphasizes the ways in which the peer element of the tutorial relationship leads to a flattening of the power dynamic. The observation of gendering of power and the pursuit of an egalitarian dynamic ideal is often the subject of feminist theory. That is, a feminist lens can help us understand the way social power is negotiated in a tutorial setting. Other works take this line of inquiry further by focusing on the ways in which writing centers can not only enact but also further feminist values. Mary Trachsel's "Nurturant Ethics and Academic Ideals: Convergence in the Writing Center," for example, argues that the writing center is an ideal site to explore and enact an **ethic of care**. This ethic of care borrows significantly from Carol Gilligan's work, most particularly *In a Different Voice*, which argues that woman's moral development focuses on caring for others rather than individual mastery. A tutorial based in this idea attends to the whole writer and his or her emotions rather than focusing only on academic dominance. In a similar vein, Jean Marie Lutes' "Why Feminists Make Better Tutors: Gender and Disciplinary Expertise in a Curriculum-Based Tutoring Program," looks to a writing fellows program to demonstrate the ways in which feminist values can provide a firm foundation to an effective tutoring program. The writing center's emphasis on interpersonal relationships, it has been argued, makes it a rich site for exploring the ways in which an ethic of care can push against the shortcomings of academic hierarchies.

Feminist analyses of the writing center don't all focus on celebrating the tutorial's potential, however. Works such as Meg Woolbright's "The Politics of Tutoring: Feminism Within the Patriarchy," show how difficult such ideals can be to enact. Providing further friction to the feminist ideal of the writing center are those works that explore the **feminization** of the writing center. Feminization in this context refers to the line of argument that claims the association of the supposedly "womanly" qualities of the writing center—the focus on the individual, on the emotions, and on the good of the other rather than the good of the self, for example—correlates with its possession of an inappropriately low disciplinary status and institutional power on many campuses. That is, even as some feminist theorists celebrate the location of the writing center outside the restrictions of credit-bearing classes and other academic hierarchies, other scholars using a feminist lens caution us about the ways in which the association of writing centers with "women's work"—those occupations based in caring for others—associate it too with low wages and minimal authority. Arguments in this vein include an early essay by Gary A. Olson and Evelyn Ashton-Jones, who polled faculty nationally to find that writing center directors are considered "a kind of wife" and whose important attributes are the need to be "nice," "supportive but not critical," "friendly, cooperative, and have lots of personality" and, as one respondent would have it, "provide chocolate chip cookies to writing center clients" (23). While some studies have suggested that the positions of writing center directors—and, thus, the writing centers they direct—have improved (see, for example Balester and MacDonald), more recently Melissa Nicolas has shown us how empirical data suggest ways in which the feminization narrative of the writing center continues.

While scholars have shown the writing center's connection to feminism and strengthened that connection through their arguments and analyses, other researchers have broadened the gendered gaze to ask what the feminized or feminist writing center might mean for men. That is, both local and national studies have shown that the majority of writing center tutors and users are women, as can be seen, for example, in a study by Lisa Leit and her colleagues. Liet et al., peer tutors at the University of Texas-Austin, describe a sex-based disparity of the usage of their center and then speculate that it may have to do with both the disparity in writing center staffing, which tends to be primarily women, and the social-emotional affect of the tutor–writer relationship, which, they conjecture, tends to be more comfortable for women than men. When inquiring in this vein, they follow up on a foundational article in this area, Margaret O. Tipper's "Real Men Don't Do Writing Centers." In this earlier study, Tipper talks about the challenges she faced leading a underused writing center at an all-boys' high school. Drawing on linguistic and cultural studies, she looks at the ways in which boys' culture and their cognitive development may disincline them to use the center's services, ultimately arguing that we need to look for writing center strategies that work for all writers, not just the predominant users of the center. In these multiple ways, feminism has had a wide-ranging impact on writing center ideals and on the ways we look at the roles and actions of tutors, administrators, and writers of both sexes.

Centripetal Theories Gaining Force: Recent Revisions to Our Theories

The theoretical lenses considered thus far have been important parts of writing center discussions for many decades. As the field has grown in recent years, however, it has developed an awareness of what our extant theoretical lenses do not help us see; what, in some cases, they help to obscure. The last section of this chapter, then, looks at recent developments that stand to make important contributions to writing center theory in the next several years.

Race and Ethnic Studies

Although early feminist studies of the writing center have drawn our attention to important dynamics of the tutorial environment, they were surprisingly consistent in their silence on issues related to race and ethnicity in the writing center. Recently, however, this has begun to change. In the introduction to the collection *Writing Centers and the New Racism*, editors Laura Greenfield and Karen Rowan point to "Blind: Talking About the New Racism," Victor Villanueva's keynote to the 2006 International Writing Centers Association Conference, as a hallmark moment in writing center studies' attention to issues of diversity. Greenfield and Rowan introduce their volume by pointing to two well-known works—Annie DiPardo's "'Whispers of Coming and Going': Lessons from Fannie" and Nancy Barron and Nancy Grimm's "Addressing Racial Diversity in a Writing Center: Stories and Lessons from Two Beginners"—and note that these works were, for a long time, among "only a handful of published writings that explicitly address race" (6). While they cite a few more recent works (Geller et al.; Condon; Denny, *Facing*), they nevertheless note the paucity of work in this area, a deficit

Greenfield and Rowan begins to address. They organize their collection into four sections: foundational theories, praxis essays, studies of individual centers, and stories of individuals' experiences. In many ways, this arrangement of contents seems to reflect the current scope of race and ethnicity studies in the writing center. In addition to calls to action, such as Villanueva's as well as Greenfield and Rowan's, the work published in writing center studies tend to be **praxis** oriented. Praxis, which is considered theory-in-action—or the embodiment of theory in productive work—is often associated with Paulo Friere's *Pedagogy of the Oppressed*, a work whose influence on the social justice movement in and out of academe has been immense. Praxis-oriented works at the intersection of race and writing center studies include studies of tutor training (see, for example, Suhr-Sytsma and Brown; Diab et al.); writing center leadership (see, for example, Condon; Geller et al.; Diab et al.); and individual tutors reflecting upon their own practice (see, for example, Town; V. Harris; Muñoz).

Some scholars in this area draw their theoretical frameworks from the field of Teaching English as a Second or Other Language (TESOL). TESOL is of perennial interest to writing center scholars because of the field's stated commitment to inclusion, and because of the ways in which individualized writing instruction is particularly well suited to assisting multilingual writers. In addition, putting the lines of inquiry about race and ethnicity in the writing center into conversation with TESOL scholarship is a productive marriage of theories and practices, for even as there is a substantial body of writing center scholarship describing strategies for working with multilingual writers, there have been increasing calls to interrogate our assumptions concerning English as a Second Language (ESL) students' roles in the writing center (see, for example, Ronesi; Bailey).Work from TESOL studies can help us further our own thinking about both writers and the strategies we use when working with them. We discuss the praxis of working with multilingual writers in Chapter 5 and some of the related research methodologies in Chapters 9 and 12.

Queer Theory

Another important development of recent years is the inclusion of queer theory among the theoretical lenses we use to explore the writing center. In some ways, the role of queer theory in writing center studies can be connected to that of feminism. Just as feminism helps us understand the ways in which our notion of "manly" or "womanly" is a cultural construct that is often unquestioningly accepted as "biology" or "nature" or even "normal," queer theory furthers this analysis and helps us understand that sexual orientation is likewise labeled. In his landmark article "Queering the Writing Center," Harry Denny explains why such theory is particularly well suited to better understanding writing center work:

> Writing centers are places overflowing with structuring binaries: directive/non-directive, editing/tutoring, expert/novice, teacher/student, graduate student/undergraduate, professional/peer, woman/man, "American"/ESL, advanced/basic,

faculty/administrator, administrator/secretary, faculty/lecturer, lecturer/teaching assistant, teaching assistant/tutor, white/people of color, Black/Asian, Latino/Black, straight/gay, etc. These binaries and their negotiations of which side is privileged and which is illegitimate are ubiquitous in sessions. Queer theory advances awareness of the presence and multiplicity of these binaries as means for constructing individual and collective existences as well as knowledge of the politics involved in navigating and subverting them. (41)

On the one hand, as Denny reminds us, labels permeate the writing center, such as "tutor," "client," and "faculty." But on the other hand, working individually with writers demonstrates to us just how insufficient these labels are to usefully describe an individual. One of the ways in which queer theory helps us better understand our work, then, is by drawing our attention to the ways in which such binaries are simultaneously constantly in play—in a one-to-one tutorial, for example, one might see a binary comprising a tutor and a writer—even as such binaries are inherently unstable and always under revision. Even as a tutorial comprises the "expert" tutor and the "novice" writer, the tutor is aware that he or she too is a writer, and the client-writer is aware that the tutor may lack some of the necessary knowledge to be the "expert" in the writing situation at hand. Thus, as Denny rightful argues, the instability of identity in the writing center makes it inherently queer.

In addition to helping us understand the innate hybridity of the writing center in this fashion, queer theory also helps us attend justly to the participation of the LGBTQ community in the writing center. That is, just as Leit at al. and Tipper argued that we need to attend more carefully to the ways in which the writing center encourages or discourages the participation of men, so too scholars are thinking about the need to attend more carefully to queer-identifying students. Tutor-researchers working in this vein have explored the dynamics that Denny describes. This volume, for example, includes "Composing Queers: The Subversive Potential of the Writing Center," in which Jonathan Doucette explores his identity as a tutor and writer. Doucette notes that, beyond Denny's work, little has been said about the writing center as a queer space, and even less has been said "from the perspective of tutors and students about the writing center's role in resisting, (re)producing, and/or remaining ambivalent towards queer writing pedagogies" (343, this book). He attempts to work toward filling this void both by drawing on queer and interdisciplinary scholars and by reading his own experiences into and through the theories he discusses. Scholars like Denny and Doucette are moving the writing center conversation forward in important ways by challenging us to work toward the inclusivity we espouse.

In some ways, then, recent developments in identity studies locate centripetal theories among the most important in the field, for this work helps move us away from oversimplified, monolithic understandings not only of writers as a group, but also of the individual writer. Such theories help us understand that individual writers are made up of multiple identities; none of us is just one thing, but we are many things, all at once. We say more about this in Chapter 5.

Multiliteracy Theory

Just as we understand that people are made up of many identities, so too we understand that each individual is communicating via a range of means to a variety of communities. Writing center theories of multiliteracy focus our attention on the ways in which we can support writers and other composers across a variety of communication situations. Drawing from such work as that of John Trimbur and the New London Group (a research collective composed of literacy scholars from around the world), this line of inquiry attends to the ways in which writing centers can move beyond the confines of the page and traditional academic prose to embrace digital, oral and visual media, becoming multiliteracy centers. That is, according to the New London Group, it's time we moved beyond our "carefully restricted project—restricted to formalized, monolingual, monocultural, and rule-governed forms of language" (61). Instead, they hold, to meet our learners' needs we must:

> [E]xtend the idea and scope of literacy pedagogy to account for the context of our culturally and linguistically diverse and increasingly globalized societies, for the multifarious cultures that interrelate and the plurality of texts that circulate. Second, we argue that literacy pedagogy now must account for the burgeoning variety of text forms associated with information and multimedia technologies. This includes understanding and competent control of representational forms that are becoming increasingly significant in the overall communications environment, such as visual images and their relationship to the written word—for instance, visual design in desktop publishing or the interface of visual and linguistic meaning in multimedia. (61)

By expanding our gaze to include a globalized idea of writing and broadening the scope of literacy, the New London Group encourages us to meet the current challenges facing writers and other composers. Starting with John Trimbur's 2000 call for multiliteracy centers, writing center scholars have increasingly embraced this vision (although, as can be seen in Chapter 7, the implementation of a multimodal, multiliterate vision varies widely from center to center—or even tutorial to tutorial).

A multiliteracy center can draw together many of the concerns of contemporary writing center studies that have been explored here. Such a center, as Nancy Maloney Grimm affirms, "works within the context of Global Englishes," valuing multilingualism and multidialecticism among its tutors as well as among its writers (20). Here, "effective tutors learn to shift perspective, to question their assumptions, to seek alternative viewpoints. These competencies are essential for ethical work, and they are practiced daily in a writing center, particularly in those writing centers that value difference and creativity more than they value sameness and standardization" (25). The multiliteracy center, then, embraces a theory that is flexible to the individual instance and values all the literacies writers bring to the center, both the traditionally valued academic forms and those other forms of literacy that students have acquired in and out of school. As David Sheridan describes it, the multiliteracy center responds to the increasing "proliferation of multimodal media . . . access to the tool of multi-modal production and distribution . . . [and] cultural acceptance of multimodal compositions as 'serious' and useful forms of communication" ("Introduction" 2). A tutorial that takes place in such a multiliteracy center might work on assignments from "project reports to poster design" ("Introduction" 4) and would place academic discourses alongside other, equally valued forms of communication.

In this chapter we have looked at several different ways of defining a writing center—as a site, as a method, as a product of historical events, and as an entity that can be defined by using theoretical lenses, and by limning the roles of the people who work and learn there. Each of these approaches emphasizes a different set of qualities, activities, and assumptions. The next section of the book, "A Tutor's Handbook," we look at the primary definitional activity of the writing center—tutoring—and spend considerable time looking at the opportunities and challenges offered to writers and tutors in the writing center.

For Inquiry

1. This chapter has laid out both a historical and a theoretical narrative of writing center studies. To relate theoretical developments to the world events in which these theories were created, make a timeline where you draw these two narratives together. Place on this timeline any world events that you think may have affected the ways in which people learned to write. Now, put important events from your writing center or program on this timeline. How does your center reflect or disrupt the account offered in this chapter?

2. In this chapter, we referred to a map of theories that have contributed to the writing center. Create a map, Venn diagram, or other visual representation of the theories describe in this chapter. Locate your own current tutoring philosophy on that map.

3. Working with your peers, create pedagogical statements for your writing center that are intended to explain to an external audience the ideals of your center and how you work to achieve those ideals. As each group shares its vision with the class, see if you can "map" them together to find areas of overlap and areas of difference.

4. Drawing only upon the knowledge you and your classmates currently possess and/or that you can find in your center or program or on the Web, write a quick history of your writing center or program as a site. Things to consider: When was it founded? Where is it physically located? Has it always been in that location? Who directs it now? Who directed it before that person? And before that? Who

founded it? Who staffs your program or center (e.g., undergraduate students, graduate students, professional staff)? Has it always been that way? What is your writing center's mission? Does it have a mission statement? How old is the mission statement? Has the mission changed at all during its existence? Which of these questions can you answer? What surprised you most about what you could or couldn't find? What else would you like to know and why?

5. Drawing only upon the knowledge that you and your classmates possess or can find in your center or program or on the Web, write a quick institutional history of individualized writing instruction as a method. If you work in a writing center, is there anywhere else students might turn for one-to-one assistance with their writing (e.g., an academic skills center, an office of disabilities services, an ESL program, a program or office for students from underrepresented groups, an athletic tutoring program, an honors program, a basic writing program, a foreign language lab)? How far back can you trace the history of individualized writing instruction on your campus? Has it changed at all during its existence? Which of these questions can you answer? What surprised you most about what you could or couldn't find? What else would you like to know and why?

SECTION II

A Tutor's Handbook

CHAPTER 3

Tutoring Practices

For Discussion

1. What specifically about the activity of tutoring excites you the most? What activity or activities related to tutoring do you find the most challenging?

2. Think about your favorite teacher or teachers. These can be teachers in the traditional sense of the classroom, or you can explore this term more broadly, thinking about the teachers you've had in other parts of your life—employers, for example, or coaches. What are the qualities or the actions that, in your estimation, made them great? What, if any, is the relationship between the way they taught and how you learn?

INTRODUCTION

New tutors are often eager to learn right away what they should actually *do* when they help other people with their writing. As a result, you might be starting this book here, with Section II, "A Tutor's Handbook," and this chapter on tutoring practices. Admittedly, we do not—and could not—cover all of the activities tutors engage in to help writers. This limitation in large part is due to the fact that tutors constantly adapt, revise, and invent in order to respond to the particular needs of the writers they're working with and in the contexts in which they're working. However, to give you a sense of some of what you need to consider and what's possible in your important work of helping other people with their writing, our discussion in this chapter presents fifteen of the most frequently used strategies that have been developed by generations of tutors and well-known writing center scholars and researchers from across the country and around the world.

If, however, you've already read one or more of the other sections in this book, you might be wondering what the focus on research there has to do with the emphasis on practical strategies here. In fact, practice and research are deeply connected in this book, just as they are in the writing center field and in many writing tutoring programs, for several reasons: first, research can support and improve practice by providing evidence of the effectiveness of tutoring choices, and as a result, the majority of the strategies we offer are supported by current research. Second, much of this research began with the questions that emerged for tutors and directors when they reflected on their practice, noticing, for example, that some ways of helping writers worked better than others. Third, tutors who are both practitioners and researchers have potentially the most to gain from and to contribute to their work because they can create new knowledge and use this knowledge to improve their programs and add to the field of writing center studies. You are starting this practice-research process now by reading this book, discussing it with others, and testing it against your experience as a tutor, writer, student, and person. Perhaps in contrast to other textbooks you've used, you might notice that throughout this section we connect writing tutoring practice with available research. We chose this approach to show the ways that research and practice can inform one another. The *For Inquiry* assignments that appear at the end of each chapter in this section will support your research process even more directly.

We explore this research-grounded approach to tutoring writing in Section II through five chapters that move from general to specific. In this chapter, we aim to provide you with an overview of the work you'll be doing, starting with general advice about tutoring and moving to discussions of strategies that are likely to work in many tutoring situations. In the following chapters, we continue to offer strategies but in the context of more detailed discussions of

- Different ways writers write, how tutors can help them with their processes, and the history of authorship that informs both (Chapter 4)
- How tutors' and writers' individual identities influence their working relationships (Chapter 5)
- Kinds of writing you'll work with and the contexts in which you'll work with them (Chapter 6)
- The impact of new media and online communication on writing and tutoring (Chapter 7)

To further emphasize the practice-research connection, each chapter is organized around a key concept aimed adding to your knowledge about tutoring and writing and therefore to give you helpful ways to think about your work. Here, in Chapter 3, for example, we focus on **reflection**. In the chapters that follow, we address the key concepts of writing processes and authorship, identity, genre, and rhetoric. In addition to noticing these concepts, you'll also observe that we've bolded and defined keywords that are central to the ideas explored in these chapters.

FOUNDATIONAL ADVICE FOR WRITING TUTORS

Below, we offer basic advice about tutoring, both to provide information that you can put to use immediately and to begin to sketch out the local and international communities of writing tutoring that you'll be joining.

Be Specific

Perhaps the most important piece of general advice we can offer is that *tutoring writing is always specific.* That is, tutors always work with unique individuals at certain times and in particular places. There are no "general" sessions that play out according to a set script. Although this chapter, for example, offers strategies you can use in many different sessions, the transcripts from actual sessions below show just how individuated each session can be. Even when tutors work with multiple students who are all writing the same paper for the same course, each writer, each piece of writing, and, therefore, each session is distinct from the others. Each one of these writers has an individual combination of strengths and weaknesses, not to mention an individual personality and set of preferences, and the work that she will have done (or not done) when she meets with the tutor will be different from what other writers will have completed.

Be Flexible

Although tutors are able to use similar strategies for many different writers, as a result of this specificity, the way they do so is probably at least slightly different each time. What might work for one person or one piece of writing will not necessary work for another—likewise, a strategy that might be highly effective for one tutor might fall flat for another. Because there is no "one-size-fits-all" tutoring, then, tutors must be flexible, continuously adapting their tutoring strategies to the situation at hand.

Be Ethical

If you are a student at the college or university where you tutor, you likely already work within a set of context-specific ethical obligations, a large portion of which probably have to do with your institution's definition of academic integrity. Undoubtedly the most important ethical question that writing tutors face has to do with how much—and what kind—of help they can give writers. In particular, there is a concern that tutors might help so much that the writing is no longer really the writer's—because tutors have given writers ideas for what to write or, in the worst-case scenarios, coauthored with or ghostwritten for them. These concerns are very serious, and tutors shouldn't do anything that would call into question the writer's, program's, or tutor's own reputation as academically honest.

Because the line between enough and too much help is not always clear, we will provide more detailed attention to these issues later on. But we can offer these two guidelines now:

- Be sure to operate within your institution's and program's policies in terms of how much help is "too much."
- Keep in mind the writer's learning as your ultimate goal, and work to find what will best support it so that the next time he faces a similar writing situation, he'll be able to tackle more of it on his own.

Tutors encounter other ethical concerns as well. Some have to do with not taking advantage of the authority, access to information, and interpersonal relationships you will have as a tutor. Writers and faculty need to be able to trust that tutors will not undermine writers' relationships with their instructors, for example, by questioning an assignment, comment, or grade or in some other way speaking inappropriately about the course or the instructor. Writers need to be able to trust that tutors will not discuss their personal information outside of the tutoring program—and that even in this context this discussion will be handled sensitively. Tutors should be clear about their program's policies concerning when, if, and how it is appropriate to "blow off steam" after a particularly challenging tutoring session or to otherwise portray a writer or her work in a light that could be considered less than positive.

And, of course, writers need to be able to trust that tutors will not take advantage of the interpersonal nature of the tutoring relationship, even inadvertently. The tutoring relationship can be an almost intimate connection, and sometimes interpersonal communication can be misconstrued; gratitude for a particularly productive tutorial can be taken for more personal feelings, for example. Know the policies of your program and your school that govern such relationships, including policies concerning workplace and sexual harassment.

Be Safe

Tutors should be able to trust that writers will not take advantage of the tutoring relationship either. Very occasionally, a writer, stressed out by academic work and the social and cultural difficulties inherent to college life, might act in a way that is inappropriate or even threatening to a tutor. Such incidents are rare. However, it is important to find out whether your program has a safety plan and how to reach the security office if need be. And each tutor should spend some time reflecting on strategies and program policies she might draw on to guide her response to a distraught writer or an irate faculty member.

Be Professional

Another aspect of tutoring ethics is the consistent practice of professionalism. The definition of professionalism for your institution or program will be expressed in its policies and expectations, but it's probable that, like many others, your program will expect tutors to be respectful of everyone they work with—writers, other tutors, program administrators, faculty, and staff. Your program will likely also expect that you will demonstrate such respect by arriving on time, making arrangements in advance if you need to miss a session, not going over the allotted time for your sessions, and completing paperwork by the due dates. Failing to do any of these can have a negative impact on your community, ranging from creating additional work for others to damaging the reputation of your program.

Learn

Tutors do not need to know everything about writing (or anything else) before they start. This statement might be surprising because it might seem that tutoring is about having all or most of the answers for writers. New tutors come to the job with a wealth of experience to draw on, which we try to help you make use of. But one of the great benefits of being a writing tutor is that you'll learn too. Writing center scholars and researchers as well as tutors themselves have known this for a long time. Kenneth A. Bruffee famously wrote in 1984 that "Peer tutoring made learning a two-way street, since students' work tended to improve when they got help from peer tutors and tutors learned from the students they helped and from the activity of tutoring itself" (325–26, this book). More recently, Anne Ellen Geller, Michele Eodice, Frankie Condon, Meg Carroll, and Elizabeth H. Boquet maintain that all members of a writing tutoring program—writers, tutors, and administrators alike—are co-learners, teaching and learning from each other to create "a learning culture" (49, 60–61, 68).

What tutors learn on the job, including professionalism and awareness of ethical complexities, not only helps them tutor but can have potentially long-term benefits. Several studies show that tutors not only develop as writers, mentors, and teachers but also enhance their interpersonal skills and abilities to work with others, their analytical and critical thinking skills, and their confidence (Dinitz and Kiedaisch; Hughes et al.). Although some of the tutor alumni surveyed for these studies did go on to pursue graduate degrees and careers in education and in writing, many went into a broad range of other fields, including economics, history, law, medicine, music, microbiology, political science, psychology, and social work. In their subsequent careers they have become administrators, analysts, business people, nurses, lawyers, physicians, psychologists, and researchers, among others (Hughes et al. 21–22; Dinitz and Kiedaisch 4–5). According to Sue Dinitz and Jean Kiedaisch, "Many tutors commented on how tutoring helped them in the hiring process, explaining that their writing expertise came in handy in writing resumes, cover letters, and application essays, while their tutoring experience prepared them for interviews" (4). In other words, because it can add a particular expertise to students' specific aspirations across fields and careers, serving as a writing tutor can be a rare professional and personal opportunity.

Reflect

Essential to such learning as well as to tutoring and positioning yourself as a tutor-researcher is the key concept of this chapter, **reflection**. According to Efrayim Clair, a former graduate student tutor in Yeshiva University's Wilf Campus Writing Center, tutors need to actively engage in such learning to receive the benefits of their jobs. Based on his years of tutoring, his wide reading in writing center studies, and his work in YU's graduate education program, Clair argued that reflection is essential to this active learning process. Donald Schön, an influential social scientist who studied how professionals solve problems, defines reflection in the workplace as a process of thinking about what we are doing, of "turn[ing] thought back on action and on the knowing which is implicit in action . . . sometimes even while doing it" (50). Similarly, for Clair, reflection is an active process of looking back. After a tutoring session, for instance, he asks himself, "What did I do right and wrong?" Indeed, post-sessions reflections are common in many programs, with tutors required to write reports on what happened (a practice we return to below). However, Clair emphasizes that it is important to engage in reflection *while* tutoring—what Schön calls "reflection-in-action"—perhaps by thinking to yourself, "This is what I'm doing and why it works." He also urges tutors to actively reflect on connections *among* sessions, which he sees not as independent but as building on each other.

Clair's advice that tutors proactively reflect on their work applies to how you might use this book and produce research yourself. As you put into action the strategies below, you might well find that not all of them will work in the way we suggest or even at all. Geller et al. argue that this is part of the job and quote Schön on this point: because with reflection-in-action, "practitioners sometimes make new sense of uncertain, unique or conflicted situations of practice," we should not "assume that . . . existing professional knowledge fits every case" or "that every problem has a right answer" (qtd. in Geller et al. 22). In other words, the process of testing out strategies might raise questions for you and point up gaps between extant research and experience. Why didn't it work? Why did this happen this way? Many of the tutor-researchers whose articles we anthologize in Section IV take such gaps as their starting points. We hope you will too.

AN OVERVIEW OF WRITING TUTORING SESSIONS

Keeping in mind our caveat above about all sessions being specific, Figure 3.1 (next page) is an overview of a writing tutoring session. We chose to represent this general tutoring session with a word cloud rather than a linear list of strategies because we wanted to give you a sense, from the onset, of how dynamic sessions can be, with most of the elements taking place at nearly any point, sometimes repeatedly. As this word cloud shows, there is a lot that happens in writing

Figure 3.1 Overview of a Writing Tutoring Session.

tutoring sessions, and if you're a new tutor, you might be nervous about all you'll need to learn how to do. But the good news is that this book and the co-learners in your program (including the writers you work with) will help you develop and refine your knowledge of tutoring and writing. And the even better news is that you probably already know a great deal about and have many of the skills you'll need to tutor:

- *Being a student and writer:* You already know what it's like to be a student and writer—about managing your time, figuring out assignments and course readings, getting started on papers, and staying on track until they're finished. Even if you haven't always been completely successful at these tasks, you've probably gained insights from your experiences that can help writers who are figuring what they need to do to succeed in college or graduate school.
- *Interpersonal skills:* You probably already know how to interact with others, to help put people at ease if they seem to be feeling unsure (which can happen when people share their writing with strangers and even people they know), to give them space or time if they need it, to listen. All the qualities that go into making you a friendly, helpful person will be an important skill set for this job.
- *The benefits of feedback:* If you've received feedback on your writing— perhaps from a teacher, another student, or a friend—that helped in some way, you probably already know that it can be useful to get another person's perspective on your work. One of the most beneficial services you'll provide is giving the writer a new way of seeing her writing.

You're probably already familiar with some of the other skills we discuss in this chapter because they are part of ordinary conversation. As a result, we've put these under the heading of "Tutoring Is Conversation" below. Some tutoring strategies, however, are specifically and directly about helping with writing and, as a result, you might have never (consciously) used them before. So we're putting them under the heading of "Tutoring Isn't Just Any Conversation." In addition, to specify these categories a bit more, we introduce the more technical terms **motivation** and **scaffolding** because they have proven to be useful ways to think about and define the individual practices of writing tutoring. Each writer is unique and each session is specific. As a result, each of these strategies won't work in every case, and we often point out the important exceptions. You'll want to test them out, reflect on them, and be flexible about trying something else when you or the writer sense they aren't working.

For Writing

1. Reflect in writing on a successful conversation you had that was purpose-driven and high-stakes, such as interviewing for a job, convincing an authority figure to allow you to do something, or asking someone out on a first date. After selecting a situation that you remember well, write a description of the conversation, paying particular attention to the ways in which you prepared for it and what strategies you used that enabled your success.

2. Make a list of ways you have motivated yourself to accomplish tasks that seem unappealing or challenging. Compare your list with those created by other members of your class or program and make note of any common categories of motivation.

TUTORING IS CONVERSATION

By saying that tutoring is conversation, first and foremost, we want to describe what tutors and writers actually *do* in tutoring sessions. Whether they're meeting face-to-face or online (especially in synchronous instant-message or video-chat tutoring), what they do, to borrow from Bruffee, is "converse" (331, this book). This means that, rather than one person talking or asking questions while the other person quietly listens or answers, tutors and writers often engage in a dynamic back-and-forth in which both of them talk, listen, ask, and answer. In fact, studies suggest that the more dynamic these conversations are, the more the writer is apt to learn (Thompson 419; Babcock et al. 99, 107–08; Babcock and Thonus 112). In addition, like many ordinary conversations from everyday life, tutoring sessions can include laughter, play, and fun. Tutoring is serious work, but personal connections can help us enjoy the process of completing it.

Tutoring Is Interpersonal

In addition, we use "conversation" to suggest the interpersonal aspects of tutoring, the ways in which tutoring involves relationship building. As Efrayim Clair, the tutor we quote above, puts it, we are "shifting . . . focus from 'tutoring writing' to 'tutoring people.'" In a talk he gave at the National Conference on Peer Tutoring in Writing, Brian Fallon, a former undergraduate tutor and now the director of the Writing Studio at the Fashion Institute of Technology, of the State University of New York, describes how much tutors in his writing studio value tutor–writer relationships:

> [T]hey see a correlation between successful tutoring sessions and the type of relationship they foster with a writer. For instance, Louisa . . . explained to me that "When I take the time to get to know how each tutee uniquely learns and reacts to what happens during a session, the session is far more valuable than ones where the tutee is treated just as the paper they bring with them." ("Why" 362, this book)

In particular, Fallon focuses on empathy, "seeing the world from other people's perspectives and doing your best to meet them where they are" (361, this book). Such empathy is especially important for writing tutors because writers sometimes share deeply personal matters (in their writing and conversations with tutors) and because writing is often seen as an expression of who a person is, his or her "self." This means that writers can feel vulnerable and even uncomfortable about sharing their work.

Tutoring Is Motivational

But as risky as it might be, getting personal can be essential in a writing center session. Fallon, for example, sees empathy as necessary for learning to occur. Helping a writer to see his personal stake in the expression of his words and ideas can help him care more about his writing and learn more from it. This brings us to the first of our technical terms in this chapter, **motivation**, which comes from the field of educational psychology.

You probably already know that it's more fun to write something you care about and easier to learn something new if you are invested in it. Writing tutors and writing center researchers and scholars recognize too how important it is for writers to be engaged and interested in their writing, to have a sense of ownership of and even pride in their work. Three of the articles that appear in Section IV of this book and that we discuss in this chapter address writer motivation in depth: undergraduate writing tutor-researcher Natalie DeCheck points out that "motivation is one of the greatest tools for acquiring new skills and knowledge" (337, this book); researchers Jo Mackiewicz and Isabelle Thompson describe it as "the drive to actively invest in sustained effort toward a goal" and essential for improving writing (422, this book); and these researchers, along with undergraduate tutor-researcher Molly

Wilder, suggest how particular tutoring strategies can help to encourage and enhance writer motivation (which Wilder calls "engagement").

Tutoring Is Time-Bound

The idea that tutors and writers use writing tutoring sessions to build deeply conversational, interpersonal, and motivational relationships might seem to run counter to another powerful motivator for many writers (although not always a positive one): deadlines and other limits on time. Tutors, too, experience these constraints, as with the expectations for professionalism that are time related, including arriving promptly and not going over the allotted time for sessions. As a result, Geller et al. find that tutors often feel a tension between "fungible time"—measured by the clock and the tutoring schedule, for example—and "epochal time"—measured by events such as writing or relationship building that "take as long as they take" (33–34, 39). No doubt tutors are especially prone to this tension because they are responsible for ensuring that they don't run out of time in their sessions and for setting aside time at the end so that writers can plan what they'll do next.

You might find that as you gain experience as a tutor, your sense of time in the session will shift. If you've never tutored before, the time allotted for individual sessions in your program (whether 30, 45, or 60 minutes) might seem lengthy, and, at this point, you might be wondering how you will fill it up. But when you have your first sessions, you might find that with some writers, at least, the allotted time won't be enough. Geller et al. report, however, that once tutors have gained experience, they are often able to "expand and contract a session with the skill and ease of an accordion-player in a zydeco band—15 minutes here, 40 minutes there" (41). Moreover, even though a program's schedule can imply a standard length for all sessions and promotional materials often encourage writers to make appointments well before their work is due, Geller et al. encourage us to be open to the possibility that quality sessions can occur in shorter lengths of time and very close to the deadline (35–37). For Geller et al., the question we need to ask ourselves is, "How do we savor whatever time we have?" (38). In other words, how do we remain flexible in the midst of such limits?

Interpersonal Strategies for Motivating Writers

We begin by offering eight strategies (seen in Table 3.1, next page) that are conversational (practices you are likely to have used already in ordinary talk with others), interpersonal (aimed at relationship building), and motivational (ways to engage writers).

Get Acquainted

Related to the tensions around time that we discuss above, because time in tutoring sessions is limited and because the writer has come to work on her writing (and not necessarily to build a relationship with a tutor), you might feel that you

Table 3.1 Interpersonal Strategies for Motivating Writers.

- Get acquainted
- Ask (and answer) questions
- Make statements
- Offer your perspective as a reader
- Take an interest
- Praise
- Listen
- Consider nonverbal cues

need to get down to business from the very beginning of the session and start working on the writing immediately. But keep in mind how Louisa, quoted above, says she adds value to her work with writers: "I take the time to get to know how each tutee uniquely learns and reacts to what happens during a session." Indeed, according to several studies, engaging in small talk can lead to greater satisfaction for tutors and writers, and not doing so can lead to unfulfilled expectations for both (Babcock and Thonus 81; Babcock et al. 51). Taking several minutes at the beginning as well as throughout the session to get to know the writer and for the writer to get to know you is essential to building a working relationship and getting the most out of your limited time together.

Ask (and Answer) Questions

A great way for you and the writer to get acquainted is to ask questions and to answer some yourself. As writing center researchers Isabelle Thompson and Jo Mackiewicz report, questions are "a major tutoring strategy" (62). Based on an empirical study they conducted of eleven tutoring sessions, they found that questions serve a number of functions, including allowing "tutors and students to fill in their knowledge deficits and check each other's understanding," helping "tutors (and occasionally students) to facilitate . . . dialogue and attend to students' active participation and engagement," and enabling tutors to help "students to clarify what they want to say, identify problems with what they have written, and brainstorm" (61). The tutors they studied used questions very frequently and much more often than writers. Interestingly, however, when writers worked with same tutors repeatedly, the writers tended to ask more questions than the tutors (61, 63).

Table 3.2 lists sample questions you might ask at the beginning and throughout your sessions. To give you a sense of the overall range of questions you might ask, these are very general. However, we offer more specific sample questions as we address particular tutoring situations later on. For now keep in mind that, as Thompson and Mackiewicz say, it's important "to tailor questions individually for each student" (62). As with all of the strategies we offer, you'll want to be flexible about how and when you use them.

Table 3.2 Questions to Build Your Working Relationship with the Writer.

Questions to get acquainted:
- How's it going?
- What program/school/class/year are you in?
- Where are you from?
- What's your major?
- How do you like your classes?
- Have you worked with a writing tutor before?

You might answer one or more of these questions yourself!

Questions about what the writer is working on:
- What do you want to work on?
- Was it assigned for a class? Or are you writing for some other context?
- What did you/do you want to write about?
- [*If the writer has writing*] How did you write this?
- What is the assignment?
- When is it due?

Questions about what the writer wants help with:
- How do you feel about the writing/ideas you have?
- Which parts/ideas seem to work well/do you like the best?
- What questions do you have about what you're working on?
- What do you mean by ["grammar," "flow," "following the assignment"]?
- Have I answered all of your questions? Do you have any others?

To show your interest and engage the writer, you might ask follow-up questions about any of the writer's answers that show her expertise.

Note that the majority of these questions are "open"—that is, aiming to "facilitate extensive and constructive responses" from the writer (Thompson and Mackiewicz 53)—and thus can be the most helpful as a motivational strategy. "Closed" questions, which require only short responses, include those concerned with the writer's background (program, major, hometown), when the writing is due, and whether the writing was assigned for a class. You might notice too that several of these questions acknowledge the possibility that writers might not yet have completed any writing for an assignment or will want to work on writing from contexts other than courses (such as an application for graduate school or an article for the school newspaper). Questions can help tutors and writers generate ideas and understand these contexts.

Make Statements

No tutoring strategy works for every tutoring situation, and questions are no exception. Indeed, some researchers have questioned the effectiveness of tutor questions. In an article we include in Section IV, Alicia Brazeau reports that many writers she interviewed felt "anxiety over questions and answers" in one-to-one tutoring sessions and seemed to prefer working in groups partly as a result (289; see also Wilder 535, this book). For one thing, overdoing questions might make the writer feel interrogated or frustrated, especially if the tutor responds to the writer's questions with more questions. In addition, through her presentation and analysis of a transcript of tutoring sessions, Molly Wilder demonstrates that questions aren't the only means by which to learn about the writer's work or to help her engage in the session. In one of Wilder's transcripts, the tutor, Derek, is unsure about a key term the writer, Heidi, has used in her paper, but he makes a statement about it rather than asks questions. As you read the short excerpt below, note that real tutor–writer dialogue, like any conversation, can be full of colloquialisms and fillers such as "um" and "like":

> DEREK: Um, so the first thing: terminology. I really like it when people like define their terms. Um, it struck me, though, that you didn't define gender.
>
> HEIDI: Oh, right. Good point. (537, this book)

Wilder argues that in this case a statement is more effective—and "more inviting"—than a question, speculating that had Derek asked Heidi why she hadn't defined "gender," Heidi might have felt that Derek was judging her negatively. This in turn might have hindered Heidi's ability to consider Derek's suggestion, or, probably more important, to benefit from "working out for herself why she didn't define gender and what she should change." Instead, in response to Derek's statements, Wilder explains, "Heidi offers a proposition for what her definition might be, and then herself decides to revise that definition" (538, this book). For Wilder, such involvement on Heidi's part is a sign of her engagement in the session and her motivation to work on her writing.

Offer Your Perspective as a Reader

In addition, the brief excerpt above reveals that tutors use different conversational strategies nearly simultaneously. While making his statement, Derek offered an implicit suggestion and employed a third strategy, that of articulating the details of his own perspective on the writing, complete with his own preferences ("I really like it when") and what this preference leads him to notice ("it struck me, though"). This personal response might well have reminded Heidi that her audience consisted of real, live readers, such as Derek (even though he wasn't the target audience for her paper). For some writers, especially successful ones, this isn't news. But for people new to college or who struggle with writing for whatever reason (as most of us do at one point or another), writing might feel like only words on the page or screen, not an act of communicating with someone else.

As a living, breathing audience, tutors can show writers that their writing does indeed matter. Writing center researcher Robert Brown holds that one reason writing can be alienating is that the writer is usually separated from the reader "by time and space." That is, as is typically the case for writing completed for school, the writer often composes his writing at one place and time and, somewhere else and later (sometimes much, much later), a reader responds to this work, without the writer nearby to guide this response, answer questions, or provide explanations. Tutors, holds Brown, can "compensate for [this] alienation" and restore "immediacy to written communication" (72). Even though a tutor like Derek is not the target audience and is, in Brown's words, "*a* reader, not *the* reader" (73), he can nonetheless do what early writing researcher Nancy Sommers identified as a crucial strategy for writing teachers to employ, to "dramatize the role of the reader" ("Responding" 148).

Sue Mendelsohn, another writing researcher, builds on Sommers' insight, applying it to writing center tutors. In fact, Mendelsohn sees "the job of dramatizing the presence of a reader" as the tutor's primary role, "performing for writers what a reader knows, does not know, expects, and wants to learn" through such strategies as **metacommentary** (82–83). In this context, "meta" means "after," "beyond," or "about," so one way to define "metacommentary" is as commentary about commentary, not only responding to a piece of writing but saying out loud how and why you are responding as you do. In this way, "metacommentary" is closely related to a keyword we say more about in the next chapter, **metacognition**, which, similarly, means "thinking about thinking." Both metacommentary and metacognition are acts of reflection, of considering what you are doing after or even as you are doing it. Moreover, metacommentary depends on metacognition; we need to think about our thinking in order to understand how we are reading the writer's text as well as to share this response with the writer. Mendelsohn explains it this way:

> When a consultant offers metacommentary on a writer's draft, she may, for example, read the piece aloud, pausing to describe the experiences and thoughts that arise. The consultant might say things like "I feel excited to keep reading in order to see how you're going to solve the problem you set up" or "I'm slowing down because I'm looking for cues about how this point connects to the previous paragraph." If the prose is muddled, she might explain "I'm not sure I understand that sentence, so I'm going to read it again." (82–83)

Sharing metacommentary can in turn motivate a writer because it can bring home for her the fact that a real reader is trying to understand what she wants to communicate with her writing. Even if, in the process of working with a tutor and the tutor's metacommentary, a writer discovers that her writing has not effectively communicated what she wants to say, this discovery can motivate her to keep trying, just as we often do in regular conversation.

Elsewhere in her study, Wilder examines another moment when a tutor shares her own perspective on a writer's work, offering the kind of metacommentary that Mendelsohn describes. Lidia, a tutor working with students in a psychology course, summarizes Marsha's paper and, rather than pointing out a specific problem, instead provides what Wilder calls "her personal reaction to the structure":

> LIDIA: . . . so I'm reading this and I'm like, oh wait a minute like, now you're not just talking about like general principles, all of a sudden you're talking about like your study. (543, this book)

Just as Derek did, Lidia not only presents Marsha with the perspective of a real, live reader; Lidia also enables Marsha to "see the problem for herself," in this case by helping "Marsha to see her writing through the eyes of her audience (the specific audience of Lidia)" (543, this book). Through her reflection and metacommentary on her reading, Lidia is able to demonstrate for Marsha how her writing appears to a reader.

Take an Interest

In "The Power of Common Interest for Motivating Writers: A Case Study," included in Section IV, undergraduate tutor-researcher Natalie DeCheck discusses a related aid in motivating writers: showing interest in them and their work. Based on her analysis of interviews of a writer and her tutor, DeCheck concludes that a tutor's "interest is a powerful learning tool that plays a large role in motivating a writer. It drives the writer to want to explore a subject and strive for a better understanding through research and writing" (341, this book). In the case that DeCheck analyzes, the tutor Charisse's genuine interest and curiosity in the writer Andrea's project in turn helped "to move Andrea from a focus on external pressures"—writing and researching because she had to—"to a place of intrinsic motivation"—writing and researching because she herself "was interested in the material and wanted to learn more" (336, 339, this book). Although DeCheck offers suggestions that are applicable across many writing tutoring sessions, she emphasizes the specific circumstances of this tutor–writer relationship that helped to enhance both Charisse's interest and Andrea's motivation. Both Charisse and Andrea were women of color "at a large, public research university whose students are predominantly Caucasian" and both "reported in interviews identifying with" and "liking each other from the start" (338, this book). Charisse and Andrea used these unique and uniquely productive circumstances to build their working relationship.

Praise

Related to interest but even more positive is the strategy of expressing praise about a particular part of the writing. Below is a longer excerpt of Wilder's transcript of Lidia's session with Marsha, which takes place slightly earlier than the part discussed above when Lidia offers her metacommentary on the structure of Marsha's paper. Again, this is far from a scripted, idealed tutoring session. Furthermore, both Lidia and Marsha use some of the specialized language of the field in which Marsh is working (psychology), including "studies"/"study," "Darly," and "social psych."

> LIDIA: Um, so, just as like an overview, like basically like, um, I thought like you obviously like had a lot of really good studies that you'd found, and like I think you talk about those really well.
>
> MARSHA: Okay.
>
> LIDIA (*NODDING*): So like that's like, that's really great, yeah.
>
> MARSHA: I wasn't sure, because I just, I had the model . . .
>
> *LIDIA NODS.*
>
> MARSHA: . . . I wanted to work off relying on Darly . . .
>
> LIDIA (*NODDING*): Mhmm.
>
> MARSHA: . . . and I'm like, okay, like they talk about this in my social psych textbook . . .
>
> LIDIA: Yeah.
>
> MARSHA: . . . and I don't just want to be like, you know . . .
>
> *LIDIA NODS.*
>
> MARSHA: . . . it is the studies that are supporting the concepts . . .
>
> LIDIA (*NODDING*): Yeah.
>
> MARSHA: . . . but I don't want to just like reiterate what they say.
>
> LIDIA (*NODDING*): Yeah.
>
> MARSHA: I want to like, you know, so, I . . .
>
> LIDIA: Yeah, definitely.
>
> MARSHA: I had to rewrite that a couple times.
>
> LIDIA (*NODDING*): Uh huh, yeah, so I think like, maybe like the direction you could go in then is like moving from the studies towards explaining your study . . .
>
> MARSHA (*NODDING*): Okay.
>
> LIDIA: . . . which is something that you like, you sort of like, you do like talk about in the introduction. (541–42, this book)

As Wilder observes, in this excerpt Lidia starts by pointing out where Marsha was successful. The advantage of doing so, says Wilder, is that Lidia is likely able to increase Marsha's "self-confidence, morale, and general goodwill towards the tutor and the conference" and "give a concrete example of what she is talking about, one that the student understands" (542, this book).

Lidia's praise is especially noteworthy because she doesn't go overboard. Rather than claiming that the entire paper is "really good," she focuses on one aspect—the studies that Marsha presents. As a result, Lidia's praise follows Mackiewicz and Thompson's recommendation that it be specific and focus on a writer's performance rather than a characteristic of the student herself (428, this book). Because Lidia's praise is so specific and concrete, it seems to be what Lidia genuinely feels about the writing rather than something she says to make Marsha feel good. As writing center scholars Paula Gillespie and Neal Lerner hold, "We all want praise, and the writers with whom you'll work make themselves quite vulnerable by sharing their writing with you. However, don't push it. Writers will know if you're being phony and will feel patronized" (35). Moreover, empty praise can mislead writers about how much work they have ahead of them. A crucial part of the tutor's job is to reflect the writer's work back to her accurately, which requires being specific and including both the positive and the negative.

Finally, note that at the end of this excerpt, Lidia uses her praise as an opportunity to make a suggestion. By doing so, holds Wilder, Lidia indicates that Marsha "already can and has done to some extent the suggested task, that it isn't a radical change or completely new idea, but rather builds on what [she] already knew to do" (542, this book). This move is an example of what Mackiewicz and Thompson call "statements of encouragement or optimism about [the writer's] possibilities for success" (428, this book), and is another means by which to motivate writers to continue their work.

Listen

Perhaps the most important of all the tutoring strategies on our list is listening. Surveying studies that emphasize its importance, writing center researchers Rebecca Day Babcock and Terese Thonus conclude that "It cannot be stressed enough that tutors must listen to tutees" (120). Just as probably everyone likes praise, it's likely that most people want to be heard. And by listening, a tutor creates another opportunity for the writer to engage in the session because it can demonstrate to the writer that she can literally have a say in the direction of the conversation. Even though Lidia clearly has her own ideas about what Marsha should work on, she is careful to listen to Marsha's particular concerns and to let her take center stage. By doing so Lidia can gain valuable insight into the particular issues in the paper that Marsha feels she needs to work on.

In addition, through verbal confirmations ("Yeah") and by nodding, Lidia uses the strategy of *active* listening to convey to Marsha that she has heard these concerns and to encourage her to continue explaining them. Elsewhere in her study, Wilder shows Lidia engaging in other active listening strategies, by paraphrasing and mirroring back to Marsha what both she and her paper say. Writing center scholars Leigh Ryan and Lisa Zimmerelli point out that such "paraphrasing accomplishes two purposes: It lets [the writer] know that [the tutor] has heard and understood [her], but it also serves as a way to check perceptions and correct any possible misunderstandings" (23). Mackiewicz and Thompson call such moves "giving the gift of understanding" (439, this book).

Wilder notes that at the end of the session, Marsha "volunteered a significant amount of positive feedback" about Lidia's tutoring (544, this book). While admitting that such feedback might be more the result of "Marsha's personality" than anything Lidia did, Wilder speculates that "the conference was genuinely successful from [Marsha's] point of view" (544, this book). The motivational strategies that Lidia employed seem to have paid off.

Consider Nonverbal Cues

Although Wilder's transcripts reveal a number of apparently successful tutoring strategies, what they don't show us are the tutors' and writers' nonverbal communication (besides Lidia's nodding). We don't know, for instance, how long the tutors or writers paused after they spoke or if there were any periods of silence during their conversations. Nor do we know if they used hand gestures to emphasize certain points or express uncertainty. Babcock and Thonus survey the research on nonverbal communication and report that when tutors and writers don't have the same expectations about such behaviors "as eye gaze, silence, and laughter," they can end up feeling uncomfortable (140). They recommend paying "attention to nonverbal cues and possible differences in interaction styles" (142). Another suggestion they offer is addressing these activities directly, for instance by saying to the writer something like, "I have a thing about being sure I'm getting across to you. So when you understand what I'm talking about, just say 'Umhmm' or look at me and nod your head. Otherwise, I'll think I'm not being clear, and I'll go on and on and bore us both to death" (Boudreaux qtd. in Babcock and Thonus 141). For a detailed analysis of how a tutor's hand gestures support his attempts to relate to and motivate the writer, see Thompson's award-winning article, "Scaffolding in the Writing Center: A Microanalysis of an Experienced Tutor's Verbal and Nonverbal Tutoring Strategies."

For Writing

1. Compare the list of motivational strategies you came up with earlier with those described in this section and in DeCheck's article in Section IV. Describe any similarities between the two lists and ways that you see to adapt motivational strategies, either from your life to your tutoring or vice versa.

2. Think or freewrite about the ways in which you and your friends motivate yourselves to tackle particularly unappealing or difficult tasks. When sharing this information with your peers, see if you can generalize motivational strategies from similar items in your lists.

3. How many possible specific meanings you can attribute to the following two statements?

   "My paper doesn't flow."

   "I need you to check the grammar and make sure everything sounds right."

4. Share your list with your peers and see how many potential meanings you can compile.

TUTORING IS NOT JUST ANY CONVERSATION

Although tutoring shares much with ordinary conversation, we would misrepresent this work if we did not discuss ways that tutoring writing requires strategies and skills in addition to those used in everyday talk. Undergraduate writing tutor Claire Elizabeth O'Leary points out in her article in Section IV that although "conferencing and conversation are intimately linked" (483, this book), they are not identical.

Tutoring Is Task Oriented

Summarizing research on the kinds of conversations that occur in writing tutoring sessions, O'Leary concludes that unlike most ordinary conversations, those between writers and tutors are "task oriented"—that is, "focused on one issue (the student's paper) and . . . one goal (improving the paper)" (485, this book). We saw this in the excerpts from Derek's and Lidia's sessions, with both clearly focused on helping Heidi and Marsha improve their writing.

Tutoring Is Asymmetrical

In addition, O'Leary holds, the "institutional aspect" of the tutor–writer relationship affects tutor–writer conversations as well (485, this book). The tutor, for instance, is usually specially selected, perhaps in a competitive process, is often trained and experienced in tutoring writing, and is compensated by her college or university with money or course credit. As a result and in the context of the tutoring session, the tutor is granted more authority and status than the writer, making the relationship unequal or asymmetrical. As Thompson argues, "Unlike peers, tutors and students are not equals because tutors bring knowledge and skills that students often lack to conferences" (419). To their credit, Derek and Lidia don't emphasize their institutionalized status as tutors in Wilder's transcripts, but they very likely didn't need to since Heidi and Marsha were no doubt well aware of their positions.

Tutoring Is Scaffolding

Such asymmetry can, in fact, be beneficial. As Thompson writes, "In this asymmetrical relationship, the more expert tutor is expected to support and challenge the less expert student to perform at levels higher than the student could have achieved without assistance" (419). In other words, tutors can use their authority and the asymmetry of their relationships with writers to make sessions more productive than they would have been had the tutors been on an equal footing with the writers and certainly if the writers had worked on their own. This brings us to our other key technical term in this chapter, **scaffolding**.

In teaching, scaffolding refers to a learning situation in which an older or more experienced person (a parent or writing tutor, for instance) guides another person (a child or a writer) through a particular task, by interesting her in it, breaking it down into doable but still challenging parts, supporting her through any frustrations, and "fading" near or at the completion of the task (Mackiewicz and Thompson 427, this book), just as scaffolding on a building is removed once the work has been completed. You might be familiar with other different but comparable uses of this term in writing classes, where teachers talk about the ways in which papers are scaffolded or structured. While these are two distinct uses of the term, they can be usefully compared. Just as teachers might be seen as authority figures in the classroom, so too do writers have (or should have) authority in their writing. And just as teachers use scaffolding to facilitate students' learning experiences, so too do writers structure—scaffold—their papers to guide the reader through their argument and evidence.

A crucial first step in scaffolding a writing tutoring session is figuring out where the writer is in terms of a particular skill set or knowledge base. For example, if a tutor notices that a writer's paper neglects to include the kind of scaffolding language that we mention above—such as topic sentences (opening sentences in paragraphs that announce what the paragraph is about) and transitions (which link a paragraph to the one that came before)—the tutor would probably want to first establish whether the writer can see the need for such language on his own and, if not, to explain why it would be helpful to readers and to suggest ways to rewrite the opening of one paragraph. Then, the tutor would likely want to find out if the writer can see where such sentences would be useful in other paragraphs, offering help, as needed, on one or two more, but then providing less and less help as the writer is able to spot when he needs such sentences and produce them on his own.

In their article on scaffolding (included in Section IV), Mackiewicz and Thompson offer specific examples from actual session transcripts. One such example involves a tutor's scaffolding of the writer's work in generating transitions in her writing. The tutor does this in part by laying out what the writer has already accomplished and then focusing the writer's attention on an abrupt shift from one part of the writing to the next. Notice that in the transcript below the tutor does not point to the lack of a transition but rather asks for more connection. (In this transcript, "T" stands for "Tutor" and "S" stands for "Student," and the gaps in individual lines show when their talk overlaps.)

T: . . . let's see here, [reading from draft] "This is the
      first year at school and I   cannot fit in. I felt fat and at this point in
S: uh-huh
T: my life and I felt like I could not take anything to heart. My second year,"
      Okay. Then you transition. Then you say, "My second year at private school
      I was considered a slut by other girls." So here you talk about not taking
      everything to heart, and here you're talking about another terrible story. So
      what's the connection between that? (1–2 seconds) Did you start to take it
      to heart here?
S: Yeah.

T: Okay. So what's a transition sentence that you could use?

S: Hum, that towards my second year of school   I started taking things to

T: yeah

S: heart.

T: Perfect! Yeah, write that here. That's the kind of thing to transition between those two ideas. (441, this book)

Scaffolding Is Motivational

Motivation is essential not only to the tutoring session generally but also to effective scaffolding in particular. Indeed, Mackiewicz and Thompson's article is titled "Motivational Scaffolding." As a result, all of the strategies we discuss earlier in this chapter can be helpful in scaffolding a writer's learning. For instance, note how enthusiastically the tutor praises the writer when she is able to generate a transition, praise that is appropriate, as Mackiewicz and Thompson point out, because "it responds to an identifiable accomplishment" (441, this book). In addition to praise, Mackiewicz and Thompson maintain that tutors need to know how "to recruit students' interest in writing tasks, to encourage students' persistence and effort in completing the tasks, to attend to students' motivation and active participation, and to minimize students' frustration and anxiety during the conference" (427, this book).

Scaffolding Is Ethical

Scaffolding can in turn provide a way to negotiate the ethical complications we mention above concerning "too much help." Scaffolding in tutoring writing is a powerful means by which to help writers build their writing themselves and to comply with your institution's and program's policies regarding academic integrity. To follow up on the metaphor that this term draws on, just as literal scaffolding is not the building itself, so too scaffolding in tutoring is not a substitute for the writer's thinking and writing but a support meant to be dismantled and removed. Moreover, scaffolding is a way of keeping in mind the goal of the writer's long-term learning. Too much help can be just as much of an impediment to learning as not helping enough (Johnson qtd. in Babcock et al. 112).

Scaffolding Strategies

In Table 3.3 (next page) we describe strategies that will help you scaffold your sessions, focusing in particular on what Mackiewicz and Thompson see as the crucial activities of making "the writing task manageable for each individual student without simplifying the outcome" and mutually defining the goals and agenda for the session (427, this book).

We present these strategies in the context of a tutoring setting in which the tutor would not have seen the writer's work or the assignment beforehand. However, if you tutor in a program where you read and respond to the text before you

Table 3.3 Scaffolding the Tutoring Session.

- Ask the writer what the agenda should be
- Analyze the assignment and context
- Read the writing
- Negotiate the priorities for the session
- If the writer has no writing, help him get started
- Wrap up
- Reflect

meet with the writer (such as a writing fellows or asynchronous online tutoring program), you should arrange these strategies in an order that's more appropriate for your tutoring process.

Ask the Writer What the Agenda Should Be

Scaffolding starts from the beginning of the session, when you ask the writer about what she'd like to work on. Such questions are crucial in recruiting the writer's interest in both continuing the writing process and in making best use of the session itself. Such a framing demonstrates to the writer, as Lidia did with Marsha, that she can take center stage and can literally have a say in the direction of the conversation. In addition, the writer's answers to such questions are valuable for you as a tutor, because they can show you what she might expect from the session and even how and whether she understands the assignment and what she's trying to accomplish with her writing.

However, figuring out this agenda with the writer might not be as straightforward as simply asking what he wants to work on. A good example of such complications can be found at the beginning of Wilder's transcript for Conference 2, with Lily and Wally. When Lily asks if there is "anything in particular you wanted to start off with talking about, about this paper?" Wilder reports that "Wally explains vaguely that he is confused, ending with a general question for Lily:"

> WALLY: I guess a lot of it is just kind of like, does it sort of make sense?
> LILY NODS.
> WALLY: And flow? And like . . . I don't know. (539, this book)

In this exchange, Wally does not give Lily much to go on. Gillespie and Lerner describe a similar scenario, in which the writer asks the tutor to "check my grammar." They offer advice about how to understand this request as well as about how to scaffold the discussion going forward:

> First, the request . . . doesn't necessarily mean [the writer] wants line-by-line editing or for you to proofread the work. It's often a matter of vocabulary that results in such requests. In our experience, "check my grammar" can mean a whole range of requests, from "give me feedback on structure and organization," to "react as a reader to my argument," to "help me interpret this

assignment." Many students . . . simply aren't well versed in the vocabulary of writing tutoring. However, for many, the association between correcting grammar and tutoring writing is pervasive. But as a tutor, you'll have the opportunity to teach . . . writers that language of tutoring, and what once was a grammar check can next time be a request to "tell me if my evidence supports my thesis." (119–20)

We should note that some writers really do want and need to go over their grammar, and we discuss how to do that below. Here, we focus on how to proceed when the writer describes an agenda that doesn't provide enough information about what she wants to work on or might possibly (as with "grammar check") stand in for quite different writing concerns.

One strategy is to ask follow-up questions that emphasize your curiosity and need to know, in the way that Mendelsohn's metacommentary does, such as, "Can you say more about what you mean by 'flow' or 'grammar'? Because sometimes these mean different things to different people, and I just want to make sure I'm clear." Along these lines, Lily might have asked Wally what he meant by "confused" and by "if the writing makes sense": What was he confused about? What does he think might not make sense to readers? Wally might have in turn been able to provide descriptions of his concerns so that Lily could meet him halfway and provide the "vocabulary of writing tutoring" that Gillespie and Lerner describe, thus scaffolding Wally's knowledge of writing.

But it might be that this more focused sense of what to work on won't emerge until later in the session, as you and the writer learn more about the writing and what he wants or needs to accomplish with it. For instance, after you and the writer go over the assignment for the writing as well as the writing itself, you might see that the paper needs to be five pages when the writer has written only two. In this case, producing more writing will likely move ahead of anything else on the agenda. We should say too that writing is something that the writer can do *in* the session, with your help, for instance in response to your questions. (We offer more strategies for such work in the next chapter.)

Related to what we say above about the tensions connected to time, you might find that the writing is due very soon or that the writer has brought in a piece of writing that is longer than you have time to address in your session. In such cases, you and the writer can work together to determine where to put your collective energies. For example, you might

- Ask the writer to pick out the one or two or three (depending on how much time there is) places that are giving him the most trouble and concentrate on those.
- Read the first few paragraphs or pages and comment on how the opening has set the rest up.
- Ask the writer to walk you through the organization, while you make notes in the margin or on a separate page to show the writer how you, as a reader, understand the overall structure.

In such cases, you might scaffold the writer's understanding of how to make optimal use of writing tutoring by suggesting that, for future writing, he might want to make an appointment earlier on or make multiple appointments for longer papers. (Of course, he might know this already and/or have good reasons for coming when he did. And either way, you won't want to make him feel ashamed.)

Analyze the Assignment and Context

Analyzing the assignment (if the writer is completing writing for a course) as well as the larger context for what she is working on is another opportunity for scaffolding. First of all, you need to figure out if the writer understands what it is she needs to write. A good way to determine this is to ask her to explain the assignment or context and to walk you through the instructor's written instructions (if there are any). Doing so will have the advantage of encouraging the writer's participation and giving both of you a sense of key requirements and areas where either or both of you might be unsure about what it is the writer is being asked to do—thus potentially minimizing future frustration and anxiety.

If the writer has a copy of the written instructions, either of you might read it aloud and both you and the writer can engage in metacommentary, discussing questions and ideas that come up for you as you work your way through. Geller et al. point out that this is an opportunity to share your own knowledge as a writer by reflecting on how you make your way through an assignment (80). Many writers draw on the strategies outlined in Table 3.4 (on the next page).

Sometimes writers don't have written instructions, perhaps because the instructor didn't provide them, because the writer forgot to bring them to the session, or because the writing is in response to a situation outside of a classroom, such as an application for a job, an article for the school newspaper, or work that the writer is pursuing for her own satisfaction. Again, in such cases you might draw on your own knowledge as a writer. Some writers find questions like those in Table 3.5 helpful (also on the next page), even when they have written instructions.

A final caveat: analyzing the assignment or the context will give you and the writer information about what the instructor or the audience wants the writer to do, but it won't necessarily tell you what the *writer* wants to communicate. This is where additionally scaffolding the writer's motivation, through extra encouragement and efforts to help her to make a personal connection to her work, as well as breaking the task down into manageable pieces can be especially important. Below, we discuss how to break down the task when the writer has brought in writing as well as when she has no writing yet: in both cases, starting with the assignment or context is a critical first step.

Read the Writing

As we suggest earlier in this chapter when we discussed sharing your perspective as a reader by engaging in the reflective practice of metacommentary, reading

Table 3.4 Strategies for Understanding the Assignment.

- Look for important words and phrases, especially verbs, that tell the writer what she should do with the writing, such as "analyze," "explain," "define," or "compare."
- Look for places in the assignment that specify the kinds of information or evidence the writer needs to draw on, such as personal experience, readings, field or lab work, or research.
- Look for special directions about the format of the writing and what the final product should look like: Should there be a thesis or argument? A specified structure? Headings? Citations? A particular length?
- Ask the writer about and look for information external to the assignment itself:
  - Is there a grading rubric or a list of evaluation criteria?
  - Did the instructor talk about the assignment in class, perhaps emphasizing key requirements?
  - Sometimes the syllabus offers clues: What are the goals of this course? How might writing this assignment at this point in the semester or quarter help students reach a particular goal? How might their writing help them show that they're doing so?
  - If there are important terms that you and the writer aren't clear on, you might look them up in a writing handbook or online, by searching for both "writing center" (in quotation marks to ensure that you'll get a writing center site) and the term you and the writer need help with, e.g.:
    "writing center" analyze
    Such search terms will help you locate a user-friendly yet academically focused handout.
- Once you've gone through the assignment, the writer might summarize it in her own words. This can solidify her understanding of it and is also a good way to check that she understands what she needs to do for this piece of writing.
- Remember that written instructions are writing too, sometimes composed quickly by faculty who are just as rushed as students, so some parts might be unclear, in which case the writer might need to go back to the instructor. Geller et al. suggest that tutors can help writers brainstorm the kinds of questions they might ask (80).

Table 3.5 Questions to Ask When There Is No Assignment.

- What should the writer accomplish with this writing? What should happen as a result?
- Who is the writing being written for? What is this audience's relationship with the writer and what he's writing about (e.g., sympathetic, antagonistic)?
- What kind of expectations does this audience have for what the writing is supposed to look like?
- Are there any materials online (including on your institution's website) that will give you and the writer clues about what to write? For instance, career services offices often have model application letters and résumés, and pre-med and pre-law offices usually have useful advice about personal statements.

is a surprisingly complex process, even more so if you're trying to work through the writing of someone who is sitting next to you and expects a relatively quick response. Here, we focus on how to scaffold this process so that you can proceed in a manner that will be most helpful to the writer.

There is a long tradition in writing centers of asking writers to read their papers out loud. This strategy has become a tradition for several good reasons: it requires the writer's active participation, and, if she has a strong grasp of Edited Academic English and a sense of what she's trying to accomplish with her writing, reading the work aloud can be a great way for her to see and correct any grammar mistakes, spot and reword sentences that don't yet convey what she means, or become aware of larger issues and start to think about how to address them. In addition, this technique has the advantage of being a useful takeaway for writers since it is something they can do on their own.

On the other hand, some writers don't have an intuitive understanding of English or they have learning differences or other specific challenges that make it difficult for them to spot and correct their errors. For these writers, reading their own writing aloud might lead to frustration rather than insight. Instead, for these individuals, it might be more helpful for tutors to be the ones to read the writing aloud. Such a process could encourage the writer's participation (she can listen and read along) and give her a sense of when the writing makes the reader stumble or proceed smoothly and easily. Tutors can also use such reading as an opportunity for metacommentary that narrates their journeys as a readers. However, you should be open to the possibility that the writer might need the tutor to read the writing to himself silently, perhaps while the writer reads along or writes down questions or thoughts she might have.

There's another tradition of recommending that tutors read the writer's entire piece of writing before figuring out what to focus on. This strategy can be useful because sometimes writers don't articulate their main focus or argument until they write the final paragraphs (since at this point they probably know the most about what they're writing), and, unless tutors read to the end, they might not perceive this main focus or argument. However, research also shows that it can be useful for tutors and writers to stop at points along the way to offer or to ask for feedback. Babcock and Thonus report on a reading method called **point-predict**, in which tutors stopped during the reading "to describe what the paper had accomplished thus far, and what he or she predicted would come next" (117). Mendelsohn links point-predict to Sommers' insight about dramatizing the presence of a reader, since this strategy can similarly help the writer "develop a sense of how to anticipate the reader's response" (82).

It's usually not possible to know in advance which method of reading will work best for a writer. Even if you've tutored the writer before, what works for one piece of writing might not work for another. We suggest explaining the different options and asking the writer what she thinks will work best for her. You can even try changing reading strategies during the session, perhaps starting out with reading the writing aloud or to yourself and, then, as you and the writer talk in depth about a particular part, asking the writer to read it on her own and perhaps aloud. This too can scaffold the writer's learning, supporting her as she tries a new way of looking at her work. Again, flexibility is key.

Finally, writing center scholar Toni-Lee Caposella reminds us that there is sometimes additional writing to make your way through as you read the writer's work: comments by the instructor. Here again, you can draw on your own experiences with working through such comments, and Caposella suggests asking the writer herself how she thinks the comments should be used. In addition, Caposella recommends helping the writer to understand any specialized vocabulary (such as "thesis statement"), connecting individual instructor comments to particular parts of the writing to provide the writer with specific examples, and distinguishing the major issues that will require substantial revision from the smaller matters that will require editing sentences (74–75). It's worth noting that Babcock and Thonus report on a study in which concentrating on teacher comments led tutors to lose "their focus on the students and their writing" and led the writers to become "more concerned with grammatical features than with the ideas in their own texts—even if their instructors had commented on content as well" (89). Depending on what the writer wants to focus on, you might want to make sure that addressing the instructor's comments doesn't crowd out her other priorities for the session.

Negotiate Priorities for the Session

Negotiating priorities for the session is not a separate step from the previous scaffolding strategies but one that begins when the writer tells you what she needs help with, the two of you analyze the assignment and/or context for the writing, and one or both of you read the writing. However, what we haven't discussed so far that is crucial to this ongoing negotiation process is how to decide on what exactly to work on in the writing. Because there are limits on both the amount of time you have with a writer and the number of issues you can discuss without overwhelming her with too many suggestions, it's essential to decide together on which one or two or three of the many issues you might address are the most important.

For instance, in Wilder's transcript of Lidia's conference with Marsha, Lidia chooses to focus on Marsha's introduction and her transition from her literature review rather than, say, punctuation or grammar or the wording of individual sentences. But what we don't know from the transcript is how Lidia and Marsha came to make these decisions. Why did they choose to focus on what they did? Since Wilder doesn't report on this aspect of Lidia's and Marsha's work together, we can't know for certain. But Lidia might have had in mind another longstanding tutoring tradition, that of starting with "global" over "sentence-level" issues in a piece of writing. Below, we outline this way of looking at writing as offering options that you can present to the writer and that, together, you can choose from. Again we want to encourage you to stay flexible and honor the writer's requests, even if her priorities do not align with those discussed here.

Start with Global Issues. **Global issues** have to do with the writing as a whole, its ability to communicate with the reader, and its overall effect. They are also known in the writing center field as higher-order concerns (HOCs), a term coined by Donald A. McAndrew and Thomas J. Reigstad, who define it as "central to the meaning and communication of the piece, . . . matters of thesis and focus, development, structure and organization, and voice" (42). These terms are contrasted with **sentence-level** or lower-order concerns (LOCs), which "are matters related to surface appearance, correctness, and standard rules of written English" (McAndrew and Reigstad 56). Gillespie and Lerner helpfully call these "*later-order concerns*," because while important, they are ideally addressed after the writer has sorted out the "big issues" (17).

There are good reasons why distinguishing global issues from sentence-level issues is a tradition in writing tutoring. Most significant, and as you might have already experienced when reading your friends', your classmates', or your own drafts, it's sometimes very hard to see beyond the surface appearance of a piece of writing to issues such as organization or argument, perhaps because error can be one of the first impressions that writing can make and therefore hard to ignore. Perhaps, too, we respond this way because this is how our own writing has been responded to (with spelling, grammar, and punctuation mistakes circled); as we describe in Chapter 2, there's a long history of teachers focusing primarily on errors in student writing. Consequently, getting in the habit of looking for global issues in writing can be a major benefit of tutoring, helping both you and the writer see important aspects of her work—and even your own writing—that you might not have otherwise. And this perspective can help you scaffold the writer's learning, helping her to isolate specific issues to work on and, therefore, as Mackiewicz and Thompson say, potentially "minimize [her] frustration and anxiety during the conference."

The problem with this tradition, however, is that it risks inflexibility, leading tutors to believe that they can't work on individual sentences or words or punctuation marks even though this is what the writer wants and, in some cases, is what can provide the highest potential benefit for the writing. Moreover, sometimes global and sentence-level issues are so deeply interrelated that it is difficult to separate them. For instance, you might come across a sentence in which a writer has difficulty clearly articulating an idea but that, if revised, could help readers understand the entire argument of the piece. In this case, working on sentence-level issues would benefit global ones.

Questions to Help You See Global Issues. With this important caveat in mind, we offer these questions to help you and the writer see global issues:

- What does the writer see as the main point or central idea of the writing? Does the writing match this summary?
- Based on your reading of the writing, do you understand what the main focus is, what the writing is "about"? Are you able to paraphrase it for the writer?

- Does the writing seem to address all the required aspects of the assignment and context?
- Do you understand how the piece is organized, how it moves from idea to idea? Are you able to walk the writer through the different steps through which the piece progresses? Can she do that for you?
- If the piece is supposed to have an argument or thesis, are the claims sufficiently supported by evidence, examples, details, and explanation?

If you or the writer answers any of these questions with "no," you likely have a global issue to work on. However, we suggest double-checking with the writer to make sure that you aren't missing something significant, for instance a convention from her discipline that you might not be familiar with. One way to do this is to share your perspective and offer metacommentary on the writing, to show exactly what you are understand and where you get stuck. You might also ask why the writer wrote the way she did; her explanation might help you. And if you simply misread a sentence or passage, don't worry; this happens to all of us occasionally.

You might combine these questions with other strategies for seeing global issues such as waiting until you've read all of the writing before offering feedback or using the point-predict method by stopping at different places in the reading to tell the writer what you anticipate will happen next. Indeed, Babcock and Thonus report that the point-predict method can lead to "a focus on global issues like content and organization" and seems less useful for locating sentence-level issues (117).

Strategies for Working Through Sentence-Level Issues. As we point out above, sometimes working at the sentence level is exactly what the writer and the writing need. We consider below a few strategies that will help you and the writer to do just that. You'll notice that these techniques use the same basic strategies as looking for the global issues described above.

- *Reading aloud*: For writers with a strong, intuitive grasp of English, reading aloud, specifically to make sentence-level changes, can be a very effective strategy. But you'll need to scaffold this work, beginning with finding out what the writer is able to do. For example, if you notice that the writer skips over problems as he reads aloud, you might say, "I'm seeing a couple of things that you're not, so why don't we try something else?" At that point, you might try the following suggestions.
- *More scaffolding*: As represented in Figure 3.2, Gillespie and Lerner describe a process of helping you get a better understanding of what the writer can do by helping the writer zero in on his errors.
- *Prioritize the errors*: If you have read the entire piece and notice that there are many errors throughout the writing, you'll need to figure out which

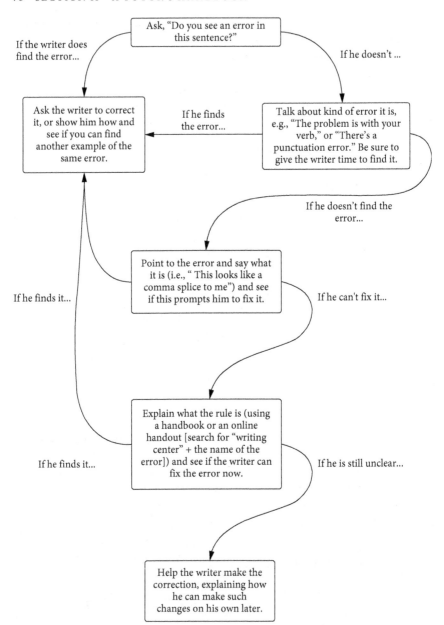

Figure 3.2 Flowchart for Scaffolding Error Correction. (Based on Gillespie and Lerner 41–42.)

ones to work on first since you might not have time to cover them all and, even if you do, covering too much ground won't scaffold the writer's learning. Here are suggestions for prioritizing errors:

1. Address errors that interfere with meaning and that prevent you from understanding what the writer is trying to say. We find that sometimes when writers talk about what they had in mind, they can clear up any problems. (And it's a good idea at these moments to have a pen in hand to write down the writer's clarification.) Sometimes, this will be a long process involving much back-and-forth between you and the writer. It is nevertheless time well spent. Clarifying ideas and sorting out appropriate vocabulary at the sentence level is a crucial part of writing.

2. Look for errors that would bother the writer's audience; find out what these might be by asking about the kinds of errors this reader (perhaps an instructor) has commented on before. Such errors include word choice, word order, and verb tenses.

3. Use Gillespie and Lerner's scaffolding strategy from the flowchart in Figure 3.2 to find patterns of error that you can comfortably address and the writer can learn to correct. You'll need to assess your own understanding of grammar and punctuation as well as work with the writer to find out what he knows. It's unlikely that you will be able to work profitably on articles or prepositions, since they are difficult even for experts to explain.

If the Writer Has No Writing, Help Him Get Started

Although working with a writer who has no draft can initially seem daunting, many tutors report that these are their favorite sessions because they get to see writers in action and help them build writing from the ground up. Generally speaking, you can draw on many of the conversational, motivational, and scaffolding skills already described in this chapter. In many cases, you'll have the assignment and in all cases you'll have a context—a reason the writer is writing. Talking about the assignment or context, while at the same time listening carefully for what the writer might be motivated to pursue, can provide useful starting points. Also helpful will be expressing your own interest, praising ideas with potential, asking "open" questions aimed at prompting the writer to flesh out these ideas (and perhaps to link them directly to the assignment or context), and paraphrasing what the writer says to confirm that you understand her (and so she herself can hear it, in a new way).

Writing can be a powerful tool during any session, whether the writer already has writing or not and whether the writer, tutor, or both write. Writing can generate new thinking, clarify ideas, raise questions, provide opportunities for experimentation, and slow the process down if the conversation is moving too quickly. And writing is all the more useful when a writer needs help getting started. You might take notes on what the writer says, or she might try freewriting or listing—writing down whatever comes to mind about the topic or about a more specific question. Perhaps under the pretense of getting a drink of water, you might leave during the session to give the writer privacy and space to do her writing. Next, you and the writer might try outlining or—because outlines don't work for everyone—in some other way representing a possible order for presenting or developing her ideas. You can find suggestions for generating ideas and writing in handbooks, online (search for "writing center" brainstorming), and in our next chapter.

Wrap Up

The end of the session is just as significant as the beginning, and is, as a result, another part of the session that you will need to be conscientious about. Just as you'll want to help the writer feel comfortable during the first few minutes about getting help from you, as the end of your time approaches, you'll want to help the writer feel good about tackling the rest of his work outside of the session. As we mention above when we address some of the tensions involved with time in tutoring writing, you will need to watch the clock to ensure that you and the writer have time to answer any final questions and map out his next steps.

Gillespie and Lerner suggest letting the writer know when there are about ten minutes left to give him a chance to raise final questions or concerns. They also recommend prompting the writer to discuss what he plans to do next with his writing (42–43). Such discussion is important because, as we address in the next chapter, some writers don't know yet how to see their writing processes in terms of doable, discrete steps, and it might not be obvious to them once they leave the session how they should get back to work. But even writers who know how to do this work will likely find it helpful to have a reminder of what they need to accomplish when they return to their project. Here too is another point when writing during the tutoring session can be extremely helpful: you might take notes on the writer's plans or you might encourage him to do so—or both.

Finally, you'll want to end the session on a friendly note, maybe with encouraging words or something else that shows you are still interested in the writer and his work, such as inviting the writer to meet with a tutor again.

Reflect

The end of the session and immediately after offer excellent opportunities for reflection that can benefit both you and the writer, as well as future writers you'll work with. As you wrap up the session, you and the writer might reflect on what you accomplished. Such reflection can help the writer feel good about his work with you and serve as a basis for his plans. In addition, it can help you formulate the knowledge that you gained from your work with this writer to apply to future sessions. As tutor Efrayim Clair points out above, it's important to reflect on what worked and didn't throughout each session and in connection with other sessions. Such reflection can greatly enhance your development as a tutor.

Table 3.6 Post-Session Reflection Questions.

- How did the appointment begin? How did you and the writer get acquainted?
- What kinds of questions did you and the writer ask? What kinds of statements did the two of you make?
- How did the two of you figure out the agenda and priorities for the session?
- How did you work through the assignment and the writing (if there was any)?
- Did you express your interest in the writer and his/her work? Did you offer your perspective on the writing? Did you listen? Did you offer praise? How? Why? Or why not?
- What did you notice about the nonverbal cues and body language of the writer? What do you think the writer might have noticed about your nonverbal cues and body language?
- Were there other ways you tried to motivate the writer or scaffold his/her learning?
- How did you and the writer wrap up the session?
- As you reflect on this session now, what stands out as interesting or surprising or noteworthy? What did you learn? What would you want to try again? What would you do differently?

To help you reflect on your sessions, we reframe the fifteen strategies we discuss in this chapter as questions for you to consider. The questions found in Table 3.6 might also offer a helpful summary of the ground we've covered so far.

In many peer writing tutoring programs, such reflection is a required part of the tutoring session, taking the form of a report that a tutor writes immediately after meeting with a writer. While session reports encourage tutors to take lessons from their work with writers, they have additional functions that are worth keeping in mind. In many programs, these reports are written not only for the tutor's benefit but to provide information for the writer's next tutor. In others, the writer and/or his instructor receive copies of the report. In still others, this year's writer might become next year's tutor, able to read the reports that tutors wrote about him in the past. In other words, because the audience for these reports isn't just the tutor herself, there is an ethical component to them. A good rule of thumb is not to write anything that you wouldn't want the writer to see. If you have serious concerns about the writer or the session, you should probably talk to your program director or administrator rather than only describing them in a report that might not be read for a while. Lastly, and touching again on the issue of timeliness, it's important to write up these reports as soon as you can after the session so that you don't forget important details. If you are as busy as the tutors we work with, it will be all too easy for other parts of your life to crowd out your memories of particular writers and assignments.

FINAL REFLECTIONS ON THIS CHAPTER

Even with all of the ground we've covered, we expect this chapter hasn't mapped out as many aspects of the tutoring session as you might like, answered all of your questions, or put all of your concerns to rest. We hope that the following chapters in this section will go a long way toward doing so. However, we would be misrepresenting tutoring if we did not acknowledge that even years of preparation won't prevent some sessions from not going very well. Experienced tutors tell us that they continue to face challenges throughout their careers and to have sessions that genuinely surprise them—perhaps because the writer or the tutor is tired or having a bad day; because neither can figure out what exactly the assignment is asking for; because the writing upsets the writer, tutor, or both, maybe due to its personal, political, or religious content; or because of a host of other reasons that are out of the writer's or tutor's control. There are so many such complications that it would difficult to cover them all here.

But we can say that it's crucial to remember in such situations that you are not alone, either in your program or in the larger writing center community. Your colleagues who have been tutoring for a while can serve as excellent resources for learning about particular challenges that they have faced and that might come up for you, and even if they did not think of effective solutions at the moment, they might be willing to share reflections on what they could have done differently. Another excellent resource from the international community is *The Writing Lab Newsletter*'s Tutor's Column, available for free in *WLN*'s online archives. Tutors, many of them undergraduates, reflect on what are sometimes very difficult tutoring situations. It's worth looking through back issues to get a sense of the range of complications that your colleagues elsewhere have dealt with, and the archives make it fairly easy to locate any relevant articles on a particular question or concern you might have. (In the search box, type in "Tutor's Column" and your topic.) Moreover, such discussions might in turn give you ways to formulate questions that you can pursue for your own writing and research.

Reflecting on the learning process of several of the tutors in his writer's studio, Brian Fallon offers remarks that make a fitting end to this chapter:

> [C]onfidence does not develop overnight, and . . . there is a process to learning how to become a confident tutor. Stephanie, a new tutor, mentioned "how important making mistakes and being in uncomfortable situations" can be for learning, and that she values "learning through experience." Being open to making a mistake is a difficult thing to do, especially when we feel there is so much at stake. Yet, this is when we have to consider the tutor as a learner. ("Why" 361, this book)

For Writing

1. If you completed the first *For Writing* prompt in this chapter, reflect on and analyze what you wrote about your successful conversation. Next, compare the qualities you attributed to your success to the tutoring strategies described in this chapter, noting any similarities or differences you see between the two experiences. Alternatively, compare your earlier description and

analysis of conversation to Kenneth A. Bruffee's description of conversation in "Peer Tutoring and the 'Conversation of Mankind,'" included in Section IV of this book. (Note: you might wish to review some of the strategies for reading theory, described on pages 211–12 of Chapter 9, before diving into Bruffee's article.)

2. Meet with someone in your program to talk about writing you've completed or writing you need to work on for any context (maybe even the writing you completed for the prompt above). Take turns trying out several of the strategies outlined in this chapter and discuss your experiences with them, both as tutor and writer. What strategies did you use that weren't described in the chapter? How did these work out? Why did you use them? If you or your partner already has experience as a tutor, discuss how (and if) these strategies work in practice. Write up your observations to share with each other and others in your program.

For Inquiry

1. With the permission of both the tutor and the writer, record a tutoring session conducted by a tutor in your writing tutoring program. Depending on the requirements of your instructor or program, you may want to review Chapter 8 for a description of the considerations related to conducting research, and you will want to consult Chapter 11, particularly pages 257–60. First transcribe the recording. Then use this data to respond to one of the questions below:

   a. Review the recording, working to identify the strategies and elements described in this chapter. What insight do these strategies give you into this tutorial element? (Hint: in reviewing the transcript, you will want to pick the element that is the most illuminating for your own practice.) You may wish to refer to Molly Wilder's "A Quest for Student Engagement: A Linguistic Analysis of Writing Conference Discourse" in Section IV for one model of how to approach such an analysis. Jo Mackiewicz and Isabelle Thompson offer another model to refer to (also in Section IV).

   b. In "It's Not What You Say, But How You Say It (And To Whom)," tutor-researcher Claire Elizabeth O'Leary concludes that "The results of my qualitative analysis suggest that gender performance by students significantly affects a writing fellow's conferencing style" (494, this book). First read O'Leary's article (included in Section IV) and then review your tutorial transcript. Finally, write an essay in which you explain the ways in which the tutorial you recorded confirms or refutes O'Leary's assertion.

2. We've covered a lot of ground very quickly in this chapter. You will find, as you progress through your tutoring career, that this is information that tutors continuously relearn and/or learn more deeply. To facilitate this process for

yourself and your community, select one portion of this chapter and read further on the topic. You might start with the relevant resources cited in this chapter, and/or you may wish to review the research strategies discussed in Chapter 1, specifically pages 6–12. Once you have deepened your knowledge through your reading, create for your community an artifact whose purpose is to increase the viewer's/reader's understanding of the concept. Depending on your context, interests, and expertise, this artifact might be an article for a tutors' newsletter, a poster for a tutor lounge, a presentation for a tutor meeting, or a web page whose link is shared with your community.

CHAPTER 4

Authoring Processes

For Discussion

1. Has anyone ever told you that you are a good writer? If so, freewrite about the situation in which you received this praise, focusing on how the term "good writer" was either implicitly or explicitly defined.

2. Create a visual depiction of your process of completing academic writing. Share your depiction with your classmates or other tutors in your program and look for ways in which your writing processes are similar or different.

3. Without consulting any sources, discuss or write about how you define (a) originality in thought, (b) originality in academic writing, and (c) plagiarism. Are there any parts of these definitions in which you and your classmates or fellow tutors disagree? Quickly review your institution's plagiarism or academic integrity policy. Does it resolve any conflicts or confusions that occur among these definitions?

INTRODUCTION

In the previous chapter, we focus on what tutors do and different strategies they can use to help writers. Here, we shift to what writers do, the activities they engage in to produce their work as well as how these activities are understood within U.S. academic culture—what are known as **writing processes** and **authorship**, the two key concepts of this chapter. But since tutors are writers too, much of what we say here might well apply to you and your writing. Indeed, you likely have firsthand knowledge of and experience with the following that you can draw on to help writers with their authoring processes:

- *Getting started on a piece of writing—and keeping going:* You might have tricks or rituals or habits that help you. You might know what it's like to struggle with this process, maybe especially when you're working on something that you don't want to do, but perhaps too with writing that's important to you and that you care about.

- *Reading:* You probably have substantial experience as a reader of both your own writing and texts by others, including reading that you need to draw on for assignments, which is very common in academic settings. You might even have a few strategies for ensuring that you read successfully.
- *Citing sources and avoiding plagiarism:* Related, you probably have experience incorporating the words and ideas of others into your own writing, giving credit where appropriate. Because using sources is a complicated task, you might have had experience engaging in a writing activity that could be considered plagiarism.

This chapter will help you build on all of this knowledge and experience. But one of the aspects of tutoring that makes it so interesting and such a rich opportunity to learn is that it's never simply a matter of convincing other people to do what you do. Each writer is unique and has different ways of learning, different strengths and areas to improve, different preferences and personalities, and different experiences with writing and school. What you do as a writer might not always be useful to the writers you tutor. They, in turn, might go about writing in very different ways from the way you do, and these ways might be effective for them even if they wouldn't be for you. So, again, flexibility is key: just as there is no one-size-fits-all tutoring, there's no one way to write.

This chapter will help you to further increase your flexibility as a tutor by developing your understanding of

- Some of the different ways people write—their writing processes—including strategies you can share with writers and use yourself as a tutor and a writer
- How these processes are part of a long history of ideas about writing and writers—a history known as authorship—that continues to influence how writing is understood
- How this history informs many ideas about citing sources and plagiarism—and how you can help writers negotiate these complexities
- How this history has influenced tutoring programs and what this influence might mean for your tutoring practices

---

For Writing

Think about two radically different writing occasions from your recent life, such as emailing or texting a friend and writing an essay for a class. Write a brief description of the ways in which you approached each of these instances and compare the processes you used to create these texts.

WRITING PROCESSES

"The" Writing Process

One of the more traditional ways that teachers and scholars have discussed how people complete a piece of writing (or how they *should* complete it) is in terms of "the" writing process—a distinct set of stages that proceed in the same order no matter who the writer is or what she is working on:

- **Stage 1: *Planning*:** This initial stage, often called "prewriting," includes figuring out what to write about, perhaps by drawing on previous experiences or readings. It can include coming up with a thesis and/or argument, organizing the order in which different parts are presented as well as understanding the purpose (what the writing should achieve) and audience (who the writing is for).
- **Stage 2: *Drafting*:** This second stage likely includes the first real writing on the topic, in which a writer might create and follow an outline and try to address the requirements of the particular assignment or other expectations.
- **Stage 3: *Revising*:** This stage involves altering the draft, from rewriting sentences to moving paragraphs around to deleting whole pages and writing new ones. Such changes might attempt to match the draft to the purpose/thesis/argument and what the audience will need in order to understand the ideas.
- **Stage 4: *Editing/Proofreading*:** This final stage aims to make sure the language is as clear as it can be and the style and tone match the writer's intention (known as editing) and to correct any mistakes with grammar, punctuation, or word choice, for instance (proofreading).

Many writing textbooks and teachers continue to present writing this way, for valid reasons. Linda Flower, an early researcher of the cognitive aspects of composing processes, points out that writing is a complex mental activity that can "easily overload the capacity of our working memory" (36). A linear model of how people write is helpful because with it writers can avoid cognitive overload by engaging in different cognitive tasks one at a time rather than attempting to complete them all at once. For someone not yet aware that writing involves many different activities, this process—with a distinct beginning, middle, and end—can be a great place to start. You might notice that distinguishing global issues from sentence-level issues, as we do in Chapter 3, closely resembles this linear writing process. In both cases, writers and tutors deal with the "higher-order concerns" before addressing the "lower-" or "later-order" ones. And in both cases, these can be useful ways of scaffolding, of breaking down into doable steps the many activities involved with writing and tutoring writing.

Writing Processes

In the 1970s and early 1980s, researchers, including Flower, began to look closely at what writers (such as professional writers and students) actually *do* when they write. These researchers gained even more insight when they asked the writers they studied to engage in a reflective process somewhat similar to metacommentary, in which writers say out loud (usually into a tape-recorder) as much as they can about everything they are thinking while writing. As a result of these "**think-aloud" protocols**, researchers discovered that instead of one uniform writing process, there are many, because, as we discuss in more detail below:

- Writing processes aren't (necessarily) linear
- Writing processes can be recursive
- Writers make meaning *as* they write
- Writing processes can involve many activities
- Writing process activities can take time to learn

Writing Processes Aren't (Necessarily) Linear

As writers move from coming up with an idea to making final touches, they don't always follow the orderly sequence of steps of "the" writing process. For instance, here's part of undergraduate writing tutor Benjy Bloch's self-portrait as a writer, in which he addresses how the beginning of his process does not follow a plan-then-draft trajectory:

> When I am in paper producing mode, I sit down at my desk, convince myself that I am not leaving for the next two or three hours, and then I write. I do not do much planning; I eschew outlines for the most part and I spurn carefully thought-out introductions. I feel that if I just get all my thoughts down on paper, even if they are incoherent and disorganized, then I am on my way to a successful paper. In essence, I am engaging in a more formalized method of pre-writing.

Instead of planning *before* writing, a writer like Bloch might start with drafting *in order to* plan and then move through a different series of stages:

- *Drafting-as-Planning:* Getting ideas on paper.
- *Revision:* After taking a break of several days, Bloch says that he returns to look "with a fresh set of eyes and a critical mindset, almost as if I was a reader and critic instead of the writer."
- *Editing-while-Revising:* As Bloch says:

    > Some writers may decide to leave the editing for the last step, only choosing to focus on grammar, word choice, and syntax after the ideas are expressed clearly and the thesis is fully supported. I do not choose this path. I edit as I read for content, fixing commas and choosing better words as I decide that I need to expand on a certain point. I think this strategy emanates from my strong feeling that correct comma placement and proper word choice help clarify the content of an essay just as much as adding a personal anecdote does.

- *Final Edits*, perhaps after another long break.

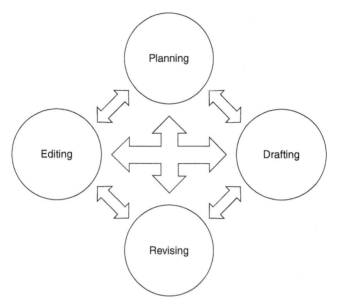

Figure 4.1 Writing Processes as Recursive.

Writing Processes Can Be Recursive

Rather than progressing sequentially from beginning to end, writing processes can repeat stages. Such repetition is what writing process researcher Nancy Sommers calls "a **recursive** process—a process with significant recurring activities" ("Revision" 386). Sondra Perl, another researcher in this area, further explains that "recursiveness in writing implies that there is a forward-moving action that exists by virtue of backward-moving action" ("Understanding" 364). As Figure 4.1 illustrates, it can be helpful to visualize recursive writing processes in terms of these possible back-and-forth movements.

In addition, Perl found that different writers repeat different activities, depending on what they are working on. For example, the most frequently recurring activity was "rereading little bits of discourse." But she studied some writers who reread "after every few phrases," others "after every sentence," and most commonly "after a 'chunk' of information has been written" ("Understanding" 364). Recursiveness, then, is a highly idiosyncratic repetition of various activities in order to move forward with the writing.

Writers Make Meaning as They Write

The discovery of recursiveness in writing processes helped writing researchers to see that, rather than figuring out all of their ideas beforehand, many writers generate ideas *as* they write—because the writing itself helps them do so. That is, writers use writing not just to represent or discover what they know but also to create this knowledge. As Flower and her co-researcher John Hayes put it, "writers don't *find* meanings, they *make* them" (21). In this way, writing is **epistemic** or knowledge producing. Here is how Bloch described this aspect of his process:

> As I write, I seem to discover new angles and fresh ideas that I would never have thought about had I not been engaged in the writing process. My writing stimulates my thinking, as I begin to automatically challenge assertions that I craft into sentences. Sometimes, I will reach the end of my time limit, and I will take a peek at the introduction and realize that I ended up in a completely different place than I thought I would. I certainly have no clear picture of the stance I will take at the outset of my writing process. Whether I need to completely revise my original introduction and thesis or simply tweak it to reflect the rest of the paper needs to be taken on a case-by-case basis, I know that I must return to the beginning and engage in some revision at least.

The epistemic nature of writing explains why, for some writers, trying to come up with a thesis and outline before starting to write can be very hard and even counterproductive. Sometimes writers cannot know what they want or need to write until they have already started or even completed the writing. In some cases, it will not make sense to try to commit to a thesis, main argument, or organization until the writer's thoughts are drafted.

Writing Processes Can Involve Many Activities

Also complicating the more orderly, linear view of "the" writing process is revision. According to Sommers, revision involves not one but four distinct "**revision operations**"—"deletion, substitution, addition, and reordering"—that happen at four different levels—"word, phrase, sentence, theme (the extended statement of one idea)" ("Revision" 380). In addition, Perl charted aspects of writers' processes that don't involve actual writing, such as the seemingly random train of thought that one writer described this way: "My mind leaps from the task at hand to what I need at the vegetable stand for tonight's soup to the threatening rain outside to ideas voiced in my writing group this morning, but in between 'distraction' I hear myself trying out words I might use" ("Understanding" 363). In addition, Perl observed student writers commenting on and interpreting the topic "to get a 'handle'" on it, talking about tentative ideas without committing themselves to them, engaging in reading related to the topic, and being silent ("Composing" 320–21). Perl found that during such silence writers seemed to be "waiting, paying attention to what is still vague and unclear. They are looking to their felt experience, and waiting for an image, a word, or a phrase to emerge that captures the sense they embody" ("Understanding" 365). Writing processes are complicated procedures that involve a wide range of activities, some of which seem to have very little to do with putting words on paper or on the screen.

Writing Process Activities Take Time to Learn

Based on their research, Sommers, Flower and Hayes, and Perl all concluded that less experienced or successful writers sometimes do not take advantage of the full range of writing activities available to them or try to make use of some at less than optimal points in their processes. Sommers, for example, discovered that experienced professional writers, who employed all of the "revision operations" that she identified, revised more deeply and more successfully than first-year college students. Similarly, Flower and Hayes found that the successful writers they studied considered more of the "rhetorical situation" or context of their writing early on. That is, rather than focusing on only the assignment and the requirements for the final text (as the less successful writers did), these writers imagined their audience, their own goals and "how they wanted to affect the reader," as well as their "personas" or how they came across in their writing (24–29). In the first study to examine the think-aloud protocols of students who struggled with their writing, Perl described the difficulties that Tony, a freshman with a multilingual background and a nontraditional entry into college, faced as a result of editing what was for him too early in his process: "From the moment Tony began writing, he indicated a concern for correct form that actually inhibited the development of ideas. In none of the writing sessions did he ever write more than two sentences before he began to edit." This in turn "interrupted the composing rhythm he had just initiated" ("Composing" 324). Although editing-while-writing can work for some writers, such as Bloch, for others, like Tony, it is a counterproductive process.

The good news about these insights about writing processes is that they show us that rather than a talent that we either are or are not born with, writing involves a set of activities that can often be learned. This is where you as a tutor can play a crucial role.

WRITING TUTORS AND WRITING PROCESSES

Being knowledgeable about writing processes has advantages for both tutors and writers (not to mention for tutors *as* writers). For example, when you tutor, you might find that some writers will bring in what will seem to be very rough or weak writing. Maybe it will be hard to tell what the focus or main idea is; maybe you won't be able to follow the flow or organization of ideas; maybe you won't see clear connections among the overall argument, individual claims, and the evidence; maybe some of the sentences won't make sense. Finding out about the writer's process of completing this work can give you a way to understand why it looks the way it does. Does this writing represent the best effort of someone who does not have much experience as a writer? Or is he usually a strong writer, but writing at 3 o'clock in the morning, he ran out of time and energy? Or could it be that the assignment asks for a kind of writing that is new to him and therefore presented additional opportunities for cognitive overload? Or is it possible that this writer prefers to share early drafts with readers in order to talk through his ideas and figure out what to do next?

In any of these cases, the writing might look the way it does because the writer planned as he drafted, using the writing to flesh out his ideas as he thought of them—in the way that Bloch describes. As a result, rather than an attempt to communicate with a reader or present a cohesive argument, the writing might be a history of the development of the writer's thinking about the topic (essentially, "first I thought this, then this, and then this . . ."). Flower calls this "Writer-Based" (as opposed to "Reader-Based") prose. But we should note that the writer might not realize that he's given you "Writer-Based" prose, so part of your job as tutor will be to show him where exactly he'll need to translate this work into something that communicates effectively to other people.

Below, we offer strategies for having these conversations with writers:

- Ask about the writer's process
- Encourage reflection and metacognition
- Remember that writers' processes are unique
- Suggest specific writing process strategies for specific writing issues
- Be aware of writing process strategies for specific tutoring situations

Ask About the Writer's Processes

To find out how the writer produced his writing, you might ask one of the questions that we mention in the previous chapter: "How did you write this?" And you might ask follow-up questions, such as, "How did you start? Did you do any planning, like brainstorming or outlining? Then what did you do? Is this similar to what you usually do?" In addition, you might share stories about your own writing processes to get the writer thinking along these lines, because reflecting on how we write isn't something most people do every day. The advantage of such a discussion for you as a tutor is that you'll have more information to help set the priorities for the session and to scaffold the session so the writer can learn more about his writing.

Encourage Reflection and Metacognition

Writers too can benefit from reflecting on their processes. For one thing, thinking back on how we've written something can help us become aware of what we do and decide whether there are changes we might need or want to make to our writing processes. A particular aspect of such reflection is **metacognition**, which you might recall from our discussion of **metacommentary** in the previous chapter. Such thinking about thinking can help writers achieve what writing center scholars Paula Gillespie and Neal Lerner see as a crucial "goal for any writer"— "to control his or her own process and to develop flexibility for approaching any writing task" (19, 13). Tutors can play a crucial role in helping writers gain this "metacognitive control" because they can interrupt writers' usual ways of thinking about their writing and encourage them to try new strategies or refine old ones (Gillespie and Lerner 19, 14).

Remember that Writers' Processes Are Unique

Gillespie and Lerner recommend too that tutors proceed with caution when suggesting new strategies because writing processes are "extremely idiosyncratic": what *you* do as a writer will not necessarily work for everyone else (14). They suggest instead that tutors try to "increase writers' options, teaching them what strategies are available, how to use those strategies, and the most appropriate time to apply any given strategy" (20). In this way, tutors can scaffold writers' writing processes.

Suggest Specific Writing Process Strategies for Specific Writing Issues

We offer the following strategies to address specific kinds of writing issues, but you might find that they will be helpful for many writers (including yourself).

Writers Who Worry Too Soon About Sentence-Level Issues

If you tutor a writer like Tony, who is so concerned about correcting grammar that he cannot produce much writing, you might encourage him to try the following:

- *Freewriting or listing:* He might try writing about or listing whatever comes to mind, without worrying about mistakes and without stopping, perhaps for a predetermined amount of time—say, five minutes. To help him avoid rereading (and correcting) as he writes, he might turn off or cover up his computer monitor. In other words, he can purposely produce "Writer-Based" prose—and take advantage of the freedom it offers "to generate a breadth of information and a variety of alternative relationships before locking himself . . . into a premature formulation" (Flower 36).
- *Talking through his ideas and taking notes:* If the writer isn't comfortable engaging in writing during your session, you might suggest that the two of you talk through his ideas as he or you take notes, maybe in the form of a list or perhaps a more visual rendering, such as a map or a chart of some kind. This too will offer both freedom and focus, since a reader (you) will be there to ask questions about anything that you don't understand or that seems worth pursuing.

These techniques wouldn't help Tony correct his errors, but they might help a writer with similar concerns put his ideas in writing so that he can deal with grammar and punctuation later, as a separate activity. We talk about this activity in more detail in the next chapter, but meanwhile what we say in Chapter 3 about working on sentence-level issues can help.

Writers Who Are Stuck

If the writer you're working with is stuck in some way—perhaps because she can't come up with additional ideas or isn't motivated by the assignment—you might keep in mind Flower and Hayes's observation that the more successful writers they studied were able to think beyond the topic and the length requirement of the assignment to consider the audience and how they wanted to present themselves in the writing. Talking through ideas with a tutor can be useful since, again, it can remind writers that there is an audience for their writing. You might also suggest these techniques:

- *Reading related material*, especially material that the audience might be familiar with, can clarify who these readers are, what their expectations might be, and how the writer might meet these expectations. Suggest that the writer take notes on his own thinking about the reading, because reading can also be a great way to generate ideas.
- *Drawing a picture of the audience, the writer, and their relationship*. When writers try to represent, in media other than writing (such as drawing or even talking), whom it is they're trying to reach and how they want to present themselves to their readers, they can sometimes gain a new perspective on the draft. We say more about other multimodal ways of approaching both writing and tutoring in the next chapter.

Writers Who Don't Know How to Revise

Writers like the first-year students in Sommers' study whose work would benefit from revision but who are not sure how to go about it might find the following strategies helpful:

- *Glossing or reverse outlining:* This process can be useful after the draft has been written, to give a writer (and a tutor) a quick overview of how the different parts are arranged so possible changes to the organization are easier to see. The writer can produce a brief summary of each paragraph in the margins ("glossing"). Or he can write out a new outline on a separate sheet (called "reverse"). If summarizing is difficult, this might mean that there are too many ideas in one section or that the writer needs to make connections among ideas.
- *Moving parts around:* As you and the writer look at the glossing or reverse outline, is the movement from one part to the next clear? If not, the writer might try literally cutting up a hard copy of the draft and arranging the different pieces in a different order, generating new transitions between the different parts.
- *Expanding on "code words or loaded expressions":* Flower says such language is a characteristic of Writer-Based prose and can make useful starting points if writers need to generate more writing. Flower asked writers to look for "expressions that might convey only a general or vague meaning to a reader" but that for the writer indicate "a large body of facts, experiences, or ideas." Then she asked these writers to pull out the "buried connections" and translate those "into a communicable idea" (32).

Be Aware of Writing Process Strategies for Specific Tutoring Situations

There are many tutoring situations in which it will be appropriate to talk with writers about their writing processes, and in each you'll want to tailor your suggestions to the individual writer's needs and motivation at the moment. Three that might require specialized tailoring on your part are

- Tutoring coauthors on one writing project
- Supporting "blocked" writers
- Helping writers with reading

Tutoring Coauthors

Some writers work together, collaboratively, on one writing project. You can get a good sense of what tutoring coauthors might entail by reading the article we've included in Section IV by undergraduate researchers Ruth Johnson, Beth Clark, and Mario Burton (who themselves coauthored their piece). Although they are ultimately less concerned with the collaborative nature of these projects than other issues, their transcript excerpts suggest that much of what tutors do with coauthors is similar to their work with individual writers: the tutor asks about the project, finds out what the writers want to work on, and offers suggestions and her perspective as a reader. However, along with needing to motivate, scaffold, and be flexible about the learning of more than one person, one key difference between tutoring individual writers and coauthors is that the coauthors might well need strategies for collaborating.

In their guides to collaborative writing, Rebecca Ingalls and Joanna Wolfe offer suggestions that you might offer to coauthors, depending on where they are in the process when you meet with them. Both recommend that before they start, coauthors should give thought to how they will work together. This reflection can include taking stock of prior experience with collaboration, structuring how the process will proceed, assigning roles, scheduling tasks, articulating group and personal goals, and understanding how to address disagreements productively. Ingalls suggests that coauthors draw up a "group contract" that "lays out the collective goals and ground rules" that ensure that everyone is on the same page in terms of the assignment, "what 'good communication' looks like," deadlines, ethics and academic integrity, and what "quality" and "success" mean for all participants (129). Along with offering more detailed guidelines for planning and project management, Wolfe usefully attends to ways coauthors can offer feedback to each other and how they might operationalize their revision processes through several technology options (59–79). By the time you meet with a group of writers, they might be well past the point of planning how they will work together, but it might still be useful to check in on how each member understands the project, the division of labor, and what will indicate to them all that the project is complete. Be sure to find out from your director or program administrator whether all group members need to be present for a tutoring session.

Tutoring "Blocked" Writers

More than being temporarily stuck on a specific piece of writing at a specific time, the term "writer's block" is most accurately used to describe writers who find it difficult, if not impossible, to complete any writing in any situation. Mike Rose, who studied blocked student writers in the 1970s and early 1980s, found that they used strategies and had "rules" about writing that hindered their processes (390), such as developing an outline that couldn't be changed or trying to finalize the first paragraph before anything else could be written. These insights confirm Perl's observation that writers who stick too closely to the linear model "find themselves easily frustrated when what they write does not immediately correspond to what they planned or when what they produced leaves them with little sense of accomplishment" ("Understanding" 368). In addition to studying blocked student writers, Rose looked at the processes of productive writers and found that they "also utilized rules, but they were less rigid ones, and thus more appropriate to a complex process like writing" (390). One of these "unblocked" writers, Susan, told Rose, "'If my original idea won't work, then I need to proceed differently'" (397).

To help a writer who is blocked, Rose recommends having the kinds of reflective discussions about writing processes that we suggest above as well as talking with her about her history as a writer and her beliefs about writing, particularly any "rules" she might follow and how she defines "'good' writing" (400). Rose says that this discussion "often reveals the rigid rule or the inflexible plan that may lie at the base of the student's writing problem" (400). But although this strategy helped most of the blocked writers he studied, it did not work with all. Once again, flexibility is key.

Helping Writers with Reading

Although helping someone with reading might not, initially, seem to be the job of a writing tutor, research has shown that writing and reading are deeply connected. As we mention above, reading is a significant aspect of many writers' composing processes since they read their own writing to produce and revise drafts. Moreover, in academic settings, writing assignments often start with reading—including the instructor's written instructions, the text or texts writers must respond to, and prior research to review and cite. There is also a strongly held belief in popular as well as academic cultures that a crucial way for people to learn how to write is by reading.

Yet as reading and writing researcher Michael Bunn has recently demonstrated, these reading–writing connections aren't always clear to college students (502). And tutors in our writing centers have been equally perplexed by reading, wondering what to do when writers have come to their sessions wanting to work on writing assignments for which they haven't completed the required reading or don't understand what they've read. We've found that tutors can help writers with reading when they are able to reflect on and share strategies from their own knowledge and experience as readers.

Bunn points out that one aspect of academic reading that can be especially confusing for inexperienced college readers is understanding the purpose of the reading and why they are doing it in the first place. Bunn offers two basic possibilities: (1) The instructor assigned the reading to provide information or content, such as historical facts or plot points, that students should in turn analyze or otherwise incorporate into their writing; (2) The reading is supposed to provide an example or model of a certain kind or form of writing, with particular structures, moves, and ways of presenting information that students comment on or should use in their own work (505–07). Table 4.1 offers questions that might be useful to tutors and writers in each situation.

Table 4.1 Heuristic for Reading for Content and/or Form.

Pre-reading questions related to content or form: These questions are especially helpful before reading, but they can be useful during and after as well.

- Who is the author of the reading and what do you know about her/him?
- Where and how was the reading published—in a book, online, in a formal or informal context?
- What can you guess about the reading from prominent aspects of the text, such as the title, the opening paragraphs, headings, bulleted lists, and final paragraphs?
- Based on what you know so far, what can you assume about the intended audience of the reading? That is, was it written for students? For scholars? For a general readers? Someone else?

Strategies related to reading for content:

- Read the whole first, relatively quickly, to get a sense of the larger argument or main idea or focus (which, in academic writing, might well be summed up at the end).
- Look for and highlight or underline what seem to be important words and phrases, reflecting on what it is about these words and phrases that indicates that they are important. If there are any that you don't understand, look them up.
- Gloss the text, writing brief summaries of the meaning of each paragraph in the margins as well as asking questions and making connections (for instance, drawing arrows) between different parts.
- On a separate sheet, write out an outline of the whole. How does this help you to understand the content?
- On a separate sheet, write out a metacommentary on the whole or specific parts, freewriting to articulate your response. Which aspects of the reading did you understand clearly? Which parts do you still have questions about?

Strategies for reading for form:

- Use the "point-predict" method to stop at what seem to be important parts. What will or should happen next? What in the text tells you this is so? Is this what happens next? How do you know?
- Gloss the text, writing brief summaries of and asking questions about what the author of the reading is doing in different parts. Make connections (for instance, draw arrows) between different parts as well.
- On a separate sheet, write out an outline of the whole. How does this help you to understand the form?
- On a separate sheet, write out a metacommentary on the whole or specific parts, freewriting to articulate your response. Which places had the most/least impact on you?

Perhaps not surprisingly, since a substantial portion of the work tutors do involves reading, you might notice that many of these strategies are similar to the tutoring strategies we offer in Chapter 3 as well as writing processes earlier in this chapter. In fact, much of what you know about writing processes can be useful in helping writers with reading. Reading researchers Robert J. Tierney and P. David Pearson argue that both reading and writing are "processes of meaning construction. Both are acts of composing" (568). In other words, as we read, we are not simply taking in the writer's meaning; as we build our understanding of the text—one that shifts as we proceed through it—we help to create this meaning ourselves. As with helping writers with their writing processes, our aim as tutors is similarly, as Gillespie and Lerner say, to help writers reflect on and develop metacognition of how they read and, in turn, gain "control and flexibility" (107).

You will find further discussion of reading especially difficult texts in Chapter 9. Often such challenges arise when we have to position ourselves in an audience role we have not previously occupied. Thus, a writer first reading scholarship in her major, first encountering a theoretical text, or first wrestling with any other unfamiliar kind of text might need to highlight words, gloss passages, and paraphrase sections to better understand the ways in which knowledge is created for this audience.

For Writing

1. Many people would argue that there are Authors and then there are student writers. What images does each of these terms conjure up for you? Write a description (or draw a picture) of these images and contrast the activities represented in them.

2. What are your school's policies about and definition of plagiarism? How do they compare to policies and definitions from other institutions and organizations? How would you paraphrase them (in your own words) and explain them to another student?

3. Complete one or both of these assignments collaboratively, with one or more coauthors. Reflect together—or separately—on how doing this work with others changed, added to, and complicated your writing processes and your ideas of authorship and even of plagiarism.

AUTHORING

Over the past forty years, writing process research has proved useful to writing tutors. However, because of the particular research questions and methodologies writing process scholars used, such research tended to focus on individual writers without consideration of the external factors that might have influenced how they wrote—including, as we address in the next two chapters, linguistic, cultural, economic, and educational backgrounds as well as the expectations of the academic fields in which they were writing. What can also influence writers, as we discuss in the rest of this chapter, are the beliefs about writing found in academic contexts. What might have particular influence on the writers you work with are beliefs about student writers, who, for a long time, were not considered to be writers at all (Grobman W179). In an article published in the journal *Young Scholars in Writing*, undergraduate researchers Heather Bastian and Lindsay Harkness trace this history and argue that "Students have often been represented as 'others' who are lacking various skills" (103). As Neal Lerner shows in "Searching for Robert Moore," included in Section IV of this book, this is a view that influenced writing centers as well.

This negative attitude about student writers has been challenged recently, particularly in the field of writing studies. Such a shift is especially evident in the many undergraduate-authored articles about writing that have appeared in publications such as *The Writing Lab Newsletter*, *Young Scholars in Writing*, and this book and that are helping to reshape the field. We can see this shift too in other contexts in which the word "writers" is used to refer to *all* people who write, whether they are students or not and whether they are published or not. Furthermore, writing tutoring programs play a crucial role in helping to "author-ize" student writers. According to undergraduate and graduate-student researchers Renee Brown, Brian Fallon, Jessica Lott, Elizabeth Matthews, and Elizabeth Mintie, whose article can be found in Section IV, writing tutoring programs can help students "to see the choices they have, to feel more confident . . . , and to identify themselves as writers" (311, this book).

Such observations about writers and authors belong to an emerging field called **authorship studies** that examines these attitudes and beliefs. This field is relevant to writing tutors because, as undergraduate researcher Jennifer Nicklay argues in her article included in Section IV, "ideals of authorship . . . are engrained in our academic lives" (480, this book). These ideals are based on a long history that continues to be foundational to how Western, and especially North American, writers in colleges and universities understand what they do when they write—and when we fail to do so. We especially appreciate Janice Haswell and Richard Haswell's term **authoring** since it includes not only this long history but also the current "physical act of generating discourse and the author's phenomenological sense of that act" (4n.)—in other words, the writer's processes as well as her reflections on and metacognition of these processes.

To help you make use of some of the insights from the field of authorship studies in your tutoring, the rest of this chapter will offer

- A brief history of Western beliefs about authorship
- A summary of how plagiarism is understood in the United States

- Strategies for helping writers with citation processes
- How beliefs about authorship and plagiarism affect writing tutoring programs

A Brief History of Western Beliefs About Authorship
In Western culture, the hallmark of a true author is that he or she produces "original" writing and ideas, and because these words and ideas are seen as originating from him or her, he or she is said to be the "owner" of this work. This wasn't always the case.

Attitudes About Authorship Have Changed Over Time
In the long history of writing, during the vast majority of which only a very small percentage of people were able to read and an even smaller percentage could write, conceptions of authorship changed dramatically. In classical and medieval times, far from being seen as originators, authors (some of whom, as part of an oral tradition, did not write) were seen as merely the vessels through which the gods or God spoke. Even at those times when originality was prized, so too other forms of writing were valued; in the Renaissance and eighteenth century, for example, imitation was a respected form of writing, both a way of learning to write and a form of authorship in which the author aimed to reflect nature (Burke 5–8, Howard 487).

However, in the eighteenth century, an idea of the author emerged that is more familiar to us now. Literacy began to rise beyond the privileged classes, which meant that money could be made by selling works to a growing reading public. But publishers wanted to ensure that their profits would not be depleted by copies made by "pirates," so they argued in several crucial legal cases (predecessors of copyright laws today) that authors were the "owners" of their work and that publishers bought the right to copy it (Mark Rose 2–6). In addition, in the century that followed, writers of this period—many of whom were known as "Romantics"—were increasingly interested in the possibility that their work originated not from divine sources or even as a reflection of the world around them but from their own minds and memories, as expressions of their unique and individual selves. Several scholars have argued that the economic incentives of the publishers combined with these Romantic notions of authorship to produce modern European and American ideas of authorial **originality**—of words and ideas originating in unique ways from individuals, as expressions of their "own" particular feelings, thoughts, and perspectives (Mark Rose 119–29).

Much has happened since the late eighteenth and early nineteenth centuries to call into question this individualistic and "proprietary" idea of authorship. In the late twentieth century, scholars interested in authorship began to demonstrate that the Romantic myth of the solitary and proprietary author is just that, a myth. For one thing, authors (and writers) do not write in isolation, even when they write alone. They learn their words and phrases and ideas from others; writing, in other words, is **social**, part of a series of networks that link all texts to other texts. We can see traces of these networks in the ways writers indicate, by citing their sources, how they draw on other writers' ideas and language—a process that, ironically, given the emphasis on originality, can, in academic contexts, help to "authorize" them as experts on their topics. Internet hyperlinks make this network more visible than ever by literally connecting online texts to each other. Moreover, much of the writing that's conducted in the workplace is produced collaboratively, sometimes by many people. Again, the Internet helps to make the collaborative nature of much writing apparent, in, for instance, the multiple, collaborative, usually anonymous authorship of Wikipedia.

What does this abbreviated history of authorship in the West have to do with twenty-first-century writers and tutors? Actually, quite a lot. For one thing, just because scholars recognize that the solitary author is a myth doesn't mean the myth isn't still alive and kicking. The emphasis on the uniqueness of each individual writer in much writing process research, in many writing tutoring programs, and even in this book is in some ways an expression of it. Collaborative writing scholar Andrea Lunsford points out that many writing centers have been "informed by a deep-seated belief in individual 'genius,' in the Romantic sense of the term" (4). As a result, and as we discuss in Chapter 2 regarding expressivist theories of writing, this model views "knowledge as interior, as inside the student, and the writing center's job as helping students get in touch with this knowledge, as a way to find their unique voices, their individual and unique powers" (5). As Rebecca Day Babcock and her colleagues suggest, this "Romantic version of the writer as all-knowing" positions "the tutor as selfless facilitator, there to draw out ideas" (111). And, as we discuss at the end of this chapter, this belief about tutors has significantly influenced the practices and theories of tutoring writing.

For Writing

1. Go to your school's website and search the phrases "student writer" and "student author." Working with the first fifteen or twenty hits for each term, describe how these terms seem to be used at your school. Contrast these usages to arrive at a theory of how your institution uses these terms.

2. Look up your school's policies about and definitions of plagiarism. Rewrite part or all of this information so that it would be readily understood by a student on your campus.

PLAGIARISM

Probably nowhere is the continuing Romantic myth of the owner-author more evident than in the ways many academic institutions in the United States understand **plagiarism**. As writing center scholar Kurt Bouman says:

> Ideas about plagiarism are driven by a particular understanding about what it means to write. Many Western cultures, for instance, place a strong value on individuality and independence, and writers are encouraged to develop and use

their "authentic voice," a way of writing that is uniquely their own. Most Western cultures expect writers to express themselves in their own voices rather than through the voices of others. So, when one considers *why* voice might matter so much in writing, one reason for strong attitudes toward plagiarism becomes clear: Plagiarism misrepresents voice, a unique, individual, and essential characteristic of a writer. (163)

Using Sources in Different Cultures

We can get a sense of how specific our ideas of plagiarism are to U.S. academic culture most easily if we think about it in a global context. As Bouman goes on to discuss, the U.S. perspective is far from universal. For instance, whereas writers in U.S. academic institutions cite sources to distinguish their ideas from what others say, writers in countries such as China, which value "communal ties rather than unique individual identities," can be "expected to suppress their individuality rather than celebrate it" (163–64). Bouman points out that Korean teachers praise students for imitating famous writers in ways that might be considered plagiarism in the United States, where, by contrast, teachers want students to produce "original" work (164, 163). Furthermore, whereas "Western academic audiences expect writers to explicitly acknowledge their sources in their texts" (as we're doing here with Bouman), in other cultures, it might be enough to simply list the sources at the end of the paper (167). These differences do not mean that plagiarism is tolerated in other cultures, only that it can be defined and addressed in substantially different ways.

Variations Within U.S. Culture

Definitions of plagiarism vary not only across countries but within U.S. culture at large and even within higher education: legal and other forms of technical writing can, from an academic perspective, look like plagiarism, because it can be standardized "boilerplate" language that is copied and pasted from document to document. Likewise, and following the conventions of corporate documents, college and university plagiarism policies often borrow heavily, and usually without acknowledgment, from policies at other institutions. Even within academic institutions, faculty from different academic disciplines might define plagiarism differently.

Nonetheless, Academic Integrity Rules Matter

By highlighting these differences in attitudes about plagiarism and citation practices, we do not want to give the impression that because the rules aren't hard and fast, there aren't any or that they're not important. As you might know from your own encounters with plagiarism policies and discussions of academic integrity, in U.S. academic institutions, showing when we draw on sources is critical, and there are sometimes serious consequences for writers who don't. Instead, what we want to make clear is how complicated and varied these ideas about plagiarism are and, as a result, how difficult they can be to learn, whether someone been educated in the United States or not. As Bouman says, "People often spend years practicing these conventions before they can use them confidently and correctly as they weave together their own thoughts with ideas from their sources" (162). Moreover, as Brown et al. assert in their article on how the plagiarism detection software Turnitin.com affected their writing center, "many students are never taught what plagiarism is or how to avoid it" (323, this book). If these assertions hold true at your school, it's likely that you too will need to work with writers on the processes involved with citing sources.

HELPING WRITERS WITH CITATION PROCESSES

Because many people have such (understandably) negative feelings about plagiarism, talking to writers about this issue might not be something you are eager to do—perhaps because you don't want to embarrass the writer or because you yourself might feel embarrassed or even offended. As Bouman says, however, "there is nothing inherently shameful in the topic, and it is both appropriate and important to discuss source use with a writer when there are any questions about whether the writer has plagiarized, intentionally or not" (168). As we suggest above, it's helpful to think about avoiding plagiarism—or, more specifically, citing sources—as yet another set of composing processes that writers in academic settings engage in. Like composing processes, citing sources involves tasks that are best dealt with one at a time, that aren't necessarily linear (and therefore are sometimes messy), that can be recursive (because citations and quotation marks can be inserted after the draft has been written), that produce meaning (by way of connections writers draw between sources and in relation to their own arguments), that involve many activities, and that can take time to learn. In this section, then, we provide strategies for ways to set aside some of the emotional baggage associated with plagiarism and help writers succeed at citation processes:

- Know the definitions and policies of your institution and program
- Be direct and explicit
- Use more specific terms than "plagiarism"
- Don't assume that citation problems are intentional
- Help the writer use sources appropriately

Know the Definitions and Policies of Your Institution and Program
There are a number of reasons why you should be aware of how plagiarism is defined and what the relevant policies are at your institution. First, this knowledge can be useful for the writer. Writers new to college and academic writing might not be familiar with the definition and policies, and, even if they are, they might find them confusing or unclear: hearing a tutor's take in a less pressured

situation than a classroom can make all the difference. Second, this knowledge can be useful for tutors, making the discussion less personal and more a matter of institutional expectations. Third, even though, as we mention above, definitions of plagiarism are often borrowed from other institutions, they can be significantly different. Some institutions might consider any failure to acknowledge a source, whether intentional or not, to be plagiarism; another might define plagiarism as only deliberate and intentional misuse; yet another might consider a student's submitting the same paper to fulfill assignments in two different courses to be a form of plagiarism; some institutions have honor codes that require students to report on violations that others commit; and in many instances the punishment can range from a lower grade on the assignment to expulsion. As a result, knowing one institution's policy or a general definition of plagiarism won't necessarily give you insight into all contexts.

Finally, you'll want to know your program's specific policies. For instance, in some writing tutoring programs, writing that misuses sources isn't considered to be "plagiarized" until it is turned in to the instructor; before that time it is still a draft and in process. And some writing tutoring program directors want to be kept informed of any source-use issues that arise in your tutoring sessions, because faculty, deans, and academic integrity boards can raise questions later—about the writer, the paper, and his or her use of the program.

Be Direct and Explicit

Bouman suggests that discussing citation issues as clearly as possible is especially important for writers educated outside of the United States who, after all, might have very different expectations about when and how sources should be cited (168). However, we believe that being direct can be useful for any of the writers you might talk with about this subject. When you notice a quotation without a citation, shifts in the language, style, or even the font, or other related issues, Bouman suggests asking, "Did you consult any sources as you wrote this paper?" You can then ask the writer if she can show you which individual words and phrases or more general ideas come from someone else's writing. If the writer indicates that none of her writing came from a source, you can offer metacommentary about which aspects of her text led you to ask the question in the first place (Bouman 168). For instance, "The reason I'm asking the question is that at this point the language sounds really different from the rest of your writing. And that made me wonder if maybe you were drawing on something else here."

Use More Specific Terms than "Plagiarism"

For a word with such potentially dire consequences, "plagiarism" is not very precise. From a Latin word meaning "kidnapping," it can be used to describe a whole range of activities that, as we suggest above, different institutions can treat very differently As a result, Bouman recommends avoiding "the 'p' word" altogether, because it might lead to more confusion than clarification (168). Luckily, authorship scholar Rebecca Moore Howard has defined (and, in the case of "patchwriting," coined) a set of terms that are much more precise alternatives:

- **Insufficient citation:** The writer might have tried to cite the source but didn't include enough information about it.
- **Failure to mark quotations:** Quotation marks might be missing and/or the writer might in some other way have failed to show that these are someone else's words.
- **Failure to acknowledge sources:** The writer used a source but didn't indicate that he did.
- **Patchwriting:** The writer includes, or "patches," relatively brief direct quotations or paraphrases from a source into his writing.
- **Fraud:** The writer intends to turn in writing composed by someone else as his own. (487–88)

Don't Assume That Citation Problems Are Intentional

Brown et al. exhort tutors not to "automatically assume that any text that imitates another text or lacks originality is a result of a criminal act." They encourage us instead to work "to understand the causes of students' plagiarism" (309, 307, this book). Toward this end, note that of Howard's categories, all but fraud can be unintentional. The other problems, by contrast, might be the result of the writer's learning process. The writer might not know yet how to cite correctly or completely; the writing might be an early draft that the writer is using to sort out what he knows; or, as Bouman points out, "what appears as plagiarism may in fact represent the beginning of [the writer's] participation in a new academic language and culture" (167). And it is always possible that, as writing center scholars Leigh Ryan and Lisa Zimmerelli suggest, the writer might be completing an assignment in which the instructor has specified that citations aren't necessary (104).

Help the Writer Use Sources Appropriately

To help a writer who hasn't cited her sources sufficiently, hasn't marked her quotations, or hasn't acknowledged her sources, you might:

- **Ask the writer what she knows about source use**, specifically quoting, acknowledging, and citing sources. This discussion can help you find out how well she understands the process.
- **Help the writer compare her source to her writing**, asking her to underline or highlight words, phrases, and passages that draw on the source (Bouman 169).
- **Show the writer how to acknowledge sources.** With the help of a handbook or an online handout (search for "writing center" "citing sources" or the name of the documentation style the writer is using, such as MLA or APA), talk about how to acknowledge sources by inserting quotation marks, the author's name, a signal phrase (e.g., "As Bouman suggests,"),

page numbers (if appropriate to the documentation style), and other information about the source listed at the end, in a works cited or reference list. Keep in mind that citation styles can be vastly different from discipline to discipline (which we say more about in Chapter 6).

Some writers need help learning to **paraphrase**, translating sources into new language that is appropriate to their writing. As Bouman points out, "paraphrasing is one of the most complex writing skills there is. To paraphrase well and correctly, writers must employ a number of high-level language skills." These skills include understanding the words and ideas of the source, being able "to accurately discern the author's tone and stance in the writing," and being able to generate "alternative words and sentence structures" (166). Brown et al. offer this strategy: ask the writer to set the source aside and tell you what she can remember about what it says. Both you and the writer can take notes on this recounting to start generating a paraphrase (318, this book).

The above strategies will likely be appropriate even if it becomes clear that the writer has *intentionally* not cited or acknowledged his sources sufficiently, not marked his quotations, or patched together his language with that of a source text. Moreover, Bouman holds that these strategies will be helpful if you believe that the student is attempting to turn in fraudulent writing—a paper written largely or entirely by someone else: "Offer to help the student understand your school's plagiarism policy, and offer to work with the student to use source texts" (170–71). We also suggest that you ask the director or administrator of your program what to do if in this situation the writer doesn't want this kind of help.

AUTHORING, PLAGIARISM, AND WRITING TUTORING PROGRAMS

As we mention above, the Romantic myth of the solitary author has influenced how writers and tutors work together in writing tutoring programs, sometimes limiting this work to drawing out ideas already inside the writer. As we discuss in here, our current (U.S., academic) understanding of plagiarism has had an impact on this work as well. Specifically, there has been a history of concerns about how tutors help writers with their writing—whether, instead of drawing out writers' ideas, tutors might be putting ideas in or, in the worst-case scenario, coauthoring with or ghostwriting for writers. These concerns run so deep that Brown et al. point out that much scholarship on writing tutoring has aimed to defend these programs against charges of "too much help" (309, this book). These concerns are indeed very serious, and you won't want to do anything that might damage the writer's or your program's (or your own) reputation as academically honest. But how should tutors make sure this doesn't happen? The answer to this question is complex and requires a bit more historical exploration.

Nondirective Tutoring vs. "Too Much Help"

In the 1980s and 1990s, as pedagogies for educating tutors about how to work with writers were being developed, it seemed as if the common-sense solution to the "too much help" problem was simply to limit how much tutors could do for or with writers. Undergraduate researcher Jennifer Nicklay traces the most salient articulations of this solution to two foundational works in writing center studies, Stephen North's "The Idea of a Writing Center" (1984) and Jeff Brooks's "Minimalist Tutoring: Making Students Do All the Work" (1991). North famously asserted that the tutor's job "is to make sure that writers, and not necessarily their texts, are what get changed by instruction" (qtd. in Nicklay 474, this book). Admittedly, in making this statement, North was addressing faculty complaints not about "too much help" but rather about students' getting too little or the wrong kind of help. However, his focus on changing the writer was quickly pressed into the service of defending against charges of "too much help" as well. As a result, holds Nicklay, "This idea has permeated nearly every theory, ideology, strategy or technique introduced within the writing center community" (474, this book). In turn, Brooks's model of "minimalist" tutoring put into action North's idea by asserting that the best way to change writers was for tutors to do as little as possible while writers did "all the work."

And to be fair, North's focus on the writer as well as Brooks's concrete suggestions for how to do that—including "sitting beside the student, having the student closer to the paper, not writing on the paper, and having the student read the paper aloud" (Nicklay 475, this book)—are all potentially useful strategies because they can motivate writers and promote their learning. Drawing on some of the same research that supports the motivational scaffolding that we outline in Chapter 3, Babcock et al. cite research that shows that when individuals receive "too much assistance," they cannot learn (112). Indeed, two of the sessions that undergraduate researchers Ruth Johnson, Beth Clark, and Mario Burton studied serve as useful illustrations of this observation. They found that when tutors "includ[ed] too much of their own knowledge when giving suggestions to the student," the student's ideas were "silenc[ed]" and she was "inhibit[ed] . . . from discovering ideas on her own" (396, this book). In addition, they raise the possibility that even when tutors feel confident about the knowledge they are sharing, this knowledge can be incorrect (393, this book).

Although many minimalist, **nondirective** strategies are useful, there can be drawbacks, especially when these rules of thumb become absolutes that must be applied to all tutoring situations. First of all, as undergraduate researcher Molly Wilder shows in the article we discuss in Chapter 3, nondirective tutoring doesn't necessarily guarantee success (which she measured by student engagement), nor does directive tutoring necessarily lead to the tutor "steamroll[ing]" the writer (544, this book). From her analysis of Derek's session with Heidi, she found that "nondirection can elicit student engagement," but she also found that it can "fall flat," as evident in Lily's session with Wally (545, this book). Moreover, Lidia's session with Marsha "shows how a more classically directive style of conferencing can also be very effective in showing student engagement" (545, this book). Wilder suggests that key differences in each of these cases were the writers themselves (Wally "does not bring his own concerns to the table," but Heidi does) as well as "the strengths of the particular tutors" (545, this book).

Nondirective, minimalist tutoring can be problematic because, especially in its absolute form, it cannot take into account such differences among writers and tutors. In addition, as Nicklay learned from surveying her colleagues in her own writing center as well as scholarship about other writing centers, tutors can be made to feel guilty whenever they use a strategy that could be considered directive, even if the strategy is appropriate to the situation (479, this book). "In using directive strategies," Nicklay holds, "it is understandable that consultants would feel guilt because they are stepping outside the expectations of the academic institution" (479, this book). This guilt is especially potent and "very difficult to overcome" because it stems from "the ideals of authorship and ownership that are engrained in our academic lives" (480, this book).

Strike a Balance: Just Enough Help

So, again, what should tutors do in this complicated situation? Along with Wilder, we want to suggest that whether a tutor is directive or nondirective isn't really the issue. We would argue instead that we should approach questions about what kinds of help to give and when to give it in terms of two other imperatives:

1. First and foremost, you don't want to do anything that will call into question the reputation of your writing tutoring program, the writer, or you yourself. To do so, you must make sure you understand and are operating within your institution's and program's policies in terms of how much help is "too much."
2. At the same time, but without contradicting the previous imperative, you need to promote writer engagement, learning, and success.

Following both of these imperatives simultaneously involves a more complicated set of processes than heeding nondirective rules. Because both are also situation-specific and our writing tutoring programs might be different from yours in this area, we're not able to tell you exactly what to do.

But we will say that the kinds of scaffolding that we address in Chapter 3 and that Mackiewicz and Thompson discuss in more detail provide a useful way to support the writer's learning, engagement, and success without giving her "too much help." Alongside the tradition of nondirective tutoring is one that honors modeling writing activities as a way of teaching writers how to eventually do them on their own. Keeping the writer's learning in mind as your ultimate goal, and knowing that this learning can be a slow process in some cases, can go a long way toward ensuring that the help you offer is just enough. In addition, Nicklay and Brown et al. offer other useful suggestions for negotiating this tension:

- *Talk with experienced tutors in your program:* Nicklay points out that "These more experienced consultants are often more comfortable with flexibility in consultations—particularly with directive methods" (480, this book).
- *Explore scholarship on the topic:* The articles by Nicklay, Wilder, Johnson et al., and Brown et al. are great places to start, and the research they cite will give you a sense of the scholarly conversation that informed their work.
- *Authorize yourself to contribute to the research:* Brown et al. recommend joining this conversation yourself: "As tutors, we see a lot that other people at our institutions either take for granted or barely recognize, but we do have the ability and opportunity to speak up on those often glanced over issues and to reach out to fellow students and our faculty" (323, this book).

For Writing

1. Writing teachers have experimented with asking students to plagiarize—by not citing or acknowledging sources, by not using quotation marks to indicate direct quotations, and by patchwriting. To develop workshop materials for tutors in your program that explore the blurred boundaries of originality and plagiarism, use one or more of these techniques, perhaps by using material in this chapter.

2. Drawing upon the discussion in this chapter, your institution's policies, and, if you completed the previous *For Writing* prompt, above, the inappropriately cited writing you produced, write a reflection describing how you might approach one or more of the following scenarios:

   - You read a paragraph or so in a three-page paper that's very different from the rest of the writing, but the writer hasn't cited any sources. What might you say?

   - The writer doesn't seem to be able to answer any questions about the paper, including how she wrote it or how she found information for it. In fact, she can't even tell you about the topic or how she chose it. As a result, you suspect that someone else wrote the paper. How would you start this conversation?

For Inquiry

1. If a history of your writing tutoring program has already been written, consider it in the context of the studies of writing processes and history of authoring that have been addressed in this chapter. How are writers and writing presented in this history of your program? You might also want to refer to Chapter 10, and particularly the discussion of Lyotard's historical narratives on pages 226–29 as well as the larger history of writing centers and writing studies outlined in Chapter 2 and in other sources.

2. If a history of your writing tutoring program has yet to be written, you might wish to refer to Chapter 10 to help you with this process. First, you'll want to survey the materials and resources you have available to you. These can include archival and administrative documents, program leaders (current and past), and the history of your institution and writing instruction there. (Remember that for any interviews you would want to conduct for oral histories, you will need to work through your Institutional Review Board. You'll want to discuss this with your program's administrator or your instructor, and you might want to refer to Chapters 8 and 10.) Writing the history of a program is potentially a very large endeavor, so, as suggested in Chapter 10 and according to the guidance of your program administrator or instructor, you might wish to collaborate with several other tutors—including future tutors who might build on your archival work later on.

CHAPTER 5

Tutor and Writer Identities

For Discussion

1. First, make a list of all the groups you belong to, interpreting the concept of "group" broadly. Include everything from the ethnic group(s) with which you identify to social circles you enjoy to academic or (pre)professional organizations you are a member of. Share your lists with your peers and discuss what groups you have in common and what groups make you distinct. Which of these group affiliations affect you as a tutor? As a writer? Why?

2. Describe to your peers a writing situation in which you wrote using a persona very different from your academic writing voice—perhaps when creating a blog post or an email or text message. What elements of your personality or experience did you include in this writing that you do not include in your academic writing? What did these elements bring to the text that is not present in your writing for school?

INTRODUCTION

Here, we focus on the work that writers and tutors do together in terms of the key concept of this chapter, **identity**. What do we mean by identity in this context? Writing researchers Elizabeth Wardle and Doug Downs define it as comprising "an individual's characteristics or personality; it consists of those factors that create a sense of 'who you are.'" They note that "individuals may not have one 'true,' stable identity but might have multiple and/or changing identities" (797). Rebecca Day Babcock and her colleagues discuss writing center scholarship that considers how distinguishing characteristics of individuals and/or groups "contribute to the creation of the tutoring session" and the relationships of tutors and writers (13). They found that these studies addressed race, sex, gender, age, language backgrounds, physical and learning abilities, and cultural identity (15–23).

In his book *Facing the Center: Toward an Identity Politics of One-to-One Mentoring*, Harry Denny adds social class as well as sexuality/sexual orientation to the list and argues that "Identity is central to writing centers" (149).

Although we will address ways in which such identity characteristics can affect tutoring sessions, the point of this chapter is not to define these identity categories or to suggest that you try to place the individual writers and tutors you work with into them. As rhetoric and diversity researcher Stephanie Kerschbaum has argued, such categorization never tells even part of the story about a person. For one thing, we are all complex conglomerations of many identities; for another, these conglomerations are dynamic and change over time and in relation to other people, partly because these other people might or might not share, understand, or be aware of our identities. And finally, although it can be useful to be familiar with how identities might influence, for example, a writer's or tutor's expectations for how the session should run or the writing they might produce, if we pay too much attention to such categories, we can end up noticing only the identity(ies) and losing touch with the writer, her uniqueness, and her own motivations. In other words, instead of asking, "What categories do individuals belong to?" or "What categories can be ascribed to particular individuals?" Kerschbaum suggests we ask such questions as, "How do individuals position themselves alongside others? How are individuals positioned by others? How do individuals acknowledge similarities and differences between themselves and others?" (631). What matters, as much as the identity categories, is the relationship—however short lived—that you and the writer form out of what the two of you have in common and what differentiates you: how you work together on building commonalities and bridging gaps (a phrase that you'll notice in many of the undergraduate tutor-researcher articles collected in Section IV and cited in this chapter).

Here, as in previous chapters, we know that you likely come to this discussion with prior knowledge, experience, and, given the nature of the topic, perhaps even concerns and hesitations. For example, you might

- *Already know a lot about identity:* You might be aware of how someone's identity can affect how she writes, reads, and interacts with others, perhaps because you are confronted with your own identity every day, or because of experiences with family or friends or a class you've taken or reading you've done.
- *Have doubts about the relevance of identity to writing and tutoring:* Even if you answered the questions that begin this chapter, you might not think of yourself as having a particular identity, or you might not understand how it could be relevant to being a student.
- *Wonder about how to address identity in a tutoring session:* Imagining doing so might feel both too personal and too political, and you might worry about making the writer or yourself uncomfortable.

• *Be concerned about tutoring someone whose identity is different from yours:* What if you can't find common ground? How will you move forward on working with the writer on his writing?

This chapter aims to address such concerns, questions, and doubts as well as help you apply what you already know about identity by expanding your repertoire as a tutor. We have organized this chapter so that it moves from general to specific, offering

- An overview of how all of us—tutors, writers, program directors, and book authors—have identities and what they can mean for tutoring.
- Additional general strategies that might be useful for any writer or tutor.
- More detailed strategies that writing center scholars and researchers have found useful for working with writers across differences of language, culture, and physical and learning abilities as well as through academic writing in the United States.

You might well note that the list of identity categories that we discuss below does not begin to cover the longer list that Babcock et al. and Denny enumerate at the beginning of this chapter. In part, this is because we are not able to address all the possible permutations of identity in writing tutoring sessions. Instead, we have chosen to focus on those categories that scholars and researchers in the field have said the most about and to offer general strategies that we think will enable you to be more flexible with your tutoring and therefore help writers across a range of identity differences. Again, throughout this chapter, we focus less on trying to define the "kinds" of writers that you'll work with and more on offering strategies that tutors and writing center scholars and researchers have found to be useful for communicating across many differences in the tutoring session. These strategies build on the tutoring practices we offer in Chapter 3 in particular. Moreover, we believe our last topic, U.S. academic writing, which is perhaps the most difficult and the most controversial since it involves a critical look at "standards," can serve as a good starting point for discussions about—and your own research into—ways identity affects writing, writers, and writing tutors in ways we do not address here.

For Writing

1. Pick one of the identity categories you listed for the first "For Discussion" question above and find two or three articles that show how this identity category has been treated in writing center studies. (For starters, search for the identity category in the online archive for *The Writing Lab Newsletter*. Next, search for "writing center" and the identity category on Google Scholar, ProQuest, JStor, and CompPile.) Summarize these characterizations briefly and describe how they compare with your firsthand experience.

2. Write a brief descriptive narrative that explains how you acquired a new discourse—a new set of vocabulary, rhetorical moves, and ways of presenting information valued by a group that you joined. This group might comprise colleagues at a new job (such as writing tutoring), at church, one of the groups you joined when you started college, a new set of friends, or a sports team. Focus on how you acquired this discourse, missteps you made as you did so, or the event(s) that made you feel like you could successfully navigate in this community. How might this compare with learning to write in a new language or dialect?

IDENTITY AND WRITING TUTORING PROGRAMS

In writing tutoring programs, "identity" as a category includes everyone and can affect many aspects of tutoring. As writing center scholars Jean Kiedaisch and Sue Dinitz hold, "tutees aren't the only ones bringing 'differences' to a session. . . . [A]ll of us, directors, tutors, and tutees alike, bring aspects of our identity to tutoring" ("Changing" 49, 44).

Identity and the Authors

We start with two examples, namely "us," the authors of this book—the abstract and disembodied "we" who have been talking to "you" in these many pages and are contained and informed by our own identities and the identities of the people we work with in the writing centers we direct:

Melissa has been aware of her differences throughout her time in university as both a student and a faculty member. As the first person in her family to go to college, she comes from a home culture that simultaneously valued higher education and devalued its use as anything but job training. Her blue-collar background contrasts with that of much of the student body of her current institution, who generally come from more affluent, educated families. She is aware, too, of the conflict between her outspoken, highly direct rhetoric and the common cultural expectations often associated with middle-aged, middle-class, Anglo womanhood. She tries to use these differences to help her tutors better understand students from the working class, to help put tutors and writers from other underrepresented groups at ease, and to open discussions about the range of real experiences that lies outside assumptions about how we "all" grew up. But she worries that she's oversimplifying the lives of the tutors and writers in her center when she compares her experiences to theirs. And she worries that she's not doing justice to her tutors or her own experiences when she "passes"—remains quiet on issues of difference and lets others assume she too is from an affluent, educated background.

Lauren directs a writing center in which identity is foregrounded every day. Because of the religious and cultural identity of Yeshiva University, the first and largest U.S. institution of higher education under Jewish auspices, all of the undergraduates on her New York City campus are Jewish and almost always Orthodox men, which means they follow biblical law concerning Sabbath, diet, interactions between men and women, prayer, and other aspects of day-to-day life. From the outside, it might be hard to imagine a more homogeneous writing center, and, indeed, tutors' and writers' shared identity can make their work together easier. Due to their religious practices, for example, undergraduate tutors and writers usually have a familiarity with one-to-one collaborative learning as well as, as tutor Efrayim Clair points out, a "larger shared vocabulary that gives us more options for communicating and making ourselves clearer to each other." On the other hand, this center is a crossroads for many different identities, in terms of class, educational background, language, nationality, race, culture, sexual orientation, learning abilities, and physical abilities. And that's just in terms of undergraduate tutors and writers. If directors (including Lauren, a middle-aged female Caucasian Protestant from Oklahoma), faculty tutors, and writers from YU's nonsectarian graduate programs are included, age and gender become part of the mix too. This intersection of identities has caused confusion, tensions, and difficulties over the years but also, as we have become more aware of them and how to build on them, insight, enlightenment, and excitement.

Identity and Tutors

In programs across the United States, undergraduate writing tutor-researchers, too, have paid attention to their own identities and how this affects their work—in terms of, for example, their economic privilege (Brecht; this book) or disadvantage (Bielski Boris), race and ethnicity (Varma), sexuality (Doucette; this book), religion (Rich), and disability (Ryan). Anita Varma, for example, reflects on times that, prompted by assumptions based solely on her outward appearance, writers have asked her when she "learned to speak English":

> [M]y physical appearance includes visual cues that telegraph "foreignness" to the all-American student beside me, who might assume that the brown-skinned woman with gold Indian jewelry and bangles must be an immigrant. In the case of immigrant families or students, appearance might also suggest bilingualism, and bilingualism might signify membership in a subaltern minority group. Therefore, it is understandable—though perhaps not entirely pleasing to the person on the receiving end of the question—that a naïve college student who has not had much exposure to members of subaltern groups might make some incorrect assumptions about a writing partner during a consultation. (32)

Discomfort and even anger can arise when assumptions are made about someone's identity based on limited (or merely presumed) information. But this isn't the only way that tutor identity can affect the tutoring session. As Claire Elizabeth O'Leary maintains in her study of the impact of gender in the writing conference, tutor and writer identities are in dialogue together in a variety of ways:

> A tutor's spontaneous conversational responses are influenced by more than the content of the conversation. . . . [T]he flow and development of the conversation are also affected by how the tutor and student enact and respond to each other's social identities. . . . [T]he social identities that could affect conversation often correspond to physically apparent characteristics that identify different persons as belonging to different social groups. Such outwardly visible characteristics lead others to make conclusions, correct or not, about an individual's status "at first glance." (483, this book)

O'Leary, like Kerschbaum, suggests that at least as important as the identity categories themselves are the relationships that writers and tutors form together, based on a range of information, assumptions, and cues.

Identity and Writing

The identities that tutors and writers share or that differentiate them affect their work together in a number of ways. The writing that a writer and tutor work on together might, for instance, look different from what might be called "Standard" English or "Academic Writing." These differences can include sentence-level matters such as grammar and vocabulary as well as more global issues such as organization, how the writer positions himself in relation to his material and addresses his audience, and, as we discuss in Chapter 4, whether and how the writer uses and cites sources. Additionally, the writer's or tutor's spoken language might not match the writing and both might not fully convey his intelligence. Therefore, assumptions we make about writers based on how they speak or write can be incorrect.

Identity and Behaviors

Another way that identity can affect the session is in terms of how tutors and writers behave during a session. When a writer and tutor have similar expectations, the session can get off to a smooth start, but when they don't, both can act in ways that might be surprising to the other. For instance, both will probably have expectations about how much authority the tutor and writer should have in determining the agenda for the session. Similarly, both will likely have expectations about personal space (how much is too much, how much too little), which might or might not align. And both might well have expectations about what constitutes politeness in this setting and whether directness, in particular, is considered impolite and to be avoided or so important that how polite it is might be irrelevant. Finally, as Anne Ellen Geller, Michele Eodice, Frankie Condon, Meg Carroll, and Elizabeth H. Boquet point out, "because time is experienced differently in different cultures, one person's timekeeping may be uncomfortable and unfamiliar to a person from another culture" (35).

Identity and the Session

As a result of these dynamics, the shape of the tutoring session might be affected too. Writer and tutor might spend substantial time at the beginning and, indeed, throughout the session getting to know each other and negotiating how their work should proceed. They might focus much of their attention on particular aspects of the writing such as sentence-level issues or organization. They might work on helping the writer understand the reading, including the instructor's assignment. The tutor might transcribe, writing down for the writer his ideas or revision plans or both.

For Writing

1. Interview one or more tutors about tutor identity: ask about the group affiliations that shape their own identities and how they see these categories affecting their tutorials. How do their identities appear to be understood by the writers with whom they work? Do they perceive their identity as affecting the tutoring session and, if so, how?

2. Using the data available from your tutoring program and from your institution, compare the demographic makeup of writers at your institution to the pool that uses your services. What groups are over- or underrepresented? Now compare this data to the demographic data of who works in your writing tutoring program. What identity categories appear to be over- and underrepresented? Reflect upon changes that might make your center more accessible to underrepresented groups.

IDENTITY AND TUTORING STRATEGIES

Because the strategies described in Chapter 3 will be useful as you work with writers across identity differences, then worth revisiting in Table 5.1 (next page). Several of these strategies can be expanded on in general ways so that they are more flexible for a wider range of writers. Following the lead of Kiedaisch and Dinitz as well as graduate student tutor-researcher Allison Hitt, whose article is included in Section IV, we reconsider these strategies in terms of a "universal design" approach to tutoring that advocates for redesigning services "so that they are suited to a broad range of users" and aims to make all tutoring sessions "accessible to the widest audience possible, reducing the need to treat any writer as having 'special needs'" (Kiedaisch and Dinitz "Changing" 50–51). As Hitt clarifies, this approach "does not eliminate the need to identify students' individual needs." Instead, it asks us "to acknowledge that *all* students have multiple ways of learning and knowing and to be flexible to those different needs" (387, this book).

Table 5.1 Revisit Tutoring Strategies from Chapter 3.

Engage in Interpersonal and Motivational Conversation
- Get acquainted
- Ask (and answer) questions
- Make statements
- Offer your perspective as a reader
- Take an interest
- Praise
- Listen
- Consider nonverbal cues

Scaffold the Writer's Learning and Decide Together on the Agenda
- Ask the writer what the agenda should be
- Analyze the assignment and context
- Read the writing
- Negotiate the priorities for the session
- If the writer has no writing, help her get started
- Wrap up
- Reflect

Ask Additional Questions to Help You and the Writer Get Acquainted

If the writer herself does not tell you about her identity and how it might affect her writing, finding out can be complicated. For instance, you wouldn't want to make assumptions based on how someone looks, similar to those made by the writer Varma worked with. Instead, Kiedaisch and Dinitz suggest adding the following questions to your repertoire because they "give every student the opportunity to share, and tutors to listen for, information that will help the tutor decide what approaches and strategies might work best for that individual"—and without requiring either of you "to directly use the language of identity or difference":

- "Before we get started, is there anything else you'd like me to know?"
- "Have you worked with a tutor before?" If the student answers yes, . . . ask what worked or didn't work . . . in those sessions. If the student replies no, ask . . . what ideas the student has for how [you] might best work together.
- "Tell me more about how you usually go about writing papers, and what parts are easy for you and what parts are difficult." ("Changing" 52–53)

These questions could be useful for your work with any writer.

Make Direct and Explicit Statements

To ensure that their sessions are effective, tutors sometimes need to be more direct and explicit than they might usually be comfortable with. Undergraduate tutor-researcher Frances Nan, whose article we've included in Section IV, points out that tutoring programs often encourage indirectness (e.g., "asking leading questions, allowing writers to say what they think rather than tutors thinking for them") and hedging ("speech that 'uses terms that soften the message such as *maybe, might, kind of, could possibly*'") (468, 464–65, this book). In the United States, certain cultural expectations can make such indirect, hedging language seem more polite and formal than direct and explicit language. In their empirical study of questions, Isabelle Thompson and Jo Mackiewicz note that although such language "implies that the tutor is aware of and respects a students' ownership of the conference agenda," such concerns must be balanced with those "for clarity and students' understanding" (62). Questions and hedging, for example, might take for granted knowledge about cultural expectations that the writer might not have. As a result, in some situations using more direct and explicit language can be helpful.

Use a Range of Communication Strategies to Engage the Writer's Learning Style

Hitt advocates for a **multimodal toolkit**, "multiple and flexible practices—that allow [tutors] to adapt to different communicative interactions" (386, this book). "Multimodal" refers to the different ways we communicate information, whether

Table 5.2 Multimodal Tutoring Strategies.

Strategies that appeal to different learning styles (from Ryan and Zimmerelli):

- *Visual strategies* for working on writing include pointing and other hand gestures, underlining or highlighting parts of the writing, taking notes or drawing maps or diagrams, and anything else that can serve as "visual reminders" for the writer after the session (60).

- *Kinesthetic strategies* highlight the physical activities involved with the visual strategies of gesturing, marking the writing, and drawing and mapping, and can include having the writer cut up a hard copy of her paper or writing out ideas on index cards or PostIts and rearranging them (60). Play-Doh, Legos bricks, and blocks can also help writers represent and physically shape their ideas.

- *Auditory strategies* include reading aloud (by the tutor or writer), repeating and rephrasing, explaining and "verbally reinforc[ing]" any visual and kinesthetic strategies you and the writer use, restating what you and the writer have discussed so far, and recording your conversation with the writer (60).

Other strategies for your expanded multimodal toolkit:

- *Make use of grammar resources,* such as handbooks and online resources, such as the Purdue Online Writing Lab. You can work through these with the writer in visual, auditory, and even kinesthetic ways.

- *Have sample student papers on hand* so you can show writers concrete examples of how information can be presented and what "good" academic writing looks like.

- *Work online,* by way of synchronous or asynchronous online tutoring (see Chapter 7) or use a word processing or text messaging program.

- *Work in small groups* rather than with individual writers, and see Alicia Brazeau's article in Section IV for a study of some writers' preferences for working in small groups over one-to-one.

through written text, visual means, or sound. (This is a concept we say more about in Chapter 7.) In this context, multimodality can include using techniques that appeal to what are commonly known as **learning styles**—visual, auditory, and kinesthetic (related to movement) summarized in Table 5.2.

In the sections that follow, we discuss in more detail strategies that might work for writers with particular identities. As we mention above, in this chapter we focus less on trying to define "kinds" of writers and more on offering a range of strategies that tutors and writing center scholars have found to be useful across several (although certainly not all) identity differences among both tutors and writers. You might find that any of these strategies might work with any writer you tutor.

For Writing

1. What language(s) have you studied or otherwise acquired (for instance, in a bilingual home)? How do you view the differences in your primary language and the other language(s) you've learned? Are there particular situations in which a language other than your home language seems better suited to your goal? What kind of "business" is best transacted in this language? What kind of social play? Family bonding? Something else?

2. What, if anything, do you know about academic writing forms other than U.S. academic prose? Read two or three articles on a form of academic writing beyond those common in the United States, such as Dirk Siepmann's "Academic Writing and Culture: An Overview of Differences between English, French and German" or Ewa Donesch-Jezo's "Comparison of Generic Organization of the Research Paper in English and Polish: Cross-Cultural Variation and Pedagogical Implications," and compare the writing you accomplish in your own courses with the forms described there.

TUTORING ACROSS LANGUAGE AND CULTURE DIFFERENCES

Of the many kinds of identity differences that tutors work across, those most often discussed by writing center scholars have to do with language and culture, and more specifically writers who are referred to as ESL (English as a second language), ELL (English language learner), NNS (non-native speaker), L2 (second-language learner), international (educated outside the United States), and "Generation 1.5" (people who are "in between" as English users, perhaps because they learned English in the United States but do not speak it at home). We prefer the term **multilingual writers** because although it's less precise than the others, it has more positive connotations; this term reminds us that knowing more about languages is a benefit rather than a deficit. For these writers, operating in more than one language is part of their identities, but because these writers or their families often come from non-English-speaking countries and because language always contains cultural aspects, cultural differences may affect their writing and tutoring sessions as well.

What Is *Your* Language Background?

How you approach working with writers across language and cultural differences might well depend on your own linguistic and cultural background(s). For instance, if you are multilingual yourself, you might be aware of language diversity, not only in terms of vocabulary and grammar, but also how speakers of a language prefer to present ideas and themselves to readers or listeners. And you likely know how writing in a second language can result in additional opportunities for cognitive overload, since making writing look like that of a native speaker can be difficult. This knowledge will serve you well as you help writers who are working to improve their English. In addition, this knowledge can help other tutors in your program if you choose to share your insights and experiences with them.

On the other hand, you might have very limited or no experience learning another language: maybe English is the only language you know and the United States the only country you've lived in, so you might be nervous about the prospect of working with someone with a different cultural background from your own who is still learning English. But there's little reason to worry, because

- *There is a lot of useful research and advice available* for helping multilingual writers, some of which we summarize below. We especially recommend the video *Writing Across Borders*, directed by Wayne Robertson, as well as Shanti Bruce and Ben Rafoth's edited collection, *ESL Writers: A Guide for Writing Center Tutors*.
- *One-to-one tutoring can help multilingual writers.* New tutors sometimes feel that the individualized help they offer will be a distant second to classroom-based instruction. But ESL researcher Ilona Leki holds that "Writing centers may be the ideal learning environment for students whose first or strongest language is not English: one-on-one, context rich, highly focused on a specific current writing need, and offering the possibility of negotiation of meaning (i.e., conversational back-and-forth that is thought to promote second language acquisition)" (1).
- *You don't have to be a grammar expert.* According to Terese Thonus, being able to correct errors and recite rules is less important than prompting multilingual writers to see their own errors, validating corrections they make, and following "through to revision of grammar, lexis [vocabulary], and discourse features" (qtd. in Babcock and Thonus 99). To learn some of the basics you'll need, you might read the ESL sections available in many writing handbooks or online, in the Purdue Online Writing Lab and other writing center websites.

Or it might be that you are somewhere between: maybe members of your family know and speak a language other than English at home that you might or might not be fluent in. Or maybe you've studied one or more languages at school and, again, have some familiarity but aren't comfortable speaking or writing in them. You might, therefore, have a good idea about how much hard work and time language learning takes, and how easy it is to make the same mistakes again and again. These experiences might give you extra patience for the time involved with negotiating meaning. The good news is that this extra time will be beneficial to the writer. As Thonus says, "research suggests [that] taking more time results in more durable and transferable language and writing skills" (qtd. in Babcock and Thonus 99).

Strategies for Working Across Language and Culture Differences

Here, we refine some of the strategies discussed in Chapter 3 as well as the "multi-modal toolkit" described above so that they are more appropriate to working with writers across language and cultural differences. Again, however, you might find that they'll be useful for a range of writers.

Get Acquainted

It won't necessarily be apparent whether a writer is or is not multilingual or, more precisely, whether his language and/or cultural background have any impact upon his writing. If the writer doesn't tell you or you don't know through some other means (such as information he included when he signed up for an appointment), perhaps Kiedaisch and Dinitz's open-ended questions (e.g., "Is there anything else you'd like me to know?") or something else later in the session will prompt the writer to talk about his background. Once a writer does so, Babcock and Thonus suggest finding out how proficient in English the writer is (or considers himself to be) (105), and Nan recommends asking about the writer's education so far (466, this book).

Consider Nonverbal Cues

Nonverbal cues are especially important to keep in mind because they too are culturally determined. Specific gestures, such as ways of nodding one's head, or matters of personal space can differ dramatically across cultures, so it will be useful to try to be aware when you are making assumptions about someone's emotional state or level of engagement based on her facial expressions and how close she sits to you. Nan points out another dimension of nonverbal cues that will be useful to be aware of. Multilingual writers, she holds, "are much more likely to pick up on the tutor's body language or tone of voice as a substitute for listening to a tutor's words. They will be able to tell when a tutor is merely being polite or when she or he is consciously trying to speak slowly" (469, this book).

Her advice is, again, to be direct and explicit:

> Rather than sugarcoat anything, a tutor must be honest and clear. Asking, "Do you need me to repeat what I just said?" is better than assuming that the writer

> does not understand unless spoken to slowly, or telling the writer that his or her English is better than it is. A lack of transparency from either tutor or writer can lead to negative results. (469, this book)

And, again, this advice might be useful for any tutoring session.

Ask the Writer What He Wants to Work on—and How He Wants to Work

Although multilingual writers might want to work on grammar and other sentence-level issues, it's important not to assume this will always be the case. As in any tutoring session, start by finding out what the writer wants to work on. If he says he wants to work on grammar, find out what he has in mind; as we discuss in Chapter 3, when writers do not have experience talking about writing, they might use the word "grammar" to describe a variety of writing issues, including vocabulary or word choice, clarity of expression, and use of idioms, punctuation, and a host of other issues that aren't, strictly speaking, related to grammar.

Also relevant here is that writers from cultural backgrounds different from your own might not share your perspective on how the session should proceed. Nan and other researchers observe that because writers unfamiliar with writing tutoring in the United States might see tutors as authority figures, they might assume that tutors will make the decisions about what to work on and not allow writers to ask questions or disagree (467, this book). As Nan goes on to suggest, this is a key area in which being direct and transparent is especially important (468–69, this book). Gillespie and Lerner recommend talking openly with writers about tutoring sessions—for instance, by explaining what expectations your program has for how tutors and writers should work together (119).

Analyze the Assignment/Context

If you are tutoring in an institution in which faculty assume that students have a strong understanding of English and familiarity with U.S. academic writing, a crucial aspect of the assignment and context will be the conventions and rhetorical features of this writing, including, as we touch on in the previous chapter, citation practices. Nan notes that U.S. academic writing "emphasizes a strict point-evidence-explain structure, as well as original thinking and creative engagement with multiple academic sources" (467, this book). By contrast, academic writing in other countries can follow other organizational structures and address readers quite differently. Chinese writers, for example, typically "do not state their thesis until the end so that readers realize the writer's intentions themselves" (Nan 467, this book).

To get a sense not only of the diverse ways cultures structure writing and social interactions through language—that is, **rhetoric**—but also some of the limitations of U.S. academic writing styles, we recommend watching the video *Writing Across Borders* (which, as of this writing, is available on YouTube). Such comparison makes up an area of study called **contrastive rhetoric**, which "suggests that writers' linguistic, cultural, and educational backgrounds may influence [their] texts in various ways" (Matsuda and Cox 44). Tutors can find it useful to know that there are differences among writing styles across cultures, not least because this knowledge demonstrates that rather than natural or universal, the conventions of U.S. academic writing are, as ESL and writing center scholar Amy Jo Minett says, "no better or worse than other conventions" (68). In addition, it's been argued that contrastive rhetoric can lead multilingual writers to "enlightenment about their writing in English, as students suddenly become conscious of the implicit assumptions behind the way they construct written ideas and behind the way English does" (Leki qtd. in Minett 68).

But in *Writing Across Borders*, director Wayne Robertson explains that the theory of contrastive rhetoric is controversial because it can serve as another way of making assumptions about writers based on their backgrounds. As ESL researchers Paul Kei Matsuda and Michelle Cox caution, we shouldn't overgeneralize about individuals' writing based on their culture or languages because "not all differences can be attributed to differences in ESL writers' native language or cultural background" (44). There might be many reasons why a writer's text does not follow a conventional aspect of U.S. academic writing, such as what was emphasized (or not) in the writer's previous education (44–45) as well as the processes he used to produce his text. Because we cannot describe the full range of culturally informed rhetorical styles without making such overgeneralizations, instead we focus below on a few key conventions of U.S. academic writing that might be useful for you and the writers you tutor to be aware of.

Characteristics of U.S. Academic Writing. By discussing key characteristics of U.S. academic writing, we don't want to suggest that it has one unified style that follows the same format no matter what the discipline or level. In fact, as you'll see in the next chapter, we believe that differences among different kinds of academic writing are crucial for tutors to know about. Here, however, we look at what these different kinds of writing often have in common—and what readers and writers of this writing tend to value—because learning to recognize the commonalities can be the first step in understanding the differences.

One generalization that tends to hold true across different kinds of academic writing in the United States is that it is **reader centered**. That is, the aim of much of this writing is to make its ideas as clear as possible to its intended readers (which we touch upon in the previous chapter in terms of Flower's valuing of "Reader-Based" over "Writer-Based" prose). Of course, what's "clear" to writers and readers who belong to a discipline that uses specialized language will not necessarily be clear to those of us outside of the discipline. But, in general, "clarity" in U.S. academic writing is achieved by focusing these ideas around a central argument that is stated explicitly at the beginning and reiterated and supported with evidence throughout. Readers are also kept on track in this writing through the presentation of distinctly delimited units of information in the form of paragraphs and/or sections with topic sentences, transitions, and headers that link these units together and move the reader forward. As a result, this writing is described as "linear" and is often contrasted with the work of writers from Asian cultures that might "withhold the thesis statement until the very end," making the reader "work harder to understand the writer's meaning" (Minett 67, 69).

Helping Writers Navigate U.S. Academic Writing. Scholars Jennifer E. Staben and Kathryn Dempsey Nordhaus offer two useful suggestions. First, they recommend discussing with multilingual writers "the directness of US culture, where phrases like 'get to the point' and 'time is money' are frequently used and show them how these values are reflected in our rhetorical choices." Doing so can be a good way to explain "why main ideas tend to be frontloaded at both the essay and paragraph level in US academic writing" (83). Second, they recommend spending time working through the instructor's written instructions as a culturally informed document. This includes alerting writers to the features we discuss in Chapter 3—key words, directions about the kinds of evidence needed and formatting, and information that's relevant to the assignment but external to it, such as a grading rubric or instructor comments. But Staben and Nordhaus point out that you might need to make clear "assumptions that are not usually directly addressed." To do this, they suggest reading the assignment, asking the writer to explain how he understands what it is asking him to do and how he tried to meet those expectations, and comparing the writer's understanding to your own: Where was he on track? What did he miss? (81). Nan cautions against lecturing multilingual writers on U.S. academic writing, suggesting that it is more productive to scaffold the discussion in the way that Staben and Nordhaus outline, "gaug[ing] the writer's level of knowledge" by asking questions about what he knows already about academic writing in the United States: "What do *you* think a thesis statement is in college writing?" (468, this book).

Read the Writing (If There Is Any)

As in any tutoring session, reading through the writer's text and encouraging the writer's participation in this process are crucial. But working through a multilingual writer's text might involve additional subtleties. First of all, as Matsuda and Cox observe, for native speakers who can draw on their extensive and intuitive knowledge of English to gauge the correctness and effectiveness of their writing, reading aloud can be a useful strategy. For writers with less than native fluency, this strategy might not be as useful. Matsuda and Cox suggest instead that the tutor try reading aloud, with the writer following along and noticing when the tutor has difficulty, adds missing words, or changes the words, as well as when the reading goes smoothly. However, they caution that "if the number of errors prevents the tutor from reading aloud without stumbling too often, it may be more effective for the tutor to read silently, focusing on sorting through meaning" (47). In addition, they strongly recommend reading the writing twice, with the first read-through reserved for getting the gist—what the writer is trying to say with her writing—and understanding "how the paper is organized on its own terms" (48).

Negotiate Priorities for the Session

As we mention in Chapter 3, negotiating priorities begins from the onset of the session, when the writer tells you why she has come for tutoring in the first place. However, after you've read through the writing and talked about it would be a good point to check in with the writer to see what she thinks she most needs help with. The following questions can provide both you and the writer with a checklist of potential areas to work on:

Are There Global Issues That Need Work? Even if the writer's work contains sentence-level issues, she might see the need to work on other matters, so it's important to find out what her priorities are. These global issues might be related to those we describe in Chapter 3, such as ensuring that the writing conveys the main point or focus that the writer had in mind, addresses the assignment, and organizes ideas and evidence. But as we explain above, these issues might include additional subtleties such as addressing both the explicit instructions and implicit assumptions of the assignment and presenting the argument and evidence in ways that meet the expectations of readers familiar with U.S. academic writing. Global issues too are culturally determined.

Are Some Sentence-Level Issues Global Issues? Another subtlety to keep in mind is that multicultural writers' texts often underscore the ways in which the sentence-level issues can themselves be global issues—and that there is sometimes not a clear distinction between them. After all, it is through a writer's individual sentences and words that readers develop a sense of the whole piece of writing, including its main focus, relationship to the assignment, and organization. To help you and the writer negotiate this subtle work, prioritizing certain kinds of errors over others can help. Below, we provide more detail about the different levels of error you and the writer might come across, starting with those that might most influence the reader's understanding of what is happening at the global level.

Are There Errors That Prevent Readers from Understanding the Meaning? Most important of the kinds of errors you might find are those that prevent the writer's intended readers from understanding what she is trying to say, errors that likely have to do with word choice, word order, and verb tenses (Matsuda and Cox 47). To locate and alert the writer to such errors, Matsuda and Cox recommend looking for and putting small marks next to "features or details that seem surprising or those that jar the reading process: the unexpected" (48). Doing so, they hold, requires an extra level of awareness of your own expectations as a reader, along the lines of the reflective work tutors do when they offer metacommentary:

> For instance, if a particular passage seems disorienting, the reader can take advantage of this situation by focusing on where he or she started feeling lost and why. What in the text caused the reader to wander? What is it about the reader's own expectations that contributed to the feeling of disorientation? The reader should also focus on areas where he or she feels "stuck"—unable to generate meaning from the text—and use this experience as an opportunity to consider what would be needed to move forward in the reading process. Does the reader need to ask the writer a question? Does the reader need to mark the area and then move on with reading, in the hope that another section of the paper will help the reader negotiate the challenging section? (48)

In an article included in Section IV, undergraduate tutor-researcher Cameron Mozafari puts this process more bluntly, holding that as tutors read multilingual writers' work, "they should avoid trying to understand what they cannot" because doing so "is equivalent to translating the text from what the student is saying to what the tutor is interpreting it as" (54). Mozafari reports on a strategy that takes Matsuda and Cox's recommendations one step further. He asked a multilingual writer, Kim, to read her text aloud and to do this prioritizing herself, by "mark[ing] only the parts of her paper that confused her or the parts where she wasn't sure if she was being clear." According to Mozafari, this process "motivated Kim to actively read her paper and look for disconnects between what she meant to say and what she was saying"—"places where she felt that her text . . . was not accurately communicating what she meant (her motive for writing the text)" (460, this book).

Are There Word Choice Errors? Carol Severino and Elizabeth Deifell argue that attention to word choice and vocabulary is especially important for multilingual writers because errors in this area are often more common than those having to do with grammar. Vocabulary is crucial for "readers' comprehension and evaluation" as well as for the writer's "ability to function successfully in a second language academic environment" (49). Their case study of a multilingual writer demonstrates that his vocabulary improved because of focused work in this area, which included both direct correction of vocabulary errors and the reflective "meta-discourse that explains them" (e.g., "Why should you use 'look at' rather than 'look'?") They argue that because these discussions can help multilingual writers become more consciously aware of their language, they can foster "explicit and purposeful learning" (49).

Are There Patterns of Error That the Writer Can Learn to Correct on Her Own? Next on the list of errors to address might come errors that appear several times in one piece of writing and that writers can correct themselves. Cynthia Linville describes these errors as usually having to do with "subject-verb agreement, verb tense, verb form, singular-plural noun endings, word form, and sentence structure" (119). She admits that the work involved with this process—for instance, asking the writer to underline each subject and verb pair—can be slow going (122–23). She recommends becoming familiar with and using relevant grammar resources, samples of which are available in her chapter (123–29) and at the Purdue Online Writing Lab.

What If You Can't Explain the Errors You See?   If you're like us and the tutors we've worked with, you might come across an error that you can't explain or find in a resource. First and foremost, and as with all tutoring situations, we have to be honest about the limits of our knowledge and admit when we don't know why a verb should take a particular form or why a particular article or preposition belongs where it does. If other tutors or administrators are around and aren't busy—and if this feels important enough to stop the session—we can ask them for help. Alternatively, we might write down the error and the writer's email address and follow up later. Or, and this might be more risky, we can offer what we *think* we know—that this part of the writing doesn't seem right to us and here's what we'd do instead—but we have to explain to the writer that we're drawing on our intuitive knowledge of the language rather than our explicit understanding of specific grammar rules. It might be that we have to admit that we just don't know, encourage the writer to ask his professor, and move on to something we can help the writer with.

If There Is No Writing, Help the Writer Get Started

To help a multilingual writer start from ground zero on a piece of writing, any of the strategies for generating ideas and writing that we discuss in Chapters 3 and 4 can be useful. You might need to highlight the cultural expectations of the assignment and help the writer work on any related reading and associated special vocabulary. Most of all, you'll want to draw on your conversational, motivational, and scaffolding skills, taking an interest in the writer's ideas, perhaps with a pen in hand so you can take notes, draw a map, or in other ways help him plan out what he'd like to say, and encouraging the writer to start on this writing during the session himself.

Wrap Up

As with all sessions, you'll want to keep your eye on the clock so that you and the writer don't feel rushed at the end, set aside the last ten minutes or so to give the writer time to address any final concerns and make a plan for what she'll address on her own. You'll also want to invite the writer to use your program again.

Reflect

During and after sessions, reflection can be especially useful when working with writers across language and cultural differences. As Severino and Deifell suggest, writers and tutors can reflect by using "meta-discourse" to describe why a language choice is the correct one. In addition, some scholars recommend that multilingual writers keep a log to keep track of these choices and reflections (Cogie, Strain, and Lorinskas 18–19, 25–28). Even if the writer is disinclined to keep such a log, simply talking about what he learned about and accomplished in the session can promote such reflection. Tutors, too, should reflect on these sessions, to consolidate their learning for themselves and for other tutors in their programs.

For Writing

1. What do you know about the way that you learn? What are your own learning differences? Are you a strong visual learner? (Do you map things out? Are you good with directions?) Are you a strong auditory learner? (Do you learn well in situations in which you hear something explained?) Are you a tactile or kinesthetic learner? (Do you learn well in situations where you move around and/or physically manipulate items to illustrate a concept?)

2. Write a brief narrative that illustrates a way in which you learn well or in which you have difficulty learning well.

3. Write a brief essay that describes as a learning environment the space in which you tutor. How, for example, does this space engage the senses? What kind of learning and learners does the configuration of space enable, encourage, discourage, and prohibit? Envision and describe the learning styles of the writer who might benefit the most from your program. Now describe a writer whose learning styles would not match well. Are there ways to adapt the program to better meet the needs of both, and if so should the program change? Why or why not?

TUTORING ACROSS PHYSICAL
AND LEARNING DIFFERENCES

How you work with writers across differences in physical and learning abilities might also depend on your own identity or background. If you have a disability yourself or know people with such differences, you will likely be well aware that disabilities make up an even bigger identity category than that of language and culture, since they include a range of both physical and cognitive impairments.

If you don't have experience with or knowledge of physical and learning disabilities and differences, the International Writing Centers Association's Statement on Disabilities might help. For one thing, it provides a sense of how wide-ranging this identity category is. Following the United Nations and World Health Assembly's definition, this statement holds that **disability** is "Any restriction or lack (resulting from an impairment) of ability to perform an activity in the manner or within the range considered normal for a human being." At least fifteen percent of the population is disabled "and people with disabilities are considered 'the population's largest minority.'" Therefore, disability "is a universal human experience and not a concern to a minority of humanity: every human being can suffer from a decrement in health and, thereby, experience some disability" (1).

The universality of physical and learning disabilities means that writers, tutors, directors, and other members of writing tutoring programs work with them every day. In addition, Babcock and Thonus point out that the accommodations stipulated by the Americans with Disabilities Act extend "to all educational contexts, including the writing center" (93). Along with being entitled to use writing tutoring programs, students with disabilities might even prefer them to the disabilities offices on their campuses, according to writing center scholar Julie Neff Lippman (Clark et al. 238). As a result, Hitt urges those of us in writing tutoring programs to be prepared to work with "*all* students" as part of our commitment to treat writers "individually and, thus, as *different* from one another in terms of what they bring to the center and how they learn and compose" (383, this book). In her award-winning article on tutoring deaf writers, Babcock holds that "tutors must respect students' abilities and realize that all students are different: some process information differently due to preference, and some, such as deaf students and students with LDs, process information differently due to differences in hard wiring" ("Interpreted" 112).

Fortunately, because writing tutors and writing tutoring programs have long recognized that there is no one-size-fits-all approach to tutoring and writing, respecting writers as individuals and tailoring our work to fit their needs is a large part of what we do in any case. This following pages will provide you with additional flexible strategies to include in your multimodal tutoring toolkit that should be especially helpful in working with writers across differences in learning and physical abilities. Generally speaking, these flexible approaches can include those listed in Table 5.3 (next page).

Below, we describe in more detail additional strategies that researchers have identified as helping work across physical and learning differences. We start with discussions of dyslexia and deafness, two disabilities that might affect the writer's text and language. Then we move to disabilities that might cause behavioral differences, including attention-deficit/hyperactivity disorder and others that result in pragmatic impairment, which can include difficulty in understanding how others are feeling or their mental states, sarcasm, irony, and jokes, as well as ambiguity and indirectness (Perkins qtd. in Babcock "When" 286, this book). We should point out that, in contrast to the relatively large amount of research and tutor-education materials on multilingual writers, there is significantly less information about tutoring writing across learning and physical differences. Below, we survey some of the research and advice currently available. We also encourage you and the other members of your program to contact the disabilities office on your campus to find out about local resources and to pursue your own research on these important topics.

Table 5.3 General Strategies for Working Across Differences in Learning and Physical Abilities.

- *Use familiar tutoring strategies*, such as getting acquainted; asking the writer what she wants to work on; analyzing the assignment or context for the writing, reading the writing (if there is any), and helping the writer get started if not; negotiating priorities, wrapping up, and reflecting.
- *Draw on strategies for working across language and cultural differences*. You might need to be more direct than feels natural or comfortable to you. You might find that reading aloud (by you or the writer) is not an effective strategy. You might need to give the writer more time to answer questions.
- *Ask the writer what works for him*. As Gillespie and Lerner suggest, the writer himself can be "your best resource in the tutorial." Along with asking the writer directly about strategies that help him succeed at various tasks, "even nonwritten ones," be sure to listen and observe the writer to find out what works. "You will need to be flexible, patient, and creative in your sessions" (170).
- *Be flexible about writing process strategies*. Gillespie and Lerner explain that for some writers with learning disabilities, brainstorming strategies such as freewriting might not be useful. They recommend instead using questions to help writers "develop their ideas. Some will need you to write down key terms or take notes as you ask them questions about the subject matter. Some may need you to help them organize their ideas into an outline" (170).
- *Support visual, auditory, and kinesthetic learning styles*. Hitt suggests using strategies that play to the writer's strengths and abilities: "If a student prefers drawing, tutors can adapt, asking the student to sketch an outline of their main ideas. Similarly, talking through a text could be more beneficial than reading it word for word" (387, this book).
- *Be prepared to not know about the writer's disability*. The writer's cognitive or physical difference might not be apparent or relevant to your work. Moreover, the writer might not want to tell you or know about it fully himself. Kiedaisch and Dinitz's opening questions that we include above can invite disclosure, but you should not ask, since doing so likely violates the writer's right to privacy.

Dyslexia

In a study for which she interviewed dyslexic students at her institution, undergraduate tutor-researcher Jennifer Wewers defines dyslexia is a broad category with "a diversity of characteristics" (230). As a "language-based processing disorder," it can include difficulties with reading (decoding words, seeing "letter-sound correspondences," and "processing the context"), "listening/comprehension difficulties," spelling, and writing processes (234, 230–31). As she is careful to point out, "dyslexia is not the result of subnormal intelligence" (230).

Wewers suggests that many of the strategies that tutors would use with any writer, such as offering their perspectives as readers and "encouraging multidrafting and revising," are useful for writers with dyslexia. She cautions, however, against viewing "dyslexic writers as 'just like' non-dyslexic writers" since this might give the impression that tutors are "delegitimizing or trivializing [their] unique problems" (232). Tutoring strategies that might be less effective for these writers include reading aloud, hedging, and even asking questions, since a dyslexic writer who has "trouble with short-term memory retention may be unable to answer the questions a tutor poses, or may need more time to arrive at an answer" (233).

Wewers urges tutors to "be flexible and creative" in their approaches, including varying "channels of communication." For instance, rather than simply repeating a question that a writer can't answer, she recommends rephrasing it in different ways "until one of them finally 'clicks'" (233–34). Tutors might also need to help dyslexic writers with reading, since one of the writers she interviewed described her struggles with paraphrasing and synthesizing material. Wewers suggests "asking guiding questions about the material and then writing down what the student says in response, following the tutee's train of thought in written form" (235). Another writer Wewers interviewed talked about her difficulties with organization and with writing that "wanders" in ways she cannot pinpoint herself (235). This writer recommended that tutors "be very specific when they are identifying aspects of a paper that are unclear or disorganized, taking care to explain exactly why they are confused" (236). Wewers suggests making a reverse outline for the writer and looking over an example of the kind of writing the writer is working on, talking over its "rhetorical moves," and highlighting the choices made by the writer of the example. "Stressing choices in this way might be helpful for the dyslexic student who has often felt that his or her choice has been taken away. With choice, tutees may feel a greater sense of control over their writing" (236).

Wewers points out too that dyslexic students might need help with grammar and spelling. Gillespie and Lerner, describing the writing of learning-disabled writers in general, explain that "The written page might not look the same to the LD writer as it does to you." This writer might not see errors in spelling or grammar. As a result, you'll need to help the writer find and correct the errors (170–71). Lippman suggests taking this process one step further. Rather than helping the writer make corrections on a hard copy, which might result in additional mistakes as the writer types in corrections later on, the tutor might work with the writer on an electronic copy, typing in the corrections as the writer says them out loud and "repeating [the writer's] words to make sure the sentences say exactly what [the writer] wants them to say"—because the writer might be able to "hear the wrong word even when he can't see it." She recommends also pointing out when a "sentence is perfect" and not treating the changes as a "big deal" (Clark et al. 240).

Deafness

Working successfully across hearing differences requires hearing tutors to reflect on several assumptions they might hold and adjust their tutoring strategies accordingly. Babcock explains that deaf people, as distinguished from the hard-of-hearing, make up "a cultural and linguistic minority who live in a society where the majority (hearing people) use speech and sound for tasks for which deaf people commonly use vision" ("Interpreted" 96). As she goes on to say,

> Deafness is a unique situation in which many commonplace ideas become problematical, such as the way we think of an author *speaking* through a text. . . . Commonly, writing and reading are described in analogies of hearing and speaking, and common tutoring practices depend on aural and oral processing of language. Deaf people, in contrast, process language through the eyes and hands, not the ears and mouth. ("Interpreted" 98)

In her longer study of tutoring deaf and hearing students, *Tell Me How It Reads*, Babcock reminds us that deaf writers cannot, of course, hear their mistakes, making reading aloud an ineffectual strategy (180). Likewise, appealing to "what sounds right" in terms of grammatical correctness is equally ineffective ("Interpreted" 115).

Instead, deaf people need to find their errors by seeing them on the page, which requires familiarity "with the conventions of print in English" (*Tell Me* 180) and particular grammar rules ("Interpreted" 115). As a result, and because it might well be "the only fully accessible, direct avenue to English for deaf people," reading is especially crucial (*Tell Me* 184). Yet because American Sign Language, the language that deaf people in the United States primarily communicate with, is distinct from written English, deaf people often have difficulties with reading. As a result, Babcock recommends that tutors "pay special attention to reading comprehension, paraphrasing, and summarizing" (*Tell Me* 180).

In addition, hearing tutors should consider how these writers take in information and what impact it will have on their own tutoring strategies. Because hearing people can process both "aural and visual message at the same time," hearing tutors might mistakenly try to communicate with deaf writers at the same time that these writers are reading over their writing. Instead, because deaf writers can process "only one visual message at a time, either the interpreter's signs or the words on the paper," Babcock reminds us that when the writer is "looking down at the text," we need to get the writer's attention first in order to communicate with her. She recommends "waving your hand in the student's field of vision" (*Tell Me* 182).

Babcock recommends two other strategies that build on deaf culture and language. First, although she acknowledges that "all writers . . . need to be pushed to find their own answers wherever possible," because deaf culture values directness, she recommends that tutors employ "direct communication" and "straight talk" when they find that leading questions and other indirect, hedging techniques aren't working (*Tell Me* 181; "Interpreted" 104). Second, although it can be useful for deaf people to produce text by writing it out, on paper or on a computer, they might find it easier to brainstorm in American Sign Language "while the interpreter interprets and the tutor takes notes," since this would avoid the additional step of translating their thoughts into written English (*Tell Me* 183).

Probably most important, since "all deaf students are different, and they know their own communication needs," Babcock suggests encouraging deaf writers to indicate which communication method is best for them. These might include making use of visual ways of communicating, including putting the text between the tutor and writer, writing on paper or online, and modeling corrections ("Interpreted" 113, 105, 115; *Tell Me* 182).

Pragmatic Impairments

In an article included in Section IV, Babcock discusses another broad category of disability, pragmatic impairment, which "is associated with diagnoses as varied as Asperger's syndrome, autism, learning disability, traumatic brain injury, and attention deficit hyperactivity disorders" (269, this book). People with pragmatic impairment might have trouble understanding why someone is asking a particular question or making a particular statement as well as using other cues such as "facial expression, pauses, [and] intonation" (272, this book). They might also use words unusually or incorrectly. Again, being direct and explicit, this time about what you want the writer to do, can "assist those tutees who do not perceive the speaker's meaning behind an utterance" (e.g., "I am asking these questions to help you come up with ideas about what to put in the paper") (272, this book).

Attention-Deficit/Hyperactivity Disorder

Undergraduate tutor-researcher Emily Ryan characterizes ADHD "as a developmental delay in self-control" with symptoms that include "impulsivity, distractibility, or excess energy" (291, Hallowell and Ratley qtd. in Ryan 290). Her article provides a largely first-person account, in part because very few students were willing to share their experiences with her, the result, she suspects, of the stigma they felt (297). Along with being sensitive to this possible "fear of being judged," Ryan suggests that tutors might need to help writers with ADHD with time management and keeping track of writing-related materials (such as the assignment) as well as organizing ideas and seeing "the big picture" (295). In addition, Gillespie and Lerner suggest that these writers sometimes need a quiet place to work (171).

We have moved quickly through a variety of physical and learning differences that can affect tutoring sessions. We should emphasize that, in addition to those we discuss here, there are many other kinds of disability and difference that can have an impact on writing tutoring sessions and that the descriptions we provide are meant as a starting place for discussion rather than a set of definitive answers. We encourage you to work with the tutors and writers in your program to broaden this conversation, by pursuing the scholarship we mention here, by talking with the staff of your campus's disabilities office, and by researching other kinds of difference that we have not named that may affect tutors' and writers' choices.

For Writing

1. Review an assignment sheet from one of your classes. Does it describe the expectations of academic writing to be completed in this assignment? If so, compare these elements described with your own understanding of academic writing. Where are these concepts the same? Different? Are there any expectations in the assignment that are implicit or missing? How do you know these expectations exist? How might the lack of this information change a writer's approach to the assignment?

2. There is a tradition of teachers saying, "Only if you truly know a topic can you write about it." Do you think this statement is true? Generally? Always? Hypothesize or write about an instance in which this was not the case.

3. Are there parts of your identity that you have left out of your own academic writing? If so, why did you make this decision? How might including these elements of your identity affect your academic writing for better and for worse?

U.S. ACADEMIC WRITING

Here, we return to a topic we touch on in our discussion of language and culture differences, U.S. academic writing. Initially, this topic might seem to have little to do with identity, and its implications for tutors might be just as unclear. For one thing, academic writing is text and not a characteristic of human beings such as those we've discussed so far in this chapter. Yet many in the writing center field, including tutor-researchers, see significant connections between academic writing and identity, in part because, when successful, this writing implies an alignment of the author's identity with expectations for community membership in U.S. colleges and universities. This is a controversial topic: you might find yourself on one side or the other, or somewhere in between. However, because it raises concerns that you might well face as a tutor, we provide information, theories, and an additional set of strategies to draw on. Moreover, as with all scholarly controversies, this topic might well present you with the kind of gap that must be filled with your own insights as a tutor and researcher.

U.S. Academic Writing, Identity, and Tutors

Academic writing in the United States can be said to "have" an identity insofar as it reflects many of the values of its home culture, with its general emphasis on efficiency and directness. Probably more important, academic writing in the United States intersects with the identities of the student and faculty writers who try to succeed at it. Such identity characteristics as language and cultural backgrounds and physical and learning differences, as well as others we do not cover here, can impede writers' individual successes with this writing.

In turn, tutors are connected to this tie between academic writing and writer identity because a large part of the work we do is to help writers achieve such success. Indeed, as we discuss in Chapter 2, this is the reason writing tutoring programs were founded in the first place, even if this is not the only reason they exist now. As undergraduate researcher Brooke Baker holds in an article included in Section IV, "It is vitally important for new writers to understand the structural and linguistic expectations of this academic discourse they are choosing to learn" (276, this book). Following Kenneth Bruffee's lead, she sees the tutor's role as one of helping writers to enter this "conversation": "Our academic literacy is one of the most important things tutors can share with our tutees. We have learned to speak the language(s) of the academy despite our divergent backgrounds, and . . . we have the ability, via peerhood, to impact the language choices of our writers" (280, this book).

Bruffee's emphasis on helping writers enter the "conversation" points up yet another way that academic writing in the United States is—or can be felt to be—linked to identity. Because for many people writing seems both to express and influence who we are, succeeding at academic writing can feel as if it comes at a cost to one's identity and how it is represented through language. Virginia Pryor, for example, an undergraduate whose discussion of academic writing appears in the tutor education textbook *Working with Student Writers*, puts the situation this way: "a large portion of student writers are faced with a constant tension between the sense of being coerced into using specific language, grammar, and style and their own compulsion to assimilate into the system by following its rules—appropriating and incorporating these standards into their own writing" (336). As a case in point, Maria E. Barajas-Román, an undergraduate researcher whose essay appears in the same collection, describes herself as "a first generation Mexican-American" and "the first in my family in over seven generations to earn a college degree." Yet as she reviewed her college writing, she found that her feelings were complicated: "Though the content in the papers is academically sound, looking back, I can read between the lines and see my intense struggle for validation. Each sentence is a shovelfull of acquiescence burying what I knew to be true about life and learning" (306). And Jonathan Doucette, a tutor-researcher whose article appears in Section IV, finds that he too had "excluded" himself from a paper he wrote as a first-year student: "writing without taking into account my own sexual identity reproduced 'appropriate,' distanced, masculine, heterosexual discourse that constrained my identity as a student writer and beyond" (346, this book). Even transferring to a new college where he was able to study the very issues of gender and sexuality that he had struggled with previously created other divisions, leading him to give up "one way of relating to the world (heteronormative) for another (queer), yet each set of discourse separated me from communities I wanted to be a part of" (347, this book).

Tutor Ambivalence About U.S. Academic Writing

This process of translating one's identity by way of academic writing has led some tutors to feel ambivalent about their roles in it. Doucette and another undergraduate tutor-researcher, Jeff Reger, whose article also appears Section IV, both express concern for "the writing center's pedagogical imperative," as articulated by Stephen North, to "change the writer" (Reger 498, this book; Doucette 351, this book). Under this imperative, Doucette holds, the writing center can be seen "as a space in which unqualified, inexperienced writers are transformed into appropriate academics" (351, this book). Tutors, in turn, holds Reger, "can inadvertently urge students to acculturate themselves into academic discourse—permanently altering the way students think and write" (498, this book). Reger extends this critique to Bruffee as well, calling into question the seeming neutrality of the re-acculturation and change of consciousness resulting from his peer tutoring model. As writing center scholar and theorist Nancy Maloney Grimm describes,

> For Bruffee, the goal of peer tutoring was to encourage students to think more like "us" (the academic community, a place not known for its racial diversity). Bruffee was interested in the "social justification of belief" rather than the negotiation of differing beliefs. His definition of community was "a group of people who accept, and whose work is guided by, the same paradigms and the same code of values and assumptions". . . . There was no discussion of what to do when paradigms, values, and assumptions conflicted. ("Retheorizing" 93)

Exemplifying this ambivalence, undergraduate tutor-researcher Mara Brecht reflects on her work with Kathy, an adult writer from a less privileged background than her own whom she tutored in a community literacy program. In the article included in Section IV, she ultimately wonders, "Did my suggestions help Kathy to write more easily and confidently about what she thought, or did my suggestions simply alter her text so it was more compatible with dominant writing styles, such as my own?" (299, this book).

Of course, you might not feel such ambivalence about succeeding at academic writing yourself, as a writer or a tutor, and you might work with writers who don't either. But because this is a concern that many in the field—including other tutors—have raised, we offer information, theories, and an additional set of strategies to draw on in case you or the writers you work with do experience such ambivalence.

Standards, Nonstandard, and a "Third Option"

One such piece of information has to do with the nature of "standard" English and standards for writing in college. As we discuss in Chapter 2, the pervasive belief in higher education used to be that there was only one way to write correctly. Whether because they learned to write in another culture, they approach writing in a particular way due to a disability, or their educational background in the United States didn't include sustained focus on such standards, people who did not follow this norm were seen as nonstandard, or "bad," writers, and perhaps not intelligent enough for college. Although this belief still has its supporters, scholars and researchers have come to see that such standards are not stable or "natural." Like authorship, they have a history that has changed over time: Shakespeare, for instance, was considered nonstandard during his day and after. And, as we have seen with citation and writing practices, these standard are far from universal. As Harry Denny puts it, academic discourse is "arbitrary, fluid, and subject to constant change. As any linguistic historian of English will confirm, the language is elastic and evolving, so for anyone to posit any common use of it as static is foolish" (*Facing* 73).

This revised view of academic discourse as arbitrary, fluid, and changing has a number of significant implications. Most important, as Denny goes on to argue, this history demonstrates that it is "wrong and unethical . . . to teach any group of students, especially those who speak and write from marginalized positions, that in order to be successful they must surrender whatever Englishes they possesses for some transitory 'standard'" (*Facing* 73). As Reger and Doucette put it, the choice between acculturating to or rejecting academic discourse is a "false dilemma." For them, there is another way, a "third option," that of "'negotiat[ing] multiple, even contradictory, subject positions while rooted in dominant discourse'" and "bridging the gap between 'home' or 'private' language and 'academic' language in ways that render the student legible to a larger academic community"(Bawarshi and Pelkowski qtd. in Reger 501, this book; Doucette 353, this book).

Writing Tutoring Programs as "Contact Zones"

This third option for a negotiated discourse in turn has implications for tutors and writing tutoring programs. As Doucette writes, "Perhaps the writing center . . . should not reject entirely the traditional codes of the academy—for the material negative effects for a student who takes such a risk would be many, not least a failing grade—nor should the center completely acquiesce to such codes either. A complex hybrid of the two approaches may be called for" (353, this book). Many of the tutor-researchers whose work we've included in Section IV promote this idea of the writing tutoring program as hybrid, calling it a "third space" (Mozafari, this book) in which tutor and writer alike enact a "critical consciousness" (Baker 279, this book; Reger 500, this book). But most often, following Grimm's lead in her groundbreaking book *Good Intentions: Writing Center Work for Postmodern Times* (57), these tutor-researchers draw on critical theorist Mary Louise Pratt's famous framework for discussing the difficulties that sometimes arise with cross-cultural interactions, the "contact zone." Reger, Brecht, and Baker all see writing tutoring programs as contact zones, places where "disparate cultures meet, clash, and grapple with each other, often in contexts of highly asymmetrical relations of power" (Pratt 34).

Tutoring writing, in other words, is not necessarily a smooth and comfortable process. As Brecht says, "Pratt highlights the idea that there is no place of neutrality or safety, even in the educational sphere. . . . The game of education is not actually a fair one" (302, this book). As a contact zone, according to Baker, the writing tutoring program can become "a place in which student and tutor could meet and clash; a space in which to try on language and form without the fear of failure" (275, this book).

In addition, these researchers demonstrate what can happen in the writing tutoring program as contact zone and offer specific strategies (Table 5.4). Identities are everywhere in our sessions and our programs, ourselves, the writing we produce, the writers we help, and the relationships we form with them. As Nancy Maloney Grimm points out, yet another of the benefits of tutoring is learning how to build such relationships across the differences that result when we do not share identities. "Whether your future workplace is a hospital operating room, an airplane control tower, or an international information systems network, your job success will depend on your ability to develop positive working relationships with people from historically, culturally, linguistically, and economically different backgrounds" ("New" 19).

Table 5.4 Tutoring Strategies for the Contact Zone.

- *Explain academic writing.* Baker describes aiming to "demystify" academic discourse for the writers she worked with in a small-group setting. Along with "playing with language, arguing about meaning, and trying on language from the outside," the group "defin[ed] good writing," explored trying "to fake this new dialect," struggled, and even "raise[d] the specter of language changing the way we think and who we are" (281, this book).
- *Analyze academic writing in terms of conventions, not absolute rules.* Reger recommends teaching writers "how to analyze writing conventions themselves so that they have the ability to understand any discourse." Specifically, he suggests explaining "that academic discourse is not necessarily the best or the ideal, but what is expected in the context of the American university." He urges tutors to steer clear of "absolute 'wrong' or 'right' judgments" by "identify[ing] errors always as what is expected by professors in academic discourse," and, consequently, "allowing ambivalence about acculturation rather than unquestioning acceptance" (501, 506, this book).
- *Identify the tensions in academic writing.* Denny argues that we should not admonish writers to "'stop writing like you speak' (as if the voice in either context is neutral and absent of deeply political referents)." Instead, we should help writers "process and name the dynamics and tensions," "understand what their professors' expectations are," and, in a manner that resembles Mozafari's work with Kim, find "ways of leveraging personal experience in occasions where professors might not otherwise allow it" (*Facing* 77, 131, 54).
- *Identify the tensions in our own programs.* In "Addressing the Everyday Language of Oppression in the Writing Center," Mandy Suhr-Sytsma and Shan-Estelle Brown provide a fruitful means of taking the discussion further, in the context of your own program. They provide strategies for dealing with "systematic inequalities and discrimination based on sites of differences such as race, ethnicity, religion, class, gender, sexuality, and/or (dis)ability" (509, this book).

For Inquiry

1. After reviewing Chapter 11, pages 261–63, design and implement a case study of writers who use your program and who represent a specific identity group. The purpose of this case study is to suggest possible resources, outreach activities, or program revisions that might better serve this group.

2. Conduct historical research into the changes over time of both your institution's student demographics and the kinds of writing education that have been available on your campus. What do these trajectories suggest about changes in your institution's concept of "student" and/or "writing"? Compare this history to the changes taking place in writing center studies and writing studies as seen in such works as Neal Lerner's *The Idea of a Writing Laboratory*, Elizabeth H. Boquet's "'Our Little Secret,'" and/or James Berlin's *Rhetoric and Reality*. Does the evidence from your institution support and/or refute these narratives?

3. Look through your institution's latest admissions pamphlet and/or prospective student webpage(s). Drawing upon identity theories such as those described in this chapter and in Chapters 2 and 9, describe the identity of students represented in these materials. How do they represent gender, race and/or class? What kinds of activities are they performing? Are they engaged in academic activities? Social? Athletic? Are they in a public forum? A private space? What stories do these pictures tell? What do these images suggest about the student identity of your institution? Compare this information with that documented by your institution's demographic data. What differences do you see? Why would your institution want to represent its students in this fashion?

4. First locate a campus group whose community is focused on an identity category—for example, the international student society or the organization for nontraditionally aged students. Next, conduct a research review in both writing center studies and writing studies to investigate literacy research pertaining to this group. Finally, investigate this group's use of your program's services and its representation among your tutoring staff. For instance, ask for an appointment with this group to interview them about their relationship to your program. (You can find information about interviews in Chapters 10 and 11.) Write a recommendation report to be shared with your program.

CHAPTER 6

Tutoring Writing In and Across
The Disciplines

> **For Discussion**
>
> **1.** Working with your peers, create a collective list of all of the writing assign-
> ments you will need to complete for your classes this semester. As you look
> over this list, discuss the writing skills that will be needed for any—or all—of
> these assignments. What writing skills are common to many of these assign-
> ments? What, if any, writing skills would be limited to only a few?
>
> **2.** Working with your peers, finish this sentence in as many ways as possible: "All
> good academic writing _____"

INTRODUCTION

By this point in your career as a student, you've probably read or composed many
different kinds of writing for a variety of courses and extracurricular contexts. As
a result, you're likely aware that the kinds of writing required for these contexts
can be diverse but that they also have features in common. And you've probably
had to figure out how to deal with these differences and similarities both as a
reader and a writer, including how to make your writing meet readers' varying
expectations. For writing in your major, about which you might well have expertise, you might have internalized these expectations so well that you don't remember how you learned them—or a time when you didn't know them. These
kinds of writing bring us to the key concept for this chapter, **genre**.

Even with all you know already about different kinds of writing in college,
the prospect of working with someone on writing for a course or other context
with which you have no experience can be intimidating. The good news is that
you're not alone. There are many accounts of tutors feeling daunted by having to

work outside of their comfort zones. For instance, in an article we include in Section IV, undergraduate tutor-researchers Ruth Johnson, Beth Clark, and Mario Burton confirm that "Although consultants work with students from a wide range of disciplines every day, informal talk . . . and formal discussions . . . frequently reveal a common insecurity about working with students in unfamiliar disciplines" (391, this book). As a case in point, they open their article with this scenario:

> *Hmm, an engineering student,* [the tutor] thinks with a little apprehension, as she prepares herself for a challenge. A group of engineering students then floods in, accompanying the one who actually made the appointment. They explain the project which they are writing—a type of project she has never written before, a type of project with which she has no previous experience. She wonders if she will give appropriate advice or if she will be able to think of anything to say at all. She wonders if she will even be able to understand the intricate, jargon-laden draft. Then she takes a deep breath, knowing that these students are looking to her for help, and starts asking questions. (391, this book)

It is true that writing in different disciplines, such as engineering or English, can be distinct in a host of ways, including subject matter, format, citation styles, organization, jargon, and even ideas about what's important or valuable to explain to readers. Both you and the writer can find it very helpful if you have experience with the kind of writing a writer is working on. On the other hand, as Johnson, Clark, and Burton. explain, the tutoring sessions they studied in which English-major tutors worked with engineering students were highly successful— indeed, more successful than these tutors' sessions with students writing for English courses. As we mention in Chapter 2 and as we say more about below, there is a long tradition of writing tutors working with writers from disciplines different from their own. Indeed, this book embodies this philosophy: even as we emphasize that each writer is unique, we offer strategies that, with adjustments and flexibility, should be useful for most writers most of the time, no matter what the field or context. Note that Johnson et al.'s hypothetical tutor begins by asking questions, and their transcripts of real sessions feature tutors doing the same as well as drawing on other strategies that will be familiar to you.

As in previous chapters, the discussion here will build on what you already know about the topic, in this case the ways in which expectations for writing in various academic disciplines, and for the courses housed within them, can sometimes be very different. Specifically, this chapter will build on this knowledge by discussing

- *Reasons for these disciplinary differences,* by way of research on writing across the curriculum (WAC), writing in the disciplines (WID), and theories of genre
- *How such differences have affected tutors and writing center scholarship,* specifically in the debate over generalist versus specialist tutoring

- *Strategies for helping writers with disciplinary writing*, whether the writer is working in a discipline that she knows but you don't, in one that you know but she doesn't, or in one with which both you and the writer are unfamiliar
- *Strategies for writing fellows*, because these tutors probably have the most experience with questions related to disciplinary writing

---

For Writing

1. Describe one of your earliest experiences with writing in school. What did this experience teach you about academic writing? About yourself as a writer?

2. Reflect upon a time when you were given a writing assignment that you did not understand. Describe the strategies that you used to figure out and accomplish the various parts. Are these strategies that you have used elsewhere? Are they strategies that might help another writer?

ACADEMIC WRITING(S)

In the previous chapter, to illustrate how writing styles can differ dramatically across cultures, we present academic writing in the United States as adhering to a uniform standard—a "point-evidence-explain" structure that's linear, front-loaded, and reader centered. However, as writing researcher Charles Bazerman and his colleagues have pointed out, there is a great deal of debate about how uniform academic writing in the United States actually is. "One enduring theoretical issue," they write, "is the degree to which academic writing is the same or different across disciplinary settings" (Bazerman et al. 85). One way to view the poles of this debate is in terms of two ways that writing in academic settings has been conceptualized in writing studies: writing across the curriculum and writing in the disciplines.

Similarities: Writing Across the Curriculum (WAC)

On one side of this debate, Bazerman et al. hold, academic writing is viewed "as singular and uniform," which is "an educationally attractive idea" since it presents "single core set of teachable language skills" (87). As we discuss in Chapter 5, much writing assigned in U.S. colleges and universities shares key features, and these similarities are in part what make it possible for colleges and universities to require students to take introductory writing courses, such as first-year composition (FYC). Students must fulfill this requirement, the argument goes, in order to prepare for the kinds of writing they will encounter later in their academic lives.

Building on such similarities, the **writing across the curriculum (WAC)** movement began in the 1970s to help faculty from disciplines outside of writing studies to use writing to support student learning in their courses. Faculty found that certain kinds of writing activities, such as reflective or personal writing, helped students to develop their knowledge and skills across vastly different disciplinary contexts. Indeed, recent researchers have found that because instructors across the curriculum sometimes share the similar pedagogical goal of helping students learn the content material, their students' writing can have much in common (Soliday 37–38; Severino and Traschel; Zawacki). This finding suggests that a course such as FYC that aims to teach students about writing in college can help them learn how to produce the kind of reflective, personal work that would help them prepare for writing in other courses. Such a course can also help prepare students to tutor other students on this writing.

Differences: Writing in the Disciplines (WID)

However, the description of U.S. academic writing as relatively uniform has struck many researchers (and students) as incomplete. For one thing, faculty assign specific kinds of writing, such as term papers, essays, summaries, lab reports, reviews, and so on, rather than generic "academic writing." And these specific kinds of writing might or might not conform to a linear, frontloaded, and argument-based format. In writing studies, this attention to the differences among kinds of academic writing is often considered part of the study of **writing in the disciplines (WID)**. One such proponent of this view is theorist and historian David R. Russell, who famously illustrated this argument by comparing writing to playing ball.

Writing in the Disciplines Is Like Playing Different Ball Games

Whether the ball is "large, small, hard, soft, leather, rubber, round, oblong, and so on," Russell holds, will ultimately depend on the game being played—volleyball, soccer, Ping-Pong, jacks, croquet, golf, tennis, squash, etc. (57). For example, although baseball and football are both played with a ball, the balls themselves are different and the games have different rules that determine how the balls must be used. Likewise, the kind of writing we produce depends on the context in which we write, whether a specific academic discipline, such as English or engineering, or some other discourse community, whether composed of stamp collectors, knitters, or heavy metal fans, all of whom have their own jargon and other ways of communicating. Each of these contexts, in other words, is a different "game," with its own rules and its own ball. And all of these contexts/games share certain commonalities, but they have many distinguishing features as well.

For Russell, a crucial implication of his analogy is that people learn to play ball games by playing the actual, individual games, not by first learning "general ball." Likewise, students learn to write for specific disciplines, such as English or engineering, only within the context of these disciplines. Therefore, according to Russell, a course in "general writing skills" such as FYC would be only as useful as "a course in general ball using" (58). Rather, students will learn the skills only when they are taught the game, because such skills only have meaning within the games that use them (58). As we discuss in more detail below, this conclusion raises important questions about how tutors outside a discipline can work with students learning to write within it.

An Example: Citation Practices in Three Disciplines

A concrete and fairly concise example of the sort of disciplinary differences Russell has in mind—and one that is useful for tutors to know about—can be found in a comparison of the ways that researchers in the sciences, social sciences, and humanities (specifically literary studies) cite their sources. The kind of documentation style they use depends on their disciplinary context or the "game" they're playing. Susan Mueller offers a helpful analysis of three major citation systems: (1) *The MLA Handbook for Writers of Research Papers,* developed by the Modern Language Association and used by students in literature and language departments, including many FYC courses; (2) *The Publication Manual of the American Psychological Association* (APA), used in the social sciences; and (3) NLM, the *National Library of Medicine Recommended Formats for Bibliographic Citation*, designed for researchers in government and academia ("Documentation" 8). According to Mueller, these professional groups developed these systems "to document and preserve those characteristics of the underlying sources that matter to the discipline." Therefore, the systems are not interchangeable because they "reflect different underlying value systems" ("Documentation" 6). For instance, take the use of quotations: because scholars in literary studies rely on written texts as their primary source of evidence, "MLA encourages the judicious use of quotations for emphasis and to lend authority to a paper." By contrast, APA "discourages the use of direct quotations" and "NLM overtly prohibits direct quotations" ("Documentation" 8), since researchers who use these systems engage in empirical research that relies on qualitative or quantitative evidence—for example, the results of experiments, case studies, and statistical analyses. For these researchers, what's important is the information itself rather than the specific language with which it is conveyed.

It's probably not possible for individual tutors to know all of the details of all of the documentation styles that writers are likely to need help with. But it can be helpful to know that there *are* key differences and, in general, what some of them are. Below is a table based on Mueller's article, as well as her later (2009) review of the revised version of the APA *Publication Manual*. Because we use MLA in this book, you'll see that we use a number of direct quotations here.

Table 6.1 Some Disciplinary Differences Expressed by Three Documentation Styles (Based on Mueller "Documentation" 6–8; Review 10).

QUESTIONS ABOUT VALUES	MLA	APA	NLM
"Time: How does the discipline view the age of a source? Does time and its passage matter?"	*Values time minimally:* "[C]onsiders ancient texts and the scholarship done upon them to be timeless."	*Values time considerably:* How current the source is matters, so emphasizes the date.	*Values time extremely:* "[S]ees itself as the documentation style of cutting edge research."
"Authorship: How is authorship determined in this discipline? Is the author the person who wrote the words? The person who did the research? The person who supervised/authorized the experiment?" "Does it use first names, first and middle initials, or first initials only?"	*Highly privileges a traditional model of authorship:* Is concerned with "recognizing and eradicating plagiarism, and maintaining fidelity to the original text and its meaning. Both of these assert the rights of the original text and its author to be absolute and unchanging over time." The author's first name is spelled out in the works cited list.	*Minimally values traditional authorship model:* Includes relatively few pages on plagiarism. Mueller suggests that "Because social sciences build on others' work, the relationship between documents is seen as more collaborative than it is under MLA." The author's first name is represented by initials in the reference list. Researchers (not just authors) can be included. Discourages first person.	*Does not value traditional authorship model:* Plagiarism not discussed. "[M]andates the use of the passive voice to emphasize the scientific tasks or findings rather than the researcher."
"Users: Who are the intended users of the documentation style? What is their level of sophistication in dealing with sources? To whom will the document (paper/article) be submitted?"	*Two user categories, professional and student:* There are separate handbooks for undergraduate students and for professional scholars.	*Directed at professionals with minimal attention to students:* One handbook, "directed at social science researchers writing articles for publication in journals," although the latest edition recognizes student users.	*Targets professionals exclusively:* "Students are sometimes required to use NLM style, but it is primarily used by medical researchers and practitioners."
"Magnitude: Is the style concerned only with documenting sources, verb tense, and overall presentation (margins, spacing)? Or does the style mandate specific headings for specific sections be included? Is the style rigid or flexible?"	*Limited focus:* Primarily focuses on documenting sources. Moderately concerned with formatting.	*Broad focus:* Concerned with much more than documentation, including style, format, headers, sections.	*Flexible focus:* "[C]oncerned with being precise, with being flexible enough to adapt to changing technology, but also being consistent enough to maintain the record for posterity."

For Writing

1. Explore connections between the citation system in your major and the kinds of writing you've read and been asked to produce in this discipline. Questions to consider include: How are sources used in your papers or in the texts you've read from this field? What information is considered consistently important when citing evidence from external sources? When writing a citation? What do your assignments and texts suggest are the values of your field? Discovery? Tradition? Reflection? Or something else entirely? Can you see these values represented by the ways sources are cited and used?

2. Look at the handbook used by a professional organization such as MLA or APA. Describe the way it is set up and any ways that it represents the values of your field. Or compare the handbook used by professionals in your field with one used by another group, looking at the ways these handbooks are meant to be used. What do their content and organization suggest about writing in this field?

3. Pick two kinds of music (e.g., hip-hop, metal, and c-pop) or movies (e.g., horror, fantasy, and indie drama). Write a brief description of each, connecting that grouping's stylistic features to the intended audience. That is, who is thought to enjoy this kind of entertainment? What values does it represent? What kind of enjoyment does it offer?

4. Pick two kinds of writing you've done for school (e.g., lab reports, informal reflection exercises, and research papers). Write a brief description of each, connecting that grouping's stylistic features to the intended audience. That is, who tends to use this kind of writing? What kinds of values does it represent? What kinds of knowledge is it used to create?

A GENRE-BASED APPROACH TO TUTORING WRITING

One concept that can help you navigate the many different kinds of writing that you might see during your work with writers is **genre**. Genre, as Elizabeth Wardle and Doug Downs point out, "comes from the French word for 'kind' or 'type' and is related to the Latin word for *genus*, which you might remember from the scientific classification for animals and plants" (796). All writing belongs to one genre category or another and sometimes combinations of more than one. It can be a difficult concept to grasp initially, but keeping in mind that "genre" is used to describe different types of music and film can help. Country, classical, and hip-hop, for example, are each types of music, but as any fan of these types would tell you, each has features that distinguish it from other types. Similarly, action adventure, horror, and romantic comedy are terms that all refer to movies, but anyone familiar with these genres will know that a romantic comedy will offer a very different outcome for the hero and heroine to that of a horror movie.

Genres Are Complex and Changing

It might seem that the simplest solution to the problem of dealing with new kinds of writing would be to give tutors and writers descriptions of the genres of writing they're unfamiliar with. In fact, if you search online for "writing center" and the name of most common academic genres (e.g., lab report, book reviews, literary analysis), you'll find many such descriptions. However, there are aspects of genres that are difficult to pin down, making such descriptions less than ideal tools for helping someone write. First, genres change over time. It's true that they offer ways to efficiently respond to situations that occur repeatedly, so that writers don't have to invent a new way of responding each and every time one is needed. But these situations aren't static or stable and writers themselves can alter genres according to their own particular needs and interests. As a result, as writing center scholar Catherine Savini holds, shifting the analogy a bit to travel, "disciplines are micro-cultures and guidelines for writing in a specific genre tend to age like travel books" (3).

Second, even at one specific point in time, there are always variations within a genre due to the different contexts in which they are used. Kerry Dirk, in her helpful introduction to genre, notes that "two texts that might fit into the same genre might also look extremely different. . . . the research paper you might be required to write in freshman composition might be completely different than the research paper you might be asked to write for an introductory psychology class" (255–56). The disciplinary context, for one thing, affects the genre in myriad ways, making it impossible to accurately describe how a "research paper" should be written in all disciplines (not to mention all levels of courses, from middle school to graduate school).

These complexities come about because genres are parts of dynamic systems. A FYC or psychology course is an example of such a system, in which the instructors' particular assignments and expectations themselves fit into genres that are part of other systems and sets of expectations, such as departments and disciplines. In other words, different disciplines and contexts correspond to the different games in Russell's ball-playing analogy. These disciplinary "games," with their specific and unique rules, expectations for players, and particular histories, in turn require different genres or balls. However, the reality is much more complex than the analogy. Unlike the official standards set for a particular type of ball (a football, say) that are agreed upon by all teams in the National Football League and that dictate how all footballs are made, genres are constantly shifting, flexible, and dynamic.

Dirk puts it this way:

> By this point you might realize that you have been participating in many different genres—whether you are telling a joke, writing an email, or uploading a witty status on Facebook. Because you know how these genres function as social actions, you can quite accurately predict how they function

rhetorically; your joke should generate a laugh, your email should elicit a response, and your updated Facebook status should generate comments from your online friends. But you have done more than simply filled in the blanks. Possibly without even thinking about it, you were recognizing the rhetorical situation of your action and choosing to act in a manner that would result in the outcome you desired. I imagine that you would probably not share a risqué joke with your mom, send a "Hey Buddy" email to your professor, or update your Facebook status as "X has a huge wart on his foot." We can see that more than form matters here, as knowing what is appropriate in these situations obviously requires more rhetorical knowledge than does filling out a credit card form. (253)

Understanding genre requires more than simply being able to reproduce the formal aspects or features of a kind of writing. You need to gauge which kind of writing to use when and what kinds of variations you can deploy while still ensuring that your writing is recognizable to your audience as the specific genre you're aiming for.

Even If You Don't Know the Genre, Knowing *About* Genres Can Help

Knowing some of the ways in which genres function can be helpful to writers because, as Dirk says, "this knowledge . . . helps us to recognize and to determine appropriate responses to different situations—that is, knowing what particular genre is called for in a particular situation" (259). Knowing about genre can help tutors as well. For one thing, even if you don't know about the specific genre the writer is working in, being aware *of* genres can give you tools for helping the writer anyway. Writing center researcher Irene Clark suggests that you and the writer can ask the following questions about any genre:

- What purpose does this genre serve?
- What are the features of this genre?
- How do its particular generic features serve its purpose?
- Whose interests does this genre serve?
- How is this genre similar to and different from other text genres?
- What creative variations on this genre are likely to enhance its effectiveness?
- Which ones will be inappropriate and therefore ineffective? (26–27)

For another thing, understanding genres can help you and the writer account for why his writing might not yet have fulfilled the requirements of a particular assignment. As genre theorist Amy Devitt holds, "When people write, they draw on the genres they know, their own context of genres, to help construct their rhetorical action. If they encounter a situation new to them, it is the genres they have acquired in the past that they can use to shape their new action" (qtd. in Dirk 259). On the one hand, this is good news: writers can apply knowledge gained from previous writing experiences to practice new ones. On the other hand, if the writer's current genre knowledge doesn't resemble closely enough the new one he's trying to understand, he might miss the boat (Clark 20–23)—or, to borrow from Russell again, end up trying to play Ping-Pong with a baseball. This is where your expertise as a writing tutor can be especially helpful.

For Writing

1. Reflect upon those traits of your personality that you think will help you in your work as a tutor. Are you outgoing, funny, excited to help people, for example? What kind of writers do these qualities best suit you to help? Now imagine a situation in which these qualities might not be an ideal match, such as an energetic and talkative tutor working with a shy writer. What are some strategies you might use to assess and adapt to this kind of writer?

2. Reflect upon any disciplinary expertise you have that you think will be helpful in your work as a writing tutor. Are you well versed in descriptive studies? Literary analysis? Lab reports? In what subjects and/or genres are you particularly well prepared to help writers? Now imagine a situation in which these qualities may not be an ideal match, such as working in a genre you have not encountered. How would you adapt to work with this kind of writing situation?

GENERALIST AND SPECIALIST TUTORING

Here, we shift the focus from the ways that different kinds of academic writing can affect the work tutors do with writers to the ways it has affected how tutors work. As WAC programs were being developed, there emerged in writing center studies a debate about the relative merits of **generalist tutors**, who lack knowledge of the writer's target discipline and genre, and **specialist tutors**, who have such knowledge because of courses they have taken in the field or their work as course-based tutors or writing fellows—or both.

Benefits of Generalist Tutoring

Given what we've described so far about the ways disciplines influence writing and, by extension, how helpful knowledge of these contexts can be for both writers and tutors, it might be surprising to learn that many writing center scholars argue in favor of generalist tutors. These scholars hold this position because they view the generalist tutors' lack of disciplinary and genre knowledge about the writer's work as beneficial to the writer: in these tutoring situations, the writer must take on the role of the expert and teach the generalist tutor. This arrangement can help the writer articulate more than he thought he knew and keep the tutor in the "nondirective" role we discuss in Chapter 4.

Although they don't use the terms "generalist" and "specialist," Johnson et al.'s study offers empirical evidence for the strengths of the generalist tutor over the specialist tutor: the English-major tutors in their study helped engineering students by using what most writing center scholars would agree are sound tutoring practices, including finding out "where the students are in the writing process" and "what they want out of the meeting," prompting the writers "to actively participate," "confirm[ing] and encourag[ing] what the students say," and acting "as equal to the students" (398, this book). Johnson et al.'s study suggests that the specialist tutor, by contrast, can follow a directive model in ways that aren't helpful. In the sessions in which the English-major tutors worked with students in English classes, the tutors' familiarity with the subject matter appeared to "become a hindrance to their ability to support and facilitate the student, allowing them to use their experience as a means of assertion and superiority" (400, this book). As we note in Chapter 4 regarding the pitfalls of directive tutoring, according to Johnson et al., the writer was silenced and inhibited as a result of the English-major tutor's use of her disciplinary knowledge.

Benefits of Specialist Tutoring

Other researchers, however, have offered reasons to support the specialist tutoring model. Jean Kiedaisch and Sue Dinitz's well-known early study of generalist and specialist tutors and Dinitz's more recent study with Susanmarie Harrington come to different conclusions from those of Johnson et al. In both studies, these researchers found that when tutors did not have disciplinary expertise (as they would if they majored in the field), they were unable to help these writers see the larger, more global problems with their drafts. Only the tutors with the disciplinary expertise were able to do so. Although Kiedaisch and Dinitz found that tutors with disciplinary and genre knowledge "may be tempted to appropriate the student's paper," the very knowledge that tempted one English-major tutor to take over the session with a non-English major writing for an English course helped at least one other tutor show the writer the process she needed "to learn to write other English papers" ("Look Back" 72, 71).

Middle Ground: Blending Specialist Knowledge with Generalist Strategies

As much as they promote the particular benefits of generalist or specialist tutoring, respectively, Johnson et al., Kiedaisch and Dinitz, as well as Dinitz and Harrington ultimately argue for a middle ground. Probably the most important reason has to do with the practical limitations of many writing tutoring programs, which "inevitably end up with both subject area 'experts' and 'non-experts'" (Johnson et al. 401, this book) and therefore can't always match up writers and tutors by disciplines (Kiedaisch and Dinitz "Look Back" 73, Dinitz and Harrington 95). In addition, Kiedaisch and Dinitz point out that the students in the sessions they studied were very satisfied with the results, regardless of their tutor's expertise ("Look Back" 73).

Also exploring this middle ground is Jill Gladstein. Gladstein focuses on **writing fellows** (called writing associates or "WAs" at her institution), about whom we say more toward the end of this chapter, but we think her observations apply to many other kinds of writing tutors as well. In particular, she questions the generalist/specialist binary, arguing that "Polarizing generalists and specialists minimizes the potential of these tutors and fails to acknowledge a level of complexity that tutors must navigate—how to work with the ideas of writing while emphasizing the process." She calls on her readers "to delve into the gray spaces to see how a WA with knowledge of a discipline can assist students effectively with argumentation or the more global issues of their writing." And she provides an example of a tutor delving into such gray spaces with Kathleen Kristian, who was able to blend her specialized knowledge with her training in generalist tutoring:

> Kathleen was a chemistry major who, left to her own devices, took what she knew about writing a chemistry lab report with what she had learned about writing strategies and combined them to help a group of students. By showing students that the lab report was not just an exercise but rather a form of argumentation, she operated within the gray space of WAC and WID, combining the disciplinary expectations of the lab report with WAC's goal of using writing as a tool for learning.

Kristian was able to use her disciplinary knowledge of a specialized genre to help scaffold writers' work and to bridge the gap between what they knew (argumentation) and what they did not (conventions of the chemistry lab report).

By contrast, the English-major tutors in Johnson et al.'s study do not occupy this middle ground because, unlike Kristian, they do not blend their specialist knowledge with generalist strategies when they work with students writing English papers. Instead, in the transcript excerpts that Johnson et al. provide, Anne and Micki seem to stick to their disciplinary knowledge exclusively, providing expert information about the novel the writers are analyzing and how the instructor will likely respond.

Further Complications with the Generalist/Specialist Binary

The opposition between specialist and generalist tutoring is further complicated by what tutors learn on the job about disciplinary writing and genres, especially if they have a chance to work with many students on the same assignment. Indeed, Yeshiva University writing tutor Ari Cuperfain discusses in the pages of *The Writing Lab Newsletter* the complications that can arise when the knowledge a tutor gains from working with one student on an assignment influences how he works with the next student on the same assignment. Although Johnson et al. don't specify whether Anne has worked with other students on the same project, it strikes us that their transcripts of Anne's sessions with the engineering students suggest just this kind of knowledge as she asks some very expert, content-based questions:

> ANNE: Alright, the Civic Hybrid, for example, how did you come up with the results you got for it? How did you look at the price? How did you look at the luggage capacity, the safety of this car, etc. . . . . Basically, because these are the cars you looked at, you've got to be comprehensive in writing your paper here; you've gotta go through each car because cars and the way you analyzed them impacted your final decision, so it's important that we see the decision-making process in the first place. (399, this book).

More important, the difference between Anne's session with the engineering students and her meeting with the English student isn't just Anne's lack of training in one discipline and expertise in the other. Rather, it has to do with how and whether she deploys such sound tutoring practices as asking questions, providing her perspective as a reader as a way to imagine how other readers might respond, and leaving the writers "in control . . . of *how* to address her concern" (399, this book).

For Writing

1. Reflect upon your own abilities as a generalist and specialist tutor. As a specialist, for what (if any) genres and subjects do you feel particularly well prepared? As a generalist, what strategies or approaches do you feel particularly confident deploying?

2. In *Language is Sermonic*, philosopher-rhetorician Richard Weaver argues that all language use is fundamentally persuasive in that it is trying to move its intended audience to action or belief. Above, Jill Gladstein's description of tutor Kathleen Kristian suggests that Kristian works from this belief as well when she describes the lab report as a form of argument. Drawing evidence from a genre with which you are familiar, such as a descriptive essay or a portfolio cover letter, argue for or against Weaver's assertion. Is all language use an argument? If so what is/are the argument(s) made by the genre you selected? What kind of evidence does it use? What are the values to which that evidence appeals?

3. Read (or reread) Johnson et al.'s transcript excerpts from Anne's and Micki's sessions with the students working on papers for English (pages 395–97). What do you think Anne's and Micki's motivations are in those excerpts? Specifically, why might they have wanted to tell the writers about the characters and historical context of the novel or about how the instructor responded to Micki's paper? To help you trace their thought processes, you might try writing an internal monologue, a set of thought bubbles, or, drawing from Chapter 4, an imaginary "talk-aloud protocol" for them.

STRATEGIES FOR TUTORING DISCIPLINARY WRITING AND SPECIALIZED GENRES

Most if not all of the tutoring strategies we discuss in Chapters 3 through 5 will be potentially useful to you in your work with writers on discipline-specific genres, whether or not this writing is something you are already familiar with because of your own disciplinary training. But we have some additional strategies for you to keep in mind as you embark on this work, the first three of which have to do with the knowledge you have (and don't have) as a student and writing tutor.

Be Provisional Rather than Certain

First of all, as Johnson et al.'s, Kiedaisch and Dinitz's, and Dinitz and Harrington's studies remind us, if you do have special knowledge about the writing, it is important not to let this expertise override your role and insights as a tutor. In the third *For Writing* prompt above, we encourage you to reflect on how you might balance and blend these two bodies of knowledge. We add now that what strikes us about the excerpts from the sessions with the English students is that Anne and Micki take on roles other than that of writing tutors; instead of focusing on the writers' learning, they seem to want to display their own knowledge as English majors, knowledge they probably worked hard to attain and were understandably proud of. Of course, there's nothing wrong with this knowledge (or pride). But it becomes problematic when it interferes with the writer's learning.

As a guard against this kind of display, Johnson et al. suggest taking on a stance of "provisionalism" rather than certainty. With provisionalism, the tutor acts "as an audience member," and her "phrasing suggests that her advice 'may be the case,' displaying her uncertainty with specific subject matter." With certainty, by contrast, the tutor acts "almost as a teacher, . . . offer[ing] definite suggestions with no room for options" (394, this book). Taking a provisional, less-than-absolutely-certain stance can be a good rule of thumb, a way of blending generalist tutoring strategies with specialist knowledge.

Be Upfront About What You Don't Know—and Try to Find Out

Second, it's important to recognize that there are disciplines and genres that you don't know about. Talking expertly and confidently about kinds of writing you don't have direct knowledge of, and perhaps misleading the writer as a result, can lead to a bad outcome for the writer and for the reputation of your program. Savini recommends being upfront with the writer when you don't know about the discipline or genre she's working in. Savini recognizes that such an admission can be uncomfortable since it can risk undermining your credibility with the writer. She suggests practicing ways to be forthcoming about your lack of expertise, such as saying, "You are working on a lab report in psychology . . . this is a genre I am not really familiar with. Could you describe it to me?" (3) However, admitting you do not know, as Johnson et al. argue, should not be the end of the discussion. Rather, they urge tutors to look up information they don't know and to encourage writers to use relevant resources themselves (402, this book).

Ask Questions About Genres in the Discipline

Third, as a writer and tutor who has (and will) work with genres in and across disciplines, you can make use of your special knowledge about writing. Savini offers questions drawn from Anne Beaufort's *College Writing and Beyond: A New Framework for University Writing Instruction*, a six-year case study of one student's learning to write in college and on the job that "breaks disciplinary expertise into five domains of knowledge: discourse community, writing process, rhetorical, genre, and subject matter knowledge" (3). As seen in Table 6.2, Savini presents

Table 6.2 Questions for Exploring Disciplinary Conventions (from Savini 4).

Discourse Community Knowledge:

Do you know what is considered "common knowledge" in this community?

What are the different genres practiced in your discipline?

What have you figured out about your discourse community? What do you feel like you still need to know?

Writing Process Knowledge:

Have you discussed this assignment with a professor/advisor? What feedback have you received?

What research, reading, and writing have you done to get to this point? What's left to do?

What do you need help with? What do you want to prioritize?

Rhetorical Knowledge:

What is the assignment? What occasion is motivating this writing task?

What is the goal of this text?

Who is the audience?

Genre Knowledge:

Do you have a model?

What is your experience with this genre?

What do you think are the expectations of this genre?

Have you written in this genre in another discipline?

Subject Matter Knowledge:

Why did you decide to write about this?

What is your experience with this subject? How new are you to the material/subject? What do you know about it? What do you still need to know?

What kind of research/work has already been done on this subject?

How are you framing your work in relation to other writers/scholars on this subject?

these questions as another alternative to the "generalist and discipline-specific tutoring" binary: by asking them, she holds, tutors can show students "how to gain access to new disciplines" (3).

There are more questions in this list than would probably be helpful for a tutor to address in one session. If there is time for only one, Savini recommends "Do you have a model?" for several reasons. First, comparing an example of the genre to any writing the writer might have done can be an efficient way to see if the work is on track. Second, and related to what we say in Chapter 4 about helping writers with reading, Savini holds that taking time to teach the writer "how to read texts as models," as opposed to solely for content, will help him "develop a sense of a genre's expectations" (4). If this process is unfamiliar to you, you might practice on one or more of the articles anthologized in Section IV of this book.

Other scholars recommend using different questions from Savini's list. Writing studies scholar Mary Soliday suggests that asking about the writer's process can be of special importance in disciplinary writing since engaging in writing from the earliest stage of data collection is both crucial and something that instructors might assume students know to do already (41–42). And undergraduate tutor-researcher Jonathan Doucette describes following up on subject-matter knowledge in a session "with a first-year pre-med student who was writing a paper concerning the legal merits of same-sex marriage for a political science course," a discipline about which neither he nor the writer had expertise:

> I felt a bit insecure and unsure of what to say. Her scientific background— apparent in her objective language and the setup of her argument—was clearly present throughout her work and I could find nothing inherently "wrong" with her research. The only thing I could think to ask was, "Why did you choose this topic?" She stared blankly at me, the dumbfounded look now on her face. For the first few minutes of our conversation, she appeared resistant to using her own "voice" in her work. Slowly, however, she began writing about her gay brother and her exposure to the queer community as a result. (352, this book)

If the writer knows about the discipline and the genre, her answers to the questions Savini provides can teach you how to work with her. But even if the writer does not know about the discipline, these questions can help you both consider your next moves, whether, as Doucette describes it, "bridging the gap between her personal and political selves" (352, this book) or talking about what the writer needs to find out from her professor and other resources.

Two Examples
Finally, below are strategies for working with writers on two kinds of writing that include a range of genres that are highly specialized and that can stump tutors unfamiliar with them, even if they are not, strictly speaking, disciplinary: creative writing and personal statements.

Creative Writing

Hans Ostrom, a published poet and fiction writer, creative writing teacher, and former writing center director, notes that tutors unfamiliar with creative writing are sometimes daunted by it. He maintains that tutors can work with writers on stories and poems just as with any kind of writing—for instance, by asking if there is an assignment and what the writer's own goals are, finding out whether she sees herself at the beginning, middle, or end of her process, and praising "what you think is good, compelling, and/or interesting about the piece" (149–54). Here is a summary of suggestions he offers that are specific to creative writing:

- *Take a genre approach:* Figure out with the writer what kind of writing he is aiming for. This kind might relate to the subject matter (e.g., a poem about love; a story about a conflict involving family), the genre or form (e.g., a coming-of-age, horror, or science fiction story; a haiku, a narrative poem), or "who 'speaks' in the poem or story" (e.g., first person, third person, many voices, reliable or not). Ostrom also suggests helping the writer identify conventions or audience expectations that are typically associated with this genre. Taking this approach will give you a context that can give both of you clues about how the writing might be revised. For one thing, just identifying the genre or type can help you both focus on larger-scale, global issues.
- *Focus on the senses:* Tell the writer "what the work makes you see in your mind" as well as what might be unclear about a scene, image, or action. Consider what the piece sounds like as well: as Ostrom writes, "Although in literal terms, poems and stories on the page are mute, they create in our minds the effect of sound." One of you might read a part out loud while the other takes notes on what works and anything that needs work, such a line "where the rhythm gets derailed, or . . . dialogue that seems out of key with the rest."
- *"Keep in mind 'radical revision'":* If the writer is comfortable with experimenting, there is no end to the kind of far-reaching revisions he can undertake, including switching genres (poem to story or vice versa), tone (comedy to serious), length (long to short), or "point of view, setting, plot arrangement, voice, beginning, ending." Ostrom sees creative writing as pleasurable "play"—as "improvisation, exploration, and trial and error"—which can be especially helpful for encouraging revision (151–56).

Personal Statements

Many of the strategies you might use to work with a writer on creative writing—or any writing for that matter—can help writers with personal statements for graduate and professional schools. However, because of the high-stakes nature of the situation, helping the writer gain a clear sense of his genre and audience is especially important:

- *Take a genre approach:* Often, as with law and medical school application essays, the writing should convey a strong sense of who the writer is—or in any case the sense of the writer that he wants to present to the admissions committee. This sense should align with the rest of the application and aim to distinguish the writer from other candidates in a favorable way. But each kind of program, and often each specific school, will have a different prompt for the writer to address. As a result, it is imperative that the writer do his own research, seeking out advice and samples online and, most important, meeting with experts, on campus and elsewhere, about the application process for this particular program to learn the rules of this particular "game." The stakes are too high for writers not to inform themselves and especially for tutors to claim expertise they do not have.

- *Dramatize the role of the reader:* What makes the process of tutoring writers on personal statements tricky is that, unlike campus and other experts who are familiar with the audiences of these documents, it's probable that neither writer nor tutor will have firsthand knowledge of these readers. This makes the strategy of dramatizing the role of the reader, which we discuss in Chapter 3, especially tricky. However, in a discourse analysis of tutors and writers working on medical school personal statements, Robert Brown suggests that this strategy might nonetheless be useful in sessions concerned with these documents. Brown observed tutors taking a range of positions in which they dramatized, or acted out, possible responses this audience might have. Sometimes the tutor did so by using the first-person pronoun, as in the phrase, "As a reader, I" (81). Even as one of the tutors he studied used "I," however, Brown maintains that she did so to "respond purposefully as *a* reader and to abandon any pretense of being *the* reader" (92). Other tutors dramatized the reader's presence by using the third person "to make their clients aware of possible objections that the target audience might have to their texts" (93)—for instance, "grammar police" who object to split infinitives or the "secular materialist" who might take issue with the writer's reference to "God given gifts" (93, 94). This third-person stance is useful, Brown holds, because

  > it allows tutors to voice [concerns] without simultaneously having to claim them for their own. Instead, they can assign an evocation to a hypothetical audience and then speculate about that audience's possible reaction to it. . . . [T]utors can *stand in* for a skeptical or judgmental reader yet not have to *stand for* what they impute to that reader. (94)

  In this way, tutors are able to be "provisional" about their advice while playing out and presenting some of the possible responses they imagine this unknown audience might have.

However, we should underscore again that it is imperative for writers of personal statements to speak with experts who know such readers and their expectations.

For Discussion

1. What experiences have you had with comments written on or about your writing? What about writing comments on other people's writing? Based on these experiences, what seem to you to be some characteristics of effective commenting?

2. Put another way, as a writer, what kinds of comments would you most like to receive on your own writing? As a writing fellow or a course-based tutor, what kinds of comments would you be most comfortable giving?

For Writing

1. Remember (or imagine) a time when an instructor wrote copious amounts of commentary on your writing. How did the comments make you feel initially? Did your attitude change at all as you absorbed what you were being asked to do? (Assuming, of course, that you could figure it out.) Alternatively, reflect upon working with an instructor who wrote very little on your text. How did that make you feel initially? Did this impression change?

2. What advice would you give a new college student about communicating with his or her instructors? Over email? During office hours? During a required conference? How much of this advice feels applicable to communicating with an instructor as a writing fellow? In what ways do you imagine that this communication might be different?

STRATEGIES FOR WRITING FELLOWS

Of all the different kinds of writing tutors, **writing fellows**—who tutor students in specific courses, often in collaboration with the instructors of these courses—are probably most likely to work continuously and in depth with disciplinary genres. The history of writing fellows is closely tied to the WAC movement, which along with influencing how writing center scholars and tutors distinguished generalist from specialist tutoring led to the development of programs that brought tutors directly into courses. Although we believe that many if not most of the strategies we've offered in this book will be useful for writing fellows, we know that they usually have additional responsibilities, often related directly to disciplinary knowledge and involvement in the discourse community of the course (Mullin et al.). We address two of the more prominent—and complex—of these responsibilities here: writing comments on student drafts and working with professors on their assignments. (We should note that we return to the complications of written comments in our next chapter, where we discuss online tutoring.)

Writing Comments

Writing comments involves many of the same motivational scaffolding strategies that talking with a writer face-to-face does, including analyzing the assignment and aspects of the context such as the discipline and genre, asking and answering questions, making statements, offering your perspective as a reader, taking an interest, praising, setting priorities, and, as always, being flexible and reflective. Nonetheless, as writing fellows scholars Emily Hall and Bradley Hughes admit, "writing smart, thoughtful comments on student papers" is a "challenging task" (29). What can make this genre especially complex, Hall and Hughes point out, is that comments from writing fellows usually have two distinct audiences with different expectations.

Multiple Audiences and Other Complications

On the most obvious level, comments that writing fellows write on student papers are written for the writers of these papers. However, in addition to this written response, fellows usually meet with students one-to-one, to discuss the draft and the comments. To avoid making this conference feel "extraneous" to the writer, Hall and Hughes recommend strategizing in advance with other fellows and your program director "about how conferences can build upon and complement comments: what advice can be 'held back' from a student until the conference, how a Fellow should negotiate the fine line between being a peer and being an authority who's written all over the paper" (31).

What further complicates the context of these comments is that there is usually a second reader. When the writer submits her final revision to the instructor, she might, in addition, be required to include her initial draft and the fellow's comments to provide evidence that she has worked through the prescribed process. But there is at least one other motive for sharing these comments with the instructor. "Well-written comments," Hall and Hughes write, "have the potential to significantly influence professors' practices and to teach faculty to take student writing more seriously" (34–35). In other words, writing fellows' comments can serve as models for faculty.

Hallmarks of the Comment Genre

Comments have special significance, then, and it's worth working to master them. Hallmarks of this genre, as described by scholars with extensive experience with writing fellows, include

- Writing in the margins (that is, on the pages themselves) and in an end note or longer final comment

- Making clear the relationship between the marginal and end comments
- In both, prioritizing global over sentence-level/local issues
- Starting end comments with praise
- Offering a limited number of suggestions for substantive revision
- Perhaps pointing out one or two patterns of error
  (Hall and Hughes 29, Soven 53; Severino and Knight 25)

We should note that the comments writing fellows compose are no longer limited to written text. It is now possible to insert audio comments into an electronic version of a writer's text, and with digital technologies constantly improving, no doubt other options will soon be available (if they aren't already).

Further complicating this process is that commenting on other people's writing is hard work even for instructors who've been doing it for years. There is a large body of scholarship on commenting that aims to balance the needs of student writers with faculty readers, especially in terms of not overwhelming either group with too much—whether too many comments or too much time per paper. You might be interested in what faculty are recommended to do in John C. Bean's well-known guide for faculty teaching writing in courses outside of writing studies. In Table 6.3 is Bean's summary of some of his recommendations, which we think serve as equally good advice for writing fellows.

Working with Faculty

At least as complicated as writing comments are tutors' working relationships with the instructors of the courses they tutor in. As Hall and Hughes put it, for

Table 6.3 Response Strategies (from Bean 335).

1. Comment first on ideas and organization: encourage students to solve higher-order problems before turning to lower-order problems.
2. Whenever possible, make positive comments. Praise strong points.
3. Try to write an end comment that reveals your interest in the student's ideas. Begin the end comment with an emphasis on good points and then move to specific recommendations for improvement.
4. Avoid overcommenting. Particularly avoid emphasizing lower-order concerns until you are satisfied with higher-order concerns. If a draft requires major revision at the level of ideas and organization, it is premature to worry about sentence errors.
5. As you read the essay, indicate your reaction to specific passages. Particularly comment on the ideas, raising queries and making suggestions on how the argument could be improved. Praise parts that you like.
6. Resist the urge to circle misspellings, punctuation errors, and so forth. Research suggests that students will improve more quickly if they are required to find and correct their own errors.
7. The end comment should summarize your assessment of the strengths and weaknesses of the writer's ideas. Challenge writers to deepen and complicate their thought at a level appropriate to their intellectual development.

this "complex teaching collaboration between faculty and Fellows" to be success-ful, fellows

> must be capable of offering tactful suggestions on assignments to a professor
> in a subject they may never have studied, able to discuss process-model phi-
> losophies of teaching writing, and willing to negotiate these philosophies in
> conversations with faculty and students. In other words, they must be WAC
> practitioners, diplomats, peer collaborators and more. (22, 27)

This is a tall order, but one major advantage you have is that you are likely a student yourself and therefore able to provide faculty with information and insights
about student perspectives that they might not otherwise have access to.

Serving as a Substitute Student in the Course

WAC and writing fellows scholars Joan Mullin, Susan Schorn, Tim Turner,
Rachel Hertz, Derek Davidson, and Amanda Baca describe the initial meeting
between faculty and fellow as a crucial stage in the process. It's at this stage
that fellows (whom their program calls "writing mentors") can "begin to 'play'
students":

> [I]n actuality, they are trying to learn about this discipline as they ask "What
> are you looking for in this assignment?" "Do students know what a literature
> review is?" "What an interesting topic! I suspect students don't know much
> about suicide in Japanese films?" . . . From their first meeting, writing mentors
> model for faculty the struggles, questions, and confusions of the novice entrant
> to the community. Faculty respond by rethinking their objectives, assignments
> and directions . . . .

In other words, an important service you can provide for faculty is to serve as a
stand-in or substitute for students in the course, responding to and raising questions about assignments and other course documents before the "real" students
see them. This role is familiar to writing tutors, who, as we mention above, dramatize or "play" the audience for writing on a regular basis.

Offer Feedback on Assignments

Because assignments themselves are written texts that might or might not fulfill
the expectations or needs of their genres and readers, writing fellows often have
to serve as tutors for these documents. Writing fellow Alex Antram describes her
experience of working with an instructor on an assignment similar to the one
Alex herself had struggled with when she took a course with the same instructor
two years earlier:

> In an essay that required creativity, I had felt stifled as a writer (and thinker)
> within an organization that left little to the imagination. As a WF, I was experi-
> enced enough to realize what had troubled me when I was his student: I hadn't
> understood how he could expect free thought in writing in such a structured

format; I didn't know what his criteria were for good writing; and I certainly didn't have the confidence at that time to question his expectations.

> As I discovered, the professor assumed his students understood that the . . . format he prescribed was only a suggestion to help them organize but not stifle their ideas. However, he hadn't conveyed this expectation well to his students. . . . Over the course of the semester, I worked with the professor to rewrite his assignments. He and I sat with two copies of his assignment and talked about what worked and what didn't and what might be misinterpreted by the students. (qtd. in Zawacki)

Antram is able to blend the disciplinary knowledge she gained from taking the course herself with her writing expertise as a fellow to help both the professor and the students in the course.

Tricky Situations with Faculty
Antram, her director, WAC scholar Terry Myers Zawacki, and another writing fellow in their program, Amaris Price, go on to describe other tricky situations involving faculty. These include occasions when the instructor knows less about responding to student writing than the tutor does or, due to disciplinary expertise, fills in "'the gaps' in a student's writing [that's] not completely coherent." In addition, some faculty might be less welcoming of a tutor's presence than others or some might change assignments or expectations for your role as the semester unfolds, even if you and your program director clarified expectations from the onset. In all of these cases, you would want to be in contact with your director to work out solutions.

However, even tricky situations with faculty offer advantages for both writing fellows and their programs. They can provide fellows with valuable experience with resolving conflicts with individuals who have more authority, and they can give both fellows and program directors chances to increase campus-wide understanding of writing and writing tutoring. Moreover, like writing in the disciplines more generally, such situations are opportunities to work outside our comfort zones. We think Jonathan Doucette's observations on the benefits of tutoring across disciplines stand as a useful summary of major points of this chapter:

> During my time as a writing associate at the Oberlin College writing center, for instance, I found myself surrounded by academics from numerous departments: from religion, English, and creative writing to clarinet performance, biology, and environmental studies. In like fashion, students who enter the writing center also run the gamut of academic disciplines. The writing center, as a place allowing a unique exchange of academic ideas (and the different ways of writing such disciplines demand), is the ideal locus for the interdisciplinary framework. . . . What better way to challenge one's (academic) assumptions about the world—one's epistemology—than to directly engage with those from different academic fields? (352, this book)

For Writing

1. Read samples of writing fellow comments. (Hall and Hughes provide an excellent example, but better would be to ask to see comments by more experienced fellows in your own program, in order to gain a sense of the context and genre expectations of your own institution.) How do these fellows negotiate the tricky situation of their double audience?

2. Practice writing comments on drafts written by other new writing fellows and talking with them face-to-face about those comments; offer each other feedback on both your written and spoken comments. What would make these written and spoken comments more effective, both for the writer and the instructor-reader?

3. Write a revision plan based on a fellow's written comments on your writing and then discuss with the fellow how close your plan came to his or her ideas about how you might revise. You might get comments on the same piece of writing by another fellow or during a session in the writing center and compare the experiences.

4. As Hall and Hughes suggest, "develop a personal philosophy of commenting" (29) and compare this to what others in your group come up with.

For Inquiry

1. Conduct a case study of the life cycle of a single assignment in a fellowed class. (You may wish to review the material on case studies in Chapter 11 to learn about what this approach might entail.) To aid in the design of your research process, we suggest that such a project might look like the following:

   - Start by reviewing the syllabus and any materials related to the assignment.

   - Next, interview the instructor, the fellow, and the student writer about the expectations and goals of the assignment. If possible, you may wish to sit in on class the day the assignment is introduced.

   - Ask for a copy of the writer's first draft, which he or she submits to the fellow, and, if relevant, observe or record the tutorial in which the draft is discussed.

   - Interview the fellow and the writer individually after the tutorial to discuss what they determined the draft's strengths and weaknesses are and what revision plan they arrived at.

   - Ask for a copy of the writer's final draft prior to grading. Discuss the draft with the writer and tutor.

   - Ask for a copy of the graded draft. Discuss with the instructor and writer.

   - When writing up the case, consider the ways in which communication did and did not work. Also reflect upon how the writer reconciled his or her own assessments with those of the instructor and the fellow.

2. Target one discipline for which you will create informational resources for both tutors and students. Your goal is to improve both groups' understanding of how writing functions in that scholarly community, and the means by which you will do so is research and effective message crafting. To aid in the design of your research process, we suggest that such a project might look like the following:

   • For research, you may wish to interview students and faculty in the discipline, and search for scholarly resources, introductory texts, and relevant writers' handbooks and style guides. You might look, too, to see if students in this discipline have won any local or national awards for effective writing, such as a best essay award, and/or ask faculty if they have model papers they share with students.

   • Draw from these diverse sources to develop your understanding of how writing functions in this discipline and what are considered the hallmarks for excellent writing.

   • Select your means of communication to reach your dual audiences. For your fellow tutors, for example, you may wish to reach them by way of an oral presentation, perhaps producing a PowerPoint or Prezi and a handout. Or you might wish to reach them by way of a newsletter for your program or a poster for the tutor break area. To reach students at your school, you might wish to create a webpage, a handout to be used in or a podcast, or a poster for your program.

CHAPTER 7

New Media and Online Tutoring

For Discussion

1. Working with your classmates, compile a list of all the composing tools you have used. Start with the earliest (such as crayons, perhaps) and be sure to include as many variations on each tool as you can think of (such as pencils—mechanical pencils, carpenter's pencils, drawing pencils, etc.). When looking at your list, do you notice any "rules for composing" that cut across multiple tools? That is, are there rhetorical principals that apply to writing on a computer or making notes with a pen or drawing with a crayon, etc.?

2. What is your earliest memory of trying to read or write with a digital technology? How did you learn to use it? What, if anything, did this teach you about learning new technologies?

INTRODUCTION

This chapter continues our exploration of different kinds of projects tutors help writers with and a range of strategies for doing this work. Here, our focus is on digital media, in terms of, first, how it influences the projects writers work on and, second, how it affects the ways tutor offer help, specifically in online contexts. To demonstrate how tutoring in this context draws on many of the same skills described in the previous chapters, we focus on the key concept of **rhetoric**, which explores the ways in which communicative acts create meaning.

We probably don't need to tell you that, nowadays, writers in college produce more than just writing. Across the disciplines and in extracurricular contexts, they work on webpages, videos, podcasts, PowerPoints, and Prezis, for example, that include text, charts, graphs, photographs, animation, audio, and much more. All of these projects and many others are considered **new media**, which we can define as digital, sometimes interactive, and **multimodal** (Grutsch McKinney 366–67, this book; Lee and Carpenter xiv). Similar to the definition we use in Chapter 5, "multimodal" concerns the different ways information can be communicated through written text, visual means, or sound by appealing to different learning styles—visual, auditory, and kinesthetic. Nearly twenty years ago, scholars in the New London Group argued that these different "modes of meaning" are "Increasingly important" and mapped out their "remarkably dynamic relationships" in a diagram similar to Figure 7.1 (80, 83). Because of this growing importance, more and more writing tutoring programs and the tutors who work in them help writers with projects that combine these different modes in technically sophisticated and dynamic ways.

Tutors not only help writers *with* technology, however; increasingly, they work with writers *through* technology, in equally sophisticated and often multimodal

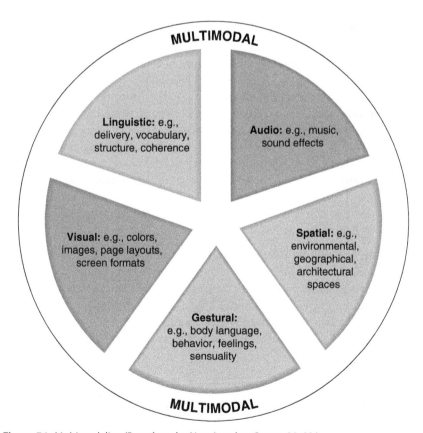

Figure 7.1 Multimodality. (Based on the New London Group, 80, 83.)

ways. Although email has been the most pervasive mode of electronic tutoring since it was first used in the 1980s, now, because of the many new communication technologies available, tutoring online is changing just as quickly as new media projects are, with tutors able to insert audio files of comments into writers' texts or to meet with writers online in real time, by way of instant messaging, video conferencing, whiteboards, and virtual environments.

As a result, writing center scholars interested in technology urge us to try as much as possible to anticipate what's coming next. In their introduction to *The Routledge Reader on Writing Centers and New Media*, for example, Sohui Lee and Russell Carpenter write that "As modes change in student composition, so will the nature of the tutorial itself. Instead of 'outlines' of essays, students may bring in storyboards of their PowerPoint presentation or video project for tutors to look at" (xviii). And in her dissertation on multiliteracy in writing centers, Sue Mendelsohn holds that "ten and twenty years from now, that work will be something else again. As the scope of the work expands to include writing, speaking, visual design, and video, centers will continue to tackle the responsibility of training consultants in visual rhetoric *and* oral communication *and* digital media *and* whatever else lies beyond those" (107). Consequently, because the technology is constantly emerging, much of the advice scholars have to offer tutors in this area is still being developed. The good news, as we discuss below, is that there is a great deal of room for tutors themselves to research and produce knowledge about this work.

At the same time, however, it is worth keeping in mind that there is much that is familiar, and in some respects extremely old, about new media and online tutoring—such as the interplay of writing and technology (as old as writing itself), the focus on helping human beings (no matter how cutting edge the technological advances), and the rhetorical (that is, audience-centered and purposeful) nature of this work. In short, even though some of what we say in this chapter might be new to you, if you tutor new media and/or online, you will likely be able to draw on your experiences with

- *Being a reader and audience member:* You know when texts communicate effectively to you and can tell writers about this communication.
- *Tutoring human beings:* New media and online tutoring have a great deal in common with writing-only and face-to-face tutoring.
- *Engaging in new media and online communication:* These technologies are increasingly part of twenty-first-century life and for most of us familiar territory.

If you don't end up tutoring new media or online, we think that learning about both is nonetheless useful because doing so can help you reflect on what you've learned so far about face-to-face tutoring of writing-only ("old" media) texts. Lee and Carpenter, for example, note that "digital communication asks us to rethink our traditional conceptions of writing, authorship, and audiences" (xv). We return to this point at the end of this chapter.

WHAT'S OLD ABOUT NEW MEDIA
AND ONLINE TUTORING?

Although there is much that is new about helping writers with and through technology, there is much that is old.

Writing Has Always Involved Technology

Technology is not a new feature of writing but has always been part of it. Mendelsohn offers the following passage by Christina Hass to make this point:

> [T]o see technology as something that is added to writing in certain situations is to misunderstand the essential relationship between writing and technology. . . . Technology and writing are not distinct phenomena; that is, writing has never been and cannot be separate from technology. Whether it is the stylus of the ancients, the pen and ink of the medieval scribe, a toddler's fat crayons, or a new Powerbook, technology makes writing possible. (qtd. in Mendelsohn 56)

As we discuss below, Mendelsohn argues that keeping the technological foundation of writing in mind can make the leap into new media tutoring less daunting.

Tutoring New Media and Online Is Still About Helping People

No matter what the degree of technological sophistication, the job of the tutor is to help human beings. Above all, as Jackie Grutsch McKinney holds in the article we include in Section IV, writing centers should secure "a spot for humans to meet other humans over texts, digital or not" (370, this book). Likewise, Beth L. Hewitt urges us to remember that in online tutoring we are "conferencing with a student, not the writing. There's a human on the other end of the computer" (97). One crucial way that this human element comes into play is in terms of access. On the one hand, the great advantage of online tutoring, for example, is that it provides more opportunities for tutoring to a broader and more diverse range of clientele—including people who aren't on campus because of work or family obligations or people who do better working with a tutor online than face-to-face, perhaps because of learning styles or certain disabilities. On the other hand, due to economic or educational disadvantages (or both), some people lack access to the technology that would enable them to receive online tutoring or to complete new media projects as easily as others. Sometimes, our jobs as tutors include helping writers negotiate this technology.

New Media and Online Tutoring Are Rhetorical

This human aspect of new media and online tutoring in turn reminds us that these processes are ultimately rhetorical in nature. That is, new media projects and online tutoring are human endeavors designed to communicate with other humans. As a body of theories, **rhetoric** helps us attend to the conditions that might enhance or detract from this communication by mapping out relationships among the speaker/writer/composer (also known as the rhetor); the audience, including the rhetor's readers, listeners, or viewers; the rhetor's purpose, what he or she is trying to accomplish; and the larger context or rhetorical situation of the rhetor, audience, and purpose, which dramatically affects what the rhetor is and is not able to accomplish. Predating writing, rhetoric is both very old and inherently multimodal, a way of accounting for not only the rhetor's words but his gestures and performance as well as how he generated his ideas in the first place ("he," because in classical times the rhetor was nearly always a man). We examine rhetoric in detail here because it is especially helpful in providing basic principles for navigating the ever-changing and always-emerging technologies of new media and online tutoring. However, as we suggest in Chapter 2 when we discuss rhetoric as a conceptual model that has influenced writing centers, you might find that it provides a useful way of reflecting on all of your tutoring.

A RHETORICAL APPROACH TO TUTORING

Rhetoric is a broad category, and there is a great deal to be said about it, but some aspects are especially useful for writing tutors to keep in mind, whether they are working with writers on new media, online, or in face-to-face sessions with writing-only texts.

Rhetoric Aims to Get Things Done

Although rhetoric helps us communicate effectively, it's about more than communicating; it's also about actively accomplishing goals. According to this famous definition by rhetorician Lloyd Bitzer:

> [R]hetoric is a mode of altering reality, not by the direct application of energy to objects, but by the creation of discourse which changes reality through the mediation of thought and action. The rhetor alters reality by bringing into existence a discourse of such a character that the audience, in thought and action, is so engaged that it becomes mediator of change. (4)

To return to the high-stakes example we discuss in Chapter 6, medical school applications aim to change the applicant's current reality (the state of being not yet accepted into the school of her choice) to one she desires (being accepted). To achieve this alteration of reality, the applicant completes and submits multiple documents (of which the statement is but one) that, when successful, compel the admissions committee to mediate, making possible the change she desires by accepting her into the school. In short, Bitzer's definition of rhetoric is useful to keep in mind because it can help tutors and writers stay focused on the ultimate goal of a project.

Rhetoric Is Situational

Bitzer is also known for demonstrating that rhetorical events, such as applying for medical school, take place not just anywhere but at a particular time and place that calls on a particular kind of response, what he called the **rhetorical situation**. Keith Grant-Davie offers this helpful explanation:

> [A] rhetorical situation is a situation where a speaker or writer sees a need to change reality and sees that the change may be effected through rhetorical discourse. Bitzer argues that understanding the situation is important because the situation invites and largely determines the form of the rhetorical work that responds to it. (265)

The rhetorical situation of a medical school application, for example, "invites and largely determines" the personal statement genre, just as, as we discuss in the last chapter, disciplines and courses define the kinds of writing scholars and students do. In fact, genres are key evidence of the importance of the rhetorical situation: genres come about because rhetorical situations repeat, and they help people (rhetors) avoid having to develop new forms of writing each time they want to communicate within this recurrent situation.

Rhetoric Fills Gaps

As Bitzer goes on to discuss, rhetorical situations are made up of several elements, a key one of which is **exigence**, which Bitzer defines as "an imperfection marked by urgency; . . . a defect, an obstacle, something waiting to be done, a thing which is other than it should be" (6). With a medical school application, the "thing which is other than it should be" is, again, the applicant's current reality of not yet being accepted to her target school. However, another relevant way in which scholars in writing studies discuss exigence is in terms of what motivates them to do their research, namely the gaps in the current knowledge that need to be filled (Jolliffe 139). As we discuss in more detail in the next chapter and in Section III, such gaps are useful for you to be on the lookout for as you consider your own research projects. Many of the tutor-researchers whose articles we collect in Section IV discuss their own research exigencies in terms of such gaps.

Rhetoric Aims to Do Things by Reaching Audiences

Another key component of the rhetorical situation that is likely more familiar is audience. In Chapter 3, we propose, with Mendelsohn and Nancy Sommers, that tutors can "dramatize the presence of a reader" (Sommers "Responding" 148), and, in Chapter 6, we discuss Robert Brown's research into how tutors of medical school personal statements "*stand in* for" the target audience (94). These activities are crucial practices in tutoring writing because they can help writers to keep in mind that they aim to communicate with other human beings and need, therefore, to anticipate the very human needs, concerns, and potential objections their audiences might have. However, as valuable as this tutoring practice is for writers, we probably all recognize, at least most of the time, that the tutor is seldom, if ever, the real audience for the writer's work. As Bitzer holds, the "rhetorical audience consists only of those persons who are capable of being influenced by discourse and of being mediators of change" (8). Tutors can act *as if* they are part of an admissions committee, for instance, in ways that can be helpful to writers. But of course they can't actually accept the writer into medical school.

Other Factors in the Rhetorical Situation

A number of rhetoricians, including Grant-Davie, argue that exigencies and audiences aren't all powerful in the rhetorical situation. Rhetors are also seen as another crucial factor and able to influence the situation as well. For instance, from the rhetor's vantage, exigence can be thought of as **purpose**, what the rhetor himself is trying to do with his writing or speaking, not just what the rhetorical situation is calling on him to do. Similarly, although rhetors need to meet the expectations of the audience by adhering to the typical features of a particular genre (such as the medical school personal statement), they usually have room to make the genre their own; indeed, for any personal statement, the writer needs to distinguish herself from other candidates as much as follow any specific rhetorical moves of the genre. Related, an aim of classical rhetoric is to help the rhetor predict some of this dynamic so that he can influence it to his advantage, by thinking about how to appeal to the audience's interests or feelings, through **pathos**, or, related to the personality the medical school applicant shows in a personal statement, how to present oneself effectively, as credible and trustworthy, through the appeal of **ethos**. Ethos is linked etymologically to "ethics" and therefore reminds us of the larger ethical issues that need to be taken into consideration when wielding rhetorical power. It would be an ethical breach, for example, to persuade people of untruths simply because one has the rhetorical ability to do so. Complaints about "political rhetoric" are often about such untruths.

Tutoring New Media and Online—Rhetorically

Below, we address important ways that tutoring new media and tutoring online are inherently rhetorical. In both contexts, writers and tutors are (or should be) concerned with audience, situation, purpose, and self-presentation. We offer strategies for helping you keep these concerns in mind.

For Writing

1. Think of a specific technology, such as a social media platform, that you use frequently. Why do you use this particular technology? What kinds of rhetorical exchanges does it encourage or discourage? How did you learn to use it effectively? Can you discern principles to compose effectively and appropriately for this venue?

2. (Re)read Jackie Grutsch McKinney's "New Media Matters: Tutoring in the Late Age of Print," included in Section IV. Using some of the concepts for discussing relationships between modes and/or principles of design that are described there, write a description of either a webpage from your own institution or a tutoring program at another institution. How is the visual message reinforced, elaborated, and/or undermined by the elements present?

TUTORING NEW MEDIA

New media projects are in several important ways very different from writing-only texts. For instance, imagine the medical school personal statement we discuss above as a new media project—such as an interactive website with writing by and photographs and video clips of the applicant as well as hyperlinks that connect these different parts so that the admissions committee members can move through the site as they wish—and such differences probably become immediately apparent. With this new media version, the applicant would have at her disposal what David Sheridan calls "a dizzying variety of semiotic [meaning-making] resources (words, graphs, music, photographs, video clips, colors, interactive components)" ("All" 79). As a result, we would want to call the applicant a "composer" rather than a "writer" for two reasons: first, "writing" would be only one part of what she would do for this new media version of her application, and, second, her processes of producing her work would be different from that of a writer since she could start with any of these resources (Mendelsohn 73). In turn, your work as a tutor would be different as well. You would have a far greater range of elements to respond to than you would with a writing-only text. Consequently, you would want to ask questions about design, visuals, and formatting that would consider these elements not as add-ons or lower-order but as essential parts of a whole project that is "greater than the sum of its parts" (Grutsch McKinney 373–74, this book; Sheridan "Words" 341).

New Media Is Rhetorical

Even with all of these very important differences, new media projects, like writing-only texts, are rhetorical. Whether the medical school applicant's personal statement is writing-only or new media, she would be responding to the same rhetorical situation (albeit one in which medical school admission boards allow multimodal new media projects), with the same goal of changing her current reality (not yet admitted) to her desired outcome (admitted). Consequently, Sheridan points out that we can ask the following questions of new media projects just as we would of any text:

- What was the rhetorical context [or situation] that gave rise to this text?
- What exigencies was it meant to address?
- Who was its intended audience?

- What strategies of persuasion are employed?
- What considerations of the ethics of persuasion need to be considered? ("All" 87)

Below, we offer additional rhetorically based questions to ask about new media projects.

Writing Is Multimodal Too

Thinking of new media in terms of rhetoric can help tutors and composers make the leap from writing-only texts to multimodal ones. What can help too is recognizing the multimodality, and especially the visual elements, of all writing-only texts. According to the New London Group, "all meaning-making is multimodal. All written text is also visually designed" (81). Mendelsohn expands on this insight, connecting it to rhetoric:

> [A] purely written document is already inherently a hybrid of language and design. Writing requires choices about fonts, colors, sizes, styles, layouts, margins, and so on. The design conventions of academic writing, reinforced by default settings, can naturalize textual design, making composers forget that choosing one-inch margins, Times New Roman font, double spacing, and so on, are rhetorical choices that make certain arguments rather than characteristics inherent in textual production. (51)

One way to "see" the rhetorical effects of these choices, Mendelsohn suggests, is to imagine what "personalities"—or ethos—different fonts have. What is the personality of **Comic Sans**, for instance? By contrast, what argument "does a font like **Times New Roman**, conventionally used in academic writing, make . . . ?" (52). To return to the example of the medical school personal statement once again, what kind of effect would be created for the admissions committee if the writer used **Comic Sans** font? How might a tutor respond to this rhetorical choice?

New Tools for Tutoring New Media

Becoming aware of these different elements, in both new media and writing-only texts, and being able to comment on the interplay between them adds to our ever-expanding repertoire of tutoring strategies in part by expanding our vocabulary. Grutsch McKinney's article provides an excellent overview of such terms that will be helpful to know when working with writers on new media projects. One such term is **juxtaposition**, a way of talking about the relationships among elements that are otherwise very different, even clashing, but together convey meaning to the project's audience in a manner that is greater than the sum of the individual parts (Schriver qtd. in Grutsch McKinney 376, this book). For example, Grutsch McKinney's analysis of a poster advertising a writing center shows how playful colors and typography can be consciously juxtaposed with a stern message ("Don't let your writing get so out of hand that it has to be put behind bars") to create an invitation to potential writing center users that effectively and appropriately combines seriousness with humor (377, this book). However, juxtaposition must be used with care. To return to the personal statement example one last time, juxtaposing its serious message with the light-hearted— and comic—associations of the comic sans font would likely undermine the writer's purpose.

Tutoring New Media Projects

Even with the new elements of and vocabulary for new media projects, you'll nonetheless want to employ many of the tutoring strategies that you would use for writing-only texts. These include

- Getting acquainted
- Asking questions about the project and what the agenda should be
- Figuring out with the composer how you should work through her text
- Motivating the composer by listening to her and attending to non-verbal cues
- Taking an interest and praising
- Being conscientious about how you wrap up
- Reflecting

However, because there will be several modalities to work with—not just writing to read but perhaps also visual images or video to look at, audio files and even the composer herself to listen to, and maybe hyperlinks to click—you will work through the text differently and likely have additional questions to ask. Below are examples of such additional strategies and questions.

Questions About the Rhetoric of New Media Projects

Given the foundational nature of rhetoric to new media texts, it makes sense to start with questions related to the rhetorical situation. Sheridan suggests the following, by way of asking composers to tell you about their projects:

- Who is your audience?
- What is your purpose?
- What opportunities are there for using images, sounds, and words to reach your audience and achieve your purpose more effectively? ("All" 75–76)

Teddi Fishman as well as Michelle A. Moreau and A. Paige Normand remind us too that we can ask questions about the applications composers have chosen, since these too are about rhetorical choices (Fishman 63, Moreau and Normand 243).

In addition, some questions you might ask about the relationship of the work to the audience can be drawn from insights from cognitive psychology that have recently been applied to designing new media texts. Moreau and

Normand use the research of cognitive psychologist Richard Mayer, whose "multimedia learning theory posits that messages are easier to retain when they engage more than one sense. Choosing graphs and pictures to accentuate a message is an easy way to make the message more engaging" (242). At the same time, however, they point out that Mayer's research shows that audiences need "multimedia messages that are free from extraneous noise, structured to emphasize the essential message, and poised to generate new ideas" (235). To help composers understand that they might be overwhelming their audience rather than conveying a central message, Moreau and Normand offer these questions:

- What information does your media convey to your audience? . . .
- Is any of your media distracting your audience from your message?
- If you had to spend a dollar for every color, font, line, movement, sound, background design or word, would you make the same investments? (245)

As a follow-up strategy, and if appropriate, they suggest showing the project on a larger screen (if you happen to have access to one) to help the composer see his work from a new perspective (244).

Strategies for Working Through New Media Projects
Because new media texts involve more than writing, responding to them requires more than simply linear, left-to-right, top-to-bottom reading (Pemberton, "Planning" 9). As a result, Grutsch McKinney maintains that it is not usually possible to "read" them in the way that we would writing-only texts. Although discussing the message the composer is trying to convey is important, it would be less than beneficial to set the work aside, as we might with a piece of writing, and focus exclusively on ideas. As Grutsch McKinney puts it,

> The intertwining of multiple modes may be lost if the tutor looks *through* the text or does not look *at* the paper or *at* the screen. Furthermore, there is no way to "read aloud" visual elements or sounds. Consequently, the tutor may just skip over these elements thereby privileging the verbal, perhaps to the detriment of the student. (372, this book)

Grutsch McKinney suggests "talk aloud" as a way of working through a multimodal text with the composer, which Mendelsohn connects to the metacommentary strategy we discuss in Chapters 3 and 6.

With talk aloud/metacommentary, Mendelsohn argues that "we can also help composers by dramatizing the presence of a viewer and a listener of multimodal compositions." In so doing, we can enable them to "develop the ability to anticipate the impact of their choices on audiences" (82). In practice, the tutor "might perform his curiosity" about hyperlinks, for example, "by going back and forth between the two pages several times, testing out the different linked passages" (104). If the tutor becomes disoriented, he would perform this experience too, to alert the composer to an effect that might or might not be what was intended (105).

Tutoring New Media Presentations

If you tutor in a program that provides help for composers of oral presentations, you might well receive specialized training in how to do this work. However, even if you work in a program whose primary (even exclusive) mission is to help *writers,* you might find yourself tutoring someone on a presentation. In such a case, since project and presentation are inextricably linked, it would be unhelpful to tell the composer that you could work with her on one but not the other. Below are suggestions based largely on Moreau and Normand's helpful discussion of oral presentations and related new media.

Most important, everything we say above about rhetoric applies to oral presentations, not least because rhetoric originated as a way to support public speaking. As a result, you'll want to help presenters anticipate the needs of their audiences. As we discuss in Chapter 4, writers sometimes need help shifting from what Linda Flower calls writer-based to reader-based prose. Similarly, Moreau and Normand point out that tutors might need to help presenters "make the transition from [a] speaker-centered presentation to an audience-centered presentation" (240). Along these lines, Russell Carpenter and Shawn Apostel suggest that it can be helpful to record the presentation so the presenter can hear (or see) what he sounds like from another perspective (163).

In addition, as described in Table 7.1, Moreau and Normand provide a number of general questions tutors can ask presenters, no matter what modalities or programs they use.

Tutoring PowerPoint Presentations

One program you might well encounter as you work with presenters is the market leader in presentation software, PowerPoint. Because this program includes several ineffective features (which have led some to call it "Evil" [Tufte qtd. in

Table 7.1   Questions for Presenters (from Moreau and Normand 243, 241).

For presenters who don't yet have drafts, ask:
- What are the main claims in your presentation?
- What visual aids do you need to support your claims?
- What is the organizational pattern? (For example, linear, specific to general, general to specific, spatial.)

For presenters with drafts, ask:
- What do you want your audience to get out of your presentation?
- How will you keep your audience engaged and interested?
- What would help your audience learn this information?

Alley 106]), we offer cautions as well as suggestions here. Related to Mendelsohn's point about program defaults and rhetorical choices, PowerPoint is notorious for making choices for presenters that do not lead to rhetorically effective presentations. Michael Alley, a professor of engineering communication who specializes in presentation slide design, maintains that the slides produced by PowerPoint's defaults "stand in direct contrast with what research has found would help audiences understand and remember the content" (108). Chief among these problematic defaults are

- Bulleted lists, which frequently do not show the connections between items listed
- Wasted space and increased "noise" created by decorative templates
- Overly large headlines that prevent composers from conveying as much information as they could in the limited space they have
- More words on individual slides than audiences can process (110, 114, 138, 111).

About this last problem, Alley cites research demonstrating that when audiences try to read a slide with too many words, they experience "cognitive overload," which leads to low comprehension "even below the comprehension rate of having no slides at all" (111). Therefore, tutors of PowerPoint presentations should suggest to writers that they not let this program make important rhetorical decisions for them and alert them to the fact that they have the power to override the defaults themselves.

An additional problem with PowerPoint is that it can tempt a presenter to use the text on each slide as notes for his talk. Moreau and Normand point out that not only does reading from a slide lead to a less than dynamic speaking style—for instance, "a lack of eye contact and flattening pitch" (240)—but it is also another potential source of cognitive overload. Drawing again on Mayer's findings as well as those of other researchers, they hold that audiences process information best when they both hear and see it—for instance, by looking at a graph while listening to an explanation about it. However, "if they see the graph, hear an explanation, and try to read the same explanation textually," they are less likely to retain the information (237).

With these limitations in mind, Moreau and Normand suggest asking the following questions of presenters who use PowerPoint:

- Is your audience going to read the text on your slide or just look at it for reference?
- Will people be able to pay attention to what you are saying while they read your slides?
- What function does the text serve?
- What does your audience need to see in order to understand your ideas? (241, 247)

While these concerns specifically address the limitations of PowerPoint, much of the advice about visual arrangement, attention to audience, and how the message of the visual text relates to the message of the presenter are equally applicable to many other multimodal programs, applications, and texts.

Concerns About Tutoring New Media

New media initially raised concerns for writing center staffs because, in the dramatic increase in modalities that these projects offer when compared to writing-only texts, some scholars felt that they threatened to make too many demands on the already limited resources of writing tutoring programs. As Michael Pemberton wrote in 2003, "If we diversify too widely and spread ourselves too thinly in an attempt to encompass too many different literacies, we may not be able to address any set of literate practices particularly well." In other words, "we have to ask ourselves whether it is really the writing center's responsibility to be all things to all people" ("Planning" 21). In addition, such diversification requires that tutors have at least some specialized knowledge, and many writing center scholars argue against this expertise for the same reason that they argue against the kind of specialist tutoring we discuss in Chapter 6, due to worries that specialized, expert tutors can end up being overly directive or forgetting the larger rhetorical concerns of the project (Mendelsohn 106).

However, in the decade since Pemberton raised these concerns, many scholars, directors, and tutors have nonetheless taken on the challenge of working with new media. Just as some writing centers and writing fellows programs offer tutoring in specific disciplines, so too do some tutoring programs, often called **multiliteracy centers**, focus on serving new media composers by providing tutoring in technology and design. Because technologies have improved so rapidly that they have increasingly large and familiar roles in all of our lives, even programs at institutions that don't have the resources to offer such specialized support can now work with composers who need help with their new media projects. Furthermore, as tutors and scholars have gained experience in this area, they have come to see that there is a middle ground just as in the disciplinary specialist/generalist debate. Mendelsohn suggests that the new media tutor's role should be "not to know how to use every piece of technology that composers walk in the door with, but to help them develop . . . strategies to answer their own questions. . . . In other words, the [tutor] needs to help the composer learn to find answers, not to have an answer" (107). Even scholars who promote technically trained tutors, such as Fishman, support generalist strategies, which tutors "can employ on the occasions when they do not know the answer to a student's technology question and must puzzle it out with them, on the spot" (67). This is similar to what we discuss in Chapter 6 about how tutors need to negotiate and be upfront about the specialized knowledge they do and don't have about writing in specific genres and disciplines.

For Writing

1. Transform a traditional writing-only text that you have produced using other modalities and media, such as a webpage, a Prezi or PowerPoint Presentation, or a podcast. Reflect (in either mode) on the ways in which the meaning of your text evolved as you transformed it.

2. Transform the discussion of one of the tutoring strategies for working with new media described above into another mode with the purpose of sharing it with your colleagues. In a mode of your instructor's choosing, explain the rhetorical choices you made to adapt the message to your specific audience.

ONLINE TUTORING

Like working with new media, online tutoring, too, has raised concerns for scholars and tutors. In this case, however, the concerns have to do with how tutors should deal with too few, rather than too many, modalities. That is, as Jeanne Smith and Jay Sloan put it,

> Within the workings of a live tutorial, both tutor and student have ready access to a complex body of information encoded in a range of communicative acts—the written text being shared, the conversational exchanges that take place, the displays of body language—all of which are more easily read and interpreted face-to-face. (5)

By contrast, depending on the method employed, online tutoring limits much of the tutor's and writer's access to the "complex body of information" found in live, face-to-face tutoring sessions. Most limited is **asynchronous tutoring**, in which the writer submits the text (for instance, by email or some other online interface) and, at a later point in time, the tutor responds with written comments that are returned to the writer, for him to read on his own. Offering a fuller range of modalities is **synchronous tutoring**, in which writer and tutor communicate together at the same time, whether by way of instant messaging or video conferencing, sometimes while both are able to view and manipulate the writer's text. However, even the best technology will impose some limits on the information that can be shared between tutor and writer. Consequently, the writer might not be able to fully articulate what she needs help with, and the tutor might not know for sure whether the writer understands his questions or suggestions. Maintaining some of the skepticism he voiced about tutoring new media, Pemberton compares the shift from face-to-face to online tutoring to "moving the writing center conference from an IMAX theater to a grainy black-and-white, thirteen-inch television screen" (Foreword x).

Advantages of Online Tutoring

At the same time that many have concerns about online tutoring, writing tutoring programs increasingly offer this service because of the advantages it provides. As we mention at the beginning of this chapter, online tutoring provides access to writing support that some writers would not have otherwise. Moreover, some tutors and writers prefer the limitations of asynchronous tutoring because it allows the writer to submit work when he is ready and gives the tutor time to think through her response and to get help from other tutors or her director if necessary. In addition, instant messaging and other forms of synchronous tutoring can encourage writers to write during sessions, which can help them generate text that they can use for their projects. Finally, online tutoring almost always produces a record of the session, giving writers notes that they can easily refer to later and providing the tutor with potential data for research projects.

Undergraduate tutor-researcher Bill Chewning explores nearly all of these advantages as he recounts his work with a writer in a hybrid of face-to-face and different kinds of online tutoring. Chewning found that the online environment was more effective at encouraging Lana, who had been struggling with several assignments, to start writing: she was able to complete freewriting toward one of these papers and submit it to Chewning through an online message board, because it was "done on her own time, 'when she felt like it'" (57). And Chewning and Lana in turn discussed this writing through email and instant messaging. It is important to note that Chewning felt that their face-to-face work gave him insights into Lana's writing process that he would not have had they worked together solely online, and, ultimately, it was the combination of both face-to-face and online tutoring that led to their success. Nonetheless, he concludes that

> [O]nline tutorials offer freedoms for both tutors and tutees, particularly in terms of when contributions to the process can be made by either party. This type of freedom is beneficial not only for reasons of scheduling, but it also allows tutors and tutees to address issues from places where and times that they feel most comfortable or "ready" to take on particular tasks. (59)

What Chewning doesn't comment on directly but demonstrates in his article is that the online component of his work with Lana also resulted in a rich set of data. As a result, he was able to go back to this writing later, both to report to his director on the results of the pilot project he conducted and to help him prepare a submission for the journal *Young Scholars in Writing*. Likewise, Beth L. Hewitt and Ben Rafoth highlight research opportunities created in this context. Hewitt, for instance, recommends that tutors use the records produced by online tutoring to conduct "self-audits" in order to reflect on their work and to develop research questions (156–57). Similarly, in his chapter on tutoring multilingual writers online, Ben Rafoth reports on the results of a study he conducted with online tutors in his center, for which Rafoth and his tutors collected writing samples from multilingual writers and asked these writers to complete a survey and participate in interviews (150).

Strategies for Online Tutoring

Depending on the kind of software and procedures that your writing tutoring program uses, some of the tutoring practices we have emphasized throughout Section II might take very different forms in online sessions from those of face-to-face tutoring. In asynchronous online tutoring, some of these practices—getting acquainted, asking questions, negotiating priorities for the session, and analyzing the assignment/context, for example—might well be initiated in a form writers complete before submitting their writing for feedback. Tutors, in turn, will need to engage in other tutoring practices on their own and in their written comments—including making statements, analyzing the assignments, reading the writing, prioritizing, offering their perspectives as readers, wrapping up, and reflecting—perhaps by following a basic template in which they identify areas of strength to praise and two or three key areas for writers to work on. In synchronous online sessions, and, again, depending on the software being used, a great many more of these tutoring practices will be possible. However, as Pemberton points out, even the best technology will impose limits—for instance, on how easily you and the writer will be able to get acquainted and negotiate priorities and how much you can understand about the writer's nonverbal cues.

Below, we describe strategies drawn from Rafoth's and Hewitt's research that apply to both asynchronous and synchronous tutoring. Specifically because of the limitations that online tutors (and writers) face, most important is being selective about and prioritizing the kinds of feedback you can offer. Also useful for dealing with these limitations is rhetoric, especially in terms of helping writers feel "listened to" (even when actual listening isn't possible), confident about the help they receive, and clear about what the tutor is trying to convey.

Be Selective and Prioritize

A major finding of the study that Rafoth and the tutors in his center conducted, which Hewitt's research supports, is that prioritizing what to work on in online, and especially asynchronous, sessions is crucial. For example, written comments—even a lot of them—can't substitute for all the information conveyed in the kind of face-to-face interactions that Smith and Sloan describe. For the writers Rafoth and the tutors in his center studied, "making lots of comments" proved to be overwhelming: "[W]here should the writer begin? What was the tutor's most important comment? The answers to these questions were hard to find in the tutors' feedback" (152, 151). After reviewing the data from their study, Rafoth and the tutors realized the value of "not merely writing less but writing more selectively" (152). Hewitt's research supports Rafoth's findings. For a variety of reasons, writers disregarded 30 to 40 percent of the online comments they received (134–35).

Based on their studies, Hewitt and Rafoth offer the kind of advice we outline in Chapter 3. Just as you might in a face-to-face session, Hewitt suggests reading for global, or higher-order, concerns first and limiting the number of issues you comment on, whether you're working in an asynchronous or synchronous environment (46, 91, 135). Rafoth holds that writers who get feedback "ranging from minor editing to global revision, often make the editing changes but not the global revisions" (156). Further, when working with multilingual writers who ask for help on sentence-level concerns, Rafoth recommends—just as we do in Chapters 3 and 5—reading the writing "more for meaning than for errors" and focusing on problems that interfere with the writer's ability to convey this meaning. "Unless a word, phrase, or sentence is clearly preventing the writer from conveying a key point, let it go and focus on those places where key points are getting lost" (154–56). If there are many points in the writing where the meaning is unclear, "pick one or two and focus on them, leaving the rest alone." And if you decide to comment on a sentence-level problem that does not interfere with meaning, be sure to tell the writer how much you would prioritize this issue in relation to others (156–57).

Rhetorical Strategies for Online Tutoring

Thinking rhetorically in the online tutoring session can be a powerful way to make up for some of the interpersonal dimensions that are lost due to the mediation of technology. Although Hewitt and Rafoth do not use this term, rhetoric is nonetheless apparent in their emphasis on communication and what Hewitt calls "practical ways . . . to enact caring and to present a human face in online settings" (61). In particular, their research-based advice about these communicative, interpersonal elements corresponds to the rhetorical appeals of pathos and ethos. In addition, their emphasis on being clear has much in common with purpose.

Pathos. As we mention above, pathos is a term from classical rhetoric used to describe how rhetors (e.g., writers, composers, and speakers) appeal to the interests and feelings of their audiences (readers, viewers, and listeners). Although the term might be new to you, the related strategies for making this appeal probably won't be since we offer many in Chapter 3 when we discuss ways to build rapport with, engage, and motivate writers. Similarly, Hewitt encourages tutors to establish a personal connection with the writer in online tutoring sessions through a number of familiar strategies, holding that we should be sure to

- Greet the writer
- Use his or her name
- Ask "open-ended and contextually genuine questions"
- Ask writers "whether they have their own questions"
- Praise "genuine strengths"

- Check in often to make sure the writer understands: "Synchronously, one might say, 'Does this make sense?' or 'Please tell me what I just said using your own words.' Asynchronously, one might say 'In other words,' and then rephrase or otherwise define . . ." (57, 92, 123).

Ethos. Perhaps less familiar is ethos, which is used to describe how rhetors present themselves in their work, particularly in terms of how they use this self-presentation to help them persuade or engage their audiences. Hewitt calls this the "conferencing voice or tone" that one can create with written comments as well as through visual and design elements (63). Visual elements and text design—such as font choices and formatting, text boxes, bullets, or numbers—can, in addition, convey the priority of your concerns and help writers with certain kinds of visual or cognitive disabilities. As Moreau and Normand do, Hewitt cautions against going overboard with these elements, however, since they can distract the writer from what you want to communicate to him about his work (131–32).

Hewitt offers additional strategies that simultaneously address self-presentation and concern for the writer. She suggests that tutors "be personable by being genuine, specific, thoughtful, and self-engaged in the conference and the student's writing" (124). Moreover, she maintains that we can show that we are attending to the writer's needs "by frequent reference to the writing, the assignment, or something that's been shared," and, when offering written comments, using emoticons and other "cues [to] designate interest" (122, 57, 63). Hewitt reminds us that a writer too can have an online ethos. She warns that when a writer's self-presentation suggests a lack of interest in the session, we should keep in mind that this effect might be created instead by limited time, discomfort with online environments, or weak typing or spelling skills. Given our usually limited knowledge about what the writer might be doing or feeling on the other end of an online session, she urges us to believe that the writer *is* interested. Such an attitude might in turn help to draw in a writer who is not (58).

Purpose. As much as you'll want "to enact caring and to present a human face" in online tutoring, you'll simultaneously need to ensure that you are clearly communicating the ultimate purpose of your feedback. As Rafoth discusses, these two goals can initially seem at odds. He describes a tutor's comment that, because it aimed to be "reassuring and comforting," distracted the writer from "the real need for revisions" (158). Reiterating a point offered in Chapter 5 about the ways that conventions of politeness and indirection that are valued in the United States are far from universal, Rafoth holds that the multilingual writers in his study heard "tentativeness or hesitation in phrases like 'you might want to think about . . .' or 'I wonder if . . .'" As he says, "We might think we sound polite and nondirective, but writers might hear wishy-washy" (157). Related, if you discuss your lack of familiarity with the topic, you might well "sow seeds of doubt in some writers' minds." Rafoth points out that "Writers assess their tutors' trustworthiness" in online sessions, and, as a result, tutors need to offer honest feedback, "plainly and confidently" (157).

Hewitt's research suggests that most writers prefer direct statements in online sessions, especially over suggestions that take the form of questions. Writers she surveyed were often confused by such suggestions-in-the-form-of-questions, which can be read exclusively *as* questions rather than as they were intended, as advice about changing the text. For instance, the suggestion-question "Have you thought about starting a new paragraph here?" might lead a writer to respond with "no" and move on, not realizing that the tutor is trying to communicate a need for revision (105–11). Instead, Hewitt maintains that tutors should state suggestions directly, with, for example, "I suggest that you . . ." (115). You might notice that this advice seems to contradict Johnson et al.'s recommendation in Chapter 6 that tutors should take a stance of "provisionalism" rather than the kind of certainty Rafoth and Hewitt suggest. In part, this difference is a function of the online session: in face-to-face sessions, especially with writers and tutors of the same cultural and linguistic backgrounds, there are more ways for both to ensure that they have communicated effectively. But as we discuss below, these online examples also reveal some important, if subtle, insights about any writing tutoring situation.

For Writing

1. If your tutoring program currently offers online tutoring, arrange to use it for a piece of your own writing. Before you do so, however, reflect on what you anticipate the differences between online and face-to-face tutoring experiences will feel like from the point of view of the writer. After working through the feedback you receive, compare your initial reflections with the actual experience. How might this experience help you and your program better prepare writers for their online tutoring sessions?

2. Perhaps as a point of comparison with the previous activity, trade hardcopy drafts with a peer and tutor each other on this writing. Afterwards, reflect on how it felt to respond and receive feedback in this manner. How did this experience differ from any tutoring sessions you have had, either with your peers or other writing tutors?

REFLECTING ON OUR CONCEPTIONS

At the beginning of this chapter, we propose that as much as new media and online tutoring take us into new territories, they also help us reflect on and gain insights into the more traditional aspects of our work. To return to the quotation we offer from Lee and Carpenter above, "digital communication asks us to rethink our traditional conceptions of writing, authorship, and audiences" (xv). Below are a few of the ways that such conceptions might be rethought.

New Insights into Writing and Authorship

New media and online tutoring enable us to reflect on and gain new insights into writing and authorship. Mendelsohn's observation about font personalities, for example, reminds us that writing is always visual, always something to see. Such visual dimensions are aspects of writing that we can attend to and alert writers to as well. Moreover, writing *is* technology and cannot exist without it. Yet some people do not have access to what might appear to some of us to be even the most basic technological understanding—of, for instance, spell check and indentations in MS Word. As people who help people with writing, we might need to help writers with technology too. Furthermore, authorship is no longer limited to writing, and new media highlights how messy and fluid composing processes are.

New Understandings of Audience and Rhetoric

The ways in which new media and online tutoring help us to reconceptualize audiences leads us to reacquaint ourselves with rhetoric, even for situations that do not feel (and perhaps ultimately are not) rhetorical. Much of academic writing does not seem to have an authentic rhetorical situation, exigence, audience, or authorized rhetor. To combat such inauthenticity, faculty sometimes assign new media projects precisely because they capture some of the rhetorical urgency that we can see in texts in the "real world." However, even when you tutor a writer who has produced a term paper simply to fulfill a requirement, you can help to create a situation that approximates an authentic rhetorical situation: as a reader and potential or stand-in audience member, you can enact a real need to understand what the writer is trying to say. And as we play this role of the reader, the rhetoric of online tutoring reminds us that we need to be aware of how we present ourselves and attend to the writer's needs in face-to-face situations as well.

New Conceptions of the Modalities of Tutoring

Both new media and online tutoring remind us of how very many modalities there are to take advantage of in our work with writers and composers. In face-to-face sessions, these include all the modalities that the New London Group says are part of multiliteracy—linguistic, visual, audio, gestural, and spatial modalities, as well as combinations of these. As we tutor, many of us speak, listen to, see, or move ourselves, each other, and objects around us in a variety of ways. These modalities include those online. If a face-to-face modality doesn't work, we might be able to shift to an online forum such as email or instant messaging as Chewning did with Lana. Likewise, in online sessions, it might be possible to shift to another mode as well—to exchange emails or set up a time to talk on the phone, to video conference, or to instant message.

For Inquiry

1. If your tutoring program uses asynchronous tutoring, in which writers submit writing that tutors write comments about, collaborate with other tutors on developing "templates" for writing comments. Hewitt suggests an overall structure might include

   1. A greeting,

   2. A statement about the strengths of the writing,

   3. Your suggestions for revision,

   4. Information related to one or more of these suggestions,

   5. A closing statement (129).

   For suggestion 4, you might interview experienced tutors about common problems they see and try to locate online resources that address them. See Kavadlo as well as Ryan and Zimmerelli (79, 86) for more extensive examples.

2. If your tutoring program offers online tutoring, research the demographics of the writers who access this service. When you compare these users to your student body demographics, who is using the service and who is not? Conduct a case study of either the most frequent users of online tutoring or a group of writers who are present on your campus but underrepresented among users of online tutoring. (You can find information on designing and implementing case studies in Chapter 11.) How can your center better meet this group's needs, either to attract new users to the service or to better serve current users?

SECTION III

Research Methods
for Writing Tutors

CHAPTER 8

The Kinds of Research—And the Kinds of Questions They Can Answer

INTRODUCTION

Imagine you go to your regional writing center conference and hear a panel of tutors give the following papers:

- Presenter One begins with an assertion that writing center tutors do not pay as much attention to grammatical issues as they should. The presenter first describes her center's policy that tutors will not proofread papers and then goes on to describe three very successful tutorials she conducted that focused on grammatical issues. These tutorials concluded, she describes, with the students learning something useful and leaving the center feeling better about their papers. From these three examples, the presenter concludes, tutors learn that we all need to focus on grammar more.
- Presenter Two argues that we need to tutor less grammar in the writing center. He describes a tutorial in which he acquiesced to the writer's insistence that they focus on grammar; the paper actually got worse because the author of the paper didn't know what she was talking about in the first place. Further, since the writer submitted the paper online, Presenter Two tells the audience, he can distribute the original to demonstrate that this paper was clearly bad and so not to the point of line editing. This presenter finishes by arguing that, because papers that are brought to the writing center are always "in process," it follows that we never should focus on grammar when tutoring writing.
- Presenter Three argues that we need to think about grammar differently in the writing center. Currently, she argues, all writing tutors address grammar only if the sentence-level errors make it impossible for the reader to

understand meaning. In contrast to degrading grammatical instruction in this way, she argues, in every tutorial we should pay attention to both global and local issues. In this way, she continues, tutors will show writers how to improve their work at multiple stages of the writing process. To demonstrate the importance of many grammatical issues in the writing process, she describes closely the contents of the grammar handbook used at her school and concludes that the length and detail of this handbook demonstrate the vast amount of grammatical information everyone needs to have at his or her fingertips.

Of the three arguments above, some, or perhaps all, could strike an audience member as unpersuasive or wrongheaded. Each one of these three presentations contains fatal flaws in terms of its **method, argument,** and/or **ethics.** Put another way, these presentations suffer from problems in the way the evidence was generated (method), what that evidence is claimed to prove (argument), or the researcher's attention—or lack thereof—to the care of the research subject (ethics). Before a tutor-researcher begins a scholarly inquiry, then, it is necessary to

- select a method appropriate to the project's goals
- check to make sure that the selected method will create knowledge that can prove the desired claims
- ensure that all researchers involved use all the ethical care called for by the research community in and out of writing center studies

Toward these ends, this chapter is meant to help you understand how to design a study. First we need to consider the idea of "method" generally. Later chapters of this section of the book focus on the concerns specific to particular methods.

LORE AND METHOD

Research studies typically start with a question—such as "Why do so few engineering students use our tutoring program?"—or with a desire to question received knowledge—such as "All writing centers employ only nondirective tutoring methods." In response to such questions or knowledge, less experienced tutor-researchers might consider as "research" the writing up of their thoughts on these issues, based on what they have seen in their program or experienced in their own tutoring. Such a firsthand account presented as evidence is illustrated by Presenter One in the opening example. In writing center studies, the knowledge created in this manner is often called *lore,* a term popularized by Stephen North in *The Making of Knowledge in Composition: Portrait of an Emerging Field.* North's book was published in 1987 and was the first attempt to systematically taxonomize the methods used to create the discipline of writing studies.[1]

Lore

Lore is still a vital, albeit contested, concept in the field and therefore one writing center researchers should be familiar with. According to North, lore is an account of successful past practice:

> [Lore] is driven by a pragmatic logic: It is concerned with what has worked, is working, or might work in teaching, doing or learning writing. Second, its structure is essentially experiential. That is, the traditions, practices, and beliefs of which it is constituted are best understood as being organized within an experience-based framework: I will create my version of lore out of what has worked or might work—either in my own experience or that of others—and I will understand and order it in terms of the circumstances under which it did so. (North, *Making* 23)

Applying North's example to the fictional scenario that opens this chapter, then, the first presentation—in which the tutor-researcher describes a series of tutorials that were, in her opinion, successful—can be seen as an example of lore. This is not to deny the impact or usefulness of lore: for a long time, it has been an effective way to create information about tutoring.

Lore is not included in the chapter-length discussion of research methods in this book, however, because its experiential nature means that the information it generates is difficult to include in a conversation focused on methods-based research. That is, methods-based research can persuade (or not) on the basis of the method used and how it was used. For example, one might be persuaded because the writer gains proficiency that is demonstrated in a study, or one might be unconvinced because the data gathered does not prove the claim made. Presenter Three from the opening scenario can be understood as illustrating a disconnect between data and claims, for while she does have a kind of dataset in her description of her institution's grammar handbook, the existence of this material does not, in fact, prove what she claims: that we should tutor grammar in every session.

Presenter Two's scenario also helps to illustrate why lore is difficult to include in evidence-based scholarly arguments. It would be difficult to disagree

---

[1]While North's book is still a valuable read for anyone interested in the development of research methods used in writing studies, some of the approaches he describes are no longer used or used in quite the way he describes and, as one should expect from a book that is over 25 years old, some of the information and examples are outdated. Thus, readers interested in such surveys of the field would do well to also consider more recent reviews of the field, such as those by Liggett, Jordan, and Price.

with her testimony that grammar instruction made for successful tutorials. As her thesis is fundamentally, "This is what I saw," it would be hard for one to say, "No you didn't!" Or, as North puts it:

> Lore's pragmatic logic and experience-based structure account for . . . its most important functional properties. The first is that literally anything can become a part of lore. The only requirement for entry is that the idea, notion, practice or whatever must be nominated: some member of the community must claim that it worked, or seemed to work, or might work. . . . Lore's second functional property is just as important as this open-door policy . . . While anything can become a part of lore nothing can ever be dropped from it, either. There is simply no mechanism for it. Lore's various elements are not pitted against one another within the framework of some lore-specific dialectic, or checked and rechecked. (North, *Making* 934)

Put another way, because lore is based on individual testimony, it is difficult to critique, test, or evaluate without personalizing that critique to the presenter's individual experience. Returning to Presenter Two, for example, if an audience member responds, "Well, I don't agree—what you describe hasn't been my experience AT ALL," neither the presenter nor her respondent can move the scholarly argument forward; they merely can state and restate their opinions and perceptions. Generating one's arguments according to a research method or methods, by contrast, will allow people to see the means by which ideas are tested and proven and so allows scholarly conversations to move forward.

Method and the Research Process
Firsthand experience might, of course, inspire a research question: the topics of the presentations described above certainly could all be used as the bases of method-based research. However, the process for conducting such research would be better served using a careful research design rather than the anecdotal writing up of experience of Presenter One, for example, or the description of a book's contents, as in Presenter Three. This section, then, focuses on research design to describe the kinds of careful planning that underlie methods-based research.

Method: Review of Research
The first step of many research processes, however, may well be familiar: the review of research. That is, typically, one might start with a review of existing research in the area to acquaint oneself with the conversation thus far on that topic. In many classes, particularly at the introductory level, this process might, in fact, be the end of the research expectation. Rather than being required to create original knowledge, in many classes, the student writer might merely need to synthesize sources and so use existing knowledge to evidence her own thesis statement. Such research demonstrate a writer's ability to find and select relevant sources, analyze them appropriately, and so demonstrate an improved understanding of the topic under consideration.

Selecting a Method

For the tutor-researcher, however, this is just the beginning. For once you have reviewed the research, noting the most relevant studies for possible inclusion in your final manuscript, it is time to think carefully about how you are going to contribute to this conversation. That is:

- What do you want to prove?
- Who do you want to prove it to?
- What kind of evidence will be found most compelling by this group?

As seen in Table 8.1, there are many, many methods of research you can use—indeed, because of space considerations, this book covers only a few—and each will result in a specific kind of evidence that will lend itself to specific kinds of arguments. In each of the following chapters in this section, we describe the considerations and direct you to resources particularly relevant to that issue, but here we introduce each method briefly to illuminate the ways in which the method you select is going to affect the kinds of questions you can answer.

While these brief discussions may make such methods sound abstract and unrelated to writing center work, it is important to note that each of these methods can be applied to the same research question, but will yield very different kinds of results. To illustrate the differences among these results, Table 8.2 picks up on the

Table 8.1 Kinds of Research.

Theoretical Research: Theoretical research consists of the application of a theoretical lens or lenses to the activities of the writing center in an attempt to gain a new perspective into writing center work, often, but not always, combined with evidence yielded by other methods to forward an argument. An example of theoretical research is Kenneth Bruffee's "Peer Tutoring and the 'Conversation of Mankind,'" which is included in the anthology section of this book. You can find a discussion of theoretical research in Chapter 9.

Historical: Historical work helps us understand the events of the past. It not only helps enrich our understanding of past practices and events but can also help us understand our present moment better and, perhaps, chart our future course of action. An example of historical work in the anthology section of this book is Neal Lerner's "Searching for Robert Moore," and you can find a discussion of historical work in Chapter 10.

Empirical: Empirical research can include both qualitative and quantitative methods. Qualitative includes attempts to understand the behavior of an individual entity or type, as in a case study, or the interaction of a group, as in an ethnography. An example of qualitative research in the anthology section of this book is Jo Mackiewicz and Isabelle Thompson's "Motivational Scaffolding, Politeness, and Writing Center Tutoring." Quantitative research, which uses numbers as a means to compare across datasets, typically deals with broader sets of data than does qualitative research. For many readers of this book, the most readily recognizable quantitative research would be statistical. In many writing centers, this is the only form of research; many centers collect and circulate quantitative information about writers' usage and satisfaction with their services. An example of quantitative research in the anthology section of this book is Alicia Brazeau's "Groupies and Singletons: Student Preferences in Classroom-Based Writing Consulting." You can find a discussion of quantitative work in Chapter 11.

Table 8.2 Research Method Heuristic.

Initial Research Question: Why do so few engineering students use our writing center?

METHOD	GENERAL KINDS OF QUESTIONS IT CAN ANSWER	SPECIFIC QUESTIONS IT CAN ANSWER FOR YOU
Lore	Drawing upon experience and stories heard from others, what is the best course of action in the present situation?	What strategies have current tutors employed with engineering students that they think work? What strategies do they think haven't worked? Why do my colleagues think so few engineering students use the center?
Theory-Based Research	How can researchers more fully understand the current situation when it is viewed through a specific critical lens? How can a specific critical lens help researchers better understand what has happened or better plan for future exigencies?	What new perspective about writing in engineering does a critical lens from writing studies yield? What new information about the writing center does a theoretical lens from engineering yield?
Historical	What precedents exist to assess options in the current situation? How was the current set of practices and/or beliefs arrived at?	Historically speaking, what has been the relationship between the writing center and the College of Engineering? Did its students ever use the center more? If so, what changed? If not, how has literacy instruction developed in that college? How, if at all, has it changed over time?
Empirical Research	How do individuals and groups interact and understand their world? How can the perceptions of others help improve practice? How does talk about writing affect writing itself?	What are the learning behaviors of those individual engineering students who use the center and what can those behaviors suggest to us about writing practices in their community? When studying a single class of engineering students, what can we learn about their disciplinary-based writing processes? How does this understanding intersect (or not) with the understanding of the writing process in our writing center? How does a survey of beliefs describe similarities and differences between frequent writing center users and engineering students?

earlier example research question "Why do so few engineering students use our writing center?" and suggests ways in which these methods might be used to address this question.

As this chart illustrates, there is a variety of ways of gathering information to help us better understand past and current practice and to help plan our future activity. We've included a template of this chart at the end of this chapter in case you wish to use it as a tool when selecting your own method. Given the diversity of approaches we might take, it could be easy to become overwhelmed, particularly if we try to look for the "right" method or the "right" answer. However, neither method selection nor the conducting of research itself looks for a single, definitive right answer. A more achievable goal is to make a contribution to an ongoing conversation and/or to create new knowledge that improves your understanding and that can improve the understanding of others as well.

Even after you "right-size" your goal, however, there is still the question of how to select a method to ground your inquiry. Often the constraints of your situation will, to some extent, help you make this determination. You may or may not, for example, have adequate data resources to ground a historical study. Similarly, you'll have to consider the timespan of the project. For example, one of the methods not covered in this text, **longitudinal studies**, observes the evolution of a group or individuals over a longer period of time. While the changes in behavior of frequent writing center users over the years of their college attendance would make for a fascinating study, it would be difficult for an individual tutor-researcher to sustain a project of the length or depth of such a study.

In addition to being aware of the limitations of their situation, researchers should also inventory the resources they have available. Some writing tutoring programs will have, for example, a rich historical archive, although these records may be considered administrative rather than historical. Or you might have access to an individual, such as a faculty member or another student, whose expertise with a method, such as statistical or archival, complements your study. You might, in fact, be that expert—many peer tutors have created important work that drew upon research methods they learned in the classes in their major, for example. Often the method we use in our research is largely the result of the kind of work we inexplicably yet inarguably gravitate toward.

ARGUMENT

Researchers also consider *whom* they are trying to convince and *what* to argue to that group. When arguing to a group of practitioners who may be less familiar with research but are well acquainted with the hard work of day-to-day instruction, lore or case study might be persuasive, but when arguing to a high-level college administrator, who quite often spends her days thinking in terms of the larger picture, large pools of quantitative data are often most effective. And if you are targeting a specific group of faculty, you may want to consider the methods used in their field. If you don't use those methods, consider what kinds of data would appeal to the **epistemologies**, the ways of thinking, common in those faculty members' fields. Put another way, and as you may have found in your coursework, the kinds of arguments made in an English literature class and the kinds of arguments made in a sociology paper can differ sharply. Thus, an audience in the humanities may be more likely to be convinced by the kinds of theoretical arguments described in Chapter 9 or the type of historical works described in Chapter 10, while a social science audience might be more familiar with, and thus more favorably inclined toward, the kinds of qualitative methods described in Chapter 11.

RELIABILITY AND VALIDITY

Once you've thought carefully about your purpose, available evidence, and audience in this fashion, you'll want to check your preliminary research plan carefully, evaluating the likely **reliability** and **validity** of this work. We're borrowing these terms from the scholarship of writing assessment, in particular the work of Kathleen Yancey, who concisely summarizes "the twin concepts validity and reliability. Validity means that you are measuring what you intend to measure, reliability that you can measure it consistently" ("Looking" 487). In other words, validity means your evidence demonstrates what you intend it to demonstrate. Reliability means that your method correctly created data appropriate to your study and would do so again for another researcher under the same circumstances.

An example might help clarify these important concepts. Imagine a tutor-researcher wishes to demonstrate the improvement of student writing by comparing the grammatical complexity of drafts written before and after a tutoring session. Such a study could yield highly reliable evidence in that properly trained readers who could identify complex sentences would consistently yield the same data in their counts when assessing the same texts. This evidence, however, would not be a valid measure of writing center overall success since complex sentences can create meaning that is highly persuasive in context or completely irrelevant to the matter at hand. Such a study then is reliable but not valid and so is unpersuasive. When designing your own research plan, you should ask yourself if the project you intend can be expected to fulfill these criteria.

AUDIENCE

Finally, it might be useful to consider where you want to share your work. You may plan to share your research only with your classmates, in which case you might only need to consider the parameters of your assignment. Even in this situation, there are elements that can affect the planning process. If your primary means of communication will be a final written paper, for example, you may be able to communicate a more detailed analysis and a larger pool evidence than if your final assignment is a presentation to your fellow tutors.

Likewise, if your research will be presented in a primarily visual fashion—for instance, by way of a poster presentation or on a website—you'll want to think about what kinds of information are persuasive in this format. An excerpt of an interview, for example, may be more powerful in a video clip shown in class than in a transcript printed on a poster board in a research fair. In addition, your research may be shared in a more public forum—a university presentation, a regional writing center conference, or a local or national publication, for example. If so, you'll want to familiarize yourself with the expectations and requirements of the final venue for your work. You may wish to think as well about what the audience in this environment will know about your topic and how you can frame your inquiry to engage their interest. Ultimately, no matter where your work will meet its audience, you'll want to plan your process with an eye to the requirements and expectations of its final environment and the ways in which you hope to appeal to that audience.

In Table 8.3, we explore how you might use the evidence to plan a research project on engineering students' underuse of a writing center. The project will be presented in a university research fair.

It may seem like there's a lot of planning that goes into method-based research before it even starts, and there is. But we've put together a template based on Table 8.3 that we've included at the end of this chapter. It's meant to help you organize this process. We think that you'll find that a well-planned research project is actually far more time efficient than just "jumping in" to research and writing.

In this chapter thus far, we've attempted to lay out a research design process that will position you well to create original research that both responds to and furthers the current conversations in writing center studies. Don't worry, though, if your research process doesn't look this straightforward—most scholars usually don't work in such neat linear fashion (we certainly don't). For one, like the writing process, the research process is usually **recursive**. Researchers move back and forth along the continuum of research—reviewing extant research, project design, data generating, analysis, and writing. There are, too, serendipitous moments in the research process that can't be planned for, when a new idea or new evidence takes you in an exciting and unforeseen direction. So while you shouldn't worry about using a process as linear as the one described here, you should make sure you've accounted for the elements we've described, including reviewing the knowledge on your topic that's already been captured in the research and planning for a method that is both reliable and valid.

ETHICS

Once you've done the necessary preliminary design and argument planning, there is one last step to take before moving forward with your work. That is, you need to evaluate any ethical considerations of your project. It may seem triply

Table 8.3 Argument Planning Brainstorm.

Research Question

Why do so few engineering students use the writing center?

What is my goal?

I would like to convince engineering faculty and students in that program that we're a great resource.

What method will I use and why?

I'll use an attitude survey administered to both frequent writing center users and engineering students, so that I can capture the opinions of a lot of people and compare the notions of people who are doing what we want (frequent writing center users) with the opinions of people who we'd like to adopt these behaviors (engineering students who don't use the center).

What is the best way to share this research?

It doesn't matter what the best way is: I'm required to share it at the university research fair. If I really like how this project is turning out, though, maybe I'll ask my director if she'd like to talk to Engineering about this work.

What are the expectations of the venue in which I'll share my research?

The university research fair takes place in a big room—it's like a science fair but for all kinds of writing research. On the plus side, you don't have to give a formal talk. On the downside, you only have a couple of minutes to talk to each group and it's really loud in there.

What audiences am I likely to reach in this venue?

Faculty, students, and administrators at my school. My project talks about engineering students but I should think about what this work might offer the other people at the research fair.

How can I best present my data?

A poster that summarizes the high points of data from the survey and a handout that explains what we do—maybe with quotes from the frequent writing center users about how come they find our services useful and similar quotes from engineering faculty on what kinds of help they think engineering students need? (Note: must add faculty interviews to IRB proposal.)

Does my planned research seem reliable?

Yeah—if someone wanted to they could give the exact same survey to the same group of people, they'd probably get the same answers.

Does my planned research seem valid?

It does to me. For one, it seems like there's a pretty straight line that can be drawn from a student's understanding of how they might learn to write better and whether or not they come to the writing center. For another, if we can find out what kinds of research faculty value, we can help their students understand how important writing is in their major. That might motivate these students to use our program, too.

---

counterintuitive to worry about ethics in a tutor's research project. For one, this is a far cry from, say, medical testing or other research traditions whose potential impact on the subject's harm or good is readily evident. For another, writing center "folks," as the cross-institutional community of individuals who work in writing centers often call themselves, strongly identify as a committed, caring community and so see themselves as unlikely to incur an ethical breach. And, finally, tutor-researchers, whose role is defined by the egalitarian nature of their relationship with the writers who often serve as the "subjects" of their research, may not seem to be in a position to do any kind of harm.

Respect, Benefice, Justice: The Components of Ethical Research

However, as can be seen in the second anecdote that opens this chapter, tutor-researchers are indeed in a position to have a negative impact on the writers with whom they work. Presenter Two has taken a writer's intellectual property—a paper—and then distributed it without securing the writer's permission. Further, this tutor's summary of the paper as "clearly bad" seems a bit unfair as a public statement, particularly when you consider that the paper is a draft meant only to be shared with a tutor. And whether or not the presenter believes that distributing a writer's paper in this manner constitutes harm, as is described below, it could nevertheless be considered as such by both your institution and the international research community.

Writing studies scholars—a group that here includes writing center researchers—have long studied both the strategies of real-world writers and the texts that these strategies yield. And yet, when compared to other traditions of scholarly inquiry, writing studies researchers and their institutions have only recently begun to see this work as having an impact on all of its human subjects. That is, since the 1970s, scientists who work with human subjects have operated under a series of guidelines that are articulated in a document called *The Belmont Report*, which outlines the ethical considerations of human subject research. More specifically, this report describes three concepts as integral to such work:

- Respect for Persons
- Beneficence
- Justice

Respect for Persons: The Cornerstone of Ethical Research

Of these three principles, *Respect for Persons* is, as Paul V. Anderson describes, "the most broadly relevant" to writing studies research (68). According to *The Belmont Report*, "Respect for persons incorporates at least two ethical convictions: first, that individuals should be treated as autonomous agents, and second, that persons with diminished autonomy are entitled to protection." Put another way, researchers are responsible for constructing studies in which participants are truly "autonomous": they have been fully apprised of their projected role in the study and have the right to opt out if they so choose. Individuals are thought to have "diminished autonomy" if their "capacity for self-determination" is missing "wholly or in part because of illness, mental disability, or circumstances that severely restrict liberty" (*Belmont*).

While this sort of diminished autonomy may seem light years away from working with writers one-to-one, as Anderson notes of the writing classroom, writers seeking assistance can indeed feel such a sense of "severely restrict[ed] liberty":

> [O]ur studies often rely on individuals who may be especially vulnerable to unintentional infringement of their rights, dignity and privacy. For example, in

> quantitative and qualitative studies, we sometimes use our own students as research participants, either by observing their "natural" behavior in classrooms, conferences, or other venues or by asking them to engage in special research activities for the sake of our projects. Students may be doubly vulnerable to us because of the trusting relationship they have with us as their teachers and because of the power our position as teachers gives us over them. (64)

Admittedly, the student–teacher relationship is different from the tutor–writer dynamic. However, not all writers may feel that difference as readily as may the tutor-researcher: many writers are new to the writing center and unsure about the power dynamic of the tutor–writer relationship. There has been a theme in writing center scholarship about avoiding the perception—or the reality—that the tutor is simply a "little teacher" to whom the writer attributes precisely the authority and responsibility connoted by the instructor's role (see, as examples, Beck et al.; Gillam, Callaway, and Wikoff; Leahy). A writer new to the writing center or from a non-U.S. educational background in which the tutor's authority is seen in teacher-like terms, for example, might imbue the tutor-researcher with the kind of authority about which Anderson cautions the teacher researcher. Even those writers who see the tutor as a helpful peer rather than an institutional authority can feel the diminished autonomy of social dynamics; they want to be helpful to the individual who is going to help them with their writing. In brief, either a sense of their obligation or the tutor's authority could make writers feel coerced into participating in research from which they would otherwise elect to opt out.

Tutor Research and Institutional Review

To make potential research subjects as comfortable as possible, there are several steps that researchers are ethically and, in fact, legally required to take. These requirements are often overseen on college and university campuses by an Institutional Review Board (IRB). You'll need to work with your instructor or program administrator to research how the IRB functions at your institution. Some schools base their requirements on the institutional standing of the researchers. The IRB might have different expectations for faculty rather than staff or students. The purposes of the research might contribute to determining the process of review as well. If your research is only to be shared in your program, for example, your project may be evaluated differently than if you want to share your work at conferences, in print, or online. This may sound a bit intimidating, but the information for what you will be required to do is usually readily available online, from an office for research, or elsewhere on campus. Your instructor, director, or faculty member is also likely to be well informed on this topic and can help point you in the right direction.

Informed Consent

Among the items tutor-researchers need to consider are how to achieve **informed consent** from your subjects and your subjects' **expectation of privacy**. Informed consent means that researchers don't just need to get participants to sign a waiver but must also

- Ensure the participants understand the research, particularly their own role as participants, and possess full knowledge of the risks and benefits of the project
- Have the right to withdraw during the research at any point in the process
- Do not feel coerced in any way to participate in the work.

According to the Conference on College Composition and Communication (a professional organization for writing teachers with which many writing center professionals are affiliated), there are several elements to informed consent. According to the "CCCC Guidelines for the Ethical Conduct of Research in Composition Studies," researchers must disclose

1. The purposes of the research and its possible benefits
2. What participants will be asked to do and how long it will take
3. What the composition specialists plan to do with the information or data they obtain from participants
4. Any potential discomforts or harms one might incur as a result of participating
5. Whether or not composition specialists intend to include information in research reports that would render participants identifiable. (Composition specialists always honor participants' requests that reports contain no personally identifiable information including information that would make them identifiable to persons familiar with the research site.)

In addition, composition specialists emphasize the following points:

1. Participation is completely voluntary.
2. Participants may withdraw at any time without penalty or loss of benefits.

As one might expect, achieving informed consent is most often a matter of careful planning and forethought. To return to Presenter Two from this chapter's opening, then, the speaker's use of student-authored texts was not done with the writer's permission and so would be considered unethical under most IRBs and *The Belmont Report*. To obtain informed consent, the researcher would have needed to tell the student of the planned use of these texts and to receive her written permission to do so. Indeed, many IRBs encourage researchers to have another individual who is not the researcher obtain the informed consent to improve the likelihood that the potential participant will not feel pressured to join the study. (While many institutions have their own forms for informed consent, we include a sample at the end of this chapter to give a sense of what one might look like.) Part of achieving informed consent focuses on communicating clearly what participants can expect regarding privacy/anonymity. Will students be named in the research? If not, how (if at all) will individual participants be identified? What is the likelihood that a reader who knows the participants will be able to identify the subjects? How will you protect your data, particularly data that identifies—or can be identified with—your subjects? Such considerations are important, not only because they will bring you in alignment with local and national practice but also—and far more importantly—because they protect the rights of the individuals involved in your work.

Research Ethics and Student Writers

While your institution may have an IRB or similar organization that you must be concerned with, scholars in writing studies have argued that those of us who work with students need to go beyond minimum compliance with regulations. Joseph Harris, the editor of *College Composition and Communication* who articulated an editorial policy concerning student work, described the reasons why we might want to take further cautions with student work and offers suggestions for what such a policy might look like:

> You should get written permission from any student whose work you wish to include in an article for *CCC* . . . Whenever possible, you should allow students to read a draft of the article in which their work appears so they can see how their writing will be quoted and what will be said about it. As with any text, you should try to reproduce student writings as exactly as you can and to make sure that their words are seen in proper context—that is, that ellipses do not distort the effect of their writing. . . . The basic issue here, it seems to me, is one of control over text. Contributors to a journal have the chance to rethink and refine their work over time, to use the comments of editors and reviewers to revise their writings before they see print. Students are rarely given quite the same opportunity. Instead what most often happens is that writings they produced for a particular teacher or class are excerpted and represented in an article written by someone else, and it is this someone else (the author of the article) who has the final say over how their views and words appear in print. ("From the Editor," 440)

In other words, researchers get the last word, so they should hold themselves accountable for presenting students' work accurately.

Guidelines such as those that Harris describes are especially important in writing center studies, for our work focuses particularly on representation of the work of others. If you look at the works included in the anthology section of this book, for example, you'll see many stories that are meant to persuade the reader, and some of the most frequently circulated texts in writing center studies focus on the representation of individuals. (See, for example, Annie DiPardo's "Whispers of Coming and Going: Lessons from Fannie," Meg Woolbright's "The Politics of Tutoring: Feminism within the Patriarchy," or in the anthology section of this book, Mara Brecht's "Basic Literacy: Mediating between Power Constructs.") Representations such as these are foundational to the discipline, and the subjects contained in such works are the very individuals we claim to help. Indeed, neither our scholarship nor our work would exist without the willing participation of these persons whose struggles and triumphs we relate in our work. As researchers, then, we bear a burden of responsibility to represent them with accuracy and respect.

Subject Privacy

Part of such respect is the attention researchers pay to obscuring identity and the ways in which we communicate clearly to the subject the likelihood and risks of identification. Questions concerning identity might include, for example:

- Do research subjects expect to be referred to by their real name?
- Should the researcher use a pseudonym, as Harris describes, or does the subject want her work to be accurately identified and her authorship of it made public?
- If a pseudonym is used, will the subject be readily identifiable nonetheless? To your intended audience or any other? If, for example, you write about a highly distinctive writer, that subject may be identifiable regardless of pseudonymity. (Think for example of an outwardly identified Muslim writer who is the only member of her religion currently using your program and is made unique among your clientele by her hijab. In a work on religious minorities in the writing center, what is the likelihood of such a subject being identified?)
- How much would such identification affect your subject?
- Have you made these risks clear?

While such risks can seem obvious to the individual who has spent much time planning the study, they will be less obvious to the potential research subject who is only being introduced to this work at the time permission is sought. And even for researchers who have long conducted research using human subjects, privacy is still a tricky issue, for technology seems to make the world smaller every day.

Such ethical concerns as we've described here can seem bothersome or even overwhelming at times. And yet, writing center research will be able to grow only if we continue to have the goodwill of the writers whom we hope to assist as well as that of our entire institutional community, including other tutors. We need, then, to take very seriously the responsibility we incur when we involve other people's lives in our work. As Anderson concludes:

> In discussing research ethics, it's easy to become focused on principles and standards in a way that seems to ask, "What can we, in good conscience, take from other people?" We should remember, instead, that in person-based research we are the recipient of gifts. The volunteers in our formal studies hand us the gift of their time and cooperation. . . . [L]et it be our goal to assure that both individually and as a discipline we treat these gifts—and their givers—justly, respectfully, and gratefully. (83)

Template 1: Research Method Brainstorm

Initial Research Question:

Method	General Kinds of Questions It Can Answer	Specific Questions It Can Answer for You
Lore	Drawing upon experience and stories heard from others, what is the best course of action in the present situation?	
Theory-Based Research	How can researchers more fully understand the current situation when it is viewed through a specific critical lens? How can a specific critical lens help researchers better understand what has happened or better plan for future exigencies?	
Historical	What precedents exist to assess options in the current situation? How was the current set of practices and / or beliefs arrived at?	
Empirical Research	How do individuals and groups interact and understand their world? How can the perceptions of others help improve practice? How does talk about writing affect writing itself?	

Template 2: Research Planning Template

Research Question:

What is my goal?

What method will I use and why?

What is the best way to share this research?

What are the expectations of the venue in which I'll share my research?

What audiences am I likely to reach in this venue?

How can I best present my data?

Does my planned research seem reliable?

Does my planned research seem valid?

Sample Informed Consent Form

Title of Project: "A Writing Fellows Case Study: Tutors' Conceptions of Tutoring Within and Outside Their Discipline"

Principal Investigator (s): Melissa Ianetta

Other Investigators: N/A

You are being asked to participate in a research study. This form tells you about the study including its purpose, what you will do if you decide to participate, and any risks and benefits of being in the study

WHAT IS THE PURPOSE OF THIS STUDY?

The goal of this project is to find out how writing fellows view the tutoring work they do with students writing inside and outside of their disciplines for future publication.

You are being asked to take part in this study because of your work as a writing fellow at the University of Delaware.

WHAT WILL YOU BE ASKED TO DO?

- You will be asked to answer four questions in writing via email for use in a future presentation and also for an article.
- The interview will take place over email, and it should take no longer than 20 minutes.

WHAT ARE THE POSSIBLE RISKS AND DISCOMFORTS?

- There are no possible risks or discomforts to participating in this study, as it is merely an opportunity for tutors to describe the work they do. However, participants should be aware that quotations from their responses may be used in future publications.

WHAT ARE THE POTENTIAL BENEFITS?

- Other than an opportunity to reflect upon the important work writing fellows do at the University of Delaware and the ability to communicate their narratives to the broader writing studies community, there is no immediate benefit for study participants. However, participation could help to shape how tutors' and fellows' work is framed in scholarly discussions and help to include fellows' voices in that work.

HOW WILL CONFIDENTIALITY BE MAINTAINED?

- Since your answers will be attached to your email and then quoted with your name in future publications, you will not have confidentiality in this study. Your responses will be stored on flash drives and computers for research purposes for an indefinite period of time to be revisited for future research projects. You will be presented with a release form when you sign this form. (See the end of the document.)

Your research records may be viewed by the University of Delaware Institutional Review Board, but the confidentiality of your records will be protected to the extent permitted by law.

WILL THERE BE ANY COSTS RELATED TO THE RESEARCH?

- There are no costs related to this research.

WILL THERE BE ANY COMPENSATION FOR PARTICIPATION?

- There is no compensation for participation in this study.

WHAT IF YOU ARE INJURED BECAUSE OF THE STUDY?

- N/A

DO YOU HAVE TO TAKE PART IN THIS STUDY?

Taking part in this research study is entirely voluntary. You do not have to participate in this research.

As a student, if you decide not to take part in this research, your choice will have no effect on your academic status or your grade in any class. The investigator would terminate a subject's participation in this study upon the subject's request.

WHO SHOULD YOU CALL IF YOU HAVE QUESTIONS OR CONCERNS?

If you have any questions about this study, please contact the Principal Investigator, Melissa Ianetta, at (302) 831–2631.

If you have any questions or concerns about your rights as a research participant, you may contact the University of Delaware Institutional Review Board at 302–831-2137.

Your signature below indicates that you are agreeing to take part in this research study. You have been informed about the study's purpose, procedures, possible risks and benefits. You have been given the opportunity to ask questions about the research and those questions have been answered. You will be given a copy of this consent form to keep.

By signing this consent form, you indicate that you voluntarily agree to participate in this study.

I, _____, hereby grant permission to Melissa Ianetta, University of Delaware, 023 Memorial Hall, Newark,

DE 19716, use of my written responses in her scholarly research, presentations, and future articles.

This permission is valid until revoked in writing by the undersigned.

Signed: _____

Dated: _____

_____   _____
Signature of Witness   Date

_____
Printed Name of Witness

RELATED WORKS

Anderson, Paul V. "Simple Gifts: Ethical Issues in the Conduct of Person-Based Composition Research." *College Composition and Communication* 49.1 (1998): 63–89. Print.

The Belmont Report: Ethical Principles and Guidelines for the Protection of Human Subjects of Research. Department of Health and Human Services, 1979. Web. 3 June 2014.

Conference on College Composition and Communication. *Guidelines for the Ethical Conduct of Research in Composition Studies.* November 2003. Web.

Harris, Joseph. "From the Editor: The Work of Others." *College Composition and Communication* 45.4 (1994): 439–41. Print.

Liggett, Sarah, Kerri Jordan, and Steve Price. "Mapping Knowledge-Making in Writing Center Research: A Taxonomy of Methodologies." *Writing Center Journal* 31.2 (2011): 50–88. Print.

North, Stephen M. *The Making of Knowledge in Composition: Portrait of an Emerging Field.* Portsmouth, NH: Heinemann, 1987. Print.

CHAPTER 9

Looking Through Lenses
Theoretically Based Inquiry

INTRODUCTION

The juxtaposition of the two passages below, we think, argues eloquently for the role of theory in undergraduate research and for the necessity of theory to understanding fully the practice of tutoring. The first, from Becky McLaughlin and Bob Coleman, argues for the role of theory in undergraduate education:

> While students may not come and go talking of [theorists] Jacques Lacan and Arthur Danto, they all possess significant practical wisdom, what the ancient Greeks called *phronēsis*, which is not mutually exclusive to the abstract wisdom and preoccupations of theoretical probing. Some or all of their experience may be un- or undertheorized; that circumstance, however, is precisely the point of their taking theory classes. As they reflect on the intersecting trajectories of theory and their everyday concerns, one possible effect is the defamiliarization of some aspects of their lives. We think of such reflection as a key point of education. (xi)

And in the second passage, Elizabeth Boquet probes her own need of a new theory—that is, a new way of seeing her writing center work:

> [M]aybe I needed to come up with a different set of questions, a different way of imagining the work of writing centers and the relationship of the work that goes on in them to students, to faculty, to . . . me. (*Noise* 3–4)

One the one hand, in the first passage McLaughlin and Coleman explore undergraduates' appreciation of theory in the framework of the classical concept of **phronēsis**. In doing so, they connect their rationale for undergraduate engagement in theory to an ancient Greek idea of "practical wisdom" that in "its most expansive context, combined elements of wisdom, knowledge, virtue and decorum"

(Gaines 601). We see such *phronēsis* at the heart of tutoring work, for to tutor effectively, one needs to possess

- an understanding of both the self and others (wisdom)
- expertise in tutoring (knowledge)
- a commitment to learning (virtue)
- an understanding of how to act to effectively pursue educational goals (decorum).

We think, too, that for tutors to improve their *phronēsis,* they sometimes need to step back and "defamiliarize" (McLaughlin and Coleman xi) the tutorial situation; in Boquet's words, they need to "come up with a different set of questions" (4). Theory can help accomplish this work by moving us to ask and answer such questions as

- What is the fundamental definition of a writing tutor and why does it matter?
- How can we understand the relationships among the writing tutor, the program, and the institution at large? How do these relationships effect writers?
- What is the relationship between one's sense of self and one's tutoring practice?

Writing center researchers already use theoretically-evidenced arguments to answer these questions. Nancy Maloney Grimm's *Good Intentions,* for example, draws from postmodern theory to argue for a fundamental change in our understanding of the writing center, one that emphasizes its "potential for more public and political action" (xvi). In a similarly theoretical vein, Nancy Welch employs the theoretical work of French psychoanalytic theorist Jacques Lacan to the relationship between the writing center and the composition program. And such scholarship as Harry Denny's *Facing the Center* and his "Queering the Writing Center" draw from identity and gender theory to help us understand the roles and contexts that enable and constrain our writing center work.

It is not only program administrators and professional scholars who have contributed to our theoretical knowledge of the writing center, however: tutor-researchers have made important contributions in this area as well. In the anthology section of this volume, for example, Jonathan Doucette, Claire Elizabeth O'Leary, and Jeff Reger, among others, show the ways in which a theoretical lens can be used profitably to enrich a peer tutor's viewpoint and so create new knowledge for the field. As these essays demonstrate, applying previously established theories to writing center work can help us gain new perspectives on both our actions and the values those actions express. These theories do not necessarily—or even usually—originate in the writing center. Often, such arguments and analyses are created by importing a conceptual framework from another field and applying it to the tutorial. Such an application is often mutually transformative, for even as you are revising a writing center perspective by applying a theory, so too you may well be revising the theory itself, adapting it to fit the context of your research. This work can be very challenging, but it is also very rewarding. To help you create and evaluate this kind of research, this chapter will first offer a definition for theoretical research and then suggest some guidelines to consider when undertaking this kind of research.

THEORIZING NOT THEORY

For most readers, the first encounters with explicitly theoretical texts can be a bit bracing. Even those students who immediately enjoy the work involved with decoding and applying theoretical texts can find a first reading of, for example, feminist writer Hélène Cixous or literary critic Walter Benjamin, off-putting. Certainly, such feelings are valid, for the intended audience of these texts would have been expected to share with the author a body of knowledge, a set of cultural references, and an understanding of the rhetorical moves appropriate to the occasion that are not familiar to the wider, unanticipated, audience these texts have reached. When Michel Foucault wrote *The History of Sexuality,* for example, he would have never imagined peer tutors applying his ideas to the writing center as Jonathan Doucette does in this volume. So if it seems unnatural to try to occupy the reader's role when first encountering a primary theoretical work such as those of Foucault, you are certainly not alone in this sentiment—the majority of readers may find that they have to work hard to adjust their reading strategies to account for the unfamiliarity of theory-dense texts.

Adapting Reading Strategies to Theoretical Texts

In part, this reading work will be well supported by the reading strategies that you already possess and that you're no doubt always refining in your work as a tutor. When you are reading a complicated theoretical text, focus on identifying and understanding the elements of the writer's argument that are relevant to your own inquiry. That is, it is usually not generative of your own ideas to focus on mastering the entirety of a theorist's body of work. Just as you do not, for example, have to understand all of Mikhail Bakhtin's work to appreciate Alice Gillam's "Writing Center Ecology," neither did the author have to master all of Bakhtin's works to write it. In some ways, then, tutor-researchers might find it helpful to remind themselves that their goal is the activity of theorizing, not the mastery of all theory. While there is a responsibility to render accurately the element or elements of another's work that you are using to better understand the writing center, such inquiry does not require total mastery of all the texts written by the individual or individuals from whom you are adapting your theoretical lens. The misconception that, to engage a theorist's ideas accurately, research must fully describe all of his or her notions in their entirety has thwarted more than one writing center researcher. More than one early draft of a project has lost its way due to an attempt to explain, for example, ALL of Roland Barthes,

Table 9.1 Theoretical Scholarship: Reader's Questions.

- Who is the original audience for the theory being used? Are there any specific differences between this audience and yourself that must be accounted for as you read?
- What original concepts or terms does the author introduce here? Are they integral to understanding this work? To understanding the element of this work that you want to apply to your own inquiry?
- What elements from the original work must you account for in order to explain this theory to your reader?
- After identifying the excerpts from the text that explain the elements in the author's words, can you then explain them in your own words in a manner appropriate to an audience of your peers?

resulting in a draft that served primarily as a description of Barthes' theory at the expense of the author's own line of inquiry. Drawing from abstract theoretical argument can be challenging, and this challenge has been known to lure researchers away from their own purpose. To combat this impulse, it is helpful to read with an eye equally to the purpose of your own research as well as to the purposes of theorists from whom you plan to borrow or develop a lens.

We think, however, that such reading is worthwhile, both for the new perspectives—the new set of questions, as Bouquet called it in the introductory passage to this chapter—this work can bring to our understanding of the center and for the ways in which these re-visionings can revitalize and enhance tutoring practice. The goal of this chapter is to support these re-viewings and, by discussing the ways in which interpreting and applying theoretical texts can be considered a research method, to introduce strategies that most profitably support this avenue of work (Table 9.1).

Before we turn to the accomplishment of that goal, though, a word on what this chapter will not do. It does not name the theories that are frequently associated with writing center work. For one reason, we already do some of this work in Chapter 2; the section "What is a Writing Center?" briefly surveys some of the theoretical perspectives commonly used to explore writing center research. You may wish to read or review that material in conjunction with your reading of this chapter, but it is not necessary to do so to engage with the material presented here. Rather than attempting to survey or summarize theories or theorists, this chapter is focused on what might be done with a theory—you might say that here we're concerned with the verb *theorizing*, the actions associated with using theory, rather than with the noun *theory*, which would entail focusing on and explaining previously existing theoretical constructs.

WHAT IS THEORY?

Before we move to theorizing as a research activity, though, it is helpful to consider what is, in fact, theory. On the one hand, tutors theorize every day and in every tutorial. When a tutor works with a writer, for example, the two collaboratively establish a theory of how they can most profitably spend a session together. Sometimes, they have to negotiate two very different theories for this to occur. Imagine, for example, the writer comes in with a theory that the definition of the writing center is "editing service," while the tutor's conceptualization of a writing center is as a place that largely focuses on global or higher-order issues. The first conversation of the tutorial, then, will be a theoretical one, in which the tutor will need to address the writer's abstract conceptualization and present her own. In this sense, then, all tutoring work is theory work.

Such activity, however, is not what most researchers associate with theory. That is, rather than the individually-formed quotidian hypotheses that get created and invoked on the fly—what McLaughlin and Coleman term *phronēsis* and what we might associate with Stephen North's concept of lore we discuss in Chapter 8—the term **theory** here is used to name an abstract conceptual lens that can be applied to a variety of occasions to foreground certain dynamics as a means of better understanding a given situation. Admittedly, this definition is, itself, fairly abstract, for the enormous variety of theories that can be applied in a writing center setting makes it difficult to offer a more specific explanation of the term. Facets of writing center work have been usefully explored using theories from education, feminism, organizational psychology, linguistics, cultural studies, aesthetics, psychotherapy, and many, many other areas of intellectual inquiry. The sheer diversity in theories, then, makes it both difficult and unnecessary to attempt to rigidly affix the notion of "theory."

WHAT IS YOUR THEORY?

Given this multiplicity in approaches, it would be reasonable to ask how to select a theory with which to view the writing center. As with any other research method, the researcher's purpose should determine the tools. Sometimes the theoretical lens is suggested readily by the area of writing center work one wishes to examine. Such a connection can be seen, for example, in O'Leary's "It's Not What You Say but How You Say It" in this volume. O'Leary's interest in the gender dynamics of a tutorial naturally connect her line of research to theories of gender and language. So, too, Doucette's interest in the intersection of identity and writing lends itself well to theoretical lenses from identity politics, in this case queer theory. If you are looking for new ways to look at your own practice and wish to draw upon the current and previous theoretical conversation in the field, you might want to read (or to review) the survey of centrifugal and centripetal theories of the writing center in Chapter 2 to see which approaches might help you answer your questions or develop new strategies to facilitate writers' learning.

Theory Work: Following the Trail

You might also want to consider using the theories referenced in those non-theory-focused essays that you encounter during your initial research review, for conducting original research is often a matter of following a trail of "citation breadcrumbs" to help develop your own ideas. Imagine, for example, that you were interested in examining the theoretical basis of using reflective writing in tutor preparation. You might start with R. Mark Hall's "Using Dialogic Reflection to Develop a Writing Center Community of Practice," which would lead you to Kathleen Blake Yancey's work on reflection and Etienne Wegner's notion of communities of practice. In Yancey's and Wegner's work, you might find elements of reflection theory that, while unimportant to Hall's project, turn out to be quite important to your work. Such reference-sleuthing often leads to finding the most useful theoretical frames.

Theory Work: (Re)Turning to the Source

Indeed, whether you're modeling your use of theory from a text in writing studies or whether you find your theoretical approach by connecting your writing center work to a theory encountered in another class, we strongly encourage you to look at the original text or texts explaining that theory. When a writer appropriates a theory secondhand from an essay, without research into the original theoretical text, mistakes often occur when representing that theory. For example, researchers typically apply only a single piece of a larger theoretical construct. By surveying the original theory, you can make sure you use the elements from that framework that best suit your goal. Further, when a theory is appropriated from a source that applies the theory rather than a text whose primary purpose is to explain that theory, the chances for a mistake in transmission increase as well. Theories alter in their application—some elements become more important and other elements less so, depending on the goals of the researcher and the selective parts of the theory they are applying. And, of course, there is also a chance that an author may simply misrepresent a theory—and you certainly don't wish to duplicate this error. By doing some research into the theoretical paradigm itself, you improve the chances that you will best use and most accurately represent the lens you've chosen.

Bringing What We Know to Theory-Based Research

Theory is often dictated by the research question. In some situations, however, a theoretical lens may give rise to a research question. This may sound surprising—that the method might dictate a research question rather than the other way around. But it makes sense if we think about the ways in which many disciplinary ways of knowing can present themselves in the writing center. Few, if any, other institutional locations will see the discipline-specific range of writing that will be present in the writing center. Such work "imports" all sorts of theory into the writing center.

And sometimes tutors will want to bring the ways of viewing their world from their majors, and this can often lead to exciting new ways of viewing tutor work. Thus in "Postcolonialism, Acculturation, and the Writing Center," included in this volume, tutor-researcher Jeff Reger notes that in tutorials his "approach occasionally—and unconsciously—integrated elements of postcolonial theory" learned in his coursework (498, this book). Noting this connection between his work in and out of the writing center, Reger then goes on to draw upon the post-colonial theory originally encountered in his classes to interrogate writing center practice. Thus the ways of viewing the world that you are learning in your academic work can enrich the ways in which you—and the audience of your research—understand tutoring practice.

WHAT CAN YOU DO WITH YOUR THEORY?

Thus far, we've associated the use of theory in research with ways of seeing the writing center. Such seeing, however, involves more than merely describing what you perceive. Rather, such a perspective creates an argument; it urges the reader to change her thinking and/or actions. In this section, then, we briefly describe some of the ways theory has been used to create such change, using essays from the anthology section to illustrate how such ends might be accomplished.

Briefly put, theory can help you do the following:

Explain the Usefulness of a Particular Practice and Demonstrate Its Connection to Scholarly Conversations in and Beyond the Field of Writing Center Studies

In tutor research, theory is often used to explain why a particular course of action might be desirable and/or effective. In this situation, theory provides a framework for presenting a practice as a coherent whole—as a reasonable and effective course of action. Further, theory helps to explore the implications of a specified action by establishing a connection of this local practice to the current scholarly conversation. Thus in Reger's postcolonial approach, he both explains his ideas and advocates for their usefulness and importance by reading tutoring practice through a lens drawn from Anis Bawarshi and Stephanie Pelkowski's "Postcolonialism and the Idea of a Writing Center." In this manner, Reger connects his argument to versions of this discussion that are happening in the wider world of writing center studies. Further, via connections he makes to, for example, Min-Zhan Lu's "Professing Multiculturalism: The Politics of Style in the Contact Zone," Reger demonstrates the relevance of his argument to debates in the wider field of writing studies. And, finally, he shows how his work participates in interdisciplinary discussions by drawing upon foundational work in postcolonial studies, such as the work of Edward Said. Such connections explain the philosophy underlying tutoring practice even while demonstrating the connection between our local writing centers and the larger conversations of the university.

Compare Two or More Things

Often theory is used to create a basis of comparison among things, such as tutoring practices, tutorial goals, or writing center philosophies. What Douglas Hesse said of teaching writing is equally true of tutoring:

> If common sense and good intentions sufficiently qualify one for teaching writing, then a master teacher in the History Department and the volleyball coach across campus are as qualified as any PhD in English. Surely they have commonsensical ideas. The moment at which a composition teacher must defend his or her common sense about writing as superior to the historian's or the coach's is the moment at which he or she must resort to theory. (231)

To prefer one tutoring choice to another or to explain the reasoning behind our pedagogy, then, we are acting on a myriad of theories: our theory of what the writing center is and is not; our theory of what good writing is and is not; our theory of the more—and less—effective ways to learn to write. Some theoretical scholarship is a reflection of these practical choices. In this volume, Claire Elizabeth O'Leary, for example, draws upon notions of gender present in the works of Evelyn Ashton-Jones and Kathleen Hunzer to compare tutoring strategies employed with a male versus a female writer and to suggest possible implications for gender-differentiated tutoring strategy. Brooke Baker likewise draws upon theory to create a comparison in this volume. While O'Leary focuses on individual interaction, Baker explores the implications of writing center philosophies, examining two common metaphors—the "safe house" and the "contact zone"—and exploring what each has to offer to the center. Thus, the theoretical can organize both local inquiries into practice, as in O'Leary, and global inquiries into the foundational philosophy of a tutoring program, as in Brooke.

Better Understand—or Understand in a New Way—Current Practice

Theory not only helps us to make decisions that will create future practice, but, equally importantly, it helps us reassess the implications of current practice. As writing center scholar Nancy Maloney Grimm has observed, "[t]heorizing itself does not solve daily writing center problems, but because it multiplies the perspectives we bring to the problems, it can change practices" (xiv). Such revision can often lead to surprising new ways of understanding seemingly innocuous practices. Grimm's *Good Intentions*, for example, describes long-cherished writing center pedagogies based on a belief in writer independence as a sort of educational bootstrapping in which the individual is the chief author of her own educational experience (i.e., it is the writer and not the tutor who decides what will take place in a tutorial). Grimm juxtaposes this faith in writer autonomy with the presumption in many tutoring programs that academic prose represents a transcendent goodness—a set of morals that focus on the universal utilitarianism of college writing. Grimm then goes on to show how these common ideological beliefs have produced a resistance to working on local issues and a disinclination to giving answers to writers. She applies lenses from literacy studies and critical pedagogy to writing center ideology and concludes that such "good intentions" may actually become coercive and unproductive tutoring practices.

In a similar vein of theoretical revision, in this volume tutor-researcher Brooke Baker draws upon literacy theory to focus attention on the power dynamics present even in a seemingly neutral tutorial situation. By looking at her own tutoring as a site of the contact zone, "a place in which student and tutor could meet and clash; a space in which to try on language and form without the fear of failure" (275, this book), Baker looks to revitalize and improve her own tutoring by connecting in a more meaningful fashion with writers. Both Baker and Grimm demonstrate the ways in which new views can lead to new actions.

Argue for a Particular Set of Values

Many of the uses of theory discussed thus far have brought critical lenses to the local tutorial setting. Another common use of theory, however, focuses on its application at a broader level, emphasizing and interrogating a concept, such as what "is" a writing center, a tutor, or a writer? In this volume, tutor-researcher Cameron Mozafari takes, in part, such an approach. Mozafari explores the essential notion of what is a writing center (or what should a writing center be) by contrasting the notion of the writing center as a "safe house" with the notion of the writing center as a "contact zone." Working at the broader levels of definition in this manner, such theory work engages our ideological values as much as our daily practice. In Mozafari's essay, for example, the reader must ask herself, what are the best ideals for a writing center? Is it writing center a "safe house," which privileges the validation of home discourses, those ways of expressing one's self that are learned in the home and local communities, as a means to supporting student success? Or should the writing center prioritize its functioning as a "contact zone," which emphasizes the conflicting discourses and, by extension, contesting values, represented by such a site? By drawing from ongoing theoretical discussions in other fields, such work helps us to understand the complex results of the ideals we engage.

Theory Can Work with Theory

Theory, then, can help us understand past and present writing center practice and determine a course for the future. Admittedly, this list is partial, for it does not cover all the things you might be able to do with a strong theoretical framework. Indeed, it doesn't even explicate the range of theoretical moves made in the essays cited. Even as O'Leary is drawing on gender theory, for example, so too is she drawing upon conversational theories, and Mozafari's argument combines the theoretical concepts described here with ideas derived from Lev Vygosky's work on cultural-historical psychology. Rather than aspiring to comprehensiveness, this brief list is meant to draw attention to some of the kinds of things that you can do with theory and, we hope, inspire you to read with an eye to how researchers use theoretical constructs in the pursuit of their research goals.

Theory Can Complement Other Methods

In addition to emphasizing the partial nature of this description, it is important, too, to emphasize that the use of a specific theory does not exclude the use of other methods. Rather, it is very common to see an essay that combines a theoretical approach with another method. Thus, Baker combines theoretical work with elements of case study by applying her understanding of safe houses and contact zones in a series of tutorials with a single writer. Jeff Reger offers a similar synthesis in his argument about postcolonialism in the writing center by applying this lens to modify his own tutoring practice.

This section has been intended to be neither a definitive nor exclusionary consideration of theory as a method; rather, it is intended to help you explore ways that theory can be used in tutor research. As a useful complement to what goals you might pursue using theory, then, we turn now to reflect upon some local qualities of theoretical essays that achieve their goal. Put another way, while this section was about your purpose, the next section will offer some strategies for implementing your theory in your research.

HOW SHOULD YOU APPLY YOUR THEORY?

As with all writing, advice about researching and writing with theory has to be offered as more of a series of guide points than as hard-and-fast rules. The assertions below, then, should be treated as probabilities—qualities that are possessed by most successful theory essays—rather than as inevitabilities.

The Best Theoretical Essays Apply Theory to Something in Order to Be Useful and Persuasive

A characteristic common among the theory-based essays in this volume is that the theory is applied to something: Baker, Brecht, Reger, Mozafari, and O'Leary all view specific tutorial situations through their different theoretical lenses. These works reflect the trend toward the individual tutorial scene as a common source of evidence/explication for the theory-based essays by tutor-researchers. Such a commonality makes sense; for one, the tutoring session is likely tutor-researchers' most common scene of activity in the tutoring program and, as such, is the place from where their questions will arise. For another, due to the constraints of the academic calendar, tutor research projects frequently must be accomplished within the space of a semester or less, and the relatively compact space of a tutoring session (or several sessions) is often manageable in that period of time.

The individual tutoring session is not the only thing that can be viewed profitably using this method, however, and writing center researchers have examined other elements as well. Researchers have examined, for example, the session report (Malenczyk), a writing center blog (Hall), and tutor education (Ronesi). While such works move the theoretical gaze away from the tutorial scene, in each case, the author gains both focus and evidence from the element of writing center work he or she is examining. Selecting a concrete element in this way brings both precision and evidence to a theoretically based argument.

The Best Theoretical Essays Have a Well-Defined Theoretical Lens

It is tempting when devising the theoretical lens to pull in all theories that might be applied to a particular element of tutor work. Such an impulse is understandable, for the creators of theory-based essays are often those individuals who find theoretical texts intrinsically interesting. Such individuals want to share the ideas and works that inspire their passion. Typically, however, the space constraints of a single project do not afford the space or time to treat adequately the many potentially relevant ideas included in such conceptually dense works, and so can result in a diffuse argument that is comprises of incomplete thoughts. By focusing the theoretical framework tightly on a single idea, however, the tutor-researcher has adequate time to investigate and reflect upon the implications of the theory under consideration and to present it fully to an audience who may not be familiar with the concept presented.

The Best Theoretical Essays Demonstrate Familiarity with Immediately Relevant Scholarly Conversation(s)

One of the challenges of work that takes a theoretical emphasis is determining what other voices need to be mapped onto the conversation. Certainly, if other researchers examining tutoring practices have used, broadly speaking, the paradigm that a tutor-researcher is employing, the final project should refer to such work. Such a citation has a twofold effect:

1. It shows the reader that the researcher is aware of the conversation in this area, thus establishing authority.
2. It demonstrates the relevancy of the researcher's ides for the ongoing concerns of the field.

Drawing in materials from other fields that are foundational for the theory being employed can be trickier. A researcher doesn't want to overload citations at the expense of argumentative focus. As seen in the anthology section of this book, such work is a balancing act, one that counterweights the importance of explaining the theoretical frame with a focus on the particulars of the writing center scenario being explored. Ultimately, however, such essays will most likely put the primary emphasis on the argument at hand. In the anthologized essays discussed in this chapter, for example, there is a brief mention of one or two seminal works related to the paradigm but little discussion of the theory's import outside the immediate argument. Such an approach maintains the focus on the research question, even while demonstrating an understanding of the works primary to the theoretical lens and offering readers a place to start if they wish to pursue research that uses a similar lens.

The Best Theoretical Essays Make Clear
Why This Idea Is Being Applied

Early on, well-crafted theoretically based inquiries include an explanation for why a concept is being applied in the manner proposed. That is, any element of a tutoring program could, hypothetically, be read through any theory and some kind of analysis would result. Whether or not that analysis has any persuasive impact or results in any changes to our understanding or practice of our work, however, is another matter. Such impact statements are often a primary element of the success of the work. So, to make clear for a reader that the tutor-researcher is proposing an idea whose analysis has real import for tutoring programs or practice, it is helpful to state in the introductory section of your essay not just what your argument does, but why it is important.

The Best Theoretical Essays Consistently
Apply the Theory Throughout the Work

Sometimes, even essays that articulate their theoretical lenses in a focused and articulate manner will have trouble incorporating the lens into the analysis part of the essay. That is, after cogently explaining the theory and clearly stating its potential for improving practice or understanding, the frame drops out of the essay and instead the work turns to offer a narrative or description that lacks analysis. Such works can leave the reader wondering how the sections of the work are related to one another.

During the drafting process, however, an unevenness of application is often less of a misstep than merely a step. That is, writers will often need to initially write down their potential material for analysis and then go back and revise this narrative or description to include an analytic element that draws upon the theoretical frame. Typically, too, the theoretical frame reappears in the conclusion to emphasize its utility for arguments such as the one at hand. In brief, then, the tutor-researcher want to make sure a theoretical frame is just that—a frame that coheres the entire work.

The Best Theoretical Essays Focus the Argument
on the Research Question, Not the Theoretical Frame

Even while making sure that an essay is consistent in its use of theory, the researcher should focus on the question rather than the theoretical paradigm. If explaining the theoretical context takes up more of a reader's time than does filling the gap in our knowledge that is named in the research question, then the manuscript may need to be revised. Such a work, after all, is intended to focus on the purpose of creating new knowledge in our field. This re-proportioning of the essay, too, is often part of the drafting process. Often a writer will have excessive explanation of his or her theoretical lens in earlier drafts. Frequently, researchers will be able to hone this material only after they have drafted their analytic material and so can determine what part of the explanation of the theoretical lens is needed to understand the argument in the work.

The Best Theoretical Essays Make Clear What Change in Action or Attitude Should Result from Their Arguments

Even the most masterful description of theory and its application to evidence will still need an explanation of how this analysis is meant to affect practice. Throughout the essay, then, the reader should be aware of what change in attitude or practice the essay is working toward. Both the introductory and concluding sections will likely forecast or summarize how this theory and this evidence combine to suggest a specific change, and the body of the text should use signposting language in such a way as to suggest how the argument is moving toward this goal.

This is not to say that every essay has to argue toward a complete reversal in practice or some other form of revolution, however. Indeed, it is often a worthwhile goal to argue merely that we need to reconsider our attitude on some topic or that we need to be more mindful of a particular element of tutoring practice. Limiting claims in this way often suits shorter works and the constraints of space and time that tutor-researchers can face if they are working on their research for a single-semester class or in the face of the many competing demands on their time. This observation is not to discourage research that pursues larger claims, for such work can be exhilarating for both researcher and reader. Of course, to make such large claims, one must plan carefully to gather data that will persuasively support them.

Adding theory to the list of tutor-researcher concerns might seem a bit overwhelming, but in many ways, the concerns of theory-based inquiry are fundamentally concerns of writing itself, including attention to your audience, fairness to others, and integrity when examining your own ideas. In other words, you will use theory not only throughout your research career, but indeed throughout your life as a writer.

RELATED WORKS

Hesse, Douglas. "Teachers as Students, Reflecting Resistance." *College Composition and Communication* 44.2 (May 1993): 224–31. Print.

McLaughlin, Becky, and Bob Coleman, eds. *Everyday Theory: A Contemporary Reader.* New York: Pearson/Longman, 2005. Print.

Yancey, Kathleen Blake. "Seeing Practice Through Their Eyes: Reflection as Teacher." In Paula Gillespie, Alice Gillam, Lady Falls Brown, and Byron Stay. *Writing Center Research: Extending the Conversation.* Mahwah, NJ: Erlbaum, 2002. 189–02. Print.

CHAPTER 10

Learning from the Past
Historical Research

INTRODUCTION

When describing the common impulse behind historical work in writing studies, noted disciplinary historian Sharon Crowley asserts:

> Few historians of rhetoric and composition, I take it, write essays or books about early nineteenth-century writing instruction for the pure pleasure of adding to the growing body of historical research in this area. Rather, we undertake our work with pedagogical goals in mind; we aim, in general, to guide teachers of composition in making pedagogical choices by acquainting them with those which have been made in the past. ("Octalog" 7)

Put another way, Crowley studies the past to better understand the present and to guide a better future. In like fashion, the introduction to research in Chapter 8 suggests that historical research can help you answer such questions as "What precedents exist for our options in the current situation?" and "How did we arrive at this set of practices and beliefs?" In this chapter, we explore the implications of looking at history in this way—what it means to read and write history as *arguments* and not just as simple descriptions of past events. Through this persuasion-based focus, we look at ways to read historical research in writing center studies as well as ways to create this kind of knowledge. To do so, we examine at both **historiography** (theories of how history can be created, interpreted, and used) as well as historical methods (the means of creating histories).

Before we move to discuss ways to read and write history, however, it might be useful to emphasize that this chapter focuses on historical methods, not on recounting the history of writing centers. You can find some of this work of historicizing writing center studies, if not individual writing centers and tutoring programs, in Chapter 2. You may find it valuable to (re)read from that chapter "What is A Writing Center? Historical Views" alongside the material here.

WHY WRITE HISTORY?

In writing center studies research, exploring history is put in the service of larger arguments about the next course of action, such as when Neal Lerner explores the history of the writing laboratory to mount an argument concerning the possibilities for "collaborating with science educators" going forward (*Idea* 6) or when Peter Carino looks at the history of writing center technologies to sound a cautionary note about the future of technology in the writing center ("Computers"). Admittedly, some early writing center historical scholarship was simply first-person accounts of life in a writing center or in the profession (see, for example, Yahner and Murdick; Summerfield; and Kinkead), and it may well be that your program has or would profit from a similar account of its own origins. However, more recent published historical scholarship, or that which otherwise intends to be useful to an audience beyond an individual program, generally takes as its goal a larger point about what collective actions we might choose as a field.

Creating such history-as-arguments offers tutor-researchers a specific set of opportunities and challenges. When reading recent histories of the field, for example, the tutor-researcher interested in history needs to attend carefully to what claims are made and what historical evidence is used to back those claims. And when both reading and writing historical research, the tutor-historian must be sensitive to overly simple stories that reduce the complexity of events into reductive cautionary tales of woe and/or feel-good "happily ever after" narratives. Indeed, an important part of contemporary historians' work is to challenge and complicate these reductive historical accounts.

As an example of a corrective history-as-argument, consider Lerner's "Searching for Robert Moore," included in the anthology section of this book. Briefly put, prior to Lerner's essay, Moore had been represented as a writing center director who employed a retrograde pedagogy focused on student deficiencies and local error correction, and so was found wanting by current, seemingly more enlightened, standards of best practice. In his essay, however, Lerner demonstrates that Moore may have been far more "progressive" than we had believed. In so doing, Lerner calls on us to question easy generalizations of writing center origins myths:

> [I]t is Moore's account and the idea of early writing centers as drill-and-practice sweat shops that has come for many to define the history of our field. The persistence of such characterizations of writing center history perhaps marks a discipline in progress, one that attempts to legitimize its future by rallying around a convenient—and frightening—version of its past. (405, this book)

This sort of explicit connection between past events, present understanding, and future choices is a characteristic trait of such historical research. That is, as can be seen in "Searching," sometimes a reader can identify a passage or passages where the author makes explicit this argument. Other times, the reader can summarize an implicit argumentative claim that the historian is asserting.

Here, Lerner describes the communal function of our disciplinary history. By viewing Moore as somehow lesser than current writing center directors, historians create a story whose plot line moves optimistically toward "better days." Further, casting our antecedents as the "bad old days" solidifies our professional identity around resisting and rejecting older "evil" pedagogies. Thus, history can be framed in a manner that lends a community a sense of optimism even as it sounds a warning note.

By offering a corrective to such easy "feel-goodism," Lerner draws our attention to the **ideological work** accomplished by seemingly straightforward accounts of events. Such ideological inquiry concerns itself with the ways that texts, as well as other communicative acts, can implicitly or explicitly appeal to and/or shape community values. That is, previous accounts of Robert Moore advanced the belief—the ideology—that we have transcended the kind of instruction Moore represents; that we are "better" than past tutors and directors. In turning over this image, Lerner offers us a new vision of history, the ideology of which is complicated by its similarity to contemporary practice. Lerner also offers us a new history of Moore that is more fully grounded in the historical record than were previous accounts, giving us better evidence to use in our assessments of the development of our field.

HISTORY, SUBJECTIVITY, AND HISTORIOGRAPHY

History, then, is not just a retelling of events but is also an argument for how things happened, the current state of affairs, or the best course of future plans. Thus **intentionality** underlies historical accounts. That is, looking closely at the arguments created in history such as Lerner's reveals that the historian has an agenda beyond mere transcription of events—historians, and thus the histories they create, have intentions; they want to convince the reader and/or move the reader to action. Such arguments draw attention to the role of the historian's **subjectivity** in research. That is, as we know, historians have personal beliefs concerning what has happened and desires for what will happen in the future. We know, too, that histories are not neutral, exhaustive recordings of events but the result of the researcher's perspective and her decisions, both about what evidence and events are relevant to her accounts and what those events and evidence mean. When writing the history of a campus writing center, for example, the researcher will have to determine the relevance and meaning of such factors as:

- The physical location of the program. (How, for example, has its physical location affected its campus visibility? If it has changed locations during its existence, how has that changed its mission and/or usage?)
- The educational background of both the tutors and the writers who use the program. (Has the makeup of the tutoring staff changed at all? Has the preparation offered to/required of tutors changed? If so, is there evidence that this has affected the program's workings?)

- The gender, socioeconomic, and ethnicity demographics of the institution, tutors, and writers. (Has the institution's student body changed during the program's existence? If so, has the mission of the center reflected those changes?)
- The impact of national conversations about literacy on the institution and the tutoring program. (What does the researcher identify as the important events in the national conversation about student writing? Are these reflected in the evolution of the program?)
- The administrative location of the program in the university's supervisory pattern. (What if any meaning, for example, does the researcher attribute to the supervision of the writing center by the English Department/Dean's Office/Provost's Office?)
- The writing culture of the institution in which the program takes place. (Has, for example, the institution's approach to writing instruction changed over the years? Often the founding of a program indicates just such a change.)
- The relationship of the center to other institutional entities. (Have other programs, departments, or services changed the way they approach student literacy? Has, for example, Career Services changed the advice they give students on writing résumés? Has the Chemistry Department started focusing on student writing? Have changes such as these had any impact on who comes to the writing center or how the writing center interacts with the campus?)
- The impact of the evolution of best practice and writing center studies. (As the field of writing center studies has evolved, has the tutoring shown evidence of a related evolution?)
- The background of program administrators, past and present (What relationship, for example, can be drawn between administrators' educational achievements and past tutoring experience on your program's mission?)
- The way that any or all of these factors have evolved over time.

Subjectivity

No single history will be able to exhaustively account for all—or many—of these elements, of course. One the one hand, it is the historian's job to sift through all the available information and determine what is relevant to his line of inquiry. On the other hand, as Lerner notes, truly exhaustive histories are unlikely because no historical record is 100 percent complete:

> Our filters as researchers work in parallel with additional filters, a veritable purification process of social forces: the choices made by those who donate institutional and personal records, the choices made by those who collect and grant access to those records and the choices we make as researchers in terms of what to examine and what motivates us to do so. ("Archival Research" 200)

We know, then, that historians weave historical accounts, selecting/emphasizing what events and evidence are important to their tale. That is, part of creating a historical account is determining what the evidence is. And here is where personal perspective—subjectivity—enters the picture. For as Lerner noted in the passage above, history is, in a sense, merely the juxtaposition of perspectives:

- Those of the historical subjects who left evidence that the present-day researcher can discern
- Those of the individuals who assemble and make available archival evidence
- Those of the historical researchers who reassemble this evidence.

This subjectivity long has been a source of discussion and debate for historians in writing center studies, in the larger world of writing studies, and, indeed, in interdisciplinary discussions of historiography—scholarship about how and why histories get made.

HISTORY, ENLIGHTENMENT, AND *THE POSTMODERN CONDITION*

Conversations about historiography in writing center studies can understood by using the work of French philosopher Jean-François Lyotard. Admittedly, there are other theorists concerned with the creation of history who might be of interest to the writing center historian, such as Hayden White, Jürgen Habermas, and Joan Scott. So, too, there is a broad range of productive historical approaches in addition to Lyotard's postmodern narrative approach, such as gender history, material history, and the history of ideas, to name but a few. We focus here on Lyotard, however, because his *The Postmodern Condition* (1979) has been widely influential on interdisciplinary understandings of historical study. This work also maps very neatly discussions of subjectivity and history in writing studies and writing center studies.

According to Lyotard, in modernity, there are two basic forms of stories, which he calls **grand narratives**. Grand narratives are those story paradigms around which groups have often organized their understanding of past events. We are inclined to synthesize such storylines from past events because of the popularity of the basic frames and because frames can create coherence and meaning in situations that might otherwise seem fragmented or like a meaningless series of unrelated events.

"It's a Great Big Beautiful Tomorrow": Narratives of Progress

The first grouping of stories is **narratives of progress**, which according to Lyotard are "success stories" about the growth of human knowledge—such as the happy ending of disciplinary improvement that Lerner critiques in "Searching." Such stories feature individuals whom Lyotard calls "heroes of knowledge." These "heroes" are depicted as increasing what we know so that as a community we reach enlightenment—that is, a higher state of knowledge and being. The story of Robert Moore that Lerner sets out to correct is an example of such a narrative of progress, for to view Moore as retrograde and to read him as representative of all of writing center practice in the mid-twentieth century allows us to see our story as one of smooth improvement and to regard present practitioners as enlightened beings who have raised writing centers from the depths that Moore represents. As Lerner demonstrates, such stories are likely to be comforting, and so influential, but are less likely to be true. In a writing center context, these stories have been called an "evolutionary model of writing center history" by Peter Carino, whose description illustrates well a writing center adaptation of Lyotardian historiography:

> The evolutionary model of writing center history goes something like this: When open or relaxed admission standards brought hordes of ungrammatical students into the academy, labs were increasingly established to teach them standard English while they learned to write in the composition class. As these labs evolved, they began to examine the writing process, the need to teach the whole of it, appropriated a piece of that mission from classrooms, matured into the type of operation North described in ["The Idea of a Writing Center"] and on many campuses today contend with classrooms as the local authority for teaching writing. ("Open Admissions" 35)

As Lerner notes, "such characterizations in writing center history perhaps mar[k] a discipline in progress, one that attempts to legitimize its future by rallying around a convenient—and frightening—version of its past" (405, this book). Progress narratives provide us with comfort and optimism by making us feel that we have, in fact, achieved advancement, both in individual tutoring programs and collectively as a field. As such, they are frequently used "to reinforce community, to argue for new agendas and to address constituencies outside the community" of writing center studies (Carino, "Open Admissions," 35).

Freedom in the Writing Center

Progress isn't the only narrative structure we have imposed on our histories, however: Lyotard also describes "emancipation narratives." Such accountings tell history as a story that moves from repression toward freedom in some sense, and the central agents in these accounts are "heroes of freedom." While at first glance it may be easier to understand how such a critique might apply to, for example, George Washington and the Revolutionary War than to your local writing center, Carino's work again helps us understand how writing center histories can be understood to enact this model. That is, Carino describes a similar paradigm for writing center history under the term "dialectical model," which he calls "a heroic tale of resistance against uninformed external forces that would reduce the lab to remedial operations established to benefit students only begrudgingly admitted to the university" ("Open Admissions" 39). Such a form of narrative can be particularly attractive to writing center professionals who often think of themselves as rebels, agents acting outside the institutional hierarchy. Steve Braye's comments in "War, Peace, and Writing Center Administration" articulate this position well:

> It seems to me that writing centers exist because there was no place in the institution, or in the spaces sanctioned by the institution, to do what centers attempt. I don't know whether this is because colleges and universities don't want to admit to teaching some of the things we do . . . or that such problems seem outside what we want the curriculum to include. But this means that centers were (are?) beating against the institutional current. (Simpson, Braye, and Boquet 66)

As Carino notes, such a "narrative is nourishing, for it reinforces centers' self-styled image as radical innovators" ("Open Admissions" 39). Further, such emancipation narratives lend themselves particularly well to biographically oriented heroes-and-villains histories that laud the impact of an individual writing center director or tutor, and such stories are often as much fun to read as they are to write. Writing center historians have to be careful about invoking such images, however, because like progress narratives, they can obscure historical detail in the service of telling a "good" story.

Little Histories: Cultural Context, Local Histories, and Thick Description

Historiography can tell us more than what *not* to do in our histories. It can be affirmative as well, helping us determine what we might do. Returning to Lyotard, for example, he urges the historian to reject the optimistic allure and generalist sweeping tales of grand narratives of progress and freedom and instead to acknowledge the diversity of history by embracing smaller, more context-bound histories (Lyotard 66). Such local histories can fulfill an important role in our understanding of writing centers, for they can offer a precision often lacking in historical accounts and help us attend to those varieties of centers—for example, centers at two-year colleges, historically black colleges and universities, tribal colleges, or community-based writing centers—often overlooked in disciplinary histories.

Here too Carino aligns with Lyotard's paradigm by calling for a "cultural model of writing center history" that would be "aware of its own role in historicizing, of representing history in language, and the need for thick descriptions of the multiple forces impacting writing centers" ("Open Admissions" 30). Such a history "would account for progress with an awareness that progress is untidy" ("Open Admissions" 30–31). Such "untidy" thick description is well suited to the local histories of writing centers that seem to be the most likely projects for the tutor-researchers for whom we wrote this book. These individuals are often most familiar with and interested in a local historical context, and their research project timelines often best accommodate a single inquiry in a single center.

From Lerner, Lyotard, and Carino, then, we learn to resist easy, feel-good historical narratives that comfort us with simple stories of linear progress or iconoclasts defying the system and to value those richly nuanced histories that are often smaller in scale but that understand that history, like writing itself, it is exploratory, recursive, messy—and fascinating.

FROM HISTORIOGRAPHY TO HISTORY: WAYS TO READ AND EVALUATE HISTORICAL RESEARCH

Understanding the ways in which history makes arguments and the ways in which histories resist or conform to overarching, overgeneralized narratives allows us to bring new lenses to our reading of historical research. If you have already read the brief history of writing center studies in Chapter 2, for example, you may wish to go back to it now and use the material discussed thus far in this chapter to read it with an eye to what we are omitting and what we are foregrounding. That is, by telling the story of writing center studies as the story of a creation of scholarly discipline, do we automatically conform to the grand narrative of progress, or do we resist it? Can you think of resistance strategies that we could have employed but did not take advantage of? Compare the individuals whose presence we include to the individuals who populate your program—tutors, writers, staff. What individuals appear in both this story and your own community? Who doesn't appear? How does our history define the field? Can you find heroes? Villains?

When we read history with an eye to how it is constructed, we are well positioned to evaluate the persuasiveness of that work. Writing studies historian Robert Connors offers a valuable approach to reading historical research:

> [D]iscrete historical facts hang in a vacuum, useless, without the interpretations that order them in all historical writing. And so the two questions that are continually argued about in historical writing are these: (1) Does this interpretation of the historical data seem coherent, reliable, interesting, useful? and (2) What can this interpretation of the past show us about the present and the future? For the first question, there are criteria that can be applied to allow us to make at least provisional answers. We can make informed judgments about any historian's basic knowledge, depth of research, imaginative facility, ideological predispositions, and writing ability to determine who writes history we will call "good." How original is the thesis? How broad the explanatory power? How many primary sources were consulted? Were any important sources missed or scanted? Are there careless generalizations? Are the assertions backed up with enough proof? Is there any attempt at explaining alternative interpretations, or is it a presentation of only one single strong side? Is the narrative written in a way that draws the reader along? Are the issues explored important or involving to the readership? These and other questions can clarify for us the "quality" of the history being presented. ("Dreams" 30–31)

Table 10.1 Historical Scholarship: Readers' Questions.

- What is the author trying to prove from this telling of history?
- Is the research presented valid to that argument? That is, does the research presented prove what the researcher claims it proves?
- Is the evidence credible? That is, do the sources seem believable? Are cited texts from reputable resources?
- Did the author gather any original data? If so, is the method for collecting that data sufficiently described to suggest it was collected in an appropriate manner? If the reader wanted to, could she access the data herself? That is, did the historian cite correctly?
- Does the author consider any counterarguments to the interpretation of the data presented in the essay? Does the author's refutation of the counterargument seem credible?
- Is there anything that seems to be left out? Any interpretation that seems an unlikely conclusion from this dataset?

Connors here compresses a broad range of evaluative criteria into a brief space. He draws our attention to the relationship between specific historical evidence and the broader claims that are made using this evidence. A well-constructed history, such as Lerner's "Searching," draws clear and direct connections among our current historical understandings, its retelling of events, and the need to revise our disciplinary narratives. By contrast, a common trait in early iterations of historical work was to tell the story of an individual writing center and then try to use that story to assert what other all writing centers are doing or should do. Such a dataset, however, is too narrow to ground such wide assertions. A canny historian, then, considers carefully what can be proven—or, at least, framed persuasively—by the evidence at hand. Or, as Connors suggests, such works consider the breadth of the explanatory powers of a single history. So, too, he draws our attention to the ways in which the historian contextualizes her argument, for such a context not only helps the reader evaluate the connection between the history being presented and current scholarly conversations, but also establishes the historian's authority by demonstrating that he or she is conversant with the works relevant to his or her line of inquiry. The questions in Table 10.1 can help you evaluate historical scholarship.

KINDS OF HISTORY

As you read further in writing center history, you'll become aware that there are several kinds of historical research, and you may find some more personally interesting or relevant to your interests than other kinds. A very simple but very usable kind of history focuses on categorizing or listing documents and/or other things that provide historical evidence. These lists can often provide resources to other historians by pointing the historian in new directions. One such aid is Lerner's "Chronology of Published Descriptions of Writing Laboratories/Clinics, 1894–1977." This bibliography is extremely useful to researchers, for it serves as a clearinghouse for early descriptions of writing centers. Similarly useful is Lerner's list of theses and dissertations on writing centers ("Introduction"). This source not only provides a **finding aid**—a resource that helps you locate relevant resources—but, as it covers dissertations from 1924 onward, also sketches the evolution of writing center research. Both of these documents serve a dual purpose, then; even as they point the reader toward other resources in the field, they also tell their own stories about early writing centers and writing center scholarship.

Reviewing the Public Record: History Using Published Texts

While such lists as those created by Lerner help to make available lesser-known resources, many historians work from readily available documents. Some of the works already mentioned in this chapter would fall into this category (Carino, "Computers," "Open Admissions"). A subcategory of histories that draw from previously published work would be the history of a single publication. Such work is often presented as a microcosm of a larger history. Michael Pemberton, for example, in his history of *Writing Lab Newsletter*, claims that *WLN* "has not only grown with and recorded the shape of the emerging writing center field over the last 25 years, but it has also been a motivating force, a primary agent of that growth" (34). In other words, by writing a history of *WLN*, Pemberton argues, he's also writing a history of the field itself.

While some scholarship thus traces the impact of a publication, other essays use such work to make an argument that is related to, but distinct from, the history of the periodical from which the evidence is drawn. Such is the case in Dana Lynn Driscoll and Sherry Wynn Perdue's "Theory, Lore, and More: An Analysis of RAD Research in *The Writing Center Journal*, 1980–2009." Here, Driscoll and Perdue trace the history of research articles in the journal to argue for an increased focus on "replicable, aggregable, and data-support[ed]" research in writing center studies (12). In other words, Driscoll and Perdue look to the history of the field to urge readers to create more data-based research that can be built upon in other settings. Whether arguing from the history of a single periodical or a broader set of records, such histories demonstrate the importance of viewing old(er) texts in new ways.

Archival History

Even as some historians create new knowledge by drawing upon previously published texts in this manner, others weave their histories from archival materials that previously have not been available to a wide audience. **Archival material**, as Robert Connors describes, consists of "primary sources, many of which exist nowhere else and were never meant to be published" ("Dreams" 18). Writing studies historian Lynée Lewis Gaillet elaborates:

> I interpret the term *archives* broadly to include a wide ranges of artifacts and documents, such as (unpublished and published) letters, diaries and journals,

student notes, committee reports, documents and wills, newspaper articles, university calendars/handbooks/catalogs, various editions of manuscripts and print documents (books, pamphlets, essays, etc.), memos, course materials, online sources, audiotapes, videotapes, and even "archeological" fragments and finds. (30)

Many of the materials Galliet names as of use to the historian of writing studies are similarly used by the writing center historian. By drawing these documents together, we can create a rich picture of a single site of writing instruction. Implicitly acknowledging the historical importance of such mundane materials, The Writing Center Research Project (WCRP), which houses the National Writing Center Archive, collects pre-1985 writing center materials similar to those described by Connors and Galliet, including:

- grant proposals
- notices to faculty
- workshop descriptions
- flyers, bookmarks
- writing center handbooks
- collections of student writing

- reports
- surveys and studies
- training materials
- constitutions
- audio—or videotaped consultations

(WCRP, n.p.)

You may well be able to look around your own writing center and see your own versions of these materials as well as other **ephemera**. In this context, ephemera means materials that were meant to be used for a specific time and function but that survived that original context. Syllabi, campus periodicals, and the like are items that can both illustrate your present practice and exhibit traces of your past.

In sum, then, a range of evidentiary materials can ground writing center histories and a variety of kinds of histories can be developed. Of course, even as we can categorize historical approaches in this manner, it's important to note that many histories will mix approaches. Quite often, for example, historians use previously published works to enrich their readings of archival texts. Indeed, historians have mixed the approaches described here with vastly different methods to great effect. In Lerner's *Idea of a Writing Laboratory*, for example, he mixes some of the approaches described here with an "observational/interview study of a sophomore biological engineering laboratory class" (10) to ground in a present-day classroom the historical arguments he traced. In other words, while it's useful to separate out methods to discuss and explore their workings, it is not necessary to do so when using them.

CREATING HISTORIES

While in designing a historical research project it is important to be aware of the approaches you might take, it is far more important to know *why* you're conducting historical research. Often, the first historical project in any writing center is a history of that center. In this situation, one of the primary purposes might be to capture its origins, both as a means of solidifying community identity by articulating the members' shared past and so that this information will not be lost to future members. Or, it may be to help the center's stakeholders understand the trajectory of its development. It may even be simple curiosity. In this section, then, we offer some specific strategies for gathering such material.

As with any other research project you might undertake, historical work in writing center studies will build upon what you know and what you know how to do. If you wish to write a history of your writing center, for example, you would want to start with a review of extant research in the history of writing centers to acquaint yourself with current approaches to this kind of work and to determine the current areas of interest that might influence your thinking and to which you could respond. The works referenced in this chapter might be a good place to start, but you'll also find more recent resources that continue this conversation in writing center studies as well as in contiguous fields, such as writing studies, philosophy, or history, that will be helpful as you formulate your research questions and make your research plan.

In all likelihood, however, the best evidence for documenting your program history will be found not in the library but in the program or its offices, and, perhaps, elsewhere in your institution. Your best first resources are program leaders, who can help you locate relevant items and understand what resources may or may not be available to you. For example, they may be able to help you locate in your center any current and early iterations of the kinds of documents collected by the WCRP, which will help you understand the story of your center. To deepen your understanding of the context in which your center has grown, you may want to look at the history of your institution, particularly the history of writing instruction at your school. Many schools have official institutional histories, which make a strong starting point, as can old school catalogs, which may show you some of the ways writing instruction has been represented over the history of the institution.

PEOPLE AS SCHOLARLY RESOURCES: CREATING ORAL HISTORIES

While these documents, if they exist, may well provide valuable insight, one of the most interesting—and most challenging—facets of creating writing center history is often the lack of a written record. Until recent years, many tutoring programs were not thought of as *having* history. They were thought of as neither distinct enough nor important enough to rate careful archiving of historical records. So the writing center historian has to be something of a sleuth, looking for available records, talking with anyone credible who might have insight, and tracing origins and evolutions through center materials.

Table 10.2 Sample Oral History Research Process.

Prior to Securing IRB Approval (if needed)
- Conduct appropriate research to understand possible interview subjects' importance to your study and to draft appropriate and useful interview questions.
- Be prepared to answer questions concerning subject selection. That is, how and why are you selecting your subjects?
- Use this research to make a list of questions appropriate for each potential research subject.
- If your subjects have photographs, records, books, or other relevant works they are willing to share, decide if you have the ability to record and/or store this information.
- Determine how you would like to record the interview. Will you use video or only audio?
- Thoroughly familiarize yourself with your recording equipment so that it will not serve as a distraction during the interview. If applicable, make sure you have extra batteries for your recording devices.
- Determine how the interviews will be stored and by what means they will be made available to other researchers.
- Compose the letter/email that will establish initial contact with interview subject(s). Make sure this message describes the project fully and includes the purpose of the interview, how the interview will be recorded and stored, who will have access to these materials, how the subject will be identified, how long it will take, and where you propose the interview will take place. A sample letter is included at the end of this chapter.
- Compose a second letter/email to be sent after a subject agrees. This communication should thank the subject, confirm the appointment, and share additional information about the interview and the study. A sample letter is included at the end of this chapter.
- Create a permission waiver for your interview subjects to sign. (Samples may be available from your institution's IRB or can be found online by searching "IRB interview release form." If your school has an IRB, however, you should consult its office, since the IRB often has institution-specific requirements.)
- Working with an appropriate faculty or staff mentor or sponsor, submit forms for IRB approval, if necessary.

After IRB Approval
- Send a letter/email to potential subjects and follow up with a phone call, office visit, or other contact.
- Set an appointment for an interview. Include start time and end time.
- Write an introduction for each interview that includes the names of the subject and the interviewer, the date time and location of the interview, and the topic, broadly construed.

During the Interview
- Start each interview with the scripted introduction you wrote.
- Even though the interview is being recorded, have a pad and pen on hand to take notes during the interview. Include in these notes anything you may wish your subject to respond to later in the interview as well as any information you think should be included with the interview recording.
- Check to make sure your technology is working correctly. Then check again.
- Work to balance your research agenda with the unexpected perspectives brought by your research subject(s).

After the Interview
- Document the research process you used to create these interviews.
- Store your materials as described in your research plan.
- Work to make your materials as broadly accessible as possible.

Often, these interviews can become resources for future researchers, particularly when collected in a careful and scholarly fashion. The Oral History Association offers useful guidelines for such interviews. Many of the items they recommend (such as making sure your subjects know what they're agreeing to) may well be required by your institution's Institutional Review Board (IRB), which on most campuses oversees research that involves live persons (see Chapter 8 for more information on the IRB). Other portions of a typical research plan will seem like simple courtesy, such as scheduling an appointment with your subjects and starting and ending on time. And yet others, such as researching your interview subject and having a set of questions to guide your conversation, may seem like duties of any researcher. However, as seen in Table 10.2, you'll want to communicate effectively and be prepared at each step in the process.

COLLABORATION, ACCESSIBILITY, AND THE CREATION OF WRITING CENTER HISTORY

As the description of conducting an oral history might suggest, creating a writing center history where there is none can be a work-intensive, albeit extremely rewarding, task. Depending on the size of your planned project, you may wish to approach it collaboratively, working with other tutors in your program to review recently published work in writing center history, to track down and catalog relevant print materials, and to conduct and make accessible oral interviews. Indeed, by housing your materials in a well-organized archive, you can, in a sense, "collaborate" with those future tutor-researchers who will learn from and build upon your work.

For your work to be part of an ongoing conversation, then, you'll want to give some thought to how it's organized and made accessible. You want to create finding aids, documents, and/or databases that help other researchers. These resources should be flexible enough that people with many different interests can find your materials. At first glance, this may seem easy. Imagine, for example, that you had an interview with the founding director of your writing center, who was an alumna of your school and has recently retired from the English Department. And, imagine too, that you're setting up an online database to help people find relevant items in your writing center records. You might tag this entry as "writing center directors." But what about later researchers who want to know about the interaction of the writing center and the English Department? Okay, then you'll have another tag for this entry: "English Department." But how will a researcher interested in the writing lives of your school's graduates find this record? You'd better label it "alumna," too. No doubt in your context there will be many other terms that might help people discover your work. This task is ideal for a group brainstorm; many people will be able to contribute to the labels you use in your finding aids, and new ones will come up as you continue to assemble your materials for future researchers. You'll want to make sure, however, that as you arrive at new useful terms the materials you've already archived are reclassified using your expanded index.

In addition to making your materials accessible in this manner, you'll also need to think about how the materials themselves are made available. Do you want to put the interviews themselves on a website, for example? If so, there are a few items you'll want to consider. For one, you'll need to have secured your subject's permission during the IRB process to make his or her words available to others. For another, you'll need to know where you can house this material online and be sure of the longevity of the site. That is, who is paying for or providing the storage, and who at your institution will be responsible for the ongoing upkeep of the site for years to come? How will your finding aids interact with this online archive?

Writing center archives that are not housed online but in physical form may sidestep some of the issue of their digital counterparts, but they have their own particular concerns, such as: How will you ensure the security and safety of these materials? How will you provide access to researchers? How will you make sure that interested researchers can find and access your materials?

FROM READING AND RESEARCHING
TO WRITING HISTORIES

You may not be gathering these materials solely for the use of others, though. Instead, you may well be creating histories of your own program. When you write your own histories, you may find it useful to be mindful of the same kinds of concerns as readers that we describ earlier in this chapter. For example:

- What biases and assumptions are you bringing to this history?
- Which of the factors listed on pages 224–25 (this book) have you determined are important to your history and why?
- What evidence is missing of your center's history? How will you account for this gap?
- What evidence do you have that you cannot account for or that you have decided is not relevant? What are you going to do with it?
- How will you make all this evidence available to other researchers, present and future?
- What kind of story are you trying to tell and why?
- Who is the audience for this history?
- What does your history offer that audience?
- Are you making an argument about how your writing center took its current shape?
- Or are you arguing for a future course of action based on your interpretation of events?
- Ultimately, who is this history for and how will it help that audience?

As we tried to communicate in this chapter, there are many ways to answer this last question. Indeed, you may find it's not hard to find a story to tell—but it's hard to tell just one. For as Connors has argued, when disciplinary historians write our histories, we realize that we are not merely telling the story of our discipline but, in fact, our own story:

> Because that is what history is: the telling of stories about the tribe that makes the tribe real. . . . Yes, the story is sometimes discouraging; yes, many false paths and useless methods were tried; yes, there were long periods of dogma and desuetude. . . . Our history is its own justification, and if our methods can grow more solid and sophisticated, our motives should not. The methods are not new, nor can they be; the effort there is to wield them with more control, more self-awareness. But out motives for writing history are what such motives have always been: we write histories to define ourselves on the stage of time. ("Dreams" 34–35)

RELATED WORKS

Connors, Robert. "Dreams and Play: Historical Method and Methodology." *Methods and Methodology in Composition Research*. Carbondale: Southern Illinois University Press, 1992. 15–36. Print.

Gaillet, Lynée Lewis. "Archival Survival: Navigating Historical Research." *Working in the Archives: Practical Research Methods for Rhetoric and Composition*. Ed. Alexis E. Ramsey, Wendy B. Sharer, Barbara L'Eplattenier, and Lisa S. Mastrangelo. Carbondale: Southern Illinois University Press, 2010. 28–39. Print.

Habermas, Jürgen. *The Structural Transformation of the Public Sphere: An Inquiry into a Category of Bourgeois Society*. Cambridge: MIT Press, 1989. Print.

Lyotard, Jean-François. *The Postmodern Condition*. Minneapolis: University of Minnesota Press, 1984. Print.

Scott, Joan. *Gender and the Politics of History*. New York: Columbia University Press, 1988. Print.

White, Hayden. *Tropics of Discourse: Essays in Cultural Criticism*. Baltimore: Johns Hopkins University Press, 1978. Print.

Sample Letter of Oral History Subject Solicitation Letter

Professor Michael McCamley
English Department
Crawford College
Boston, KS 12434

12 October 2015

Dear Professor McCamley,

I write today in the hopes of securing your cooperation with a research project currently being conducted in the Crawford College Writing Center. Several other peer tutors, including Carolyn Clark, Joseph Turner, and Rachael Zeleny, and I are working to create a history of our writing center. As part of that project, we are scheduling interviews with individuals who were influential in the origin and evolution of our center. As you were the chair of the English Department who collaborated on the founding of our center, we are hopeful that you would be willing to meet and describe your recollection of that event.

As we envision it, the interview would take no more than one hour of your time. Having reviewed the available materials related to the center founding, I would hope to discuss the reasons why the center was founded, the role it was originally intended to play in campus writing culture, and the evolution of that mission during your time as chair. As well, of course, as any additional insight into the growth of our writing center that you might offer!

This study poses no directs risks or benefit to its subjects and has been approved by the Crawford College's Institutional Review Board. I will be happy to answer any questions, as would Professor Elizabeth Keenan Knauss, who directs the writing center and who is mentoring our research.

I will contact you early next week to see if you have any questions and, if, you are amenable, to set an appointment.

Sincerely,

Heather Schulze

Follow-up Email

Professor Michael McCamley
English Department
Crawford College
Boston, KS 12434

28 October 2015

Dear Professor McCamley,

This letter follows up on our phone conversation of October 26.

Thank you for agreeing to serve as interview subject for the Crawford College Writing Center History. As you proposed, I will meet you in your office at 3:30 on Wednesday, November 15. This interview will be audio recorded and will focus on the evolution of the writing center from 1987–1993.

If you have any materials related to the center—annual reports, proposals, etc.— that you would be willing to share with our archive, I would be most happy to make a copy immediately following our meeting and return the documents that afternoon. As with the recording of our conversations, documents related to the history of our writing center will be digitized and indexed, and physical documents will be housed in the locked filing cabinets in the writing center conference room. Therefore, while all Crawford College community members have access to these records, they are being kept in a secure environment. Of course, if you have any digital resources, we will gratefully accept those as well. These documents are being kept on a password-protected server, and the history that comes from this work will be publicly available on the writing center website.

I'm greatly looking forward to our conversation. Thank you again for your time and assistance.

Sincerely,

Heather Schulze

CHAPTER 11

Show Me
Empirical Evidence and Tutor Research

INTRODUCTION

Imagine you are working in a writing center and, one day in the tutor lounge, you overhear the following joking exchange among three tutors, Kelly, Rita, and Erec.

> RITA: "Hey, the compilations of the week's writer-feedback forms are in our mailboxes!"
>
> KELLY: [Walks over and looks at her own evaluations.] "Nice! I'm the best tutor we've got!"
>
> RITA: [Laughing] "And what is THAT supposed to mean?"
>
> KELLY: "Well, look at the numbers, I have the best averages in the center."
>
> RITA: "Whatever. You tutored, like, five people last week, and I tutored, like, a dozen. That's got to count for something. Also, I have way more perfect scores than you do."
>
> EREC: "Pffft. Numbers don't mean anything in a writing center. Listen to these comments: 'I had no idea how to approach this paper until Erec talked me through it. Now I know just what to do.' 'He's the best—really cares and knows his stuff.' 'Erec is THE MAN.' Those are the words of writers who worked with our best tutor. Me. I am a case study in awesome."
>
> RITA: "You want to hear the words of writers who work with our best tutor? Listen in sometime when I'm tutoring. You may learn something!"

While this chapter will not resolve the friendly dispute described above, it will help you understand the means that would allow us to test the claims Rita, Kelly, and Erec make. That is, this chapter focuses on **empirical research**, those methods through which the scholar "amasses, analyzes and interprets data" (Lauer and Asher 6) using the five senses. Whether that data is gathered via statistical analysis, as Kelly and Rita initially suggest in the vignette above, or by textual or discourse analysis, as Eric and Rita describe in the conclusion to the scene, all these forms of empirical study are united by the use of an **inductive approach**.

TYPES OF EMPIRICAL RESEARCH

An inductive approach builds analysis from individual pieces of data to form a theory or create an argument for the reader. Thus, in our opening example Rita and Kelly use the individual pieces of data from their client feedback forms to build humorous arguments about their tutoring excellence. By contrast, a **deductive approach** works from the global to the particular by using a preexisting theory and applying it to a given situation. The research process for a theory-based essay might progress deductively by starting with a broadly framed theoretical lens from, for example, feminism, and then moving to the specifics of a given tutorial or program. For the purposes of this chapter, however, it is less important to be able to identify or design research that is purely deductive or inductive than it is to know that empirical research is primarily inductive and focuses on using data that can be apprehended by the five senses. In other words, empirical researchers use methods that allow them to gather individual pieces of data (survey responses, for example), which in turn serve as the building blocks for arguments.

This chapter investigates a range of these methods and includes both **qualitative** and **quantitative** approaches to research. Quantitative methods are those that use numbers to explore the similarities, differences, and/or patterns appearing in datasets. Qualitative research takes as its goal "to answer the *whys* and *hows* of human behavior, opinion, and experience . . . [by] collecting and/or working with text, images or sounds" (Guest, Namey, and Mitchell 3). This chapter begins with an exploration of some of those basic statistical concepts that help tutors to understand the presentations of numerical data that they most often encounter, such as in writer feedback forms or numbers of sessions. After discussing quantitative research, this chapter covers some of the more common qualitative means of investigating the writing center, such as

- Survey
- Case study
- Discourse analysis
- Ethnography

WHAT CONSTITUTES EMPIRICAL RESEARCH?

Given the range of data-gathering techniques that make up this chapter, a reader might wonder what such various means of inquiry might have in common—that is, what makes them all "empirical research." After reading this chapter, however, we think you'll see that these methods are united by their reliance on

research design. That is, empirical research often begins with a question, and the researcher then carefully designs a process to gather the data that will allow him or her to answer this question. Such design is intentional and has a keen eye toward the **reliability** and **validity** of the study (two concepts that are discussed on page 196, this book).

This approach may contrast with historical or theoretical research you have done. For an historical inquiry, for example, you might need to revisit an archive to address questions later raised in an oral interview. So too, in a theoretical piece, you might decide, after reflection and writing, that a theoretical lens different from the one with which you began your inquiry might better serve your argument—you might decide to draw upon Elizabeth H. Boquet's description of the writing center rather than Nancy Maloney Grimm's concept, for example. In an empirical study, however, once you have begun your work, it can be very difficult to alter substantially the means by which you are gathering data. For example, it would be no small matter to decide halfway through gathering survey data that your inquiry would have been better advanced by an ethnography. For one, you may well have needed institutional approval for your work, as described in Chapter 8. Any changes to your research may need to be resubmitted for this approval before you can proceed. At best, then, altering your research design will mean delaying your work while you wait for permission to move forward. At worst, faulty design might derail your study. If you receive survey data that suggests your respondents did not understand your question(s), for instance, it can be difficult or impossible to go back and re-ask your respondents to elicit the desired information. The survey population may have dispersed or you may have run out of time for data gathering and analysis. Accordingly, heavy emphasis in all these methods is placed on careful and extensive planning prior to data gathering. You want to choose a method that will illuminate directly your area of inquiry, and once you have selected a method, you want to make sure your data-gathering techniques will generate the kind of information that will, as precisely as possible, address your concern.

ON MIXING METHODS

While the remainder of this chapter focuses on empirical methods, it is worth keeping in mind that doing so is not an implicit argument against the combination of methods in a study. By contrast, researchers are not only likely to combine qualitative and quantitative methods in their work, but they often also draw upon theoretical and historical research traditions when framing their studies. So, too, researchers whose primary contributions are to historical and theoretical conversations will use empirical methods. Thus you will find a description of an empirical method—interview—in the discussion of oral history in Chapter 10 on historical research. It is typical for researchers to contribute simultaneously to multiple avenues of inquiry. For example, Janet Bean's "Feminine Discourse in the University: The Writing Center as a Site of Linguistic Resistance" first draws upon Muriel Harris for a theoretical conception of the tutor and Susan Miller for the historicizing of the ways in which writing instruction has long been associated with women's work. Bean next complicates Harris's and Miller's work with tools from linguistics by incorporating the research of Deborah Tannen and Robin Lakoff. Bean then turns to qualitative research and interviews tutors to explore the gendering of tutor language. And, finally, she moves on to the language of tutorials themselves, comparing the balance of talk between tutor and writer in a series of tutoring sessions. Even in a relatively short work such as an essay-length argument, then, a single researcher can apply many methods effectively. Ultimately, Bean's goal is to examine the presence and impact of gendered language in the writing center tutorial, and this range of methods—theoretical, historical, empirical—helps her to do so.

In undergraduate research, too, you will find that this mixing of methods is both common and useful. In the tutor research included in this volume's anthology section, for example, it would seem that tutor-researchers often pair the kinds of theoretical work we discuss in Chapter 9 with the empirical methods discussed here. Claire Elizabeth O'Leary's article combines gender theory with discourse analysis, and Natalie DeCheck's essay reads the data from her case study through a lens developed from motivation theory borrowed from educational psychology. Likewise, Jennifer Nicklay reads tutor interviews through a lens built from early work in writing center studies, namely Stephen North's "The Idea of a Writing Center" and Jeff Brooks' "Minimalist Tutoring: Making Students Do All the Work." As these examples suggest, when designing an empirical project, you should attend to devising a method that will answer your research question in an accurate and useful manner, and not worry if that means drawing together tools from different research methods.

READING EMPIRICAL RESEARCH

For someone not used to reading empirical scholarship, it can initially seem uninviting, particularly when compared to much of the theoretical or historical research published in writing center studies. For one, empirical research offers a reading experience unlike that provided by those academic essays encountered and produced in many undergraduate classrooms. That is, the familiar academic essay form is thesis-driven and so announces the importance of its contribution in the introduction. Further enticing the reader to pursue the argument, such essays follow a readily identifiable and easily discerned organizational pattern, one that likely uses strong topic sentences and signpost language to move the reader through the discussion. Finally, in the conclusion, the academic essay will often simultaneously touch back to the central point announced in the introduction and close on a note that allows the essay to look forward to the larger implications of the work. The ideal of such an essay is that its form appears organic, shaped by the intended audience and the writer's purpose in addressing that audience—although as writers and tutors we know in reality this structure can seem artificial during the writing process.

The academic essay might seem like the natural form for an argument, particularly if it is the form of research you have primarily read in the past. By contrast, initial encounters with empirical research might make you a bit uncomfortable. To gain a sense of this distinction, you may wish to compare essays from each tradition that we've included in the anthology section, such as Kenneth Bruffee's "Peer Tutoring and the 'Conversation of Mankind'" with the empirically organized "Finding Harmony in Disharmony: Engineering and English Studies" by Ruth Johnson, Beth Clark, and Mario Burton. If you do so, you may notice that the construction of an empirical research essay is dictated by the method itself; the regular readers of empirical research will expect, roughly speaking, a manuscript to contain some or all of these elements:

- *Statement of problem/exigency and review of research:* In this section, the reader would expect to find an explanation of the situation in which the researcher is attempting to intervene, a review of available work in this area, and a rationale for why the contribution of the current project is potentially significant.
- *Description of method:* Here, the reader should expect to find a description of the method used and an explanation of how this method addresses the research question/problem introduced in the previous section; it possibly elaborates the relation of the research question to the research design. This discussion also includes a description of how subjects were selected for inclusion in the study. Both the design and the method of analysis should be explained in sufficient detail that a reader could reproduce the study in a new context.
- *Results:* This portion of the essay presents data generated from the study. The reader expects to understand how the relevant data was generated and how representative data from the study was selected for inclusion in the final manuscript.
- *Discussion of data:* The segment of the essay explains the manner in which the data contributes to the knowledge of the field and argues the significance of the study.
- *Implications and limitations:* This section both specifies the limits of the work's application and conjectures ways in which future research might extend this study.

The new reader of empirical research, perhaps used to the thesis-driven, essay-form research tradition that is represented by many undergraduate writing assignments, might be surprised at the way in which such work is constructed and wonder what reading strategies best address these texts. As in other reading situations, how one reads is, in part, a result of the text and in part a result of the reader's purpose. That is, when reading an empirical study while looking for a research design to model upon, a researcher might focus most closely on the methods section. By contrast, a researcher primarily interested in the area of knowledge to which the study contributes might focus on the statement of the problem and the discussion of results. The researcher puzzled or intrigued by the conclusions at which such an essay arrives might be best served by attending most closely to the ways the work reports on the data and its analysis. Table 11.1 offers some questions that might be helpful when reviewing empirical scholarship.

Table 11.1 Empirical Scholarship: Readers' Questions.

- Is the problem framed in a productive and appropriate manner? Are the implied or stated relations of cause and effect well reasoned?
- Does the review of research seem timely and appropriate?
- Is the method described well positioned to yield data that will address the research question? Is the method adequately described to enable the reader to replicate the study?
- Are the data and analysis directly the result of the method described? Are the results a complete accounting of the data yielded by the research? If not, is it clear how the data was selected for inclusion?
- Does the discussion tie the data meaningfully to the research question?
- Does the discussion of limitations and implications seem to contextualize adequately the contribution of the study?

QUANTITATIVE RESEARCH

Because writing center studies is a field that grows out of the scholarly tradition of the humanities, and as its earliest advocates were often themselves trained in literary studies, writing center researchers sometimes tend toward number phobia ("I'm a words person! I don't do math!"). And sometimes this fear expresses itself as a sense of superiority ("What we do in the tutoring program can't be reduced to MERE numbers!"). We're hopeful, however, that the field is moving away from these kinds of narrow mindsets, for such a shift is in the best interests of the writers we serve. For one, in higher education, most institutional decisions are driven by numbers. Partially this has to do with pure practicality—it will be difficult, for example, for your school to decide your program is worth funding if you cannot give the kind of wide-angle view that numbers can allow. And partially this has to do with the kinds of stories numbers can help us tell and the hard choices they can help us make. That is, numbers are an efficient way to describe, compare, and/or look for patterns in many kinds of data.

Birds of a Feather: Using Numbers to Identify Similarity

Perhaps the most familiar quantitative numbers in everyday life are those that help us look at the similarity among items or persons. In this chapter's opening anecdote, for example, the tutors are comparing the similarities among the feedback they have received from the writers who have visited their center. Each tutor in the opening scenario introduces a different kind of evidence to support his or her claims, and quantitative analysis gives them some of the tools they need to do so. Kelly and Rita, for example, are drawing from numbers that describe the **central tendency** of the responses.

Central tendency emphasizes the commonality in a dataset or datasets by looking at the place where the data "clusters"—that is, where there are strong similarities among the data. When Kelly argues that she is the best tutor because she has the highest averages, she is invoking the most common statistical analysis of central tendency, which in quantitative research is the **mean** and in everyday life is frequently referred to as the average. This number is likely the most common statistic reported from writing center surveys.

However, the mean is not the only way of looking at the central tendency, nor is it necessarily the most accurate. As Rita points out, another way of evaluating this feedback data is to focus on the score that appears most frequently. This number is called the **mode**. If we accept Rita's assertion that the best tutor is the one who can receive the most perfect scores, then we would look at the mode as evidence.

Another way to look at the scores (albeit not one that is relevant to the tutors' friendly dispute) is to look at the **median**. The median is the midpoint piece of data. These three terms—mean, median, and mode—are the most common concepts used to look at similarities in data and are of great use in looking at many different kinds of writing center surveys. As seen in Table 11.2, for example, they can be productively applied to the feedback given to Kelly and Rita.

Table 11.2 Examples of Central Tendency.

	KELLY'S SCORES (n = 5)	RITA'S SCORES (n = 12)
	5	5
	4	5
	4	5
	4	5
	4	5
		5
		3
		3
		3
		3
		2
		2
Mean	4.2	3.8
Mode	4	5
Median	4	4

How we interpret this table will depend on how we understand the relationship between "best tutor" and writer feedback forms. Kelly is indeed correct when she says that on average she is more highly rated than Rita. But Rita is also correct when she points out that she has tutored more, as expressed by $n = 12$. (In empirical research, a lowercase italicized n is frequently used to show how many data items are under consideration.)

But What Does It Mean in Context? Understanding What Numbers Can and Can't Tell Us

The differences among mean, median, and mode in this dataset foreground the question of what is "best" in tutoring practice. Is it the tutor who helps the most writers and does so well? Or is it the tutor who, on average, is the most highly rated by writers, however many writers that might be? We could even argue for "best-ness," as does Erec and as we describe later in this chapter, by using data that is not numerical at all. However, for a study to be well designed and persuasive, the researcher would need to determine a definition of excellence at the outset and make plain why the kind of data gathering will document that definition. A definition of excellence, then, is context dependent—there might be writing centers whose mission is to reach as many students as possible and who therefore might look for their definition to Rita's model: serving many students and serving them well. And there may also be centers whose ample staff hours and/or lower usage prioritizes in their assessments each individual writer's enthusiasm at the end of the tutorial rather than considering the number of writers assisted. (To better understand the relationship between a specific context and the statistics a researcher investigates, it might be helpful at this point to reflect upon your own tutoring program and which of the information discussed here would help your community ascertain how close you come to achieving its ideal.)

The data itself, of course, isn't going to settle Rita and Kelly's argument, nor will it tell your program what to do next. But the concepts of mean, median, and mode do provide a concise way of surveying trends in the data. To use these trends as evidence in an argument, however, Rita and Kelly or your own program would need to define at the outset what "best" means for a specific argument and why that definition is the most relevant. Thus in a review of research, statistical analysis might be effectively framed by published conversations in writing center research or, at least, by relevant local conversations, whether those "conversations" are in staff meetings, tutor education materials, or other materials specific to the writing center, such as tutoring practicum materials or a shared program blog. To review an essay whose literature review synthesizes the local knowledge of one writing program with the wider conversation represented by the published work of writing, you might want to (re)read Jennifer Nicklay's "Got Guilt? Consultant Guilt in the Writing Center Community," which is included in the anthology section of this book.

Seeing Difference: Standard Deviation

In addition to building these arguments on similarities among data, we also can—and often must—look at differences—also referred to as variance—among the data. Sometimes a researcher isn't focusing on common practice but is questioning the lack of common practice, for example. Typically, the most important way of looking at these differences is **standard deviation** (SD), which tells us how far, on average, a score diverged from the mean—how far each piece of data is from the mean.

Standard Deviation and the Creation of Meaning

Without SD, the mean can be very deceptive. Assume, for example, that two tutors, Chris and Pat, have the following scores on the writer feedback item "The tutor was polite and welcoming":

Table 11.3 Tutor Scores on "The tutor was polite and welcoming."[1]

	CHRIS'S SCORES (n = 11)	PAT'S SCORES (n = 11)
	4	5
	4	5
	4	5
	3	5
	3	5
	3 <= median	4 <= median
	3	2
	3	1
	3	1
	3	1
	2	1
Mean	3.18	3.18
Mode	3	5
Median	3	4

[1] In both Table 11.3 and 11.4, numbers have been rounded to the second decimal place.

If only the mean is examined for each tutor, or even the mean and the *n*, these tutors will look the same: both Chris and Pat tutored 11 students, after all, and the mean of both their score sets is 3.18. But if we dig further into the data, by incorporating the other measures of central tendency discussed (median and mode), we might start to arrive at the conclusion that Pat consistently achieves higher scores on this item than does Chris. Pat's mode and median are 5 and 4, after all, while both Chris's mean and median are 3. Looking at the entire dataset, however, we realize that these numbers are telling only part of the story because the two sets of scores, on the whole, look very different.

As seen in Table 11.4, by using SD a clearer picture of these scores emerges:

Table 11.4 Tutor scores on "The tutor was polite and welcoming."

	CHRIS'S SCORES (*n* = 11)	PAT'S SCORES (*n* = 11)
	4	5
	4	5
	4	5
	3	5
	3	5
	3 <= median	4 <= median
	3	2
	3	1
	3	1
	3	1
	2	1
Mean	3.18	3.18
Mode	3	5
Median	3	4
Standard Deviation	0.60	1.94

The SD captures for the reader a fuller story of this feedback. An SD of 0.6 means that Chris's scores cluster more tightly, suggesting a far greater consistency in writers' perceptions than is suggested in the scores of Pat, who appears to be assessed as either extremely polite and welcoming—or quite the reverse. An SD of 1.96 on a five-point scale means that Pat's scores are either two above or two below the mean. In other words, on average, Pat's scores are virtually spread as far apart as possible. So while there is a median to these scores, that median does not describe any consistency in Pat's reception by writers. If you look back at the individual scores themselves you can see that Pat's scores span the highs and lows of the scale in a fairly equal distribution.

Standard Deviation and Context
The important thing to note here is that SD gives us a single number that summarizes these differences among the dataset. And again, by itself, this piece of evidence is not definitive: there could be a variety of pedagogical, personal, and cultural reasons for the difference between the two tutors' score sets. But this data does show us why the mean itself, so common in many writing center reports, doesn't tell a complete story. For a mean to be part of a meaningful argument, we need to know the *n* (how many individual pieces of data the average represents) and the *SD* (what the range of the difference is among these individual pieces).

Given the importance of SD, you may be wondering how to calculate the SD of your own dataset. This is certainly a useful skill to have, and the works by

Lauer and Asher, Nunan, and Johanek listed in the Related Works at the end of this chapter explain how to arrive at this number. When considering using tools such as SD in your own research, however, it is less important to know how to conduct these analyses firsthand than it is to understand what kinds of data these analyses yield. Many schools have offices and/or labs that offer statistical analysis services, and there are many readily available calculators online that will instantly analyze your data in this manner. What it important, however, is to know the ways in which your data can be manipulated and what kinds of information these manipulations will yield. A researcher who was unaware of the importance of SD, for example, might have merely looked the averages of Pat and Chris and inaccurately assumed they had almost identical tutorial effects. This would be a misleading story to tell.

Other Quantitative Measures

There are other ways in which to look at data using statistical analysis. In other scholarly communities, for example, it is common to use numerical descriptions to look at patterns in data and to create comparisons among these patterns, and to compare the characteristics among datasets. Common analyses used to pursue these kinds of work include the *t*-test, chi-square, and the ANOVA (analysis of variance). However, these tests lie beyond the introductory scope of this chapter and are not formulas commonly used in writing center research. Tutor-researchers interested in learning more about these tools, however, might look to the essays by Rowan and by Bromley, Northway, and Schonberg for recent models of the application of statistical methods in writing center studies, or for further explanations of quantitative research, consult Nunan, Johanek, or Lauer and Asher.

Quantitative Research in Writing Center Studies

Given the power of quantitative arguments in institutional discourse, there are surprisingly few examples of quantitative research popular in the writing center literature. Aside from those studies already mentioned, the most commonly cited works using this method are Neal Lerner's "Counting Beans and Making Beans Count" and "Choosing Beans Wisely." While "Choosing," in fact, repudiates the larger argument of "Counting," the set of articles is nonetheless worth reading by the researcher looking for quantitative models, even though the two essays taken together strike a cautionary note about what numbers can and cannot do—particularly when they are used, as Lerner describes in "Choosing," to advance faulty arguments. Even with the considerable methodological and logical flaws described in its counterpart, "Counting" remains a good read and a useful model, not only of how statistical analysis works but also for how to structure an empirical argument in a manner that combines a collegial tone with the typical parts of a manuscript that presents this kind of research.

QUALITATIVE RESEARCH

While quantitative research may be new, and, we hope, exciting, to some tutor-researchers, qualitative methods might seem more familiar. Tutor-researchers who have worked or studied in the social sciences may already know some or all of the methods discussed here. And even for those individuals who have studied in, for example, the business and/or humanities traditions, the emphasis on narrative in qualitative research may seem familiar. As Rebecca Day Babcock and Theresa Thonus note:

> *Qualitative* data analysis . . . focuses on qualities, non-numerical patterns in the data. Much qualitative data analysis is rooted in *grounded theory* first codified by the sociologists Glaser and Strauss in 1967. Researchers examine their data iteratively, coding them and allowing theory to emerge from the data. There are no preconceived categories for coding; rather the researcher notes tentative codes and writes coding memos describing the issues rising to the surface. (43)

Put another way, the researcher systematically gathers descriptive data about the phenomena and/or individuals he wishes to investigate and then repeatedly reviews information looking for trends. In many ways, such an approach seems to align well with the pedagogical and cultural values of many writing centers. For one, **grounded theory**, with its emphasis on what is occuring and what appears to work, appeals to the practical inclinations of many tutor-researchers as well as other writing center scholars, most of whom want to know how their investigations can immediately improve practice. For another, the narrative emphasis of much qualitative research often appeals to the storytelling urge of many writing center studies participants. Qualitative methods can help channel this narrative into forms that are understood by a broad audience and therefore make our knowledge available to new readers. Finally, grounded theory, with its emphasis on what is happening in the present, is particularly useful for instances in which there is very little preexisting literature, allowing the tutor-researcher to create new knowledge by observing what is happening in the present moment. Additional information on grounded theory can be found in Corbin and Strauss and in Glaser and Strauss.

WHAT'S HAPPENING NOW: SURVEY METHOD

In writing center practice and scholarship, a common use of quantitative analysis is to analyze results from a **survey**. Indeed, in some ways surveys can be seen as a bridge from quantitative to qualitative methods, for surveys are interpreted by using the kinds of quantitative tools discussed above. Surveys are frequently used by writing centers to inquire into their performance and are particularly useful for giving a "snapshot of conditions, attitudes and/or events at a single point in time" (Nunan 140). It is important to keep in mind, however, that a survey is not necessarily a report on actual conditions, but a report on respondents' views.

That is, a writing center user feedback survey including the item "The writing center tutor helped me improve my paper" will not, by itself, yield data concerning the improvement of the paper. Rather, it helps the researcher understand whether or not the respondents think tutors helped in this manner. To ascertain whether or not conversation with the tutor actually did have a positive impact on the paper, a researcher would need to define "improvement" and then look at other evidence that would document improvement—analyzing the writer's text, for example, and/or interviewing the instructor.

Surveys are, however, a useful tool for gathering data about respondents' opinions and so are the most common form of empirical research in most writing centers. In addition to the kind of writer feedback survey already discussed in this chapter, many writing centers survey the various stakeholders on their campus—instructors, students who have or have not used the writing center, administrators—to determine how their services are perceived. And, quite often, national and international surveys are posted on WCENTER, the writing center administrators' listserv, by researchers hoping to gather information about a particular kind of tutoring program (such as a community college writing center, a graduate student writing center, or a discipline-specific tutoring program) or looking to generate data concerning a particular issue common to many writing centers (such as how writing centers deal with habitual no-shows or what print and/or electronic resources are commonly used by tutors of writing).

Crafting a Survey

At first glance, survey creation may seem quite easy: simply ask the question and see what answers roll in. However, as anyone who has dealt extensively with this method will attest, creating questions that will elicit precisely the information you wish to gather can actually be far more difficult than it first appears. After settling upon your line of research, then, there are several other questions for you to consider, such as the following.

What Survey Population Will Provide the Best Data to Explore Your Research Question?

For some research questions, the appropriate population may be readily apparent. If, for example, you wanted to examine the differences between the ways in which first-year students and seniors view your tutoring program, you would ask first-year students and seniors. And yet, even a research question such as this one raises questions about the populations to be surveyed. That is, which first-year students and seniors will you query? How will you ensure that the responding populations are representative of the student body? How will you define the student body for this study? Will it include both full- and part-time students, for example? Will you compare the gender, ethnic identity, and/or grade point average for respondents to data representing the entire student body? If not, how will you know that the respondent pool is representative? If so, to assure adequate representation you will need to gather this data from or about survey respondents. In brief, you will need to define carefully both your research question and the audience for your survey instrument.

What Number of Respondents Are You Targeting?

This question is sometimes self-answering. For example, if you are comparing attitudes about the writing center among students in a first-year writing class that requires visits to the center with the attitudes of students in a first-year writing class where such visits are encouraged but not required, you might hope to elicit full participation, or at least close to it. If, however, you are looking at a larger population or populations—comparing, for example, attitudes about the writing center among the 10,000 students who take first-year writing at your institution versus those students who are either exempted or take the class elsewhere—you will need to determine what sample size you will need to evidence your claims.

When determining this number, you will want to consider the size of the group that the survey population is meant to represent as well as how much you will want to **granulate** the responses—how far you will wish to drill down into the responses by respondent demographics to add further detail to your analysis. In the last scenario, for example, if the group of students who do not take first-year writing at your school is large, you may be satisfied with a fairly small response rate among this group: 10 percent of 10,000 students is still a very large group. But if only 250 students didn't take first-year writing, ten percent will represent a much smaller data set.

If you are going to want to delve more deeply into this data by granulating the responses—to separate out respondents by class standing or major, for example—you will need a larger number of respondents for your survey data to maintain its argumentative force. And if the size of your potential respondent pool is extremely small, you may need to rethink your avenue for inquiry or the method you are using to answer that question. That is, if your likely number of respondents is, for example, nine individuals, you may well generate more meaningful research using the case study method described below.

Unfortunately, given the potential range of survey-based research projects, we can't give you a simple number or rule—such as, don't do a survey less than 32. Much like writing itself, you will need to think about what you want to prove and whom you want to prove it to as you think through your survey design.

How Will You Incentivize Participation?

You may encounter among your target population a resistance to participate in your survey. Sometimes this resistance is due to apathy but increasingly it is due to **survey exhaustion**. Institutions want to know as much as possible about their members, and with the advent of online survey resources, it has become very easy to create and administer surveys. Unsurprisingly, college students and other university members increasingly are disinclined to respond to such requests.

Accordingly, you want to do everything possible to motivate your target respondents. Researchers sometimes use tangible goods such as gift cards or a raffle to motivate respondents. If you wish to incorporate such items, they should be included in both your research design and your IRB application; in some institutional cultures this will not be possible.

In creating your survey, however, you can do other, nontangible, things that can motivate participation, such as the following:

- *Identify yourself as a student.* In "De-centering Peer Tutors: Research Applications for Undergraduates in the Writing Program," Skyler Konicki reports an unusually high response rate to a student-authored survey and suggests that many students were willing to participate because they identified with the researcher as a peer (80). Such affiliation between you and your target audience can help your survey stand out from those from residence life, the dining hall, academic services, etc.

- *Assert the benefit of your research early in your appeal.* In the initial email or letter to your targeted audience, frame your request in terms of how it stands to benefit others rather than yourself. For example, rather than stating, "I am a student in the tutoring writing course, and I am hoping you will participate in my research," it might be more productive to write, "So that we can improve the services we offer you, I am researching student use of the writing fellows program."

- *Keep both your solicitation message and the survey itself as concise as possible.* By sending a survey, you are asking people to, in effect, give you their time. One of the best ways to show you value their contribution is to use this time efficiently and meaningfully. You may also find it is effective to demonstrate that you value their time by including in the solicitation message an estimate of how long the survey should take (such as "This survey should take no longer than 10 minutes to complete").

- *Ensure that the survey is clearly worded, that it does not indicate researcher bias, and that the questions are as easy to respond to as possible.* Taking care when creating a survey instrument is another way you can demonstrate to your target population that you respect their time. Piloting your survey, as is described below, is a way to help ensure that your questions are readily understood.

What Kinds of Questions Will Best Support Your Research?

When creating your survey, think about what kinds of questions will yield the most meaningful data in your research context. **Closed-form questions** are those in which the respondent must select from pre-established answers (e.g., Yes or No; rank on a scale of 1 to 5). Such questions yield data that is easily manipulated, even when using a large number of respondents, and that can often generate meaningful results when viewed through the kinds of quantitative analysis described earlier in this chapter. However, such questions must be crafted carefully, anticipating, for example, that some of your respondents will have absolutely no familiarity with the item under consideration. When creating such questions, then, you may inadvertently leave out the most meaningful option your respondents would select, "I am unfamiliar with ___" or "I neither agree nor disagree with ____."

Open-form questions allow the respondents to answer in their own words. Such questions yield data that may provide an entirely new perspective on the research question, but the results are more unwieldy to analyze than closed-form questions. When dealing with open-form questions, researchers typically review the data multiple times, first looking for patterns in the responses and then reviewing the answers repeated times to code the responses for these patterns.

Whatever kind of questions you ask, craft them with as much precision as possible. Don't ask multiple questions in the same item. "Were you happy with the time and location of your appointment?" would rightly be two questions, not one. Review the questions carefully for unstated assumptions that your respondent may not share. For example, "The new writing center is more useful to students than the prior location. Agree/Disagree" would not only assume that all respondents had visited the old location but also that they shared the researchers' idea of what constitutes writing center "usefulness," be that better-trained tutors, more writing technology, or a new coffee machine.

How Will Your Respondent Pool Interpret Your Questions?

It is often difficult to anticipate how your respondents might interpret your questions. To decrease the chances of miscommunication, craft your instrument carefully. After initially drafting it, you may want to discuss your instrument with one of the other tutors in your program to get an idea of how an individual external to your research project might interpret your questions. Once you've revised it in response to any peer response, you will want to **pilot** your survey—that is, try it out with a small group that represents your target population. responses can show you where you might need to rephrase and/or add or delete a question to best achieve your research goals. To this end, you may wish to conduct a **cognitive review** of your survey. That is, you may wish to ask students piloting our survey to read each question out loud and then to tell you in their own words what the question means to them If the question is a closed question, as the student to tell you if the choice make sense to them and if they think any choices have been left out. Such introspection can help you improve your instrument substantially before data gathering begins.

How Will You Interpret Your Respondents' Answers?

Your analysis of responses will depend on your context, the purpose of your research, and the kinds of questions you have chosen to ask. That is, while questions on a 1-to-5 scale might be best expressed via numerical analysis, open-ended questions respond best to the recursive search for trends in data described earlier in this chapter. Such inquiry looks for similarities in responses that can be tentatively categorized and then applied to the data set to see if a meaningful pattern or themes emerge. Such a comprehensive reporting of data is in contrast to the "cherry picking" involved in reporting only data that supports the immediate argument, such as Erec's report of his most glowing writer feedback in the opening of this chapter. Admittedly, these kinds of testimonial highlight reports can be rhetorically useful (e.g., in writing center publicity), but in research a balanced picture of results is expected and so is ultimately more persuasive.

Surveys in Writing Center Research

Surveys have not only been a popular way for individual writing centers to conduct research concerning their institutional contexts, but they have also provided the basis for prominent published writing center research as well. Well-known surveys in the field include the 2007–08 and the 2009–10 international writing center surveys by the Writing Center Research Project. Some of the results from that study are reported in "Local Practices, National Consequences" by Jo Ann Griffin et al. Surveys have also compared the working conditions of writing center directors with other writing program administrators (see, for example, Balester and MacDonald; Charlton and Rose; and Gladstein and Regaignon) and to investigate tutoring practice (see, for example, Schendel; Robinson; Severino, Swenson, and Zhu; Thompson et al.). More recently, in "How Important Is the Local, Really? A Cross-Institutional Quantitative Assessment of Frequently Asked Questions in Writing Center Exit Surveys," authors Pam Bromley, Kara Northway, and Eliana Schonberg use surveys administered at three sharply different institutions—a large public university, a medium-sized private university, and a small private liberal arts college—to compare the similarities among writer experiences in these three sites to challenge the common cliché that "every writing center is different."

Tutor-researchers, too, have often used surveys to explore their research questions. In the anthology section of this book, for example, Jennifer Nicklay's "Got Guilt? Consultant Guilt in the Writing Center Community" surveys tutors to examine what behaviors and attitudes cause tutors to feel guilt. Drawing across these responses allows Nicklay to offer some insight into trends among consultants' emotions. In like fashion, in "Groupies and Singletons: Student Preferences in Classroom-Based Writing Consulting" Alicia Brazeau surveys first-year writing students to investigate trends in student preferences for group tutorials versus one-to-one writing conferences. As these works suggest, surveys are often a useful way for the tutor-researcher to investigate some element of local practice.

IT'S NOT JUST WHAT YOU SAY, IT'S HOW YOU SAY IT: DISCOURSE ANALYSIS

While surveys currently might be the most common method of empirical research in the tutoring of writing, discourse analysis is among those research methods most directly connected to the work of a writing tutor. That is, while a writer's text or writing ability might form the central concern in a tutorial, that concern is explored via conversation; even in an online tutorial, the writer and tutor interact via synchronous or asynchronous "talk." **Discourse analysis** is the means by which researchers explore the many different elements of communication that are occurring simultaneously in any communication event by focusing on "'naturally' occurring language as opposed to . . . more 'artificial' contexts, such as formal interviews, and aim to extract social and cultural meanings and phenomena for the discourse studied" (Guest, Namey, and Mitchell 34).

More specifically, discourse analysis inquiry can yield insight into how individual concepts, such as invention or style, have been addressed during a tutorial. Discourse analysis can also help the researcher investigate the impact of elements of conversation, such as

- Turn-taking
- Questions
- Politeness
- Validation
- Rejection (Babcock and Thonus 49–50; Nunan 160)

Critical Discourse Analysis

In addition to examining both the topics (such as invention) and the elements of discourse (such as turn-taking), researchers have looked to discourse analysis to study the power dynamics at play. Thus, Janet Bean analyzed the discourse of a series of writing center tutorials "[t]o study the relationship between gender and talk" (133). As she describes, there is a connection between the amount of time spent talking and tutorial power relationships:

> My analysis of talk in writing center conferences is based on a model of conversational symmetry that connects balance in features of conversation—interruptions, amount of talk, and topic selection, for example—to balance in the power relations of the participants. Conversational asymmetry can signal a power relationship where one speaker is dominant over the other, for example, when one speaker monopolizes the talking time or controls the topic selection. (Bean 136–37)

Put another way, Bean looks at discourse transcripts to evaluate where conversational control resides. Such "conversational symmetry"—or the lack thereof—can provide the basis for an inquiry using **critical discourse analysis** (CDA), which Babcock and Thonus identify as studying "the relationship between form and function in language and attempt[ing] to reveal the hidden assumptions and power relations in discourse contexts. CDA is not neutral because it attempts to improve social relations through detailed analysis of language use" (47). Such approaches can help us explore the impact of nondirective tutoring, gender dynamics, and other elements that affect the ebb and flow of authority and control in tutorials.

Speech Events

There are other ways of looking at the discourse in tutoring programs. In their discussion of writing center research, for example, Paula Gillespie and Neal Learner discuss two additional approaches. The first, based in the work of sociolinguist/anthropologist Dell Hymes, looks at interactions as "speech events," those exchanges that are defined, at least in part, by the conventions and expectations of the speech that will occur. Such an approach, according to Gillespie and Lerner, is concerned with "uncovering th[e] social rules we largely adhere to unconsciously. By exposing these rules, we can begin to see the logic behind our behavior and particularly why miscommunication can occur" (Gillespie and Lerner 132). Such miscommunication is common: what a tutor might interpret as resistance or disinterest, for example, might in fact be shyness or fear. Hymes' model gives a highly structured way for looking at discourse in this manner.

Feedback Sequences

In addition to looking at the Hymes structuring of discourse analysis, Gillespie and Lerner also examine tutorial discourse using the lens of feedback sequences. Feedback sequences are exchanges in which information is first elicited and then assessed. And as, Gillespie and Lerner note, such units are a primary part of the tutoring exchange:

> In our study of tutoring, we often see how a writer seeks the tutor's feedback on how to best proceed with the text, whether this advice is on a word, paragraph or whole-text level. Thus most tutoring sessions can be seen as chains or requests for feedback. Some are started by writers, some by tutors. . . . Whatever the focus and whoever begins the sequence, either the tutor or writer closes the sequence by giving an evaluation or offering a correction, and then the other participant states it's time to move on. . . . In many ways, entire tutoring sessions can be seen as one large feedback sequence. (137)

Analyzing Discourse

Regardless of which focus of discourse analysis is most appropriate to a research inquiry—be that an investigative lens oriented to topic, for example, or one attuned to conversational elements and/or power dynamics—there still several further questions for the researcher to answer during the research design process.

What Are You Looking for? How Will You Know It when You See It?

Admittedly, there is a tension in discourse analysis between defining a research question with sufficient precision to allow for the design of a research plan and maintaining sufficient flexibility to learn new, exciting things from the observed interactions. A research project would not be well positioned for success if, for example, the researcher decided to use discourse analysis to look for good tutoring—despite Rita's claims to that effect in this chapter's opening. The researcher would need to have defined what discourse element(s) of tutorial exchange were being identified as good tutoring; otherwise it would be difficult to gather data in a systematic and useful way. Thus a tutor-researcher might stipulate that good tutoring involves the use of generative questions, and would decide to use discourse analysis methodology to examine the kinds of questions tutors ask and the kinds of information shared in writers' responses. On the other hand, as empirical research is about the observation of data, the researcher must be open to the data present. Therefore, a study intending to look at the ways in which questions yield writer response might, once the transcripts have been iteratively reviewed, morph into a study of, for example, the ways tutors use silence to generate writer response. Ultimately, the researcher must identify the focus of the inquiry, yet be sufficiently flexible to discern its presence in unanticipated forms.

How Will You Record the Interactions?

The technology one uses to record interactions will be, in part, dictated by the research question. If, for example, a researcher wanted to investigate the ways in which writers communicate resistance during a tutorial, it might make the best sense to videotape tutorials to observe nonverbal resistance cues. (Isabelle Thompson's "Scaffolding in the Writing Center: A Microanalysis of an Experienced Tutor's Verbal and Nonverbal Strategies" is notable for its use of discourse analysis methods when rendering a tutor's physical gestures.) But the environment in which the interactions take place and the comfort level of the participants need to be considered as well. A crowded writing center might not be the best place for video recording, for example, or participants in your context may be more comfortable with audio rather than video recording.

How Will You Transcribe Your Recordings So That They Can Be Coded?

One of the labor-intensive elements of discourse analysis is the transcription of the recording. The practicalities of a short- to medium-term research project (one that occurs over the course of a semester, for example, or even an entire academic year) often mean that you will experience significant time constraints. Accordingly, you should consider how much of the data will be transcribed for analysis and inclusion in your study. How long it takes to transcribe your research into a written text will depend in part on the clarity of the recording, the expertise of the transcriber, the kinds of information included in the transcript, and the technology used to transcribe. A highly expert transcriber working in ideal conditions might be able transcribe at a 2:1 rate (i.e., two hours of transcribing for each hour of recording). A novice transcriber working with hard-to-hear audio inflection, talking over one another, physical cues, etc.—can take much, much longer, so you will want to scale your project and budget your time and/or money accordingly. That is, you can pay people to transcribe your research, but many researchers who use discourse analysis as a research method argue that the best way to explore the data is to transcribe it themselves: such engagement with the discourse will allow the researcher to discern previously overlooked information. Also, transcription by a reputable professional will become expensive very quickly.

Keep in mind, too, that adequately transcribing discourse means including more than just the words. Noises of assent and other filler are an important part of the communication act, as Magdalena Gilewicz and Terese Thonus argue. Further, Gilewicz and Thonus demonstrate that merely writing the word "misrepresents the temporal place of speaker contributions, and it 'edits out' linguistic and nonlinguistic contributions . . . relating them to the category of 'conversational dust' to be swept under the carpet" (26). We only have to think of the effect of an enthusiastic "uh-HUH!" or an awkward pause to see the validity of Gilewicz and Thonus's claim. Including such conversational indicators can increase the time of transcription, yet they are a vital part of the record.

What Kind of Coding System Will You Use when Analyzing Your Data?

Transcribing data and reviewing the transcripts multiple times helps a researcher to establish relevant themes in the research. After the first reviews of the transcript, a researcher might begin to code the data, in a systematic yet tentative and conditional fashion, making note of each instance of the feature or dynamic under consideration. Whether you use one of the discourse analysis models described above or another system entirely, you will want to process your transcripts in a consistent manner that will be transparent for your reader.

How Will You Render Your Transcripts in Your Final Manuscript?

To answer this question, you need to consider not only what parts of your transcripts provide the most illuminating and accurate data in support of your argument and analysis, but also how that data can be effectively communicated to your reader. You need to consider what patterns of pauses, inflections, and overlaps, for example, need to be incorporated into those passages of the discourse you share with your reader, and you need to make sure that the coding is consistent, accurate, and easy to understand.

Discourse Analysis in Writing Center Studies

Due to the centrality of discourse to tutorial work and the immediate applicability of its results to practice, discourse analysis is both a popular method in writing center studies and one of the methods that is most likely to be used when writing center scholarship appears outside of the specialist journals of the field (e.g., *Praxis* and *The Writing Center Journal*). Discourse analyses of tutoring have appeared in venues focused on linguistics, education, and the teaching of English as a second or other language (TESOL) (as representative examples see Thonus "Acquaintanceship;" Bell, Arnold, and Haddock), Discourse analysis has also proven to be a popular method for dissertations in the field. Such large-scale projects offer the researcher the opportunity to analyze for the reader large data-sets and to incorporate discourse analysis with other methods (see, for example, the studies by Babcock and Fallon).

As with the other methods discussed, discourse analysis has been used to great effect by tutor-researchers. Several examples of this work can be found in the anthology section of this book. In "Finding Harmony in Disharmony: Engineering and English Studies," for example, tutor-researchers Ruth Johnson, Beth Clark, and Mario Burton use discourse analysis to look at the intersection of writing center pedagogy and tutor disciplinary expertise, or lack thereof, in a paper's content area. So, too, Molly Wilder's "A Quest for Student Engagement: A Linguistic Analysis of Writing Conference Discourse" uses linguistic analysis to find in tutorial transcripts instances of writer engagement. In "It's Not What You Say, But How You Say It (and to Whom): Accommodating Gender in the Writing Conference," Claire Elizabeth O'Leary performs an analysis of tutorial transcripts, yielding features that she then correlates to gender.

ISN'T THAT JUST TYPICAL! CASE STUDY

Case study is a term that is often used in writing center studies in a fairly casual manner to identify a genre of stories that encapsulate tutor lore as described in Chapter 8. While they are engaging and often illuminating, as Liggett, Jordan, and Price explain and Babcock and Thonus concur, such informal retrospective retellings do not fall under the definition of the case study methodology:

> [The] designation 'case study' is sometimes (mis)applied to pure description, ranging from status-type reports on specific writing centers (the services they offer, their physical locations, their funding and administrative allocations, and so forth) to depictions of a particular person or activity (such as a single tutorial session or an incident that provoked subsequent research of other types). MacNealy cautions that a case study should not be equated with 'a retrospective or anecdotal report on some procedure or event'; rather 'The value of a case study depends on good design. . . . The difference is preplanning' (196). (Liggett, Jordan, and Price 71)

Erec's claim to be "a case study in awesome" in the opening of this chapter, then, may be correct in the everyday use of the term, but his claim is not persuasive as an example of the case study method. Rather, the **case study method** focuses on a single instance or multiple examples of a specific group or phenomenon (e.g., student athletes who use the writing center) in a natural context to improve understanding of the group of phenomena or group represented in the case study.

What Are the Benefits of the Case Study Method?

Babcock and Thonus identify case studies as a likely growth area in writing center research (42), and we agree. As described by Adelman, Jenkins, and Kemmis, the benefits of such an approach are well suited to the research interests of many tutor-researchers; they list the following among its advantages:

- *The case study method is "strong in reality."* The real-world framing of case studies means that practitioners whose primary or exclusive interest is the improvement of practice will find the immediate focus and experiential orientation of case study attractive. Any tutoring strategies and successes represented in a case study, for example, might be quickly implemented by the reader.
- *Case studies can represent simultaneously a variety of perspectives and therefore are open to multiple interpretations.* In tutoring sessions, multiple points of view—tutors, writers, and instructors—can often collide. The case study method can depict together all of these perspectives.
- *Case studies are a particularly accessible form of research.* Tutor-researchers and writing center administrators come from a wide variety of intellectual and cultural backgrounds. In their reliance on the data presented and narrative, Adelman et al. argue, case studies "reduce the dependence of the reader upon unstated assumptions . . . and make[s] the research process itself . . . accessible" to a wide audience (149).

What Are the Processes of the Case Study Method?

As with other empirical methods, a case study begins with a research question, such as "How well does our writing center's current pedagogy address the instructional needs of nontraditionally aged, returning students?" The case study researcher would then design a plan that covers a relatively short period of time, such a few weeks to a semester. During this time, the researcher builds a profile of an individual or individuals. To these ends, the researcher works to gather data from a preplanned variety of sources, such as tutorial observation, session reports, surveys of faculty and students, and interviews. The case study method, then, draws upon evidence yielded by other methods discussed in this chapter. From these materials, the researcher builds a narrative, being careful to demonstrate to the reader the ways in which the events of the narrative and the importance ascribed to these events are evidenced in the data gathered.

How Do Case Studies Differ from Ethnographies?

Ethnographic research, the in-depth study of a community over an extended period of time, has much in common with case studies: both are studies that are based on observing individuals and situations in context. The distinction between the two approaches, however, has much to do with the depth and breadth of the research. Broadly speaking, ethnography is longer term and far more data-rich than a case study. Furthermore, as ethnographers are in the community they study for a sustained time, they often either are or become members of the community they study; therefore they carefully document and reflect upon their own role in the group. Also, while coping with the amount of data gathered can be a challenge when a case study or ethnographic approach is used, it is an area for particular concern when using the latter due to the vast amount of data collected.

In addition to the scope of research, ethnographies typically differ from case studies in focus. That is, a case study, as its name describes, is an investigation of a particular case—be it an individual (such as a specific tutor or writer) or a particular situation (such as working with second-year geology majors). By contrast, an ethnographer will study group interactions, looking broadly at the function of a community. For these reasons, ethnographies of the writing center are typically dissertations and similarly long-term projects.

Case Studies, Ethnography, and Writing Center Research

While it is not uncommon for writing center scholarship to self-describe as case studies, there are surprisingly few true case studies to be found in the published research. Among well-circulated writing center research, "Whispers of Common and Going: Lessons from Fannie" by Anne DiPardo is the best-known case study. DiPardo draws upon a variety of resources—interviews with writer-student Fannie and her tutor Morgan, recorded tutorial sessions between the two women, drafts of Fannie's work, comments and evaluations from Fannie's writing instructors, and other sources. DiPardo uses these materials to offer an argument about sensitivity to cultural difference that has long resonated with tutors.

A FINAL WORLD ON METHOD

This chapter has been an empirical buffet of sorts, for its goals have been to offer small tastes from a range of empirical methods by presenting the kinds of questions you might answer using each approach, some of the considerations you might encounter, and a few models demonstrating how each of these approaches has been applied in writing center studies. We want to end this chapter, and this section of the book, by emphasizing that the point of any research method is not to demonstrate that you can use it, but to actually use it to answer your question in a reliable and valid manner. The question, then, is not whether you are using a research method correctly, but whether you are using it in the manner that will create the knowledge you want and need.

RELATED WORKS

Babcock, Rebecca Day, and Terese Thonus. *Researching the Writing Center: Towards an Evidence-Based Practice*. New York: Peter Lang, 2012. Print.

Corbin, Juliet M., and Anselm C. Strauss. *Basics of Qualitative Research: Techniques and Procedures for Developing Grounded Theory*. Thousand Oaks, CA: Sage, 2008. Print.

Gilewicz, Magdalena, and Terese Thonus. "Close Vertical Transcription in Writing Center Training and Research." *The Writing Center Journal* 24.1 (2003): 25–50. Print.

Glaser, Barney, and Anselm C. Strauss. *The Discovery of Grounded Theory: Strategies for Qualitative Research*. New Brunswick, NH: Aldine Transaction, 1999. Print.

Guest, Greg, Emily E. Namey, and Marilyn Z. Mitchell. *Collecting Field Data: A Manual for Applied Research*. Thousand Oaks, CA: Sage, 2013. Print.

Johanek, Cindy. *Composing Research: A Contextualist Research Paradigm for Rhetoric and Composition*. Logan, UT: Utah State University Press, 2000. Print.

Lauer, Janice M., and J. William Asher. *Composition Research: Empirical Designs*. New York: Oxford University Press, 1988. Print.

Nunan, David. *Research Methods in Language Learning*. Cambridge University Press, 1992. Print.

SECTION IV

Readings from the Research

When Something Is Not Quite Right: Pragmatic Impairment and Compensation in the College Writing Tutorial[1]

Rebecca Day Babcock

Rebecca Day Babcock is a professor at the University of Texas of the Permian Basin. This article was originally published in the periodical *The Writing Lab Newsletter*.

Like all talk, tutoring talk follows unwritten rules of pragmatics. Pragmatics is "[the study of] the use of linguistic and non-linguistic capacities for the purpose of communication" (Perkins, *Pragmatic* 10). Since the tutoring session is not a "regular" conversation, conversational rules apply in a non-conventional way. Many times, even in non-directive tutoring,[2] the tutor wants to direct the tutee to provide some information or to do something, but the directive can be either directly or indirectly stated ("Read this." vs. "Would you mind reading this?"). It's important to keep in mind the difference between non-directive (or Socratic) tutoring, in which the tutor attempts to draw ideas out of the student, and indirect speech acts, which are actually requests for information or behavior couched in language that is conventionally polite. Since the participants in a tutoring session are purportedly engaged in a mutual goal-oriented, cooperative behavior, the concept of the Cooperative Principle is relevant: "Make your conversational contribution such as required, at the stage at which it occurs, by the accepted purpose or direction of the talk exchange in which you are engaged" (Grice 26). If the principle is violated, it is up to the interlocutors to figure out why the other party is being indirect, ambiguous, or obscure and to play along accordingly.

For some, this capacity to "play along" is impaired. This state of "something not being quite right" with language in use is known as pragmatic impairment,[3] and is associated with diagnoses as varied as Asperger's syndrome, autism, learning disability, traumatic brain injury, and attention deficit hyper-activity disorders (Perkins, "Pragmatic Ability" 367; van Balkom and Verhoeven 289). Definitions of pragmatic impairment are often vague, such as "problems with language use" (Perkins, "Pragmatic Impairment"). Perkins notes some specific features that may be present with pragmatic impairment, but the reader must be aware that people with pragmatic impairment don't necessarily exhibit every feature: "problems understanding sarcasm . . . indirect requests, irony, and punchlines of jokes . . . indirect replies . . . lies . . . ambiguity resolution . . . text and discourse processing . . . and others' mental states, attitudes and emotions" ("Clinical" 11).

Since tutoring sessions involve talk, pragmatic impairment can influence the interaction. According to Perkins, the unimpaired individual will often compensate to help the other person and create equilibrium. This may cause a complication in the tutoring session if such compensation goes against "rules" of tutoring. For instance, if a person in a non-tutorial situation has problems with word retrieval, the conversational partner may offer up possible words, while in a tutoring situation, a tutor may have been trained not to provide words for a tutee.

There have been no previous studies of pragmatic impairment in writing centers. Also, studies of pragmatics involving non-impaired individuals in writing centers are few in number and have usually concentrated on politeness (Thonus; Young; Murphy) or non-verbal behavior, also an aspect of pragmatics (Boudreaux). Research studies of students with disabilities in the writing center have been done by Jean Kiedaisch and Sue Dinitz and by Jennifer Wewers. In both these studies, students with learning disabilities were surveyed or interviewed, resulting in similar findings. Although pragmatics was not the focus of either study, tutees with dyslexia told Wewers they needed more time to answer questions and tutors should rephrase questions when necessary. They wanted tutors to meet their problems head on—but with tact. Kiedaisch and Dinitz found that tutees with learning disabilities rated tutoring sessions lower than any other group. Students reported the need for more precise assistance from tutors. As I have suggested elsewhere ("Research-Based"), tutors, when working with deaf tutees, should consider pragmatics, particularly the types of questions they ask and the appropriateness of directive and non-directive tutoring styles.

Perkins claims the cause or definition of pragmatic impairment is not as important as the actual behaviors observed. So rather than list the behaviors and definitions found in other studies, I will focus on two sessions I observed, explain my observations, and when appropriate, compare those instances to what other researchers have found. It should not be inferred that these are all or the only aspects of pragmatics or pragmatic impairment, but simply the ones observed occurring between a particular tutee and her tutor.

I observed two tutoring sessions involving a 21-year-old white woman—a musical theater major with a diagnosed learning disability—and her tutor, an older African-American woman with a Master's degree in Special Education. The tutee informed both researcher and tutor about her learning disability. When asked to explain it further, she preferred not to speak to me directly, instead referring me to her mother, explaining that her mother is her spokesperson in these matters. Her mother wrote to me that the student has a specific learning disability affecting her receptive and expressive language abilities (the terms "specific language impairment" or "pragmatic impairment" were not used). Her mother, who is an educator, explained that the student "has receptive and expressive language deficits. These impede her ability to read and express herself orally in a clear, concise, grammatically correct manner. She has difficulty decoding nuances of social language."

People with pragmatic impairment have trouble with inference, which involves understanding the reasons behind why a person might make a particular statement or ask a particular question, and as a result, the impaired person may take requests quite literally. In cases of pragmatic impairment, the "inferential burden must be taken on by the interlocutor, who is required to expend greater effort in being more linguistically explicit and leaving less to infer" (Perkins, *Pragmatic* 20).

In the case of this tutee, the following exchange illustrates just that, her lack of understanding of the reason behind a question. The tutee and tutor are discussing *Giovanni's Room* by James Baldwin:

TUTOR: David, the story's about David, right? Was David a straight guy or a gay guy?
TUTEE: We don't know.
TUTOR: Did David know?
TUTEE: No.
TUTOR: Did he know in the end?
TUTEE: I don't think so, no.
TUTOR: Why didn't he know?
TUTEE: I don't know, you gotta read the story.
TUTOR: I don't have to read the story, I have to read your paper.
TUTEE: I don't remember. Ask [the teacher]. She'll tell you. I don't know.
TUTOR: Come on . . . let's stop that.

In this case, the tutee misunderstands the intention of the tutor, seeming to think the tutor is genuinely interested in the plot of the novel and the sexual orientation of the main character. We know, through our knowledge of tutoring and our pragmatic understanding, that the tutor is trying to elicit ideas from the tutee to enhance the argument of her paper or perhaps to help her generate examples that she can use as evidence to support her points. Instead, the tutee answers the tutor's questions with suggestions that she read the book herself or ask the teacher to get the answers she seems to want. The tutee refers the tutor to the book or teacher several more times during the tutoring session.

At one point, the tutee shows the tutor the book and says, "There you go, you can read this stuff here." The tutor responds, "You need it for your paper. I don't need to read it." And then the tutee responds, "Yes, you do, cause you want to know these things." In a related example given by Perkins, a teacher and student are looking at slides:

TEACHER: What can you see?
ROSIE: And they're going in the sand.
TEACHER: Mm?
ROSIE: You have a look.
TEACHER: Well you have a look and tell me.
I've seen it already.
I want to see what you can see. (*Pragmatic* 78)

Perkins explains the impaired person is not able to conceive of the task, a display task not very common outside the classroom or tutoring situation. In most real-life situations when a person asks for information, she genuinely wants it, so a suggestion about how to get that information (have a look, ask the teacher, read the book) would be appropriate. However, the tutor, like the teacher above, attempts to explain the task ("I don't have to read the book, I have to read your paper"), but then gets frustrated with the tutee as if she is intentionally trying to be difficult ("Come on . . . let's stop that").

In another instance, the tutee again takes the tutor literally:

TUTOR: OK. Where you have "and" here and someplace else. How would those sound if, if you took those "ands" out and made two independent sentences? [falling intonation]
TUTEE: I don't know.
TUTOR: It's kind of long. [reads] I think you can put a period over here [reads]. Take out the "and."

The falling intonation indicates that this is not a literal question, but a suggestion for revision. If it were a literal question, the intonation would be rising. The tutee does not perceive this and answers as if it were a request for information. She literally does not know how it would sound if the sentence were revised thusly. In a related example given by Perkins, a speech therapist is working with a child with autistic spectrum disorder:

T: Can you turn the page over?
C: Yes. (No sign of continuing)
T: Go on then. (points)
C: (turns the page over) (*Pragmatic Impairment* 67)

In this case the therapist compensated for the lack of understanding by becoming more directive. Since the tutor's tutor training encouraged her to be non-directive, she was hesitant to take on this more directive role, even when misunderstood. Instead she answers with another comment—"It's kind of long,"—presumably a hint to revise the sentence, and then compensates for the tutee's lack of understanding by directing her on how to revise the sentence. Even then, though, she does so indirectly ("I think you can . . . ").

Pragmatic impairment can also involve unusual or incorrect use of words. In the following excerpt, the tutor compensates for the tutee's semantic slip when talking about the analysis of the book she was reading:

TUTEE: It wasn't vague enough.
TUTOR: I'm—It was vague?
TUTEE: It was.

The tutor at first begins speaking, realizes what the tutee has said, and then compensates by reformulating the utterance correctly. Often the tutee attempts to get what she needs by asking questions, such as turning the tutor's statements around into questions. For instance,

TUTOR: You're not making it clear.
TUTEE: Well, how can I make it clear?

She does this several times, and sometimes gets real answers that help her write her paper. Perkins indicates that this type of repetition, or "echolalia," is actually a very productive device. Also in the session they engage in meta-discourse about how to proceed, and the tutee begins to explain her problem and what she needs:

TUTOR: I'm trying to help you. . . . What would you have me do?
TUTEE: I don't know. Just read it and let me know what you think or something.
TUTOR: I'm, I'm trying—
TUTEE: You're not telling me, though.

Perkins does not mention the capacity of the impaired person to be able to step back and explain the type of interaction and compensation that would be most useful. In an interview, the tutee told me that she asked questions because she wanted to learn and that she liked it when the tutors would give "tips," and she wished the tutor would "explain more." She told me she liked the way her other tutors would push her and give her lots of ideas to write about. With this tutor, she said, "Like if she's not, like, explaining stuff to me, I get kind of like, confused." Meta-discourse— either during or after the session—surrounding odd or frustrating tutoring sessions would be productive, as would tutors realizing that an impaired person was not trying to be difficult or resistant but simply had difficulties communicating.

Again, in normal conversation, the unimpaired partner will likely compensate for the impaired member of the pair. However, in tutoring, tutor training may pro-scribe these behaviors. In most cases in my observed sessions, the tutor compensated for the tutee's impairment, but could have been more direct in her explanations of *what* she wanted the tutee to do and *why* she was asking particular questions.

Perkins makes some suggestions about ways that an interlocutor can scaffold for a person with discourse-related pragmatic impairment:

- Provide backchannel feedback and encouragement
- Ask questions to help person focus
- Reformulate utterances to provide model sentences
- "Provide a linguistic formulation when [the person] is only able to produce a gesture." (*Pragmatic* 137)

The tutor compensated in several ways, such as asking questions, although she could have explained better to the tutee what the questions were for. And she did help the tutee reformulate an utterance from "It was too vague" to "It was vague." I did not observe much backchannelling,[4] except for a few instances of "OK," and the tutor did not provide any linguistic formulations in response to a gesture.

Terese Thonus, in an article on tutoring second-language writers in the writing center, introduces a concept that I recommend for tutors working with students with disabilities that interfere with pragmatic understanding. This is the Illocutionary Force Indicating Device (IFID). Thonus found that with non-native speaking tutees and native speaking tutors, the use of IFIDs "may increase the comprehensibility of tutor suggestions" (275), since non-native speakers may misunderstand pragmatic cues due to cultural differences (rather than impairments). In traditional linguistics, these devices include facial expression, pauses, intonation, and discourse markers. But since individuals with pragmatic impairments have difficulty understanding these aspects (Perkins "Pragmatic Impairment" 229), tutors can use an explicit IFID. Some of the more explicit IFIDs that Thonus observed native-English speaking tutors using with non-native English speaking tutees were, "I have to recommend that you do it this way," and "That's just a suggestion" (274).

In the tutoring sessions I observed, when the tutor asked the tutee to tell her what happened to David, and the tutee answered, "You have to read the story," the tutor replied, "I don't have to read the story, I have to read your paper." This response is still rather indirect and leaves the interlocutor to infer that she, as the writer, needs to determine the needed material and then put the material into the paper. The tutor could have explained, "I am asking these questions to help you come up with ideas about what to put in the paper." Although this may seem obvious to people with un-impaired pragmatic processing abilities, these types of statements will assist those tutees who do not perceive the speaker's meaning behind an utterance.

Oftentimes, in the name of "non-directive" tutoring, tutors will utter open-ended questions, but the actual intention is directive. This can be seen in the following example when the tutor says, "Why do you think David lied to Joey?" She is not curious, but she is attempting to direct the tutee to write the answer in her paper. The tutor goes on to say, "That's an analysis, telling me why." She could have also added, "You need to take the answers to these questions and write about them in your paper." This would have explained to the tutee explicitly what the questions and answers were for. In the actual tutorial, the tutee insisted on referring the tutor to the book to read the answers to her questions. This caused the tutor frustration, and perhaps even caused her to misinterpret the tutee's misunderstanding as outright sassiness:

> TUTOR: [reads from Squirt's paper] Why? Why do you think David lied to Joey? That's an analysis, telling me why.
> TUTEE: Well, because they're not friends anymore.
> TUTOR: Why are they not friends anymore?
> TUTEE: Because, you know, about that incident that they had. You know, it's on the first page.
> TUTOR: I know. But [name, name], stop, stop, stop, stop. OK. We gotta get through this.

For people with unimpaired pragmatic processing it's hard to comprehend how frustrating it must be to be on the other end of non-directive tutoring.

I recommend that tutor trainers explain what pragmatic impairment is and for tutors to be on the lookout for tutees taking statements and questions extremely literally or using words in ways that seem wrong or strange from a semantic or syntactic standpoint. In this way, tutors can be aware of sessions that seem frustrating, where the tutee gives odd answers or seems resistant to give the type of answers the tutor is trying to elicit.[5] In these possible cases of pragmatic impairment, the tutor can try an explicit Illocutionary Force Indicating Device or other compensatory moves and tell the tutee the intent behind the utterance in addition to engaging in meta-discourse about the communication in the tutoring session. Finally, tutor trainers should be aware that sometimes compensation for a disability will involve offering a word or words for a tutee or being very direct about what needs to happen in the tutoring session. Consideration of these factors will help immeasurably in meeting the needs of tutees with pragmatic impairment and others who learn differently.

NOTES

1. This research was funded in part by grants from IWCA and Rock Valley Foundation.
2. Non-directive tutoring as writing center lore has been discussed by Isabelle Thompson and colleagues, and the practice has been problematized by Linda Shamoon and Deborah Burns.
3. It is also known as pragmatic disorder, pragmatic disability, and semantic-pragmatic disorder.
4. Backchannels are short responses in conversation that do not involve a conversational turn, but rather provide encouragement to the speaker or confirm that the listener is following along. Common backchannel responses are "Right," "OK," or "Yeah."
5. Tutors should use caution and tact, and remember that only trained professionals may attempt to diagnose a disability. People interested in learning more about this topic should read *Pragmatic Impairment* by Michael Perkins.

WORKS CITED

Babcock, Rebecca Day. "Research-Based Tutoring Tips for Working with Deaf Students." *Kansas English*, 93.1 (2009): 73–98. Print.

Boudreaux, Marjory A. "Toward Awareness: A Study of Nonverbal Behavior in the Writing Conference." Diss. Indiana University of Pennsylvania, 1998. DAI 59.1145. Print.

Grice, [H.] Paul. *Studies in the Way of Words*. Cambridge: Harvard UP, 1991. Print.

Kiedaisch, Jean and Sue Dinitz. "Learning More from the Students." *The Writing Center Journal* 12.1 (1991): 90–100. Web. 26 May 2010.

Murphy, Susan W. "Politeness and Self-Presentation in Writing Center Discourse." Diss. Texas A&M University. 2001. DAI 62 (11A) 3766. Print.

Perkins, Mick [Michael]. "Clinical Pragmatics." *Handbook of Pragmatics*. Ed. Jef Verschueren, Jan-Ola Blommaert, and Chris Bulcaen. Amsterdam: John Benjamins, 2001. 1–29. Print.

———. "Pragmatic Ability and Disability as Emergent Phenomena." *Clinical Linguistics & Phonetics* 19 (2005): 367–77. Print.

———. *Pragmatic Impairment*. Cambridge: Cambridge UP, 2007. Print.

———. "Pragmatic Impairment" *The Handbook of Language and Speech Disorders*. Ed. Jack S. Damico, Nicole Müller, and Martin J. Ball. West Sussex, UK: Wiley, 2010. 227–46. *Google Books Search*. Web. 20 April 2010.

Shamoon, Linda K. and Deborah H. Burns. "A Critique of Pure Tutoring." *The Writing Center Journal* 15.2 (1995): 134–51.

Thompson, Isabelle, et al. "Examining Our Lore: A Survey of Students' and Tutors' Satisfaction with Writing Center Conferences." *The Writing Center Journal* 29.1 (2009). 78–105.

Thonus, Terese. "How to Communicate Politely and Be a Tutor, Too." *Text* 19.2 (1999): 253–79. Print.

van Balkom, Hans and Ludo Verhoeven. "Pragmatic Disability in Children with Specific Language Impairments." *Classification of Developmental Language Disorders: Theoretical Issues and Clinical Implications*. Ed. Ludo Verhoeven and Hans von Balkom. Mahwah, NJ: Lawrence Erlbaum, 2004. 283–305. *NetLibrary*. Web. 15 April 2010.

Wewers, Jennifer. "Writing Tutors and Dyslexic Tutees: Is There Something Special We Should Know?" *Working with Student Writers*. Ed. Leonard A. Podis and JoAnne M. Podis. New York: Peter Lang, 1999. 229–37. Print.

Young, Virginia. "Politeness Phenomena in the University Writing Conference." Diss. University of Illinois Chicago, 1992. Print.

Safe Houses and Contact Zones: Reconsidering the Basic Writing Tutorial

Brooke Baker

Brooke Baker was an undergraduate at the University of Michigan–Flint when she wrote this article. It originally appeared in the journal *Young Scholars in Writing*.

In addition to conventional one-on-one tutoring, the University of Michigan–Flint writing center is involved in a second kind of tutorial with our basic writing program, English 109. Students in English 109 are generally unprepared for the writing tasks expected from the university. These students register for three credits of English 109 and meet with an instructor twice weekly in a classroom setting, which is supplemented with four hours spent in the writing center tutorial. Students work with the same tutor throughout the semester, creating a portfolio of writing that is specific to the writing center (that is, not the work done in the classroom component of English 109), which is then graded by the tutor, in conjunction with the center's manager and director. These students are what the discipline tends to call "basic writers."

I have spent five years as a writing tutor at the University of Michigan–Flint. There is an advantage to this longevity in that I have learned a great deal about writers and writing, and I have become comfortable with the ways and processes of tutoring that new tutors are still learning. The disadvantage is that while I have become comfortable in this space, I have also become, to an extent, complacent. This complacency manifests itself, at times, as both rigidity and authority—in the sense that I know how to do this, I know how it has always been done, and I am, therefore, the one who knows all about tutoring. Because I began to see these thoughts and behaviors affecting my tutorials, I started looking for new ways to approach the tutorial, particularly in the work that I do with basic writers.

One of the ideas that appealed was that of the contact zone—a place in which student and tutor could meet and clash; a space in which to try on language and form without the fear of failure that often accompanies these students, who are new to the formal expectations of academic discourse. In particular, I wanted an approach that would be applicable to those basic writers who come into the academy knowing intuitively, if not overtly, that they are underprepared for college writing. These are the students who often speak and write in a home dialect, and usually have little experience with the more formal language expected from the academy. My experience has shown that for these writers, the voice of the learned peer is of particular value. Our peerhood positions us somewhere between the voice of authority that is the classroom instructor and the more equal place of the peer responder who comes to a response group wary of making enemies. Our value in the tutorial comes from the fact that although we are students, we have gained some mastery of the conventions of formal writing.

Given that this learned peer status gives us some small authority, and given that I think it is vitally important for new writers to understand the structural and linguistic expectations of this academic discourse they are choosing to learn, simply offering a safe place to try new moves and strategies isn't always enough. Instead, we need to demystify just what this language is, and one of the ways of doing this is through using a contact zone strategy.

BASIC WRITING AT UNIVERSITY OF MICHIGAN–FLINT

At my university, students are placed into English 109 based on their performance on the Writing Proficiency Exam (WPX). WPX readers evaluate student essays based on certain criteria, including organization (how thoughts are organized around the central idea), coherence (the ability to smoothly connect thoughts from sentence to sentence and paragraph to paragraph), development (ability to thoroughly explain an idea in writing), and control (ability to successfully manage the rules of basic written English).

Although our placement criteria are standard, definitions of basic writers are manifold and often in conflict. One of these is set out by Linda Stine, who argues that "[b]asic writing students [are] typically older, poorer, less apt to come from stable, highly educated families, and more apt to have learning disabilities" (51). This contrasts with Kenneth Bruffee's description: "The common denominator among both the poorly prepared and the seemingly well-prepared [is] that . . . all these students seem to have difficulty adapting to the traditional or 'normal' conventions of the college classroom" (85). While my experience with basic writers in the 109 tutorial suggests that these are both true, neither seems wholly definitive. In my experience, the first is too narrow, the second too broad.

One of the advantages of being a tutor rather than a teacher is that the tutorial can engender a relationship that allows us to get to know our students' histories and goals. What I have observed over time is that although each of these writers comes with unique skills and backgrounds, there are two primary camps. The first is made up of those who come from homes, often nontraditional, often working class, in which they are the first to graduate from high school, and don't have family or peers who understand the drive toward higher education. The second is comprised of those who don't want to attend college, but have families who have pushed them in this direction.

Not surprisingly, the challenges facing these writers are wildly divergent. The first group faces the difficulty of learning this new discourse without a place outside of the university to practice it. The second resists the discourse because they aren't where they want to be—they need to be pushed toward this thing that they don't really want, and their motivation for doing so is primarily external, meaning that the tutors who work with these students often face struggles simply getting them to try to write.

Regardless of a student's goals and background, the primary goal of English 109 has traditionally been to give writers a space in which to practice writing. During the course of the semester, students generate a large quantity of writing, some of it in essay form, some in less traditional academic forms. Because tutors work in small groups, we have the advantage of guiding each writer according to his or her needs. In this process, we have typically followed a fluid sequence of assignments in our 109 tutorials. We begin with what we call fluency—the act of simply getting the words onto the page, without focusing too narrowly on grammar, mechanics, or specific language issues. The reasoning is that if we can get our writers to just *write,* then we have opened one of the first channels of thinking in written language—a Peter Elbow concept that very often works in the tutorial.

Once we are convinced that our writers are capable of and confident about putting thoughts on paper, we move into summarizing short stories or articles. From here, we progress to analysis, and somewhere in the mix we talk about thesis statements, textual support, and other features of good academic writing. Our primary argument for following this format is that each type of assignment builds on the previous so that by the end of the semester the student has created a portfolio of increasingly more complex writing.

THE BASIC WRITING TUTORIAL AS A SAFE HOUSE

In our tutor-training seminar, we read and discuss composition and collaborative theory in preparation for the work we do with writers. At the time that I went through the training, our dominant pedagogical focus was on the process and practice of appointment tutoring. The ways and ideas of the 109 tutorial were handed down from mentor-tutor to new tutor in a predominantly oral tradition.

The focus, then, was on how we could make the writing center a safe space for practicing writing. The basic writing tutorial was process-focused and heavily reliant on a drawer full of writing prompts like "My Mother's Kitchen," which asked for lots and lots of detail about one's mother's kitchen. Descriptive assignments like this one would lead, eventually, to other, more complex writing tasks. In this kind of tutorial, it was the tutor's primary responsibility to encourage writing, to point out positive aspects of the writing, and to foster a sense of success in her writers. I have often thought of myself as a cheerleader, motivating new and often cautious writers to keep trying new things as I avoided being particularly critical about what they had done before. Many, possibly even most, students tutored under this approach leave the center feeling that they have gained, if not a complete mastery of the writing process, at least a reduction in the panic they feel when faced with a new writing task.

Why, if this approach to tutoring seems to help many new writers, do I feel compelled to move away from it? The answer comes when I look at my notes from earlier tutorials and find that creating a strictly supportive environment can sometimes fail my writers. They may pick up some grammar skills, may learn to write an effective short essay, may gain some mastery of writing more complex texts, but more often than not, it seems to be a stopgap measure in that their fundamental thinking about writing, and particularly about the writing expectations of the university, still remains unchanged.

The potential weakness of a purely supportive approach, then, lies in its inability to get at some of the deeper issues that basic writers confront. Although many of these students face some larger, deeper challenges rooted in their socioeconomic and cognitive backgrounds, the ones that I, as a tutor, am most equipped to address are primarily superficial and related to language usage. These include limited linguistic acclimation to the institution, limited understanding of one's audience and that audience's expectations, and still-limited experience with formal written English. The latter particularly concerns me because there is the sense, often, that there is a particular educated discourse "that classifies non-standard dialects as incorrect and that positions non-standard speakers as not competent, uneducated, wrong, or even cognitively deficient" (Maxson 27). I begin to feel that in order to move toward larger academic expectations of competency we must move away from being merely supportive in the tutorial.

In truth, I struggle against my own inclinations. The literature of composition offers many debates about home dialect, particularly as it detracts from the acculturation of basic writers to the writing expectations of the university. Some compositionists, such as Linda Adler-Kassner and Susanmarie Harrington, Jeffrey Maxson, Donald McCrary, and Mike Rose, make a compelling argument that expecting new writers to fully embrace this new academic dialect is tantamount to requiring that they remove themselves from the things that tie them to their homes and cultures—giving up the home dialect in favor of one that is more academic changes more than just the words we speak. It changes who we are.

From a purely rhetorical perspective, I embrace this idea, this understanding that unsophisticated writing does not equal unsophisticated thought. I have spent too many hours in too many tutorials with writers who could speak articulately and in depth about a subject which, when the pen is in hand, or the fingers are on the keyboard, escapes capture into written form. What these writers are keenly aware of, and what I, from my position as a tutor who has read many assignment sheets from many professors cannot ignore is that while this home dialect is all well and good, the inescapable expectation is that students will come into their history or biology or nursing class with the ability to write and speak and think in formalized, academic language.

THE BASIC WRITING TUTORIAL AS A CONTACT ZONE

The contact zone, as Mary Louise Pratt defines it, is a place where "cultures meet, clash, and grapple with each other, often in contexts of highly asymmetrical relations of power" (34). Its application in the classroom has been documented by compositionists such as Patricia Bizzell, Mark Williams and Gladys Garcia, and Jeffrey Maxson, each of whom notes the value of this approach in helping underprepared students find their place in and master the literacy of the contemporary academy. For Bizzell, the contact zone manifests itself in a Friereian push toward critical consciousness, while Williams's focus is more closely linked to breaking down the insider/outsider distinctions that lie in much of the discourse. For each, one of the unexpected consequences of using the contact zone in the classroom has often been a challenging of authority and the notions of critical consciousness. As Maxson points out, "the contact zone can open up clashes between teacher and student cultures" (2).

Because contact zone pedagogy so clearly opens up lines of confrontation, I initially didn't see its application to writing center practice. It was only after discovering Maxson's approach of solicited oppositional discourse, or a modified variant of the contact zone, that I began to consider its application to the tutorial. In his "'Government of da Peeps, for da Peeps, and by da Peeps': Revisiting the Contact Zone," Maxson suggests ways to make oppositional discourse less personal, thereby reducing the potential for confrontation. The benefits of this approach, he suggests, are first, that it allows basic writers to "tell the stories of their encounters with formal language and how they have or have not made places for themselves in settings where formal language is the norm" and second, that, as Pratt suggests, this approach creates a place where "language users [can] write (or talk) themselves into and through unfriendly language environments" (25). When we work with basic writers in the intensely personal tutorial, these are two things that we can do, and do well. We have the time and the involvement to listen even as we encourage and direct. My faculty advisor argues that good teachers will do the same, and while I know experientially that this is true, I suggest that the tutor-tutee relationship is different in that even the most involved teacher cannot develop the same close relationship that we can.

We have in this tutor-tutee relationship the unique advantage of being learned peers, rather than teachers. The "learned" distinction is an important one in that, as Muriel Harris points out, "[t]utors are supposed to be . . . better acquainted with the conventions of academic discourse . . . but the more skilled tutors are, the further they are from being peers in a collaborative relationship." Although we are peers, we are seen by our writers as "knowledgeable insiders" despite our continuing struggles to master the language of the academy (379).

Like our basic writers, we still wrestle with academic language and "ways of knowing." "Education," as Bruffee insists, "properly speaking, is an initiation into the skill and partnership of [an academic] conversation in which we learn to recognize the voices, to distinguish the proper occasions of utterance and in which we acquire the intellectual and moral habits appropriate to the conversation" (87). As tutors, we are learning to enter the conversation, and we consistently work toward this entrance by writing and talking about writing among ourselves and with other writers. Certainly, we tutors have gained more experience and have had more practice with the expectations of the academy. And because we are still working toward entrance into this knowledge community, we are positioned to help facilitate the basic writer's transition into formalized language usage. We are close to the process.

Our academic literacy is one of the most important things tutors can share with our tutees. We have learned to speak the language(s) of the academy despite our divergent backgrounds, and because we speak and write the language, and because we work so closely with our writers, we have the ability, via peerhood, to impact the language choices of our writers.

Pratt visualizes a classroom that examines differences rather than marginalizes them, a place that is nonauthoritian, in which students with different ideas, different languages, and different voices come together in often conflicting ways. Her argument is that by giving each voice "air," collective, collaborative meaning can be made. Often the meaning may not be what the authoritarian teacher would choose or suggest or advocate, but it is meaning nonetheless, and therefore of value. Also, because these conversations lead to collective (socially constructed) meaning, participants in the conversation come away with a deeper understanding of those meanings. And if we are examining ways of making collective, socially constructed knowledge—as Bruffee tells us we must—then the collision course that can be the contact zone is one such place for this meaning making.

I first attempted this contact zone strategy during the winter of 2006—the same time that I began grappling with my own questions about the effectiveness of safehouse tutoring. As I was researching the ideas of academic languages and university expectations, my ideas began to take shape and become part of my practice. The advantage of winter is that it is a slow 109 semester, and I had only one student with whom I started discussing my research and my questions. I was fortunate in that she was amenable to trying new, potentially useless ideas, and that she was willing to openly discuss her ideas and reactions to these new assignments.

In this section, I will discuss how I approached the tutorial with this student, as well as how I have begun trying new kinds of writing assignments with my writers in fall 2006. This practice is evolving as I take what I am learning from the tutorials and constantly searching for ways to adapt new strategies.

From my early experience, I decided that there are three interrelated elements that should be addressed in the tutorial: playing with language, arguing about meaning, and trying on language from the outside. Much of my reading has pointed toward these elements, and because I am compelled to translate theory into practice, a series of different writing assignments was born.

In particular, I began by modeling an assignment created by Maxson in his basic writing classroom. Maxson asked his student to read and then translate into home dialects passages from well-known literature: the balcony scene from *Romeo and Juliet*; Dr. Martin Luther King's "I Have a Dream" speech; Lincoln's "Gettysburg Address." What the results of this assignment showed was that many of Maxson's basic writers were wholly capable of understanding nuance and meaning, and adapting these "lofty" texts into familiar language.

In my tutorial, I asked the writer to read and translate a passage from compositionist Richard Fulkerson into everyday English. With a dictionary in hand and two hours to work on it, she ended the session by handing me a completed, readily accessible version of what was originally a heavily academic and jargon-laden text.

Taking the assignment a step further, I asked her to reverse the process with the lyrics to 50 Cent's "That Ain't Gangsta." This, curiously, was both more difficult and wholly frustrating for her. When we discussed it afterward, she explained that the first assignment was easy, that it was nothing more than "looking it up and understanding it." When it came to working with what she classified as "her" language, elevating it to something readily understood by a reader unfamiliar with that language, it proved so difficult that she gave up. The why of this leads me to questions that I have not yet been able to answer, but which I think about as I keep working with students on this contact zone strategy.

In our discussions about language, particularly the issues of academic language, my tutee remarked once, "I need you to teach me to fake it. I don't know how to write this stuff, but if I can learn to pretend to do it, I might get through." For me, this was a turning point in that I had been thinking about the idea of fakery, suspecting that if we could show our writers how to fake this new dialect, it would eventually lead to familiarity, from familiarity to comfort, and thence ultimately to knowledge. It was David Bartholomae's argument that we are expecting these new writers to speak with authority and in an unfamiliar language that had sent me in this direction—I wondered how we could have these expectations without handing over the proper tools to help writers meet them. This writer, then, gave me permission to work with her in this new direction, and this has informed much of my practice in this new semester.

To return to those ideas of playing with, arguing about, and trying on language, I began this semester by discussing the ways in which we use language, and the ways in which home and academic dialects differ. I had my writers start by defining "good writing" and then examine their own writing to determine whether it meets their criteria. From here, I asked if the way they talk in school is the same way they talk to their friends and family. The answers have been interesting.

According to one group, the features of good writing include good grammar, an interesting opening, and words that "flow." When asked if their own writing includes these elements, most answered "no." More tellingly, one answered, "I thought [my writing] was good, and I made good grades in high school English, but I don't know what my teachers here want." This points again to the need to demystify the expectations of academic writing.

The second part of my inquiry about if and how their school language is different than their home languages offered further insights. Each writer, when first asked if his or her language was different, initially answered "no." Upon further reflection and much hemming and hawing, most said, "Well, yeah. It's a lot easier to talk to my friends. I'm not worried that they'll think I'm stupid." Many expressed frustration with the fact that they hadn't yet learned to talk—and write—in the two different dialects.

Approaching this tutorial from the contact zone requires that I open a dialogue about code-shifting and academic expectations. It requires that I raise the specter of language changing the way we think and who we are. It also requires that I accept the protestations that academic discourse is boring and repetitive, and push forward regardless.

Lately, I've been having my writers create textbook entries because I think of textbooks as student-centered examples of what academic discourse looks like. I begin by having my writers list the features of textbook entries, and their lists look like this: boring language, big words, index, study questions. We then pick a topic for each writer—something he or she knows something about—and then they begin crafting their entries, with the understanding that when they are complete, they will be distributed and others will write about that entry.

As they are writing, we are talking about why the language seems dry, about why sometimes one big word is more effective than a lot of small ones that don't quite hit at the meaning they want. They are writing with dictionaries in hand and with an ear to their future readers.

In this case, the writing becomes more than just writing for writing's sake; rather, it is an exercise in meaning making, in applying new language to familiar subjects, and in learning to use this language from the outside in. What has been gratifying for me is what these writers are saying: "This is the hardest thing I've ever done. But I'm really happy with it. I didn't know I could do this." When they ask, "Do you think the others will understand what I mean by this?" I send them to the rest of the group for the answer even when I think I already know, because this writing must focus on the audience, and in the contact zone, I am not the authority. This isn't the traditional fluency-to-analysis path that we have traditionally taken, and I have had to step way back and let them figure things out for themselves, but what I see happening is a new mastery and understanding of academic dialect that I hope will translate into greater mastery in future classes.

CONCLUSION

In reality the tutorial is not, nor should it be, all contact zones all the time. Every writer needs a safe space in which to practice this craft, and the writing center should offer this, too.

Instead, contact zone elements should be part of the whole experience. As a peer, not a teacher, it falls to me as a tutor to be willing to practice the same things that my writers are doing, and when it comes to giving up authority, this isn't always easy. Handing over control of text and language is a struggle because, due to my learned peer status, I know how to write formally, I know how to construct arguments and responses. It is infinitely more comfortable to take on the supportive "Let me show you what I know" role than it is to watch writers struggle. And yet when our writers struggle with this new language, when they talk among themselves about how and why academic language and writing are so "weird and different," they begin to understand the very nature of that difference. With this understanding comes new competence.

Last winter, I dared to say, "I don't know. Let's hash this out together." In the end, I changed as much as the writer did. I knew then that I was opening myself up to a relationship with the potential to affect my tutoring. At times, I struggled to let go of my own knowledge and let the student find her own way through formal writing. In the end, she left the center not only better and more confident as a writer, but also more assured of her own ability to navigate the university.

WORKS CITED

Adler-Kassner, Linda, and Susanmarie Harrington. *Basic Writing as a Political Act.* Cresskill, NJ: Hampton, 2002. Print.

Bartholomae, David. "Inventing the University." Wiley, Gleason, and Phelps 460–79. Print.

Bizzell, Patricia. "Contact Zones and English Studies." *College English* 56 (1994): 163–70. Print.

———. "What Happens When Basic Writers Come to College." *College Composition and Communication* 37 (1986): 294–301. Print.

Bruffee, Kenneth. "Collaborative Learning and the 'Conversation of Mankind.'" Wiley, Gleason, and Phelps 84–97. Print.

Elbow, Peter. *Writing without Teachers.* Oxford: Oxford UP, 1973. Print.

Harris, Muriel. "Collaboration Is Not Collaboration Is Not Collaboration: Writing Center Tutorials vs. Peer-Response Groups." *College Composition and Communication* 43 (1992): 369–83. Print.

Maxson, Jeffrey. "'Government of da Peeps, for da Peeps, and by da Peeps': Revisiting the Contact Zone." *Journal of Basic Writing* 24 (2005): 24–47. Print.

McCrary, Donald. "Represent, Representin,' Representation: The Efficacy of Hybrid Texts in the Writing Classroom." *Journal of Basic Writing* 24 (2005): 72–91. Print.

Pratt, Mary Louise. "Arts of the Contact Zone." *Profession* 91 (1991): 33–40. Print.

Rose, Mike. *Lives on the Boundary: A Moving Account of the Struggles and Achievements of America's Educational Underclass.* New York: Penguin, 1989. Print.

———. "Remedial Writing Courses: A Critique and a Proposal." *College English* 45 (1983): 109–28. Print.

Stine, Linda. "The Best of Both Worlds: Teaching Basic Writers in Class and Online." *Journal of Basic Writing* 23 (2004): 49–69. Print.

Wiley, Mark, Barbara Gleason, and Louise Wetherbee Phelps, eds. *Composition in Four Keys: Inquiring into the Field.* Mountain View, CA: Mayfield, 1996. Print.

Williams, Mark T., and Gladys Garcia. "Crossing Academic Cultures: A Rubric for Students and Teachers." *Journal of Basic Writing* 25 (2005): 93–119. Print.

Groupies and Singletons: Student Preferences in Classroom-Based Writing Consulting

Alicia Brazeau

Alicia Brazeau was an undergraduate at Grand Valley State University when she wrote this article. It originally appeared in the journal *Young Scholars in Writing*.

At Grand Valley State University, the writing center offers its services in two ways: both in the actual center and in the entry-level writing classrooms themselves.[1] In the writing center, students have the opportunity to meet with writing tutors in an academic environment outside of the classroom. Some students come because their professors have requested that they workshop a paper or have offered special credit to those who make use of the writing center. Most students, however, come voluntarily, either for a weekly one-hour tutorial with a specific consultant or for a brief session with a consultant during the time designated for "walk-in" appointments. Both types of tutorials offered in the writing center are open to all students, regardless of the type of class they are taking.

Within the classroom, writing consultants' time is split between one-on-one consultations and group tutorials. Once each week, consultants work with students in the computer lab while they are engaged in the writing process. During the other class session, consultants meet with small groups of students to discuss their writing and coordinate peer response groups. As a result of the class structure, some writing students have the chance to work on their papers in both environments.

For me and other consultants, working with first-year writing students both in groups and on an individual basis during class time can often feel like two completely different tasks; the group dynamic varies greatly, thus altering the manner in which students and consultants approach the writing session. A student may react one way to response given by the consultant during a group session, then react in another way to similar response given by the same consultant during an individual meeting. While certain students seem to respond more positively to group meetings, where the advice of the consultant is tempered by discussion and opinions of a group of fellow classmates, other students prefer to work privately with a consultant and may in fact be quieter and less inclined to participate during a group tutorial.

As a writing consultant who works with students in both settings, I wanted to explore how students' preferences for individual or group tutoring might affect their experiences with writing consultants. Since student participation is an important component of any successful writing tutorial, I wondered to what degree student perceptions of group and individual meetings might alter the usefulness of those sessions. I reasoned that the difference in the nature of group and individual settings might also affect the type of response offered, whether content, focus, organization, or mechanics. More specifically, I wanted to discover if students felt that group sessions handled a certain kind of response more effectively than an individual tutorial. Interestingly, there is little research on this topic.

In this article, I discuss the findings of my research into these significant questions.[2] The responses I received demonstrate that students' experiences with writing consultants correlate directly with their perceptions of both the manner in which the tutorial is conducted and the possible success of that writing session. Thus, there was little agreement as to which setting focused more successfully on which type of response or which setting was more dependent on consultants' questions. Each student's preference, borne out of previous experience, consistently paralleled his or her belief in the make-up of writing tutorials. In short, the results from the surveys and interviews seemed to indicate that both in-class programs offered meaningful writing support.

BACKGROUND

In GVSU's required, entry-level writing course, Writing 150, consultant visits are arranged according to each professor's preference. Writing consultants can take part in small group meetings during classroom time, assist students during the class's period in the computer lab, or both. The small group sessions, though chosen by the professor, are mandatory for students. Generally meeting for an hour each week, these group meetings vary according to paper topics and the individuals forming the group, but they often involve brainstorming; reading and discussing drafts for content, structure, and mechanical issues; or discussing citation guidelines or course assignments.

Because the students and consultant meet regularly and each session is discussion-based, these group tutorials allow for the development of peer relationships. Although her focus is on individual writing tutorials, Muriel Harris addresses the importance of peer and consultant interaction with writing students as a means of promoting writing-based discussion in an environment free from the higher authority of the professor, claiming that "writers both need and want discussion that engages them actively with their ideas through talk and permits them to stay in control" (31). These weekly group meetings in Writing 150, then, create a setting where students, currently sharing a similar writing experience in the classroom, can wield control over the discussion and formulate responses integral to the writing process. At the same time, they have the guidance and advice of the consultant who "inhabits a world somewhere between student and teacher" (28). Indeed, as a group tutorial is constructed around the conversation of its members, students retain a great degree of control over the meeting; the personality of the group as a whole often determines the manner in which the sessions are run and can influence the students' and the consultant's experience and comfort level. Shyer students, for instance, can open up more to discussions and become more willing to share their papers as the members of the group begin to develop a relationship and the group as a whole begins "to talk more freely and more honestly because they are not in the confines of a teacher/student relationship" (28). Ultimately, this group dynamic plays a critical role in the writing tutorial, causing some students' experiences in writing groups to differ widely from one-on-one conferences.

The consultants' time in the computer lab, on the other hand, is generally spent in impromptu one-on-one tutorials and, perhaps more often, in simply answering students' questions and talking with them about various aspects of their papers and assignments. While some students seek out help in the lab on a voluntary basis, consultants more frequently have to approach many students to offer help because students do not always initiate conversations. Nonetheless, consultants' presence in the lab allows them to aid students during the actual composing process and, due to the informal nature of the meeting, engage in open and personal interaction with the students. It is this flexibility of interaction that Harris argues "permits a close look at the individual student" (29). Harris views this from within the confines of the writing center itself, but the consultants' time in the computer lab only serves to further expand the possibility for this type of interaction: students and consultants are able to meet much more frequently and on a regular basis and in the immediacy of writing for class. Moreover, students who might not be inclined to go to the writing center are given the chance to work with a consultant on an individual basis and, as with the group meetings, develop a relationship with that consultant.

The time with the consultants in computer labs and in group meetings also supports Kenneth Bruffee's concept in "Peer Tutoring and the 'Conversation of Mankind'" of the relationship between reflective thought as a part of writing and social conversation. Bruffee argues that this writing-oriented peer conversation, which is "emotionally involved, intellectually and substantively focused, and personally interested," ought to be employed at "as many points in the writing process as possible" (91). Thus, both group and individual conferences with the writing consultants in the classroom allow students to engage frequently in the kind of conversation to which Bruffee refers. Clearly, tutorials in the classroom and labs offer the same type of conversation Bruffee advocates is an integral part of work in the writing center; the consultants' presence in the classroom increases the frequency and alters the nature of the interaction. The labs, especially, allow the consultants to draw students into conversations about their writing while they are in the process of composing, thus blending reflective thought and conversation.

METHODOLOGY

Because the Writing 150 students who took part in this study worked with consultants in small groups during their class time and also met with consultants during their time in the computer lab, they experienced both environments. Each of the three

Writing 150 classes I surveyed consisted of approximately 28 students; five consultants worked with groups of approximately five students. There were also two consultants during the lab time each week. For two of the classes I researched, the two consultants present in the lab were also group leaders in the same class. My survey focused on students' experiences working with consultants in their classrooms. The survey not only addressed each student's preference but also sought information on their most successful writing tutorial: the setting, the focus of the response, and the effect of the setting on the session. Additionally, the survey inquired about the type of help offered most often in individual and group sessions, the environment in which the student felt more comfortable reading his or her paper and most actively participated, and in which setting the consultants asked more questions. Ultimately, seventy Writing 150 students completed the survey. (See Appendix A for a copy of the questionnaire.)

I also conducted follow-up interviews with five students to obtain more in-depth answers to their survey questions.[3] Finally, my observations, coupled with my own experience working with students both in groups and in individual tutorials, provided a foundation for this research.

RESULTS AND ANALYSIS

Significantly, 45% of the students in the survey specified that they found both environments—group and one-on-one consultation—to be equally helpful. Still, 58% indicated that they preferred to work in consultant-led groups and 41% stated that they would rather work with the consultant individually. Citing their most successful or influential session with a writing consultant, the students' responses correspond, almost exactly, with their preferences: for 56% that session took place in a group setting and for 44% that session took place working individually with the consultant. In fact, 75% of the students who prefer to work in groups indicated that their most successful writing session took place in a group; 71% of the students who prefer to work individually likewise indicated that their most successful writing session took place in a one-on-one tutorial. In addition, 76% of the students felt that the setting influenced the success of the experience.

Survey results also highlighted students' perceptions of the type of feedback offered in both individual tutorials and groups. Referencing their most successful experience with a writing consultant, whether in a group or individual setting, 34% of the students responded that the session focused on content, while 65% indicated that the session centered on organization and focus, and only 1% answered that it focused on grammar and mechanics. Interestingly, both the group and individual sessions maintain these same percentages: 32% of the most successful group session focused on content, while 67% focused on organization and only 5% focused on mechanics, and 31% of the most successful individual tutorials focused on content, while 68% focused on organization. That the results for the type of response offered in the most successful sessions in both group and individual settings so closely parallel the general results for the type of response offered in successful writing tutorials implies that, for this group of students, both group and individual tutorials offer substantive feedback.

Likewise, in the interviews, there was no agreement on which environment better concentrated on which type of feedback, but rather, as with the surveys, all students seemed to find that their preferred setting best offered the type of help they most needed. One student, Jane, for example, who prefers to work individually, expressed that one-on-one tutorials frequently focused on organization, the issue with which she felt she most often needed help.[4] Conversely, Jennifer, another student who is partial to working alone with the consultant, asserted that individual sessions better concentrate on the area of content, but that this was by her choice.

The same pattern held true for the students who prefer to work in groups. These students indicated that the group setting allowed them to get feedback and ideas, not just from the consultant, but from their peers as well, which they found particularly helpful. One student argued that the group setting is better because it "seems to generate more ideas [and] it's easier for a group of kids to talk together with the consultant keeping them on topic and giving them questions so they have more to talk about." This belief was echoed by many other students, who similarly commented that they felt the "group setting is more successful because everyone views the writing from a different perspective," and they liked the "multiple ideas from diverse students."

The multiplicity of perspectives and ideas present in the group was acknowledged in the survey by the students who preferred to work individually, but they all agreed that working with the consultant individually helped them to avoid the distractions and the feelings of being overwhelmed with the responses they found in many of their group meetings. These students repeatedly stated that they felt the individual sessions allowed them to stay focused on the details of their essay; in fact, the words "focus," "specific details," and "personal" were echoed in the statements of the students who preferred to work individually. One student remarked that "with the individual session I got feedback on just my paper and was able to ask more specific questions on my paper."

The interviews also echoed the comments written on the surveys about the nature of the environment created by group and individual meetings. The students interviewed consistently maintained that the group meetings often felt more informal while the individual tutorials were more formal and focused more closely on the paper itself. The students who prefer working individually liked the closer focus, frequently mentioning that this close attention prevented them from feeling distracted. Jennifer, for example, felt that in an individual tutorial she "got more work done because [she] actually did the work instead of talking with [her] friends . . . [she] got more attention." Jennifer, as well as Jane, also claimed to prefer the individualized attention on the specific style of writing and personal challenges.

Likewise, the students who prefer group sessions stated that they enjoyed the more informal environment because they found it more comfortable. Anne, for example, expressed that these meetings are "not always by the book, [they are] more informal." Anne and the other interviewed students emphasized that in groups the attention and focus is more broadly based; they felt that the group meetings tended to be more discussion oriented, with several peers all participating and sharing the attention, rather than focused on any single person. The students who prefer groups noted that they appreciated receiving many different points of view and benefited from the sense of shared experience that permeated the group sessions. One student, Lindsay, stated that the relationships built in the small groups helped her to share her paper; she claimed that it helped if those around her knew her personally and already had an understanding of what she was trying to say so that they could offer advice for how to explain her ideas to others.

Another important finding is that 58% of the students most actively participate in the setting of their preference. It is reasonable to conclude that the willingness of the student to participate affects not only the success of the writing tutorial but also the content on which that session focuses. It is probable that a session with a consultant, in either setting, will more likely focus on the type of help the students themselves feel they need the most if those students actively participate in the meeting. Harris cites the importance of this active participation on the part of the student and the focused attention on the part of the consultant in her assertion that during writing tutorials, "the conversation is free to roam in whatever direction the student and tutor see as useful" (29).

Interestingly, while 41% of the students who took the survey claimed to prefer to work with the writing consultant on an individual basis, most do not frequently seek out the consultant in the writing labs; 45% of all students admitted that they almost never asked for help and 50% only do so sporadically. Nonetheless, according to these students' written comments, the participation of the writing consultant in the class and lab is most beneficial to them.

Additionally, most of the students surveyed indicated that they felt that the consultant asked more questions in the setting of their preference. 82% of the students who preferred to work individually with the consultant felt that consultants also asked more questions in an individual setting. Similarly, 67% of the students who prefer to work in groups feel that consultants asked more questions in a group setting.

However, all the students interviewed agreed that consultants asked more questions during an individual tutorial. Significantly, a few students remarked that consultants asked a great many questions in all situations but that they felt that these questions were more noticeable during an individual meeting. A number of the students who would rather work in groups stressed that the questions asked during individual tutorials were often not as helpful for them because they were so busy trying to find the "right" answer that they could not pay close attention to the discussion of their paper. Here, Lindsay admitted that when alone with the consultant she found that "if they ask [her] questions, [she's] just going to try and come up with something that will make [her] sound smart or something, and [she's] not even trying to think at all." Adam, likewise, when asked how he felt about consultants' questions in an individual tutorial, responded, "sometimes, it's like, I'm not ready to go that far right now." Students like Lindsay and Adam preferred the questions be aimed at prompting group discussion rather than be directed to any individual. The students who favor individual tutorials, on the other hand, stated that the questions helped them to think about the specifics of their own paper. Indeed, Jane claimed that the consultants "really ask you for your ideas . . . [They] help [me] get ideas by the question that they ask."

IMPLICATIONS

Based upon the results of the survey and the follow-up interviews, it appears that neither the group sessions nor the individual sessions offer any type of response or focus better than the other, but that students consistently find the kind of help they feel they need most—whether content, organization, or focus—in the setting they prefer. Since the students who participated in this study indicated that they often do not initiate writing tutorials themselves but rather rely on consultants approaching them first, the incorporation of writing center services within the classroom itself is a necessary step to expand on the number of students who benefit from working with writing consultants. These findings provide clear evidence that classroom-based writing tutoring can contribute to the development of students' writing and revising abilities. As a result, writing center directors, writing program administrators, and writing faculty should consider using both kinds of in-class tutoring in writing classes and other classes in which writing takes place.

My research has other noteworthy implications. While the classes I researched used the same consultants in weekly groups in the classroom, other arrangements might be equally helpful and allow for a greater variety of environments in which students and writing consultants could work together. In some classes, for example, consultants and group members could rotate weekly so that students get the chance to work with different peers. In other classes, consultants could be available for one-on-one consultations outside of the group at certain times. Similarly, during lab time, students' meetings with writing consultants could be incredibly casual and brief or more formalized; consultants may even have the opportunity to form a small, impromptu group within the writing lab according the immediate situation. Experimenting with different formats could provide students the opportunity to experience several different kinds of writing tutorials to find which type of session works best for them and to explore different ways of approaching the writing process with consultants and their peers.

Another option, of course, would be to incorporate group tutorials into writing centers. My research shows that for some students, group sessions are more helpful than individual conferencing. While adding group tutorials to writing center practices would only benefit those students inclined to actively seek help with their writing, it would, nonetheless, provide students not enrolled in a writing class with the opportunity to discuss their work with their peers in an academic environment. Moreover, at the times when there are more students requesting help in the center than the present consultants can handle, the use of group sessions might be a way to allow as many students as possible to receive help with their writing.

While consultants cannot necessarily change students' preferences for group or individual tutorials, consultants can listen to students' needs and partialities and fit the tutorial to address those factors. When working in a group setting, writing consultants can make a point of mentioning the availability of the writing center so that students who prefer to work alone with a writing consultant may seek out individual help on their own. Likewise, in one-on-one tutorials, consultants should keep in mind one of the main advantages of peer groups that the writing students in this study consistently mentioned: the presence of diverse ideas and responses. In this situation, consultants can suggest that students either discuss their papers with friends and peers or seek out the help of another writing consultant in order to gain a number of different perspectives. Additionally, the student and consultant could work to together to imagine ways in which other readers (their grandparents, their high school teacher, their favorite pop star) might view the writing so that, even when working individually, that student is able to benefit from multiple perspectives which are present in the group setting.

Furthermore, while Harris asserts that the interaction between consultants and students creates an environment free from "penalties for asking what [students] perceive as 'dumb' questions (the penalty being that the teacher will find out how little they know or how inept they are in formulating their questions)" (28), for some students, this anxiety over questions and answers is not completely dispelled during a conference with a consultant. Consultants should be aware of the comfort level of the students with whom they are working. Especially in an individual setting, it may be helpful for consultants to pay attention to students' reactions to questions and alter their approach accordingly. If a particular student seems to be struggling to come up with answers, it might be useful to say that the purpose of the question is to think about their paper topic or writing process. Again, if the questions do not seem to be helping a student, perhaps the concept brought up by the question could be rephrased into a statement or example.

While the data regarding the number of questions consultants ask in group and individual sessions is inconclusive, it would appear, based upon the survey at least, that consultants do not usually ask more questions individually than they do in group meetings. Perhaps it is not a matter of quantity but of prominence. Anne, in her interview, for instance, claimed that consultants ask many questions all the time, but "when they have more students to worry about, [the questions] are more like broad, a discussion." Overall, student interviews stressed the more informal and discussion-based nature of group meetings and also indicated that discussion topics and questions are generally aimed at the group as a whole rather than focused on an individual's essay. With this in mind, questions in the group setting may tend to be more rhetorical, thus causing the questions to seem fewer and less prominent because they do not necessarily require the individual student to formulate an answer. Perhaps in both settings a better way for consultants to handle questions would be to first assure students that they do not need to find a "correct" answer, or indeed any answer at all, and that all questions are merely attempts to promote thoughtful discussion.

CONCLUSION: PREFERENCES AND PERCEPTIONS

That student preferences and perceptions are not easily categorized or understood appears quite obvious and simplistic. Nonetheless, the students' responses in this study suggest that they have been influenced by their previous experiences with writing consultants, and that, respectively, this history has shaped their perception of the content and helpfulness of group and individual tutorials. For example, 80% of the students who prefer to work in groups and whose most successful session focused on content also believe that groups generally offer more help with content. Likewise, 96% of the students who prefer to work in groups and whose most successful session focused on organization also believe that groups offer more help with organization and focus. The results among students who prefer to work with the consultant individually follows suit: 78% of those whose most successful session focused on content likewise indicate that they believe that individual sessions generally offer more help on content, and 74% of those whose most successful session focused on organization feel that individual sessions generally offer more organization and focus.

It might even be deduced that these preconceptions about time with consultants influence students' willingness to participate in tutorials, which further reinforces their original opinions. This cycle of reinforcement, between experience, preference, and participation, only emphasizes for writing center administrators and scholars the importance of offering a range of approaches to writing tutorials. Constant exposure to different kinds of consultation methods might compel students to reevaluate their perceptions. Ultimately, when there are diverse options available to students for engaging with writing consultants, there is a greater chance that students will discover new ways of looking at their writing and their writing process(es).

With special thanks to Professors Ellen Schendel and Victoria Brehm for all their help on this project.

NOTES

1. In-class peer tutoring is an emerging practice in composition studies. For three interesting discussions of this practice, see Soliday; Soven ("Curriculum-Based Peer Tutoring Programs"; "Curriculum-Based Peer Tutors and WAC").
2. I received permission to conduct this research from the Human Research Review Committee at GVSU. All participants gave informed consent.
3. By coincidence rather than design, four of the five interviewees were female. This may have influenced the results of the interview in respect to the fact that, as volunteers, these particular students may have been more likely than their peers to feel comfortable working with a consultant and more willing to discuss their writing experience.
4. All names have been changed in order to protect the identity of the students I interviewed.

WORKS CITED

Bruffee, Kenneth A. "Peer Tutoring and the 'Conversation of Mankind.'" *Landmark Essays on Writing Centers.* Ed. Christina Murphy and Joe Law. Davis, CA: Hermagoras, 1995. 87–98. Print.

Harris, Muriel. "Talking in the Middle: Why Writers Need Writing Tutors." *College English* 57 (1995): 27–42. Print.

Soliday, Mary. "Shifting Roles in Classroom Tutoring: Cultivating the Art of Boundary Crossing." *The Writing Center Journal* 16.1 (1995): 59–73. Print.

Soven, Margot. "Curriculum-Based Peer Tutoring Programs: A Survey." *WPA: Writing Program Administration* 17.1–2 (1993): 58–74. Print.

———. "Curriculum-Based Peer Tutors and WAC." *WAC for the New Millennium: Strategies for Continuing Writing-Across-the-Curriculum Programs.* Ed. Susan H. McLeod, Eric Miraglia, Margot Soven, and Christopher Thaiss. Urbana: NCTE, 2001. 200–32. Print.

APPENDIX A

Survey Questions

1. Do you prefer to work with the consultant:
   a. in the group session
   b. individually

2. Based on the papers you have written and discussed thus far, which has been most helpful:
   a. working in the group
   b. working individually with the consultant
   c. both equally

3. Think back to your most successful writing session with a consultant or suggestion from a consultant that has most influenced your writing. Did this occur in:
   a. group session
   b. one-on-one with the consultant

4. Thinking back to your most successful or influential writing session with a consultant, what did the feedback/discussion focus on?
   a. content
   b. focus/organization
   c. grammar and language

5. Thinking back to your most successful or influential writing session, do you think the success of the session was influenced by the setting (group or individual)? Explain.

6. How often do you seek out one-on-one help in the lab?
   a. every class
   b. sporadically
   c. almost never

7. Do you feel more comfortable discussing your paper:
   a. in the group
   b. individually

8. In your group, which do you receive more help on:
   a. content
   b. organization/focus
   c. language/grammar

9. In the lab, which do you receive more help on:
   a. content
   b. organization/focus
   c. language/grammar

10. Where do you find it easier to actively participate:
    a. the group
    b. with the consultant individually
    c. no difference

11. Do you ever feel overwhelmed with response:
    a. in the group
    b. with the consultant alone
    c. both
    d. neither

12. Are you asked more questions by the consultant:
    a. in the group
    b. individually

Basic Literacy: Mediating Between Power Constructs

Mara Brecht

Mara Brecht was an undergraduate at Oberlin College when she wrote this article. It originally appeared in the journal *Young Scholars in Writing*.

INTRODUCTION: MOVING INTO THE PROJECT

I attend Oberlin College, which is located in Lorain County, in Northern Ohio. Lorain County, like many counties in the United States, has a program for adult education. Lorain County's Adult Basic Literacy Education classes (also known as ABLE) reach throughout the community. There are classes in church basements, schools, prisons, community centers, and health facilities; they occur anywhere people are able to gather and usually are held in the evenings. Adults who attend these programs are most often pursuing their General Education Degree (GED); some English as a Second Language (ESL) speakers come seeking help with English; and some already have a high school diploma and just want to "brush up." The ABLE classes are free; the programs are funded by the state, and, consequently, are strictly regulated and budgeted.

I am involved with an ABLE program at Lorain County's Joint Vocational School (JVS) every Tuesday and Thursday evening. During these evenings, there are three levels of classes. The students in the most advanced classes need about three to sixth months to prepare for the GED test itself. The next level class members usually need six to twelve months of preparation for the test. I work with the most basic level class. Most ABLE programs simply cannot afford to fund the level class that I tutor. My position is set up through Oberlin College; Oberlin funds most of my wage and helps buy materials for these classes. Without Oberlin College's involvement, there would be no basic level classes.

The students whom I tutor need help with very basic skills: reading, writing, and arithmetic. There is a significant gap between my class and the other two classes, as it is not uncommon for my students to work on reading a Dr. Seuss book, for example, while the students of the other classes are writing five hundred word essays and doing geometry. My class is unique.

Most of my students are middle-aged men, though I have some women and some younger students who recently left high school. They come every Tuesday and Thursday night, and we work diligently on different assignments. The work is mostly one-on-one. For example, I sit with a student, and she/he reads out loud to me. In the sessions, the differences between us become quite clear; many jokes fly around the room as they laugh, observing that I "can read" and they "cannot." There is an acute gap between my students and me. I am a student from an elite educational institution, tutoring others in the least elite educational institution. My education is valued in American society, and their education is not. This is an incredibly daunting situation. I have attempted to bridge this gap, to find creative ways for interactive learning, and to open communication about "difference." Yet, everything I do only seems to highlight the great educational and social disparities. The following paper discusses one particular learning venture I attempted in my ABLE class. I will evaluate this venture, "Literacy Letters," through various lenses: as a tutor at ABLE classes, as an Oberlin College tutor, and as a student of rhetoric and composition. In this, I have gained an interesting perspective on the interplay among writing, tutoring, and power.

DEVELOPMENT AND THEORY OF LITERACY LETTERS

For the most part, really effective writing and reading materials are hard to come by for this kind of tutoring. I find myself struggling to create interesting and helpful writing assignments. I have tried various strategies, from writing a paragraph about a newspaper article we read together to writing paragraphs using new vocabulary words to writing journal entries. The response I hear most to these ideas is, "I don't have anything to say." I want to say, "OF COURSE you have something to say. You always have something to say!" But that is a statement that is very far from being fair and one that would probably make my students more self-conscious than they already are. They do, in fact, have something to say, plenty to say. The issue is instead a matter of having something to write or the ability to write. Thus, I was searching for a writing project that could be interactive, engaging, and helpful.

Linda Brodkey documents the use of "Literacy Letters" as a helpful and interesting task for basic writers. In Brodkey's essay, "On the Subject of Class and Gender in 'The Literacy Letters,'" literacy letters are a series of written exchanges between an ABLE student and a community member. Brodkey's scholarly work deals with the unwritten ideas contained in the literacy letters. Brodkey wants to make clear that there is always a power dynamic, even in a place that is often considered neutral or exempt from oppressive hierarchy. She deconstructs the common notion that educational spaces are neutral spaces by examining closely the "asymmetrical relationships between [education's] knowing subjects, teachers, and its unknowing subjects, students" (656). She would, for instance, say that there are more than only intellectual assumptions behind the statement that "the teacher knows more than the students." As in my case, I am the advantaged individual (Caucasian, educated, middle class); race, class, and gender, for example, all play a part in educational settings.

I began a letter exchange between a junior at Oberlin College, Mae, and a middle-aged student at ABLE classes, Kathy. The letter authors shared their gender, female, and their homes, Ohio; beyond those commonalties, the authors were very different. In this essay, I have transcribed a portion of the exchanges almost exactly as they were written. Spelling, capitalization, word choice, and format remain as they did in the letters; the only difference is that the ABLE student handwrote her letters. I use Brodkey's general method of examining the project based on theories in rhetoric, composition, and tutoring.

HELPING WITH WRITING: TAKING RISKS AND STEPPING BACK

Choosing material for a student like Kathy was difficult because it involved both functional and ethical choices. In the essay, "Ten Lessons in Clarity and Grace," author Joseph Williams asserts, "An action is ethical when as its agent, we would in principle be willing to trade places with the person who is its object, or vice versa. Writing in particular is ethical when, as a matter of principle, we would be willing to trade places with our intended reader" (222). Because Kathy felt intimidated by the materials we worked with, I, as the tutor, had a functional obligation to choose writing and reading exercises that would not totally alienate her. My intent in the Literacy Letter project was to choose a medium that would be non-threatening. Letters seem to be a positive medium for writing, because letters are extemporaneous by nature. Yet they are still inscribed with messages about power, which I will explore later in the paper.

Just as it is unethical to write to intimidate our readers, is it also unethical to choose an assignment which highlights disparities between the author and the reader? Is it a tutor's position to decide what material is "appropriate"? I was the first agent of authority in this project; I chose the project and asked Kathy and Mae to participate. However, my authority was much more complicated than I originally thought. Though the class setting that I tutor in is not structurally similar to a conventional classroom (that of, say, a fourth grade classroom), my "authority" is a factor for the students. Brodkey states, "Educational discourse grants teachers authority over the organization of language in the classroom, which includes allocating turns, setting topics, and asking questions" (644). What I do in the classroom is inscribed with my own biases and agendas. Williams sees ethical issues involved when tutors choose assignments. Tutors are obliged to think critically about the way the assignments, which they choose, affect their students.

To start, I asked Kathy to write a letter to an unknown friend. She and I talked together about some ideas that she might like to include in the letter. I helped generate ideas, but Kathy composed the letter alone:

> *Dear Mae,*   *Oct 31, 2002*
>   *Well, I be around horses all my life. I have a qater horse. she is a Brown horse, she still about 15 hand, high. My Brother has high Bloodpressure, since we got our horse Ace, his Bloodpessure has come down.*
>
> > *Thank you your friend*
> > *Kathy*

Kathy worked for about an hour handwriting the first letter. Although Mae was unaware of it, Kathy was responding directly to my prompts. She and I began talking about horses, and I said to her "Why don't you tell Mae about that?" Her sentences are a typical length for students in my class. Although her writing makes leaps, it was obvious to me (as we talked) that her thought process was very clear as she easily connected the relationship between her horse and her brother's blood pressure when she explained orally. However, when she wrote, she lost that connection.

From the beginning, I placed Kathy in a disadvantaged position. I asked her to move out of her comfort zone and write to a stranger. For me, this was a casual sort of thing. For Kathy, it was exactly the opposite. As Kathy wrote the letters, I helped her through the process: working on structural issues (capitalization, punctuation, subject-verb agreement) and developmental issues (expressing ideas, voice). In the following section, I explore the complicated issues that underlie tutoring form and/or content; I am still unsure if the tutoring choices I made were good—both effective and ethical.

Tutoring in composition must progress toward both a final piece and improved writing skills. The work of Nancy Sommers guided me as I gave Kathy feedback. Offering suggestions on her individual letters and on her writing as a whole, I navigated between helping Kathy to find her own voice in writing and helping Kathy to form grammatically correct sentences. I also knew that when responding to writing, questions of authority enter the discourse: who decides what a "final piece" is or what "better writing" is? For this first letter, I intentionally chose to avoid helping with spelling, grammar, or style, unless Kathy specifically asked. I wanted the letter to be a sort of pure form of communication, not one where I, as the teacher, intervened. I wanted to remove myself from the process as much as possible. In the later letters, however, I did work with Kathy occasionally on her writing. In her essay, "Responding to Student Writing," Sommers believes that "we need to develop an appropriate level of response for commenting on a first draft, and to differentiate that from the level suitable to a second or third draft" (345). When working with very basic writers, it is important to view their writing as a part of a larger process, just as I view my own writing as process oriented. Though Kathy did not compose a series of drafts for each letter, the array of letters themselves are a series of drafts. When I did work with her, I addressed concerns that could be applied to a later draft. For example, I suggested always using a capital letter to begin a sentence and a period (or other punctuation) to complete a sentence rather than focusing on particular sentences or word choice. I wanted my suggestions to be helpful for the later process.

Sommers also believes in the responsibility of the teacher/tutor "to show them [our students] through our comments why new choices would positively change their texts, and thus show them potential for development implicit in their own writing" (346). I chose to give Kathy comments about capital letters and periods because I thought it would be helpful. But I am left asking if this was positive change for Kathy or for me? Did my suggestions help Kathy to write more easily and confidently about what she thought, or did my suggestions simply alter her text so it was more compatible with dominant writing styles, such as my own? I thought that it was important not to tip the scale too drastically in either direction. I wanted Kathy to be truly confident in her writing, but I also wanted to give Kathy what she came to classes for—the ability to write in a "correct" way, the skills to write complete sentences on a job application, and the know-how to use capital letters and exclamation marks on a birthday card.

Mae responded to Kathy's first letter, in typed format:

Dear Kathy,   November 5, 2002

    My name is Mae, and I'm a friend of Mara's. I go to school at Oberlin and I study Chemistry. Do you like science? Mara sure doesn't. I thought your letter was very interesting. I especially like hearing about your horse. What is its name? My cousin shows horses with her 4-H group, and I always want to talk about it with her. And that's great about your brother lowering his blood pressure! Do you think it's because of him spending time with your horse? I think it's really amazing how animals affect our health.

    So, where is your son now? Is he stationed somewhere with the Navy? A friend of mine from high school is in California with the Marine Corps. I think she likes it all right. It must be very hard for you not to see him, though. Does he come home for the holidays?

    Speaking of holidays, what do you do for Thanksgiving? I always spend Thanksgiving with my parents, my aunts, my grandma, and lots of cousins. There are usually about fifteen of us all altogether. Thanksgiving may just be my favorite holiday!

    Well, Kathy, I hope to hear back from you soon. I hope you have fun with Mara in the meantime.

        Your friend,
        Mae

Mae begins by introducing herself and emphasizing the connection among herself, Kathy, and me. Mae's first letter focuses mainly on responding to ideas brought up in the letter or ideas that she had previously heard about Kathy through me. At the end, Mae reveals the importance of her family by speaking about Thanksgiving. Kathy wrote back to Kari:

Dear Mae,   Nov, 5, 2002

    How are you doing? Do you like going to Oberlin? Yes I like chemistry. Mara is a good teacher. My horse named is Aces. She is a Quarter horse. Will you please asked our cousin about how old you have to be to in 4-H. Yes, I think it is because He spending time around her. animals make people feel good, is make your health Best. My son may not be going home for thanksgiving, I'm do no know if he get to go home for Christmas. My twin miss he a lot. the holidays make them sad, But that uncle JR take them that be around faimily is good. Will I like hear from you. Thank you for writing to me. Mara's and your firends are nice people.

        Thank you have a good Day
        Kathy

I was excited about Kathy's response. This was most writing I had ever seen her complete, especially at a single time. She wrote a great deal and answered Mae's questions clearly. When Kathy brought her own ideas to the letter (those that were not formatted around Mae's questions), her language was confused. Notice the sentence, "My twin miss he a lot." The sentence has correct capitalization and punctuation. The suggestions I made to Kathy makes her sentences *look* correct, yet the grammar and language are incorrect.

Some types of writing pedagogy find little room for tutoring proper grammar; thus, structural issues become edged out or eclipsed by focus on only the written content. While I do not adhere to this philosophy of tutoring writing wholesale, theories such as these allowed me to ask myself if I was paying enough attention to content. In his "Reconceptualizing Grammar as an Aspect of Rhetorical Invention," David Blakesley presents the argument that "knowing and saying, conception and delivery, thought and language-each opposition describes in reality what is a united, living process. . . . [W]riters need to learn *how to know* by knowing *how to say,* then to say what they know by saying it so that others know it" (195). Is this to say that, because Kathy writes, "My twin miss he a lot," her language really does not convey her intention? When she writes "my twin" she does not actually mean her own twin, but is referring to one of her twin sons who misses his twin brother a great deal. But her sentence does not really express this idea.

Blakesley would criticize my suggestion to Kathy to work on capitalization and punctuation. He believes that tutoring pedagogies whose "purpose [is to manipulate] surface structure is reader-based and whatever consequences these skills have for the writer's competence (potential for generating deep structure) remain unarticulated" (198). According to this model, as I attempted to help Kathy deal with simple structural issues (like capitalization and punctuation), which I thought could be helpful for future work, I was actually avoiding dealing with larger issues. Perhaps I should have been helping Kathy to learn how to know rather than to make her writing compliant with the standards of grammar.

Whether she realized it or not, Kathy recognized standards of language and grammar and mimicked them. Kathy's second letter (above) was patterned almost exactly around Mae's. She answered each of Mae's questions directly, and asked one of her own. Like Mae, Kathy reveals aspects of herself through details of her family. Kathy "knows" about her family. Mae only provides a format for Kathy to express in writing what she already knows. As a tutor, I could never really teach Kathy "how to know" about her family. She, not I, experiences her family and her life. Kathy and I are in a situation where I am supposed to teach her what or how to know, but there are limits to this instruction: I could never teach Kathy about her own experience. I could—at best—provide a framework for expressing her knowledge or give her a different lens through which to view/interpret her experience. There were many things I was able to teach Kathy, and, importantly, there were plenty of things Kathy could teach me. Simply because her knowledge was not about grammar or language did not mean she did not "know" anything.

Tutoring is a balancing act: in this situation, I negotiated between attention to form and attention to content, between my goals as a tutor and Kathy's needs a student, between Kathy's confidence in writing and Kathy's "rightness" in writing. There was one more negotiation, which was perhaps the most important negotiation, that between power/authority and subordination/subjectivity. In "Arts of the Contact Zone," Mary Louise Pratt writes about the encounter between the person(s) of authority and the person(s) of subordination. She states, "The idea of the contact zone is intended in part to contrast with ideas of community that underlie much of the thinking about language, communication, and culture that gets done in the academy" (179). Pratt highlights the idea that there is no place of neutrality or safety, even in the educational sphere. I would be ignoring the contact zone of education to assume that Kathy, in Pratt's words, "was engaged in the same game and that the game is the same for all players" (181). The game of education is not actually a fair one. As a rule, "When speakers are from different classes or cultures, one party is exercising authority and another is submitting to it or questioning it" (181). I exercised my social and intellectual authority, unwittingly, in tutoring situations. Mae, also obliviously, exercised her social and intellectual authority. Thus, an authority/subordination relationship was especially prominent in the letter exchanges. Kathy mimicked Mae's format and style, which was the dominant and acceptable way of writing. Pratt terms this process "transculturation" and defines it as "[the process] whereby members of subordinated or marginal groups select and invent from materials transmitted by a dominant . . . culture" (178). Teaching Kathy how she "should" know happened inevitably in this contact zone situation. It was not my, nor Mae's, intention to have Mae do exactly as we did. The literacy letters were supposed to be a medium through which both Kathy and Mae could express themselves comfortably. But I am left with questions of how anything can be comfortable in the contact zone.

The contact zone is tricky but not useless; in this contact situation, formidable problems surfaced. The difficult questions about pedagogy, power, and authority became formative. The contact zone challenged me to think about my role in tutoring and allowed me to alter practices and shift my emphases. The following exchange, in particular, challenged me to consider the ways my personal values entered into my tutoring, perhaps overstepping my role as a tutor.

Dear Kathy,   *November 21, 2002*
    It seems like you really like animals—I think Petland is a great place for you to work. What do you do there? Do you like your coworkers? I hope you'll have a chance to ride Ace this weekend. I think the weather is going to be a little bit better. And who are Steven and Jarod? Are they relatives or just friends?
    Cambridge is a pretty nice city. There really isn't much to do, but I like my house a lot. I live outside of the town, near a lot of farms. Ohio is lovely in the fall. The colors of the leaves make nice landscapes. Sometimes I like to just drive around and look at the leaves. It's very relaxing.
    I'm glad that you like going to class with Mara. She talks about you and your classmates a lot. She really enjoys it. I hope you have a good weekend, Kathy. Don't work too hard!

    Your friend,
    Mae

Kathy replied:

Mae,   Nov. 21
    I work in the Back with the Dogs. Yes, I Like the coworkers, they are very good people to work with. Maybe I will have a chane to Ride her. The weather man said on the T.V. we may get snow this weekend. Steven and Jarod, they are my twin boys. I like being outside a lot. I like writing to you.

    Mara and her friends are very good teachers. I hope you have a good weekend too. no I am not married. I am to fat for that.

    HAPPY HOLIDAYS
    from,
    Kathy

The final lines in Kathy's response are strikingly personal, and when I read them, I felt very uncomfortable. I did not really know if I should pursue Kathy's idea of being "to *[sic]* fat" for marriage or if I should just let it drop. I was uncomfortable because I assumed this statement to be self-degrading; perhaps I also reacted because Kathy went "too far," shared too much personal information. However, was it possible to see Kathy's statement as an example of her expressing herself to a friend, Mae? Was it really my position at all to discuss what I saw as the implication of Kathy's assertion? When working with Kathy, I often found it hard to recognize where any lines were. I was unsure if I would be crossing boundaries by asking Kathy why she felt the way she did or by saying something like, "Oh, don't say that Kathy!" I did not want to encourage self-effacing writing, but at the same time, it was her writing, not mine. My values were not Kathy's values, and my tutor position did not grant me authority to alter Kathy's values. In her article, "What Line? I Didn't See Any Line," Molly Wingate hands over her piece of knowledge: "My rule of thumb is this: If you think you have stepped over the line, you probably have" (12). Wingate also states, "It is not exactly reassuring to realize that the line always moves and that tutors find it by crossing it" (14). True, but where did that leave me when I tutored Kathy? Even now, I am unsure of what is and is not acceptable. This experience pushed me to evaluate the boundaries of the tutor-tutee relationship.

Even before the questions of language and codes of authority surface, I am still unsure if my choice of Mae as correspondent was appropriate. Was writing to Mae at all natural for Kathy? Why would Kathy have something, anything at all, to write to a stranger, particularly to Mae, who existed in a very different world?

Brodkey examines how the authors of the letters represent themselves. Mae, certainly, never identified herself as an authority figure. Yet, Mae was represented not only through her language, but also through her word choice, her grammar, and her method of writing. Kathy, too, represented herself directly and indirectly. The simple fact that she was writing *with* a tutor *in* an ABLE class demonstrated her position: educationally, socially, and economically. Mae's writing spoke to Kathy and Kathy's writing spoke to Mae about their respective positions in society.

Brodkey also examines actual written language; she states "each institutionalized discourse privileges some people and not others by generating uneven and unequal subject positions as various stereotypes and agents" (641). Brodkey would say that Mae's subjectivity was "positively produced" and thus she accepted and even embraced standard "discursive practice." Mae was able to express herself clearly and paint the portrait she wanted to paint. She had command of the English language and could thus positively show, or produce, herself. She was comfortable representing herself. Kathy, on the other end of the spectrum, could not describe herself as she might desire. She could only describe herself with the language she could access. She was negatively represented in the writing process, and she therefore resisted the methods. Resists, has resisted, will resist?

Kathy resisted the institution every time she said to me, "I have nothing to say." She was at first very uneasy about the idea of writing, and this comes through in her first letter. She did not ever introduce herself. Instead she wrote according to my prompt. Under Brodkey's model, Kathy and Mae both wrote as a result of their personal subjective representations. Is this why Mae was typing from her personal computer at an elite Oberlin College and Kathy was printing on a legal pad just a few miles down the road at the county's JVS?

IMPLICATIONS FOR TUTORING
AND TUTORING PRACTICES

I wish that I could say that the letter exchanges are the least institutional and the most pure method of communication; however, I find myself realizing that the power inscriptions are always unavoidable. Kathy and Mae did not escape the inscribed power structures, though their exchanges were seemingly successful and comfortable. These letters, like Brodkey's, "[ultimately challenge] the ideology that class, and by extension race and gender differences, are present in American societies and absent from American classrooms" (657). These differences permeate all aspects of life *including* learning. The rhetorical practice of letter writing seems to be casual, and thus would not be politically and socially charged. Yet, Kathy was unable to assert herself as an agent of the process. Rather, she used Mae's letters and positive representation as a template, one that she attempted to follow. Mae's template operated in a very specific space, leaving little room for spontaneity. This method does not truly support new ideas for someone who is uncomfortable in the medium. These letter exchanges are incredibly complicated and deserve great attention and thought.

Nancy Grimm works with ideas of power and domination in her article "Toward a Fair Writing Center Practice." Grimm states, "Members of the dominant group have difficulty conceptualizing oppression because it lies outside their lived experience. They tend to minimize its effects because they confuse it with the injustice of domination" (103). I must evaluate how I dominate in the tutoring situation. Do I dominate because of the nature of my position? I was the tutor; Kathy was the student. Or do I dominate because of my social position? Grimm encourages tutors to recognize their own agency in the process of educational oppression. For example, when I asked Kathy the question, "What do you think we should work on?" she shrugged and shied away. Kathy did not have the vocabulary to talk about "proofreading" or "sentence level errors." By trying to have her decide what to edit, I only widened the gap between her understanding and "acceptable" writing practices. Instead of having her decide what to work on, I used my authority as tutor to choose what we worked on. I decided that Kathy should work on capitalization and punctuation in her letters. My intent was to make her comfortable writing and, eventually, to improve her skills. Grimm would suggest, however, that my choice left Kathy out of the process and only catered to the dominant way of thinking. I was using my privileged position as an authoritative tutor *and* as a member of the dominant social group. I was, in fact, encouraging Kathy's denigrated status in the educational sphere. Grimm also writes, "Students from underrepresented groups experience oppression in classrooms and writing centers every day. They experience it bodily and intellectually and because the dominant group doesn't *intend* it, because underrepresented students do not feel prepared to take on the social arguments against it, they remain silent" (107).

Kathy is not an underrepresented group within the ABLE basic level classroom, since the class is designed for the most basic level of students. She is, however, underrepresented in the educational system as a whole. According to Grimm, although neither Mae nor I were trying to assert our authority and high position in the educational system (and society), we did. We participated actively and passively in this "unjust structural oppression" (107). As I tutor I must realize "how systems function, how language influences the construction of Self and Other, how literacy as cultural and social practice, how political action produces social change" (110). Because Mae could write clearly and use language "correctly," she was able to define herself through her writing. Kathy could not do this, and thus became the opposite. Kathy was relegated to "Other" status. Both Mae and I needed to evaluate the way in which we were affecting Kathy's ability to write.

In "P is for *Postmodernity* and for Possibilities," Grimm asserts, "Postmodern thinking provides no easy answers to these questions, but it does hold in check our assumptions about the neutrality of the critical stance expected in academic discourse" (23). She believes that postmodern thinking can transform and reevaluate a person's ideas about power structures. For example, Grimm states, "a postmodern framework . . . encourages me to think of students not as isolated individuals but as members of communities and families" (20). It was important for me to think of Kathy outside of the classroom experience. Kathy was a member of a community and family that was entirely separate from the ABLE classroom. She was not simply the "Other." In her own life, Kathy lives as "Self."

Another avenue to postmodern thought is the ability to "simultaneously maintain multiple viewpoints, to make quick shifts in discourse orientation, . . . to negotiate cultural and social differences, to handle the inevitable blurring of authorial boundaries, and to regularly renegotiate issues of knowledge, power, and ownership" (2). Grimm's suggestions keep the authority of the tutor in check. The postmodern tutor should be willing to learn from her students, to try new approaches, and to view her students through different lenses. The postmodern tutor should also realize that her authority as a tutor should come from her knowledge of the subject material, not from her social position: her power is limited.

The composition and tutoring theories I chose to work with in this paper center around boundaries, power, and constructs. Through examining these theories and my own experience of tutoring, I realize more and more that there is no neutral zone. I play a part, Kathy plays a part, Mae plays a part. We all come to the table with our own backgrounds, our own beliefs, and our own agency. Though Kathy and I may have used the same pencil and may have written on the very same pad of paper to compose and refine letters to Mae, we wrote in very different ways. Our language is charged with our background.

I strongly believe that in order to establish a successful tutoring session, the tutor must be willing to recognize some of the influencing factors when working with basic literacy students. I do not believe that I now or will ever totally understand the impact of my language, my tutoring style, and my authority. Furthermore, I cannot fully understand Kathy's reaction to my language, tutoring style, and/or authority. Tutoring in this capacity could be seen as climbing a slippery slope. To recognize the risks involved is to take a step in the right direction. It must be a constant process of locating comfort zones, tweaking, and adjusting those comfort zones. Tutoring must not establish a singular set of rules, or an understanding of all students as "Kathy." Just as there is no neutrality, there is no one way to tutor.

WORKS CITED

Blakesley, David. "Reconceptualizing Grammar as an Aspect of Rhetorical Invention." *The Place of Grammar in Writing Instruction: Past, Present, Future*. Ed. Susan Hunter and Ray Wallace. Portsmouth: Boynton/Cook, 1995. 191–203. Print.

Brodkey, Linda. "On the Subjects of Class and Gender in the 'Literacy Letters.'" *Cross-Talk in Composition Theory: A Reader*. Ed. Victor Villanueva, Jr. Urbana: NCTE, 1997. 639–58. Print.

Grimm, Nancy Maloney. *Good Intentions Writing Center Work for Postmodern Times*. Portsmouth: Boynton/Cook, 1999. Print.

Pratt, Mary Louise. "Arts of the Contact Zone." *Negotiating Academic Literacies: Teaching and Learning Across Languages and Cultures*. Ed. Vivian Zamel and Ruth Spack. Mahwah: Lawrence Erlbaum Associates, 1998. 171–86. Print.

Sommers, Nancy. "Responding to Student Writing." *The New St. Martin's Guide to Teaching Writing*. Ed. Robert J. Connors and Cheryl Glenn. Boston: Bedford/St. Martin's, 1999. 339–47. Print.

Williams, Joseph M. *Style: Ten Lessons in Clarity and Grace*. 6th ed. New York: Longman, 2000. Print.

Wingate, Molly. "What Line? I Didn't See Any Line." *A Tutor's Guide: Helping Writers One to One*. Ed. Ben Rafoth. Portsmouth: Boynton/Cook, 2000. 9–16. Print.

Taking on Turnitin:
Tutors Advocating Change[1]

Renee Brown, Brian Fallon, Jessica Lott, Elizabeth Matthews,
and Elizabeth Mintie

Renee Brown, Jessica Lott, Elizabeth Matthews, and Elizabeth Mintie were undergraduates at Indiana University of Pennsylvania when they wrote this article, and Brian Fallon was a graduate student at the same institution. This article
originally appeared in *The Writing Center Journal* and won the 2007 Outstanding Article Award from the International Writing Centers Association.

Like many writing centers, ours trained us to respond to writers whose papers might
involve plagiarism; we learned to show students how to use various paraphrasing
techniques and how to cite sources. In staff meetings, we talked about why it was
more important to understand the causes of students' plagiarism than to judge them
for it. Then one day, a student walked into our writing center and said that she had
submitted a paper to her professor online, as required, only to learn a little later that
her paper had been reported to her professor as plagiarized. Visibly upset, this student
asked that we help her with this paper so that she could resubmit it and avoid failing
the course. She also showed us this statement in the course syllabus: "Students agree
that by taking this course all required papers/reports/test may be subject to submission for textual similarity review to Turnitin.com for the detection of plagiarism."
This was the boilerplate language recommended to professors at our institution who
chose to use Turnitin.com, a web-based plagiarism detection service, in their courses
(Sherwood). Before our tutors had time to decide how best to respond to this experience, other panicked students came in with similar stories. We felt helpless to do
anything for these students because we understood so little about Turnitin or their
professors' literacy expectations and values. Were the students really plagiarizing?
Could Turnitin point the finger at them and cause them to fail the course? How does
Turnitin work? The answers to these questions, we discovered, were not to be found
easily. Our director, Ben Rafoth, suggested that we investigate and then share what
we learned with others at the university and in the writing center community.

As both students and tutors, we had concerns about the Turnitin software being
used at our university. It was easy for us to identify with students who felt helpless
when dealing with a software program that could seal their fates. We found it harder
to identify with the values of their professors and of the Turnitin officials who made

students use the program without providing important background information and without helping them to interpret the results. As we began to learn more about the program—more, actually, than we suspected even the faculty knew—we had to confront another question: How much should tutors tell students about Turnitin? If we decided to say nothing, we were tacitly supporting the way Turnitin was being used. If we told what we had learned, we were entering a realm of discourse that we might not be able to sustain and could even get in trouble for. With some encouragement, we decided to keep investigating and to go wherever our search led us.

We began our mission with two goals: What did our writing center staff need to know about Turnitin? and, How could tutors help students who must deal with Turnitin and the professors who require it? As we delved into these questions, we felt a growing sense that we were looking at very different values and expectations when it comes to student writing than we had learned during our training and our combined years of experience. We combed through websites and talked to students and faculty, collecting evidence that was sometimes technical, frequently changing, and often confusing. Our aim was to learn as much as we could about Turnitin and how it affects our peers so that we could tell students, faculty, and others in the writing-center community what we had learned and how it might affect them. Although the students who visited the writing center concerned about Turnitin prompted our inquiry, we felt that our findings were best used when we considered the pitfalls and possibilities for tutoring involved. As a foundation for the work we embarked on, we held to some notions about plagiarism, writing centers, and tutors that we feel are important for grounding this discussion.

PLAGIARISM, TUTORS, WRITING CENTERS: A COMPLICATED TRIO

Our research began with the practical challenge of what to say to students who brought papers to us that had been identified by Turnitin as containing plagiarized material. In some cases, students had received papers back from their professor because Turnitin had flagged them as plagiarized, and they were now being asked to correct plagiarized passages and submit revised versions. These students came to our writing center and said, "Here's what Turnitin said I plagiarized, so how do I fix it?" In other cases, students were about to submit their finished papers to Turnitin as they were required to do, and were worried that the program would accuse them of plagiarism. This challenge, though, soon led us in a number of directions that would help us to offer the best advice possible to students and to discover what kinds of roles we as tutors and the writing center play in campus conversations on plagiarism. In order to find the right words to say to students who visit with Turnitin concerns, we had to understand plagiarism better, the stance writing center literature takes on plagiarism, and what kinds of institutional roles tutors can play.

As students, we began to feel that our own perceptions on plagiarism, mainly that it is academic dishonesty, were problematic because what Turnitin had flagged as plagiarism didn't seem to suggest that students were intentionally being dishonest. With the help of our assistant director, we looked to composition studies for some answers and considered some of Rebecca Moore Howard's thoughts on plagiarism. Through an exploration of her work, we began to expand our understanding of plagiarism by taking into account Howard's attention to patchwriting in her *Standing in the Shadow of Giants: Plagiarists, Authors, Collaborators*. Students are often criminalized for being patchwriters, Howard argues, when, in actuality, even the most professional writers are merely sophisticated patchwriters. She establishes a pedagogical space for patchwriting, which she refers to as, "a process of evaluating a source text, selecting passages pertinent to the patchwriter's purposes, and transporting those passages to the patchwriter's new context" (xviii). Furthermore, Howard, elsewhere, calls for the replacement of plagiarism with the categories of *fraud, citation,* and *repetition* ("Sexuality, Textuality" 488). In addition to Howard, Kurt Bouman has strongly suggested that differences in cultural and academic expectations can lead some students, particularly international students, to make choices that would be deemed wrong by an American academic audience. Given what we learned from our initial exploration into discussions of plagiarism in composition studies and what we've witnessed from students with Turnitin concerns, we have decided to reserve the term *fraudulent plagiarism* for instances in which there is, beyond a doubt, true intent by writers to submit work that is not their own. We have made this decision primarily because any discussion on plagiarism should not automatically assume that any text that imitates another text or lacks originality is a result of a criminal act.

With a better sense of how experts in the field define plagiarism, we began to think carefully about what the writing center's stance is when it comes to plagiarism. As we noted at the beginning of this article, an issue for us as tutors centered on what we would say to a student whom we knew was plagiarizing. Luckily for us, this scenario has not happened very often, but we still had to consider what kinds of positions we could possibly take on this issue. Would we establish a set of procedures like tutors Jennifer Herrick and Mark Niquette did in their "Ethics in the Writing Lab: Tutoring under the Honor Code"? Would we casually take a walk with the writer and describe to them what's at stake by choosing to plagiarize? As our research developed, we realized that we had to take a step beyond our training, that our response to such a situation had to be informed by what scholars were saying about the writing center's tempestuous past and present relationship to plagiarism. In their "Plagiarism, Rhetorical Theory, and the Writing Center: New Approaches, New Locations," Linda Shamoon and Deborah H. Burns provided not only a history of this relationship, but some answers to the questions we had about how the writing center might approach the issue of plagiarism in general.

According to Shamoon and Burns, the writing center literature mainly focuses on defending our institutional spaces against accusations that writers receive too much help when they visit. They present three responses to charges of plagiarism that the writing center literature has provided: "[W]e recount the nature of the writing process, we explain the importance of feedback for all writers, and we offer pointers about how peer tutors can negotiate the border between the 'legitimate' practice of giving advice and the 'illegitimate' practice of writing too much on the paper" (184). However, Shamoon and Burns are quick to point out the philosophical discrepancies inherent in these three responses when they are measured against our beliefs about writing and the realities we face while tutoring. The perspective they ultimately endorse is a *social-rhetorical* one that "would make interpellation more conscious because it articulates the constructed nature of subject matter, of disciplinary thinking and questioning, of the related features of the discourse (including paper features), and of the values and expectations of a specific reader or audience" (191). In line with their recommendation to approach tutoring from this perspective, we believe that our job as tutors is to help students come to new meanings, understandings, and ideas through their writing and to do so while situating themselves in the kinds of disciplinary conversations their teachers expect of them.

This is not an easy task, but what we've learned about plagiarism, particularly in Howard's explanation of patchwriting, tells us that complicated plagiarism issues most likely happen in the writing center more frequently than we may have thought. That is, if all writers are essentially patchwriters and if students are particularly prone to having their patchwriting critiqued as cheating, then we, as tutors have a dilemma on our hands every time we work with students who are already under suspicion for plagiarizing. Since our job entails walking the line between what type of writing is expected in the student's discipline and how the student is prepared to meet those expectations, we may find ourselves wandering into disciplinary conversations about plagiarism that aren't so pretty. In taking this approach how we respond to plagiarism cannot be framed in terms of ethics or a misconception of writing center practice, as Shamoon and Burns suggest, because a *social-rhetorical* approach to writing center pedagogy "views the issue of plagiarism as a social and rhetorical construct, and rather than sidestep the issue of plagiarism by claiming to build a fence around collaboration and tutoring, such a writing center inserts itself into a conversation about the rhetorical and social nature of the disciplines" (192). We are left to ponder how tutors, as the main practitioners in our writing centers, might insert themselves into such a conversation, especially now that Turnitin has presented us with new challenges to our tutoring and to our institutional positions.

Of course, the time we spent researching Turnitin was extensive, and we had the opportunity to present our findings both locally and nationally, but the persistent issue of who is really listening to us, the tutors, kept nagging us throughout this project. During our first presentation to the English faculty here at Indiana University of Pennsylvania (IUP), we became aware that showing professors what Turnitin is all about and how it is influencing their teaching could potentially put us in the political hot seat. How would they respond to us, their students, but also their other students' tutors? At the end of the day, the information we had to share was well received and the faculty in our audience were there because they wanted to hear what we had to say, but this was the first time we had to ask ourselves about the potential risks involved in becoming advocates for students who have had bad Turnitin experiences. In considering a political and pedagogical space for our research, we found it necessary to step outside the traditional roles of writing center tutors in order to make claims about how Turnitin was influencing teaching on our campus. Thinking about Shamoon and Burn's social-rhetorical approach to writing center work led us to the conclusion that there was, or at least should be, an arena for tutors to discuss campus-wide issues that affect tutoring. In Harvey Kail and John Trimbur's "The Politics of Peer Tutoring," they argue that, "[l]ocating the sources of knowledge in the social fabric rather than in the power lines of generation and transmission offers a way to talk about peer tutoring that goes beyond the operational model of plugging tutors into the grid" (207). We began to consider the kind of knowledge we could bring to the social fabric of our institution and other ways that Kail and Trimbur's statement informs our situation almost twenty years after they originally made it.

We are not interested in being plugged into the Turnitin grid just because some faculty and administrators on our campus have chosen to use the program. Instead, we would like to offer up our voice along with the voices of students who have been informed about this decision as a way to cautiously approach what Turnitin means for learning and teaching on our campus. Although the debates about peer tutoring may have focused on collaborative learning in the university, we have reinterpreted our goals in line with Kail and Trimbur in that "[t]he experience of co-learning changes students and helps them to see that the power ascribed to the faculty depends on the students' own sense of powerlessness and [the faculty's] need for omnipotent authority" (209). What we came to recognize at our writing center is that we had an opportunity to inform students about what Turnitin does and how their teachers are using it so they could make informed decisions on how to approach their professors and engage their own texts. If we took the time, together, with students to pose problems with what Turnitin said they plagiarized and explained why it had said so, then we'd be doing productive work in our writing center rather than working to just fix the supposed problem areas of flagged texts. We would, in a sense, have to forgo how the institution intended to use Turnitin and help students in these situations to see the choices they have, to feel more confident in how they use sources, and to identify themselves as writers who intricately manipulate and synthesize texts for their own purposes.

With this complex nexus of plagiarism, writing centers, and tutor roles as a base, we will now turn our attention to how Turnitin works from technological, legal, and ethical perspectives; how students seem to be responding to the increasing use of plagiarism detection services; and how Turnitin limits pedagogical options and opportunities. Finally, we will offer some perspectives on what tutors can do both in their sessions and on their campuses to have their voices heard in a discussion on plagiarism detection services.

HOW TURNITIN WORKS

Understanding how Turnitin functions and the purposes for which it is used by an institution proved vital to any discussion we had about the program. We should note, however, that Turnitin updates the information it provides online regularly, and has done so since we first began our research. The information provided from Turnitin's web site in this article was collected in March 2006. Likewise, the information we present throughout this section is also influenced by the kinds of programming parameters set for our institution, which means that different institutions can customize aspects of the program for their own purposes. What we present in this piece demonstrates the issues that we have dealt with here at Indiana University of Pennsylvania (IUP) with our new subscription to Turnitin.

For starters, we found that the corporation behind Turnitin claims to have an educational purpose. In fact, banners on their website tout that they are "focused on education" ("Products and Services"). Turnitin's website hosts an online interface where students can submit work to professors, comment on their peers' work, and review their grades. Although these services are similar to those provided by other educational resources such as WebCT and Blackboard, Turnitin is unique because as "the standard in online plagiarism prevention," Turnitin also claims to "help educators and students take full advantage of the internet's educational potential" by scanning every paper submitted for "measurable rates of plagiarism" ("Plagiarism Prevention").

Bill Marsh's "Turnitin.com and the Scriptural Enterprise of Plagiarism Detection" offers a thorough description of how Turnitin operates, specifically dealing with the way Turnitin "maps identity, codes writing, and manages transgression in the service of broader, historically entrenched values of authorial propriety and educational achievement" (427–28). Our analysis echoes much of the work done by Marsh, and we recommend his article for those who are investigating Turnitin, but we have included our observations since they were not only the results of researching the Turnitin web site but also our own experimentation with the program.

Turnitin's capacity to detect plagiarism is actually based on the matches it makes between similar sequences of text ("Product Tour"). When students or professors submit work on Turnitin's interface, proprietary algorithms convert the text into what Turnitin calls a "digital fingerprint," a unique sequence of code that has meaning only within Turnitin's technological interface. Turnitin's web crawlers compare these "fingerprints" to the 4.5 billion student papers and archived websites Turnitin claims to have in its proprietary database. The database then retains a copy of the "fingerprint" to compare against future student submissions. When the code sequence of a submitted paper matches a file within Turnitin's database, Turnitin highlights the matching text and creates a link to the source in its database. The instructor receives an originality report with a color-coded Similarity Index that shows the total percentage of text in the submitted document that matched text from sources in the database. (Again, see Marsh's article for a thorough explanation of Turnitin's scriptural similarity and originality reports.)

Once a paper is submitted to Turnitin, its "fingerprint" remains in the proprietary database indefinitely ("Product Tour"). This feature distinguishes Turnitin from other plagiarism prevention programs, such as Essay Verification Engine and Integri-Guard, because other programs do not maintain a database of student work. Turnitin claims that retaining these fingerprints does not infringe upon students' copyrights because the proprietary algorithms it applies convert the text into a new product, the fingerprint, even though they convert it back to its original format to produce originality reports ("Legal Document"). Turnitin's lawyers explain this sleight of hand as follows: "The fingerprint is merely a digital code, which relays the unprotectable factual information that certain pre-defined content is present in the work . . . the fingerprint does not include any of the work's actual contents, and is therefore neither a copy nor a true derivative of the original text" ("Legal Document"). In other words, according to Turnitin's legal team, the code products of Turnitin's algorithms contain information about the text rather than the actual text, just as a physical fingerprint contains information about a finger rather than the actual finger. This analogy is questionable, however. A student's text can, and is, reconstructed from Turnitin's "digital fingerprint," whereas a physical finger cannot be reconstructed from a fingerprint.

This reconstruction of text poses an ethical dilemma pertaining to students' ownership of their work, as well as a privacy issue. Tutors in our writing center found that students who are enrolled in classes using Turnitin are not always aware that the database retains a fingerprint of their work. When we experimented with the program in December 2005, we created a fictional student and then later submitted a small portion of an actual paper that was written for a graduate-level criminology course in April. When we obtained consent to use the paper, we asked the writer whether her professor used Turnitin. She replied that to the best of her knowledge, none of her work had ever been submitted to Turnitin; she had never even heard of the program. However, this was not the case because her professor had submitted her work to Turnitin without her knowledge, and, in submitting her paper for our experiment, we had unwittingly alerted her professor to the possibility that she might be attempting to submit the same paper for another course. To prevent his misconception, we contacted the professor to explain that we had used the student's paper with permission as part of our research on Turnitin.

In this situation, the originality report flagged 24% of the student's text as matching a document within the database. After selecting Turnitin's option to obtain more information, we received an e-mail message stating that the professor from the course in which the matching paper had been submitted granted permission for Turnitin to send us the original paper from which our submission had ostensibly been "plagiarized." Turnitin forwarded us a copy of the entire paper, including the personal information the writer had included in her heading, specifically her full name and course number. In many courses students are required to put their identification numbers, e-mail addresses, and even contact numbers on their papers; *we* had now discovered that this student information can be forwarded by Turnitin to third parties as long as the original professor—not the student author—grants permission. We had not only obtained the student's entire original paper without her knowledge or permission, but also her full name and course number.

In addition, Turnitin claims to save professors time ("Plagiarism Prevention"). Instructors who use the program still must look at Turnitin's report of the student's paper because this report does not distinguish between properly and improperly cited information. While the option exists to omit marking material within quotation marks and in the bibliography, Turnitin cannot verify that citations are formatted correctly or that students have quoted correctly. As we have noted, Turnitin is able to detect only copy-and-paste plagiarism from within its database; the instructor must still check for copy-and-paste plagiarism from outside of the Turnitin database. Turnitin, however, is not clear about these limitations in the scope of its database, simply stating that it uses "exhaustive searches of billions of pages from both current and archived instances of the internet, millions of student papers previously sub-mitted to Turnitin, and commercial databases of journal articles and periodicals" ("Plagiarism Prevention"). Furthermore, since Turnitin detects only this type of plagiarism, professors must scrutinize papers for other types of plagiarism on their own. Therefore, the timesaving claim made by Turnitin is dubious.

The more we delved into the institutional aspects of Turnitin, the greater our con-cerns became. The money that institutions use to pay for the license to use Turnitin can come from various sources, depending on the institution. At our university, the funds come from the technology fee that all students are required to pay. This fee is meant to enhance student learning, provide equitable access, and make graduates competitive in the workplace ("Pennsylvania"). Turnitin charges between $4,000 and $10,000 a year for the use of their program, depending on the institution's enroll-ment. Bigger schools pay more for the service because it is expected that they will submit more papers to the program. In 2004–05, with approximately 13,500 students, our university paid $8,100. Meanwhile, Turnitin is a for-profit company that charges licensing fees to institutions that want access to their program. Turnitin's parent company, iParadigms, had 3,500 member institutions in 2004 and earned $10 million in annual revenue (Dotinga).

iParadigms reports that it receives over 20,000 papers on a peak day from users in 51 countries ("About"). iParadigms' other services include iThenticate, a commer-cial version of Turnitin; plagiarism.org, a website that provides information about online plagiarism and Turnitin; and Research Resources, a website about plagiarism and the Internet ("Products"). Turnitin, backed by its ever-expanding proprietary database, is the star of iParadigms' corporate agenda. Every new subscription not only generates revenue for the company through licensing fees; it also increases the size of its proprietary database and thus the market value of its product. Student papers remain in the database even after students graduate or schools cancel their sub-scriptions, so that every paper that enters the database puts iParadigms a step ahead of aspiring competitors. iParadigms' CEO Tom Barrie boasts, "In very short order, we'll have it all wrapped up. We'll become the next generation's spell checker . . . There will be no room for anybody else, not even a Microsoft, to provide a similar type of service because we will have the database" (Masur).

"Having the database" is crucial to Turnitin's business model, which depends upon adding value to its product by continuously expanding the amount of original work it collects from students and other sources and then holds forever. Each sales transaction to a college or university then creates a dependent economic relationship between Turnitin and the university, leaving institutions that might want to choose a different software company to decide between losing access to all of their students' papers and renewing their licenses with Turnitin.

Furthermore, the legal issues surrounding Turnitin concern the Copyright Law and the Fair Use Law. The Copyright Law covers items such as literary works, musical compositions, musical records, screenplays, and works of art. Items not eligible for protection under the Copyright Law are ideas, facts, titles, names, short phrases, and blank forms. The Fair Use Law determines whether the use made of a work is fair, and several factors are considered in this decision. One is the purpose and character of the use, such as whether the item in question is being used for commercial or nonprofit purposes. Another is the nature of the copyrighted work and includes the amount and substantiality of the portion of the work in question relative to the copyrighted work as a whole. Finally, there is the effect of the use upon the potential market for or value of the copyrighted work. Turnitin argues that the purpose of the digital fingerprint is to enable the evaluation of works for plagiarism; the purpose of the work itself is to express an idea or information for an academic purpose. Therefore, the purposes of use are not prohibited under the Fair Use Law. This also means that the use of the students' work will not affect its potential market value.

As of December 2005, there was no clear legal precedent for the situation created by Turnitin. Turnitin, however, markets itself largely as an educational tool. It is conceivable that Turnitin attempts to use its affiliations with educational institutions to gain leniency in copyright and fair use laws. Programs affiliated with educational pursuits often argue that special circumstances are required to fulfill their educational mission. Actions that are used to advance that goal are often able to infringe on possible copyrights and are justified because the purpose is the greater goal of education. Turnitin proclaims to be working for education, and the company claims that it should be able to make use of these legal leniencies; others contest the view that Turnitin has the educational system in its best interests.

On its website, Turnitin publishes a statement by its law firm, Foly & Lardner, to reassure readers that Turnitin infringes on no copyrights ("Legal Document"). The statement claims that using Turnitin "does not pose a significant risk of infringement of any copyright in written works submitted to Turnitin for evaluation." Perhaps in anticipation of questions about the violation of copyright laws, Turnitin defends their program on their website in a section called "Legal Document," where they pose a series of questions. The first one asks: "Does Turnitin infringe on student's [sic] copyrights to their work?" Their response to this question is as follows:

> Determining whether a copyright exists in a particular work or is infringed by a particular use of the work is difficult [. . . .] [C]asual analysis of these issues will not suffice, especially when the use in question is novel, as is the Turnitin system for plagiarism detection. For that reason, iParadigms [. . .] sought expert legal advice before launching the Turnitin system, and have continued to do so during its operation. Based on extensive analysis of all aspects of the Turnitin system, we have concluded that its use does not pose a significant risk of infringement of any copyright in written works submitted to Turnitin for evaluation. ("Legal Document")

Readers of this response may agree with us that it is vague and evasive, relying mainly on reassurances that the company has received expert legal advice and conducted an extensive analysis, but offering no supporting evidence. The evasiveness continues on page three of their legal document, when Turnitin poses the question, "Is Turnitin's use of student work ethical?" They respond first by noting:

> Each faculty user of the Turnitin system must decide whether the advantages of detecting plagiarism quickly and efficiently, coupled with the ability for peers to efficiently and anonymously review each others' work, is outweighed by any reservations the faculty user may have about how Turnitin accomplishes those goals. ("Legal Document")

This statement seems to ignore the question of using students' original work and focuses instead on the convenience afforded to faculty, suggesting that students will simply have to defer to their instructors' wishes about handling their work. Students' rights are often subordinated to the decisions of teachers and administrators, and Turnitin may believe it has the backing of most legal opinions. The question of whether or not it is ethical for Turnitin (and the faculty and institutions who subscribe to it) to use students' work in the way that Turnitin seems to encourage is left unanswered. The "Legal Document" goes on to state:

> In that respect, we believe it helpful to bear in mind that academic institutions and their teachers are not only entitled, but obliged, to award grades to student work based on student input, rather than the intellectual contribution of others. Students should know that not only the content, but also the integrity of their work is subject to evaluation.

Once again, we see Turnitin shifting the focus of the question to what they believe students must do, namely, maintain the integrity of their work. The integrity of students' work is precisely what is at stake, however, when Turnitin encourages faculty to require that all students submit their work to Turnitin's proprietary database and holds these works there indefinitely, even sending out copies of the students' work with personal, identifying information to those who wish to examine it, as we found in our research.

STUDENT PERCEPTIONS ON TURNITIN

What do students think about Turnitin? In addition to the panicked writers we met with and the students whose frustration we've discussed thus far, we visited an online conversation forum called "Students Hate Turnitin.com." Some of the posts were supportive. One student wrote, "I think the concept of Turnitin is good—as somebody who doesn't plagiarize then I've got nothing to worry about. What don't like though is the thought of my work being kept on file for future comparison." Another student believed that if people were against Turnitin, it must be because they themselves plagiarize. "Why else would anyone complain about such a service?" she asked. Also surprising was the seemingly low regard students had for their own work. At least three posts indicated feelings of surrender, suggesting that the moment they submit their papers, the work is no longer theirs. After all, they said, the papers were never copyrighted or protected in any way, and whatever the professors decide to do with the papers is fine with them; this, they felt, was the "cost" of the grade they received in return. On the other hand, there were two responses expressing dislike for Turnitin. One student wondered what happened if "[a] student isn't comfortable with their assignment being put through this system?" Another student observed the long-term effects of submitting work and "how the information can/will be used."

Students who deliberately choose to plagiarize are often well aware of Turnitin's shortcomings. Some of our tutors who are English education majors doing their student teaching had the opportunity to speak with a number of the high school students in their classes about their thoughts on Turnitin. One fifteen-year-old student told us that due to "the paper mill plagiarism problem," his high school required students to submit all papers through Turnitin. We asked if the requirement had stopped students from downloading papers, and he laughed. He explained:

> Really, it's so worthless. Everyone knows how it catches you, so it's easy to figure out how not to get caught. All you have to do is move things around in a sentence to change the order, or put in some extra words, or put in words that mean the same thing. They say a lot of times it fixes the paper up, actually, because those papers you get online aren't so good when it comes to grammar or using vocabulary. (Anonymous)

So perhaps, after all, Turnitin leads some students to edit their plagiarism more carefully, even as it poses little obstacle for determined plagiarists.

We wonder whether students realize the full extent of the obstacles Turnitin creates. Consider students who feel attached to their work, whether it is creative or research based. Do they understand how Turnitin benefits financially from having their work in the database? Or, do they realize that their work is easily reproduced whenever a paper is submitted that matches what they've written? We found few who expressed serious reservations about Turnitin and what it might mean for them in the future. Those who favored Turnitin seemed to do so because they respected those who do not plagiarize and wanted people who *do* to get caught. There were occasional complaints on student blogs about the unauthorized retention of student work, but they were relatively mild.

If these scant complaints have failed to get much attention, a 2004 court case involving a student at McGill University in Montreal seems to be having an impact. College sophomore Jesse Rosenfeld failed his assignments when he refused his professor's instructions to submit his work to Turnitin, citing "ethical and political problem[s]" with the system (Grinberg). "I was having to prove I didn't plagiarize even before my paper was looked at by my professor," Rosenfeld stated. A Canadian court sided with the student, and many authorities agreed with his position. Ian Boyko, national chairman of the Canadian Federation of Students, stated, "Of the 20 Canadian universities currently using the site, not one consulted with students in the decision-making process when signing on with Turnitin.com . . . that in itself shows a lack of respect for students' rights" (qtd. in Grinberg). Boyko further states that students, as authors, should be able to decide where their work goes, period, especially considering that the company makes money from the submissions. This last piece of evidence may be the most damaging to the credibility of Turnitin, which bases the legality of its operation on its purported educational mission.

Tom Barrie, founder and president of Turnitin.com, had strong reactions to the accusations: "This is the first time since our inception in 1998, since millions of papers have gone through our site, that this issue has come up . . . we are following the letter of the law, and not one of the 3,000 universities who use our service would have signed contracts with us if we weren't" (qtd. in Grinberg). He also disputes that Turnitin withholds student work. Because the papers are imprinted digitally into the system, rather than in written form, he says there is no need for concern. "We don't harm the free-market value of the work—a student can take their Macbeth essay to the market and make millions," argues Barrie. But the claim is at least debatable because once a work is in the database, its content is available to others, even unscrupulous users who could claim the work as their own and take it to the market. Whether the input of the saved work is manifested digitally or otherwise seems beside the point if it is being stored against the will of the writers who crafted it.

Given the responses we've provided from students and the scenarios offered that led to poor solutions to plagiarism issues in student writing, we do not believe the program actually helps to solve the problem of plagiarism. Boyko argues that it does not: "We see the use of sites like Turnitin.com as means of cutting corners . . . we think they are a poor substitute for trained individuals" (qtd. in Grinberg). Most teachers feel an obligation that goes beyond producing graduates who have simply met the requirements; writing teachers and tutors, in particular, believe that each student's experience with writing is at least as important as the ability to follow the rules of writing. And yet the sheer power of electronic solutions is hard to match. Turnitin's president says there is little choice but to rely on a digital solution because "[h]uman beings cannot detect plagiarism . . . unless you apply a digital solution, it's impossible. We have 13 seven-foot, computer racks to determine if a student has lifted one line in an essay from the internet" (qtd. in Grinberg).

Turnitin does make a compelling argument when it observes that human brains do not have the capacity to scan billions of pages to detect every instance of plagiarism; on the other hand, detection is not a simple matter of matching. Whether or not a student has plagiarized requires knowledge of the student, the assignment, and other factors for which human judgment trumps computer power. The controversy over Turnitin will likely continue, and it is bound to find its way back to the courtroom, and much more research is needed on how students perceive and are being informed on Turnitin at their schools. For now, we'd like to take the controversy to spaces where writing is taught, learned, and done.

SOME PEDAGOGICAL LIMITATIONS OF TURNITIN

In a typical session dealing with the topic of plagiarism, tutors at most writing centers try first to understand what students do and don't know about the topic. They explain what plagiarism is and how to avoid improperly using the words, ideas, and research of others. The session might last thirty minutes to an hour. The tutor and writer review when information should be cited, how to handle direct quotes, and how to acknowledge someone else's words or ideas. Tutors show students how to do relatively easy things like using signal phrases and harder ones like creating summaries and paraphrases. While we may not always be experts on the pedagogy of teaching citation, tutors have developed effective skills for teaching skills related to the use of sources. Sometimes we ask writers to read the original source aloud, and then we use this as a basis for teachable moments, as when a writer struggles to read passages he or she did not write. Sometimes tutors remove the original text by minimizing the computer screen or turning over the paper and asking the writer to recap what he or she has just read. Tutors write or have the student write notes based on what the student is able to remember. These strategies, which Howard advocates in her work on helping students to learn paraphrasing skills, provide students the opportunity to expand how they think about incorporating sources into their own writing ("Plagiarisms" 801).

At the same time, tutors are trained to steer students away from certain practices. Tutors generally do not teach students to use the computer's thesaurus as a paraphrasing tool. We do not encourage them simply to substitute words like "splendid" for words like "great" to create an acceptable paraphrase. Avoiding the thesaurus becomes problematic once students understand how Turnitin defines and detects "plagiarism," however. While most people would agree that a thesaurus can be helpful, it becomes downright essential to using Turnitin when writing something that involves a set of standard or agreed-upon terms that professional writers repeat without quoting or citing. We discovered this as we spoke to students who were required to submit papers to Turnitin and had figured out that a thesaurus was almost essential. We wrote and submitted a passage to Turnitin (in December 2005) that used standard terms to define a concept: "Freud discussed hidden emotions and drives as a person's libido, a type of psychic energy." When we made minimal changes to the sentence— "Freud talks about concealed emotions and drives as a person's libido, a kind of psychic energy"—and resubmitted it, Turnitin did not recognize the text as plagiarized. Similarly, we found that changing the syntax of the sentence could also outwit the software. "As defined by Freud, the id is the psychic energy that . . ." was not flagged as being plagiarized from the original, "The id, as defined by Freud, is the psychic energy that. . . ."

Turnitin is marketed as a campus-wide "technological solution," so various departments in schools, colleges, and universities across the nation ask students to submit their papers to their instructors through the program. Many instructors use Turnitin to compare "textual similarity," meaning identical or nearly identical strings of words and phrases, which they believe is a key step in the detection of plagiarism (Sherwood). Considering only textual similarity as a way to identify plagiarism is a limited way of looking at the problem, however, and causes distress for students who seek to learn the appropriate discourse practices of their field of study and the writing center tutors trying to support them. In our writing center, we have met several students who were writing field-specific papers in the sciences and social sciences. These papers relied heavily on precise definitions and standard vocabulary. In a paper on Attention Deficit Disorder that one of our tutors wrote in December 2005, the three types of ADD, as defined by the DSM-IV (American Psychiatric Association), a widely accepted psychological manual for diagnosing disorders, were listed. The section of text that Turnitin flagged as plagiarized was, "the DSM-IV: predominantly inattentive, predominantly hyperactive-impulsive, and combined." This string of words matches other strings of words that exist with high frequency in cyberspace because these are the precise names of the subcategories of the disorder ADD, in the order in which they appear in the DSM-IV. The paper was not plagiarized, but the terminology being used was too specific for the software to interpret intelligently. Tutors and students will continue to struggle through sessions with papers like this one because concerned students have determined that they must change the order in which the subcategories are described in order to circumvent the identical binary coding that Turnitin matches and mark for "textual similarity." Should students have to change what they know is right because their institution's computer software does not?

Even when students deliberately copy text from another source, Turnitin does not consistently identify this type of fraudulent plagiarism. Kurt Bouman points out that there are many levels of plagiarism. There is a clear difference, for example between a student who inadvertently paraphrases a source incorrectly and a student who fraudulently downloads a paper from a paper mill and submits it as his or her own writing. Since Turnitin cannot distinguish a student's intent as it scans the paper, the program often marks appropriate paraphrasing as inappropriate and lets inappropriate paraphrasing slide. As part of our investigation, we conducted a test to determine whether we could submit a plagiarized text without being detected by Turnitin. We began with a text from DigitalTermPapers.com, an online paper mill. We were able to view, on the mill's website, the first 150 words of a sample essay written on *The House on Mango Street,* and so we copied and pasted this publicly available text into a word processor and submitted the document to Turnitin in February 2005. Surprisingly, the originality report came back with only the first sentence flagged and a similarity index of 10%. When we clicked on the highlighted text to see what Turnitin had matched to our text, it displayed a page of nonsensical strings of words and sentences from an obscure website. An instructor evaluating the originality report would not have been able to determine that we had directly copied the text from a publicly available Internet paper mill, even though that is the type of website Turnitin claims to target with its web crawlers.

Most paper mills require accounts and passwords, thereby placing them beyond the reach of Turnitin's web crawlers. Turnitin claims that this is not a significant weakness of their program since it retains a copy of every paper submitted within its database. As soon as a student submits a paper purchased from a paper mill, that paper can be compared to future submissions ("Turnitin Virtual Tour"). In response to this, paper mills have begun to offer custom-written papers that are guaranteed not to be detected by services such as Turnitin. The website EssayMall.com advertises "original, well-balanced, and thoughtfully-written custom essays" which are checked by a "licensed plagiarism detection program to ensure one hundred percent originality and authenticity of work" ("Custom Essay Value"). Prices range from $11.79 per 330-word page with five days' notice to a steep $29.79 per page for twelve hours' notice; however, the company assures prospective buyers that the quality of its products, coupled with its originality and confidentiality guarantees, is worth the price. As long as the company is true to its guarantees, students who fraudulently plagiarize through custom paper mills such as EssayMall.com are safe from Turnitin detection.

Thus, we question Turnitin's ability to be a campus-wide "technological solution" to plagiarism, which brings us to even more serious questions about the program's pedagogical limitations. From the information we've presented here, the program itself is in no way a panacea for plagiarism issues. From our discussion throughout this section, we would like to point out two major differences between students who accidentally plagiarize and those who, as in the cases of students who buy papers off the Internet, fraudulently plagiarize. Believing that Turnitin will function as a "cure all" detracts our attention from asking why or how students plagiarize and places an emphasis on what they plagiarize. The danger in such a focus is that the teaching of proper paraphrasing may be overlooked for the simplest solutions to preventing plagiarism that we've demonstrated, such as using the thesaurus function in Word. This approach may not happen in composition classrooms, but we wonder about those students with whom we met who were simply required to fix the problems rather than being told how to paraphrase and cite properly. Turnitin offered no advice to these students on how they might begin to cite and paraphrase properly. Furthermore, in our more extreme example of fraudulent plagiarism, Turnitin failed to catch the work that was purchased from paper mills. The question for us, then, is whether or not Turnitin actually has any pedagogical purposes on its own? A teacher can surely use the program to some pedagogical ends, but what does it say about the pedagogical claims being offered by Turnitin when the program is more than likely going to flag issues of accidental plagiarism and totally miss cases of severe fraud? The point is that we cannot and should not forget about the kinds of responsibilities we have to young writers as tutors and teachers just because we now have the ability to compare cases of textual similarity.

WHAT'S A TUTOR TO DO? SOME THOUGHTS ON PRACTICE AND ADVOCACY

Back in the comfort of our own writing center, we pondered one more question: To what extent can the writing center change the momentum when an institution has decided to adopt a program like Turnitin? At the very least, tutors and directors can try to make their faculty aware of the limitations of Turnitin and the need to interpret its reports carefully.

Tutors who begin to learn about Turnitin software soon confront the question of what to tell others. To what extent, for example, should tutors become a political voice for or against the program? Arguably, knowing more precisely what Turnitin can and cannot do could strengthen its support among faculty, students, and perhaps even tutors. Some might say that it is helpful to know that Turnitin cannot determine fraudulent from inadvertent plagiarism, and that it cannot even be counted on to help detect fraudulent plagiarism. And then there is the cost. Is it appropriate for tutors who learn the price their institutions pay for a Turnitin license to share this information with their peers? Are the stakes in this debate higher if Turnitin is funded entirely through student fees?

At times, we felt it was our duty to take what we had learned, and the discourse we had developed to articulate it, and become politically active on our campus. The more students who go to their professors and complain about Turnitin, we reasoned, the more likely the professors would be to unite and to ask the university to curtail its use or at least to request better training measures that critique the use and implications of Turnitin. On the other hand, many of the students using Turnitin are first- or second-year undergraduates. Is it appropriate for their tutors to increase the anxiety level of these students by telling of *potential* horror stories about the "plagiarism detector"? At our university, as in many others, tutors are employees of the school. As university employees—and without tenure—do we have license to speak against an institutional practice? If we were to publicly oppose Turnitin, how might this impact the writing center and the broad support our center enjoys from faculty and administrators? Would we reduce ourselves to "bitching buddies," willing to bash professors who use Turnitin and possibly creating the misconception that we believe plagiarism should be tolerated?

What we found in our own tutoring was a space for honest discussions about the program and approaches to dealing with a professor who may not be entirely aware of how the program works. Initially, during sessions that dealt with Turnitin issues, we told students everything we had learned about the program; we told them as we have addressed earlier, how it works and what this means for the work that they are doing. There was something empowering about these conversations because students were given the kind of information they needed to address seriously how they were being implicated in the mix between their writing, their teachers' beliefs about plagiarism, and the use of the program. We shared the stories and the information we had collected not to strike fear in the hearts of anxious students but to give them a sense of what they're really dealing with and the kinds of options they had. As we saw more students with similar issues, our Turnitin information blitzes turned into focused pieces of advice that worked well for students at our university.

In efforts to be both honest and supportive to students, we first told them that it was important to speak with their professors about the situation. Beyond teaching students how to properly paraphrase and cite, the students here needed to know that it was ok to ask professors questions to point out that Turnitin was flagging parts of their papers that they had merely cited or in which discipline specific discourse was being used that would represent common knowledge in their field. In addition to trying to open up lines of communication between students and teachers, we also encouraged students to share their stories about Turnitin with other students, to let others know that there's much more than meets the eye with this program and that students have a stake in how this program is being used because it affects them both scholastically and financially at our institution. Our approach, in a nutshell, was to create avenues for discussions on Turnitin that tutors and other students could take in discussing problems of plagiarism and plagiarism detection services with faculty and other members of the University community.

As for us, we dealt with the questions we articulated earlier about the political implications of our exposé of Turnitin, our outreach to faculty, and our relationship to other students with the utmost seriousness. With our initial questions about the program and how it was used answered, we decided to become intellectually engaged with what we had learned. We presented our findings to faculty and students at our institution, and in doing so, we posed ethical, legal, and financial problems with the program that prompted faculty to think carefully about how to use Turnitin in their classes. In addition to the outreach we did locally, we brought what we had learned to the IWCA/NCPTW[2] conference in Minneapolis, where we heard even more stories about Turnitin, both positive and negative, that have helped shape our current approaches to the Turnitin dilemma on our own campus. We would recommend that other tutors do the same—to find out more about how things on their campuses work and to become engaged in conversations about various campus issues at both local and national levels. As tutors, we see a lot that other people at our institutions either take for granted or barely recognize, but we do have the ability and opportunity to speak up on those often glanced over issues and to reach out to fellow students and our faculty.

Coming back to our own research, we think that writing centers have a greater obligation to the Turnitin debate, however, which begins by acknowledging that many students are never taught what plagiarism is or how to avoid it. Many high school teachers decide that citation skills can be taught in college, while many college teachers outside of English departments decide it is not their responsibility to teach writing. For students who have had little or no instruction on how to cite sources, Turnitin is not the answer. Writing center staff should press their faculty and administration to offer all students the opportunity to learn how to document their sources before they require them to use Turnitin. Second, writing center staff should promote in-service education for all instructors who use Turnitin so that they are familiar with the program and learn to use it in limited, pedagogically sound ways. And, finally, we believe that all members of the writing center community need to keep up with technological innovations related to plagiarism detection so that faculty can be warned against and tutors can be prepared to deal with programs that are potentially detrimental to the educational process in composition.

NOTES

1. We would like to thank our writing center director Ben Rafoth for his support and guidance while we researched, wrote, and presented this piece. We would also like to thank our fellow tutors Anna Bloom, Gretchen Burger, and Jon Derr who embarked on this research project with us and have since graduated. Their efforts set the foundation for our presentations and this publication.
2. IWCA/NCPTW is the joint conference of the International Writing Centers Association and the National Conference on Peer Tutoring in Writing. [Editors' Note]

WORKS CITED

Anonymous. Personal Interview. 3 Oct. 2005.

"About Us." *iParadigms.* 2005. Web. 9 Dec. 2005.

American Psychiatric Association, *Diagnostic and Statistical Manual of Mental Disorders DSM-IV* 4th ed. Washington, D.C.: American Psychiatric Association, 1994. Print.

Bouman, Kurt, "Raising Questions About Plagiarism." *ESL Writers: A Guide for Writing Center Tutors,* Ed. Shanti Bruce and Ben Rafoth. Portsmouth: Boynton/Cook, 2004. 105–16. Print.

"Custom Essay Value." *Essay Mall.com.* Web. 3 December 2005.

Dotinga, Randy. "Electronic Snoops Tackle Copiers." *Wired.com.* 2 Apr. 2004. Web. 14 Feb. 2005.

Grinberg, Emanuella. "Student Wins Battle Against Plagiarism-Detection Requirement." *CNN.com.* 21 January 2004. Web. 3 Oct. 2005.

Herek, Jennifer, and Mark Niquette. "Ethics in the Writing Lab: Tutoring under the Honor Code." *The Writing Lab Newsletter* 14.5 (1990): 12–15. Print.

Howard, Rebecca Moore. "Plagiarisms, Authorships, and the Academic Death Penalty." *College English* 57.7 (1995): 788–806. Print.

———. "Sexuality, Textuality: The Cultural Work of Plagiarism." *College English* 62.4 (2000): 473–91. Print.

———. *Standing in the Shadow of Giants: Plagiarists, Authors, Collaborators.* Stamford, CT: Ablex, 1999. Print.

Kail, Harvey, and John Trimbur. "The Politics of Peer Tutoring." *Landmark Essays on Writing Centers.* Ed. Christina Murphy and Joe Law. Davis, CA: Hermagoras, 1995. 203–10. Print.

"Legal Document." *Turnitin Legal Information.* 2005. Web. 10 Oct. 2005

Marsh, Bill. "Turnitin.com and the Scriptural Enterprise of Plagiarism Detection." *Computers and Composition* 21 (2004): 427–38. Print.

Masur, Kate. "Papers, Profits, and Pedagogy: Plagiarism in the Age of the Internet." *Perspectives Online.* November 2001. Web. 8 November 2005.

"The Pennsylvania State System of Higher Education Technology Policy." *Indiana University of Pennsylvania.* 3 Sept. 2002. Web. 9 Dec. 2005.

"Plagiarism Prevention." *Turnitin.com.* 2006. Web. 6 March 2006.

"Privacy Pledge." *Turnitin.com.* 2006. Web. 6 March 2006.

"Products and Services." 2005. *iParadigms.* Web. 9 Dec. 2005.

"Product Tour." *Turnitin.com.* 2006. Web. 6 March 2006.

Shamoon, Linda, and Deborah H. Burns. "Plagiarism, Rhetorical Theory, and the Writing Center: New Approaches, New Locations." *Perspectives on Plagiarism and Intellectual Property in a Postmodern World.* Ed. Lise Buranen and Alice M. Roy. Albany: SUNY P, 1999. 183–92. Print.

Sherwood, Kenneth. "Syllabus-ENGL 202-Research Writing-Fall 2005." *Indiana University of Pennsylvania.* August 2005. Web. 5 April 2005.

"Students Hate Turnitin.com." *Webhosting Talk.* Web. 3 Oct. 2005.

Turnitin.com. 2006. iParadigms. Web. 15 March 2005.

Peer Tutoring and the "Conversation of Mankind"

Kenneth A. Bruffee

Kenneth Bruffee was a professor at Brooklyn College when he wrote this article. It originally appeared in the collection *Writing Centers: Theory and Administration.*

The beginnings of peer tutoring lie in practice, not in theory. A decade or so ago, faculty and administrators in a few institutions around the country became aware that, increasingly, students entering college had difficulty doing as well in academic studies as their abilities suggested they should be able to do. Some of these students were in many ways poorly prepared academically. Many more of them, however, had on paper excellent secondary preparation. The common denominator among the poorly prepared and the apparently well prepared seemed to be that, for cultural reasons we may not yet fully understand, all these students had difficulty adapting to the traditional or "normal" conventions of the college classroom.

One symptom of the difficulty was that many of these students refused help when it was offered. Mainly, colleges offered ancillary programs staffed by professionals. Students avoided them in droves. Many solutions to this problem were suggested and tried, from mandated programs to sink-or-swim. One idea that seemed at the time among the most exotic and unlikely (that is, in the jargon of the Sixties, among the most "radical") turned out to work rather well. Some of us had guessed that students were refusing the help we were providing because it seemed to them merely an extension of the work, the expectations, and above all the social structure of traditional classroom learning. And it was traditional classroom learning that seemed to have left these students unprepared in the first place. What they needed, we had guessed, was help of a sort that was not an extension but an alternative to the traditional classroom.

To provide that alternative, we turned to peer tutoring. Through peer tutoring, we reasoned, teachers could reach students by organizing them to teach each other. Peer tutoring was a type of collaborative learning. It did not seem to change what people learned but, rather, the social context in which they learned it. Peer tutoring made learning a two-way street, since students' work tended to improve when they got help from peer tutors and tutors learned from the students they helped and from the activity of tutoring itself. Peer tutoring harnessed the powerful educative force of peer influence that had been—and largely still is—ignored and hence wasted by traditional forms of education.[1]

These are some of the insights we garnered through the practical experience of organizing peer tutoring to meet student needs. More recently, we have begun to learn that much of this practical experience and the insights it yielded have a conceptual rationale, a theoretical dimension, that had escaped us earlier as we muddled through, trying to solve practical problems in practical ways. The better we understand this conceptual rationale, however, the more it leads us to suspect that peer tutoring (and collaborative learning in general) has the potential to challenge the theory and practice of traditional classroom learning itself.

This essay will sketch what seems to me to be the most persuasive conceptual rationale for peer tutoring and will suggest what appear to be some of the larger implications of that rationale. The essay will begin by discussing the view of thought and knowledge that seems to underlie peer tutoring. Then it will suggest what this view implies about how peer tutoring works. Finally, the essay will suggest what this concept of knowledge may suggest for studying and teaching the humanities.

CONVERSATION AND THE ORIGIN OF THOUGHT

In an important essay on the place of literature in education published some twenty years ago, Michael Oakeshott argues that what distinguishes human beings from other animals is our ability to participate in unending conversation. "As civilized human beings," Oakeshott says,

> we are the inheritors, neither of an inquiry about ourselves and the world, nor of an accumulating body of information, but of a conversation, begun in the primeval forests and extended and made more articulate in the course of centuries. It is a conversation which goes on both in public and within each of ourselves. . . . Education, properly speaking, is an initiation into the skill and partnership of this conversation in which we learn to recognize the voices, to distinguish the proper occasions of utterance, and in which we acquire the intellectual and moral habits appropriate to conversation. And it is this conversation which, in the end, gives place and character to every human activity and utterance.[2]

Arguing that the human conversation takes place within us as well as among us and that conversation as it takes place within us is what we call reflective thought, Oakeshott makes the assumption that conversation and reflective thought are related in two ways: organically and formally. That is, as the work of Lev Vygotsky and others has shown,[3] reflective thought is public or social conversation internalized. We first experience and learn "the skill and partnership of this conversation" in the external arena of direct social exchange with other people. Only then do we learn to displace that "skill and partnership" by playing silently, in imagination, the parts of all the participants in the conversation ourselves. As Clifford Geertz has put it, "thinking as an overt, public act, involving the purposeful manipulation of objective materials, is probably fundamental to human beings; and thinking as a covert, private act, and without recourse to such materials, a derived, though not unuseful, capability."[4]

Since what we experience as reflective thought is organically related to social conversation, the two are also related functionally. That is, because thought originates in conversation, thought and conversation tend to work largely in the same way. Of course, in thought some of the limitations of conversation are absent. Logistics, for example, are no problem at all; I don't have to go anywhere or make an appointment to get together with myself for a talk. I don't even need to dial the phone, although I do sometimes need a trip to the coffeemaker. And in thought there are no differences among the participants in preparation, interest, native ability, or spoken vernacular. On the other hand, in thought some of the less fortunate limitations of conversation may hang on. Limitations imposed by my ethnocentrism, inexperience, personal anxiety, economic interest, and paradigmatic inflexibility can constrain my thinking just as they can constrain my conversation. If my talk is narrow, superficial, biased, and confined to cliches, my thinking is likely to be so, too. Still, it remains the case that many of the social forms and conventions of conversation, most of its language conventions and rhetorical structures, its impetus and goals, its excitement and drive, its potentially vast range and flexibility, and the issues it addresses are the sources of the forms and conventions, structures, impetus, range and flexibility, and the issues of reflective thought.

The formal and organic relationship I have been drawing here between conversation and thought illuminates, therefore, the source of the quality, depth, terms, character, and issues of thought. The assumptions underlying this argument differ considerably, however, from the assumptions we ordinarily make about the nature of thought. We ordinarily assume that thought is some sort of "essential attribute" of the human mind. The view that conversation and thought are fundamentally related assumes instead that thought is a social artifact. As Stanley Fish has put it, the thoughts we "can think and the mental operations [we] can perform have their source in some or other interpretive community."[5] Reflective thinking is something we learn to do, and we learn to do it from and with other people. We learn to think reflectively as a result of learning to talk, and the ways we can think reflectively as adults depend on the ways we have learned to talk as we grew up. The range, complexity, and subtlety of our thought, its power, the practical and conceptual uses we can put it to, as well as the very issues we can address result in large measure (native aptitude, the gift of our genes, aside) directly from the degree to which we have been initiated into what Oakeshott calls the potential "skill and partnership" of human conversation in its public and social form.

To the extent that thought is internalized conversation, then, any effort to understand how we think requires us to understand the nature of conversation; and any effort to understand conversation requires us to understand the nature of community life that generates and maintains conversation. Furthermore, any effort to understand and cultivate in ourselves a particular kind of thinking requires us to understand and cultivate the community life that generates and maintains the conversation from which a particular kind of thinking originates. The first steps to learning to think better are to learn to converse better and to learn to create and maintain the sort of social contexts, the sorts of community life, that foster the kinds of conversations we value.

These relationships have broad applicability and implications far beyond those that may be immediately apparent. For example, Thomas Kuhn has argued that to understand scientific thought and knowledge, we must understand the nature of scientific communities.[6] Richard Rorty, carrying Kuhn's view and terminology further, argues that to understand any kind of knowledge, we must understand what Rorty calls the social justification of belief; that is, we must understand how knowledge is generated and maintained by communities of knowledgeable peers.[7] Stanley Fish completes the argument by positing that these "interpretive communities" are the source not only of our thought and the "meanings" we produce through the use and manipulation of symbolic structures, chiefly language; interpretive communities may also be in large measure the source of what we regard as our very selves.[8]

CONVERSATION, WRITING, AND PEER TUTORING

The line of argument I have been pursuing has important implications for educators, especially those of us who teach composition. If thought is internalized public and social talk, then writing is internalized talk made public and social again. If thought is internalized conversation, then writing is internalized conversation re-externalized.[9]

Like thought, therefore, writing is temporally and functionally related to conversation. Writing is in fact a technologically displaced form of conversation. When we write, having already internalized the "skill and partnership" of conversation, we displace it once more onto the written page. But because thought is already one step away from conversation, the position of writing relative to conversation is more complex than even that of thought. Writing is at once both two steps away from conversation and a return to conversation. By writing, we re-immerse conversation in its social medium. Writing is two steps removed from conversation because, for example, my ability to write this essay depends on my ability to talk through with myself the issues I address here. And my ability to talk through an issue with myself derives largely from my ability to converse directly with other people in an immediate social situation.

The point is not that every time I write, what I say must necessarily be something I have talked over with other people first, although I may well often do just that. What I say can originate in thought. But since thought is conversation as I have learned to internalize it, the point is that writing always has its roots deep in the acquired ability to carry on the social symbolic exchange we call conversation. The inference writing tutors and teachers should make from this line of reasoning is that our task must involve engaging students in conversation at as many points in the writing process as possible and that we should contrive to ensure that that conversation is similar in as many ways as possible to the way we would like them eventually to write.

PEER TUTORING AS SOCIAL CONTEXT

This practical inference returns us to peer tutoring. If we consider thought as internalized conversation and writing as re-externalized conversation, peer tutoring plays an important role in education for at least two reasons—both resulting from the fact that peer tutoring is a form of collaborative learning. First, peer tutoring provides a social context in which students can experience and practice the kinds of conversation that academics most value. The kind of conversation peer tutors engage in with their tutees can be emotionally involved, intellectually and substantively focused, and personally disinterested. There could be no better source of this than the sort of displaced conversation (i.e., writing) that academics value. Peer tutoring, like collaborative learning in general, makes students—both tutors and tutees—aware that writing is a social artifact, like the thought that produces it. However displaced writing may seem in time and space from the rest of a writer's community of readers and other writers, writing continues to be an act of conversational exchange.

PEER TUTORING AS A CONTEXT
FOR "NORMAL DISCOURSE"

The second reason is somewhat more complex. Peer tutoring, again like collaborative learning in general, plays an important role in education because it provides a particular kind of social context for conversation, a particular kind of community: that of status equals, or peers. This means that students learn the "skill and partnership" of re-externalized conversation not only in a community that fosters the kind of conversation academics most value, but also in a community like the one most students must eventually write for in everyday life—in business, government, and the professions.

It is worthwhile digressing a moment to establish this last point. Ordinarily people write to inform and convince other people within the writer's own community, people whose status and assumptions approximate the writer's own.[10] That is, the sort of writing most people do most frequently in their everyday working lives is what Rorty calls "normal discourse." Normal discourse, a term of Rorty's coinage based on Kuhn's term "normal science," applies to conversation within a community of knowledgeable peers. A community of knowledgeable peers is a group of people who accept, and whose work is guided by, the same paradigms and the same code of values and assumptions. In normal discourse, as Rorty puts it, everyone agrees on the "set of conventions about what counts as a relevant contribution, what counts as a question, what counts as having a good argument for that answer or a good criticism of it." The product of normal discourse is "the sort of statement that can be agreed to be true by all participants whom the other participants count as 'rational.' "[11]

The essay I am writing here is an example of normal discourse in this sense. I am writing to members of my own community of knowledgeable peers. My readers and I (I suppose) are guided in our work by the same set of conventions about what counts as a relevant contribution, what counts as a question, what counts as an answer, what counts as a good argument in support of that answer or a good criticism of it. I judge my essay finished when I think it conforms to that set of conventions and values. And it is within that set of conventions and values that my readers will evaluate the essay, both in terms of its quality and in terms of whether or not it makes sense. Normal discourse is pointed, explanatory, and argumentative. Its purpose is to justify belief to the satisfaction of other people within the author's community of knowledgeable peers. Much of what we teach today—or should be teaching—in composition and speech courses is the normal discourse of most academic, professional, and business communities. The "rhetoric" taught in our composition textbooks comprises—or should comprise—the conventions of normal discourse of those communities.[12]

Teaching normal discourse in its written form is thus central to a college curriculum because the one thing college teachers in most fields commonly want students to acquire, and what teachers in most fields consistently reward students for, is the ability to carry on in speech and writing the normal discourse of the field in question. Normal discourse is what William Perry calls the fertile "wedding" of "bull" and "cow," of facts and their relevancies: discourse on the established contexts of knowledge in a field that makes effective reference to facts and ideas as defined within those contexts. In a student who can consummate this wedding, Perry says, "we recognize a colleague."[13] This is so because to be a conversant with the normal discourse in a field of study or endeavor is exactly what we mean by being knowledgeable—that is, knowledge*able*—in that field. Not to have mastered the normal discourse of a discipline, no matter how many "facts" or data one may know, is not to be knowledgeable in that discipline. Mastery of a "knowledge community's" normal discourse is the basic qualification for acceptance into that community.

The kind of writing we hope to teach students in college, therefore, is not only the kind of writing most appropriate to work in fields of business, government, and the professions; it is also writing most appropriate to gaining competence in most academic fields that students study in college. And what both kinds of writing have in common is that they are written within and addressed to a community of status equals: peers. They are both normal discourse.

This point having, I hope, been established, the second reason peer tutoring is important in education becomes clear. As a form of collaborative learning, peer tutoring is important because it provides the kind of social context in which normal discourse occurs: a community of knowledgeable peers. This is the main goal of peer tutoring.

OBJECTIONS TO PEER TUTORING

But to say this only raises another question: how can student peers, not themselves members of the knowledge communities they hope to enter, help other students enter those communities? This question is of course a variation of the question most often raised about all kinds of collaborative learning: isn't it the blind leading the blind?

One answer to this question is that while neither peer tutors nor their tutees may alone be masters of the normal discourse of a given knowledge community, by working together—pooling their resources—they are very likely to be able to master it if their conversation is structured indirectly by the task or problem that a member of that community (the teacher) provides.[14] The conversation between peer tutor and tutee, in composition or for that matter any other subject, is structured by the demands of the assignment and by the formal conventions of academic discourse and of standard written English. The tutee brings to the conversation knowledge of the subject to be written about and knowledge of the assignment. The tutor brings to the conversation knowledge of the conventions of discourse and knowledge of standard written English. If the tutee does not bring to the conversation knowledge of the subject and the assignment, the peer tutor's most important contribution is to begin at the beginning: help the tutee acquire the relevant knowledge of the subject and the assignment.

What peer tutor and tutee do together is not write or edit, or least of all proofread. What they do together is converse. They converse about the subject and about the assignment. They converse about, in an academic context, their own relationship and the relationships between student and teacher. Most of all they converse about and *pursuant to* writing.

PEER TUTORING AND THE HUMANITIES

The place of conversation in learning, especially in the humanities, is the largest context in which we must see peer tutoring. To say that conversation has a place in learning should not of course seem peculiar to those of us who count ourselves humanists, a category that includes many if not most writing teachers. Most of us count "class discussion" one of the most effective ways of teaching. The truth, however, is that we tend to honor discussion more in the breach than in the observance. The person who does most of the "discussing" in most discussion classes is usually the teacher.

Our discussion classes have this fateful tendency to turn into monologues because underlying our enthusiasm for discussion is a fundamental distrust of it. The graduate training most of us have enjoyed—or endured—has taught us that collaboration and community activity is inappropriate and foreign to work in humanistic disciplines. Humanistic study, we have been led to believe, is a solitary life, and the vitality of the humanities lies in the talents and endeavors of each of us as individuals.[15] What we call discussion is more often than not an adversarial activity pitting individual against individual in an effort to assert what one literary critic has called "will to power over the text," if not over each other. If we look at what we do instead of what we say, we discover that we think of knowledge as something we acquire and wield relative to each other, not something we generate and maintain in company with and in dependency upon each other.

TWO MODELS OF KNOWLEDGE

Only recently have humanists of note, such as Stanley Fish in literary criticism and Richard Rorty in philosophy, begun to take effective steps toward exploring the force and implications of knowledge communities in the humanistic disciplines and toward redefining the nature of our knowledge as a social artifact. Much of this recent work follows a trail blazed a decade ago by Thomas Kuhn. The historical irony of this course of events lies in the fact that Kuhn developed his notion about the nature of scientific knowledge after first examining the way knowledge is generated and maintained in the humanities and social sciences. For us as humanists to discover in Kuhn and his followers the conceptual rationale of collaborative learning in general and peer tutoring in particular is to see our own chickens come home to roost.

Kuhn's position that even in the "hard" sciences knowledge is a social artifact emerged from his attempt to deal with the increasing indeterminacy of knowledge of all kinds in the twentieth century.[16] To say that knowledge is indeterminate is to say that there is no fixed and certain point of reference against which we can measure truth. If there is no such referent, then knowledge must be a made thing, an artifact. Kuhn argued that to call knowledge a social artifact is not to say that knowledge is merely relative, that knowledge is what any one of us says it is. Knowledge is generated by communities of knowledgeable peers. Rorty, following Kuhn, argues that communities of knowledgeable peers make knowledge by a process of socially justifying belief. Peer tutoring, as one kind of collaborative learning, models this process.

Here then is a second and more general answer to the objection most frequently raised to collaborative learning of any type: that it is a case of the blind leading the blind. It is of course exactly the blind leading the blind if we insist that knowledge is information impressed upon the individual mind by some outside source. But if we accept the premise that knowledge is an artifact created by a community of knowledgeable peers and that learning is a social process not an individual one, then learning is not assimilating information and improving our mental eyesight. Learning is an activity in which people work collaboratively to create knowledge among themselves by socially justifying belief. We create knowledge or justify belief collaboratively by cancelling each other's biases and presuppositions; by negotiating collectively toward new paradigms of perception, thought, feeling, and expression; and by joining larger, more experienced communities of knowledgeable peers through assenting to those communities' interests, values, language, and paradigms of perception and thought.

THE EXTENSION OF PEER TUTORING

By accepting this concept of knowledge and learning even tentatively, it is possible to see peer tutoring as one basic model of the way that even the most sophisticated scientific knowledge is created and maintained. Knowledge is the product of human beings in a state of continual negotiation or conversation. Education is not a process of assimilating "the truth" but, as Rorty has put it, a process of learning to "take a hand in what is going on" by joining "the conversation of mankind." Peer tutoring is an arena in which students can enter into that conversation.

Because it gives students access to this "conversation of mankind," peer tutoring and especially the principles of collaborative learning that underlie it have an important role to play in studying and teaching the humanities. Peer tutoring is one way of introducing students to the process by which communities of knowledgeable peers create referential connections between symbolic structures and reality, that is, create knowledge, and by doing so maintain community growth and coherence. To study humanistic texts adequately, whether they be student themes or Shakespeare, is to study entire pedagogical attitudes and classroom practices. Such are the implications of integrating our understanding of social symbolic relationships into our teaching—not just into *what* we teach but also into *how* we teach. So long as we think of knowledge as a reflection and synthesis of information about the objective world, teaching *King Lear* seems to involve providing a correct text and rehearsing students in correct interpretations of it. But if we think of knowledge as socially justified belief, teaching *King Lear* involves creating contexts where students undergo a sort of cultural change in which they loosen ties to the knowledge community they currently belong to and join another. These two communities can be seen as having quite different sets of values, mores, and goals, and above all quite different languages. To speak in one of a person asking another to "undo this button" might be merely to tell a mercantile tale, or a prurient one, while in the other such a request could be both a gesture of profound human dignity and a metaphor of the dissolution of a world.

Similarly, so long as we think of learning as reflecting and synthesizing information about the objective world, teaching expository writing means providing examples, analysis, and exercises in the rhetorical modes—description, narration, comparison-contrast—or in the "basic skills" of writing and rehearsing students in their proper use. But if we think of learning as a social process, the process of socially justifying belief, teaching expository writing is a social symbolic process, not just part of it. Thus, to study and teach the humanities is to study and teach the social origin, nature, reference, and function of symbolic structures.

Humanistic study defined in this way requires, in turn, a reexamination of our premises as humanists and as teachers in light of the view that knowledge is a social artifact. Since to date very little work of this sort has been done, one can only guess what might come of it. But when we bring to mind for a moment a sampling of current theoretical thought in and allied to a single field of the humanities, for example, literary criticism, we are likely to find mostly bipolar forms: text and reader, text and writer, symbol and referent, signifier and signified. On the one hand, a critique of humanistic studies might involve examining how these theories would differ from their currently accepted form if they included the third term missing from most of them. How, for instance, would psychoanalytically oriented study of metaphor differ if it acknowledged that psychotherapy is fundamentally a kind of social relationship based on the mutual creation or recreation of symbolic structures by therapist and patient? How would semiotics differ if it acknowledged that connecting "code" and phenomenon are the complex social symbolic relations among the people who make up a semiotic community? How would rhetorical theory look if we assumed that writer and reader were partners in a common, community-based enterprise, partners rather than adversaries?

And having reexamined humanistic study in this way, we could suppose on the other hand that a critique of humanistic teaching might suggest changes in our demonstrating to students that they know something only when they can explain it in writing to the satisfaction of the community of their knowledgeable peers. To do this, in turn, seems to require us to engage students in collaborative work that does not just reinforce the values and skills they begin with but that promotes a sort of resocialization.[17] Peer tutoring is collaborative work of just this sort.

THE LAST FRONTIER OF COLLABORATIVE LEARNING

The argument I have been making here assumes, of course, that peer tutors are well trained in a coherent course of study. The effectiveness of peer tutoring requires more than merely selecting "good students" and, giving them little or no guidance, throwing them together with their peers. To do that is to perpetuate, perhaps even aggravate, the many possible negative effects of peer group influence: conformity, anti-intellectualism, intimidation, and the leveling of quality. To avoid these pitfalls and marshal the powerful educational resource of peer group influence requires an effective peer tutor training course based on collaborative learning, one that maintains a demanding academic environment and makes tutoring a genuine part of the tutors' own educational development.

Given this one reservation, it remains to be said only that peer tutoring is not, after all, something new under the sun. However we may explore its conceptual ramifications, the fact is that people have always learned from their peers and doggedly persist in doing so, whether we professional teachers and educators take a hand in it or not. Thomas Wolfe's *Look Homeward, Angel* records how in grammar school Eugene learned to write (in this case, form words on a page) from his "comrade," learning from a peer what "all instruction failed" to teach him. In business and industry, furthermore, and in professions such as medicine, law, engineering, and architecture, where to work is to learn or fail, collaboration is the norm. All that is new in peer tutoring is the systematic application of collaborative principles to that last bastion of hierarchy and individualism, institutionalized education.

NOTES

1. The educative value of peer group influence is discussed in Nevitt Sanford, ed., *The American College* (New York: Wiley, 1962), and Theodore M. Newcomb and Everett K. Wilson, eds., *College Peer Groups* (Chicago: Aldine, 1966).
2. Michael Oakeshott, "The Voice of Poetry in the Conversation of Mankind," in *Rationalism in Politics* (New York: Basic Books, 1962), 199.
3. For example, L.S. Vygotsky, *Mind in Society* (Cambridge, Mass.: Harvard University Press, 1978).
4. Clifford Geertz, "The Growth of Culture and the Evolution of Mind," in *The Interpretation of Cultures* (New York: Basic Books, 1973), 76–77. See also in the same volume "The Impact of the Concept of Culture on the Concept of Man" and "Ideology as a Cultural System," Parts IV and V.
5. Stanley Fish, *Is There a Text in This Class? The Authority of Interpretive Communities* (Cambridge, Mass.: Harvard University Press, 1980), 14. Fish develops his argument fully in Part 2, pages 303–71.

6. Thomas Kuhn, *The Structure of Scientific Revolutions,* 2nd ed., International Encyclopedia of Unified Science, vol. 2, no. 2 (Chicago: University of Chicago Press, 1970).

7. Richard Rorty, *Philosophy and the Mirror of Nature* (Princeton, N.J.: Princeton University Press, 1979). Some of the larger educational implications of Rorty's argument are explored in Kenneth A. Bruffee, "Liberal Education and the Social Justification of Belief," *Liberal Education* (Summer 1982): 8–20.

8. Fish, 14.

9. A case for this position is argued in Kenneth A. Bruffee, "Writing and Reading as Collaborative or Social Acts: The Argument from Kuhn and Vygotsky," in *The Writer's Mind* (Urbana, Ill.: NCTE, 1983).

10. Some writing in business, government, and the professions may of course be like the writing that students do in school for teachers, that is, for the sake of practice and evaluation. Certainly some writing in everyday working life is done purely as performance, for instance, to please superiors in the corporate or department hierarchy. So it may be true that learning to write to someone who is not a member of one's own status and knowledge community, that is, to a teacher, has some practical everyday value; but the value of writing of this type is hardly proportionate to the amount of time students normally spend on it.

11. Rorty, 320.

12. A textbook that acknowledges the normal discourse of academic disciplines and offers ways of learning it in a context of collaborative learning is Elaine Maimon, Gerald L. Belcher, Gail W. Hearn, Barbara F. Nodine, and Finbarr W. O'Connor, *Writing in the Arts and Sciences* (Cambridge, Mass.: Winthrop, 1981; distributed by Little, Brown). Another is Kenneth A. Bruffee, *A Short Course in Writing* (Cambridge, Mass.: Winthrop, 1980; distributed by Little, Brown).

13. William G. Perry, Jr., "Examsmanship and the Liberal Arts," in *Examining in Harvard College: A Collection of Essays by Members of the Harvard Faculty* (Cambridge, Mass.: Harvard University Press, 1963); as reprinted in Bruffee, *Short Course,* 221.

14. For examples and an explanation of this process see Kenneth A. Bruffee, *Short Course,* and "CLTV: Collaborative Learning Television," *Educational Communication and Technology Journal* 30 (Spring 1982): 31ff.

15. The individualistic bias of our current interpretation of the humanistic tradition is discussed further in Kenneth A. Bruffee, "The Structure of Knowledge and the Future of Liberal Education," *Liberal Education* (Fall 1981): 181–85.

16. The history of the growing indeterminacy of knowledge and its relevance to the humanities is traced briefly in Bruffee, "The Structure of Knowledge," 177–81.

17. Some possible curricular implications of the concept of knowledge as socially justified belief are explored in Bruffee, "Liberal Education and the Social Justification of Belief," *Liberal Education* (Summer 1982): 8–20.

The Power of Common Interest for Motivating Writers: A Case Study[1]

Natalie DeCheck

Natalie DeCheck was an undergraduate at the University of Wisconsin-Madison at the time she wrote this article. It originally appeared in *The Writing Center Journal*.

Andrea, a doctoral student in education, has a demanding schedule. She has a young child, a job, a house on the market, and a spouse who travels so much that she can only see him on certain weekends. To cope with these unavoidable distractions to her research, she found the writing center and was paired with a fellow graduate student, Charisse.[2] Andrea claimed, "Even though I haven't had a chance to just really sit and think and write the way I would like to, meeting with Charisse, at least that's one hour a week that I get to dedicate to that. I'm at least moving forward in that respect." Meeting with Charisse gave Andrea the opportunity to move ahead when she may have otherwise been at a standstill with her writing. In turn, Charisse supported Andrea and helped her manage her research at a time when it seemed nearly impossible. In order to draw our attention to the role of motivation in tutoring, this article shows how Charisse's interest in Andrea and in her research served as a powerful motivating force by helping to move Andrea from a focus on external pressures to a place of intrinsic motivation where she could express excitement for her writing and research. As a case study, this research is limited in scope, but seeks to explain why a tutor's interest—that is, deep curiosity in a writer's work—is so important in writing center tutoring.

Writing center sessions are described as some of the most meaningful educational experiences for both writers and tutors. For instance, in reporting the findings of the Peer Writing Tutor Alumni Research Project, Paula Gillespie, Brad Hughes, and Harvey Kail demonstrate that, through writing center work, tutors deepen their writing and critical thinking skills and learn to "work with others collaboratively and effectively" (41). Beyond these benefits for writing, thinking, and interpersonal relationships, writers and tutors also gain confidence, a powerful motivating force. As Harvey Kail argues, "Many former tutors write about gaining confidence in themselves through a new intimacy with and understanding of the writing process." By working with others, tutors gain the skills necessary to better develop their own ideas and compositions. Writers, in turn, gain reassurance that their work is meaningful—that others see value in their work.

Drawing on and extending these claims as to the benefit of writing center work, I examine how a tutor's interest leads to a motivated writer and so may serve as a powerful learning tool. I draw on research in educational psychology that focuses on what motivates students and the impact of students' goals on motivation (Grant and Dweck). Through analysis (qualitative coding) of interviews with the writer Andrea and the tutor Charisse, I examine why writing conferences are considered meaningful by the participants involved and by researchers such as Gillespie, Hughes, and Kail. This analysis yields explanations of a tutor's role in increasing the writers' frequency in writing and in reciprocal, shared interest in building upon ideas under discussion during sessions. Further, I draw on research by psychologist Carol Dweck that finds that motivation is one of the greatest tools for acquiring new skills and knowledge, and I argue a deeper understanding of motivation can be used by tutors and incorporated in tutor education. Ultimately, I investigate what types of intrinsic and extrinsic motivation the writer experiences in and extending out of writing center sessions and the role the tutor plays in motivating the writer.

In addition to drawing upon the work of the Peer Tutor Alumni Research Project and Dweck's research, my argument also builds upon a previous study by R. Evon Hawkins. Hawkins argues that students must be motivated to regulate, plan, and monitor their own writing processes to build intrinsic motivation for writing. Hawkins offers strategies for tutors to build this motivation and instill confidence in writers. Through my case study, I extend her findings by focusing on how the tutor's interest in the writer's work can improve the writer's motivation. I begin by explaining different types of motivation and the design of my case study and then provide a description of the writer and tutor and provide analysis of their relationship. This analysis concludes with a brief consideration of possible pedagogical implications of this work.

RESEARCH METHODOLOGY

Research Context

I came to this project as an undergraduate research scholar interested in both the humanities and social sciences. My research mentor had collected a large data set of writing center conferences and interviews with both writers and tutors. As I stepped into the project and began transcribing interviews, I became particularly interested in how tutors described their interest in writers' projects. Specifically, when transcribing interviews with one writer, Andrea, and tutor, Charisse, I noticed the importance of motivation. This analytical observation led to my own study of these interviews, which I pursued over an academic year. Specifically, my qualitative study seeks to answer two questions:

- What types of motivation can occur in writing center sessions?
- What role can the tutor's interest play in motivating the writer?

The interviews were semi-structured and focused on Andrea's and Charisse's relationship, learning, and evolution of their sessions over a period of almost one year in which they worked together weekly in a writing center at a large, public research university whose students are predominantly Caucasian. They are both women of color and reported in interviews identifying with each other based on similar experiences with discrimination throughout their schooling. Though they were studying in different departments and their research was quite different, they reported liking each other from the start, and the tutor Charisse said she learned from Andrea's research and found that their discussions helped her think more critically about her own research as well.

Data Analysis and Coding Categories

As I transcribed the audiotaped interviews and then read and reread the transcripts, a set of categories emerged through a process of qualitative coding. Qualitative coding involves an iterative process of reading and annotating the transcripts, noting patterns and exceptions. As I reviewed the categories with my research mentor and presented this research for feedback from other undergraduate researchers and audiences on campus, I collapsed and expanded sub-codes within three larger categories of motivation, assurance, and lack of motivation. I borrowed these largest coding categories from Vassilis Barkoukis et al. and Marylène Gagné and Edward L. Deci who describe the three types of motivation: amotivation, extrinsic motivation, and intrinsic motivation. Often one code was related to several types of motivation, so I found myself applying multiple codes to a single line of transcript and then redefining and eventually collapsing sub-codes. This analytical process allowed me to see the usefulness of Barkoukis et al.'s and Gagné and Deci's definitions, which eventually became my largest coding categories and helped me to interpret the patterns I identified in the interview transcripts. The following definitions describe the three types of motivation Andrea and Charisse discuss as impacting and emerging from their writing conferences:

Amotivation is a lack of motivation. Barkoukis et al. describe four types of amotivation: the belief in the lack of ability to perform an activity, the belief that adapted strategies will not produce a desired outcome, the belief in an activity is too demanding, and the belief that high effort is not adequate for a successful performance (40). An example of amotivation in the interview data arises when Andrea reported feeling pressure from a grant proposal deadline while managing other demanding aspects of her life and so avoided writing altogether.

Extrinsic motivation is centered around what motivates the writer externally. In other words, extrinsic motivation takes place when the writer is motivated by someone or something. External regulation, the type most often associated with extrinsic motivation, happens when the writer participates or does an activity to get a reward or to avoid punishment (Barkoukis et al. 40; Gagné and Deci 334–36). An example of this occurred when Andrea had to finish her grant submission by a deadline and used the deadline as a motivating factor. Integrated self-regulation, another type of extrinsic motivation, differs because the action is considered part of the self but is still performed for external reasons, as when Charisse got Andrea excited about her work by sharing personal anecdotes related to Andrea's research, which, in turn, helped to fuel Andrea's writing. Extrinsic motivation and its derivatives were the most frequent codes.

Intrinsic motivation covers the opposite side of the spectrum, relating to motivation the writer feels internally. Intrinsic motivation is defined as doing an activity for "the pleasure and satisfaction of performing it" (Barkoukis et al. 39). Gagné and Deci similarly state, "Intrinsic motivation involves people doing an activity because they find it interesting and derive spontaneous satisfaction from the activity itself" (331). When Andrea wrote and researched because she was interested in the material and wanted to learn more, she was intrinsically motivated. This is also a specific example of intrinsic motivation to know, which Barkoukis et al., quoting Vallerand et al., define as "engagement in an activity 'for the pleasure and satisfaction that one experiences while learning, exploring, or trying to understand something new'" (40).

ANALYSIS

Andrea came to the writing center looking for someone to help her with the process of writing her dissertation proposal and related funding applications. She was looking to develop consistency in her research. She had been to the writing center twice before but found both sessions to be unhelpful. On her third visit, however, she was paired with Charisse, a graduate student with similar interests in education and shared experiences negotiating the large, predominantly white university. Charisse explained that she aimed at helping Andrea by facilitating brainstorming sessions, by asking her to "push further" and to elaborate on theories. Andrea reported that after sessions she had a better idea of where to go next with her research and that she tried to repeat what she'd learned in the writing center sessions when writing at home. Andrea continued meeting with Charisse for almost a year, finding value in their writing relationship and responding to Charisse's interest in her school experiences and in Chicana feminism, a topic connected with her identity as a woman of color and central to her proposed research.

Writing center sessions seem to be linked with intrinsic and extrinsic motivation—and in this way seem to counter amotivation. When Andrea first worked with Charisse toward a deadline for her grant proposal, she felt frustrated with writing. Her concerns seemed to be centered around her deadline rather than interest in her project. It was a task rather than something she had interest in doing. Andrea said, "I felt anxious because I didn't have anything written" and was "frustrated because I could not get work done." Initially after finishing her proposal, Andrea felt anxious because she did not have anything written, another form of "pressure" contributing to amotivation. As Andrea felt more comfortable "brainstorming" with Charisse, their writing center sessions became more conversational. I see these sessions linked with intrinsic and extrinsic motivation, as they often consisted of casually chatting about the topics of Andrea's project, sharing anecdotes with one another, and brainstorming how to elaborate on key points of Andrea's project. Andrea's move from a feeling of anxiety to one of comfort reflected the move from having a deadline to not having one, from writing for external reasons to writing to write.

Charisse's informal tutoring strategies also facilitated Andrea's movement from amotivation to intrinsic and extrinsic motivation. Charisse showed a genuine interest in her project, one factor that boosted Andrea's confidence. Charisse claimed, "There was a huge common interest for me there because I'm very passionate about educa-tion, as is she . . . I shared anecdotes of my own, and she shared anecdotes of hers." Through these sessions, Andrea was extrinsically motivated by knowing that another person (Charisse) found value in her work, and she also gained intrinsic motivation as a result of conversing about her topic. Andrea's description of the writing confer-ences aligns with those of Charisse, as Andrea said she experienced the most changes when she and Charisse chatted and brainstormed during sessions with "little to no agenda." Charisse explained that after several months, conferencing "was more brainstorming which [Andrea] said she found really helpful." Andrea similarly re-ported, "I usually come away from [these sessions] feeling good about myself. I usu-ally come away feeling like I have good ideas." This sense of self-worth led her to experience integrated self-regulation, a form of extrinsic motivation. Charisse de-scribed these sessions as "not pressure filled," which increased their effectiveness by lessening the chance of Andrea experiencing amotivation due to pressure. She may have felt an increased motivation to write because Charisse's interest helped her feel that she had valid ideas. Arguably, Charisse's interest in Andrea's project seems to have been the most important motivating factor for Andrea. As Charisse said, "I ac-tually was interested in her project and wanted to talk about it. I think having those same specific common interests helped us both be more interested in both of our projects." This interest seems to have motivated Andrea to think more about her proj-ect and to write outside of sessions. This self-initiated writing can be described as intrinsic motivation to know and integrated self-regulation.

The role of interest connected with shared experiences and comfort suggests the importance of common backgrounds among writers and tutors. Based on this one case study, we might ask in writing centers, how do we work toward a diverse tutoring staff so that all writers are ensured of finding a tutoring partner with genu-ine interest in not only their writing (their research and ongoing projects) but also their experiences in the university and in navigating the complex writing situations we find ourselves in? Tracing movement from amotivation to extrinsic and intrinsic motivation—in this case, from avoiding writing to writing because another person cares about the work—calls attention to the role of the tutor's interest in tutoring success.

CONCLUSION

For those of us working in writing centers, additional attention to motivation can help us to improve writing sessions. From my results, I have concluded that fostering motivation involves providing a writer with direction for where to go next, helping a writer improve his or her writing process, and showing the writer that his or her project is meaningful or interesting. These strategies go beyond what Hawkins pro-posed, as these strategies focus on long-term tutoring relationships, suggesting the importance of meeting over time and helping writers and tutors build on the one-time session. Charisse particularly motivated Andrea when she helped Andrea elabo-rate on her own ideas and to continue writing on her own and so get out of a cycle of avoiding writing altogether. In addition, she helped Andrea further her interest in a subject in which she already had a strong interest. Based on the interviews, Charisse accomplished this through informal talk and the interest she herself had in Andrea's topic. Charisse succeeded in motivating Andrea because she informally discussed troubles Andrea had with writing and asked her a range of questions about her project. Often, these questions were based on Charisse's personal interest in Andrea's project and made Andrea think about additional ways to approach what she was trying to say. Charisse's interest played a vital role in helping Andrea submit multiple grant proposals and move much closer to completing her dissertation proposal. This movement suggests that writing centers can increase their effectiveness by matching tutors and writers with similar interests or even by asking tutoring partners to consider their interests during conferences.

This project brings to writing centers both a framework and vocabulary for talking about the power of motivation in writing conferences. We often think of extrinsic and intrinsic motivation, but there's an equally important and complimentary concept of amotivation that helps enrich our understanding of motivation. As shown in this case study, interest is a powerful learning tool that plays a large role in motivating a writer. It drives the writer to want to explore a subject and strive for a better understanding through research and writing. Writing center tutors play a role in heightening extrinsic and intrinsic motivation by talking with writers and encouraging them to go deeper into their projects. As I model here, we can trace the power of writing centers by observing how ongoing partnerships develop in them and how ongoing meetings provide the structure for tutors to inspire and motivate writers, facilitating movement from amotivation to extrinsic and intrinsic motivation.

NOTES

1. I would like to acknowledge Beth Godbee, my research mentor, and the Undergraduate Research Scholars Program at the University of Wisconsin–Madison for their resources, help, and encouragement throughout this research project.
2. Andrea and Charisse are the participants' chosen pseudonyms. This research received IRB approval, and I completed IRB training when I began analyzing interview data already collected as part of a larger study in my campus writing center.

WORKS CITED

Barkoukis, Vassilis, Haralambos Tsorbatzoudis, George Grouios, and Georgios Sideridis. "The Assessment of Intrinsic and Extrinsic Motivation and Amotivation: Validity and Reliability of the Greek Version of the Academic Motivation Scale." *Assessment in Education: Principles, Policy & Practice* 15.1 (2008): 39–55. Print.

Dweck, Carol S. "The Perils of Promise of Praise." *Educational Leadership* 65.2 (2007): 34–39. Print.

Faye, Cathy, and Donald Sharpe. "Academic Motivation in University: The Role of Basic Psychological Needs and Identity Formation." *Canadian Journal of Behavioural Science* 40.4 (2008): 189–99. Print.

Gagné, Marylène, and Edward L. Deci. "Self-determination Theory and Work Motivation." *Journal of Organizational Behavior* 26.4 (2005): 331–62. Print.

Gillespie, Paula, Bradley Hughes, and Harvey Kail. "Nothing Marginal About This Writing Center Experience: Using Research About Peer Tutor Alumni to Educate Others." *Marginal Words, Marginal Work?: Tutoring the Academy in the Work of Writing Centers.* Eds. William J. Macauley, Jr., and Nicholas Mauriello. Cresskill, NJ: Hampton, 2007. 35–52. Print.

Grant, Heidi, and Carol S. Dweck. "Clarifying Achievement Goals and Their Impact." *Journal of Personality and Social Psychology* 85.3 (2003): 541–53. Print.

Hawkins, R. Evon. "From Interest and Expertise: Improving Student Writers' Working Authorial Identities." *The Writing Lab Newsletter* 32.6 (2008): 1–5. Print.

Kail, Harvey. "Situated in the Center: The Peer Writing Tutor Alumni Research Project." 2006. *The Peer Writing Tutor Alumni Research Project.* 13 May 2011. Web.

Composing Queers: The Subversive Potential of the Writing Center

Jonathan Doucette

Jonathan Doucette was an undergraduate at Oberlin College when he wrote this article. It originally appeared in the journal *Young Scholars in Writing*.

Reflecting upon my first year as a writing associate in the Oberlin College writing center, I have found myself questioning the ways in which I have been taught to write academic discourse, how certain writing functions and ways of knowing have been normalized, and what possibilities might exist beyond the borders of normative pedagogical practices. In attempting to think through these theoretical ideas, I have sensed an ominous (though, until this moment, unknown) gap in both scholarly literature and practical applications surrounding conversations in the field of composition studies and academia in a broader context. This lack—or rather oversight—has found iteration through thinking about my own identity in relation to writing and the writing center as an institution: both are pretty straight (or, to use a more suitable academic term, "heterosexual"). Through my research, therefore, I hope to find ways in which to queer[1] theoretical pedagogical approaches to writing, looking towards the writing center as a potential site for such queering. While many scholars in the field of rhetoric and composition have addressed the (in)visibility of queerness, both as a theoretical framework for engagement in composition studies and as a suitable topic for academic discussion amongst students and educators, little has been said from the perspective of tutors and students about the writing center's role in resisting, (re)producing, and/or remaining ambivalent towards queer writing pedagogies (or a complex combination of the three). Scholars do cite two specific explanations for a lack of queer engagement: the "compulsory heterosexuality" and heteronormativity that institutions and American society at large demand for students' sexual identity and the historical amnesia of the histories surrounding the LBGTQ movement. I hope to expand upon these thoughtful preliminary conversations of queerness in composition studies and academic institutions, exploring and critically engaging with the ways scholars have attempted to combat such normalizing pedagogies, which ultimately work to hinder (indeed, silence) many students' voices. In understanding how and why queerness is noticeably absent in composition studies, I hope to offer ways to resist normalizing discourses, looking towards the writing center as a potentially subversive queer space. By employing an interdisciplinary framework both within and beyond the borders of the writing center, I hope to create space in academia through which queer (and queer-minded) students and educators might find ways to claim a sense of agency in and through writing.

"COMPULSORY HETEROSEXUALITY": (SEXUAL) ASSUMPTIONS IN COMPOSITION STUDIES

In John Goshert's article "Reproductions of (Il)Literacy: Gay Knowledge and First-Year Composition Pedagogy," he articulates the ways in which students are neither compelled on their own nor institutionally encouraged to apply queerness—or any form of sexual iteration—in their writing. Goshert describes this phenomenon as linked to the implicit (and overt) heteronormative structure that exists in much of academia. As he states:

> The connection between developments in LBGT/q studies and composition lies in the assimilation into academe of mass culture's normative values and practices. In both instances that assimilation is predicated on the suppression of critical inquiry, and on allowing students to simply consume and reproduce the discursive products of dominant culture in the classroom. (18)

In other words, true academic critical inquiry is replaced with assimilation into "the discursive products of dominant culture." The classroom and the students who enter it are enmeshed in the (hetero)normative discourses prevalent in American society, which are reinforced as students are in turn taught that writing means assimilating to the sexual status quo. Indeed, as Jessie Blackburn articulates in her book review of Jonathan Alexander's *Literacy, Sexuality, Pedagogy: Theory and Practice for Composition Studies*, "one of the most important assumptions we can examine with students . . . is the assumption that a classroom is a value-free or neutral space" (229). The cultural laws that govern American society are still present within the classroom.

The lack of a queer framework within the field of composition studies also brings to light the various assumptions academics have about the very nature of what composition studies *is*. In her essay "I Thought Composition Was about Commas and Quotes, Not Queers," Danielle Mitchell speaks of the resistance she encountered from colleagues upon attempting to introduce issues of queerness in a first-year rhetoric class. Though some of her colleagues applauded her efforts, many felt "that writing courses [were] about punctuation, spelling, grammar, and sentence structure" (27). Mitchell found unique ways to combat such discourse, claiming that she was training her students to become "critical citizens" both within and beyond the academy, and that her course goals "revolve around reading, writing, thinking, and public discourse" (27). Mitchell uses queerness as a way to engage her students actively and critically with pertinent political topics and "texts" in both an academic and "public" forum, challenging them to think of the ways reading and writing can *produce* ideas or mobilize action. In their analysis "The Queer Turn in Composition Studies: Reviewing and Assessing an Emerging Scholarship," Jonathan Alexander and David Wallace highlight the importance of looking at the intersections of queerness and composition studies, pointing to the ways sexual difference influences both "literacy and political efficacy" and "our ability to speak about our lives," thus impacting "our sense of freedom to participate in [American] society" (W304). Queerness not only has a place within composition studies, it is crucial: it gives students a sense of agency and a way to write themselves into American society. Alexander and Wallace's arguments challenge me, as a writing associate, to think of how my own position(ality) occupies this important and emerging intersection in either supportive or oppressive ways; as a writing tutor, I have the opportunity (indeed, the obligation) to create an open, low-stakes, and welcoming environment where students are able to uncover the ways they might see their lives communicated through writing. Ensuring the availability of this open environment where students are allowed to take such personal risks is, in essence, a queer practice, one that, until recently, has remained unseen in institutional contexts.

As a transfer student, I have had the opportunity to witness the ways in which these theoretical arguments play themselves out in different academic institutions. When I was a first-year student at a conservative liberal arts college in upstate New York, heteronormativity left its invisible mark on my identity as a student writer. For example, in my first-year, writing-intensive seminar, Introduction to Poetry, there were many classroom discussions about "human nature." These conversations often rested on assumptions about the essential nature of human identity, present "since the beginning of time" with little regard for differences in cultural and historical moments. One such assumption was the belief that monogamous, presumably heterosexual relationships were both appropriate and "natural." The discursive techniques utilized by both students and professors lacked the "critical inquiry" of sexuality studies Goshert sees as absent in academic institutions more broadly. How, then, did this moment influence my own identity as a student writer?

If I looked at identity as a rigid, confined, ahistorical, and unchanging entity, my ability to change and grow as a writer was stalled; as my classroom disallowed an academic discourse to legitimize and make sense of sexual identity (or rather, *my* sexual identity), I found difficulty in placing myself within my writing. Thus, my first-year work shows an objective distancing. Such use of distancing and objectivity, it has been argued by numerous scholars, is a distinctly masculine trait. According to Donovan Hohn, for instance, in his essay "'The Me Experience': Composing as a Man," the adoption of such a masculine voice "can result only in a narrowing of possibilities, can produce only a fiction of authenticity and wholeness, a hegemony of one 'style' or voice over the many other voices each of us can and do speak" (288). Indeed, as is the case with many first-year writers, this masculine voice seeks authority at the expense of understanding how one's subjectivity (as informed by one's sexual identity) may influence writing.

Embedded within these notions of masculinity, I argue, is the implicit assumption of heterosexuality. In ignoring or silencing the possibility of sexual discursive practices within academic writing, as Mitchell attempts to resist through her pedagogical practices, a challenge to hegemonic sexual identities (or even the understanding that such identities *exist*) remains difficult. As an excerpt from one of my first-year papers demonstrates, my attempt to speak in objective, masculine (heterosexual) ways disallowed understandings of the "human condition" in different historical and cultural moments: "For countless generations, beginning with the earliest philosophers, man has constantly questioned his reason for roaming the Earth. This journey has led many of these thinkers, writers, and poets, such as the twelfth-century Afghani poet Rumi and the English poet William Blake, not only to question man's existence, but to understand his true nature." As an objective writer, I was unable to account for historical specificity ("For countless generations") except in ways that reproduced hegemonic, masculine notions of "human nature." The "trueness" of such nature implies an essential understanding of maleness as both an identity category and a way of understanding and approaching the world. Being a queer, male-bodied, male-identified first-year writer, I excluded myself from my writing insofar as I assumed a masculine position; as one of the tenets of the masculine identity is distinct, compulsory heterosexuality, I disallowed myself the ability to account for my own positionality within my writing. By discursively reproducing knowledge about maleness (and the "trueness" of such a category) and by using the male pronoun to account for humanity in a broader sense, I was unable to work through how my own positionality may have influenced my understanding of the world. As my first-year experience helps illuminate, writing without taking into account my own sexual identity reproduced "appropriate," distanced, masculine, heterosexual discourse that constrained my identity as a student writer and beyond. I silenced my own voice in this first-year classroom, viewing my sexual identity as distinct from—indeed, as irreconcilable with—my academic writings.

Upon transferring to a more politically conscious institution in my sophomore year, I found that topics of sexual inquiry were considered appropriate modes of understanding my identity as a writer. My worldview was dramatically expanded in informative ways; identity politics jargon became, as if overnight, a part of my every-day repertoire. I scoffed at my pre-Oberlin self, self-assuredly (and surprisingly non-reflexively) mocking the fact that I had once submitted to the gender binary or thought "gay" was an easily defined, essential category. For my winter-term break, I went back to my first-year institution, an air of (moral?) superiority in my wake, a knowing smirk on my face. When asked by my former classmates about the course of my academic life, I told them I was a "comparative American studies major," relishing the dumbfounded, confused looks on their faces when I began to describe my new-found academic self. I peppered each conversation with jargon ("heteropatriarchy," "imaginings of transgender identities," "queer") and, dare I say, pretention. As the weekend progressed, the dialogue had ended between my friends and me. Through both my airs and highly specified language aimed at capitalizing on my friends' un-familiarity with such discourse, I had created two divisions: I had isolated myself from my friend group while simultaneously distancing my peers from topics of gender and sexual inquiry. Once again I was left with feelings of isolation. I had found a niche within academia to explore that part of myself previously left unspoken, unre-solved, and yet the discourse I was attempting to appropriate (and the ways I mobi-lized such discourse) separated me from my peers in detrimental ways.

I was once again left without a place to reconcile my academic and personal selves. Looking back, it seems as though I was engaging with what David Bartholomae describes as "inventing the university"; in his article of that title, Bartholomae addresses the many ways students attempt to adopt "academic" discourse. Through my unfamiliarity with the discourse present in the academic (inter)discipline of comparative American studies, I was "trying on" these languages, "learn[ing] to speak [the] language" of scholars I had become fascinated by (605). My "air of authority" on gender and sexuality studies was, in reality, an "approximation of" jargon, rather than a true understanding (if such is possible) of this discourse (607). My attempt to write through these ideas in this very article stands as yet another testament to the various ways liberal arts students attempt to maneuver through multiple academic disciplines, each with distinct forms of languages and ways of knowing. I had forfeited one way of relating to the world (heteronormative) for another (queer), yet each set of discourse separated me from communities I wanted to be a part of. How to reconcile my two (or more) discourse communities?

Perhaps the answer might be found in Goshert's analysis. His article concludes that the lack of queerness within academia (and the field of composition studies) is due to—ironically—a lack of critical engagement with *straightness*. In other words, sexuality in general is rarely a "suitable" topic for academic discussions and writings. Sexuality, as Goshert would argue, is ubiquitous in American society, and yet is often relegated to the "private" sphere. This results in a lack of critical engagement with sexuality of any sort. In order to remedy this lack of engagement, Goshert calls upon his students to "develop a more critical literacy about gender and sexuality, and about social structures that place such a high premium on gender/sexual conformity" (18). Goshert's model has students look beyond their own sexual identity to uncover the power structures embedded in American society that construct sexualities, valuing certain sexual expressions while marginalizing others. As scholar Robert Toynton states in his article "'Invisible Other': Understanding Safe Spaces for Queer Learners and Teachers in Adult Education," a piece examining queer pedagogy techniques for adult learners, "Only through challenging and making visible the heteronormativity of the environment can the queer student (or teacher) be allowed to feel they belong" (187). By allowing students to think through these various (often invisible) structures of privilege and oppression *through writing,* it may be that both the field of composition studies and academia at large will open up space for nonnormative (or, indeed, normative) sexual expressions. It may offer students a place to belong. In making explicit the intersection of composition studies and queerness, I feel that, as a writing center associate, I am finding both a productive method and a physical context to bring such discussions of sexuality into the realm of academic discourse more broadly.

What Goshert and others are less successful in articulating, however, are the ways in which heteronormative discourses may be combated (or, at the very least, called into question). According to Gillian Rose in her work *Visual Methodologies,* discourse finds its power through its productivity. In other words, discourse is powerful because it produces subjectivities. The heteronormative discourse in American society disallows the queer subject a voice—it works to render queer subjectivities invisible. As Rose describes, however, such discourse is not absolute:

> Discourse disciplines subjects into certain ways of thinking and acting, but this is not simply repressive; it does not impose rules for thought and behaviour on pre-existing human agents. Instead, human subjects are produced through discourses. Our sense of our self is made through the operation of discourse. (137)

Mirroring Michel Foucault's discussion of power,[2] discourses do not operate in a top-down power hierarchy, but rather in a complex web of power, oppression, and privilege. When students write discourse, they are, in a sense, writing themselves. Despite the power of heteronormativity in American society, such discourse does not always produce repressed subjects: moments of subversion can and do exist. Scholar Harry Denny uses queer theory as a way to mobilize such subversion in his article "Queering the Writing Center," describing such theory as analyzing "practices that inscribe meaning, making certain bodies and ways of doing visible and marked and others illusory, invisible or unmarked" (42). Like Denny, I see the writing center as a space to make the invisible (the queer body) visible.

What continues to trouble my own academic and sexual identity, however, are the ways academia has taught me to appropriately engage with sexual identity. As my experience attempting to navigate two academic and personal spheres can attest to, sexual discourse within academia offers the space for both empowerment and new forms of distancing. Even now, as a third-year (and more seasoned) comparative American studies major, I hear from my peers at Oberlin how inaccessible and shaming "my" discourse sounds to those unfamiliar with the tricky terrain of intersectional identity politics. What is the point of gender and sexuality discourses if not to create and make change while building community? How can change commence when such discourse is at best alienating for some, at worst shaming and exclusionary?

HISTORICIZING THE QUEER BODY: AMNESIA AND HOMONORMATIVITY

Academics, students, and institutions must now look for ways to create more accessible discourse(s) in terms of sexuality and gender studies, bridging the gaps between queer, academic, and more "normative" communities. How such a discourse may take shape, however, is difficult to determine. While there are academic spaces where lines of sexual inquiry may be addressed, they are often relegated to a few distinct disciplinary categories (most generally found in the humanities and, occasionally, the social sciences), thus offering inclusion for some while excluding others. Who, for instance, has access and the ability to read Foucault's *History of Sexuality* in a productive classroom environment? Unless students and/or educators actively seek out ways to incorporate topics of sexual and gender engagement within writing, heteronormative assumptions will continue to remain unquestioned across other academic institutions and disciplines. Instead of thinking of queer history as relegated to specific communities, educators must start seeing sexual diversity as part of *all* of our histories, not a select view.

Goshert's article notes the ways in which queerness, both in practice and theory, remains invisible in academic spheres due to the lack of a queer historical framework. He shifts his focus from a (hetero)normative audience to that of queer youth deliberately studying queer literature. Goshert relates that while teaching John Rechy's 1963 novel *City of Night* to (supposedly queer) students, he was met with resistance to concepts such as public sex and other markers of radical queer culture in the 1960s and 1970s. Rechy describes his own reaction to queer youth in academia: "Most gay people think history begins the last time they had sex with somebody. I've pointed out that our history is very long, but the record of it is very short" (Goshert 16). The lack of an archival memory for queer history results in a historical amnesia, both within and beyond the queer community. Queer radicalism of the past has been replaced with a homonormativity, or the desire for LBGTQ individuals to "claim their normalcy within dominant culture" (Goshert 16). The desire to learn of queer culture and history, then, is replaced by a desire to fit in, rather than push against, normative society.

The lack of archival memory and validity for LBGTQ history is also present (or rather, absent) within the field of composition studies and the writing center. Given the implicit heteronormative nature of academia described by Goshert above, one way to combat such normalizing powers is to teach, learn, and—perhaps most importantly—*value* the voices of queer authors and activists of the past. As Jonathan Alexander and David Wallace state, LBGTQ narratives and experience must become a part of academia in a *"proactive* way," beginning "with the premise that queer people need to have their lives and perspectives represented substantively on their own terms and not only as an aberration from some mythical norm" (W309). By employing a critical (queer) pedagogy, students are able to "examine how dominant cultural norms about sexual orientation shape our sense of self" (W309). By demanding the recognition of sexual identity (specifically queer representations) in academia, students and educators will begin to develop an institutional history, which will in turn challenge students to examine the ways we organize our identities around sexual expression.

Thinking again about my own relationship to academic institutions: I assumed as a first-year student that my history as a queer male was *supposed* to be absent from standard academic classes. Queer histories had been simultaneously silenced and actively overlooked by educators in my high school—why should college be any different? Given that I am unable to find a place for myself within the history of American society, it should come as no wonder that writing queerness into academia is a difficult feat. Indeed, in attempting to write through this paper, I find myself grasping at rhetorical straws, paralyzed both by the lack of research on this topic and by my insecurities, feeling as though queerness may not have a place within my identity as a student writer. And yet I cannot help but feel as though something within me (as a result of my sexual identity) pushes me to examine the unspoken heteronormative assumptions within my writing that create my identity as an academic.

MINDING THE GAP: INTERDISCIPLINARITY AS QUEERING ACADEMIC WAYS OF KNOWING

How do we bring queerness into theories of composition? How can we ensure that academic institutions (in this case, the writing center) remain accessible both for queer students and queer academic approaches? While queerness is entering conversations among scholars and teachers in the field of composition studies, I would like to propose that the concepts of interdisciplinarity and intersectionality can be useful tools to further the process of queering academic discourse.

Philip Deloria, an American studies scholar, defines interdisciplinarity as an academic approach that allows one to engage a text in multiple, intersecting ways. As he states:

> One may enter a project at the level of the text, the context, or the theory. In other words, questions may come from registers ranging from the material to the abstract, and one can weave analyses among these three registers. In doing so, one utilizes different disciplinary methodologies, blurring them together in true interdisciplinary form. (15)

In looking at a text as originating from a specific historical and cultural moment ("the context"), students can better understand their own positionality and identity as directly influencing their writings. Applying a theoretical framework to a text *within* a certain context also adds another layer of analysis that challenges the assumptions implicit in a singular disciplinary framework. Approaching a text in multiple and varying ways not only queers the academic notion of "disciplinary" study as the only legitimate form of articulating knowledge, but acts as a way to check the student's own assumptions in terms of methodological approaches to texts. In articulating the "context" of their writing, students are encouraged to think about how their own cultural and sociopolitical stance in society may influence their findings. This, in turn, may lead to further engagement with the concept of identity in a broader sense, potentially challenging the normalizing discourses that construct hegemonic identities.

In order for such engagement to take place, "writing across the curriculum" (WAC) endeavors that seek to advance the importance of disciplinary writing in universities may benefit from thinking beyond, across, and between the lines of disciplinarity. In writing this article I am attempting in some way to begin to bridge the gap between composition and queer studies. How would biology papers, for instance, benefit (or at the very least change) from a queer approach in what students choose to write about? Disciplinarity frames not only the way students write, but the way they think, understand, and engage with the world and their identities. Similar to teaching queer histories (again, assuming that such a history is integral to "straight" histories, not separate from them), intersectionality offers space for such engagement between and beyond disciplines.

THE SPACE WE OCCUPY: ACCESSIBILITY
IN THE WRITING CENTER AS INSTITUTION

The largest gap in the scholarly literature of composition studies concerns the physical space we, as tutors, occupy in the writing center. How do our identities resist and/or engage potentially oppressive normative ways of being and writing? How does the atmosphere we create as a unit and institution offer space for students to either challenge or reproduce dominant hegemonic (academic) discourses? In a very practical sense, how do we ensure that students feel safe to express non-normative sexual identities?

In attempting to queer the ways in which we think about and do writing, we must also queer the writing center as an institution that occupies physical space within a structure of power, oppression, and privilege. Indeed, a queer student may not find the necessary support within a writing center that does not recognize his/her/hirs[3] identity and/or ways of thinking about writing as legitimate or a cause for serious academic engagement. This "queering," as I see it, rests on the shoulders of tutors. We must be continually aware not only of the various ways we interact with tutees (and the power structures laden therein), but of how we engage with one another.

In order to think of the writing center as a potentially subversive queer space—employing the aforementioned interdisciplinary/sectional framework—it is important to note both the constraints and the possibilities of the writing center as an institution. In other words, we must first identify the purpose of a writing center and the tutor's role in creating such a space. As Stephen North's influential 1984 essay "The Idea of a Writing Center" famously states, "in a writing center the object is to make sure that writers, and not necessarily their texts, are what get changed by instruction. In axiom form it goes like this: Our job is to *produce better writers, not better writing*" (438; emphasis mine). The burden placed upon the writing tutor, therefore, is to usher a "novice" writer into the realm of the experienced through taking a holistic view of the writing process, using a "participant-observer methodology" (438–39). The process North proposes operates under the assumption that students seeking guidance from the writing center are genuinely interested in becoming better writers and have both time and resources to commit to their writing. Many scholars in the field of rhetoric and composition, however, have challenged North's idealized vision of a writing center. Indeed, North himself responded with his own critique in his 1994 essay "Revisiting 'The Idea of a Writing Center,'" paying closer attention to institutional, cultural, and political barriers that may prevent tutors or students from being "changed." In very practical terms, a given writing center may be constrained by a lack of funding and institutional support, engagement on the part of those entering the writing center, time commitments/constraints on the part of both student and tutor, and the murky relationship between student tutor and tutee. All of these issues highlight the rift between scholars' theoretical hopes for a writing center and the practical realities student tutors often face.

What is interesting about North's original ideal, however, is his call for the writing center to create "better writers"; that there exist constraints upon the writing center is clear, yet the notion that such a space has the potential to change writers, "not writing," is certainly intriguing. I am left wondering, however, what a "better writer" looks like and how a student tutor and tutee must work together in order to create such change. Rather than think of the writing center as a space in which unqualified, inexperienced writers are transformed into appropriate academics—all the while assuming that student tutors are the gatekeepers to such academic discourse—I would like to see the writing center as a queer institution, challenging academic ways of knowing in place of reproducing suitable hegemonic academic writing styles. For as Denny states, the temptation to reproduce these norms is always already ingrained in those walking into and working for the writing center: "[C]odes of privilege and their rules of usage are often natural to or already learned by us"; "successful academics and students" are successful because of the ways they have (unconsciously) subscribed to such "normalized" writing functions (51). Denny describes this phenomenon as "passing," stating that those in the "margins" (such as queer people, people of color, first-generation students, and others) are able to negotiate their stance between "margin and center" in adopting specific types of "appropriate" academic discourses. How, then, might we ensure that the writing center does not succumb to this temptation?

Though these normative realities exist, the central construction of the writing center has, in many ways, queer elements already ingrained into its structure. During my time as a writing associate at the Oberlin College writing center, for instance, I found myself surrounded by academics from numerous departments: from religion, English, and creative writing to clarinet performance, biology, and environmental studies. In like fashion, students who enter the writing center also run the gamut of academic disciplines. The writing center, as a place allowing a unique exchange of academic ideas (and the different ways of writing such disciplines demand), is the ideal locus for the interdisciplinary framework. As Linda K. Shamoon and Deborah H. Burns state in "A Critique of Pure Tutoring," an article addressing the "hands-off" method espoused by North, "[M]ost of us sometimes have difficulty seeing alternatives to our own ways of thinking. . . . [W]ithin a strong system generally held notions and behaviors so permeate our lives that only they seem legitimate or make sense, which all other notions and behaviors seem illegitimate" (140). What better way to challenge one's (academic) assumptions about the world—one's epistemology—than to directly engage with those from different academic fields?

As a writing tutor in the Oberlin College writing center, I have witnessed first-hand how students (both tutor and tutee) have their ways of knowing the world challenged in thinking interdisciplinarily. For instance, one evening I was working with a first-year pre-med student who was writing a paper concerning the legal merits of same-sex marriage for a political science course. Though neither the student nor I were well versed in "political science discourse," we were now asked to work with one another in the late evening hours the day before her paper was due. As we read her paper out loud together, her strong, informative writing style was instantly apparent; the paper was riddled with statistical facts, legal precedence, and historical dates worthy of the work of a seasoned academic. By the conclusion of her paper, I had learned about the political history of same-sex marriage through a lens—namely, the academic style she was adopting—that was entirely foreign to me. I was left a bit dumbfounded by the end, as she eagerly looked towards me for advice, her eyes begging for some sort of constructive criticism or critique. I felt a bit insecure and unsure of what to say. Her scientific background—apparent in her objective language and the setup of her argument—was clearly present throughout her work and I could find nothing inherently "wrong" with her research. The only thing I could think to ask was, "Why did you choose this topic?" She stared blankly at me, the dumbfounded look now on her face. For the first few minutes of our conversation, she appeared resistant to using her own "voice" in her work. Slowly, however, she began writing about her gay brother and her exposure to the queer community as a result. Her paper began to take an entirely different approach to the matter of same-sex marriage, bridging the gap between her personal and political selves. She left the writing center with a new lens through which to understand how to write about the topic of same-sex marriage (by writing about herself), while I had learned a new approach to discussing the future of the LBGTQ movement. Through the writing center, as a result of the interdisciplinary dialogue we participated in, both of our assumptions about writing were shifted in profound ways.

Reflecting on this experience, I have begun to think about the implications for future tutoring moments or (a grander idea) for the future of academic discourse. As I have argued throughout, I see the writing center as a potential interdisciplinary, queer, safe space that may encourage students to take personal and academic risks through writing. While certain disciplines currently frown upon (or actively resist) the inclusion of personal narrative within academic writing, such experiences are crucial in uncovering the way a student knows the world, as evidenced by my exchange with this young woman. Interdisciplinary dialogue opens up space in academic discussions to show the way our identities act as organizing structures that shape the way we view the world and, ultimately, the arguments we make about it. As Denny states, "Tutorials become spaces where students and tutors alike shore up, build anew, and deconstruct identities and the ways of knowing that are sutured to them" (45–46). In having the writing center act as a space to share and critically think about our identities (both of tutor and tutee), we may be able to queer the way academic fields write about our (subjective) experiences in the world. This queering brings to light not only *how* we come to know the world, but *who* is allowed to know and under what circumstances. Perhaps the writing center, as it seeks to create its subversive potential, should not reject entirely the traditional codes of the academy—for the material negative effects for a student who takes such a risk would be many, not least a failing grade—nor should the center completely acquiesce to such codes either. A complex hybrid of the two approaches may be called for. Denny calls this the "third" type of communication, one that encourages students to "invoke dialects as part of introductions and descriptions of personal experiences," bridging the gap between "home" or "private" language and "academic" language in ways that render the student legible to a larger academic community (54). These maneuvers may, perhaps, begin the process of queering academic discourse in a broader sense.

Though the writing center has the potential to act as a queer academic space, its physical environment continues to be enmeshed in the (hetero)normative values of American society (and, more specifically, the academic institution to which it is attached). Though interdisciplinary exchange creates possibilities for queer voices to be heard, without institutional support and training for rising tutors that address issues of accessibility for historically marginalized students (queer students included), the writing center may not fully become a place for queer students and queer-minded academics. Just as a feminist composition pedagogy asks its students to "see how the larger culture positions [students] as gendered," the writing center must also employ a queer pedagogy, one that challenges students to see themselves as distinctly sexualized subjects (Alexander and Wallace W304). In doing so, students will be challenged to see themselves as subjects influenced by normative societal values, subjects whose voices, writing styles, and methodological frameworks are influenced by the ways they are shaped as sexual beings.

CONCLUSION

I came to this research topic with the hope of finding a way to reconcile my academic and personal selves: to find a way to bridge the gap between the academic disciplines of composition and queer studies, while also attempting to place myself personally within certain academic spaces. In short, this paper is an attempt at belonging.

In considering more broadly the ways academic institutions produce ways of knowing the world, I am challenged to think about what it means to write sexuality into the field of composition studies. This paper arguably stands as one of my most personal to date. The final product feels at once the most uncomfortable yet surprisingly authentic academic paper I have produced. The emotional investment I have made demands not only a certain level of recognition—not simply visibility—but an institutional support that addresses and encourages the types of risks queer students take in writing about sexuality. As Toynton points out, "While being both other and invisible, [the queer student] is subjected to a burden of emotional work of a different order of magnitude to that of the privileged majority" (187). While the emotional work of the queer student may be different than that of those more in line with normative sexualities, it remains clear that sexuality in general continues to be the source of much anxiety both within and beyond the academy. Through combating heteronormative discourses (in writing), addressing and valuing the histories of LBGTQ persons, and using the writing center as a queer, interdisciplinary space, however, perhaps queer voices (and, in turn, all voices) will find safe spaces of iteration within academia. For indeed, the writing process can be a profoundly personal, emotional task for any student; until we begin to validate such emotional investments, we cannot queer, alter, shift, and/or call into question normative pedagogical writing practices.

NOTES

1. By "queer," I refer not only to a nonnormative sexual identity, but to a process by which academic, political, and/or cultural normativities are defamiliarized, shifted, altered, and seriously called into question. "Queer" as used throughout my analysis can be understood, then, as an adjective (a "queer" person) or a verb (to "queer," or to make the familiar unfamiliar).
2. For more in Foucault's discussion of discourse as it relates to sexuality specifically, see Foucault (18).
3. "Hir" is a third-gender pronoun. "He/him/his" would be assigned for male-bodied individuals, just as "ze/hir/hirs" would be for those who do not conform, either physically or politically, to the gender binary. "Third-gender" does not necessarily imply an essential "third" category of gender, but rather works as a disruption to the gender binary.

WORKS CITED

Alexander, Jonathan, and David Wallace. "The Queer Turn in Composition Studies: Reviewing and Assessing an Emerging Scholarship." *College Composition and Communication* 61.1 (2009): W300–20. Web. 26 May 2010.

Bartholomae, David. "Inventing the University." *When a Writer Can't Write: Studies in Writer's Block and Other Composing-Process Problems*. Ed. Mike Rose. New York: Guilford, 1985. 134–66. Rpt. in *The Norton Book of Composition Studies*. Ed. Susan Miller. New York: Norton, 2009. 605–30. Print.

Blackburn, Jessie. Rev. of *Literacy, Sexuality, Pedagogy: Theory and Practice for Composition Studies,* by Jonathan Alexander. *Journal of International Women's Studies* 10.2 (2008): 226–30. Print.

Deloria, Philip J. "Broadway and Main: Crossroads, Ghost Roads, and Paths to an American Studies Future." *American Quarterly* 61 (2009): 1–25. Print.

Denny, Harry. "Queering the Writing Center." *The Writing Center Journal* 25.2 (2005): 39–62. Print.

Foucault, Michel. *The Will to Knowledge: The History of Sexuality, Part 1*. London: Penguin, 1998. Print.

Goshert, John. "Reproductions of (Il)Literacy: Gay Cultural Knowledge and First-Year Composition Pedagogy." *Composition Studies* 36.1 (2008): 11–27. Print.

Hohn, Donovan. "'The Me Experience': Composing as a Man." *Working with Student Writers: Essays on Tutoring and Teaching*. Ed. Leonard Podis and JoAnne Podis. New York: Peter Lang, 2005. 285–99. Print.

Mitchell, Danielle. "I Thought Composition Was about Commas and Quotes, Not Queers: Diversity and Campus Change at a Rural Two-Year College." *Composition Studies* 36.2 (2008): 23–49. Print.

North, Stephen M. "The Idea of a Writing Center." *College English* 46.5 (1984): 433–46. Print.

———. "Revisiting 'The Idea of a Writing Center.'" *The Writing Center Journal* 15.1 (1994): 7–19. Print.

Rose, Gillian. *Visual Methodologies: An Introduction to the Interpretation of Visual Materials*. London: Sage, 2007. Print.

Shamoon, Linda K., and Deborah H. Burns. "A Critique of Pure Tutoring." *The Writing Center Journal* 15.2 (1995): 134–51. Print.

Toynton, Robert. "'Invisible Other': Understanding Safe Spaces for Queer Learners and Teachers in Adult Education." *Studies in the Education of Adults* 38.2 (2006): 178–94. Web. 26 May 2010.

Why My Best Teachers
Are Peer Tutors

Brian Fallon

Brian Fallon is a professor at the Fashion Institute of Technology–SUNY (FIT). This text was delivered as a keynote speech at the 2011 National Conference on Peer Tutoring in Writing (NCPTW).

I would like to begin by thanking Paula, Shanti, and Kevin for inviting me to speak to you today.[1] NCPTW is a very special part of my academic life, and it's a great honor to have the opportunity to share my thoughts on peer tutoring with you.

I'll start with a quick story about a former peer tutor who visited me a few weeks before this semester started. Joylene, who was one of the first tutors I hired to help start the Writing Studio at FIT, stopped by to say hello and tell me what she's been up to. She now works at the Children's Museum of Manhattan, which may seem unusual for a graduate of the Fashion Institute, but it actually fits her perfectly. Her major was History of Art and Museum Professions, and she was hired to work in the Museum's education department. In a few short years, she has become one of the head teachers at the museum. I, of course, was very pleased by this news, especially since Joylene explained to me that she relies on her experience as a peer tutor to work with the other educators and the children who visit. Joylene's story is impressive to me. As a graduate of a school with no courses or formal training in education, she's managed to become a head teacher at a New York City museum. Her talent and drive have a lot to do with her success, as does her disposition. She's pretty much the nicest person you could ever meet. But I think what strikes me is how she's used her peer tutoring experience to position herself in such a way.

Peer tutoring provided her valuable insight into how people learn and how to operate with patience and understanding when working with others. And the more I thought about what Joylene has been able to accomplish as a result of her time as a peer tutor, the more I wanted to hear from her about what she learned at the Writing Studio. And I ask myself, as a writing center director and a teacher, how do I educate and mentor another Joylene?

In order to get at what I think might be the answer, I'll begin by addressing what I believe is a critical issue for both tutors and tutor educators: reconciling the representation of tutors in our scholarly work with the daily pedagogical and institutional demands writing center tutors experience. Scholarship is meant to inform practice, to assist in uncovering the dynamics that influence every session that tutors have, and it often does this without considering the perspective of one key figure—the tutor. This is not a new problem. It is one that has developed over time, and we can trace it back to at least 1984, and possibly even earlier than that. But we know for sure that in 1984 Stephen North told us, "our job is to produce better writers, not better writing" (438). And in that article, an article that has been afforded a special place in writing center history and lore, there is actually very little talk of tutors—they are part of the collective 'our,' but not singled out as the individuals charged with the task of producing better writers. North certainly provided writing centers a sense of mission, but a great cost comes with such a handy statement.

So, I have come to a place in my career, a career that began my sophomore year in the writing center at the University of Kansas, where I'd rather make my idea of a writing center a place where we produce better tutors, not just better tutoring. And, if like North, I am focused on promoting intellectual growth in students rather than helping them produce prepackaged and predictable assignments, then I think that makes me more interested in learning than it does in writing. This is not to say that making decisions based on the needs of writers is unimportant or that writing itself does not hold a significant place in the work we all do. But I do think the time has come for us to pay more attention to peer tutors, to what they tell us about learning, teaching, and writing, and to what they bring to our scholarly conversations in the writing center and composition studies fields. With this in mind, I will speak about peer tutor representation in writing center scholarship and what I learned about confidence, empathy, and learning relationships from some of the peer tutors at FIT.

A notable call for including peer tutor voices in our literature came a few years ago from Sue Dinitz and Jean Kiedaisch who noted the absence of tutor voices in writing center scholarship. They discuss that a number of scholars from Muriel Harris to Kenneth Bruffee to Nancy Grimm envision the writing center as a place where particular theories meet and become practice, but, they write, "Largely left out of these constructions of writing centers are tutor voices" (63). Dinitz and Kiedaisch attempt to close the loop on the interaction between theory and practice by using tutors to respond to best practices and to issues in writing center theory. This is an exciting move for many reasons, but most importantly, it brings our attention back to the heart of the work done by writing centers: the work of tutors.

I have been using the word "tutor" more generally at times because it's easier. The politics of tutoring, of who does the work and how well they do it, is tricky and has been discussed over the years in a number of articles and at conferences like the one we're at. However, I do believe that whether you are an undergraduate student, graduate student or a professional tutor, there are significant lessons in peer tutoring that cut across age and institutional rank. So many of the lessons I'm referring to have been buried over the years due to how the writing center field progressed from the mid 1980s onward, particularly when in the early 1990s, we began to see the literature using critical theory as a lens for our work. But if we look back to the late 1970s and the early 1980s, we see a literature invested in the social dynamics of peer tutoring (see Bruffee, Hawkins, Kail, Warnock and Warnock). In fact, peer tutors were the result of and the cause of much of the theory then. In many cases, the friendship between tutor and writer became a hallmark of what makes learning to write in a writing center fundamentally different from learning to write in any other academic setting. These discussions, however, were not about friendship, I believe, as much as they were about authority, power, and institutional norms. It seemed that the peer tutor provided the perfect solution to the problem of a teacher-centered, authoritative classroom, and not only was the peer tutor a solution to this problem but also a symbol of collaboration and the changing landscape of teaching and learning. Sounds almost too good to be true, doesn't it?

To be honest, it was a little too good to be true, but there were a lot of good reasons to focus on the social dynamics of tutoring and to argue that peer tutoring in writing was helping us to rethink traditional relationships in teaching and learning. And the fact that so many of these early scholars who discussed and promoted peer tutoring were eager to talk about tutors and writers in terms of friendship probably had more to do with the realization that peer tutors bring something to the table that they couldn't. Specifically, peer tutors have an intrinsic understanding of how social and academic expectations influence one's ability to learn and to become comfortable with writing. We might now be wary to think about tutors and writers as friends, although I know many tutors who have befriended tutees, but it's not a stretch for us to be concerned with relationships: how tutors foster positive relationships with tutees, and, as a result, how they pave the way for student writers to enter into new relationships with teaching and learning. But I suspect that there is much more to this than what I've said so far, and I'm even more interested in how tutors' relationships with learning and writing are influenced by their experiences in a writing center.

Harvey Kail and John Trimbur discuss the type of relationships I'm talking about in "The Politics of Peer Tutoring." They write: "To reorganize the relationship among students is simultaneously to probe the traditional relationships of teaching and learning" (10). What strikes me most about this quote is that it means so much for all of us involved in writing center work, and for me, it becomes the number one reason why writing centers need peer tutors. When Kail and Trimbur penned this line, they were pointing to the influence that peer tutoring potentially has on our traditional educational values and our understanding of how knowledge is constructed and consigned in the academy. Leading up to this statement, Kail and Trimbur note that, "Locating the sources of knowledge in the social fabric rather than in the power lines of generation and transmission offers a way to talk about peer tutoring that goes beyond the operational model of plugging peer tutors into the grid" (10). They continue to argue that, "Peer tutoring, in this view, is not a supplement to the normal delivery system but an implicit critique of gen/tran ideology and the official structures of curriculum and instruction" (10). What is so fantastic about this for all of us working in writing centers today is that Kail and Trimbur set the stage for discussing peer tutoring not in terms of institutional rank or age or in terms of friendship but rather in terms of how peer tutors beg the academy to rethink how it manages information and knowledge.

We owe Harvey Kail even more applause for his work in 1983 when he so eloquently discussed the nature of peer tutoring and collaborative learning. Kail asked readers of *College English* whether or not the academy was ready for the intellectual shift collaborative learning in the form of peer tutoring would make on our campuses. To me, the argument Kail makes in his 1983 article is far more significant and important for writing centers than North's assertion that we make "better writers not better writing" (438) in 1984. More than a mantra, Kail teaches us why the peer tutor's intellectual role in the academy is important. It's work like his that inspires me to revisit what peer tutor supporters and educators were writing about in the late '70s and early '80s to inspire tutors in the 21st century. Simply stated, these scholars worked hard to position peer tutors in an intellectual arena, which is an effort that deserves more of our time and attention.

So, the reason I'm sharing this with you is to set the groundwork for what I think we should be thinking about when it comes to tutors, tutoring and the teaching of tutors. We must look back to look forward and shift the way we think about peer tutoring. We must think of peer tutoring as a pedagogy driven by the belief that co-learning and collaboration have meaningful places in our writing centers, and that without these, student writers who visit our centers are missing out. We must consider how peer tutors shed new light on the ways we learn and teach, and through this consideration, we must begin to identify the values of peer tutoring that we can all engage and implement during our interactions with writers. I believe that we can all have a "peer moment," regardless of our education, our identity, our age, or our experience. A peer moment is not something easily defined. I see them as those moments when we find an opportunity to connect with a writer during a session. My guess is that the peer tutors in this room would be able to describe moments such as these in far more interesting and compelling ways than I can, and this is part of the reason why we need to listen to peer tutors and what they have to say about our work.

So, much like Dinitz and Keidaisch, I think it is time we move tutors toward the center. We must listen to them carefully and take their everyday interactions into consideration, just as the authors of *The Everyday Writing Center* encourage us to do (Geller et al.). So with that, I argue the teaching of tutors must be and can only be accomplished by learning from tutors.

To support this position, I don't need to go much further than speaking to tutors about what they've learned or taken away from their time at the writing center. I'm certainly not the only one who is involved in this type of investigation. In fact, projects like Paula Gillespie, Brad Hughes and Harvey Kail's Peer Writing Tutor Alumni Research Project provide a model on how to go about this business. And others are working with their tutors to learn about their experiences. One great example is in Clint Gardner of the Salt Lake City Community College Student Writing Center. Gardner highlighted a dilemma for tutor education during a presentation at the Conference on College Composition and Communication last spring. While trying to examine what tutors at his writing center were learning, Gardner was surprised to discover that despite all of the wonderful academic and pedagogical skills directors feel tutors benefit from, tutors reported that empathy was one of the most important things they learned. So, this begs the question as to whether or not empathy is an intended outcome of tutor education or if it's a byproduct of the type of environment peer tutors are able to create. I can find examples in tutor training manuals and other writing center texts that encourage tutors to find common ground, to tell a story to break the ice, to establish rapport, or even to be aware of social, political, or economic differences, but I have not found the article or chapter that dives extensively into empathy. Is it because empathy doesn't have an academic appeal or is it because tutors don't typically write these chapters? So, I started wondering: what other things do tutors learn that might not be so well documented in our scholarship, and are these the types of things that should be inspiring chapter headings in training manuals or in tutor education courses?

In my own research, I have learned from tutors that confidence and risk taking are essential to their everyday interactions with writers. What if we had a more comprehensive theory of tutoring based in confidence or risk taking? Elizabeth Boquet has clearly outlined this kind of a theory in *Noise from the Writing Center* when she asks tutors to take a higher risk/higher yield approach to tutoring by operating on the edge of their expertise. But what is expertise in peer tutoring? I think Boquet is right to look to tutors for answers to this question. And what I would like to do is not only try to come to some consensus on this with the help of tutors, but to then use the information that tutors provide us to guide everything from the teaching of tutors to the teaching of writing.

At the beginning of this semester, I was considering some ice-breaker activities for our first staff meeting. We decided to go with the classic "Find Someone Who . . ." activity, and we adjusted some of the questions to make them writing center friendly. One of the questions was: "Find someone who has had a tutoring experience that changed them for the better." I threw what I thought was a cheesy question on the list without thinking about the responses it would get, and as tutors told their stories, we as a group started to notice that the work we do is powerful. The best I could gather from this experience, though, is that FIT writing consultants saw their experiences in terms of confidence and empathy, two themes that seem to come up again and again in my conversations with peer tutors. And tutors extend these two terms to both their own experiences and to the experiences of the writers with whom they work. At times, they come together as they did for Lina, who in commenting about non-native speaking international students told me, "Their stories are inspirational in a way, brave even, throwing themselves into a new environment, not knowing how they were going to come out on the other side." The bravery Lina sees in these students is interesting. She sees a possibility for being inspired by the students with whom she works. But I also think of tutors the way that Lina thinks about these students. You don't know what's going to happen; you have to be brave in approaching a new person or a new idea; and you have to adapt to new social and academic environments from one person to the next. You as tutors are aware of the relationships you build with students, but you have no idea what that relationship will or can be until you're in the midst of working with a writer.

Beyond the confidence that it takes for writers to be open to our feedback, confidence must also grow in tutors. The unknowns of a session become less of a place riddled with tension and uncertainty and more of a place for play and growth. Another tutor, Yecca, who is at her third NCPTW, tells me that "With each assignment I become increasingly aware of the unknown, the sum of unfamiliar topics, unsolved problems, and blank stares I have yet to encounter. Usually my first reaction is a quick pang of anxiety, followed by confident realization that I will find a way." It's so impressive to think, as Yecca points out for us, that our awareness of the unfamiliar, the unknown, becomes a source of strength. Many new tutors I have worked with over the years—and this happened to me, too, when I first started tutoring—often tend to focus on grammar in their early sessions. I suppose this could be due to the ways we were taught to write from a young age, but I often wonder if it has more to do with our confidence level. Can I tell this writer I disagree with her main argument? Am I ready to suggest a complete overhaul of the introduction? Am I prepared to challenge homophobia, racism, sexism, or any kind of bigotry during a session? It takes a strong tutor to take action on these things and to push writers to broaden their understanding of audience. I also think it has to do with being confident in what you know will help the writer learn.

But, of course, confidence does not develop overnight, and as Yecca points out, there is a process to learning how to become a confident tutor. Stephanie, a new tutor, mentioned "how important making mistakes and being in uncomfortable situations" can be for learning, and that she values "learning through experience." Being open to making a mistake is a difficult thing to do, especially when we feel there is so much at stake. Yet this is when we have to consider the tutor as a learner. Since Stephanie has helped establish that learning through experience is key, we might see in her comments an interesting quandary in that one must be confident enough to make mistakes in order to gain more confidence. What's more is that Stephanie's thoughts suggest that a tutor's comfort during a session might not be the most productive for teaching and learning. It might be comfortable to stick with grammar when a text is fraught with issues ranging from a troubled personal history to ideas about the world that challenge your own. But what are we learning and what is the writer learning when we do not challenge ourselves to engage the text as a true reader?

And don't think that this only about challenging someone else's political stance or argument. It's also about acknowledging someone else's experiences and seeing them as more than just words on the page that line up to make meaning. This brings me to the second theme that I noticed in tutor responses to my question: empathy. In my opinion, empathy in tutoring is about making a connection and building a relationship. It means seeing the world from other people's perspectives and doing your best to meet them where they are. I mentioned earlier that Clint Gardner learned from his tutors that empathy was a key value they took away from their writing center work, and FIT tutors echoed these values. Jessica, who is at her first NCPTW, told me that "the social aspect of tutoring is also important—dealing with people and establishing some sort of connection." Jessica continued by saying, "that tutoring is also about real life experiences because you never know who is going to walk through the door." The connections that Jessica points to and the acknowledgement that we are dealing with all kinds of people make a case for empathy in tutoring. Jessica shared a tutoring experience about a young woman who made it to college with no concept of how to use punctuation. The student had gone to school in NYC, a school system that faces many challenges, and was simply not provided the same access to education that Jessica had received because of socioeconomic differences. Jessica explained, "This [situation] made me extremely grateful for the education that I received, but it also made me more mindful and compassionate to all of the people who did not have the chance to learn what I was able to learn." Tutoring begs us to see the world through another person's eyes. Recognizing differences, like Jessica has done, is the first step in understanding them, why they exist, and what we can do to work toward tolerance and change. What I think I'm learning is that empathy has the power to ignite our curiosity and can challenge us to question the status quo.

If what we learn as tutors and from tutors is that empathy drives the learning and writing process, then we ought to focus our attention on what it is about empathy that makes us better tutors. I suspect that it has something to do with relationships— empathy allows us to understand and share the feelings of another, a strong foundation for any relationship. But I'm not just taking a stab in the dark here. I've heard that relationships are important from a number of tutors, and I've also witnessed how tutor-tutee relationships influence what happens during a session (Fallon). In fact, when I asked FIT tutors about their experiences, most of them discussed the importance of the tutor-tutee relationship. And they see a correlation between successful tutoring sessions and the type of relationship they foster with a writer. For instance, Louisa, whose brother also happens to have been a peer writing tutor, explained to me that "When I take the time to get to know how each tutee uniquely learns and reacts to what happens during a session, the session is far more valuable than ones where the tutee is treated just as the paper they bring with them."

Emma described to me a relationship she has developed with a writer over time and what it is like to be able to celebrate successes with that writer. Her thoughts are that, "The tutor-tutee relationship is a personal one and, just like any relationship, laughter and enjoyment are an important part of the dynamic. In my experience having a good time also results in better work." What I think interests me in Emma's response is that the relationship she refers to is one that is mutually established over time. It's not forced or scheduled for them; there's something organic to it, and as a result, Emma notices that they do better work together.

So, what I think I'm learning from peer tutors is the importance of learning relationships, and how confidence and empathy play into building genuine and beneficial experiences between tutors and writers. And I can't help but to think back to what I learned about peer tutoring from people like Kenneth Bruffee, Harvey Kail, Muriel Harris, John Trimbur, and Thom Hawkins, that the peer tutor really does have us rethink traditional learning and teaching relationships. That the very existence of peer tutors gives us new ways to think about how people learn, what motivates learning, and why collaborative learning in the form of peer tutoring is productive, fun, powerful, and meaningful. But what 21st-century peer tutors bring to 20th-century conversations about tutoring has the capability to dramatically change not only how tutors are educated but also how we teach writing, how we think about learning, and how we value our relationships with each other and the knowledge we build together.

Peer tutors, in that case, teach all of us how to meet our students where they are, how to celebrate in that space, and how to be open to learning from moments that present great challenges. I really do believe that in writing centers, peer tutors are my best teachers, and their experiences echo from one generation of tutor to the next.

And because I believe this, I asked Joylene, the former tutor I mentioned at the beginning of this address, to come speak with the current FIT peer tutors at one of our staff meetings. I feel compelled to share with you what she shared with us because it reflects the qualities I've discussed today. She said,

> I think one of the main things I took away from working with the writing of others was that nobody's first language is writing. Writing is something that is constantly evolving, expanding and changing with time throughout our lives. What I read in one text will most likely be very different than what someone else understands, which can also be entirely different from what the writer intended. This is not to say that writing is full of miscommunication but rather that there are many opportunities for various interpretations and that is what makes writing such a rich and wonderful thing. It can't help but inspire conversations, whether they are ones that are internal and personal or ones that are held with a larger audience.

Joylene reminds me that writing is about conversation; that it involves reaching out, trying to grasp what others mean, and using this conversation to shore up our ideas and our relationships to one another. And this process is what I've been trying to do with peer tutor voices this evening. Thank you to the peer tutors who have lent me their voices for this talk, but there is more to come. Peer tutors' roles in teaching and learning will continue to expand, especially as we work to create more opportunities to include peer tutor voices in scholarly conversations. And I can't think of a much better place to get to work on this than right here in Miami at NCPTW. You peer tutors will teach all of us gathered here about your work, and I for one will be listening closely, doing my best to be your co-learner.

Thank you.

NOTE

1. Paula Gillespie, Shanti Bruce, and Kevin Dvorak were the co-chairs of the 2011 National Conference on Peer Tutoring in Writing.

WORKS CITED

Boquet, Elizabeth H. *Noise from the Writing Center.* Logan, UT: Utah State UP, 2002. Print.

Bruffee, Kenneth. "The Brooklyn Plan: Attaining Intellectual Growth through Peer-Group Tutoring" *Liberal Education* 64 (1978): 447–68. Print.

———. "Two Related Issues in Peer Tutoring: Program Structure and Tutor Training." *College Composition and Communication* 31.1 (1980): 76–80. Print.

Ceballos, Joylene. Personal interview. 30 Sept. 2011.

Dinitz, Sue, and Jean Kiedaisch. "Creating Theory: Moving Tutors to the Center," *The Writing Center Journal* 23.2 (2003): 65–76. Print.

Fallon, Brian. "The Perceived, Conceived, and Lived Experiences of 21st Century Peer Writing Tutors." Diss. Indiana University of Pennsylvania. 2010. Print.

Gardner, Clint. "A Culture of Learning: The Effects of Working in a Community College Writing Center on Peer Writing Tutors." Atlanta, GA. 62nd Conference On College Composition and Communication. Conference Paper. 18 April 2011.

Geller, Anne Ellen, Michele Eodice, Frankie Condon, Meg Carroll, and Elizabeth H. Boquet. *The Everyday Writing Center: A Community of Practice*. Logan, UT: Utah State UP, 2007.

Harris, Muriel. "Talking in the Middle: Why Writers Need Writing Tutors." *College English* 57.1 (1995): 27–42. Print.

Hawkins, Thom. "Intimacy and Audience: The Relationship between Revision and the Social Dimension of Peer Tutoring." *College English* 42.1 (1980): 64–68. Print.

Hayon, Jessica. Personal interview. 20 Sept. 2011.

Hughes, Bradley, Paula Gillespie, and Harvey Kail. "What They Take with Them: Findings from the Peer Writing Tutor Alumni Research Project." *The Writing Center Journal* 30.2 (2010): 12–46. Print.

Kadar-Penner, Emma. Personal interview. 20 Sept. 2011.

Kail, Harvey, "Collaborative Learning in Context: The Problem with Peer Tutoring." *College English* 45.6 (1983): 594–99. Print.

Kail, Harvey, and John Trimbur. "The Politics of Peer Tutoring." *The Writing Center Journal* 11.1–2 (1987): 5–12. Print.

Morse, Stephanie. Personal interview. 13 Sept. 2011

North, Stephen M. "The Idea of a Writing Center." *College English* 46.5 (1984): 433–46. Print.

Riveros, Lina-Paola. Personal interview. 23 Sept. 2011.

Trimbur, John. "Peer Tutoring: A Contradiction in Terms?" *The Writing Center Journal* 7.2 (1987): 21–28. Print.

Wakefield, Louisa. Personal interview. 23 Sept. 2011.

Warnock, Tilly, and John Warnock. "Liberatory Writing Centers: Restoring Authority to Writers." *Writing Centers: Theory and Administration*. Ed. Gary A. Olson. Urbana, Illinois: NCTE, 1984. 16–23. Print.

Zeng, Yecca. Personal interview. 14 Oct. 2011

New Media Matters:
Tutoring in the Late Age of Print

Jackie Grutsch McKinney

Jackie Grutsch McKinney is a professor at Ball State University. This article originally appeared in *The Writing Center Journal*.

At the turn of the century, John Trimbur predicted that writing centers would become "Multiliteracy Centers," drawing on the terminology of the New London Group (30). These re-envisioned centers, he suggested, would provide help for students working on a variety of projects: essays, reports, PowerPoint presentations, web pages, and posters. His prediction has proved true to some degree—most notably in the state of Michigan. The University of Michigan's Sweetland Writing Center opened a Multiliteracy Center in 2000 within its writing center, a place where students "could receive one-to-one support as they worked on digital projects such as websites, PowerPoint presentations, and other forms of communication that depend on multiliteracies" (Sheridan, "Sweetland" 4). Additionally, at Michigan State, digital writing consultants worked with students on digital texts as early as 1996 (see Sheridan, "Words" and DeVoss). Institutions outside of Michigan have responded to new media writing also. The Worcester Polytechnic Institute—where Trimbur works—renamed its writing center the Center for Communication Across the Curriculum, with "workshops" in writing, oral presentation, and visual design (Trimbur 29), and the Center for Collaborative Learning and Communication was created at Furman University (Inman). Many other centers have not changed names but have begun tutoring students on a variety of texts.

However, in one of the few published articles on writing centers and new media, entitled "Planning for Hypertexts in the Writing Center . . . or Not," Michael Pemberton asks if writing centers should open their doors to students working on hypertexts. Although he answers "maybe"—he believes directors should decide based on their local needs and constraints—the bulk of his argument seems to say "no" more loudly than "yes," as seen here:

> Ultimately, we have to ask ourselves whether it is really the writing center's responsibility to be all things to all people. There will always be more to learn. There will always be new groups making demands on our time and our resources in ways we haven't yet planned for. And there will never be enough time or enough money or enough tutors to meet all those demands all of the time.

If we diversify too widely and spread ourselves too thinly in an attempt to encompass too many different literacies, we may not be able to address any set of
literate practices particularly well. (21)

Now—twenty years after Stephen Bernhardt urged us to *see* student texts; after
Craig Stroupe, more recently, argued for the visualization of English studies; after
Diana George showed us how visual literacy has been a part of writing instruction
since the 1940s; and after Gunther Kress argued convincingly that the revolution in
writing dominated by the image is not coming, it is already here—the writing center
community seems divided on whether writing centers should work with new media.

Though at first blush I thought that Pemberton's argument was shortsighted,
upon reflection, I think this sort of response actually speaks to an understandable
uncertainty. We are fairly sure that we do good work with paper essays, pencils, and
round tables. We are just not sure that we can do good work when those things
change into new media texts, computer screens and speakers, mice and keyboards,
and computer desks. The argument follows that if we are not certain we can do good
work, then we should not do it at all.

I agree with Pemberton that we shouldn't take on work that we are not prepared
for. But our agreement only goes so far, because I *do* think it is our job to work with
all types of writing in the writing center—including new media. In this article, then,
I suggest that writing centers need to offer tutoring in new media texts, but not the
same tutoring we've always done. I begin by briefly defining *what* new media are (or,
really, how I will use the term) and outlining *why* I think writing center tutors should
work with new media texts. The bulk of this essay is devoted to *how* to tutor new
media, since I see that as the crux of the issue, so in the last part, I describe the ways
that writing center directors and staffs wanting to work with new media can evolve
their practices to do so.

WHAT IS NEW MEDIA?

Scholars use the term "new media" in a handful of ways that both overlap and diverge, which can make matters complicated. Are new media texts digital? Can they
be print? Are they the same as multimodal texts? Or are they employing a different
rhetoric? Cynthia Selfe, Anne Wysocki, and Cheryl Ball each offer definitions of new
media that I find helpful, not because they agree with one another, but rather because I can see from the sum of their individual definitions the exciting range of new
media texts.

For Cynthia Selfe, new media texts are digital. She defines new media texts as
"texts created primarily in digital environments, composed in multiple media, and
designed for presentation and exchange in digital venues" ("Students" 43). Although
such texts contain alphabetic features, she claims that "they also typically resist con-
tainment by alphabetic systems, demanding multiple literacies of seeing and listening and manipulating, as well as those of writing and reading" ("Students" 43). She
would use "new media" to describe a web portfolio or another text viewed on screen
that would contain alphabetic texts and other modes, too.

Anne Wysocki, though, sees new media as any text that in its production calls attention to its own materiality:

> I think we should call "new media texts" those that have been made by compos-
> ers who are aware of the range of materialities of texts and who then highlight
> the materiality: such composers design texts that help readers/consumers/view-
> ers stay alert to how any text—like its composers and readers—doesn't function
> independently of how it is made and in what contexts. ("Openings" 15)

This attention to materiality means the text might or might not be digital. As Wysocki writes, "new media texts do not have to be digital; instead, any text that has been designed so that its materiality is not effaced can count as new media" (15). An example of a new media text that isn't digital is Wysocki et al.'s *Writing New Media* itself. Design choices in this text, such as the horizontal orientation of the page numbers, make readers "stay alert" to how the writers are playing with the usual conventions of a book. The key term for Wysocki's conception of new media, then, is materiality.

A third definition of new media comes from Cheryl Ball in "Show, Not Tell: The Value of New Media Scholarship." She writes that new media are "texts that juxtapose semiotic modes in new and aesthetically pleasing ways and, in doing so, break away from print traditions so that written text is not the primary rhetorical means" (405). For Ball, then, like Selfe, new media is multimodal and digital. Unique to Ball's defi-nition, however, is that what's "new" in new media is the way in which these texts make arguments—the primacy of non-textual modes. New media texts make funda-mentally different types of arguments. She illustrates this difference in her article through analysis of two web texts. One relies on print conventions to make its linear argument; the other radically departs from print conventions as it asks readers to compose the argument by dragging and dropping audio, still images, and text to play together in an order determined by the viewer/reader.

Combined, the three definitions show a range of texts that are "new" in signifi-cant ways: 1) their digital-ness; 2) their conscious materiality or form; 3) their multi-modality; and/or 4) their rhetorical means. Of course, texts that fall under the category of *new* media by one or more of these definitions have existed for some time, but it is only recently that students, especially in writing classrooms, have been regu-larly asked to read or compose new media texts. The norm in colleges and universities for decades has been typed, double-spaced, thesis-driven texts on 8½-by-11-inch, stapled, white paper. Thus, in this article, when I say that we should train tutors to work with new media, I mean the sorts of texts that would fit any of the three (Wysocki's, Selfe's, or Ball's) definitions outlined above. Practically speaking, this would mean that tutors would also be trained to work with texts that are not traditional, paper, alphabetic, text-only, academic print essays or assignments. Increasingly common, new media assignments in first-year composition (FYC) include PowerPoint presen-tations or slidecasts; video essays and documentaries; audio essays or podcast series; posters, collages, and other visual arguments; websites or hypertexts; and comic books, animations, or graphic novels. These are the sorts of texts we must be prepared to work with in the writing center in the twenty-first century in addition to the more traditional texts that have been the norm.

WHY TUTOR NEW MEDIA?

Pemberton suggests four ways of dealing with new texts in writing centers: 1) ignore them since they will rarely appear; 2) use specialist tutors; 3) treat new media texts like other texts; or 4) train all tutors to work with them.[1] The last of these is the approach I will argue for; I believe the writing center is the place to tutor students with their new media texts. I think all tutors should be trained to work with these texts and that these texts have unique features, which means some of our traditional tutoring practices will not work (more on this later). Here, I will briefly defend my belief that we should take on the task of tutoring new media. Many readers, I imagine, will not need convincing, as writing centers around the country already work with new media writing. For these readers, this section might help them articulate this new work to colleagues or administrators who question the evolution of their writing centers. Other readers might find themselves more resistant to offering what they perceive as yet another service when demands on their resources and time are already too high. I can empathize with this position but do my best to articulate how I do not think tutoring new media is something we can or should opt out of. It is not another thing—it is *the* thing we have always done, just in new forms, genres, and media.

Reason #1: New Media Is Writing

Writing has irrevocably changed from the early days of writing centers. Early writing centers in the 1960s and 1970s developed peer tutoring techniques when student texts were written by hand or with typewriters. Adding another mode—even a simple image—to paper texts was difficult and usually avoided. The 1980s and 1990s brought us personal computers with word processing, but for the earlier part of this period, the texts writing centers worked with did not radically change. Word processors made texts that looked like they came from typewriters; texts were composed on screen but printed and distributed on paper.

Fast forward to the 2000s. Student texts now are nearly always composed on screen. Most students have their own computers—laptops are popular. Many texts that students compose, even for FYC, never leave the screen. Students write reading responses in a course management system, like BlackBoard. They post the response to the course discussion board where the instructor and other students respond. Likewise, longer writing assignments—essays and web pages—can be "turned in" and "turned back" without ever being printed out. In fact, when Microsoft Word 2007 was released, it sported a new default typeface created for onscreen viewing, replacing the long-reigning Times New Roman, because of the frequency with which texts—even word-processed texts—were viewed on screen.

In these ways, we have witnessed a fundamental change in the textual climate. Before, putting a text on paper—and writing for that linear, left-to-right, top-to-bottom, page-to-page form—was *the* way to write. That has changed. Now, there are many ways to communicate through writing; consequently, putting a text to paper is now a rhetorical choice that one should not make hastily. We ought to really think through whether a paper essay, say, is the best way to reach our audience or purpose. If we decide to compose paper essays knowing we have the wide range of available textual choices, we are deeming the paper essay the best way to meet our rhetorical ends. Many of us, perhaps, have spent our lifetimes writing paper essays because that was how arguments were made—academically if not otherwise. The paper essay was the default. This is no longer the case even in academic circles. Many academic conference presentations are not paper essays read to the audience but arguments presented with PowerPoint slideshows, videos, animations, and print or digital posters, suggesting that many academic writers, upon weighing their rhetorical choices, are no longer choosing paper essays.

I think it is unreasonable to grant that writers have a wide range of options for meeting their rhetorical ends—even academically—yet to insist that we will only help with those texts that writing centers have historically worked with, namely, paper essays and assignments. New media is "new," as the earlier definitions show, yet it is still writing. More than that, it is a type of writing that academia and the greater public value more and more.

Sending students with new media texts to another center or a specific tutor, as some centers have done, could give the message that new media is not writing, that it is not something the writing center values. Some universities might be in the position, as the University of Michigan was, to create a separate center for new media texts. But many of us struggle, annually, to keep one center open. Many of us also struggle to run one center, and most of us would not find additional compensation for willingly increasing our workload, I imagine. However, preparing all tutors to work with new media texts requires no second space or additional staffing. It does not necessarily require great investments in new technology or technology training. Most writing centers are likely adequately outfitted with at least one, if not several, computers on which to view digital texts. We might very well want to acquire large monitors or projectors to enable viewing of certain texts (e.g., slidecasts, video essays, or PowerPoint presentations), but these texts can be viewed on small screens for the purpose of tutor response.

Reason #2: The Line Between New Media and Old Media Is Blurry

Though I attempted a clear-cut definition of new media texts in the previous section, it is often the case that a text straddles the old media/new media line. A writing center that officially works with only essays, reports, and other such alphabetic texts will increasingly, if not already, find multimodality and digitality a part of such texts. Pemberton's question about hypertexts is a good example. He meant, I think, to question whether writing centers ought to work with digital texts composed in HTML and viewed in web-browsers, otherwise known as web pages. Yet many programs now, including Microsoft Word and PowerPoint, allow for hypertext links (not to mention color, images, charts, sound, animation, and video), so traditional essays are quickly becoming less, well, traditional. If we say we do not work with hypertexts, would we then not work with essays that contain links? Or what of a webpage that contained an essay with no links? When is it an essay and when is it hypertext?

I think a writing center that sets out to determine when a traditional essay becomes a new media text—in order to say "yes" we work with these or "no" we don't work with those—will find this an increasingly difficult task. Likewise, a writing center that asserts that it can only help with the "writing" part of a new media text is also on shaky ground. The alphabetic text in a new media text is subsumed into the whole and must be read in context of the whole composition.

Reason #3: If We Don't Claim It for Writing, Others Will Subsume It as Technology

If we surrender the composition of web texts or other new media texts to computer science or another department on campus, we allow new media composition to be lost to the technology. As Dànielle DeVoss writes, "Writing center theory and practice must . . . evolve so we can situate ourselves as crucial stakeholders, working towards more complex and critical use of computing technologies and computer-related literacies" (167). If composing new media texts are just about mastering the technology, then we can be convinced (or others will try to convince us) that new media is better left to those on campus who know the most about technology. For example, if creating a website is only about learning HTML or CSS, then we could let the computer science department teach it. Yet, if we consider new media as texts composed consciously in multiple modes, we would have to acknowledge that we are responsible for and good at teaching composing.[2] We ought to speak up about how creating digital texts involves more than mastering a software program just as loudly as we speak up about how writing in general is more than mastering MLA format or rules for comma usage.

New media texts are texts—written for particular occasions, purposes, and audiences. As such, writers of new media still need human feedback. Related to this, the "CCCC Position Statement on Teaching, Learning, and Assessing Writing in Digital Environments," a guide for classroom instruction of digital writing, advises, "Because digital environments make sharing work especially convenient, we would expect to find considerable human interaction around texts; through such interaction, students learn that humans write to other humans for specific purposes." The statement reminds us that digital texts are rhetorical and therefore need rhetorical feedback—of the ilk a writing center typically provides—not just technical troubleshooting. The evolved writing center secures a spot for humans to meet other humans over texts, digital or not. Working with students on their new media texts asserts our stake as composing professionals in the new media age.

HOW TO TUTOR NEW MEDIA

In the previous two sections I argued, perhaps paradoxically, that there is something new and different about new media writing, yet that it is writing and therefore we should tutor writers working on it. For me, there is enough that is "new" about new media that I had to ask myself how well our traditional tutoring practices address it. Trimbur is clear, too, that the change in types of projects we see in the center will change our tutoring. He writes,

> The new digital literacies will increasingly be incorporated into writing centers not just as sources of information or delivery systems for tutoring but as

productive arts in their own right, and writing center work will, if anything, become more rhetorical in paying attention to the practices and effects of design in written and visual communication—more product-oriented and perhaps less like the composing conferences of the process movement. (30)

I have to agree with Trimbur that it would be foolish not to prepare my tutors to work with these texts. What I have come to believe is that accepting new media texts necessitates rethinking our dominant writing center ideas and revising our common practices. Practices vary from center to center, from tutor to tutor. Still, there are some practices espoused repeatedly in the literature of the field and tutor training manuals that seem to compose our general tenets. Many of these practices will have to change. Although such radical re-imaginings of writing center work may seem daunting, we could see this as an occasion to reconsider how well we are responding to all texts, to all writers—an occasion to improve the work we do.

Up to this point, I have been concerned with arguing that we ought to work with new media; now I complicate that. I think it would be irresponsible not to think through (and follow through with) consequent changes to our practices. In what follows, I look at the often-espoused practices for tutoring writing, particularly the ways we read student texts and the ways we respond.

How We Read Student Texts

Ever since Stephen North published his writing center manifesto, "The Idea of a Writing Center," writing center scholars and practitioners have been guided by this statement: "in a writing center the object is to make sure that writers, and not necessarily their texts, are what get changed by instruction. In axiom form it goes like this: our job is to produce better writers, not better writing" (438). What follows this writing center mantra is important; he writes, "In the center, we look *beyond* or *through* that particular project, that particular text, and see it as an occasion for addressing our primary concern, the process by which it is produced" (438, emphasis added). This idea has been translated into practice in various ways. For one, Christina Murphy and Steve Sherwood, in *The St. Martin's Sourcebook for Writing Tutors*, describe tutoring in terms of "pre-textual," "textual," and "post-textual," where the goal of tutoring is, indeed, to get beyond the text. In these three stages, the tutor is to first talk about the paper with the client, then read the paper with the client, and finish by moving from the paper and dealing with the client's issues in writing in general.

Another way to "look beyond" particular projects is to not physically look at them. This comes in the form of a hands-off policy in relation to student texts. We train our tutors to leave the text in front of the client or between tutor and client. As Leigh Ryan and Lisa Zimmerelli suggest in *The Bedford Guide for Writing Tutors*, "Give the student control of the paper. Keep the paper in front of the student as much as possible. If you are working at a computer, let the writer sit in front of the screen as well as control the keyboard" (19). When a student hands a tutor a paper, the tutor often quickly puts it down on the table. Irene Clark and Dave Healy note that this practice, which they call the pedagogy of noninterventionalism, exists because of an ethical concern in some centers. If tutors hold the paper, write on the paper, or otherwise "own" the paper, they may be unwittingly helping the student too much, i.e., plagiarizing or editing. Linda Shamoon and Deborah Burns, in turn, call this hands-off practice "The Bible," an orthodoxy that has attained the force of an ethical or moral code within writing center studies (175).

Likewise, tutors are encouraged to use a read-aloud method for tutoring. Tutors read the student text aloud to the client or request the client to do so. However, this common approach of reading texts in writing centers might not be helpful for students with new media texts. The intertwining of multiple modes may be lost if the tutor looks *through* the text or does not look *at* the paper or *at* the screen. Furthermore, there is no way to "read aloud" visual elements or sounds. Consequently, the tutor may just skip over these elements thereby privileging the verbal, perhaps to the detriment of the student.

For example, several years ago one of my composition students, "Amy," took her final project to the writing center for help. She was working on her "book," a type of portfolio project that asked students to rethink their semester's work in terms of a consistent theme and design. She had decided to use divider pages featuring Winnie the Pooh throughout her book. It was an odd choice as a design feature that became downright inappropriate when one of her "chapters" was an essay on Hitler. The baffling juxtaposition of Pooh and Piglet and the horrific details in her essay surely did not escape her tutor; however, the tutor did not say anything to Amy about this choice quite possibly because the tutor was working under the typical assumption that the alphabetic text was her domain, or because the tutor never even saw this visual element since Amy held the book and read aloud to the tutor. Amy might have received a similar silence had she used certain types of online tutoring which ask writers to cut and paste their text into email forms or whiteboards, allowing tutors to see only the alphabetic text.

How we read texts in writing centers is especially problematic for certain new media texts, such as digital texts, which offer the reader a choice in navigation—where to start, when to go back, where to go next. A tutor must look at a hypertext and interact with it to read it, which begs the question: how would one—or why would one—read aloud a website? The first step in evolving writing center practice, then, is insisting that tutors look at texts to *see* student writing. Stephen Bernhardt's suggestion to composition teachers that they ought to look *at* student texts instead of *through* them seems just as important for writing centers now. If we don't, Bernhardt warns that we are ensuring our own irrelevance as the gap widens between the literacies we have traditionally taught and the ones students need: "Classroom practice which ignores the increasingly visual, localized qualities of information exchange can only become increasingly irrelevant" (77). Doing so, we ask tutors to consider the materiality of texts from the resolution of images to the quality of paper for a resume.

Secondly, instead of asking tutors to read aloud, we can ask tutors to talk aloud as they negotiate a text—a subtle yet important change. In reading aloud, the tutor may be tempted to skip over nonverbal elements since the elements are, well, not verbal. In fact, in my own tutoring experience, I have worked with students who quickly turn the page past charts or graphs as if they are inconsequential to the text at hand. However, if the tutor talked through the text, he or she would instead render a reading of it, showing the student how it could be read in its entirety. For instance, imagine Amy taking her book to a talk-aloud session. The tutor right away would begin with the materiality of the text. "Wow, this is quite a big document. I see it has lots of pages. This, here, seems to be a title. Is this a collection of writings of sorts?" And then, "I'm noticing as we go through this that you've used Winnie the Pooh on each divider page. Why is that?"

This tactic would be immensely helpful for hypertexts, too. The tutor could talk through the links and her expectations for how to negotiate the pages. "OK, we've read through this page on Senator Clinton. I'd like to go back to the page on Moveon.org, but I don't see how I'd do that." Or, "The first thing I notice is these images changing—fading into one another. They all seem connected by their subject—all protesters of sorts? This makes me think this website is about protesting even though the title says, 'Citizens of America.'" This sort of talking aloud would let students see how a reader makes meaning by reading the various modes in the text: images, text, layout, color, movement, and so forth.

How We Talk About Student Writing

In a typical writing center session, tutors are trained to read through the student's text and then to set an agenda on what issues to tackle during the remainder of the session. Many tutors are trained to focus the tutorial on higher order concerns (HOCs) first. These are defined as "the features of the paper that exist beyond the sentence-level; they include clarity of thesis or focus, adequate development and information, effective structure or organization, and appropriate voice and tone" (McAndrew and Reigstad 42). Only after working through the "higher order" issues does the tutor turn to lower order concerns (LOCs), which primarily manifest on the sentence level. All in all, this practice makes sense. It is only logical to work students through revisions that might necessitate substantial changes first before tackling what is happening on a micro-level.

Nonetheless, there may be a problem with this practice for new media texts since tutors are not trained to see other modes, such as visual elements, as contributing to the overall meaning of the text. That is, they are not trained to see that visual elements can be and often are a higher order concern and should be attended to as such. For instance, a tutor, Bryan, told me last year of a student he worked with who was composing a scholarship essay. The student had selected an apple clip art border for his text that he felt was fitting for the type of scholarship—a scholarship for future teachers. These apples, which Bryan felt inappropriate for the genre, were really the only thing he remembered about the essay, yet were not something he discussed with the student since he said he wanted to discuss "the more important issues" first. Clearly, this is just one example, but I believe it does speak to the way we set agendas— what we decide to talk about with writers.

Tutors do not typically broach the subject of formatting without direct questioning from the student because issues of formatting, if they are seen at all, are seen as LOCs or because tutors usually work with drafts and may assume the students will know how to "fix" such elements by the final copy. The visual aspects of a text may not even be on the tutor's radar, let alone other modes such as sound, color, or motion.

In numerous tutoring manuals, there is little acknowledgement that visual elements or document design are important for tutors to read and discuss with students. The closest are Ryan and Zimmerelli's *Bedford Guide,* which states that lab reports should have headings, includes a page on PowerPoint presentations, and asks tutors to consider if resumes are "pleasing to the eye" (87), and Bertie Fearing and W. Keats Sparrow's "Tutoring Business and Technical Writing Students," which focuses mainly on issues of voice, diction, economy, emphasis, and parallelism, but also devotes one paragraph to typography, headings, and lists. Beyond this, there is little about the multimodality of academic essays and more often than not nothing about considering the multimodality of any other type of assignment. Even when telling tutors how to work with typically visually-heavy forms—manuals, instructions, memos, proposals, progress and feasibility reports—McAndrew and Reigstad do not show tutors how to give feedback on the non-verbal elements. Obviously, if writing centers are going to work with new media texts—those texts which purposely employ various modes to make meaning—tutors will have to be trained to know when and how the interaction of various modes are HOCs.

Furthermore, unless trained otherwise, tutors might not suggest the use of non-textual modes in revision planning with the student. There are moments as readers when the use of a diagram, illustration, or image could help with our comprehension of ideas, and there are times when the use of a bulleted list, graph, or chart allows a writer to present ideas succinctly. Tutors, as readers of and responders to texts, need to be able to describe to clients their expectations in terms of verbal and other elements and plot out the tutoring sessions to reflect that. Tutors need to be able to talk about new media texts, which requires both a broader understanding of rhetoric (of how new media texts are rhetorical) and a new set of terms about the interactivity between modes and the effects of that interactivity.

Several composition scholars have theorized how we might respond to or assess classroom-assigned new media writing. Several of them emphasize the rhetorical nature of new media, thereby arguing that we can respond to new media in ways similar to how we respond to other texts, as they are all rhetorical. For example, in "Looking for Sources of Coherence in a Fragmented World," Kathleen Blake Yancey argues that we need new ways of talking about digital writing: "Without a new language, we will be held hostage to the values informing print, values worth preserving for that medium, to be sure, but values incongruent with those informing the digital" (89–90). To that end, she offers a heuristic for readers to ask of digital texts: What arrangements are possible? Who arranges? What is the intent? What is the fit between intent and effect? (96) Though she sees digital composition as different, she sees rhetoric as "being at the heart" of all the writing composition teachers assign and assess (90).

Likewise, Madeleine Sorapure's "Between Modes: Assessing Student New Media Compositions" suggests teachers look for the use of the rhetorical tropes of metaphor and metonymy when assessing students' new media compositions, thereby focusing on the relationship of modes. She writes,

> Focusing assessment on the relations of modes might alleviate part of what Yancey described as the "discomfort" of assessment: that part that comes from

our sense that we are not the most qualified people on campus to judge the effectiveness of the individual modes of image, audio, or video in a multimodal composition. But I think we are indeed qualified to look at the relations between modes and to assess how effectively students have combined different resources in their compositions. (4)

I think Sorapure's idea is on the right track. We don't need to be, say, filmmakers to respond to video in new media compositions. However, we do need to be able, at a minimum, to respond to how the video relates to the whole of the text. As Yancey, Sorapure, and others suggest, new media texts are rhetorical. We can talk about how the text is motivated, how it is purposeful, how it is written to a particular audience. These conversations can be similar to the conversations we have about old media texts.[4] Yet if we do read rhetorically to determine how well a text meets its ends, our tutors need to be able to explain how a text has or has not done so. I do not think our language for talking about texts is adequate in and of itself for this task.

Instead, I have increasingly drawn on other fields to give tutors ways to talk about the interactivity of modes and their sense of the gestalt in students' new media texts. Teaching tutors these terms will give them a vocabulary to describe the relationships between modes; without such an understanding, many times students and tutors assume that images, graphics, animation, or other modes are decoration or supplementation (although they probably won't use that term) for the real mode of writing: the words. I've tutored more than one student who assumed that visuals always make sense to readers, that other modes don't need interpretation like words do.

As a start, I think it is appropriate to teach tutors Karen Schriver's terms for the relationships between modes, Robin Williams's principles of good design, and Cynthia Selfe's criteria for visual assessment. Each of these, I believe, gives more concrete language for tutors or teachers responding to new media. The space of this article will not permit me to draw out extended examples of each of the terms; I hope that readers interested in these ideas will look to the primary texts. However, I will briefly look at a sample new media text to see how this terminology as a whole might help a tutor respond to such a text.

Relationships Between Modes: Karen Schriver

Schriver's terms were intended to describe how visuals work with alphabetic text, though they easily translate to the relationships between different modes, too, such as sound, video, and color.

Redundant:	"substantially identical content appearing visually and verbally in which each mode tells the same story, providing a repetition of key ideas" (412)
Complementary:	"different content visually and verbally, in which both modes are needed in order to understand the key ideas" (412)
Supplementary:	"different content in words and pictures, in which one mode dominates the other, providing the main ideas, while the other reinforces, elaborates, or instantiates the points

made in the dominant mode (or explains how to interpret the other)" (413)

Juxtapositional: "different content in words and pictures, in which the key ideas are created by a clash or semantic tension between the ideas in each mode; the idea cannot be inferred without both modes being present simultaneously" (414)

Stage-setting: "different content in words and pictures, in which one mode (often the visual) forecasts the content, underlying theme, or ideas presented in the other mode" (414)

Principles of Design: Robin Williams

Williams's four basic design principles come from her work *The Non-Designer's Design Book,* where she tries to simplify design concepts for those who must design on paper or screen but do not do so as their primary occupation. Using this sort of text draws on the field of graphic design, which has multimodal composition at its heart.

Contrast: Difference created between elements for emphasis; elements must be made quite different or else the elements simply *conflict* with one another (63)

Repetition: How consistently elements (e.g., typeface, color, pattern, transition) are used; repetition unifies (49)

Alignment: How elements line up on a page, the visual connection between elements; "every item should have a visual connection with something else on the page" (31)

Proximity: How closely elements are placed on page or screen: related items should be close to one another, unrelated items should not be (15–17)

Visual Assessment Criteria: Cynthia Selfe

The last set of terms comes from a chapter of *Writing New Media* in which Selfe, drawing on the work of Gunther Kress and Theo van Leeuwan, gives assignments and rubrics for helping writing instructors incorporate new media into their classes. This set of terms is helpful in looking, literally, at the gestalt of a new media text.

Visual impact: "the overall effect and appeal that a visual composition has on an audience" ("Toward" 85)

Visual coherence: "the extent to which the various elements of a visual composition are tied together, represent a unified whole" ("Toward" 86)

Visual salience: "the relative prominence of an element within a visual composition. Salient elements catch viewers' eye [*sic*]; they are conspicuous" ("Toward" 86)

Visual organization: "the pattern of arrangement that relates the elements of the visual essay to one another so that they are easier for readers/viewers to comprehend" ("Toward" 87)

Using the New Terminology to Respond to a New Media Text

Figure 1 is a grayscale reproduction of a poster created by the Writing Center staff at Clarion University. They produce these posters collaboratively as a staff and sell customized versions via their website. This one, the "Criminal Justice Poster," is one of my favorites. I selected this text to model a new media response because it fits within the very general definition of new media that I have used throughout this article, because it consciously takes advantage of its materiality as a poster, and because it relies on multiple modes to make its argument. It also is exchanged as a digital text first—composed digitally and bought from digital previews before it is printed poster-size. In addition, I wanted to select a text which a reader of this article could see in its entirety (though my response is to the original full-color file which can be viewed at http://www.clarion.edu/80053.jpg).

So, first off, what kind of relationship do we see between the modes here? The composer has used text, photograph, color, and typography to make this text. The image of the handcuffed person is in a *complementary* relationship with the text,

Figure 1 Clarion "Criminal Justice Poster."

"Don't let your writing get so out of hand it has to be put behind bars." The image helps give the reader context. Though the text is a threatening command (do this or else), the orange, bright blue, and green colors and typography are more playful than foreboding. Perhaps this *juxtaposition* is purposeful to play up the humor of the poster, or perhaps it takes away from the effect. This could be something to discuss with the writer.

We can also look at the principles of design at work here. *Contrast* is evident in the change in typeface. The composer wanted to emphasize the word "Don't," so it appears larger than the other words. The different colors, sizes, and weight of the other words and background signal difference, perhaps of importance. "Don't let your writing" is in one typeface; the rest of the text is in a very similar sans serif typeface, which makes for a *conflict*. *Repetition* is evident in the color choices; the background colors are also used for the type. The words "Don't" and "writing" are actually repeated and faded into the background. There are varied *alignments* here. Mostly, the text is center-aligned and shares the same base line. However, "Don't" and "let your" don't share a common baseline. The (mostly) center alignment makes the words on the left margin and right margin nearly line up. Further, there is no consistent alignment within the colored blocks; the text sits near the bottom in blue and green squares but floats to the top in orange. There are two sentences here, and the *proximity* is very close between them, signaling to the reader that these ideas are closely related. The image breaking through the first sentence makes the reader understand the picture as part of the message of that first sentence.

Finally, we could look at this as a visual argument. Using Selfe's terms, we would probably acknowledge that the overall *visual impact* is quite striking. This is a poster that stands out because of the image and bright (though not garish) colors. The purpose of a poster is to call attention to itself, and this poster has the potential to do that. The *visual coherence* is also quite strong because of the repetition of colors and type. The poster will be customized in the white box with the purchaser's logo or information. There is a possibility that there will be less coherence when that element is introduced if there are different types or colors. The elements that are *visually salient* are the word "Don't" and the photograph. Both hold key positions—one in the top left corner and one across the center of the poster. The quick in-a-glance message provided by these two elements is, "don't end up in cuffs"—pretty powerful! The placement of the prominent "Don't" at the top invites the reader to start there and move down; thus the *visual organization* of elements tells the reader how to use the text.

At this point, I should mention two things. First, I am not implying that a tutor would or should go through reading/responding to a text as extensively as this during a session. Like other sessions, the tutor and student would discuss what seems most pressing. I, for one, would probably talk to this composer about how color and type relate to text and image and the overall alignment—another tutor might focus on other elements. Which brings me to my second point: not everyone using these terms is going to come to the same reading. The reader's job with new media is still interpretation. Responding to new media requires close interaction with the text and ways to talk about what we read/view/interact with.

SUMMARY AND CLOSING THOUGHTS

This article has been about reconsidering how we train tutors to read and respond to texts. The subject here has been new media texts. I've asked us to reconsider how we tutor and how we talk to students about their writing. The impetus for these evolved practices is the arrival of increasing numbers of new media texts assigned in university classes. As new media texts consciously and purposefully employ multiple modes to make meaning, they require us to direct our attention to texts differently. Current practices won't suffice, as they limit us to the alphabetic text. Thus, I believe it is imperative to train all tutors in these evolved practices because they will change the ways we respond to all texts, considering more than we have before, perhaps in significant ways. In short, here's the 28-word, visually-arranged version of this article:

TWENTIETH-CENTURY TUTORING	TWENTY-FIRST-CENTURY TUTORING
Read aloud	Talk aloud
Getting beyond the text	Interacting with the text
Zoomed in: talk about words	Zoomed out: talk about whole

It strikes me that writing center studies is at a crossroads, a moment in time where tough decisions regarding the scope of our practices need to be made. Certainly, changes in composing technologies have asked us to push beyond the writing center practices that developed in the 1970s writing center boom. I, for one, do not think this is a time for conservatism, for preserving the tradition for the sake of tradition. Though I understand the impulse as a writing center director to say, "Not one more thing! We do enough!" to me, tutoring new media is not another thing. Writing has evolved with new composing technologies and media, and we must evolve, too, because we are in the writing business. A radical shift in the way that writers communicate both academically and publically necessitates a radical re-imagining and re-understanding of our practices, purposes, and goals.

Finally, I want to address one of the concerns that I discussed earlier: that we are not sure that we can do a good job of tutoring new media, so perhaps we shouldn't try. I think we need to remember that writing centers are largely based on the idea that talk among peers will help. We've never been concerned about expert tutors or perfection, and our feathers get ruffled when others (students or professors) expect this. If we evolve the practices in the ways I suggest, tutors will not be experts in new media composing, but they will be able to offer a response. And that is what we do.

NOTES

1. Pemberton focuses exclusively on hypertexts, not all new media.
2. For more on this, see Grutsch McKinney.

3. This could also hold true for tutoring via email or chat. The texts may be copied and pasted into an email and the tutor will not see the text as it will materialize for its intended audience, for example, how it prints out on the page.

4. For example, see JoAnn Griffin's schema in "Making Connections with Writing Centers" for discussing audience, purpose, form, context, organization, unity/focus, detail/support, style, and correctness of alphabetic essays, audio essays, and video essays (155–56).

WORKS CITED

Ball, Cheryl. "Show, Not Tell: The Value of New Media Scholarship." *Computers and Composition* 21.4 (2004): 403–25. Print.

Bernhardt, Stephen A. "Seeing the Text." *College Composition and Communication* 37.1 (1986): 66–78. Print.

Conference on College Composition and Communication. "CCCC Position Statement on Teaching, Learning, and Assessing Writing in Digital Environments." Adopted 25 Feb. 2004. Web. 15 Dec. 2007.

Clark, Irene, and Dave Healy. "Are Writing Centers Ethical?" *WPA: Writing Program Administration* 20.1/2 (1996): 32–48. Print.

DeVoss, Dànielle. "Computer Literacies and the Roles of the Writing Center." *Writing Center Research: Extending the Conversation.* Ed. Paula Gillespie, Alice Gillam, Lady Falls Brown, and Bryon Stay. Mahwah, NJ: Erlbaum, 2002. 171–90. Print.

Fearing, Bertie E., and W. Keats Sparrow. "Tutoring Business and Technical Writing Students in the Writing Center." *Writing Centers: Theory and Administration.* Ed. Gary A. Olson. Urbana, IL: NCTE, 1984. 215–56. Print.

George, Diana. "From Analysis to Design: Visual Communication in the Teaching of Writing." *College Composition and Communication* 54.1 (2002): 11–39. Print.

Griffin, JoAnn. "Making Connections with Writing Centers." *Multimodal Composition: Resources for Teachers.* Ed. Cynthia Selfe. Kresskill, NJ: Hampton, 2007. 153–66. Print.

Grutsch McKinney, Jackie. "The New Media (R)evolution: Multiple Models for Multiliteracies." *Multiliteracy Centers: Writing Center Work, New Media, and Multimodal Rhetoric.* Ed. David Sheridan and James Inman. Cresskill, NJ: Hampton, 2010. 207–23. Print.

Hassett, Michael, and Rachel W. Lott. "Seeing Student Texts." *Composition Studies* 28.1 (2000): 29–47. Print.

Inman, James. "At First Site: Lessons From Furman University's Center for Collaborative Learning and Communication." *Academic Writing 2* (2001): n. pag. Web. 15 Dec. 2007.

Kress, Gunther. *Literacy in the New Media Age.* New York: Routledge, 2003. Print.

McAndrew, Donald, and Thomas J. Reigstad. *Tutoring Writing: A Practical Guide for Conferences.* Portsmouth, NH: Boynton/Cook, 2001. Print.

Murphy, Christina, and Steve Sherwood. *The St. Martin's Sourcebook for Writing Tutors.* 2nd ed. Boston: Bedford/St. Martin's, 2003. Print.

North, Stephen M. "The Idea of a Writing Center." *College English* 46.5 (1984): 433–46. Print.

Pemberton, Michael. "Planning for Hypertexts in the Writing Center . . . or Not." *The Writing Center Journal* 24.1 (2003): 9–24. Print.

Ryan, Leigh, and Lisa Zimmerelli. *The Bedford Guide for Writing Tutors.* 4th ed. Boston: Bedford/St. Martin's, 2006. Print.

Schriver, Karen A. *Dynamics in Document Design.* New York: Wiley Computer, 1997. Print.

Selber, Stuart. *Multiliteracies for a Digital Age.* Carbondale, IL: Southern Illinois UP, 2004. Print.

Selfe, Cynthia. "Students Who Teach Us: A Case Study of A New Media Text Designer." Wysocki et al. 43–66. Print.

———. "Toward New Media Texts: Taking Up the Challenges of Visual Literacy." Wysocki et al. 67–110. Print.

Shamoon, Linda K., and Deborah H. Burns. "A Critique of Pure Tutoring." *The Writing Center Journal* 15.2 (1995): 134–51. Rpt. in Murphy and Sherwood. 174–90. Print.

Sheridan, David. "The Sweetland Multi-Literacy Center." *Sweetland Newsletter.* Oct. 2002. Web. 15 Dec. 2007.

———. "Words, Images, Sounds: Writing Centers as Multiliteracy Centers." *The Writing Center Director's Resource Book.* Ed. Christina Murphy and Byron Stay. Mahwah, NJ: Erlbaum, 2006. 339–50. Print.

Sorapure, Madeleine. "Between Modes: Assessing Student New Media Compositions." *Kairos* 10.2 (Spring 2006): n.pag. Web. 15 Dec. 2007.

Stroupe, Craig. "Visualizing English: Recognizing the Hybrid Literacy of the Visual and Verbal Authorship on the Web." *College English* 62.5 (2005): 607–32. Print.

Trimbur, John. "Multiliteracies, Social Futures, and Writing Centers." *The Writing Center Journal* 20.2 (2000): 29–31. Print.

Williams, Robin. *The Non-Designer's Design Book.* Berkeley, CA: Peachpit, 2003. Print.

Wysocki, Ann Frances. "Opening New Media to Writing: Openings and Justifications." Wysocki et al. 1–42. Print.

Wysocki, Ann Frances, Johndan Johnson-Eilola, Cynthia L. Selfe, and Geoffrey Sirc. *Writing New Media.* Logan, UT: Utah State UP, 2004.

Yancey, Kathleen Blake. "Looking for Sources of Coherence in a Fragmented World." *Computers and Composition* 21.1 (2004): 89–102. Print.

Access for All: The Role of Dis/Ability in Multiliteracy Centers

Allison Hitt

Allison Hitt is a graduate student at Syracuse University. Her article originally appeared in *Praxis: A Writing Center Journal*.

In David Sheridan and James Inman's 2010 edited collection, *Multiliteracy Centers: Writing Center Work, New Media, and Multimodal Rhetoric,* Inman discusses designing a multiliteracy center.[1] He writes, "A final, but vital, consideration should be the accessibility of any zoned space for individuals with disabilities. In this pursuit, the idea is not just to make spaces minimally accessible, but instead to consider how the disabled may be able to most fully participate in the uses for which the spaces were designed" (Inman 27). This comes as the last "special issue" of consideration for design (28). Though Inman highlights disability and access, these issues are not taken up further as pedagogical considerations. I believe that we need to explore and broaden our understandings of disability as more than a physical design issue and of accessibility as more than an issue for students with disabilities. The creation of multiliteracy centers, spaces "equal to the diversity of semiotic options composers have in the 21st century" (Sheridan 6), presents an opportunity to position disability within the larger context of diverse learners in order to better understand how we can create more accessible multiliterate spaces and pedagogies.

A writing pedagogy that supports multiliteracies must be spatially and pedagogically accessible to a diverse range of students. In many ways, a multimodal pedagogy[2] supports accessible practices through its attention to multiplicity in various modes and media and in its focus on flexibility in processes and products. Disability studies offers two lenses that are also valuable for supporting writing pedagogies: Universal Design (UD) and Universal Design for Learning (UDL). UD is a spatial theory, articulated by architect Ronald Mace in 1988, which emphasizes the importance for all spaces to be physically accessible to all people. UDL, developed by the Center for Applied Special Technology (CAST) in 1994, extends UD in order to create equitable and flexible pedagogies. A multiliteracy center that applies principles of UD and UDL can support students' different physical abilities, modes of learning, types of knowledge, and literacies. Despite advances in accessibility, however, disability remains a troubling binary that creates an us/them framework, undermining the inclusive spirit of multiliteracy centers. I argue that we need to reposition representations of disability in both writing center scholarship and tutoring practices.

INCLUDING DISABILITY IN SCHOLARSHIP

One of the first steps in recognizing and respecting disability is including it in writing center scholarship and dialogue. Despite several notable contributions to this dialogue (see, for example, Babcock "Tutoring"; Babcock "When"; Hamel and Hewett), both disability and access are largely undertheorized with regard to composition. Often, disability is positioned as something that tutors must cope with and that sometimes cannot be helped at all. For example, in her anthologized essay, Julie Neff suggests practices that could help LD students but nevertheless positions such students as Other: "Although learning-disabled students come to the writing center with a variety of special needs, they have one thing in common: they need more specific help than other students" (382). This cues tutors that they need to treat students with disabilities *differently* than other writing center patrons, which can create frustrations that lead to failure. In a reflection of a failed session, Steve Sherwood writes, "I had no training in helping students cope with learning disabilities, much less with the effects of a severe brain injury" (49), concluding that we will continue to encounter LD students who "despite our best efforts, we can't help" (56). Sherwood makes the argument that tutors are not trained for working with LD students, while he simultaneously argues that writing centers are incapable of helping students with LD. Tanya Titchkosky identifies this impasse as a "You can't accommodate everybody" attitude that identifies some students, particularly those with disabilities, as "'naturally' a problem for some spaces" (35).

All students who enter a writing center are treated individually and, thus, as *different* from one another in terms of what they bring to the center and how they learn and compose, so the issue is not seeing students with disabilities as different. Rather, the issue is to position students with disabilities as so *radically* different from other students that they are beyond help—that they require too much time, resources, or special knowledge. A disability studies perspective asks us to interrogate our centers and practices: What makes it culturally or pedagogically acceptable to say "no" to students with disabilities? Why would we, as people with a shared sense of social justice, contribute to the rhetoric that students with disabilities are beyond our help?

Turning to disability studies scholarship is critical as centers move toward multiliterate and multimodal practices that push against the "'natural' exclusion" (Titchkosky 6) of disability within academia. Jean Kiedaisch and Sue Dinitz borrow from disability studies in their article about Universal Design, which they describe as "an approach advocating for the design of products and services so that they are suited to a broad range of users" (50). They recall a moment in tutor training when a disabilities specialist came to talk to their tutors, "encourag[ing] tutors *not* to think of how they might adapt their tutoring for students with disabilities" because *all* students come to writing centers with different types of knowledge and abilities (50). Such a differentiation is an example of treating students as *different*, but not treating students with disabilities *differently*. Kiedaisch and Dinitz do not argue that individual needs should not be met; rather, they advocate adjusting our assumptions about students' particular abilities and engaging in more accessible practices. Rebecca Day Babcock similarly argues that meeting deaf students' learning needs can help writing center tutors "rethink their practices in light of others who learn differently" ("Tutoring" 28). This shifting of assumptions and practices benefits students with disabilities, but it also accounts for *any* diverse, twenty-first-century learner who enters the multiliteracy center.

Shifting assumptions about disability is increasingly important as disability diagnoses rise.[3] In a 2010 report, Melana Zyla Vickers claims that two percent of college students have a documented learning disability, not including students with intellectual disabilities, autism, or other "severe" diagnoses (3). It is estimated that only half of college students report their disabilities, and many forego accommodations for fear that they will be treated *differently* by their instructors and peers (Walters 427). These increases in disability, labeled or not, may indicate a larger problem. Cathy Davidson argues that we are more likely to label a student as LD if she fails to fit into our educational system or is unresponsive to our particular pedagogical practices (10). To address this, then, we need to evaluate our writing center practices: How do our current pedagogical practices exclude particular students? How can we make our writing pedagogies more inclusive to diverse student populations?

CREATING ACCESSIBLE SPACES AND PRACTICES

More than a decade ago, the New London Group recognized multiliteracies as an opportunity to move beyond the dominating limitations of print- and word-based literacies, to reach other modes of representation such as visual, aural, gestural, spatial, and multimodal (28). Gunther Kress argues that these other modes are embodied, that "[h]uman bodies have a wide range of means of engagement with the world" that occur in various and multiple ways (184). A multiliteracy pedagogy, then, encourages practices that relate to students' different bodily experiences and promote student agency (New London Group 31). Similarly, a multimodal pedagogy recognizes students as "agentive, resourceful and creative meaning-makers" (Stein 122). This agentive learning is valuable for students of all abilities to take control of what and how they best receive and create knowledge. And indeed, writing centers have traditionally been known for flexible pedagogies that support multimodal practices and active student-centered learning. A writing center reflects a different space than the classroom, one that both physically and pedagogically encourages alternative modes of communication and composition. Yet even as writing centers create these *different* spaces and practices, students with disabilities are still often treated *differently*. In order to truly support students' different bodily experiences and embodied writing practices, multiliteracy centers must be both spatially and pedagogically accessible.

Universal Design and Spatial Accessibility

Universal Design is useful for considering how to make multiliteracy center spaces more accessible to wider populations. Before a center can support accessible practices, it must be free of spatial features that could disable users from interacting within that space. Bertram Bruce and Maureen Hogan note that physical environments construct disability because, as tools and technologies become naturalized, people who cannot use them are positioned as disabled (297). If we think of chairs as a natural part of the writing center environment, then they disable students who are unable to use them. A universally designed chair has wheels to support mobility and flexibility, allowing students to more easily use the chair or to push it aside if it is a hindrance.

Stairs are one of the most common examples of inaccessible spatial features, for they construct disability by disempowering wheelchair users (Bruce and Hogan 297). However, adding a ramp just for these users would be a retrofit—the act of adding a component to an already-built space (Dolmage 20). Often, these retrofits are forced: they occur only after someone recognizes that the space does not meet standards or is inaccessible. Retrofits also force students to access spaces differently. Rarely do we see ramps at the entrances of buildings; rather, they are on the side or in the back, reinforcing the idea that disability is an "afterthought" (Dolmage 21). UD encourages us to build writing center spaces that are accessible from the beginning, although many centers may retrofit because they lack the finances to design a new center. In this case, it is still beneficial to change inaccessible features. If we return to ramps, a Universally Designed approach to ramps helps everyone: wheelchair users, people who limited mobility, even strollers and rolling backpacks. The push toward multiliteracy centers provides opportunities for spatial reconsiderations of how well centers support accessible literacy practices.

Though some multiliteracy centers are completely redesigned to support multiple rooms and new technologies, a center does not need to change completely to implement accessible practices. This can be seen with the multiplicity and flexibility of different spatial configurations: long tables, clustered desks, overstuffed chairs, and computer stations. Even something as simple as furniture arrangement is multimodal. Stein writes, "The classroom is itself a multimodal place with visual displays and the arrangement of furniture in space that realizes particular discourses of English" and shapes the way students create meaning (122).[4] Mobile furniture, technologies, houseplants, windows, and wall décor work to create an environment that is accessible, encouraging students to learn and compose in the ways that most benefit them.

While spatial elements are important, they cannot be separated from a multiliteracy center's pedagogical goals. Inman writes, "Many centers appear to have been designed around furnishings and technologies, rather than what clients will actually be doing. This approach poses a problem because any center exists to provide effective services for clients, not to have the grandest furnishings and technologies" (20). As spatial theorist Henri Lefebvre argues, the physical spaces we inhabit affect our actions within those spaces; in turn, our actions and social practices impact those spaces. Thus, the material spaces of writing centers greatly impact what kind of pedagogy those spaces can enact.[5] Even if a center is physically accessible, students cannot benefit from inaccessible pedagogy.

Universal Design for Learning and Pedagogical Accessibility

UDL offers a way to apply the equitable and flexible spatial principles of Universal Design to writing pedagogies. According to CAST, UDL pushes against a "single, one-size-fits-all solution," advocating instead for approaches that are flexible, multiple, and adjustable. The principles of UDL—multiple means of representation, actions and expression, and engagement—can help expand our teaching, learning, and composing practices. They can also help us to configure multiliteracies more inclusively. Often, multiliteracies refer to the different technological abilities, or literacies, that a person has for communicating through electronic means. We see this wealth of abilities represented in centers that house computer labs, specialized video and editing software, and OWLs. However, if we conceive of multiliteracies more broadly, as *embodied* practices, we can engage with multiliterate practices that are more inclusive to students with a range of abilities.

A more accessible multiliteracy pedagogy provides multiple and flexible options for all students, including those who may be constrained to particular modalities or have preferred learning styles. Jody Shipka argues for a broader understanding of multimodal texts within our pedagogical frameworks, expanding the definition to include print and digital texts, embodied performances, photographs, videos, physical objects, and repurposed or remediated objects (300). This definition speaks to the multiplicity of UDL and allows for a richer understanding of pedagogical accessibility: if students want to compose essays, collages, videos, or webtexts, these all fit within multimodal pedagogies. Similarly, if students with disabilities are limited to particular modalities—e.g., a blind student who relies on auditory or sensory modes to write or a deaf student who relies more heavily on visual modes—a multimodal pedagogy more easily adapts to these needs, incorporating rather than accommodating them.[6] Broader understandings of multimodality also extend to multiliteracies, encouraging students to engage with their various literacies, such as traditional writing, technology, music, and visual or studio art.

A typical writing center session inherently encourages a multiplicity of communicative and learning styles: students enter a center, meet with a tutor, and engage with texts in a variety of ways. These interactions could include engaging in verbal discussions, collaboratively drafting, looking up information in books, working on computers, and participating in online appointments. Still, working with such a diverse group of students on widely varying rhetorical projects can be difficult. Patricia Dunn and Kathleen Dunn De Mers admit, "Coming up with alternate strategies that simulate (and stimulate) the complex brain work involved in writing is very difficult—partly because we're so steeped in 'writing' as a heuristic for other writing, and partly because in this society we're so steeped in a narrow view of what is 'normal.'" For a tutor or consultant, developing these strategies can be particularly difficult if they have never experienced similar pedagogies. Therefore, it is crucial for writing center tutors and workers to develop multimodal "toolkits"—multiple and flexible practices—that allow them to adapt to different communicative interactions.

Developing a multimodal toolkit involves developing rhetorical strategies that push against fixed communicative interactions and present more opportunities for students. The idea is not to max out all sensory options but to provide flexibility. Shoshona Beth Konstant suggests using multiple channels: "Use combinations of visual, auditory, and kinesthetic techniques—the multisensory approach. Say it and draw it; read text aloud; use color to illustrate things" (7). Konstant takes an early cue from UDL when she argues that *everyone* has learning practices that work best for them (6). Similarly, Dunn and Dunn De Mers promote using a "variety of visual, aural, spatial, and kinesthetic approaches to tap into the intellectual chaos that goes into writing." This means pushing against singular notions of how to interact with both students and texts, and it requires a negotiation between tutor and student. In her work with deaf students, Babcock suggests explicit dialogue: "Most of all, try to find out what the deaf person needs and wants out of the session, and gear your tutoring toward that" ("Tutoring" 35). If students are unaware of what they want or need, knowing some multimodal practices can be useful.

A multimodal toolkit does not eliminate the need to identify students' individual needs, just as UDL does not eliminate the need for accommodations. Instead, both multimodality and UDL ask us to acknowledge that *all* students have multiple ways of learning and knowing and to be flexible to those different needs. If a student prefers drawing, tutors can adapt, asking the student to sketch an outline of their main ideas. Similarly, talking through a text could be more beneficial than reading it word for word. Grutsch McKinney encourages talking—rather than reading—as a way to interact more holistically with all features of a multimodal text ("New Media Matters" 39). This practice is useful for texts that consist of more than just alphabetic text, but it could also benefit students with disabilities. For example, reading a paper aloud for errors may not be as effective when working with deaf students, students with ADHD, or students with pragmatic language impairment (PLI).[7] By talking *about* a text, students have more opportunities to engage with the text in ways that reflect overall comprehension and understanding of their particular rhetorical choices.

To engage in accessible multiliterate practices, tutors must adapt to students' different embodied practices, recognizing that all students who enter the multiliteracy center will learn and compose in different ways for different purposes. Tutors should not be expected to be technology experts to engage in these practices, but they should have basic understandings of different modes and media for rhetorical communication. Because many multiliteracy centers support various technologies, it is useful to know how to locate resources online, work with software to compose and edit multimedia texts—or to communicate with students who use assistive technologies—and even create audio recordings of sessions that students could replay once they leave the center. Beyond available technologies, however, Teddi Fishman reminds us that "the ability to adapt [is] more critical than any particular or specific accommodation" (65).

All students have a variety of rhetorical, intellectual, and physical abilities, and multiliteracy center spaces and practices must be ready to *adapt* to students' various needs.

ACCESS FOR ALL

Writing centers need a new approach for working with students of *all* abilities as we continue to see advances in technologies, changes in educational practices, and increases in disability diagnoses. I believe that implementing the principles of Universal Design and Universal Design for Learning can help make multiliteracy centers more accessible. Applying UD can create a physically accessible space for a diverse student population, establishing a foundation for flexible tutoring, learning, and composing practices. Similarly, UDL promotes the understanding that all students have diverse needs that writing pedagogies need to address. By applying UD and UDL to multiliteracy pedagogies, we incorporate the important work of disability studies and broaden our understandings of both disability and accessibility.

Providing students with the resources to communicate within different modes, to practice and learn new literacies, and to harness their rhetorical abilities should be the goal of all multiliteracy centers. When we adopt multiliterate and multi-modal pedagogies that support these resources, we acknowledge two things. First, *all* students have different abilities, types of knowledge, and literacies. Second, *all* students can benefit from engaging with texts in different ways—visually, aurally, and kinesthetically—and in different contexts. Applying the flexible principles of UD and UDL can make multiliteracy centers more accessible both spatially and pedagogically, allowing us to better prepare students to become effective twenty-first-century communicators.[8]

NOTES

1. I use writing center and multiliteracy center almost interchangeably throughout this paper because, as I will argue, all writing centers support multiliterate practices.
2. The term "multiliteracies" refers, in part, to a multiplicity of communication modes and media (New London Group 9). Similarly, multimodality refers to the multiple modes that we use to represent information, and as Kress reminds us, "textual objects—spoken, signed, written, drawn—always occur in a multiplicity of modes" (199). Because multiliteracies and multimodality are so interrelated, it is necessary to discuss both.
3. According to the CDC, one in six children has a developmental disability—e.g., autism, ADHD, cerebral palsy, or intellectual disabilities—a 12–15% increase from 1997 (Boyle et al.).
4. At my institution's writing center, for example, there is a small room of cubicles at the center's entrance that can be used for quieter sessions, which could benefit students with ADHD who may be more distracted in larger settings or students with autism-spectrum disorders who prefer to be in less populated areas. Students also have the option to work in a large open room where there are multiple tables, chairs, and computer stations arranged for tutoring.
5. For a more in-depth discussion of how writing center scholars engage with spatial theory and how space can affect pedagogy, see Fishman; Hadfield et al.; Kinkead and Harris; and Grutsch McKinney, "Leaving".
6. For example, Shannon Walters reminds us that technology can be harmful if it is positioned as an impairment-specific approach. Audio- or image-only accommodations not only exclude other audiences, they often oversimplify and generalize the person with the disability (439).
7. Students with PLI may struggle with reading and expressing themselves, which can affect listening comprehension (Babcock, "When" 7).
8. I would like to thank Patrick Berry, Jay Dolmage, and Jason Luther for reading multiple drafts of this article and for providing invaluable feedback.

WORKS CITED

Babcock, Rebecca Day. "When Something Is Not Quite Right: Pragmatic Impairment and Compensation in the College Writing Tutorial." *The Writing Lab Newsletter* 35.5-6 (Jan/Feb 2011): 6-10. Print.

———. "Tutoring Deaf Students in the Writing Center." *Disability and the Teaching of Writing: A Critical Sourcebook.* Ed. Cynthia Lewiecki-Wilson and Brenda Jo Brueggemann. Boston, MA: Bedford/St. Martin's, 2008. 28-39. Print.

Boyle, Coleen A., et al. "Trends in the Prevalence of Developmental Disabilities in US Children, 1997-2008." *Pediatrics* 127.6 (2011): 1034-42. Web. 19 Jan. 2012.

Bruce, Bertram C, and Maureen P. Hogan. "The Disappearance of Technology: Toward an Ecological Model of Literacy." *Handbook of Literacy and Technology: Transformations in a Post-Typographic World.* Ed. David Reinking, Michael C. McKenna, Linda D. Labbo, and Ronald D. Kieffer. Florence, KY: Routledge, 1998. 269-82. Print.

CAST. *The National Center of Universal Design for Learning.* Center for Applied Special Technology. 2012. Web. 26 Oct. 2011.

Cope, Bill, and Mary Kalantzis. *Multiliteracies: Literacy Learning and The Design of Social Futures.* London: Routledge, 2000. Print.

Davidson, Cathy N. *Now You See It: How the Brain Science of Attention Will Transform the Way We Live, Work, and Learn.* New York: Viking, 2011. Print.

Dolmage, Jay. "Mapping Composition: Inviting Disability in the Front Door." *Disability and the Teaching of Writing: A Critical Sourcebook.* Ed. Cynthia Lewiecki-Wilson and Brenda Jo Brueggemann. Boston, MA: Bedford/St. Martin's, 2008. 14-27. Print.

Dunn, Patricia A., and Kathleen Dunn De Mers. "Reversing Notions of Disability and Accommodation: Embracing Universal Design in Writing Pedagogy and Web Space." *Kairos* 7.1 (2002). Web. 10 Oct. 2011.

Fishman, Teddi. "When It Isn't Even on the Page: Peer Consulting in Multimedia Environments." Sheridan and Inman 59-73.

Grutsch McKinney, Jackie. "New Media Matters: Tutoring in the Late Age of Print." *The Writing Center Journal* 29.2 (2009): 28-51. Print.

———. "Leaving Home Sweet Home: Towards Critical Readings of Writing Center Spaces." *The Writing Center Journal* 25.2 (2005): 6-20. Print.

Hadfield, Leslie, Joyce Kinkead, Tom Peterson, Stephanie H. Ray, and Sarah S. Preston. "An Ideal Writing Center: Re-Imagining Space and Design." *The Center Will Hold: Critical Perspectives on Writing Center Scholarship.* Eds. Michael A. Pemberton and Joyce Kinkead. Logan, UT: Utah State UP, 2003. 166-76.

Hamel, Christine M. "Learning Disabilities in the Writing Center: Challenging Our Perspectives?" *The Writing Lab Newsletter* 26.8 (2002): 1-5. Print.

Hewett, Beth L. "Helping Students with Learning Disabilities: Collaboration between Writing Centers and Special Services." *The Writing Lab Newsletter* 25.3 (2000): 1-5. Print.

Inman, James. A, "Designing Multiliteracy Centers: A Zoning Approach." Sheridan and Inman 19-32.

Kiedaisch, Jean, and Sue Dinitz. "Changing Notions of Difference in the Writing Center: The Possibilities of Universal Design." *The Writing Center Journal* 27.2 (2007): 39-59. Print.

Kinkead, Joyce A, and Jeanette Harris, eds. *Writing Centers in Context: Twelve Case Studies.* Urbana, IL: NCTE, 1993.

Konstant, Shoshona Beth. "Multi-Sensory Tutoring for Multi-Sensory Learners." *The Writing Lab Newsletter* 16.9–10 (1992): 6–8. Print.

Kress, Gunther. "Multimodality." Cope and Kalantzis 179–99.

Lefebvre, Henri. *The Production of Space.* Trans. Donald Nicholson-Smith. Cambridge, MA: Basil Blackwell, 1991. Print.

Neff, Julie. "Learning Disabilities and the Writing Center." *The Longman Guide to Writing Center Theory and Practice.* Eds. Robert W. Barnett and Jacob S. Blumner. New York, NY: Pearson, 2008. 376–90. Print.

New London Group. "A Pedagogy of Multiliteracies: Designing Social Futures." Cope and Kalantzis 9–37.

Sheridan, David M., "Introduction: Writing Centers and the Multimodal Turn." Sheridan and Inman 1–16.

Sheridan, David M., and James A. Inman, eds. *Multiliteracy Centers: Writing Center Work, New Media, and Multimodal Rhetoric.* Cresskill, NJ: Hampton Press, Inc., 2010. Print.

Sherwood, Steve. "Apprenticed to Failure: Learning from the Students We Can't Help." *The Writing Center Journal* 17.1 (1996): 49–57. Print.

Shipka, Jody. "A Multimodal Task-Based Framework for Composing." *College Composition and Communication* 57.2 (Dec. 2005): 277–306. Print.

Stein, Pippa. *Multimodal Pedagogies in Diverse Classrooms: Representation, Rights, and Resources.* New York: Routledge, 2008. Print.

Titchkosky, Tanya. *The Question of Access: Disability, Space, Meaning.* Toronto: U of Toronto P, 2011. Print.

Trimbur, John. "Multiliteracies, Social Futures, and Writing Centers." *The Writing Center Journal* 20.2 (2000): 29–31. Print.

Vickers, Melana, Zyla. "Accommodating College Students with Learning Disabilities: ADD, ADHD and Dyslexia." *PopCenter.org.* The John William Pope Center for Higher Education Policy. 25 March 2010. Web. 12 Dec. 2011.

Walters, Shannon. "Toward an Accessible Pedagogy: Dis/ability, Multimodality, and Universal Design in the Technical Communication Classroom." *Technical Communication Quarterly* 19.4 (2010): 427–54. Print.

Finding Harmony in Disharmony: Engineering and English Studies

Ruth Johnson, Beth Clark, and Mario Burton

Ruth Johnson, Beth Clark, and Mario Burton were undergraduates at the University of Alabama–Huntsville when they wrote this article. It originally appeared in the journal *Young Scholars in Writing*.

A consultant walks into the University of Alabama–Huntsville Writing Center, sets her books on the desk in the back, and finds an unoccupied computer station to check her schedule for the day. She clicks on the name of her first client and glances down at the summary section of the dialogue box: "I need help with my ISE paper," the student has written. *Hmm, an engineering student,* she thinks with a little apprehension, as she prepares herself for a challenge. A group of engineering students then floods in, accompanying the one who actually made the appointment. They explain the project which they are writing—a type of project she has never written before, a type of project with which she has no previous experience. She wonders if she will give appropriate advice or if she will be able to think of anything to say at all. She wonders if she will even be able to understand the intricate, jargon-laden draft. Then she takes a deep breath, knowing that these students are looking to her for help, and starts asking questions.

This is a hypothetical example of how a writing center consultant might feel about working with a student from an unfamiliar discipline. Although consultants work with students from a wide range of disciplines every day, informal talk among consultants and formal discussions at monthly staff meetings frequently reveal a common insecurity about working with students in unfamiliar disciplines. However, since writing centers rely on building successful relationships with students, consultants must understand how to initiate effective interaction with all students, even those with subjects outside their comfort zone. Because UAH has a large engineering college and because many of our writing center consultants are English majors, we decided to focus on the relationship between these two disciplines. Although various articles discuss the writing center's significance in merging the gap between the engineering and English departments, very little research exists on the interpersonal relationship that develops between writing center consultants and engineering students, and even less on the strategies used by consultants within these relationships. Therefore, we decided to conduct research to explore the similarities and differences in consulting strategies when working with engineering and English students. Although we expected consultants to communicate more effectively with students from English classes than with engineering students, we found the opposite. While the consultants we observed exhibit the supportive behaviors central to writing center pedagogy, their familiarity with English papers lets them be controlling and assertive with English students. Conversely, their lack of familiarity with engineering forces them to remain engaged in an open and equal dialogue with those students. By relying on questions, the consultant in our opening scenario does exactly what consultants should do with any student. While we do not suggest that lack of knowledge or expertise itself produces effective consultants, our counterintuitive discovery does remind us that emphasizing supportive consulting strategies during consultant training is crucial; moreover, in light of this conclusion, we may need to train subject-area "experts" differently than "non-experts."

LITERATURE REVIEW

Our study required background research on writing in the engineering discipline, the role of writing centers, and the Gibbs Communication Model of consulting with students. Since our goal is to help bridge the gap between engineering and writing, which is usually associated with English courses, we must establish some background on writing in the field of engineering and define the gap between the two disciplines.

Current scholarship explains that engineering as a discipline and career involves a good deal of writing. For instance, Stephanie Nelson claims that writing can help engineers "think, act, and evaluate" tasks in their field (2). However, Charlotte Brammer and Nicole Ervin indicate that engineering courses may not always prepare their students for the writing they'll do on the job. Their article establishes the need for engineers to develop better writing skills. Carol Kramburg-Walker reiterates this need and goes further to point to English departments' obligation to help "provide writing support for academic engineers" (130).

With this need in mind, some writing centers and English departments collaborate with engineering departments. Most recent scholarship on such collaboration focuses on college-, department-, or faculty-level programs rather than on interaction between students and consultants. For example, Elisabeth Alford discusses the University of South Carolina's program working with faculty and staff to design coursework and with students in groups or one-on-one to improve individual projects. Also, Erik Fisher, Michael Ursey, and Heather Beasley show how the University of Colorado–Boulder implemented university-wide strategies to increase effectiveness of engineering writing assignments and improve engineers' writing skills. And Meredith Green and Sarah Duerden describe an Arizona State University program that implemented more writing into the engineering curriculum through problem-solving exercises involving teamwork. Although these articles demonstrate ways opportunities are increased for engineering students to practice writing and receive feedback and support, the research does not discuss interaction *strategies* for providing this feedback and support to engineering students.

However, one in-depth analysis on "writing tutors' comments" by Jo Mackiewicz does discuss consulting strategies during four consultations—three involve writing tutors who have no experience with engineering writing and one involves a tutor with twenty years' experience in engineering writing (318). The study showed that the tutor with engineering experience not only gave useful advice on writing but also established rapport with the student. On the other hand, the other three tutors focused only on mechanical elements of the students' work, confidently giving incorrect advice. Mackiewicz therefore concludes that experience in the field allowed the first tutor to respond more effectively than those without experience (326). If nonexperienced tutors had more training in engineering writing, she claims, their comments would improve.

Our research revisits Mackiewicz's study by analyzing how consultants interact differently with English and engineering students. We noticed that besides the difference in expertise among the tutors in Mackiewicz's study, there was also a difference in consulting strategies: the effective tutor was also an effective communicator. Paulo Freire explains why effective communication is so crucial in such settings: "Authentic thinking, thinking that is concerned about *reality*, does not take place in ivory tower isolation, but only in communication" (58). In writing centers, this communication involves both the inquiry and guidance of the consultant and the input of the student. Freire offers a reason why using an inquiry model is so important in writing centers: "Any situation in which some individuals prevent others from engaging in the process of inquiry alienate[s] human beings from their own decision-making" (66). As consultants, we do not want to hinder students' decision making but guide it.

To assess whether or not our consultants are using this inquiry model to guide students, we chose to apply the Gibbs Communication Model to several consultations because it explicitly draws distinctions between supportive, assisting behaviors and defensive, controlling behaviors and helps us see if we follow our own definition of effective consulting. In *The Writing Lab Newsletter*, Beverly Menassa lists and explains six sets of contrasting behavior outlined in the Gibbs model: evaluation versus description, control versus problem orientation, strategy versus spontaneity, neutrality versus empathy, superiority versus equality, and certainty versus provisionalism—each set naming an unsupportive behavior and its supportive contrast (4–5). For example, to support the student, the consultant should *describe* what a student is doing in a paper and respond to it rather than *evaluate* it. We should identify the *problem* and offer suggestions rather than *control* the solution. We should *spontaneously* and openly respond to the student's ideas rather than *manipulate* them. We should approach students with *empathy* rather than *indifference*. We should present ourselves as equals to the students rather than superiors. We should present our suggestions as one option rather than the only course available for revision.

METHODOLOGY

Data Collection

To analyze differences in how consultants interact with engineering and English students, we recorded and transcribed four half-hour consultations—one of each field with two different consultants—to compare how each consultant works with both an English and an engineering student. We selected participants by randomly choosing two engineering student groups from the fall 2006 Engineering Economy (ISE 321) class who had made writing center appointments. We then recorded the two consultants who worked with these groups in English consultations. While separate, both English consultations happened to be with the same student, which did narrow our sample. However, both consultants happened to have written papers for the student's instructor on similar topics, so we could specifically consider how their familiarity influenced their interaction with the student and how it differed from their interaction with the engineering students. One consultant was an undergraduate with approximately two months' experience in the writing center, and the other was a graduate with approximately two years' experience there. With only two consultants, we cannot account for how differing consulting styles may affect their interaction, but having consultants with different levels of experience helped us speculate about how much training may affect interaction. Future research could easily broaden this sampling to include different personalities, cultural backgrounds, educational backgrounds, and fields of study among consultants and students, but this research offers us sufficient data to begin questioning how familiarity affects consulting strategies. These four consultations provided two solid hours of conversation in which we could look very carefully and analytically at specific moments of student-consultant interaction.

Procedure

After recording and transcribing the tapes, we analyzed the data using the Gibbs Communication Model. Although we were unable to observe nonverbals such as tone of voice and body language, which can influence supportive environments as much as what consultants say, we were able to closely analyze verbal interaction. We used four of the model's comparative components to decide whether consultants' strategies fostered an environment that was supportive and advantageous for feedback or

Table 1   Defensive and Supportive Communication Strategies

DEFENSIVE	SUPPORTIVE
Control—the consultant says, "Don't do that, do this"	**Problem orientation**—the consultant gives students general advice and suggestions on content issues
Superiority—the consultant provides the material rather than prompting students to generate the ideas themselves	**Equality**—the consultant asks for information and encourages students to participate in finding solutions
Indifference—the consultant lacks interest in the students' ideas	**Empathy**—the consultant is supportive and confirms the students' ideas
Certainty—acting almost as a teacher, the consultant offers definite suggestions with no room for options	**Provisionalism**—acting as an audience member, the consultant's phrasing suggests that her advice "may be the case," displaying her uncertainty with specific subject matter

Adapted from the Gibbs Communication Model.

one that was defensive and discouraged adequate responses. We began coding the transcripts separately; however, we continually had to compare notes because terms often bled into one another and became open to interpretation. Consequently, we decided to articulate more specific definitions upon which we all agreed (see Table 1). After defining exactly what type of interaction should characterize each strategy, we reread the transcripts together, coding instances of each. When we cite specific examples in our discussion, we will use pseudonyms to refer to consultants, calling the undergraduate Anne and the graduate Micki.

RESULTS

English Consultations

The student in the two English consultations is constructing an argument essay on *Joseph Andrews* for her eighteenth-century literature class. Although she doesn't have a draft yet, she comes in for help with brainstorming to formulate her ideas. The student consults with Anne, who is currently taking the same class, and Micki, who had previously taken a related class from the same instructor. Consequently, both consultants are familiar with the novel, period, and teacher. During the consultation, the student's main concern is finding a focus; essentially, both meetings involve brainstorming and discussing possible directions for the essay.

Both Anne and Micki initially respond with supportive empathetic behavior. They tend to reply with affirmations such as "Right" and "Okay" when listening to the student's ideas, showing interest in what the student has to say. Micki also uses supportive equality behavior when first interacting with the student by asking her thought-provoking questions to encourage the student's participation in the meeting. She tells the student, "So, if that's a workable thesis, which I think it is, then how are you going to talk about that so you prove that?" Anne exhibits this same behavior, but she uses it less often and toward the end of the session. At the beginning, Anne mostly affirms the student's explanation. Near the end, she does ask questions to prompt her to find her own solutions. When the student asks questions or *invites* suggestions, Anne and Micki provide advice (problem orientation). Anne tells her student, "We'll try and come up with a kind of outline." However, they qualify their advice so the student is the ultimate decision maker. They make suggestions for revision, but they moderate these suggestions with phrases such as "What you could do is . . . ," "I think . . . ," "You could look at . . ." to make sure the student selects all final decisions.

Conversely, despite Anne and Micki's use of supportive behaviors, they also employ defensive behaviors with this student, specifically superiority. At times, they include too much of their own knowledge when giving suggestions to the student. This technique silences the student's ideas and shifts ownership of the paper from the student to the consultant. For example, in Anne's session, she corrects the student's ideas, adding her own knowledge rather than prompting the student to generate those ideas on her own:

> STUDENT: I think Fanny's well bred. What about her station? Is that right?
> ANNE: Fanny is . . . not well bred.

Here, because the student asks the consultant's opinion, Anne becomes the responder and contradicts the student's ideas. She closes off the interaction instead of inquiring or probing into why the student thinks Fanny is well bred. The conversation continues with the student asking:

> STUDENT: She's not well bred?
> ANNE: No, she's . . . Fanny's kind of an issue there too in a lot of ways because she's . . . been . . . she comes from humble origin. She didn't even know who her parents are. Um, and, and, she's relatively common, but she's in a noble's household.
> STUDENT: Right.
> ANNE: Um, and she's a . . . I believe she's a lady's maid in a noble household, which gives her a certain knowledge of breeding, so she'll, she'll have picked up on and learned the behaviors of a well-bred woman.
> STUDENT: Okay.

In this exchange, the two speakers switch roles. The student questions, and the consultant answers. Such behavior illustrates the consultant's superiority because she imposes her knowledge and ideas of the novel on the student. Rather than asking the student what Fanny's origins are or what the character knows about her parents, Anne provides that information, no longer using assisting behaviors that encourage the student's participation. Instead, the student uses the supportive behaviors Anne should be using, such as questioning and affirming Anne's statements with "Right" and "Okay." After this exchange, Anne immediately moves from this issue about Fanny to suggesting how to address these ideas in the paper:

> ANNE: . . . um, you, a good way to incorporate her would definitely be to talk about, um, the similarities between Leonora and Fanny.
> STUDENT: Okay.

Again, in this situation, Anne tells the student how she should put these ideas into the paper instead of asking questions to get a sense of what points the student wants to convey or how the student might want to address them. By simply telling her what to do, Anne controls the situation, and like the former exchange, the student is the one affirming ideas and saying "Okay." Anne's defensive strategies are problematic because they can make the student feel inferior to the consultant and inhibit the student from exploring ideas or possible ways of articulating them.

Like Anne, Micki utilizes her own knowledge and inhibits the student from discovering ideas on her own. For example, Micki uses her experience with the instructor to control the direction of the consultation: "When I had him, I wrote on Landers, and he took exactly the opposite view that I did, but it didn't hurt my grade." Micki's advice in this instance positions her as superior to the student and an authority on the instructor. Moreover, Micki also employs her knowledge about the time period:

> MICKI: Right, another reason, and yours is justifiable. I'm trying to remember—this is the 1700s?
> STUDENT: Yeah, 1700s, eighteenth century.

MICKI: Ok, right, there you go. So, in that time period, they were big into the pure versus the people that did things wrong.

STUDENT: Right.

In this passage, Micki again asserts her own knowledge rather than encouraging the student to supply ideas herself. Micki starts by asking the student the time period of the text, to which the student responds. However, instead of asking another question that allows the student to explore the time period's influence on the text, the consultant tells the student her own perspective of the era and how it might affect the content. Once more, the dialogue's structure illustrates the two switching roles: the consultant delivers information and the student confirms it, rather than vice versa. Besides using her knowledge of the time period, the consultant also shares her knowledge about the author of the text rather than asking for the student's ideas:

STUDENT: So why does he want to show you this? You get the story of this woman.

MICKI: And just knowing Fielding from *Tom Jones*, he loves that bad stuff. Here, he's painting that person who's really good, but for some reason, and I think it's because he likes it and the people like it too—commercialism, that he's trying to make people keep reading it. You can only read so much about a good person and then say okay. You know?

STUDENT: Right. It's like could you please shut up about Joseph?

In this role switch, the question the student asks—"Why does he want to show you this?"—is central to the assignment. The student's job is to develop an analytical response to this question; the consultant needs to help the student understand this task and generate her own answer rather than immediately providing one. Micki could remind the student that this question is the assignment and that as such, it could have a variety of valid answers. After agreeing with the student that this question is a great place to start brainstorming, the consultant could discuss different possibilities and allow the student to choose an answer on her own.

Overall, the consultants use a variety of supportive strategies with the English student—empathy, equality, problem orientation, and provisionalism—which help prompt the student's participation and facilitate her writing process. However, the surprising discovery here is that the consultants *also* exhibit superior communication strategies, which foster a defensive climate and defeat the writing center's goal of providing students with a supportive audience.

Engineering Consultations

The engineering students whom we recorded scheduled appointments to work on their final research projects for Engineering Economy (ISE 321)—writing a final report for a hypothetical client that includes their recommendation for the most economical solution to a real-world problem. Throughout the semester they had deadlines for portions of the research, all of which they needed to compile in the final report. Anne worked with students who brought in a draft from a previous project but had not started drafting the final report. Micki worked with students who brought in an actual draft of the final report. Both consultations followed the same general pattern of opening remarks, establishing what the assignment was, offering suggestions, and answering questions.

Through the first several lines of the consultations, Anne and Micki use equality strategies by asking questions to prompt the students to explain their project and discuss their ideas. For example, Anne begins the consultation:

> ANNE: Okay, uh, what's your project on . . . before we . . .
> STUDENT 1: We had to evaluate several cars that we . . .
> ANNE: Okay . . . and you came up with the rating system and . . . um, well, do you have some kind of like setup or anything or, ooh, a draft . . .
> STUDENT 1: Yeah, this is [. . .] what we turned in for the previous part of the assignment . . .
> ANNE: Okay.
> STUDENT 1: . . . but we were, didn't know what direction to go in from here.
> ANNE: Alright, so in developing it into a final . . .
> STUDENT 1: Yeah.
> ANNE: . . . copy.

Here, Anne asks a series of questions to learn more about the assignment and where the students are in the writing process. These position her as equal to the students and prompt them to actively participate in the consultation. Encouraging their participation helps the consultant find out what the students' needs are. Similarly, Micki asks a question to assess the students' needs:

> MICKI: [. . .] The people who have come in the last week basically hadn't written the paragraphs that go with their analysis. Have you done that?
> STUDENT: Yes, we've got pretty much the final report written.

With this exchange, the consultant learns that the students have a draft of their assignment. Both consultants, then, use questions to establish where the students are in the writing process and what they want out of these meetings. Whereas Anne discovers that the group has pieces of data and needs to work toward a draft, Micki discovers that her group has actually written a draft and wants her feedback on it. Throughout the meeting, they also confirm and encourage what the students say (empathy) with words such as "Okay" and "Right."

As the English student does, the engineering students ask the consultants for advice or suggestions. The difference here is that Anne and Micki avoid appearing superior to the students by replying with provisional suggestions or more questions, rather than telling the students how they should handle their problem. As Micki reads through her students' draft, she points out specific statements and asks questions about them. She reads aloud, "'It's not as safe as it used to be'" and then asks, "Has it ever been safe? I've been here nineteen years, and it seems like it's gotten worse." Here, Micki addresses a statement that concerns her. With her question "Has it ever been safe?" she asks them to reevaluate this point because she has a different perspective. By telling them she's been here nineteen years and by using the provisional term "seems," she presents this as one perspective, not a fact, leaving it up to them to decide how to address her question. Later in the draft, Micki points out another issue about which she has a question:

> MICKI: Oh, and I don't know if this matters, but if you're trying to stick to the point, "the job is demanding on his vehicle." Do we really care if it's demanding on him?
>
> STUDENT: No, not really. It's just extra.
>
> MICKI: Yeah.
>
> STUDENT: I could cut that.

Here, she points out text that does not seem relevant, but she does not simply tell the students to delete that sentence. Instead, she asks and leaves it up to them to answer if "we," the audience, need this information (problem orientation). Micki leaves it as a question, and the student concludes, "I could cut that," demonstrating that he, not the consultant, is in control.

Anne also uses provisional statements demonstrating her uncertainty, position as an audience member, and willingness to let the students decide what choice to make. For instance, in the following interaction, Anne follows a suggestion with a concrete example:

> STUDENT 2: You're saying, like, should we put how we rate the cars and in this paragraph, talk about his car.
>
> ANNE: Alright, the Civic Hybrid, for example, how did you come up with the results you got for it? How did you look at the price? How did you look at the luggage capacity, the safety of this car, etc. . . . Basically, because these are the cars you looked at, you've got to be comprehensive in writing your paper here; you've gotta go through each car because cars and the way you analyzed them impacted your final decision, so it's important that we see the decision-making process in the first place. Alright. Does that kinda make sense?

With this explanation, Anne provides the group with a list of questions and then explains why she thinks they're important—the readers need to see how these decisions impacted their final decision. She does tell them that showing their "decision-making process" is necessary, but she still asks them questions (equality) and leaves them in control (problem orientation) of *how* to address her concern. Later, Anne includes a similar series of questions to suggest what the group can add to clarify their ideas:

> ANNE: You need to tell us what it was you were looking for in the first place. [. . .] You give us the scenario in the introduction and what it was you were looking for, but what exactly did you decide would . . . what attributes did you decide would fit that solution? For example . . . alright, you need a car. What kind of car is it that you were looking for?
>
> STUDENT 1: We're looking for a compact car, that, car with, that has a good gas mileage.
>
> ANNE: Okay. You're looking for a compact car with good gas mileage. What is it that makes a good compact car, and how did you decide that? You've cited

luggage capacity, safety, horsepower, reliability, and warranty were the important factors, and miles per gallon, were the important factors in a compact car. How did you come to the decision that those were the attributes you would use in your rating system?

Anne begins this conversation by recounting what the students have already done in the paper—describing the scenario—and then asking how they moved from identifying the problem to identifying what would solve it. After the student tells her what kind of car they are looking for, she then lists questions that will help them discuss how and why they came to that decision. Her questions demonstrate equality—as she does not act as a superior by asserting her own knowledge—and problem orientation—as she notes a portion of the text that concerns her and offers suggestions on how the students might revise it. Furthermore, when the students ask Anne a question about how to write as a group, she hedges her comments, giving several options rather than the one "right" way to do it: "You could do it both ways and kind of blend methods and, you know, get together as a group and then assign each [. . .] person to write a certain thing." Here, she uses "could" to present her comment as a suggestion, not a mandate.

With the engineering students, the consultants use supportive communication strategies rather than defensive ones. By demonstrating equality, empathy, provisionalism, and problem orientation, they do not position themselves as superior to the students as they sometimes did with the English student.

DISCUSSION

These results suggest that the consultants' familiarity with English topics can become a hindrance to their ability to support and facilitate the student, allowing them to use their experience as a means of assertion and superiority. By stating that they know or are familiar with a specific topic, the consultants attempt to persuade the students that they know the best way to interpret the text. This approach is particularly problematic because, as the Gibbs model suggests, it promotes dependency and discourages responses from the student. Although the consultants are sometimes empathetic and supportive, their experience usually becomes a means of dictating, via superior communication strategies, that there is a right way to interpret a text and they know how best to do so.

Because the consultants are less familiar with engineering topics, their approach to engineering students' questions and comments during consultations demonstrates more equality and support. The consultants' lack of familiarity with engineering topics allows them to ask questions that are consistent with Gibbs's "equality." When Anne asks several questions about how the students got their results, her asking a question instead of providing the answer, as she does with the English student, positions her as an equal and not a superior. Uncertainty with the topic also allows the consultants to use "provisional" language to navigate through specific areas. Interaction with engineering students is less "manipulative" than with the English students and more "spontaneous." Therefore, both participate in ensuring that the consultation is effective.

Ultimately, the consultants' familiarity with the English topics becomes a temptation to control the interaction. Since they have knowledge of or experience with the topic, they *can* use it, whereas in the engineering consultations, they are forced to question instead of answer because they lack familiarity and experience with the topics. Writing center theory constantly reminds us that consultants should use an inquiry model in which they remain equal with and supportive of students (Kinkead and Harris; North; Olson). Consequently, whatever amount of experience they have with a topic, they should replicate the questioning format that Anne and Micki use with the engineering students. In practice, writing centers inevitably end up with both subject area "experts" and "non-experts." This situation is not necessarily problematic if writing centers learn how to address it: since everyone cannot be an expert, centers must develop effective training for both roles. It may be telling that although both Anne and Micki use controlling techniques during their consultations with the English student, Micki uses them less. Perhaps extra years of experience and training have helped Micki communicate more supportively—suggesting that training might be the key to addressing this potential problem.

For both groups, we want to stress using questions and suggestions to create the supportive climate of the Gibbs Communication Model. We want to warn subject area experts about the potential problem of using their experience to create a defensive climate, and provide ways to avoid this situation. For instance, instead of responding to a student's question with a definitive answer, like both Anne and Micki do with their English student, consultants could respond by rephrasing the question back to the student or by providing several options for answering the question. And while acknowledging that lack of expertise may not be the best-case scenario, we can show non-experts how it can be used to their advantage. Specifically, when they are unsure about a subject, they can ask the students to clarify their point, which is the strategy consultants *should* use in any situation. By asking questions, they use the problem-orientation strategy instead of controlling the situation by solving the problem themselves. Non-experts naturally question the students because they are uncertain about the subject matter, but experts should question as well because they need to assist, not control, students.

Even though expertise can be problematic, we must admit that uncertainty can be problematic as well. While showing the students that consultants are equals, and therefore often uncertain, is a positive outcome of non-expertise, the consultants do not need to allow this conclusion to stop them from answering students' questions. For example, this conversation between Micki and an engineering student is problematic:

MICKI: Up to the number nine, you spell it out. Since this is a technical paper, I don't know.

STUDENT: That's the way I've always done it.

MICKI: However, technical papers may be different. I can't say. I would think that they'd rather see the numbers because it's an analysis.

In this instance, Micki admitting that she is unsure is better than covering uncertainty by confidently providing incorrect answers (as the inexperienced consultants did in Mackiewicz's work); however, letting an answer stand as "I don't know" is not particularly helpful for the student. Consequently, we should remind non-expert consultants to follow up such uncertainty by looking up information in writing center resources and encouraging students to utilize these resources themselves.

Moreover, using resources can also bridge between subject area experts and non-experts. Both groups need to make use of resources for several reasons. First, consultants should use resources in front of the students to be good writing models. Second, consultants should use them to remind students that they must support their ideas. When Anne tells her English student that Fanny is not well bred, she lists several reasons. Instead of this assertion, Anne could have disclosed that she had a different perspective and suggested they return to the novel to find more solid evidence. Third, consultants should use resources to check themselves on grammar, citation, and style conventions in different genres. When Micki tells her engineering student that she does not know whether technical writers use figures or words for numbers, she could have looked it up in a technical writing manual.

CONCLUSION

Through this research, we have discovered as writing center consultants that our consulting strategies may be more supportive with engineering students than with English students. The very uncertainty that concerns us may actually help us remain more supportive and less controlling during our interaction. Our knowledge and familiarity give us confidence that can easily translate into superiority, but in situations when we are not familiar with a topic, we have no choice but to use supportive communication strategies and follow the inquiry model we should follow at all times in the writing center. This gives us insight into the role of familiarity within a consultation and provides a basis to acknowledge the potential of using familiarity as a controlling tool. While writing center researchers should continue collecting more data to test this conclusion with a larger, more varied sample, seeing that these two consultants act superior in familiar situations warns us that subject area experts have more potential to succumb to using superior consulting strategies than do non-experts. This conclusion illustrates that non-experts can still be a valuable resource to students while subject area experts should be careful not to let their knowledge inhibit the learning process and critical thinking of their students.

We would like to thank the students and consultants who allowed us to record and analyze their sessions and our advisor, Dr. Diana Calhoun Bell, who supported us with guidance and feedback through the entire process from idea development to revising our final manuscript.

WORKS CITED

Alford, Elisabeth M. "Writing Center Programs for Engineering." *Frontiers in Education Conference, 1996* 1.1 (1996): 7–10. *IEEE Explore.* IEEE, UAH Library, Huntsville, AL. Web. 13 Sept. 2006.

Brammer, Charlotte, and Nicole Ervin. "Bridging the Gap: A Case Study of Engineering Students, Teachers, and Practitioners." *Communication Jazz: Improvising the New International Communication Culture* (1999): 251–56. *IEEE Explore*. IEEE, UAH Library, Huntsville, AL. Web. 25 July 2007.

Fisher, Erik, Michael W. Ursey, and Heather A. Beasley. "OWL: A Wise Way to Enhance Engineering Students' Writing Skills." *Frontiers in Education, 2003* 2.1 (2003): 16–21. *IEEE Explore*. IEEE, UAH Library, Huntsville, AL. Web. 14 Sept. 2006.

Freire, Paulo. *Pedagogy of the Oppressed.* 20th Anniversary Edition. Trans. Myra Bergman Ramos. New York: Continuum, 1997. Print.

Green, Meredith, and Sarah Duerden. "Collaboration, English Composition, & the Engineering Student: Constructing Knowledge in the Integrated Engineering Program." *Electronic Proceedings for Frontiers in Education Conference.* Session 6a1 (1996): 1–4. Web. 25 July 2007.

Kinkead, Joyce A., and Jeanette G. Harris. *Writing Centers in Context: Twelve Case Studies.* Urbana: NCTE, 1993.

Kramburg-Walker, Carol. "The Need to Provide Writing Support for Academic Engineers." *IEEE Transactions on Professional Communication* 36.3 (1993): 130–36. *IEEE Explore.* IEEE, UAH Library, Huntsville, AL. Web. 25 July 2007.

Mackiewicz, Jo. "The Effects of Tutor Expertise in Engineering Writing: A Linguistic Analysis of Writing Tutors' Comments." *IEEE Transactions on Professional Communication* 47.4 (2004): 316–28. *IEEE Explore.* IEEE, UAH Library, Huntsville, AL. Web. 14 Sept. 2006.

Menassa, Beverly Neu. "Training Writing Consultants to Utilize Supportive Behaviors." *The Writing Lab Newsletter* 24.8 (2000): 1–5. Print.

Nelson, Stephanie. "Teaching Collaborative Writing and Peer Review Techniques to Engineering and Technology Undergraduates." *Electronic Proceedings for Frontiers in Education Conference.* Session S2B. (2000): 1–5. Web. 25 July 2007.

North, Stephen M. "The Idea of a Writing Center." *College English* 46 (1984): 433–46. Print.

Olsen, Gary A., ed. *Writing Centers: Theory and Administration.* Urbana: NCTE, 1984. Print.

Searching for Robert Moore[1]

Neal Lerner

Neal Lerner is a professor at Northeastern University. His article originally appeared in *The Writing Center Journal*.

Little did Robert Moore realize that he would help to create an entire academic discipline when he declared in a 1950 *College English* article that "writing clinics and writing laboratories are becoming increasingly popular among American universities and colleges as remedial agencies for removing students' deficiencies in composition" (388). Yet for Stephen North in 1984, Christina Murphy and Joe Law in 1995, and Robert Barnett and Jacob Blumner in 2001, Moore represents a writing-center past against which the writing-center future—whether of individual writing centers or of the discipline itself—should be defined. North sees Moore's account as evidence of a "limited conception of what such places can do—the fix-it shop image" ("The Idea" 436). Murphy and Law note in the introduction to *Landmark Essays on Writing Centers* that Moore "typifies [a] conservative attitude, which views the writing center exclusively as a site for diagnosing and removing language deficiencies" (xi). In the *Allyn and Bacon Guide to Writing Center Theory and Practice*, Barnett and Blumner write that Moore's "definitions and concerns still reverberate in our field today" (1). Thus, Moore has come to be essential reading in the post-World War II history of writing centers: a benchmark for how far the thinking in our field has come and a shadow presence of what the contemporary writing center might return to lest we relax our theoretical and pedagogical vigilance.[2]

Complicating this conclusion, however, is a great deal of documentary evidence. For instance, a 1941 University of Illinois survey described the writing laboratory concept as "one of the more popular methods" of teaching writing and that "sometimes it is provided outside the composition course as a convenient place where students may write, under guidance, for any course" (Howard 25). Even Robert Moore himself, in a 1948 piece published in *Illinois English Bulletin*, described the Illinois Writing Clinic in far more student-centered ways than he would two years later. Moore wrote that "the counselling in the Writing Clinic attempts to be invariably friendly and sympathetic. To allow the student to feel stupid or unwelcome or badgered is fatal to the securing of the voluntary and persistent effort" ("The University of Illinois Writing Clinic" 11). Furthermore, Peter Carino ("Early Writing Centers"; "Open Admissions") and, more recently, Beth Boquet have presented accounts of writing centers past that displayed considerable diversity and, in many instances, a set of practices and challenges similar to contemporary ideas. Still, it is Moore's account and the idea of early writing centers as drill-and-practice sweat shops that has come for many to define the history of our field. The persistence of such characterizations of writing center history perhaps marks a discipline in progress, one that attempts to legitimize its future by rallying around a convenient—and frightening—version of its past, what Peter Carino labels the "Evolutionary Model" of writing center history ("Open Admissions").

In what follows, I show that the reality of Robert Moore and his Writing Clinic is far more complex than previously assumed. In fact, the history I offer is a familiar narrative about the politics of writing centers and writing programs designed to meet the needs of under-prepared students. It is also a "survivor" story about a Writing Clinic that existed for nearly 40 years, far outlasting other components of a remedial program because it served certain rhetorical, political, and pedagogical needs. While the familiarity of this narrative—its ordinariness—seems antithetical to the "uniqueness" of writing center identity and thus claims for disciplinarity, the similarities between writing centers past and writing centers present offers a disciplinary history that is built upon continuity and persistence rather than upon antagonism. Thus, the story of Robert Moore and the University of Illinois Writing Clinic might be far more emblematic of our field than Moore's detractors realize.

MEETING ROBERT MOORE

Let me start with what I know about Robert Hamilton Moore, culled from archival records at the University of Illinois[3] and at George Washington University, email with Moore's GWU colleagues, and various publications: He was born in St. Matthews, Kentucky, on January 3, 1913, received his B.A. in English from Indiana University in 1934, then worked as a newspaper reporter in his hometown of Louisville, KY, before returning to Indiana in 1937 for his M.A., which he received the following year, writing a thesis titled *Anthony Trollope's Treatment of the Novel.* Moore then started an eleven-year association with the University of Illinois, coming to Urbana-Champaign for his Ph.D. in English in 1938 and completing his dissertation, *Victorian Religious Liberalism Reflected in Autobiography,* in 1948. Moore's teaching career at Illinois included the position of Assistant in English from 1938 to 1943 and Instructor in English from 1943 to 1949. In 1948, Moore was named the Director of the Illinois Writing Clinic, reviving an entity that was created in 1944 but had languished following World War II. Moore then left Illinois in 1949, Ph.D. in hand, and was hired at George Washington University at the rank of Associate Professor. He was Chairman of Composition from 1949 until 1977 and became emeritus in 1978. Moore died of cardiac arrest on December 31, 1984, four days shy of his 72nd birthday.[4]

In terms of Moore's academic publishing, once he settled into GWU, Moore began a long career of textbook writing, starting with *Plan Before You Write,* which was published in 1950, and then with *Effective Writing,* which was first published in 1955 and then updated with subsequent editions in 1959, 1965, and 1971. All of Moore's textbooks were published by what was then Rinehart and later became Holt, Rinehart and Winston.

I have a few more documents, sent to me by the archivist at George Washington University. One is a photograph, my only photo of Moore, taken in May, 1964. Moore would have been 51, but in this photo he appears much older, a gaunt man in a dark, loose-fitting suit and a bow tie. His graying hair is kept short and combed straight back, exposing a high forehead. Moore is pictured giving "congratulations" to "Miss Emily DeHuff, a Fairfax High School senior," who "recorded the first perfect score in the seven-year history of the University's annual English competition for Metropolitan area high school juniors and seniors."

That capsule is pretty much what I know about Robert Moore. I have read *Plan Before You Write* and the first two editions of *Effective Writing*. Nothing particularly earth-shattering there. In his introduction to *Effective Writing*, Moore's rationale to the student writer is that "your composition course is specifically designed to teach you efficient language habits. Insofar as a two- or three-semester course can, it is designed first to correct unconventional habits you may bring with you to college, since uneducated speech and writing can be the biggest obstacle to advancement in any career to which college graduates might aspire" (3). Thus, Moore's approach is akin to what Sharon Crowley identifies as the "moral language" of the originators of the required composition course at Harvard, where "the point of the required course is not to acquire some level of skill or knowledge that can be measured upon exit; it is instead to subject students to discipline, to force them to recognize the power of the institution to insist on conformity with its standards" (74). Moore's texts, large sellers that they were, broke no new ground nor advanced any new approach or theory of composition,[5] nor did they make much mention at all of his experience in the Illinois Writing Clinic. It is only the preface to *Plan Before You Write* in which Moore invokes his clinic experience to note that "even the college student may have less knowledge of technicalities than he should" (v).

This is a story, then, that seems familiar: A graduate student is given an opportunity to run a writing clinic (or lab or center), parlays that opportunity into a couple of academic publications and, ultimately, a faculty position. And once established in that position, he would leave the writing center world far behind.[6] As far as the Illinois Writing Clinic is concerned, its origins and development and its rhetorical and political role within a larger writing program also seem like a very familiar tale, despite its relative obscurity. Indeed, its familiarity makes one wonder just how many times it has been repeated in the last 50 to 75 years.

THE CREATION OF THE UNIVERSITY OF ILLINOIS WRITING CLINIC

The narrative of the Illinois Writing Clinic starts in a familiar place—in a report of a "crisis" in students' literacy skills. In the spring of 1940, the Illinois Board of Trustees authorized an investigation into "the problem of improving students' use of English" after various Trustees "had found through their contacts with alumni and through criticisms which they received from those who had business and other dealings with former students that too many graduates of the University used poor English in their oral and written expression" (Potthoff, "The Graduation Requirement" 1). The three-part solution was one that also seems familiar: (1) the institution of a writing competency exam for students after their sophomore year; (2) the addition of an upper division course, Rhetoric 200, for students who failed this exam; and (3) the creation of a Writing Clinic "open on a purely voluntary basis and without fee to any student in the University" (Potthoff, "The Graduation Requirement" 4).

According to archival records at the University of Illinois, the specific design of the Writing Clinic evolved directly from a 1941 survey that Jessie Howard and Charles Roberts published in *The University of Illinois Bulletin*. Indeed, the March 13, 1942, minutes of the Committee on Student English, of which both Howard and Roberts were members, indicate that Howard and Roberts began a series of reports on the use of writing clinics and laboratories at the institutions that had responded to their earlier published survey. It also seems that Howard and Roberts represented different sides of this approach, Howard taking up the Writing Laboratory cause, which would substitute one-to-one and small-group instruction for sections of remedial writing, and Roberts championing the Clinic, which would provide diagnostic measures and referrals more than any direct instruction. Despite a majority faculty vote for the laboratory approach, at their April 3, 1942, meeting, the committee voted to establish a Writing Clinic, open three days per week and staffed one-half or one-third time by one instructor, someone already part of the Rhetoric staff, a much less expensive proposition than a full-blown writing laboratory.

The earliest published report of this Clinic comes from its first director, W. G. Johnson, in a 1945 article in the *Illinois English Bulletin*. Johnson presents the "charge" of the Clinic, as described by H. N. Hillebrand, the Head of the English Department, in a 1944 letter to Illinois faculty:

> The Writing Clinic is designed to analyze the writing difficulties which the student encounters, to provide the advice necessary for him to remedy them under his own "power," and to determine the effectiveness of his remedial efforts. The general purpose is to help the student up to the point where he can exercise intelligent self-direction in overcoming his own difficulties; *the clinic does not supervise writing or provide tutoring.* (emphasis added 9)

This language—and the contrast to a writing laboratory which *would* "supervise writing" and "provide tutoring"—speaks to the power of Charles Roberts' design for the initial Clinic and echoes Roberts' Clinic description from his 1941 survey: "The clinic, as usually set up, is simply an office in which a student's writing difficulties are diagnosed and prescribed for" (89). Indeed, similar descriptions would appear continually in committee minutes, promotional materials, and outside publications, including Moore's two published descriptions of the Clinic. For instance, in its December, 1943, report, the Senate Committee on Student English recommended that "a writing clinic should be established in the University to guide students toward intelligent self-direction in overcoming their own difficulties. The Clinic would not supervise writing or provide tutoring, but it would diagnose weaknesses and suggest corrective procedures." Edward Potthoff, the chairman of the Committee on Student English, described the Clinic in very similar—if not identical—terms in a 1945 *College English* article:

> [The Writing Clinic], which is open on a purely voluntary basis to any student in the university, is designed to analyze the writing difficulties which he encounters, to provide the advice necessary for him to remedy them under his own "power," and to determine the effectiveness of his remedial efforts. In general, the clinic seeks to help the student up to the point where he can exercise intelligent self-direction in overcoming his difficulties; it does not supervise writing or provide tutoring. (161–62)

The role of the Writing Clinic, then, was to provide instructional support up to a point—it would provide the "volunteer" student an idea as to what the problem might be and would let him or her know if those problems persisted, but it was the student's responsibility to find the proper long-term instruction, whether that meant additional coursework or tutoring. W. G. Johnson points out this role in his 1945 description, offering the suggestion that "since the Writing Clinic is not a tutoring agency . . . [and] if the counsellors in the clinic are not only to analyze the student's difficulties but also to suggest remedies, the Senate Committee on Student English and the Department of English will need to provide the students with means for overcoming their difficulties" (11). Furthermore,

> many of our students are unable to remedy difficulties "under their own power." With the exception of some of the foreigners, none of the students who came to the Clinic had been trained to exercise intelligent self-direction. If the University does not want to deny such students degrees because of poor English, it should supply them with means for removing their difficulties. (13)

The contradiction here is that one would think that these "means for removing their difficulties" would be put into place at the same time the Clinic was established, but this evidently was not the case. Perhaps the true motivation for the creation of the Clinic comes from Edward Potthoff's description of the entire program, one in which the Clinic is offered as the "carrot" to counter the "stick" of a required proficiency exam: "The clinic was established partly in order that students who have difficulty in meeting the graduation requirement already discussed would have no ground for objecting that the various facilities necessary to enable them to meet it are not available to them" ("The Program for Improving Students' Use of English" 162). Thus, in the scheme of the entire Rhetoric program, the Clinic played a rhetorical role, one that was not necessarily about ensuring literacy standards, nor was it about "punishing" under-prepared writers. As noted in the November 14, 1951, Committee on Student English meeting minutes, "It was observed that it has been past policy not to make the Committee a disciplinary agency, but to use the Clinic, in conjunction with the Qualifying Examination and Rhetoric 200, as motivational devices." Instead, the intent was to create a powerful symbol of student support—a function that will seem quite familiar to contemporary writing center directors.

While the Clinic was "allowed to lapse during the confusion of post-war expansion" (Moore, "The University of Illinois Writing Clinic" 9), by 1948 the Committee on Student English "expressed the desire to see the Writing Clinic again in operation. Professor Roberts explained that it can be revived whenever room and personnel are available." That personnel would come in form of Robert H. Moore, a long-time instructor in English who was just short of completing his dissertation. Moore was one of a stable of Rhetoric instructors led by Charles Roberts, whose influence must have been considerable. Roberts had introduced a graduate course on "The Theory and Practice of English Composition" in 1945 (see Roberts, "A Course for Training Rhetoric Teachers"), and Moore had served Roberts and the Committee on Student English previously, not just in his publications in *Illinois English Bulletin,* but as a researcher of "the standards used in the grading of papers in the Qualifying Examination in English," for which Moore was paid $2.25 per hour.

By April, 1948, the Committee minutes report that the Clinic was to be reopened, and on May 13, 1948, "the Committee discussed ways of publicizing the newly revived Writing Clinic." One method was to run an article in the June, 1948, *Faculty Bulletin,* which echoed familiar language for its faculty audience:

> The clinic, designed for students whose written English is unsatisfactory, will have three major objectives. They are to analyze the writing difficulties, to provide the advice necessary to remedy them, and to determine the effectiveness of remedial efforts. . . . The clinic will not supervise writing or provide tutoring. However, it may, in some cases, advise a student to enroll in some particular course or to employ a tutor. ("English Department Clinic Re-established" 5)

By October of 1948, the Clinic blurb in the *Faculty Bulletin* seems to have softened its tone, perhaps in an effort to draw more students: "Students may come to the Clinic at any time during the semester and may cease to attend whenever they feel they have secured all the assistance they need. There are no classes, and no credit for attendance. All the work is handled through individual conference and individual recommendation of work designed to remove the student's deficiencies" ("Writing Clinic" 9).[7]

Once he had completed his Ph.D., Moore would stay on as Director of the Writing Clinic, a one-person operation open 10 hours per week, and his publications of these experiences would largely continue to deliver the Committee on Student English message. In a 1948 account of the Rhetoric Program, he wrote, "[The Writing Clinic] is not a tutoring bureau, and it is only incidentally a writing laboratory. It attempts to discover the student's chief weaknesses and to suggest remedial measures he himself may pursue" ("The University of Illinois Rhetoric Program" 5–6). In "The Writing Clinic and the Writing Laboratory," Moore seems to be presenting an amalgamated description of clinics and laboratories nationwide. However, his descriptions particularly apply to the Illinois Clinic, at least in terms that were endorsed by the Committee on Student English. For example, Moore writes that "the clinic is not, as a rule, concerned with the direct supervision of remedial efforts, with providing extensive tutoring; it is therefore most satisfactory as a supplement to a wider remedial program" (390).

What has made Moore's article the focus of so much vitriol is his specific terminology. Moore's descriptions are repeatedly "clinical" in the medical sense: "removal of specific deficiencies," "diagnosis and prescription," "remedial treatment" all call to mind the white-coated and white-masked technician fighting the "disease" of bad student writing. Such language, Peter Carino writes, "degrades students by enclosing them in a metaphor of illness" ("What Do We Talk About" 33). The other disturbing aspect of Moore's *College English* article is its repeated jabs at students themselves: their motivation, their commitment, their skills. For instance, he writes, "The more intelligent and eager the student, of course, the easier it is to discover the difficulty in the first place and to determine means to enable him to remove it" (390), and "the laboratory is a highly successful remedial device for those students who are willing to make intelligent use of the assistance provided" (392). These claims are consistent with the design of the Illinois Writing Clinic—one that ultimately placed the responsibility for improvement on students themselves, whether that meant hiring a private tutor or completing grammar and usage exercises. The approach says a great deal about the university's disdain for the entire enterprise of remediation, despite the extensive machinery put into place to combat the "problem" of poor student writing.

It is not surprising, then, that in 1956, Charles Roberts announced in *College Composition and Communication* (of which he was editor from 1950 to 1952 [Goggin]) that by fall 1960 the University would discontinue offering sections of Rhetoric 100, its "sub-freshman, non-credit course in English fundamentals," required of students who scored below a certain level on the university's writing placement exam ("CCCC Bulletin Board" 50). Despite nearly 15 years of work by the Committee on Student English, the "problem" of students' poor writing performance persisted, and the solution for Roberts was a sink-or-swim approach and an attitude reflected in Moore's 1950 article. In his article on the Illinois decision, Harris Wilson writes, "The sad fact is that studies show that four out of five of the students originally sent to Rhetoric 100 are out of the university on academic deficiencies by the end of their third semester. Consequently, for many students Rhetoric 100 would seem merely to postpone an inevitable and tragic consequence" (71). As has always been true for most institutions' relationship with under-prepared students, responsibility for student success was shifted from the institution to the individual. Certain machinery constructed in the name of "salvation" was disassembled, the missionaries retreated, and the natives were left to languish in their error-filled lifestyles.

Still, the Illinois Writing Clinic lived on, and Moore's 1948 description and subsequent reports by Moore's successor, Albert Tillman, give some indication as to the reasons for its endurance. Moore's *Illinois English Bulletin* account of the Writing Clinic, as I noted previously, is quite a contrast in tone, if not in content, to his *College English* piece.[8] We first find that the Clinic was not necessarily a field hospital for the least prepared writers. As the Committee on Student English minutes described, the Clinic played a middle role between the English Qualifying Examination, given to students after their sophomore year, and Rhetoric 200, the course to which students who failed the EQE were assigned. As Moore noted in a paragraph worth quoting in its entirety,

> Although [the Writing Clinic] is open to all students, including graduate students, it is primarily designed to provide assistance to upperclassmen whose deficiencies in writing skills are not sufficiently great to justify them a degree until they have successfully passed a three-hour remedial course—Rhetoric 200—but who are yet unsatisfied with their own ability to express themselves clearly and effectively in their course examinations or papers. Such students are customarily aware of their own weaknesses. They are weak in punctuation, or they spell badly; their writing is habitually too general, or they do not know how to organize their term papers or examination answers. Their course grades, consequently, suffer, and they want to know what to do about it. The Clinic attempts to provide them with suggestions for constructive self-help. ("The University of Illinois Writing Clinic" 9)

In his 1948 article, Moore's tone toward students and their responsibility is also much softer than would appear eighteen months later. He notes that "consultation with the Clinic is voluntary, and this is perhaps its strongest point. . . . Some have been advised to come in by their instructors or the deans of their colleges; if they come reluctantly, little good, perhaps, results, though even here informality and sympathetic friendliness sometimes transform reluctance into willingness and potentially successful effort" (9). As anyone who has worked in a writing center where compulsory attendance is the norm can attest, Moore's description is right on target. This way of thinking is also the ingredient that would allow the Writing Clinic—or any clinic, laboratory, or center—to survive, if not thrive. After all, one major flaw in the belief that early writing centers were all about quarantined students endlessly filling out drill-and-practice worksheets is that if attendance were voluntary—as was true in Illinois and other places—students would simply vote with their feet and not visit. If a writing center is to thrive, as any contemporary writing center director knows, its primary constituents, students, must be satisfied with its services.

Still, based on his published writing, Moore was not exactly a champion of the cause of under-prepared students. In his earliest published piece in *Illinois English Bulletin,* the same issue in which the Writing Clinic was first described by W. G. Johnson, Moore characterized the "problem" of student writing in fairly harsh terms:

> In spite of the requirement of six hours of elementary rhetoric, too many of our students, after having been passed as competent, write a semiliterate gibberish in term of papers or discussion examinations in their advanced courses, or in business letters and reports after graduation. . . . As all English teachers know, most students write "English" only for their English classes, and for the rest of their communication needs use whatever form of pidgin comes natural to them. ("The Upperclass Remedial English Course" 5)

Later in the article, when comparing the high-school sophomores and college sophomores, Moore writes, "The basic troubles of the semi-literate student seem pretty much the same at both stages—except that in college they are by four years more firmly rooted in the student's own despair" ("The Upperclass Remedial English Course" 6). Yet this attitude was by no means unique at the time, nor, perhaps, is it unusual today. The entire enterprise of remediation is often cast in such terms, an elitist disdain for students' lack of mastery of the high style of "educated" English and a grumbling among English faculty that they need to soil themselves by working on such issues. Susan Miller traces such thinking back to the original purpose of college composition "as a consciously selected menu to test students' knowledge of graphic conventions, to certify their propriety, and to socialize them into good academic manners" (66). One strand of the history of writing clinics, laboratories, and centers is a history that implicates these entities in this larger status-quo-preserving enterprise (Grimm). Yet another strand, one evident from the accounts of the Illinois Writing Clinic after Moore had left, indicates a place that is much less driven by rigid ideology toward student error but instead one that is shaped by those very students who came seeking instruction.

LIFE AFTER ROBERT MOORE

As I have noted, Robert Moore left the Illinois Writing Clinic before the fall of 1949. Taking over was Albert Tillman, a fellow English Ph.D. student and member of the Rhetoric staff. Tillman dutifully filed annual reports of the Writing Clinic (records exist from 1951 until 1968), and from these reports one can see that the Clinic's original intent *not* to provide tutoring but only referrals was challenged by the reality of student need and available resources. Tillman noted in his 1951–52 report that "the English Writing Clinic has been conducted during the 1951–52 year according to the policies stated by Mr. Robert Moore in the *Illinois English Bulletin* of November, 1948." However, Tillman commented that

> the clinic went beyond its intended function and worked with twenty-one students who were registered in Rhetoric courses. . . . Nine came either because their teachers were not available, even during scheduled office hours, or because the teachers made the students feel that they were unwelcome or insignificant. . . . These students voluntarily came to the clinic for many appointments and all of them improved in their writing. These facts indicate that the low grades which the students had received were more a measure of the teachers' indifference to the students than of the students' lack of interest and ability.

Tillman, as many current writing center directors would understandably do, shifts responsibility for students' writing back to the classroom teachers, becoming an advocate for students. In this report, he noted, "Probably the most valuable asset of a service such as the writing clinic is a group of satisfied, grateful users of that service. The clinic strives to make every caller feel that he is welcome and that a sincere effort will be made to help him overcome any difficulties which he may have in his writing. With such an informal, friendly approach, the clinic can accomplish much." We also learn that year that the Clinic met with 84 students for 388 appointments or an average of five appointments per person, certainly not the kind of contact one would expect if the Clinic was only concerned with "diagnosis" and "follow-up."

The pattern of usage would remain fairly consistent over the 17 years for which records exist. The number of students who visit the Clinic would rise and fall, growing to 297 in 1954/55 but dropping to 89 in 1957/58, and reaching a peak of 316 in 1965/66. The number of sessions per student was consistently between 4 and 6 over this period, and these usage patterns were a function of several factors: (1) Tillman consistently noted in his annual reports that the Clinic was overloaded at various times or by students working on particular tasks, and staffing was consistently one person at a time though total hours varied from 10 hours per week in the early 1950s to 40 hours per week by the mid 1960s. (2) A large number of appointments in the early years of the Clinic were to help students prepare for the English Qualifying Examination. During a short period, students who failed the EQE also used the Clinic to review their results, but this taxed the available resources and was dropped. In the mid 1960s, usage went up when the university no longer required students who failed the English Qualifying Exam to take Rhetoric 200; instead, they were urged to attend the Writing Clinic before re-attempting the exam. Finally, the exam itself was dropped in the late 1960s, and one must imagine that business at the Writing Clinic dropped off as a result. (3) Increases in business were also seen from occasional programs aimed at targeted students, whether that was athletes in 1960–61, law students in 1962–63, or other targeted graduate programs throughout the years.

Overall, Tillman seemed to run an operation that would sound quite familiar to most contemporary writing center directors. In his 1953–54 report, he noted that

> the Writing Clinic is an ideal teaching situation—one teacher and one student sitting down informally to talk about writing, or a piece of writing, because both see a need for improvement. Therefore, it should not be surprising (although it is pleasantly so) that students rather frequently comment that they have learned more in a few visits to the Clinic than they have in a whole semester of Rhetoric. Such expressions, true or not, are warm compensation for long hours at the Clinic desk.

Albert Tillman long sat at that desk, from 1949 until 1982. The endurance of the Writing Clinic might come as a surprise to most contemporary writing center directors who see their budgets and existence continually threatened. However, the Illinois Clinic took advantage of the fact that it was a small, low-profile, relatively inexpensive operation. Tillman always had a partial appointment in the Clinic and other instructors came from the pool of graduate students who were teaching rhetoric classes. According to the Illinois Board of Trustees Records for the last year of his appointment, 1981, Tillman had the lowest salary among English Department faculty, little more than one-third of the highest paid faculty member even though Tillman by this point had been with the English Department for over 30 years.

One other constant that kept costs down was that the number of students who used the Writing Clinic was never particularly high, not for a state institution that had nearly 17,000 total students in 1950 and nearly 28,000 in 1965 (University of Illinois at Champaign–Urbana). As a result, it likely was easy to keep the Clinic going; after all, English Departments and most universities are essentially conservative places: when entities such as writing clinics are established, particularly if they continue to play a certain rhetorical or political role and they do not take up too many resources, they will tend to stick around for a long time. Perhaps this longevity can also be explained by the mutual relationship between the Writing Clinic and the Rhetoric Program. Nancy Grimm, drawing upon family systems therapist Harriet Goldhor Lerner, sees such relationships as long-standing, a result of Modernist assumptions, and antithetical to the development of either entity: "As long as writing centers enable students to get through the system, the system has no reason to change. Conforming to the system and seeking approval from it does not result in improved relationships or improved practice" (85). By all accounts, practice in the Writing Clinic was quite consistent for a very long time.

SURVIVING THE SIXTIES

According to Albert Kitzhaber, by the early 1960s, writing clinics nationwide were closing, particularly as under-prepared students were being redirected toward two-year colleges, and many four-year institutions became more selective. As Kitzhaber notes, "Mainly because of the much diminished interest shown by the better colleges and universities in this kind of student in the last few years, writing clinics and laboratories are on the decline" (121; see also Boquet 471–72).[9] This brief hiatus occurred before the advent of open admissions would bring about a new "crisis" in students' literacy skills and a renewed interest in the concept of a Writing Laboratory (Boquet; Carino "Early Writing Centers"). Nevertheless, as I noted earlier, of the three components created in 1942—(1) the English Qualifying Exam; (2) Rhetoric 200, the course for students who would fail that exam; and (3) the Writing Clinic—it is only the Clinic that would survive the scrutiny of the late 1960s and live into the 1980s. Rhetorically, it was hard to argue with, financially it used few resources, and politically it would continue to send a message that something was being done about students under-prepared for writing at the University.

By the late 1960s, amid new pressures and a new "crisis" in literacy, it is interesting to note that it was *not* the Writing Clinic that was turned to; instead, the Committee on Student English created a subcommittee to study the feasibility of creating a Writing Laboratory, one that would co-exist with the Writing Clinic but be primarily dedicated to working with disadvantaged students admitted through the University's Student Educational Opportunities Program. By the 1968–69 academic year, the Writing Laboratory was in full force, a much larger operation than the Clinic ever was or ever would be, but also a set up quite differently, being established as a one-credit pass-fail class rather than a place for drop-ins or referrals. And like the Writing Clinic, the Writing Laboratory had a long life, existing in the *Course Catalog* until 1996 and being renamed "Rhetoric Tutorial" the following year when the EOP Rhetoric Program was renamed the "Academic Writing Program," which it remains today (Pemberton). As for the ultimate fate of the Writing Clinic and Albert Tillman, it is clear that the Clinic disappeared once Tillman retired in the early 1980s. Dennis Baron, a current member of the Illinois English Department who had some overlap with Tillman, responded to my email inquiry to fill in the pieces of the last days of the Writing Clinic. He writes,

> Until the 1980s, the Writing Clinic remained a well-kept secret in the English Department. It was always too small to serve general university needs, or even

general department needs. Under Al, it was probably a one-man show run out of his office. When he retired, it was staffed by one or two part-time graduate students, and was still hidden away in a small office. . . . The Clinic was considered by TAs to be a plum assignment, since there was little in the way of preparation, no take home work, and when they were not seeing students they could read or work on their dissertations.

Thus, from 1944 until 1982, with a couple of years hiatus following the end of World War II, the University of Illinois Writing Clinic plugged along, never growing much in size, but always serving a certain political and rhetorical purpose. For a long while it was the good cop to the bad cop of the English Qualifying Exam, but when that requirement was eliminated in 1968, the Writing Clinic persisted, filling a comfortable niche, expending few resources, ruffling few feathers. In its Summary Report of April, 1969, the Committee notes that "the long established Writing Clinic, directed by Prof. A. C. Tillman, 311 English Building, no longer tutors persons for the [English Qualifying Exam], but serves mainly counseling referrals and a few thesis writers." And that is what Albert Tillman would do for another 13 years.

THE IDEA OF ROBERT MOORE

I am not above criticism for allowing my initial reading of Moore's article to reinforce my notions of writing center history. Like many, I read and re-read North's "Idea" article, where I first came upon his reference to Moore. For my dissertation literature review, I then tracked down Moore's article, pulling that dusty bound copy of *College English* from the library shelf. My use of Moore's ideas was no less emphatic than North's, as I show in the following excerpt:

> Moore's article represents a turning point of sorts in writing center literature. Writing labs had become fully associated with "drill-and-practice" remediation . . . and would spend the next forty years trying to escape this "stigma." . . . Moore's presentation of survey results is filled with an attitude toward remediation that can only be called "regretful." Though Moore aims to give an overview of what services are available for students in need, he discounts the potential effectiveness of these methods "since only the intelligent and eager student can be wholly successful in applying even the best self-help measures" (390). This transfer of responsibility upon the "motivated" student conveniently removes responsibility from the institution. In the best case, as Moore claims, "the laboratory is a highly successful remedial device for those students who are willing to make intelligent use of the assistance provided." (392)

Thus, what I thought then was that my search for Robert Moore was complete, that Moore was yet another (or perhaps the most important) in a long line of narrowminded academics whose characterizations consign writing centers to basements and marginality. In other words, the evidence I gleaned from Moore's article fit my "theory" of writing center history, just as they did for North.[10] However, my search for Robert Moore complicates my neat theory, my notions of linear writing center history.

The misuse of writing center history is also marked by a reluctance to acknowledge that the history even exists. As I pointed out earlier, despite the work of Peter Carino ("Early Writing Centers"; "Open Admissions") and Beth Boquet, the prevailing notion found in a great deal of writing center scholarship is that the history of our field is one best written after 1970. It is not difficult to find statements written in the last 15 years such as "Once a rare phenomenon limited to a few innovative schools, the writing center or writing lab is now a common program in colleges and universities" (Haring-Smith, et al. 1), or "If you look back at the history of writing centers, you will discover that few existed before the 1970s" (Bower, et al. 1).[11] In a recent thread on the listserv WCENTER, readers were asked to report on the age of their writing centers. Eighty-two institutions were accounted for, and the average starting date was 1987. The most common starting decade was the 1980s with 28 centers, followed closely by the 1990s with 25 centers starting then. Only one center reported a lineage back to the 1950s and only one back to the 1960s. Certainly many of these centers *in their present form* were started within the last 15 years, but many, such as the one at Illinois, have a much longer history, one of which current directors are only rarely aware. By most contemporary accounts, it would seem a very young field indeed.

This fountain of youth, however, is not supported by the historical record. One need only to go back to Moore's 1950 *College English* article when he reported that "70 percent of the colleges indicating the nature of their remedial work either now use or are considering using the clinic or laboratory in the solving of students' writing difficulties" (388). While this claim was based on a survey conducted in the 1940s, the relative visibility of writing laboratories and clinics was clear well into the 1950s. Of the first seven years of the Conference on College Composition and Communication— 1950 to 1956—workshops on writing clinics or laboratories were held at six of them and reported on in the pages of *College Composition and Communication*. Furthermore, during the decade of the 1950s, specific references to writing clinics, writing laboratories, or tutoring programs akin to writing center work (including peer tutoring) appeared in the pages of *College English* and *College Composition and Communication* twenty-five times. The attitudes toward such entities were not always positive, such as Herbert Creek's 1955 comment that "Writing clinics for feeble students were established here and there" (9). However, the greatest testament to the prevalence of the writing clinic "phenomenon" was that it could be satirized in James Ruoff's 1958 *College English* piece "The English Clinic at Flounder College," where we find that

> this new approach has enabled our English instructors to so reduce their teaching responsibilities that their students no longer interfere with their work. Liberated at last from any compulsory responsibility to meddlesome, inquisitive students, they are free to devote as much time as they wish to more important activities like questionnaires, committee meetings, conventions, hiring interviews, and research. (351)

Perhaps the invisibility of this history is a testament to its ordinariness. Descriptions of the Illinois Writing Clinic never trumpeted a "new" innovation in the teaching of writing, a superiority over classroom methods, or the clinic as a safe-house for the beleaguered student, as many writing center accounts after 1970 do. If anything, it simply made sense to teach writing one-to-one just as it does now. Of course we created a Writing Clinic and then a Writing Laboratory. How else were we to deal with the issue of helping students to improve their writing? Early writing clinics don't merit bronze plaques or window displays in university libraries. They are places where learning and teaching went on, just as might happen in the classroom, the faculty office, the cafeteria, or the poolroom.

Our field's historical amnesia is also, perhaps, a function of our growth as an academic discipline. Lepenies and Weingart note that disciplinary histories "serve the function of legitimation" (xv) of that discipline. Furthermore, "Histories of disciplines are being written and rewritten, to extend the present (or what is to become the future) as far as possible into the past, thereby constructing an image of continuity, consistency and determinacy" (xvii). In this way, believers in a writing center field created largely after 1970 extend their belief that contemporary developments in what we know about student writing and learning—the process movement of the 1970s—best inform current writing center practice. What occurred prior to 1970 was surely tainted by the stain of "current-traditional rhetoric," a veritable (James) Berlin wall of belief. Consider the "call to arms" issued in 1980 by Lil Brannon and Stephen North in their editorial for the inaugural issue of *The Writing Center Journal*:

> Writing centers are at crucial junctures in both their political and scholarly growth. Perhaps it would be most apt metaphorically to say that in both contexts writing centers are adolescent, and that while the future is bright with promise, it is full of deadly threats as well. (1–2)

The sense of newness and its concomitant instability and urgency serve well the notion that writing center directors must be ever vigilant to ensure their survival. To believe that writing centers are long-standing, fully enmeshed in the fabric of teaching and learning at many institutions, threatens an identity that is the warp and woof of most contemporary writing centers. Certainly, writing centers continue to confront their enemies and challenges. However, my reading of writing center history indicates that enemies and challenges are long-standing as well. Some writing clinics close; most plug on in relative obscurity; and many others live multiple cat-like lives.

So has this article been my attempt to "remediate" Robert Moore's reputation? I suppose in the most obvious sense I am working on the presumption that writing center history is much more complex than many contemporary writing center theorists, directors, and tutors acknowledge. Rather than a period of darkness followed by an age of enlightenment or an age of youthful idealism followed by a contemporary world of cynicism and "accountability," the history of writing centers, labs and clinics—and of those who create, direct, work in, research and write about them—is a history that is best written as an always incomplete narrative. Moore's 1950 *College English* article seems to say more about those who have used it as an example than it does about the reality of labs and clinics at the time or about Moore's attitude and beliefs. Moore's first sentence—"writing clinics and writing laboratories are becoming increasingly popular among American universities and colleges as remedial agencies for removing students' deficiencies in composition" (388)—particularly those final eight words and the attitudes and practices implied, are thoroughly intertwined with contemporary writing center practice, as a sort of "ghost dance" we perform against the powerful forces aligned against us. What I would like to see is that our practices be shaped by rich historical accounts, not reactionary movements based upon "us-versus-them" dichotomies.

Writing center history as a means of validating contemporary beliefs will always be subject to overgeneralization and distortion. Instead, the search for Robert Moore and other figures in writing center history shows that what we know now is contingent upon a partial knowing of what has previously occurred. We must continue to piece together this history, to write the narratives that tell us where our field has been and where it might be heading, but at the same time we must realize that these narratives like all narratives (like this narrative) are subject to the perspectives, desires, and goals of those who tell them.

NOTES

1. This research was partially funded through a grant from the International Writing Centers Association. Thanks to William Maher, Robert Chapel, and Ellen Swain of the University of Illinois Archives, to Evelyn Schreiber and Lyle Slovick of George Washington University, and to Libby Miles and Robert Schwegler of the National Archives of Composition and Rhetoric/Richard S. Beal Papers at the University of Rhode Island. Thanks also to Beth Boquet, Anne Ellen Geller, Jon Olson, and two *WCJ* reviewers for their comments on earlier drafts of this article.

2. The earliest misuse of Moore's article came in 1956 when Stanton Millet and James Morton reported on their Writing Laboratory at Indiana University and took umbrage at Moore's alignment of writing labs and clinics with remediation. They note, "Instead of compulsory work for the poorest students, [our lab] offers informal supplementary help for the great middle class of composition students, those who are doing only average work and want to improve" (38). What they did not know was that the University of Illinois Writing Clinic was not targeted at the "poorest" students—they were required to enroll in a class—nor was it compulsory. For its entire life, nearly 40 years, attendance at the Writing Clinic was voluntary. An additional irony is that Moore received his B.A. and M.A. from Indiana and was an English tutor there.

3. All references to records in the University of Illinois Archives come from Record Series Numbers 4/2/823 and 4/2/23, the records of the Senate Committee on Student English.

4. Another irony of this narrative is that Moore died of a heart attack just three months after North singled him out in "The Idea of a Writing Center"!

5. Moore identifies this "middle-ground" approach in his introduction to *Effective Writing,* noting that the handbook section "attempts to find a compromise between the liberal and the conservative positions" (v). Indeed, Richard S. Beal, an English professor at Boston University and Holt, Rinehart's primary reviewer of textbooks, noted in his comments on the original manuscript that Moore's text was marketable because of its middle-of-the-road approach.

6. Moore may have been involved in previous incarnations of the current Writing Center at George Washington University, but none of his contemporaries who responded to my

inquiries indicated such. Moore did chair a 1965 CCCC workshop on "New Approaches in Teaching Composition" in which writing laboratories were offered as "the best way to teach composition" (208). However, the published account of that workshop does not mention any contribution by Moore on the topic.

7. The consistency in the ways that the Clinic was described in "official" publications is remarkable over the course of its existence. Compare the 1948 blurb ("Students may come to the Clinic at any time during the semester and may cease to attend whenever they feel they have secured all the assistance they need. There are no classes, and no credit for attendance. All the work is handled through individual conference and individual recommendation of work designed to remove the student's deficiencies.") with this brief description from the 1982 university catalog: "Any University student who has a writing problem (organization, punctuation, grammar, and usage) may consult the English Writing Clinic. . . . All the work in the clinic is done in individual conferences and attendance is voluntary. Students may seek help on their own or they may be referred to the clinic by their instructors or by the deans of their colleges." It is perhaps most interesting to note that deleting the phrase of contention—"designed to remove the student's deficiencies"—has been the only significant change.

8. It at first seemed mysterious to me why Moore published his account in *College English* and not in *College Composition and Communication,* of which Charles Roberts was editor. The answer was, most likely, one of timing. Moore left Illinois in the fall of 1949, and the GWU press release of September 16, 1949, notes that Moore's article would appear in a subsequent edition of *College English.* That article came out in April, 1950; the first edition of *CCC* was March, 1950, and it's likely that Moore simply wrote and submitted his piece before *CCC* was created at the 1949 NCTE convention (Goggin 43). During the period when Moore placed several articles in *Illinois English Bulletin,* Roberts was the editor of that journal.

9. Kitzhaber's comment comes in the context of his report on the writing program at Dartmouth, which had maintained a writing clinic since the early 1940s, one that is cited as a model in Charles Roberts' 1941 survey. However, by the early 1960s, Kitzhaber saw that the Dartmouth Writing Clinic was underutilized and allowed faculty outside of English to confirm "their belief that good writing is solely the business of the English department, and that they themselves need assume no responsibility for helping to maintain acceptable standards of writing in their courses, except to send the worst offenders among their students to the clinic" (115). As a result, Kitzhaber's recommendation was that the Dartmouth Clinic be closed.

10. When I asked Stephen North why he chose Moore's article, he wrote to me that he "simply turned up that piece because it was in a relatively major journal. And since it articulated what I understood then—and now, for that matter—to be a widely held view of labs/centers and their functions, I adopted it for emblematic purposes" ("Re: Historical Question").

11. As far as I could trace, the history of writing clinics as a recognized entity goes back to 1929, when Warner Taylor of the University of Wisconsin found that six institutions had created English "clinics"; however, Taylor notes that "in theory the project is excellent; in practice it may prove of little value through the lack of cooperation accorded by departments other than English" (31).

WORKS CITED

Barnett, Robert W., and Jacob S. Blumner, eds. *The Allyn and Bacon Guide to Writing Center Theory and Practice*. Boston: Allyn and Bacon, 2001. Print.

Baron, Dennis. "Re: A Question about Department History." E-mail to the author. 7 June 2001.

Berlin, James A. *Rhetoric and Reality: Writing Instruction in American Colleges, 1900–1985*. Carbondale: Southern Illinois UP, 1987. Print.

Boquet, Elizabeth H. "'Our Little Secret': A History of Writing Centers, Pre- to Post-Open Admissions." *College Composition and Communication* 50.3 (Feb. 1999): 463–82. Print.

Bower, Virginia, Charlene Kiser, Kim McMurtry, Ellen Millsaps, and Katherine Vande Brake. "The Writing Center: Past and Present." *Tutor.edu: A Manual for Writing Center Tutors*. 2000. 19 July 2001. Web.

Brannon, Lil, and Stephen North. "From the Editors." *The Writing Center Journal* 1.1 (Fall/Winter 1980): 1–3. Print.

Carino, Peter. "Early Writing Centers: Toward a History." *The Writing Center Journal* 15.2 (Spring 1995): 103–15. Print.

———. "Open Admissions and the Construction of Writing Center History: A Tale of Three Models." *The Writing Center Journal* 17.1 (Fall 1996): 30–48. Print.

———. "What Do We Talk About When We Talk About Our Metaphors: A Cultural Critique of Clinic, Lab, and Center." *The Writing Center Journal* 13.1 (Fall 1992): 31–42. Print.

"CCCC Bulletin Board." *College Composition and Communication* 7.1 (Feb. 1956): 49–50. Print.

Creek, Herbert L. "Forty Years of Composition Teaching." *College Composition and Communication* 6.1 (Feb. 1955): 4–10. Print.

Crowley, Sharon. *Composition in the University: Historical and Polemical Essays*. Pittsburgh: U of Pittsburgh P, 1998. Print.

"English Department Clinic Re-established." *University of Illinois Faculty Bulletin* 1.4 (June 1948): 5. Print.

Goggin, Maureen Daly. *Authoring a Discipline: Scholarly Journals and the Post-World War II Emergence of Rhetoric and Composition*. Mahwah, NJ: Lawrence Erlbaum, 2000. Print.

Grimm, Nancy Maloney. *Good Intentions: Writing Center Work for Postmodern Times*. Portsmouth, NH: Boynton/Cook, 1999. Print.

Haring-Smith, Tori, Nathaniel Hawkins, Elizabeth Morrison, Lise Stern, and Robin Tatu. *A Guide to Writing Programs: Writing Centers, Peer Tutoring Programs, and Writing-Across-the-Curriculum*. Glenview, IL: Scott, Foresman & Co., 1985. Print.

Howard, Jessie. "The Problem of English Composition in American Colleges and Universities: Part I—A Summary of Recent Literature on the Teaching of *Composition*." *University of Illinois Bulletin* 38.48 (July 22, 1941): 9–62. Print.

Johnson, W. G. "A Report on the University of Illinois Experimental Writing Clinic." *Illinois English Bulletin* 33.1 (Oct. 1945): 9–13. Print.

Kitzhaber, Albert R. *Themes, Theories, and Therapy: The Teaching of Writing in College*. New York: McGraw-Hill, 1963. Print.

Lepenies, Wolf, and Peter Weingart. Introduction. *Functions and Uses of Disciplinary Histories, Volume VII.* Ed. Loren Graham, Wolf Lepenies, and Peter Weingart. Dordrecht, Holland: D. Reidel Publishing Co., 1983. ix–xx. Print.

Lerner, Neal D. *Teaching and Learning in a University Writing Center.* Diss. Boston University, 1996. Ann Arbor: UMI, 1996.9622601. Print.

Miller, Susan. *Textual Carnivals: The Politics of Composition.* Carbondale: Southern Illinois UP, 1991. Print.

Millet, Stanton, and James L. Morton. "The Writing Laboratory at Indiana University." *College English* 18.1 (Oct. 1956): 38–39. Print.

Moore, Robert H. *Plan Before You Write.* New York: Rinehart, 1950. Print.

——. "The University of Illinois Rhetoric Program." *Illinois English Bulletin* 36.2 (Nov. 1948): 1–6. Print.

——. "The University of Illinois Writing Clinic." *Illinois English Bulletin* 36.2 (Nov. 1948): 9–11. Print.

——. "The Upperclass Remedial English Course of the University of Illinois." *Illinois English Bulletin* 33.1 (Oct. 1945): 5–9. Print.

——. "The Writing Clinic and the Writing Laboratory." *College English* 11.7 (Apr. 1950): 388–93. Print.

Moore, Robert Hamilton. *Effective Writing.* New York: Rinehart, 1955.

Murphy, Christina, and Joe Law, eds. *Landmark Essays on Writing Centers.* Davis, CA: Hermagoras P, 1995. Print.

"New Approaches in Teaching Composition." *College Composition and Communication* 16.3 (Oct. 1965): 207–08. Print.

North, Stephen M. "The Idea of a Writing Center." *College English* 46.5 (Sept. 1984): 433–46. Print.

——. "Re: Historical Question." E-mail to the author. 12 December 2000.

Pemberton, Michael. "Re: Questions!" E-mail to the author. 22 June 2001.

Potthoff, Edward F. "The Graduation Requirement Relative to Proficiency in Written English at the University of Illinois." *Illinois English Bulletin* 33.1 (Oct. 1945): 1–5. Print.

——. "The Program for Improving Students' Use of English at the University of Illinois." *College English* 7.3 (Dec. 1945): 158–63. Print.

Roberts, Charles W. "A Course for Training Rhetoric Teachers at the University of Illinois." *College Composition and Communication* 6.4 (Dec. 1955): 190–94. Print.

——. "The Problem of English Composition in American Colleges and Universities: Part II—A Survey of Requirements in English Composition." *University of Illinois Bulletin* 38.48 (22 July 1941): 65–94. Print.

Ruoff, James E. "The English Clinic at Flounder College." *College English* 19.8 (May 1958): 348–51. Print.

Taylor, Warner. "A National Survey of Conditions in Freshman English." *University of Wisconsin Bureau of Education Research Bulletin,* No. 11. May 1929. Print.

Tillman, Albert C. "Report of the English Writing Clinic, 1951–52." University of Illinois Faculty Senate Committee on Student English. nd. Print.

University of Illinois at Champaign-Urbana. "Spreadsheet of Historical Enrollments." 6 July 2001. *UIUC Student Enrollment.* 23 July 2001. Web.

Wilson, Harris W. "Illinois vs. Illiteracy." *College Composition and Communication* 7.2 (May 1956): 70–73. Print.

Motivational Scaffolding, Politeness, and Writing Center Tutoring

Jo Mackiewicz and Isabelle Thompson

When this article was published, Isabelle Thompson had recently retired from Auburn University, where Jo Mackiewicz was a professor. Professor Mackiewicz has since moved to Iowa State University. This article originally appeared in *The Writing Center Journal*.

Writing center tutors know that improving writing skills requires sustained effort over a long period of time. They also know that motivation—the drive to actively invest in sustained effort toward a goal—is essential for writing improvement. However, a tutor may not work with the same student more than once, so tutorials often need to focus on what can be done in a single 30- to 60-minute conference. Further, although tutors are likely to attempt to motivate students to invest time and effort in improving their writing, when writers leave the writing center, tutors' influence might end with the conference. Therefore, tutors must work to develop and maintain students' motivation to participate actively during the brief time they are collaborating in writing center conferences.

Such concern about motivation is well placed. Because motivation can direct attention toward particular tasks and increase both effort and persistence, it can lead to improved performance and so is important for learning, Motivation is both reflected in and enhanced by students' active participation and engagement in learning and is particularly well supported in collaborative environments such as writing center conferences (Bransford, Brown, and Cocking; Hidi and Boscolo; Hynd, Holschuh, and Nist; Lepper et al. "Motivational"; Maclellan). Although motivation is a complex phenomenon with affective, perceptual, and cognitive components, we focus here on how tutors attend to the affective component. Specifically, like many studies of educational settings (e.g., Kerssen-Griep, Hess, and Trees; Legg and Wilson; Wilson), we investigate how tutors enhance students' motivation to learn by generating rapport and solidarity with them.

Our purposes are first to review research about motivation, scaffolding, and politeness theory. Then, based on this research, we draw upon two tutoring sessions to illustrate tutors' enhancement of students' motivation through encouraging solidarity and rapport in writing center conferences. Although all aspects of the writing center context may influence a tutor's ability to develop rapport and solidarity with a student, here we focus on tutors' available linguistic resources. Well known in educational research, scaffolding refers to those tutoring strategies used to support students' efforts to arrive at their own solutions to problems or, in the case of writing center conferences, to decide on topics and revisions of existing drafts. According to Jennifer G. Cromley and Roger Azevedo, motivational scaffolding is the feedback tutors provide to promote students' active participation in writing center conferences. To define and describe with accuracy the verbal behaviors that make up motivational scaffolding, we use Penelope Brown and Stephen C. Levinson's politeness theory, a linguistic framework familiar to some writing center researchers. Linguistic politeness refers to the language individuals use to meet the face (i.e., the self-image) needs of their interlocutors. Such analysis seems particularly promising because politeness theory explains how rapport and a sense of solidarity emerge from certain verbal (and potentially nonverbal) conversational strategies—in other words, politeness strategies. The goal of this article is to provide a theoretical foundation contributing to both research and practice in writing centers by describing and showing some examples of tutors' possible language choices that may enhance students' motivation and active participation in writing center conferences.

Our review and subsequent discussion of tutoring strategies are focused and limited in scope. As previously stated, we consider only what happens during writing center conferences; we do not report on what students do after they leave the writing center. Further, although we speculate about students' responses based on commonly used measures for participation, such as the number of words students or tutors contribute to a conference, we are concerned primarily with tutors' linguistic choices as they attempt to develop rapport and solidarity with students. Such a focus on discrete institutional events and on the facilitators of those events is common in investigations of classroom discourse (see, for example, Cazden; Mehan; Nassaji and Wells). Focusing on the facilitator's role in meaning–making and in learning can bring a tutor's behavior to the forefront for observation and, hence, for analysis and critique. Finally, because we are concerned with students' affect, we do not consider cognitive scaffolding or direct instruction, common and vital aspects of writing center tutoring (see our works cited for articles with more comprehensive treatments). With direct instruction, tutors give students suggestions about their writing, explain those suggestions, or ask leading questions. With cognitive scaffolding, tutors list alternatives, prompt, paraphrase, or read aloud to help students arrive at their own answers.

POLITENESS AND STUDENTS' COMFORT IN WRITING CENTER CONFERENCES

Empirical research has analyzed writing center conferences not only to determine how tutors convey their suggestions for improving students' writing, but also to consider students' affect and comfort. This research has analyzed the conversation of writing center conferences for a variety of linguistic and rhetorical expressions, including interruptions, closed or open questions, echoing, qualifiers, directives, mitigation strategies, volubility, backchannels, and overlaps (see Blau, Hall, and Strauss; Davis et al.; Severino; Thonus, "Dominance," "How," and "Tutor"; Wolcott). Student contributions have been analyzed according to number of words, amount of time the student held the floor, questions the student asked and those the student answered, interruptions, and topics raised. Including surveys as well as analyses of writing center conferences, some empirical research has yielded findings relevant to our study. For example, students' reports of their "comfort" in conferences has been shown to be important to their conference satisfaction (Thompson et al.), and returning for future conferences has been shown to correlate with students' confidence as writers (Carino and Enders). In a 2001 review of empirical research about writing center conferences, Teresa B. Henning concluded that students' perceptions of conference success relates in part to students' feelings of rapport with tutors and to the occurrence of mutual negotiations during agenda setting. Further, in an empirically developed "profile" (Thonus, "Tutor and Student Assessments") of successful writing center conferences, six of the ten "necessary but not sufficient conditions" (126) related to rapport and solidarity: the student and tutor agreeing on a diagnosis of how to improve the writing, turn structure resembling real conversation, frequent "interactional features" (127); the student and tutor "achiev[ing] some degree of intersubjectivity" (129), or mutual understanding of each other's intentions; and the tutor's willingness to accept negotiations of evaluations or directiveness. Hence, previous research has touched on notions of rapport and solidarity in writing center conferences, but no one has considered rapport and solidarity as they relate to motivation.

A fair amount of empirical research in writing centers has also employed Brown and Levinson's framework to examine tutoring interactions, sometimes for the effect of contextual variables such as tutor and student gender (e.g., Black). However, most of the research on politeness in writing center conferences has focused on tutors' use of politeness to mitigate the threats to students' face that tutors carry out while they are trying to achieve a successful interaction (in whatever way "success" might be defined). In so doing, writing center researchers have focused mainly on how tutors use so-called negative politeness, particularly diminutive hedges like *a little,* as in *This paragraph seems a little unfocused* and modal-verb hedges like *could,* as in *You could move this section to the end of the paper* (e.g., Mackiewicz, "The Effects" and "The Functions"; Thonus, "Dominance" and "How"). In terms of scaffolding, these studies of politeness in writing center conferences help explain how tutors express negative feedback and give suggestions in ways that do not threaten students' motivation to participate actively in collaboration—the learning that takes place as tutors modulate their direction and student writers take control of their own writings through decision making.

But in examining how tutors mitigate their advice to students to balance their own directiveness with student control, most writing center research has largely glossed over the importance of investigating how tutors' politeness, particularly positive politeness, supports motivational scaffolding for students. Positive politeness strategies—such as noticing a person's accomplishment (i.e., giving praise), joking, and being optimistic—generate rapport and a sense of solidarity, but they can be difficult to identify and classify systematically. Susan Wolff Murphy's study of eight writing center conferences is an exception to the rule; she discusses how tutors used the pronoun *we* to include both conversational participants in the activity.

In addition to the difficulty of understanding their use among American-English speakers, analyzing positive politeness strategies can involve another level of complexity: positive politeness can be particularly difficult for speakers in cross-cultural interactions to use effectively and to comprehend easily. For example, studies of humor in cross-cultural communication show that joking can fail for a number of reasons beyond the hearer's failure to comprehend the word meanings, syntax, or the utterance's force (e.g., failure to recognize irony). Jokes can fail when a hearer does not recognize the frame of the joke or the incongruity that creates the humor (Bell and Attardo). Joking can therefore be a tricky or even a risky politeness strategy to use in cross-cultural exchanges because one or more participants may misinterpret a speaker's intent.

In writing center research, Diane C. Bell and Madeleine Youmans, studying L1–L2 conferences, examine how the positive politeness strategy of praise can generate miscommunication and confusion. This finding is supported by cross-cultural linguistic research on Chinese compliments and compliment responses (Yu; Yuan), on compliments in Arabic (Farghal and Haggan; Mursy and Wilson), and on interactions between British English speakers and Spanish speakers (Lorenzo-Dus). They found that an L1-speaking tutor may consider praise such as *This is a good place to start* as a "springboard" to further discussion for how the student might improve the paper, while the student might "focus primarily on the compliment itself" and wonder why he or she would need to change the paper at all if it were worthy of praise in the first place (43–44). In short, the important motivating function of positive politeness merits more attention.

In planning our study, we recognized the challenge of accounting for cross-cultural differences in intention to use politeness and in uptake of politeness strategies. We thus limit our analysis here to L1–L1 (American English) writing center interactions. We focus on the substantial role that tutors' positive politeness plays in creating a sense of connection and thus in contributing to tutors' ability to develop students' confidence and curiosity along with students' ability to work at the appropriate level of challenge and to control their own writing and their tutoring interaction (Johnson and Rizzo). But we also note that tutors' negative politeness contributes to motivational scaffolding as tutors use it to demonstrate their willingness to make way for and their interest in students' decisions and contributions. By defining and describing tutors' motivational scaffolding in terms of the politeness strategies they use, we hope to develop a robust system for identifying, analyzing, and improving tutors' discourse—what tutors can say to assist students' motivation to participate actively in writing center conferences.

MOTIVATION

As noted above, motivation is "the desire to achieve a goal, the willingness to engage and persist in specific subjects or activities" (Margolis 223). It influences the time and effort that students are willing to invest in completing a task and to some extent the possibility of transferring learning from one environment to another (Bransford, Brown, and Cocking). Further, the active participation associated with motivation provides an important diagnostic tool for tutors in writing center conferences (Evens and Michael). The more dialogic writing center conferences become, the better tutors can determine what students need to know and what they already understand; hence, tutors may be more effective in individualizing instruction for students (Puntambekar and Hubscher). Moreover, this dialogue, or "collaborative contextualizing" (Fox 1), also situates writing assignments for both tutors and students. In the same way that knowledge is constructed through social interaction, motivation is constructed through "mutual reciprocity" between students and their environments (Meyer and Turner 112). Therefore, as a substantial part of the environment, a tutor can exert a strong influence on a student's effort and willingness to participate in a writing center conference. According to recent research about writing and motivation (Hidi and Boscolo; Pajares and Valiante; Boscolo and Hidi; Zimmerman and Kitsantas), motivation influences and is influenced by three major components: interest in the writing task, self-efficacy concerning successfully completing the task, and the ability to self-regulate performance.

Interest can result in increased attention, concentration, and enjoyment of learning (Hidi and Boscolo). Individual interest, which is associated with intrinsic motivation, has been shown to influence learning (Bye, Pushkar, and Conway; Lepper and Henderlong). However, some researchers (see Hidi and Harackiewicz; Hynd, Holschuh, and Nist) argue that situational interest, which is associated with extrinsic motivation, can enhance learning as well. For example, grades are commonly considered extrinsic motivators, with interest limited to the particular situation that the grade results from. Although students are usually very interested in getting good grades on their writing assignments, writing center tutors usually want to inspire a different type of interest, a more lasting individual interest related to intrinsic motivation. Although not directly connected with individual interest, good grades correlate with students' perceptions of self-worth and confidence (see Van Etten et al.)—important influences on intrinsic motivation. Extrinsic motivators, such as feelings of rapport and solidarity and wanting to please the tutor, may lead a student to invest more effort during the short time spent in a writing center conference and, pushing this possibility even further, may eventually facilitate the improvement of the student's writing and increase student interest in writing over the long run.

Also influenced by feelings of rapport and solidarity, self-efficacy and self-regulation are mutually dependent. Self-efficacy, or self-confidence, relates to "individuals' beliefs and personal judgments about their abilities to perform at a certain level and affects their choice of activities, effort, and performance" (Hidi and Boscolo 148). It influences effort and persistence and willingness to persevere in difficult tasks (Pajares and Valiante). Identifying successes, connecting these successes with personal control or effort, and cultivating "students' beliefs in their own capabilities" all influence self-efficacy (Pajares and Valiante 160). Self-regulation relates to the control students have in achieving their goals (Zimmerman and Kitsantes; Zimmerman and Schunk). A self-regulated writer is aware of his or her ability to manage the writing process and to find assistance when it is needed. High self-regulation increases self-efficacy and may stimulate a writer's interest in a particular writing task and in writing generally (Hidi and Boscolo). Students are likely to be intrinsically motivated to improve as writers when they attribute their potential for improving a draft (and future drafts) to something they can control and believe in their abilities to make necessary revisions.

MOTIVATIONAL SCAFFOLDING

The term "scaffolding" was first coined and defined by David Wood, Jerome S. Bruner, and Gail Ross in a 1976 article analyzing the effectiveness of certain collaborative behaviors mothers use in teaching their children. When providing children a task to build a block structure that was slightly too difficult to accomplish on their own, one of the researchers (Ross) provided the one-to-one assistance each child needed to complete the building. This assistance was called "scaffolding," which referred to how the adult structures the task, motivates the child to participate in the task, and sometimes performs those parts of the task that the child cannot perform, hence allowing the child to concentrate on what he or she can do. Success is guaranteed, and the child is expected to eventually perform the task on his or her own—competently and willingly. When the child is ready to perform the task independently, the adult tutor fades and requires the child to assume responsibility for the task. In a related study published in 1975, David Wood and David Middleton explain that scaffolding is successful only within the students' "region of sensitivity to instruction" (181), defined as the students' "readiness" (181) for a particular task. Later, the region of sensitivity became correlated with the "zone of proximal development," the well-known Vygotskian concept defining learning potential as a variable affective and cognitive range with boundaries determined by what a student can do independently and what a student can do with assistance.

Over the past thirty-five years, Wood, Bruner, and Ross's concept of scaffolding has been adapted to classroom instruction and especially to tutoring. It has found instructional relevance with many different age groups, including college students being tutored in math, science, and other disciplines (Azevedo, Cromley, and Seibert; Chi; Chi et al.; Cromley and Azevedo; Fox; Graesser et al.; Graesser, Person, and Magliano; Hume et al.; Merrill et al.; VanLehn et al.). However, only a few studies of scaffolding in writing center conferences have been published (see Thompson; Williams), and its potential for understanding and improving writing center tutoring is largely untapped. For tutors to effectively support students' learning through scaffolding, they need to know how to make the writing task manageable for each individual student without simplifying the outcome, to mutually define the goals and establish the agenda for the conference, to recruit students' interest in writing tasks, to encourage students' persistence and effort in completing the tasks, to attend to students' motivation and active participation, and to minimize students' frustration and anxiety during the conference (Clark and Graves; Daniels; Gaskins et al.; Palincsar; Puntambekar and Hubscher; Stone). Because scaffolding can influence solidarity and rapport with students and, at the same time, according to its definition, guarantee in-the-moment success as long as the tutor is present, writing tasks undertaken in writing center conferences should be less frustrating, less anxiety-provoking, and, as Wood, Bruner, and Ross say, "less dangerous" (98) for students than those undertaken in working alone. By building a caring emotional environment, tutors can decrease students' anxiety (Bruning and Horn).

Motivational scaffolding, in part, is the feedback that tutors use to build rapport and solidarity with students and to engage students and keep them engaged in writing center conferences. Tutors in writing center conferences can use motivational scaffolding in ways Brown and Levinson ascribe to positive politeness in conversation—as "a kind of social accelerator" where the speaker indicates he or she wants to strengthen the connection he or she has with the hearer (103). Based on research about motivation and scaffolding, we can describe five types of motivational scaffolding that we later connect with politeness strategies:

- *Praise*—to point to students' successes; to praise them for specific achievements. Praise should focus on the students' performance (process praise) and not on their innate, unchangeable characteristics, such as intelligence (person praise) (Dweck; Maclellan), and it should be specific (e.g., *Nice catch!* when pointing to a misplaced comma identified by the student) rather than general (e.g., *Good draft*) (Mackiewicz, "The Functions"; see also Hancock).
- *Statements of encouragement or optimism about students' possibilities for success*—to build confidence; to reduce stress; to directly encourage agency, usually with reference to effort and persistence.
- *Demonstrations of concern for students*—to build rapport by showing caring; to assure students that the tutoring environment is safe and positive. Among other expressions, caring can be demonstrated through questions about students' welfare (Cooper).
- *Expressions of sympathy and empathy*—to express understanding of the difficulty of the task, often through confessions about one's own writing difficulties.
- *Reinforcement of students' feelings of ownership and control*—to increase students' developing self-regulation; to increase students' confidence in their potential for success (see Lepper et al., "Motivational"; Lepper et al., "Self Perception"; Lepper et al., "Scaffolding").

POLITENESS AND MOTIVATION

The linguistic framework of politeness theory provides a detailed description of the types of rapport and solidarity building important for motivational scaffolding.

Positive Politeness Strategies

Brown and Levinson outline a variety of specific politeness strategies, and those relevant to writing center interactions fall into three broad categories. First, tutors can give understanding and sympathy. They may do so by articulating understanding of student writers' situations and by acknowledging that they wish challenging situations were otherwise (thus conveying sympathy).

Second, tutors can notice or attend to students' accomplishments or conditions. A tutor may employ the strategy of noticing by offering praise (e.g., *That's a good change*) but may also claim common ground by demonstrating concern that a shared understanding of the task-at-hand exists. For example, a tutor might ask a student *Do you see what I mean?* to ensure that the student understands what the tutor has said and, therefore, to ensure that the two are on "common ground." A tutor might also use repetition, which demonstrates engagement in what the student has said and signals agreement, or he or she might use the strategy of avoiding candid disagreement. With this latter strategy, a token agreement (e.g., *OK but*) is used, even though the speaker does not necessarily agree with his or her interlocutor. Table 1 also exemplifies how a tutor can use the positive politeness strategy of asserting common ground by joking. Brown and Levinson write that "since jokes are based on mutual shared background knowledge and values, jokes may be used to stress that shared background or those shared values. Joking is a positive-politeness technique, for putting [the hearer] 'at ease'" (124). Thus, as a kind of shibboleth, jokes convey solidarity and generate rapport—as long as the speaker and the hearer share the appropriate experience.

Third, tutors can convey that they and the students are cooperators. Brown and Levinson explain this broad category of showing cooperation, which appears to be a critical one for writing center tutors, this way: if two people are conversationally cooperating, "then they share goals in some domain" (125). This category includes four specific strategies that tutors can use when providing motivational scaffolding: (1) assert or presuppose the tutor's knowledge of and concern for the student's wants; (2) be optimistic; (3) include the tutor and the student in the activity; and (4) give reasons.

Negative Politeness Strategies

Negative politeness strategies involve carrying out a speech act that threatens face, called a face-threatening act—such as when a tutor makes a suggestion or states a criticism—but simultaneously acknowledging the interlocutor's (the student's) want to be independent and free from imposition (131). Thus, tutors can use questions (e.g., *Do you think you should find a few more sources to back up this claim?*) rather than declaratives to state their suggestions (and criticisms) politely. They can also use hedges (e.g., *You could maybe connect these two paragraphs with some transition phrase, like "In contrast."*). With these politeness strategies, tutors acknowledge students' desire to control themselves and their work.

Finally, tutors may avoid the pronoun *you* or impersonalize the face-threat (e.g., a suggestion) by stating it in passive voice. Tutors also subjectivize their suggestions, stating what they would do if they were in the student's position. So, instead of saying *You should connect these two paragraphs with a transition phrase*, a tutor might say, *I would connect these two paragraphs with a transition phrase*. Discussing editing sessions about technical writing, Jo Mackiewicz and Kathryn Riley found this negative politeness strategy particularly effective in balancing the need to be clear with the need to be polite.

As noted above, writing center research has focused on negative politeness strategies because of their ability to mitigate the force of speech acts that threaten face. We argue, though, that negative politeness also signals a tutor's willingness to maintain good relations because it acknowledges and demonstrates interest in a student's decision-making and ideas.

As shown in the following section, the verbal behaviors described in detail by politeness theory operationalize (i.e., express) motivational scaffolding through their shared goal of solidarity and rapport-building.

MOTIVATIONAL SCAFFOLDING THROUGH POLITENESS

Table 1 shows the correspondence of specific politeness strategies (Brown and Levinson) to the motivational scaffolding strategies.

Table 1 Motivational Scaffolding Expressed through Politeness (P is an abbreviation for "positive politeness," N for "negative politeness," T for "tutor," S for "student," and "FTA" for "face-threatening act.")

TUTORS' MOTIVATIONAL SCAFFOLDING STRATEGIES	POLITENESS STRATEGIES THAT OPERATIONALIZE MOTIVATIONAL SCAFFOLDING	EXAMPLE
(1) Praise (general and specific)	• (P) **Notice S:** T positively evaluates S's work	• T: *This was a good idea.* • T: *Perfect! Yeah, write that here. That's the kind of thing to transition between those two ideas.*
(2) Encouragement/ optimism	• (P) **Be optimistic:** T minimizes the difficulty of a complex situation (or of a face-threatening act like a criticism), such as the task of revising a paper. T implies that S will rise to the challenge.	• **Be optimistic:** T: *I think you can do it though. I mean I think you can. It will take a lot of work, but I think that.... I think that it will be worth it though.*
	• (P) **Joke:** T calls attention to the background knowledge or values T and S share through humor.	• **Joke:** T: *Oh, teachers can be so difficult.*
(3) Demonstration of concern for student	• (P) **Attend to S:** T inquires about the extent to which the S understands or is satisfied.	• T: *Do you feel comfortable with the topic you're going for?*
(4) Statements of sympathy or empathy	• (P) **Give the gift of sympathy or understanding:** T satisfies S's want to be cared for, listened to, or understood.	• **Give the gift of sympathy/ understanding:** T: *I mean this is difficult. Don't think that I don't realize that it is.*
	• (P) **Include T and S in the activity:** By using the inclusive "we" form, T conveys that T and S will take on the task at hand together.	• **Include T and S in the activity:** T: *It seems to me, after reading your paper what's missing is focus. So if we put a check mark next to the things that are not related.*
	• (P) **Assert concern for S's wants:** T implies knowledge of and caring for S's feelings, concerns, and interests.	• **Assert concern for S's wants:** T: *O.K. So now you're feeling overwhelmed with everything that you have to do, but you'll be fine.*

(5) Reinforcement of student's ownership	• (P) **Use repetition:** T repeats in whole or part what S said to validate it and show attention.	• **Use repetition:** T refers back to something the student has said earlier in the conference: *Kind of what you said about the business man, you know?*
	• (P) **Give reasons:** T justifies his or her suggestion or explains the payoff.	• **Give reasons:** T: *So that would be a good progression. . . . That giving up and that not being yourself is what she's [the instructor is] asking for here when she talks about why it's important.*
	• (P) **Avoid candid disagreement:** T avoids a strongly stated no response by beginning the response in a neutral or even affirmative way.	• **Avoid candid disagreement:** S: *So I can't develop it [the topic] anymore.* T: *O.K. Tell me what you think. Let me go back here. [Begins reading the paper.]*
	• (N) **Mitigate the FTA:** T eases a suggestion through the use of hedges and passive voice and other linguistic forms to avoid imposing on S's views.	• **Mitigate the FTA:** T: *You might want to think about if there are some examples in here that are kind of repetitive.*

In order to facilitate the application of this knowledge in a variety of writing center settings, through the rest of this article we examine excerpts from two writing center conferences to show how possible attempts at motivating students can be described linguistically in terms of scaffolding and politeness theory. The conferences excerpted here were chosen from a corpus of 51 writing center conferences, consisting of more than 30 hours of student-tutor conversation, and recorded with permission from the Institutional Review Board at a large Southeastern university. At the time the conferences were recorded, the writing center (called the English Center) was a unit in the English Department. The center served only undergraduates enrolled in first-year writing and world literature, both required university core courses. More than half of the tutors were English graduate students, serving in the center to fulfill part of the requirements for their graduate teaching assistantships. Advanced graduate student tutors also taught first-year writing and world literature. The rest of the tutors were undergraduates from a variety of majors. The undergraduates were rigorously screened, and each was recommended by an English instructor, interviewed, and required to pass a proofreading test. During their first year, all tutors were required to attend a weekly training practicum, which not only presented curricular-based information about the common assignments in first-year writing and world literature but also considered pedagogical issues such as how to encourage student engagement and how to scaffold or lead students' thinking. Although tutors were instructed to follow students' agendas, they were also shown how to lead by introducing the possibility of expanding an agenda with student permission. Tutors were told to ask for instructors' assignment handouts as soon as possible in conferences so that they could better understand what students were supposed to do. The tutors in the conferences excerpted below follow this guideline, likely to the benefit of the students they work with.

The conferences excerpted in Examples 1 and 2 were video recorded, and the tutors and the students filled out matching surveys indicating conference satisfaction. As soon as possible after the conferences, one of the researchers conducted a retrospective interview with each tutor, by playing back the recording of the conference and asking questions. We chose these two conferences to excerpt because they show tutors who appear to take advantage of opportunities to build rapport and solidarity, and in the surveys administered after the conference, both students rated the conferences as highly satisfactory. In their interviews, tutors discussed their attempts to motivate students to trust their goodwill and expertise and to participate actively in the conferences.

Example 1: The Unconfident Student

In this section, we show how a tutor through politeness, particularly positive politeness, attempts to move the student writer from frustration to interest, self-efficacy, and to some extent self-regulation of her learning. Although this tutor does not take advantage of every opportunity to attend to the student's motivation (nor could any tutor), he appears to be actively looking for those opportunities and, when possible, he creates them.

The Example 1 excerpts were taken from a 31-minute conference between an experienced undergraduate male tutor and a traditional-aged female first-year student. The tutor is pursuing a psychology major and English minor and at the time of the tutorial, his second year as a tutor, worked 15 hours per week. He has consistently received high evaluations for his skill as a tutor. The student has come for help with a position paper requiring her to argue that a certain problem exists, to address counterarguments, and to cite sources that agree and disagree with her position. Her classmates have already reviewed the paper, and as the conference proceeds, it becomes apparent that during the peer review, which occurred in front of the class, her draft was severely criticized by both the instructor and the class. Before coming to the English Center, the student has revised her draft according to the directions she received during the peer review. The tutor believes that her new draft does not meet the requirements of the assignment and, based partly on his previous experience with other students from the same instructor, thinks that the student has been subjected to harsh and embarrassing treatment. In the retrospective interview, the tutor says that he is concerned about the student's self-confidence (self-efficacy) as well as her writing ability.

At the beginning of the conference, the tutor asks the student what she needs help with and reads through the instructor's assignment handout. The student confirms that she has followed the instructions and tells the tutor that her argument—the topic of her position paper—is that people need to be informed about cell phone manners. The tutor realizes that this is not a strong argument. He tells the student as much, using politeness (hedges like *maybe* and the minimizer *one thing*). As he says in his retrospective interview, he deliberately mitigates his criticism that her thesis is not arguable: *But that's one thing that I think maybe I see as a problem before reading it. You have to have a black-and-white contrast for arguments.* The tutor's use of negative politeness at the outset likely avoids shaking the student's confidence any further and improves the chances of motivating her to participate actively in the conference.

After this exchange, the tutor reads the draft silently, stopping to ask questions about the class discussion of position papers, trying to help the student identify the weaknesses in her thesis statement herself. Finally, the student tells the tutor about her humiliation in the class peer review—that she had originally written a more argumentative thesis statement, but her classmates provided many counterarguments and suggested that her thesis statement be confined to informing people about cell phone manners. According to the student, the instructor agreed with her classmates' suggestion. During the retrospective interview, the tutor says that just before the dialogue in Excerpt 1.1 began, he realized that the student had received bad advice and was feeling frustrated. In the conference, he uses a variety of positive politeness strategies to convey solidarity and, thus, increase the student's confidence.

Excerpt 1.1

1 T: How about we kind of (1–2 seconds) And I'm not saying we'll have to get rid
2   of all of this. Some things we'll kind of take out but a lot of this we'll still be
3   able to use. From what I got, (1–2 seconds) kind of the message that came
4   across to me in the paper was "be quieter when you use cell phones."
5 S: And I know on that position as far as like
6 T: [Interrupts] Yeah. You're kind of like telling me like "Be quiet. Don't do
7   this, don't do that," and it was like less of a strong argued (1–2 seconds) you
8   know (1–2 seconds) a position paper, than a just "these are the guidelines
9   to follow."
10 S: Yeah. I know I did for some reason. [inaudible]
11 T: And now I (4 seconds) Now what happened in class, I mean I'm sure that
12   happened for a reason, but maybe we can work with that original argument
13   and then take it (1–2 seconds) kind of take it down a notch. Maybe they
14   disagreed with that so much (1–2 seconds). I take it that they disagreed a
15   lot with it and came up with countless counterarguments?
16 S: Umm. I was going to set limits both the places. [inaudible] People should
17   know that there are places where people can't talk on cell phones. And then
18   there are places where they can clearly talk in a low tone. And then a girl
19   came up with "What is a low tone?" And then we got into needing to define
20   what a low tone was. What kind of voices, and then I think
21 T: [Interrupts] Which can be done. I mean don't think that would be impossible,
22   you know? There are numerous things that (3 seconds) society imposes upon
23   the public that are kind of iffy. For instance, you should dress appropriately.
24   How is appropriately defined?   By a code, by a dress
25 S: uh-huh
26 T: code and all businesses. So a tone could very easily be defined. You
27   know, you can start off with the broad (1–2 seconds) you know, (5 seconds)
28   a decibel level or a loudness level that does not interfere with the conver-
29   sations or (1–2 seconds) does not, the conversations around you does not
30   (1–2 seconds) what? You tell me.

The tutor begins his motivational scaffolding with the positive politeness strategy of optimism, conveying that although the thesis must change, much of what she has already written can be salvaged (line 1: *And I'm not saying we'll have to get rid of all this*). He acknowledges that the essay needs revising and alludes to the fact that the revision will likely be substantial and, therefore, difficult, but he also assures the student that she will not have to start the writing process over completely.

The tutor continues motivational scaffolding with several other politeness strategies that might bolster the student's confidence. First, with his use of *we*, including both he and the student in the activity, he signals solidarity right at the start. Although she may feel demoralized, he is on her side, and they will work together to revise the paper. The assurances that the more expert participant will support the less expert participant and that during the time they work together he will ensure success are critical to fostering the student's self-efficacy and defining characteristics of scaffolding. In addition, the tutor uses negative politeness. He minimizes his assessment by limiting its scope (*Some things*) and by hedging the action to be carried out (*kind of*) (line 2). His negative politeness, then, again can reinforce his positive politeness because it contributes to the optimism he conveys about her chance for success in formulating a viable position.

The tutor switches back to positive politeness, using the strategy of repetition (line 12), repeating the student's word *reason* and thus likely validating her claim that she had followed some line of reasoning when she changed her thesis. By acknowledging the difficulty and assuring the student that she will not have to start over, the tutor conveys solidarity and attends to the student's motivation.

After the student explains the counterarguments that her classmates and instructor generated, which she has used to temper her original argument, the tutor again conveys optimism, telling the student that defining a low tone (and thus prescribing cell phone etiquette) is indeed feasible (line 21: *Which can be done*). At this point, the tutor interrupts the student for the second time in this excerpt (see also line 6). Although these interruptions suggest the tutor's dominance, they may also demonstrate his commitment to help the student through his support of her original position, no matter what counterarguments her classmates have given. The tutor also does most of the talking in this conference, particularly at the beginning, again signaling his dominance. However, like his interruptions, the tutor's talk is directed at helping the student. He does not appear to interfere with the student's ownership of her ideas, but instead prompts her in defending and expanding those ideas. The tutor follows up with yet another positive politeness strategy, using *you know?* as a tag question (as opposed to a hesitation as he used it previously, e.g., lines 7–8) to increase the student's interest and, thus, involvement. Indeed, in the retrospective interview, the tutor says that he is at this point trying to get the student to talk to him. As he points out, he is "going to throw the hook out and see if she bites. And maybe say something I can praise her for and break down the barrier." The tutor believes that the student has a lack of motivation to work with him and that she expects strong criticism: "She is expecting me to say, 'This is wrong. This is wrong.' [Tutor hits the table with his fist]. And I am trying not to do that." Thus, the tutor seems aware that conveying solidarity with the student by being optimistic and generating rapport and by facilitating the student's participation are important for conference success.

Later in the conference, the student finally becomes engaged, and the tutor says in the retrospective interview that he feels "energized." The tutor jokes with the student while providing a mitigated suggestion that moves the student toward a viable thesis:

Excerpt 1.2

1　T:　OK. Let me propose this to you. And everything I say you're free to say,
2　　　"John, that's just horrible. Why would you think that?" What if we change
3　　　one of the awkward verbs in your thesis, you know, "should be informed"?
4　　　How about we change it to something like (5 seconds) What I'm going
5　　　for maybe is "should adhere to rules of cell phone etiquette." You know?
6　　　Because there are certain rules that are understood with cell phones.

When the tutor jokingly says that the student is free to tell him that his idea is horrible (line 2), he conveys a positive attitude toward the student, a move that—at least in this L1-L1 interaction—builds rapport and increases the likelihood that the student will be encouraged to continue and perhaps even increase her participation. (Because this joke depends on the shared frame of deference to instructors and tutors and the incongruity of explicitly criticizing one's instructor or tutor—a frame that is common across cultures—this joke might very well work in cross-cultural inter-actions too.)

After the tutor's joke, the student begins taking notes for the first time, a signal that she is engaged and likely understanding what the tutor is suggesting. Indeed, as the tutor says later in the retrospective interview, they have at this point "totally revolutionized the paper." In Excerpt 1.3, the tutor continues to try to convince the student that cell phone manners can be enforced. He gives examples of places where cell phone use has been prohibited and the prohibition has been enforced (airplanes) and mentions places that have been somewhat successful in enforcing prohibitions against cell phones (the English Center and the university library).

Excerpt 1.3

1　S:　So I was hoping I'd pick out a topic where it's more along the lines where
2　　　it aggravates me, which would be in the hallway, or in the classroom, or
3　T:　OK.
4　S:　But, I don't see that being a great position. And I don't see anybody (3
5　　　seconds) adding cell phone rules to more public places (1–2 seconds) like on
6　　　the transit for instance. I think it's rude for people to shout on their cell
7　　　phones, which disrupts everybody else who's on the transit.
8　T:　That could be wonderful for a topic, you know? What you could do is (1–2
9　　　seconds) The addition of cell phone policies to places that don't have them.
10　　　And that's very much what you're interested in, is it not?

After the student articulates her interest—cell phone policies (lines 4–7)—the tutor praises her idea and caps that gift of praise with a tag question that intensifies interest (line 8): *That could be wonderful for a topic, you know?* In the retrospective interview, the tutor says that he has been looking for an opportunity to praise the student, and it is worth noting that he uses process praise—praise for the student's accomplishment—rather than person praise.

At this point, the student has asked questions to develop the new thesis and has stated her preference for an arguable thesis. Therefore, returning back to the argument she put forth to her class and instructor but now more sophisticated and refined, she appears more interested and engaged in the process of revising her paper. In Excerpt 1.4, the conference begins to wind down. The tutor checks the student's outlook on revising:

Excerpt 1.4

1 T: Do you feel comfortable with the topic you're going for?
2 S: Uh-huh. I think there's a paper that I went out in front of the class was (1–2
3   seconds)   "I would like to limit and restrict the use of cell phones in
4 T: uh-huh
5 S: public places" was what I started off with. I think when I got up there I (3
6   seconds)
7 T: Did what you (1–2 seconds) you got to shifting a little? OK, kind of like,
8   "Well, I don't know" that kind of thing?
9 S: Uh-huh.

The student responds positively and summarizes why she changed her thesis in the first place. By the end of the conference, she is reflecting back on what had occurred in class and how she had reacted to the advice she had received there. The student has already demonstrated that she is able to regulate her writing process to some extent by choosing to come to the English Center for assistance. The student appears motivated to make the revisions discussed during the conference, even though she will return to her original, much criticized topic. She also seems less frustrated than she was at the beginning of the conference. Politeness strategies such as being optimistic can nurture a positive affective environment by conveying solidarity and rapport and, thus, can facilitate motivational scaffolding.

Example 2: The Complaining Student

The excerpts in this section are intended to show how a tutor's positive politeness, particularly her use of optimism, sympathy, expressions of caring, along with her concern not to take control from the student, help move the student toward a revision that should not overwhelm her. Like the tutor in Example 1, this tutor does not take advantage of every opportunity to attend to the student's motivation, but she works hard so that the student can leave the conference with an achievable revision goal. The excerpts are taken from a 32-minute conference with a female tutor, a graduate teaching assistant pursuing an MA in English, and a traditional-aged first-year female student enrolled in first-year writing. The tutor has almost four years of experience in the English Center—two years as an undergraduate and two years as a graduate student. Partially because of her demonstrated positive attitude and caring, this tutor was selected as assistant coordinator of the Center. She has also been teaching first-year writing for almost two years. The student came to the writing center to get help in revising an essay that has received a grade of C.

In addition to experiencing the anxiety and frustration provoked by revising an essay that has received a grade she perceives as unsatisfactory, the student is writing about unpleasant memories of high school, where she reported that she was shunned and mocked by her classmates, an emotionally laden topic. The assignment that the student wants to revise requires her to write about a change in her life. The conference begins with the tutor asking the student for the instructor's assignment handout and then asking about the instructor's criticisms of the essay. In response, the student states that the instructor did not mark the essay but instead returned it with a copy of the departmental rubric with the grade and grade's description circled. The tutor immediately begins using the positive politeness strategy of giving sympathy, by reading the description of the C grade aloud and saying, *It's pretty sad how this C paper is a pretty good paper. When I first read this, I was like "Man, that's tough."*

After asking if the student has revised the essay since it was returned and learning that the student *ha[s]n't had time,* the tutor scans the draft. However, rather than focusing entirely on the paper, the tutor continues to attend to the student. She leans over to keep the essay between the two of them instead of moving it in front of her. She also summarizes and responds as she reads the student's unpleasant memories of her private high school: *An enchilada right on your head! Really? Wow!* and a minute or two later, *Goodness gracious! What kind of school was this?! These people sound terrible.* When asked about these comments in the retrospective interview, the tutor says that she is trying to keep the student engaged to "let her know where I am and that what I am reading is interesting." The tutor appears to be trying to build rapport and solidarity by showing her agreement with the student that her treatment in high school was awful. She is validating the student's viewpoint.

In the retrospective interview, the tutor says that as she scanned the essay, she realized that rather than one life change, the student is writing about two changes— she transferred from a public high school to a private one and then made the change to college. In addition, the writing switches back and forth from the first change to the second and, thus, lacks coherence. The tutor suggests that the student choose one change to write about:

Excerpt 2.1

1   T: And I think that talking about those transitions is making your paper seem
2   a little unfocused. And so I think what I would think about is which of these
3   you would like to focus on? You want to focus on what you learned from this
4   change, or do you want to focus on what you learned from that change?

The tutor's questions signal that she has refrained from presuming what the student wants to do, thus reinforcing the student's control over her writing with this negative politeness strategy. Moreover, the tutor uses politeness to deliver the necessary criticism, softening the blow with hedges (lines 1–2: the verb *seem* and the diminutive *a little*). The student chooses to write about the change from her private high school to college, which had a positive effect on her.

The conference proceeds, and throughout the student talks a great deal about her painful private school experiences: *when I came here no one liked me, so I couldn't. No one would be friends with me.* The tutor continues to show sympathy about the student's bad treatment: *Yeah, of course, yeah. I mean you had some really difficult situations in that new school.* In the retrospective interview, the tutor says that she thought the student might be embarrassed by having the tutor read about such humiliating experiences. Therefore, the tutor says, she showed "extra sympathy" because she was "trying to make [the student] feel like it's okay."

What appears to be the turning point in the conference—the point at which the tutor and student determine the paper's focus—occurs across the excerpts below (Excerpts 2.2–2.5). The tutor has been giving advice about how to revise the essay so that it clearly focuses on one change, from private high school to college. She suggests that the student read through the essay, putting check marks by information irrelevant to that change. When Excerpt 2.2 begins, the student has realized that no small amount of work will be involved:

Excerpt 2.2

1 S: I guess it's going to get hard now changing it   from public to private
2 T: yeah
3 S: because
4 T: [Interrupts] Right, that was your whole focus really.
5 S: Yeah.
6 T: Because it was how when you changed into the private it was so different.
7 S: Yeah.
8 T: So it will be
9 S: [Interrupts] I have a feeling that I'm going to be writing it all over tonight.
10 T: Yeah, you probably will be, you know. And with these revisions it always
11   ends up being (1–2 seconds) You know, it's always a lot of work in order to
12   try to get a to better (1–2 seconds) to try to write a better paper.
13 S: Yeah. I just spent like all last night revising it, a whole new paper, because
14   I'm doing two papers at once for   the same teacher.
15 T: oh
16 T: I see. So this is taking more time than you had originally expected?

The tutor responds to the student's assessment that changing the focus of the paper will be difficult by agreeing with her and summarizing why the change would be difficult (line 6: *Because it was how when you changed into the private it was so different*). The tutor's response constitutes what Brown and Levinson would call giving the gift of understanding (129). That is, by summarizing or paraphrasing what students say, tutors show that they understand. Indeed, after the student again states that the effort required for revising the paper will be substantial (line 9: *I have a feeling that I'm going to be writing it all over tonight*), the tutor (in line 10) agrees with her again. Rather than minimizing the time required for the revision, the tutor agrees with the student, demonstrating her concern not to mislead. Further, by acknowledging the difficulty required for such an extensive revision, the tutor also sympathizes with the student. In addition, in lines 11–12, the tutor tries to encourage the student by helping her make the connections between writing improvement and effort, possibly to convince the student that the quality of the essay—and the grade—are under her control.

The tutor conveys understanding again after another complaint from the student (lines 13–14), using an explicit marker of understanding: *I see* (line 16). With her confirmation question in line 16 (*So this is taking more time than you had originally expected?*), the tutor employs yet another positive politeness strategy: she asserts knowledge of and concern for the student's wants. That is, the tutor's questions signal her understanding of what the student is thinking—that revising the paper has taken up a lot of time already, making spending more time on it particularly troublesome. With this signal of shared knowledge, the tutor conveys solidarity with the student and, in a sophisticated move, shifts her expression of sympathy about the student's terrible experiences in the private high school to focus entirely on revising the essay.

A few turns later, the discussion of the assignment continues. In Excerpt 2.3, the tutor conveys optimism about the student's ability to revise.

Excerpt 2.3

1 S: Yeah.   She's giving me the extension on the other one.   I was like,
2 T: okay   okay
3   "Oh man."
4 T: I think you can do it though. I mean I think you can (1–2 seconds) It will take
5   a lot of work, but I think that (1–2 seconds) I think that it will be worth it
6   though. I think if you take out these things that focus on the transition from
7   public to private and mainly focus on the negative things at your private school,
8   and then focus on your transition to college, I think you can do it.
9 S: Yeah, I hope so.

After the student explains how it is that she has two papers to revise in a small amount of time, the tutor employs optimism. With *I think that you could do it though* (line 4) and *I think you can do it* (line 8), the tutor builds the student's confidence without denying the extensive changes that the student needs to make or the time those changes will require. In lines 4–6, as in lines 11–12 of Excerpt 2.2, the tutor again correlates effort with writing quality and states explicitly that the effort is worthwhile. Thus, in terms of motivational scaffolding, the tutor continues to provide comfort without misleading the student about the difficulty of the revising task.

Even so, a few minutes later, it seems that the student is still frustrated, as she complains that the revision will require writing a new introduction, one of her self-proclaimed weaknesses. Therefore, the tutor proposes a quite different possibility for the revision.

Excerpt 2.4

1 S: So I'm going to edit that whole thing out and just say I went from the guys
2   (1–2 seconds) because that's going to be so hard.
3 T: Well, how about this then? Would you rather focus it on this? [points to
4   draft] Even though this change is kind of a negative one, but she didn't say
5   it had to be positive.
6 S: Exactly.
7 T: She just said it had to change you in some way.
8 S: Okay. I'd rather do that then.
9 T: Okay. Well, then what you need to do is (1–2 seconds) the same kind of
10   thing, but it might be a little easier, but go through and take out the stuff
11   about the transition [to college. Yeah. And really focus on what you learned
12 S: [to college
13   from this transition.
14 T: (3 seconds) So yeah, let's go find it. Where, where is it at about college?
15   (30 seconds)

This excerpt includes the tutor's questions to the student about the paper's focus (line 3: *Well, how about this then? Would you rather focus it on this?*). Such questions indicate that the tutor is not presuming to know what the student wants to do and that the tutor is concerned that the student remain in control of her own writing and the agenda for the conference. Moreover, as she has done previously when the student complained that she would be *writing it all over tonight* (Excerpt 2.2, line 9), the tutor uses the strategy of avoiding candid disagreement, refusing to contradict the student's assessment that the revision would be *so hard*. Instead, she gives the student another option and in doing so conveys that she is trying to cooperate.

The other option the tutor has in mind is that the student focus on the negative change from the happy time at a public high school to the unhappy time at the private high school—rather than the positive change from the unhappy time at the private high school to the happy time in college. With this hedged suggestion, the tutor generates what appears to be a turning point in the conference, showing she is willing to discard the work they have done and move to what she refers to in the retrospective interview as "Plan B." Typical for this conference, the choice of how to focus the draft belongs to the student. At the end of Excerpt 2.4, the tutor demonstrates her concern for the student by offering her help in finding the information to be deleted from the draft. Indeed, she uses the strategy of including both the tutor and the student in the activity in her use of *let's* (line 14), signaling her intent to help the student.

In the retrospective interview, the tutor says that she was willing to accept the student's rejection of her advice and move to Plan B because the student seemed frustrated. Earlier in the retrospective interview, the tutor discussed the importance of calibrating feedback according to the student's motivation. She says that when the student told her she did not have time to make the suggested revisions, "I tried to go smaller, and say, 'Okay, if you don't want to do that, what do you think would be the next best thing?'" Rather than pushing the student to make the revisions she believed would most improve the essay, the tutor decides to focus first on lowering the student's anxiety. The tutor's decision may have been important in enhancing the student's motivation to participate actively in the conference. As the tutor says in the interview, "I try to pay more attention to the text, but some students' personalities are such that you can only work with them if you work with them." The conference continues, with the tutor and student working on the new revision, a revision that details the loneliness and desperation of her experience in her first two years at private school.

Excerpt 2.5

1	T:	Does that make sense? And let's see here, [reading from draft] "This is the
2		first year at school and I cannot fit in. I felt fat and at this point in
3	S:	uh-huh
4	T:	my life and I felt like I could not take anything to heart. My second year,"
5		Okay. Then you transition. Then you say, "My second year at private school
6		I was considered a slut by other girls." So here you talk about not taking
7		everything to heart, and here you're talking about another terrible story. So
8		what's the connection between that? (1–2 seconds) Did you start to take it
9		to heart here?
10	S:	Yeah.
11	T:	Okay. So what's a transition sentence that you could use?
12	S:	Hum, that towards my second year of school I started taking things to
13	T:	yeah
14	S:	heart.
15	T:	Perfect! Yeah, write that here. That's the kind of thing to transition between
16		those two ideas.

By this point, it seems that enough trust has been established to allow the tutor to read aloud embarrassing details from the student's draft without stopping to show sympathy. Hearing these details does not appear to affect the student's motivation to participate in the conference. The tutor is also able to insert specific praise for the student (lines 15–16: *Perfect!. That's the kind of thing to transition between those two ideas*). The praise is particularly strong because it responds to an identifiable accomplishment, creating the transition sentence.

As the conference winds down, the tutor continues to sympathize with the student about the difficulty of the writing task. She also uses optimism to encourage the student to continue: *Okay. So now you are feeling overwhelmed with everything that you have to do, but you'll be fine.* The conference ends with the student again complaining about the deal she cut with her instructor that allows her to revise two papers simultaneously and the enormous workload it caused:

Excerpt 2.6

1   T: Oh man, that's difficult.
2   S: It was really crazy.
3   T: [joking tone] Well, go hurry! Work on it. Don't waste any time.

Even at this point in the conference when the student has moved away from the draft she and the tutor were working on and is complaining more generally about all the work she has to do, the tutor uses positive politeness, specifically, by giving sympathy (line 1: *Oh man, that's difficult*) and by jokingly issuing a directive to the student (line 3: *Well, go hurry!*).

CONCLUSION

Motivational scaffolding strategies operationalized through politeness provide a means for identifying, analyzing, and discussing an important aspect of writing center tutoring—tutors' linguistic resources for building rapport and solidarity with students and attending to their motivation during writing center conferences. Affective connections are essential to these conversations, which, at their most successful, require high levels of cooperation among participants. Motivational scaffolding reflects tutors' care for students. When carried out via positive politeness, it can do more than save face for students. For example, praising students for specific achievements can not only point to behaviors that students should reproduce but also build students' confidence and self-regulation. Avoiding candid disagreements with students can enhance their ownership of their writing and acknowledge their primary role in agenda-setting throughout the conference. Further, by directly expressing concern and sympathy, tutors can emphasize students' importance. Because "notice," "attend," and "give" strategies may in particular get lost in teachers' classroom comments, it is important that tutors focus their full and caring attention on students, work to develop rapport and solidarity, and demonstrate their respect for them. Through reinforcing the students' ownership, tutors also emphasize students' responsibility for their writing.

Empirical research based on our investigation about motivational scaffolding and politeness in writing center conferences might consider the effects of these tutoring strategies on students' and tutors' satisfaction and conference success, however success may be defined. By recording conferences and then conducting retrospective interviews during which tutors and students are asked to recall their responses to certain comments or circumstances, we can consider the effects of motivational scaffolding as it is operationalized by politeness in a particular writing center context, with a specific tutor and student, and at a certain time in composing. We can also count how frequently tutors use motivational scaffolding strategies in writing center conferences considered satisfactory by both tutors and students. However, because, in most cases, we cannot define in-the-moment conference success except in terms of satisfaction, measuring frequency of occurrence may be misleading. It is possible that tutors can be too polite and try so hard at motivating that students will be turned off.

Further research might also consider writing center conferences with participants differing according to race, ethnicity, cultural background, and other characteristics. Even though all four participants in the two conferences excerpted here are white, American-English speakers, one of the tutors is male while the other is female. Both tutors are knowledgeable about the typical assignments and about the attitudes and quirks of instructors in first-year writing and world literature. They also demonstrate their caring for students and use many of the same politeness strategies, including mitigation, optimism, and joking. However, the tutors also show some differences. Whereas the male tutor in Example 1 helps the student develop her revision and improve her confidence by giving her examples to convince her that the first topic is better than her current one, the female tutor in Example 2 also gives the student advice, but she does not try to persuade the student to adopt a certain topic. In fact, the student changes her topic in the middle of the conference. Along with her flexibility and her commitment to the student's control of her own writing, the tutor in Example 2 loads the conference with sympathy for the student—for the student's difficulty in revising two essays simultaneously as well as for her awful experiences at the private school. Although the different approaches used by the two tutors in these two conferences seem to lead to good outcomes for the students, in other conferences, we might find more complexity and confusion in the tutor and student dialogue. We need to be able to discuss some potential problems with attempting motivational scaffolding when the student and the tutor do not share the same cultural background.

Although this article focuses on verbal tutoring strategies, future research might consider how tutors' nonverbal strategies—for example, hand gestures, eye contact, and posture—can enhance rapport and solidarity in writing center conferences. According to Adam Kendon and Geoffrey Beattie, body posture, hand gestures, and other forms of nonverbal communication show how people feel about each other and how willingly they invite relationships. Janet Beavin Bavelas et al. identify two categories of hand gestures: topic gestures, which are representational and "depict semantic information directly related to the topic of discourse" (473), and interactive gestures, which are not representational of topics but "refer instead to some aspect of the process of conversing with another person" (473). Tutors' interactive gestures may allow tutors to reach out to students and draw them into the conversation.

Probably most important, based on this review, we can now identify a range of linguistic alternatives to inform the tutoring strategies available for use in writing center conferences, and we can describe these alternatives in our training for new tutors. Hence, we can help tutors to become more aware and make more conscious choices about what they say to students. Research has shown that without training, tutors are not likely to use strategies that attend to students' motivation (see Graesser, Person, and Magliano). The more we know about the linguistic possibilities available in writing center conferences and the more often we pass that knowledge on to tutors, the better we can serve students.

WORKS CITED

Azevedo, Roger, Jennifer G. Cromley, and Diane Seibert. "Does Adaptive Scaffolding Facilitate Students' Ability to Regulate their Learning with Hypermedia?" *Contemporary Educational Psychology* 29.3 (2004): 344–70. Print.

Bavelas, Janet Beavin, Nancy Chovil, D. A. Lawrie, and A. Wade. "Interactive Gestures." *Discourse Processes* 15.4 (1992): 469–89. Print.

Beattie, Geoffrey. *Visible Thought: The New Psychology of Body Language.* London: Routledge, 2004. Print.

Bell, Nancy, and Salvatore Attardo. "Failed Humor: Issues in Non-Native Speakers' Appreciation and Understanding of Humor." *Intercultural Pragmatics 7* (2010): 423–47. Print.

Bell, Diana C., and Madeleine Youmans. "Politeness and Praise: Rhetorical Issues in ESL (L2) Writing Center Conferences." *The Writing Center Journal* 26.2 (2006): 31–47. Print.

Black, Laurel Johnson. *Between Talk And Teaching: Reconsidering the Writing Conference.* Logan, UT: Utah State UP, 1998.

Blau, Susan R., John Hall, and Tracy Strauss. "Exploring the Tutor/Client Conversation: A Linguistic Analysis." *The Writing Center Journal* 19.1 (1998): 19–48. Print.

Boscolo, Pietro, and Suzanne Hidi. "The Multiple Meanings of Motivation to Write." *Writing and Motivation.* Ed. Suzanne Hidi and Pietro Boscolo. Boston: Elsevier, 2007. 1–14. Print.

Bransford, John D., Ann L. Brown, and Rodney R. Cocking (Eds.). *How People Learn: Brain, Mind, Experience, and School.* Washington: National Academies, 2000. Print.

Brown, Penelope, and Stephen C. Levinson. *Politeness: Some Universals in Language Usage.* Cambridge: Cambridge UP, 1987. Print.

Bruning, Roger, and Christy Horn. "Developing Motivation to Write." *Educational Psychologist* 35.1 (2000): 25–38. Print.

Bye, Dorothea, Dolores Pushkar, and Michael Conway. "Motivation, Interest, and Positive Affect in Traditional and Nontraditional Undergraduate Students." *Adult Education Quarterly* 57.2 (2007): 141–58. Print.

Carino, Peter, and Doug Enders. "Does Frequency of Visits to the Writing Center Increase Student Satisfaction? A Statistical Correlation Study—or Story." *The Writing Center Journal* 22.1 (2001): 83–103. Print.

Cazden, Courtney. *Classroom Discourse: The Language of Teaching and Learning.* 2nd ed. Portsmouth, NH: Heinemann, 2001. Print.

Chi, Michelene T. H. "Constructing Self-Explanations and Scaffolded Explanations in Tutoring." *Applied Cognitive Psychology* 10.7 (1996): 33–49. Print.

Chi, Michelene T. H., Stephanie A. Siler, Heisawn Jeong, Takashi Yamauchi, and Robert G. Hausmann. "Learning from Human Tutoring." *Cognitive Science* 25.4 (2001): 471–533. Print.

Clark, Kathleen F., and Michael F. Graves. "Scaffolding Students' Comprehension of Text." *The Reading Teacher* 58.6 (2005): 570–80. Print.

Cooper, Bridget. "Care—Making the Affective Leap: More Than a Concerned Interest in a Learner's Cognitive Abilities." *International Journal of Artificial Intelligence in Education* 13 (2003): 3–9. Print.

Cromley, Jennifer G., and Roger Azevedo. "What Do Reading Tutors Do? A Naturalistic Study of More and Less Experienced Tutors in Reading." *Discourse Processes A Multidisciplinary Journal* 40.2 (2005): 83–113. Print.

Daniels, Harry. *Vygotsky and Pedagogy.* New York: Routledge/Falmer, 2001. Print.

Davis, Kevin M., Nancy Hayward, Kathleen R. Hunter, and David L. Wallace. "The Function of Talk in the Writing Conference: A Study of Tutorial Conversation." *The Writing Center Journal* 9.1 (1988): 45–51. Print.

Dweck, Carol S. "The Perils and Promises of Praise." *Educational Leadership* 65.2 (2007): 34–39. Print.

Evens, Martha and Joel Michael. *One-on-One Tutoring by Humans and Computers.* Mahwah, NJ: Erlbaum, 2006. Print.

Farghal, Mohammed, and Madeline Haggan. "Compliment Behavior in Bilingual Kuwaiti College Students." *International Journal of Bilingual Education and Bilingualism* 9 (2006): 94–118. Print.

Fox, Barbara. *The Human Tutorial Dialogue Project: Issues in the Design of Instructional Systems.* Hillsdale, NJ: Erlbaum, 1993. Print.

Gaskins, Irene W., Sharon Rauch, Eleanor Gensemer, Elizabeth Cunicelli, Colleen O'Hara, Linda Six, and Theresa Scott. "Scaffolding and Development of Intelligence Among Children Who Are Delayed in Learning to Read." *Scaffolding Student Learning: Instructional Approaches and Issues. Advances in Teaching and Learning Series.* Ed. Kathleen Hogan and Michael Pressley. Cambridge, MA: Brookline, 1997. 43–73. Print.

Graesser, Arthur C., Cheryl Bowers, Douglas J. Hacker, and Natalie Person. "An Anatomy of Naturalistic Tutoring." *Scaffolding Student Learning: Instructional Approaches and Issues. Advances in Teaching and Learning Series.* Ed. Kathleen Hogan and Michael Pressley. Cambridge, MA: Brookline, 1997. 145–84. Print.

Graesser, Arthur C., Natalie K. Person, and Joseph P. Magliano. "Collaborative Dialogue Patterns in Naturalistic One-to-One Tutoring." *Applied Cognitive Psychology* 9.6 (1995): 495–522. Print.

Hancock, Dawson R. "Influencing Graduate Students' Classroom Achievement, Homework Habits and Motivation to Learn with Verbal Praise." *Educational Research* 44.1 (2002): 83–95. Print.

Henning, Teresa B. "Theoretical Models of Tutor Talk: How Practical Are They?" Conf. on Coll. Composition and Communication. Denver, 15 Mar. 2001. Presentation.

Hidi, Suzanne, and Pietro Boscolo. "Motivation and Writing." *Handbook of Writing Research.* Ed. Charles A. MacArthur, Steve Graham, and Jill Fitzgerald. New York: Guilford, 2006. 144–57. Print.

Hidi, Suzanne, and Judith M. Harackiewicz. "Motivating the Academically Unmotivated: A Critical Issue for the 21st Century." *Review of Educational Research* 70.2 (2000): 151–79. Print.

Hume, Gregory, Joel Michael, Allen Rovick, and Martha Evens. "Hinting as a Tactic in One-on-One Tutoring." *The Journal of the Learning Sciences* 5.1 (1996): 23–47. Print.

Hynd, Cynthia, Jodi Holschuh, and Sherrie Nist. "Learning Complex Scientific Information: Motivation Theory and Its Relation to Student Perceptions." *Reading and Writing
Quarterly: Overcoming Learning Difficulties* 16.1 (2000): 23–57. Print.

Johnson, W. Lewis, and Paola Rizzo. "Politeness in Tutoring Dialogs: 'Run the Factory,
That's What I'd Do.'" *Intelligent Tutoring Systems*. Ed. James C. Lester, Rosa Maria
Vicari, and Fábio Paraguaçu. 206–43. Berlin: Springer-Verlag, 2004. 67–76. Print.

Kendon, Adam. *Gestures: Visible Action as Utterance*. Cambridge: Cambridge UP, 2004.
Print.

Kerssen-Griep, Jeff, Jon A. Hess, and April R. Trees. "Sustaining the Desire to Learn: Dimensions of Perceived Instructional Facework Related to Student Involvement and
Motivation to Learn." *Western Journal of Communication* 67.4 (2003): 357–81. Print.

Legg, Angela M., and Janie H. Wilson. "E-Mail From Professor Enhances Student Motivation and Attitudes." *Teaching of Psychology*, 36.3 (2009): 205–11. Print.

Lepper, Mark. R., Lisa G. Aspinwall, and Donna L. Mumme. "Self-Perception and Social-
Perception Processes in Tutoring: Subtle Social Control Strategies of Expert Tutors."
Self-inference Processes: The Ontario Symposium. Ed. J. M. Olson and M. P. Zanna.
Hillsdale, NJ: Erlbaum, 1990. 217–37. Print.

Lepper, Mark. R., Michael F. Drake, and Theresa O'Donnell-Johnson. "Scaffolding Techniques of Expert Human Tutors." *Scaffolding Student Learning: Instructional Approaches and Issues*. Eds. Kathleen Hogan and Michael Pressley. Cambridge, MA:
Brookline, 1997. 108–44. Print.

Lepper, Mark. R., and Jennifer Henderlong. "Turning 'Play' into 'Work' and 'Work' into
'Play': 25 Years of Research on Intrinsic Versus Extrinsic Motivation." *Intrinsic and
Extrinsic Motivation: The Search for Optimal Motivation and Performance*. Ed. Carol
Sansone and Judith M. Harackiewicz. San Diego: Academic, 2000. 257–307. Print.

Lepper, Mark. R., Maria Woolverton, Donna L. Mumme, and Jean-Luc Gurtner. "Moti-
vational Techniques of Expert Human Tutors: Lessons for the Design of Computer-
Based Tutors." *Computers as Cognitive Tools*. Mahwah, NJ: Erlbaum, 1993. 75–105.
Print.

Lorenzo-Dus, N. "Compliment Responses Among British and Spanish University Students:
A Contrastive Study." *Journal of Pragmatics* 33.1 (2001): 107–27. Print.

Mackiewicz, Jo. "The Effects of Tutor Expertise in Engineering Writing: A Linguistic Analysis of Writing Tutors' Comments." *IEEE Transactions on Professional Communication* 47.4 (2004): 316–28. Print.

———. "The Functions of Formulaic and Nonformulaic Compliments in Interactions
About Technical Writing." *IEEE Transactions on Professional Communication* 49.1
(2006): 12–27. Print.

Mackiewicz, Jo, and Kathryn Riley. "The Technical Editor as Diplomat: Linguistic Strategies
for Balancing Clarity and Politeness." *Technical Communication* 50 (2003): 83–94.
Print.

Maclellan, Effie. "Academic Achievement: The Role of Praise in Motivating Students."
*Active Learning in Higher Education: The Journal of the Institute for Learning and
Teaching* 6.3 (2005): 194–206. Print.

Margolis, Howard. "Increasing Struggling Learners' Self-Efficacy: What Tutors Can Do and
Say." *Mentoring and Tutoring: Partnership in Learning* 13.2 (2005): 221–38. Print.

Mehan, Hugh. *Learning Lessons: Social Organization in the Classroom*. Cambridge, MA:
Harvard UP, 1979. Print.

Merrill, Douglas C., Brian J. Reiser, Shannon K. Merrill, and Shari Landes. "Tutoring: Guided Learning by Doing." *Cognition and Instruction.* 13.3 (1995): 315–72. Print.

Meyer, Debra K., and Julianne C. Turner. "Discovering Emotion in Classroom Motivation Research." *Educational Psychologist* 37.2 (2002): 107–14. Print.

Murphy, Susan Wolff. "'Just Chuck It: I Mean, Don't Get Fixed on It': Self Presentation in Writing Center Discourse." *The Writing Center Journal* 26.1 (2006): 62–82. Print.

Mursy, Ahmad Aly, and John Wilson. "Toward a Definition of Egyptian Complimenting." *Multilingua* 20.2 (2001): 133–54. Print.

Nassaji, Hossein, and Gordon Wells. "What's the Use of 'Triadic Dialogue'?: An Investigation of Teacher–Student Interaction." *Applied Linguistics* 21.3 (2000): 376–406. Print.

Pajares, Frank, and Gio Valiante. "Self-Efficacy Beliefs and Motivation in Writing Development." *Handbook of Writing Research.* Ed. Charles A. MacArthur, Steve Graham, and Jill Fitzgerald. New York, NY: Guilford, 2008. 158–70. Print.

Palincsar, Annemarie Sullivan. "Keeping the Metaphor of Scaffolding Fresh—A Response to C. Addison Stone's 'The Metaphor of Scaffolding: Its Utility for the Field of Learning Disabilities.'" *Journal of Learning Disabilities* 31.4 (1998): 370–73. Print.

Puntambekar, Sadhana, and Roland Hubscher. "Tools for Scaffolding Students in a Complex Learning Environment: What Have We Gained and What Have We Missed?" *Educational Psychologist* 40.1 (2005): 1–12. Print.

Severino, Carol. "Rhetorically Analyzing Collaboration(s)." *The Writing Center Journal* 13.1 (1992): 53–64. Print.

Stone, C. Addison. "The Metaphor of Scaffolding: Its Utility for the Field of Learning Disabilities." *Journal of Learning Disabilities* 31.4 (1998): 344–64. Print.

Thompson, Isabelle. "Scaffolding in the Writing Center." *Written Communication* 26.4 (2009): 417–53. Print.

Thompson, Isabelle, Alyson Whyte, David Shannon, Amanda Muse, Kristen Miller, Milla Chappell, and Abby Whigham. "Examining Our Lore: A Survey of Students' and Tutors' Satisfaction with Writing Center Conferences." *The Writing Center Journal* 29.1 (2009): 78–105. Print.

Thonus, Terese. "Dominance in Academic Writing Tutorials: Gender, Language Proficiency, and the Offering of Suggestions." *Discourse & Society* 10.2 (1999): 225–48. Print.

———. "How To Communicate Politely and Be a Tutor, Too: NS–NNS Interaction and Writing Center Practice." *Text* 19.2 (1999): 253–79. Print.

———. "Tutor and Student Assessments of Academic Writing Tutorials: What Is 'Success'?" *Assessing Writing* 8.2 (2002): 110–34. Print.

Van Etten, Shawn, Michael Pressley, Dennis M. McInerney, Arief Darmanegara Liem. "College Seniors' Theory of Their Academic Motivation." *Journal of Educational Psychology* 100.4 (2008): 812–28. Print.

VanLehn, Kurt, Stephanie Siler, Charles Murray, Takashi Yamauchi, and William Baggett. "Why Do Only Some Events Cause Learning During Human Tutoring?" *Cognition and Instruction* 21.3 (2003): 209–49. Print.

Williams, Jessica. "Tutoring and Revision: Second Language Writers in the Writing Center." *Journal of Second Language Writing* 13.3 (2004): 173–201. Print.

Wilson, Janie H. "Predicting Student Attitudes and Grades From Perceptions of Instructors' Attitudes." *Teaching of Psychology* 33.2 (2006): 91–95. Print.

Wolcott, Willa. "Talking It Over: A Qualitative Study of Writing Center Conferencing." *The Writing Center Journal* 9.2 (1989): 15–29. Print.

Wood, David, Jerome S. Bruner, and Gail Ross. "The Role of Tutoring in Problem Solving." *Journal of Child Psychology and Psychiatry* 17.2 (1976): 89–100. Print.

Wood, David, and David Middleton. "A Study of Assisted Problem-Solving." *British Journal of Psychology* 66 (1975): 181–91. Print.

Yu, Ming-chung. "On the Universality of Face: Evidence from Chinese Compliment Response Behavior." *Journal of Pragmatics* 35 (2003) 1679–1710. Print.

Yuan, Yi. "Compliments and Compliment Responses in Kunming Chinese." *Pragmatics* 12.2 (2002): 183–226. Print.

Zimmerman, Barry J., and Anastasia Kitsantas. "A Writer's Discipline: The Development of Self-Regulatory Skill." *Writing and Motivation*. Ed. Suzanne Hidi and Pietro Boscolo. Boston: Elsevier, 2007. 51–69. Print.

Zimmerman, Barry J., and Dale H. Schunk. *Self-Regulated Learning and Academic Achievement: Theoretical Perspectives*. 2nd ed. Mahwah, NJ: Erlbaum, 2001. Print.

Creating Third Space: ESL Tutoring as Cultural Mediation

Cameron Mozafari

Cameron Mozafari was an undergraduate at University of Maryland–Baltimore County when he wrote this article. It originally appeared in the journal *Young Scholars in Writing*.

When Stephen North laid the foundations for the modern university writing center in his 1984 article "The Idea of a Writing Center," he proclaimed that "in a writing center the object is to make sure that writers, and not necessarily their texts, are what get changed by instruction" (38). That is, the writing center should focus on the process of writing and not the produced text. While it may be easy for tutors to follow this guideline in general, the task becomes much more daunting when tutors deal with tutees whose first language and style of thinking are different from their own. When the tutor and tutee are separated by a language barrier—and a difference in cultural and historical context—North's collaborative process tutoring is nearly impossible.

I have noticed that this is a large problem in the writing center at the University of Maryland–Baltimore County where I work. All of us tutors were required to take an extensive course in tutor training and tutoring theory in which we were reminded time and again that a writing center is not what North calls a "fix-it shop"—ESL tutoring scenarios were especially highlighted—but I still frequently find myself and my fellow tutors doing nothing more than proofreading the papers of ESL students when a session becomes difficult. In this situation, tutors are given the task of helping tutees transform their "unofficial" product into Standard English prose. In addition, since these students usually appeal to the writing center because their produced texts were rejected—by teachers or their own insecurities about the quality of their writing—tutors feel pressure not to aid in the writing process but to translate the troubled text into their own versions of academic prose.

When an ESL student comes into the writing center, an inherent contradiction arises between what the writing center is supposed to do and what the writing center does for this sort of writer, in particular. A difference in expectations manifests; the tutee expects to have his paper proofread or to be taught why his problems persist, while the tutor does not know what to expect from such a difficult session. Thus, the tutoring session turns into a somewhat nebulous proofreading session, since the tutor's and tutee's exigencies are competing rather than communicating or collaborating. The tutee and tutor both expend a lot of energy on parallel paths because

449

their starting points and end points are not common. If intersection—or effective communication—does not occur, a common goal cannot be met. The efforts of the session result in parallel objectives, both of which remain unfulfilled. In my article, I plan to show how a tutor can work to solve this contradiction by creating a "third space" within the tutoring session, a theoretical space where the tutor's and the tutee's expectations meet and negotiate. As I will go on to show, third space is not only a space that helps bridge the gap between the unofficial ESL bank of knowledge and the official academic bank of knowledge, but it can also change and shape participants' identities to become more active and, thus, more apt to change. Furthermore, when such a negotiation is reached, tutors are able to conduct sessions consistent with Stephen North's idea of a writing center: one where the focus is on a person's writing process, not the product.

CULTURAL HISTORICAL ACTIVITY THEORY AND THIRD SPACE

A fundamental problem that writing center tutors face when working with ESL students concerns the notion of understanding what language is. Before tutors can fully understand an ESL student's language usage, they must first ask themselves where both they and their tutees fit into the larger academic tapestry and how their different understandings of culture play a role in how the two parties can negotiate the writing process. Here, the Russian philosopher Mikhail Bakhtin notes, "The word in language is half someone else's" (293). By this, Bakhtin means that an individual is not accountable for how his utterances are understood. No one is independent of society; it is society that determines the words used and understood in communication. From this frame of reference, because the tutee is not independent, society must provide him with the cultural knowledge needed to negotiate successful acts of communication.

While ESL students would seem to be the ones most in need of this cultural knowledge, many times their acts of communication are overlooked or ignored because of how they compose their speech. This is where a tutor can be beneficial to a tutee. If tutors know the rules of academic discourse within the English-speaking culture, they should be better guides in helping their tutees to abide by the proper rules of this new Standard English academic community. But here, two problems arise: First, do such rules of academic discourse definitively exist? Who legitimizes these rules? And second, if tutors could get their tutees to immerse themselves in the Standard English academic culture, does this overlook or undervalue the knowledge a tutee already has from a different cultural framework? For my purposes, I refer to Cultural Historical Activity Theory (CHAT), a sort of meta-theory that can be helpful in showing the cultural significance in the motivations and historically situated thought processes behind given actions. CHAT can help tutors to see exactly where motives of their tutee's utterances do not align with the objectives they are trying to carry out with their texts.

CHAT derives from Lev Vygotsky's dialectical materialistic psychology. Vygotsky sought to create a shared-tool model of learning to map and analyze any activity and qualitatively assess how subjects and objectives or goals change depending on the mediating tool used. Vygotsky notes that these tools, too, are changed when used. They present a dialectical relationship within any given activity between subjects and objectives, as well as the tools used to obtain an objective. For example, looking at Vygotsky's model in terms of communication, learning occurs when a sender uses a mediating tool or sign system to communicate her intended message to a receiver: in this simple instance of communication, the received message depends on the success or failure of the sender's use of mediating tools. If the tool fails, the sender's message is lost, and the sender must think of another tool to use (Vygotsky 40). Here we see how the relationship between senders (subjects), the words or symbols they use (the mediating tools), and receivers (the people responding to what the sender is trying to communicate) are all components affecting one another.

By applying Vygotsky's theory to a student's composing process, one can model the relationship between subject, mediating tool, and response. The subject (the student) uses different tools (rhetorical maneuvers and word choices) to reach an objective (to communicate the intended message to an audience). However, while the student's intentions should be communicated in the produced text, this is not always the case. ESL students in particular often miscommunicate their intentions, confusing their audiences. While Vygotsky's model is useful for organizing factors that play a role in successful communication, in certain unsuccessful situations such as these, his model merely shows that something strange is happening with the use of the mediating device but can't fully account for what the problem is, i.e., the ESL student's situation of coming from a foreign community with foreign rules. Vygotsky's model does not account for an audience or rules of communication; it only shows how communication and learning are interwoven.

There seems to be more behind an activity system than just subjects, mediating tools, and objects; and, indeed, Yrjö Engeström's expanded model of an activity system takes into account the shortcomings of Vygotsky's initial model. Engeström's model shows how any act of communication, as Bakhtin had inferred, is dependent on society, or an audience. Engeström's model keeps Vygotsky's initial model intact (subject, tools, object) but adds another layer, elucidating other factors that go into activity systems (see Figure 1). In order to legitimize and assess standards of communicability,

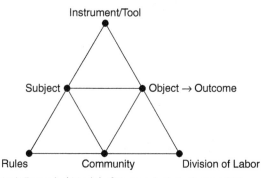

Figure 1 Engeström's Extended Model of Human Activity System (36).

there must be a community. And with this community comes the rules of communicability it creates. Division of labor, too, must be involved in order to place the subject into a role within the community.

Applying Engeström's extended model of an activity system to the ESL student's composing process, it becomes clear where his actions are coming from and how he justifies these actions to himself. It also becomes evident how the larger academic community interacts with his text (the object produced in the activity system), either accepting or rejecting it based on the standards that academia holds. When an activity system does not produce a text that reflects the tutee's intended motives, it reveals a disconnect between the tutee as an individual within his own activity system and the academic community. This disconnect is due to the tutee having a different understanding of audience, community, rules, and division of labor (elements that reflect the student's unrecognized cultural background knowledge). The academic community with which the tutee is attempting to communicate, in this sense, is essentially foreign to him, and he cannot adequately articulate and structure his text because the process of structuring is based on assumptions of what Standard English academics are seeking.

When the ESL student is psychologically alienated from the community she is trying to communicate with, Engeström's model shows us that there is also disconnection between the student and the rules, as the rules are connected with the community, too. And when the rules also become disconnected from the student, she has trouble successfully recognizing and utilizing the appropriate mediating tools—rhetorical devices, structures, information, etc.—for the objective of producing a text that reflects her motives. The student ultimately becomes isolated from the rules of communication and the community that she is trying to communicate with, as the figure below illustrates (see Figure 2). In order to find out the rules, the student must go through a guess-and-check process, where she chooses arbitrary mediating tools to create an object—in this case, a paper—in order to see how that object will be received by the community. Through the reception and response of the community, the student then sees the rules. However, since she is separated from the rules to begin

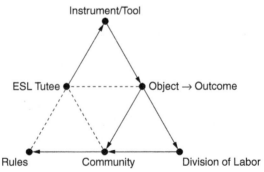

Figure 2 Representation of an ESL Student's Activity System in Relation to Writing. The Dashed Lines Signify Disconnects.

with, there is a disconnection between the subject (the student) and the object (the text)—or at least the process of creating a text here is unnatural and riddled with guessing games as to what tools the student should use to compose her message. In many ways, the student is isolated, prevented from communicating through the writing process. As a result, many of the guesses she makes seem to disconnect and estrange the student from the academic community or any of its representatives.

But—bringing Bakhtin's expression "The word in language is half someone else's" back into the picture—while the ESL student feels psychologically alienated from the society he is trying to address, he still has to get his means of communication—his system of figuring out what to guess for the appropriate mediating tools, rules, and perspective of audience—from somewhere within society, perhaps based on how he views the academic community or perhaps based on background knowledge from his own culture. The student is lost somewhere between that legitimized, official academic activity system and the unofficial, unrecognized activity system of his mother culture. The space where the student's activity system is located, a space halfway between the official and the unofficial, is what scholars like Kris Gutiérrez have termed "third space" (see Figure 3). By learning how to compose within third space, an ESL student can find more effective and productive means of communicating motives derived from that unofficial body of knowledge (such as background knowledge stemming from a different culture) to the community of an official and legitimized body of knowledge (such as that of academia). This, however, means strengthening and making conscious the third space activity system within which these special cases are operating (Gutiérrez, Baquedano-López, and Tejeda 289–90).

It is here, in third space, where tutors can help their tutees to modify their composing processes. Tutors become better able to help reconcile the individual and academic motives of their tutees. In the context of CHAT, this means producing a healthy link between the subject (the tutee) and the community (the teacher or the academic community at large), thereby creating a healthy activity system where the

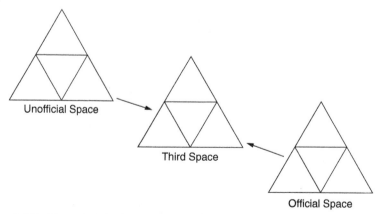

Unofficial Space

Third Space

Official Space

Figure 3 Third Space Activity System Where Official and Unofficial Spaces Meet (Gutiérrez, Baquedano-López, and Tejeda 292).

motives of the tutee reflect the exigence of the text the tutee produces. By using what Gutiérrez and her colleagues term "third space discourse practices," a tutor can help situate the tutees' own knowledge into the context of academia and thus legitimize it. In an article entitled "Rethinking Diversity: Hybridity and Hybrid Language Practices in Third Space," Gutiérrez and her coauthors Patricia Baquedano-López and Carlos Tejeda explain that using third space discourse practices means using "multiple, diverse, and even conflicting mediational tools [to promote] the emergence of 'Third Space,' or zones of development, thus expanding learning" (286). Such mediating tools range from the use of different languages (e.g., Korean vs. English) to different means of communication (e.g., writing vs. speaking) to the use of different tutoring techniques (e.g., different scaffolding techniques). By using such tools within a tutoring session and encouraging conflict, tutors can better examine the root of such conflicts and better see how their tutees' societal views differ, thus giving the tutor a launching point for understanding the tutee's thought process. Here, tutors can work with tutees to make motives and texts match and ultimately to let the tutee's unofficial knowledge be successfully communicated to the academic community. The result of such communication can in turn legitimize unofficial cultural knowledge, allowing for more intellectual and intercultural freedom within academia. Thus, the purpose of third space discourse practices is not to encourage students to move away from familiar, foreign cultural bodies of knowledge to more academic bodies of knowledge—these practices bring aspects of both official and unofficial into a third space, producing an area where unofficial utterances can in turn be understood and legitimized.

THE PROOFREADING TRAP

However, when third space discourse practices are not employed in a tutoring session, and the tutor submits to the role of proofreader, the tutor risks setting the official space at odds with the unofficial space, leaving the third space a no-man's-land between. The tutee's unofficial goals are subordinated to the tutor's official view of what these goals should be. And this is where tutors become complicit in what Jane Cogie and her colleagues Kim Strain and Sharon Lorinskas refer to as the proofreading trap. In their article titled "Avoiding the Proofreading Trap: The Value of the Error Correction Process," proofreading is viewed as something to be avoided in writing center sessions, as it inhibits language acquisition on the part of the ESL student. The trap can be seen as a set of two conflicting activity systems: one that knows not to proofread (the tutor) and one that seeks proofreading with the motive of passing a class (tutee). Although the mediating tool (writing) and the object (the text) are shared between the tutor and tutee, the two have very different goals or objectives, and, therefore, must have very different notions of the rules, community, and division of labor that justify their activity systems. Writing center pedagogues have, for some time now, been aware of both the problems and the advantages of ESL proofreading activities in the writing center. While tutors think that they are being helpful by proofreading their ESL tutees' papers, they are actually stunting language and culture acquisition. Cogie and her colleagues note that ESL tutees, "[w]ith their many cultural, rhetorical, and linguistic differences, . . . often lack the knowledge to engage in the question and answer approach to problem-solving used in most writing centers." Cogie et al. insist that tutors should make their tutees painfully aware of their differences in culture and the way their culture determines legitimate ways of communicating; then, tutors should act as cultural informants and show how, in Standard English, the rules of legitimization differ. Tutoring sessions should focus not on sentence-level errors and proofreading but on "sharing information about English [that] these students have no way of knowing on their own" (7). Cogie and her colleagues go on to suggest the importance of self-editing for ESL students, minimal marking during an ESL tutoring session, and the use and implementation of error logs, among many other proposals.

The problem with this line of tutoring, as Sharon A. Myers points out, is that in a sense it ignores errors or makes them secondary to learning new ways to successfully communicate. In her article "Reassessing the 'Proofreading Trap': ESL Tutoring and Writing Instruction," Myers critiques almost every aspect of the self-reflective tutoring suggested by Cogie and her associates. Myers, instead, argues for tutors to pay attention to errors instead of logging errors to help tutees to correct their reoccurring errors when they arise (288). Proofreading, for Myers, is not a trap, per se. It is a starting point from which a tutor a can begin the transference of Standard English onto a tutee. Myers concludes, "A much more relaxed attitude about 'error,' one reflecting an appreciation of second language acquisition processes, and better training in the pedagogical grammar of English as a second language would go a long way toward preventing either student or tutor from feeling frustrated or 'trapped' in any part of the tutoring session" (233).

While I feel that Myers's critique is very revealing, that focusing both on language acquisition and on sentence-level errors only when they come up is the most appropriate course of action for ESL tutoring sessions, Myers's tutors are perhaps unrealistically well prepared. Unlike most peer tutors, they are people who have been trained in language acquisition—people with a firm grasp of both common ESL errors and Standard English. These are not the types of tutors who work here at UMBC's writing center, tutors who—for the most part—fall back into the "proofreading trap," as they are unaware of the ways in which the trap may be beneficial as well as inhibiting for language acquisition.

There is a general assumption running through the work of Cogie et al. and Myers that ESL student and tutor are both viewing language in the same light, as professional and experienced ESL pedagogues. This is, however, often not the case, and this lack of experience leads to the proofreading-as-tutoring practices that I have described. For example, in Lucille McCarthy and Stephen Fishman's article "An ESL Writer and Her Discipline-Based Professor: Making Progress Even When Goals Don't Match," the subject of their article, a twenty-three-year-old Indian immigrant named Neha Shah at the University of North Carolina at Charlotte, notes that she made good use of the writing center, a place where Neha's papers were contorted into ones that granted her an A in her composition class (203). Later, when Neha joined Stephen Fishman's Introduction to Philosophy class, she did not attend sessions at the university's writing center as frequently, and her work shows a considerable barrier between her and the professor's understandings of the ways of communicating in Standard English. In the article, McCarthy argues that, to some extent, it was the mismatch of goals and motivations that led to Neha's poor writing (202). What Neha produced was not what Fishman expected, and as Neha realized this (through poor grades and suggestions to go to the writing center) she began to focus more on her writing and became aware of her problems arising from her inadequate acquisition of Standard English. Ultimately, Neha saw Fishman's class as an obstacle in a process to get her diploma, so her motivation was to pass the class. Fishman, on the other hand, wanted to see Neha produce critical thought and understanding of basic philosophical texts; since he did not understand what Neha was writing, his expectations were not being met.

While Fishman told Neha to go to the writing center because he did not know how to address her problems in language acquisition, I would feel that it is fair to say that the writing center tutors at the University of North Carolina at Charlotte probably knew even less than he did on the topic of language acquisition. That is why the tutors, when Neha took her composition class papers to the writing center, ended up rewriting her texts and, according to her, suggesting how to compose her paper. Neha was ultimately the victim of these corrections and suggestions as she lacked the problem-solving skills necessary to successfully compose appropriate Standard English prose in subsequent writing contexts. She thought that if she turned in proofread papers she would pass the class and come one step closer to her diploma. Indeed, it seems that Neha's activity system usurped the tutor's because, while the tutor knows not to proofread, the tutor does not actually know what to do in situations like Neha's and in the end succumbs to what Neha wants. That is, tutors generally are not the ideal experts that Myers assumes them to be; therefore, they default to proofreading because they do not know how to benefit tutees other than by participating in the proofreading of sentence-level errors.

But in the conflict between the tutor's and tutee's activity systems comes the relevance of the tutor as a cultural mediator. Tutors, by creating a third space for relevant language acquisition, can act as more than just a stand-in for a university professor. They can and do represent the official body of knowledge, yes, but they are also freer to help address specific problems they notice tutees having than a professor who teaches a class of twenty-five students. The recognition of an ESL student's problem is only the first step in creating a third space, and, arguably, due to the limitations of classes and the heterogeneous nature of classrooms, teachers cannot move past this first step and begin creating a third space. Tutors have the liberty, as Gutiérrez and her colleagues suggest, to participate in third space discourse practices to set up and utilize a third space zone of developing ideas that links unofficial knowledge to the official knowledge expected in academia. While it may be hard for tutees to transcend their motives of getting good grades, it is possible, as I will show, to get them to participate in a third space tutoring session, one that employs use of multiple means of communication to help them learn how to communicate their intentions to the representatives of unfamiliar and official discourse communities. Ultimately, with a shift in identity from unofficial space to third space, ESL students can act as cultural mediators themselves, mediating the ways in which discourse is legitimized in their unofficial way to the legitimized and official community. Thus, an ESL student who acts as a cultural mediator is in a position to eventually legitimize and incorporate the unofficial into the official.

TUTORING AS A MEANS OF CULTURAL MEDIATION

While peer tutors are appointed to their role of tutor by the academic community, and while tutors, in this sense, represent the official bank of learning and activity, tutors are freer to bend the official rules and focus on the unofficial due to their peer and student roles. Tutors are not academics, though they act as stand-ins for academics. They have background knowledge and know how to produce activities that will grant them recognition by the official, but they are still not part of the community that creates and governs rules or divides labor; in the eyes of academia, peer tutors are still students. This technicality of the peer tutor's role in academia makes the tutor best suited to participate in third space discourse practices. While tutors do not have the authoritative power of teachers, they represent and reflect this power in a tutoring session. Tutors, in being given the role of tutor, have both a teacher's authority in a tutoring session and a student's role in the academic division of labor, community, and rule usage. Knowing that tutors hold the power in tutoring sessions and, thus, can negotiate the power between tutor and tutee is essential for understanding how tutors can diverge from their normative tutoring session when dealing with special-case tutees like ESL students. In such collaborative sessions, however, tutors need to be extremely aware of what they are doing and saying in order to create—as Gutiérrez and her colleagues suggest—consciousness of competing socially and historically situated and legitimized activity systems.

One way a tutor can create such a consciousness is to focus on difference and conflict. But this is a tricky game. As Linda Flower, in her article "Intercultural Knowledge Building: The Literate Action of a Community Think Tank," notes, "The conflict among these representations [culturally situated realities] is a tangled web: the counter-productive aspect of conflict (e.g., misunderstanding, competition, and anxiety) may co-exist with the generative potential of difference (e.g., with the possibility of altering perspectives, rival hypotheses, competing conceptualizations, and an expanding division of values and priorities)" (239). These sorts of coexisting contradictions—the ESL student's knowledge and the tutor's knowledge—act as a launching point from which tutors can focus on difference and show the enriching qualities that their diversity brings to any collaborative tutoring session. Flower also notes that the interesting and productive value of CHAT is that it focuses on transcending "the dualisms of the individual self and its social, material circumstances, of mind and behavior" (241). Using CHAT to analyze culturally situated activity systems and the conflict between these activity systems, for this reason, can be a helpful tool in strategizing ways for tutors and tutees to transcend their social and material circumstances.

What I am suggesting is that tutors should not begin tutoring sessions looking for what they know and understand, but rather, they should avoid trying to understand what they cannot. To try to understand and interpret an ESL student's difficult text is equivalent to translating the text from what the student is saying to what the tutor is interpreting it as. That is, when tutors attempt to understand their ESL tutees' texts, they often end up viewing the text through their own interpretations and contriving their own intended messages, which may not be the same as the tutees'. The tutor and tutee may come from two entirely different cultural backgrounds, and, thus, the writing process works differently for them. By assuming what the tutee's message is, the tutor removes the tutee and the tutee's goals from the tutee's writing activity system and replaces them with her own goals. In this case, the tutor is directly manipulating the tutee's activity system, rather than helping the tutee to do this (in third space). As a result, the tutor can never truly understand an ESL student's original goal or meaning in her text. Likewise, academia begins not only by declaring that the ESL student's text is wrong and must be mechanically modified, but also by looking for ways to modify the meaning of the text to something more standard or presentable—here we see a tutoring situation similar to Neha's interaction with the writing center for her English composition class. A writing center is supposed to focus on the process of producing text, not the text itself.

However, the text can be a valuable launching point for beginning to conduct third space discourse practices. The degree to which the tutee is conscious of the rules that govern his use of writing, the acceptance of his text in the academic community, and his position as a student all factor into his troubles writing texts in standard academic prose. These are all problems in social consciousness that inhibit the writing process, an inherently culturally legitimized process within a given community. Tutors can help solve these problems by first acknowledging the differences between the ESL student's text and a standard academic text. Tutors can ask questions about the cultural motivations, histories, and backgrounds that led their tutee to produce his written text in the way he did. Here, tutors can prod their tutees to understand how they interpret all the factors that go into producing the objective outcome of successfully communicable academic text. In analyzing the outcome from a text, tutors can see the inherent activity system involved in their tutees' writing processes. In the activity system of producing text, the subject, mediating tools, and object are given (the tutee, his writing, and his text, respectively), but the degree to which the tutee understands the rules, community, and division of labor vary, and this locates the ESL student in the writing process.

I argue that, if ESL tutees knew the full extent of their cultural marginalization and the attempt of academia to enculturate them into its Eurocentrically established community, these tutees would show some level of resistance to mere proofreading. This, however, relies on the assumption that ESL tutees know that the writing center is a place to learn and not a mediating tool to use in the larger objective of getting a diploma. This is why it is important, as I stated earlier, to prod a tutee—in the most polite and nonconfrontational way, of course—to find out her true intentions in seeking help at the writing center. The motivation for going to the writing center must be to learn, and the tutoring session objective must fulfill this need. Tutors have the power to proofread just as much as they have the power to redirect the tutoring session away from the text and into third space, meaning tutors can help raise consciousness of differences in their unofficial ESL students' identities and the contradictions that lead to their poor writing in an official academic context. While tutors are placed in a position of power due to their legitimization in academia, they do not have to cooperate with the academic structure and reproduce the marginalization that accompanies proofreading and so-called suggestive structuring of texts.

Focusing on the CHAT-based components that govern the activity of production (the dialectical relationships between subject, mediating tool, object, rules, community, and division of labor) means first recognizing that the response to the object is not equivalent to the response to the ESL student's intentions. Culture is necessarily linked to the process of text production, in that each community views the object through its own culturally and historically situated lens. Staying true to Stephen North's idea of a writing center, a tutor who helps an ESL student to realize the complexities of his culture in relation to the culture he is writing to/in will help not only language acquisition but also the writing process as a whole. That is, when ESL students realize the differences and importance of successful communicative habits both in their culture and the culture they write to, the significance of the historically situated pragmatic context of words and their associated outcomes is given a purpose: to communicate the unofficial to the official, thus granting a place for the unofficial within the official. Tutees are given an answer to the question "Why learn to learn?" Their learning will be directed and molded for the sole purpose of giving themselves, and others like them, a place and voice within academia.

THIRD SPACE TUTORING IN PRACTICE

Tutors may have their own motives; ideally, they will have the motive of creating a third space tutoring session that helps ESL students to acknowledge their position in academia, ultimately encouraging ESL students to actively learn and successfully communicate their nonofficial exigencies to an official academic audience. In this section, I will give an example of a successful third space tutoring session with a twenty-one-year-old Korean second-year female student whom I will call Kim. Kim is part of UMBC's English Language Center (ELC), a center that teaches ESL students English and the professional skills needed in the workplace. Though the ELC has highly trained teachers and tutors who deal specifically with English language acquisition, Kim came to the writing center because she wanted to know if her work was comprehensible. She was, in essence, using the writing center as a way of measuring her ability to communicate in English.

The work Kim brought with her to the writing center was a research paper she was composing on healthy eating habits for her ELC 051 class. When we first sat down, I asked her what she was expecting from our tutoring session. "My English writing is not very good," she told me, "and I am not sure what I am to write." Her spoken English was not actually poor at all, as she was able to clearly speak and make evident what her difficulties were. However, she was having trouble identifying what she was supposed to write and how she was supposed to write it. Clarification of what and how Kim was supposed to write on the topic of healthy eating was her motive for coming to the writing center. I told her that, while the writing center often proofreads papers and looks for sentence-level errors, I would not do this in our tutoring session.

I wanted to see how clearly she could communicate her intentions, and I made this known to her from the start.

Kim had been to UMBC's writing center before, so she knew the standard way in which most tutors begin their sessions: a read-aloud method that is designed to enable tutees to catch their own mistakes. Our session was no different in this respect; I had her read her paper aloud, but before she began reading, I asked her to mark only the parts of her paper that confused her or the parts where she wasn't sure if she was being clear. "If you don't mark anything," I explained, "then I'm not going to be able to help you." This motivated Kim to actively read her paper and look for disconnects between what she meant to say and what she was saying. While reading aloud, Kim vigorously marked phrases and words about which she was uncertain.

Kim caught many of the syntactic and semantic errors she was making during the read-aloud section of our session, and this is, in part, why UMBC tutors use this method. However, what I was interested in seeing, as I made clear to her before she began reading, were places where she felt that her text (the object) was not accurately communicating what she meant (her motive for writing the text), thus resulting in an improper or ambiguous interpretation of what is written (the outcome). By having Kim find and highlight her perceived trouble areas—be it how to compose a research paper, the topic of healthy eating in the United States, why healthy eating is important, or her understanding of what Americans must do to achieve healthy eating— I could, in a sense, move backwards in Kim's writing process and see how the composition of text represented her unique ESL activity system; that is, I could help Kim to recognize not only the text (the object), which was to portray a certain message (the outcome), but also: herself (the subject) in relation to her text, her use of resources (mediating tools) to compose the text, what it meant to eat healthy (the rules), whom she was writing to (the community), and what power her own opinions held in her text (the division of labor). All of these components went into Kim's writing of her research paper, as well as the overwhelming uncertainties she had about them, which made her understandings of academic research (the official body of knowledge) unclear and which made her feel lost and confused in her own paper. Furthermore, Kim did not know her audience or where she fit into her research, which created a text that did not clearly connote her motives for writing.

I began using third space discourse practices by focusing first on the areas that Kim highlighted; most of them had to do with certain foods, eating habits, and health terminologies with which she was unfamiliar. For example, at one point during the read-aloud section of our session, Kim struggled saying words like "celery" and "obesity." When she was done reading, I went back to the text and pointed out that she had not highlighted the word celery and asked her if she knew what celery was. She did not until I drew a picture of a stalk of celery. She did not know many of the vegetables— from Brussels sprouts to stringbeans—she cited in many of her sources. I asked her, then, why she would include information in her paper that she was unfamiliar with, to which she replied, "For the research paper, this is important for American health." This got us into a discussion about what exactly she knew about American health issues. My intentions were to show Kim that, while she did not know or fully understand the official knowledge she was citing, she did in fact know more than she believed she did. By opening up a space for Kim to recognize herself and her unofficial knowledge of Korean eating habits, she could then draw this information into how she understands the official knowledge. In other words, by helping Kim to recognize herself in third space, she would be able to culturally bridge what she already knows is typical of her Korean heritage to the American academic information she doesn't fully understand.

Kim was in no way naive about the general concerns in American health, even though she did not know some of the terminology. She knew about the food pyramid, about McDonald's, about cholesterol, about heart disease, about what she called "people dying of eating fat," etc. These were also concerns that she grew up hearing about in Korea, though the foods, statistics, eating regimens, and suggestions for exercise were notably different, judging by what Kim told me. Her understanding of American health issues in eating habits was not fully American, as she acknowledged the problems to be similar but more extreme forms of the ones Koreans faced, and her understanding also was not based on the official academic information she had acquired in her research: Kim's understanding—as her paper certainly signified—was centered in a confusing tug-of-war between two cultural banks of knowledge regarding the issue. By highlighting the cultural contradictions she was feeling toward the issue of healthy eating habits, I was asking her to recognize herself as writing in third space, between the official academic American body of knowledge and the unofficial Korean body of knowledge.

To help Kim recognize her writing as being influenced by both American academic and Korean cultural motivations, and thus to recognize herself within third space, I used a scaffolding technique: I instructed Kim to write down, in three columns, what she felt the differences in eating habits were between first Americans, then Koreans, and lastly herself—a Korean living in American culture. In the section under Korean diet, she noted that most Koreans eat mainly vegetables, but as fast food chains are becoming more and more popular, there are increasing health issues. In the section under American diet, she noted that Americans eat mostly high-fat foods, "box foods" (processed foods), and fast food, which lead to unhealthy eating habits. In the section under her own eating habits, she noted that she eats a lot of Korean food (meaning foods like vegetables, fish, and tofu) but when she doesn't have time to get Korean food, she eats fast foods, which are unhealthy.

I then led her back into her text to a certain passage she cited and was unsure about regarding a healthy eating program. I asked first if she understood what the source was stating (which she did to some degree) and next if the healthy eating program applied to her and her diet (which it also did). In this instance, I am trying to show Kim that there are connections between the official research information she gathered and her own Korean-American identity that Kim may have overlooked when writing her text. This way, Kim can relate to the official information more so than when she first wrote her text; before, she saw the research as a generalization about the American population, a population within which she did not identify herself. By recognizing herself within the American population through her Korean identity, she could think more freely and connect ideas between herself and her research data. She was also then able to better understand the official community through understanding how her eating habits differed from and were similar to those of the general Americans represented in the statistics. Immediately, she reanalyzed how she was using her resources (the mediating tools) to create her text; for instance, in the section where she offered alternative eating habits, she asked me if she could use traditional Korean foods like kimchi in place of what she had previously written down—things that were foreign to her, like granola and beans. I replied that of course she could and stressed to her that, though she was writing a research paper for her teacher, she was ultimately the author of her piece.

The notion that Kim could incorporate her Korean diet information into her paper made thinking about the relevance of eating habits easier for her to understand. While there were still many words and terms that she did not know, she could understand the general ideas promoted in the official research sources and see where her background information could be useful in giving tips—for example, on what sorts of low-cholesterol foods people should eat and how foods should be prepared. Kim left the center feeling that she could synthesize in her paper her Korean knowledge with the official body of research on eating habits. In this sense, Kim is not only making learning from her research practical to her own life, but is also making room for Korean-Americans within her paper on American eating habits, thereby using third space to enhance her original research.

There was definitely a change in the way Kim looked at her research before our session and after it, and I argue that this change came from learning within her third space identity. While she still does not fully understand the academic health regimens included in her paper, she told me at the end of the session that she understands them much clearer now that she can see her relationship to them. Once she arrived at a clearer motive through recognition of herself within the activity she was to write about, her writing (the object) was less confusing and more informative (the outcome) to both her and others.

CONCLUSION

Third space tutoring does not always work, as I have come to realize. But the reason why is situated in how the writing center is viewed within the university: as a kind of fix-it shop or a place for last-minute proofreading before an assignment is due. Many of the instances where third space tutoring did not work in my experience were a result of differences in expectations between me and my tutee. Students, peer tutors included, need to understand that writing centers are meant to be places where tutees can work on process and not product, and this means that the university at large needs to stop thinking of writing centers as proofreading services. Writing centers have the ability—and, in my view, a very unique one—to change and shape academia. They can help the university to become more democratic by helping marginalized students to clearly communicate their meanings and contributions. This does not mean that tutors should help their tutees to structure their papers and does not mean that tutors should try to even interpret their tutees' papers. It means tutors should help tutees recognize what factors go into their writing and where they stand in the larger official structure of academia.

While the writing center is just one of many components in a complex university student support system, it definitely can be a very convenient tool for helping marginalized ESL students' voices to be heard. Compared to other components of academia, the writing center seems to be one of the most free places for ESL students to express their ideas without unwarranted scrutiny—that is, if their tutors let them. Walk-in writing centers, like the one I participate in, cannot fix all of a tutee's problems in one sitting, granted, but in one sitting, we can at least analyze, identify, and address problems in cultural misunderstandings and miscommunication that complicate and confuse the reader and writer alike. One way of addressing misunderstandings and miscommunications is by utilizing third space discourse practices. Third space tutoring means stepping out of the controlled and rationalistic environment of academic discourse and working on uncovering and making conscious the conflicting cultural bodies of knowledge that go into ESL students' writing processes. The writing center, then, can be something closer to what Stephen North envisioned: a place that truly does focus on process and not product. In a way, the writing center is a unique place for tutors and tutees alike to discover active, intellectual, and intercultural communication skills and ways of learning that, in time, have the ability to shape the university's body of knowledge into a democratic, multicultural, and multifaceted reality.

WORKS CITED

Bakhtin, Mikhail. "The Problem of Speech Genres." *Speech Genres and Other Late Essays.* Ed. C. Emerson and M. Holquist. Trans. V. W. McGee Austin: U of Texas P, 1986. 60–102. Print.

Cogie, Jane, Kim Strain, and Sharon Lorinskas. "Avoiding the Proofreading Trap: The Value of the Error Correction Process." *The Writing Center Journal* 19.2 (1999): 7–31. Print.

Engeström, Yrjö. *Learning by Expanding: An Activity-Theoretical Approach to Developmental Research.* Helsinki: Orienta-Konsultit, 1987. Web. 29 Feb. 2008

Flower, Linda. "Intercultural Knowledge Building: The Literate Action of a Community Think Tank." *Writing Selves/Writing Societies: Research from Activity Perspectives.* Ed. Charles Bazerman and David R. Russell. Fort Collins: WAC Clearinghouse, Colorado State University, 2003. 239–79. Web. 18 Apr. 2008

Gutiérrez, Kris, Patricia Baquedano-López, and Carlos Tejeda. "Rethinking Diversity: Hybridity and Hybrid Language Practices in Third Space." *Mind, Culture, and Activity* 6.4 (1999): 286–303. Print.

McCarthy, Lucille, and Stephen Fishman. "An ESL Writer and Her Discipline-Based Professor: Making Progress Even When Goals Don't Match." *Written Communication* 18.2 (2001): 180–228. Print.

Myers, Sharon A. "Reassessing the 'Proofreading Trap': ESL Tutoring and Writing Instruction." *The St. Martin's Sourcebook for Writing Tutors.* 3rd ed. Ed. Christina Murphy and Steve Sherwood. Boston: Bedford/St. Martin's, 2008. 219–36. Print.

North, Stephen. "The Idea of a Writing Center." *The St. Martin's Sourcebook for Writing Tutors.* 3rd ed. Ed. Christina Murphy and Steve Sherwood. Boston: Bedford/St. Martin's, 2008. 32–46. Print.

Vygotsky, Lev S. *Mind in Society: The Development of Higher Psychological Processes.* Cambridge: Harvard UP, 1978. Print.

Bridging the Gap: Essential Issues to Address in Recurring Writing Center Appointments with Chinese ELL Students

Frances Nan

Frances Nan was an undergraduate at Pomona College when she wrote this article. It originally appeared in *The Writing Center Journal*.

As the population of international—and particularly Chinese—students grows in U.S. academic institutions, it is critical that writing center tutors be able to address these students' needs. However, whereas writing tutors at my institution are often taught to be indirect and focus on higher order concerns, such strategies are not always practical for working with English Language Learners (ELL), who may have writing experiences different from those of native speakers or may have brought perceptions of tutor-tutee roles from their home countries. This essay therefore focuses on suggestions that tutors might consider bringing to their work with Chinese ELL students during "writing partner consultations," my institution's term for weekly, one-on-one meetings between a writer and the same writing tutor for the entirety of the semester. Effective writing partnerships are particularly useful when working with Chinese native writers, for they allow tutors and writers to focus on both individual papers and long-term improvement. By drawing upon a literature review and a study of two writing partner dyads over a semester, I conclude that the level of understanding, directness, and transparency between tutor and student affect the success of writing partnerships. By incorporating such suggestions into tutor training, I believe writing partnerships between tutors and ELL writers can improve.

The population of international students increases annually on U.S. college campuses, and Chinese international students comprise the largest group of international students (Inst. of Intl. Educ.). Based on my review of the literature, the training for leading one-on-one consultations at my institution—which prioritizes asking leading questions and "hedging"—may not be as effective for ELL consultations as with native speakers. By "hedging," I mean speech that "uses terms that soften the message such as *maybe, might, kind of, could possibly*," rather than direct speech in imperative forms: hedging would sound like, "You might want to make all your verbs past tense" rather than, "Put all verbs in the past tense" (Baker 76). Second, as a result of the language barrier, when working with non-native writers, tutors may feel more limited in what they say, how they say it, and even in their body language. Nevertheless, there are suggestions tutors can implement before and during the appointment to help ELL writers to feel comfortable and engaged, to understand what is going on, and to be motivated to continue revising post-consultation. At the same time that I want to add to our knowledge of these cross-cultural exchanges, I hope my attention to two individual pairings helps erase any blurred misconceptions and mutual misinformation among Chinese ELL writers and the writing center.

In the 2009–10 and 2010–11 school years, during which my study was conducted, new international student enrollment in undergraduate colleges nationwide increased 6.5 percent, from 79,365 to 84,543, continuing a general upward trend since 2004–05 (Inst. of Intl. Educ.). In 2009–11, China was also the leading place of origin for international students. The population of undergraduate Chinese international students increased 42.7 percent, from 39,921 to 56,976, while graduate student enrollment increased 15.6 percent, from 66,453 to 76,830 (Inst. of Intl. Educ.). While previous articles are ambiguous about the exact number of ELL students who visit writing centers (see, for example, Griffin et al. 16), the increasing population of international, ELL students reflects a forthcoming study's conclusion that at least at one large public, one medium private, and one small liberal arts college, writing centers "see more ELL students than their campus demographics would suggest" (Bromley et al.).[1] To best help and remain relevant to the needs of this expanding group, it is important to learn to address the expectations and challenges ELL student writers face compared to native speakers.

For context, this study took place at a highly selective liberal arts college. On our campus, the peer tutoring writing center is the sole support center for ELL writers. During the 1,189 appointments in the 2010–11 school year, all writers were asked to complete an evaluation of the writing center and 28 percent (n=330) did so. Of the writers that completed the survey, 15 percent reported that English is *not* their first language, while 19 percent reported that English is one of their first languages. I interviewed the tutors and freshman Chinese ELL writers in two of the eleven writing partnerships during the fall semester, seven of which were with freshmen and three of which were with Chinese ELL students. Based on these demographics, it is clear that freshmen and Chinese students make up a large part of our institution's writing partnerships.

In this essay, I combine existing theory and research with my individual interviews to arrive at specific, useful advice about comportment and interaction. First, I address issues that tutors should be aware of prior to consultations and offer suggestions about how to run their initial consultations in order to present these issues openly. Then I describe what tutors and writers might address in their partnerships and methods of follow up and evaluation.

KEY CONSIDERATIONS FOR TUTORS
TO ADDRESS WITH CHINESE WRITERS

Before their first consultations, tutors can better prepare by exploring the cultural differences between themselves and the writers with whom they work and by considering how these differences affect their writing consultations.

Writing Experience

In general, Chinese international students arrive at college from high schools with very different standards of writing (Scordaras 190). The two Chinese ELL writers that I interviewed said they arrived at college with little knowledge of American writing, and their peers probably "have similar high school experiences" (Zhu, 28 Sept.). One writer received his only introduction to writing in English through preparing for standardized tests such as the TOEFL and SAT (Zhang, 5 Oct.). While the latter demands five-paragraph essays, the TOEFL asks for a paragraph of 500 to 600 words maximum (Zhang, 5 Oct.) in response to sample prompts such as, "Would you agree/disagree that parents are the best teachers?" or "Would you agree/disagree that television has destroyed communication among friends and family?" and to be written in 30 minutes (Educational Testing Service).

As Myers writes, Chinese ELL students "may have 'studied' English . . . in their home countries, but that 'study' may have consisted of rote memorization of isolated words in vocabulary lists and 'grammar' tests" (287). In the words of an ELL writer, English classes in Chinese high schools are "so easy" (Zhang, 5 Oct.), and "grammar practices [were] multiple choice questions [that were] pretty easy" (Zhu, 28 Sept.). A typical writing prompt would read something like, "Write a letter to your friend in the United States describing how you feel about your courses this semester," with a 200-word maximum (Zhang, 5 Oct.). In the U.S., such prompts would be found in a first semester university-level foreign language course. Therefore, there is an obvious lack of preparation among many ELL students when it comes to composing the argumentative, highly analytical essays that their college courses demand.

In addition to struggling with academic assignments in American universities, Chinese ELL writers may be unfamiliar with negotiating the difference between the Chinese and U.S. structure and style of argumentation. In terms of content, an essay in Chinese may have many or no arguments: one Chinese writer described how prompts in China asked him to analyze a metaphor, and the teacher expected his essay to interpret the poem from different angles, such as how the poet wrote the poem or how the metaphor can be applied to life. Graders in China are more concerned with the beauty of a student's language—his or her ability to "employ some flowery words to make [the writing] fancy"—and his or her ability to demonstrate extensive knowledge about Chinese literature and culture (Zhu, 28 Sept.). Thus, citing "a lot of ancient poems [would] give you a lot of advantage" in a Chinese classroom (Zhang, 5 Oct.). One tutor observed that, for his writing partner, forming an argument that "goes a step further" than what he had read in class "was a really new concept for him [in contrast to China, where teachers] ask you to play within the boundaries [of] what's already in the canon" (Demski, 2 Dec.). In China, there is obviously more of an emphasis on synthesizing other authors' works, compared to the U.S. focus on making unique arguments.

The U.S. writing style emphasizes a strict point-evidence-explain structure, as well as original thinking and creative engagement with multiple academic sources. In contrast, Chinese essay writers do not state their thesis until the end so that readers realize the author's intention themselves (Zhang, 5 Oct.). Minett, paraphrasing Hinds, writes, English writing is "reader friendly in its directness and clarity" (68). Chinese writing, like the Japanese style that Minett and Hinds discuss, can be described as *"writer* friendly [since] it's mainly the reader's job to determine the writer's intention" and to "anticipate with pleasure the opportunities that such writing offers them" (Hinds qtd. in Minett 68). The rationale behind the Chinese method of writing is best described as a "spiral"—one likes to "talk around" a point before arriving at the "center" (i.e., one's thesis). Consequently, writers put their thesis at the end of a paragraph or paper (Zhu, "The Article"). For example, whereas a sentence in English may state outright that "soccer is a difficult sport" and then describe reasons why, in Chinese, the descriptions would come before the conclusion that soccer is difficult ("英汉表达差异"). ELL students' contrastive rhetoric, namely "the ways that cultures differ in their expectations about rhetorical patterns or logical organization of a text," may heavily influence how ELL students write in English (Hayward qtd. in Bruce 228). Thus, they may be unprepared for the U.S. focus on innovative arguments in a direct writing style.

Perceptions of Tutor-Tutee Roles

Chinese ELL writers may misunderstand how much authority their tutors have; many come from diverse cultures with "rules of speaking that may conflict with those of U.S. classrooms, [which influences] the students' perceptions of their and their teachers' roles in a conference" (Goldstein and Conrad 456). Such students may have preconceived notions about how to approach conferences with someone seen as an authority (Goldstein and Conrad 457). For instance, students may be accustomed to dynamics wherein the teacher initiates and questions (Goldstein and Conrad 456), and the student responds or is not allowed to ask questions. If a student believes she or he cannot or should not argue with the tutor, he or she may feel uncomfortable questioning suggested revisions, which could lead to further misunderstanding.

SUGGESTIONS FOR IMPROVING ELL WRITING PARTNERSHIPS

Tutors themselves must have a meta-awareness of their consultation style to be able to work effectively with ELL writers. Like teachers, tutors must be aware that their (mis)informed assumptions about a writer's ability may influence how the conference is run. Once tutors observe writers' behaviors, and subconsciously behave "in ways consistent with [their] expectations" (Goldstein and Conrad 456), they may accept less participation from these writers from the beginning of their writing partnership, without allowing writers to showcase just how active they could be. Second, a tutor should not be "blinded by the [tutor's] own conference objectives . . . regardless of the [writer's] reactions" (Han 259). In other words, sometimes tutors may be so concerned about improving their partner's paper that they forget that it is their partner's paper, not their own.

ELL writers must understand the slow process that writing partnerships may take and that tutors as well as ELL writers themselves should prioritize higher order concerns, rather than focusing on those lower order concerns for which professors may penalize them more heavily. Some tutors tell their partners from the beginning that their partnership will be a long-term progression, wherein they may not be able to immediately fix everything in every essay (Goldman, 29 Sept.). In order to keep one's position credible, the tutor should be clear that, whereas the writer's professor will be grading the essay compared to the writer's peers, the tutor will focus solely on helping the writer develop.

Assess Where the Writer Is Now

A tutor attempting to develop a course of action for a semester-long writing partnership should set aside the task of examining individual papers and instead ask the writer how much he or she knows about U.S. academic writing. Rather than sermonizing *at* the writer on the difference between U.S. and Chinese writing styles, the tutor should gauge the writer's level of knowledge by transforming the session into a collaborative, questioning one: "What do *you* think a thesis statement is in college writing?" As one tutor noted, tutors must understand that they may have to begin "from the foundations [or] spend the first month going through, 'What is a paper in a U.S. college? What are they asking for? What are the different pieces of a paper? And here's why [U.S. professors expect] you to do these things'" (Demski, 2 Dec.). In this way, tutors can assess their writing partner's background in writing.

Be Direct

Tutors must be direct in order for ELL writers to realize that they too can shape the consultation. Tutors in my writing center are taught that indirectness—e.g., asking leading questions, allowing writers to say what they think rather than tutors thinking for them—will help writers learn better because it allows them to learn from their own mistakes. However, for ELL writers, more initial direction may be necessary. Tutors, like teachers, should "suspend politeness (indirect speech acts and hedging) in favor of clarity (direct speech acts) when working with non-native speakers of English" (Baker 77).

Tutors must be prepared to first make direct changes for writers while modeling specific examples before expecting them to flourish under the usual indirection. ELL writers "need to get a sense of what such texts look like and 'sound' like" (Myers 298), since they are often less familiar than native writers with what is expected. One tutor found when he was "very generous with examples," his writing partner could "hear archetypes, such as how to use words like 'however,' 'in addition,' or 'by contrast'" (Goldman, 30 Nov.). Similarly, an ELL writer was adamant that tutors should be direct rather than indirect: he seemed confused to hear that tutors expected writers to know what to correct without being told. When I posited the fear in existing literature that writers would become too dependent on tutors to point out their errors, he shook his head and said, "Still you should point out, and then correct it, and then next time I'll know what word to use. . . . Because, *I don't know,* I actually don't know, so I wouldn't come up with an idea" (Zhang, 4 Dec.). As Myers writes, "if [ELL writers] don't have the appropriate word or lexical phrase, no editing will provide it" (291). Therefore, tutors should feel comfortable taking a more direct approach with ELL writing partners.

Be Transparent

At the same time, transparency is still important: ELL writers must know what to expect of the writing consultation dynamic. With explicit direction, tutors must also include their reasons. Instead of beating around the bush, tutors should, depending on their assessment of an individual writer's reaction, be honest. As one tutor described, a tutor should remember that, "a sentence is never just 'bad,' it's 'bad because'" (Goldman, 29 Sept.). Han suggests that transparency from the tutor will encourage the ELL writer to direct the consultation by increasing the writer's "metacognitive awareness" about consultation strategies (Han 258). Tutors need to show ELL writers that tutors are certainly not perfect when it comes to giving suggestions or running consultations and that writers are encouraged to make suggestions or queries.

Notice Body Language

Transparency is also necessary in the tutor's body language during a consultation (Belhiah). Because there may be more of a language barrier with ELL writers, they are much more likely to pick up on a tutor's body language or tone of voice as a substitute for listening to a tutor's words. They will be able to tell when a tutor is merely being polite or when she or he is consciously trying to speak slowly. Rather than sugarcoat anything, a tutor must be honest and clear; asking, "Do you need me to repeat what I just said?" is better than assuming the writer does not understand unless spoken to slowly, or telling the writer that his or her English is better than it is. A lack of transparency from either tutor or writer can lead to negative results. For instance, when I met with an ELL writer who was a little difficult to read in terms of body language, I was unsure if he valued my suggestions or would follow up on them afterwards. In my reflection on the consultation, I noted my increasing uncertainty about giving the writer suggestions, since I could not tell if I was offending him. Tutors can encourage writers to speak and be engaged in the consultation by asking direct, specific questions that writers can answer in order to combat their possibly quiet or seemingly standoffish nature.

Engage in Meta-talk

One way to make writers comfortable asking questions of the tutor and even begin to direct the consultation is to make them comfortable speaking in the first place, through chitchat and "meta-talk." De Guerrero and Villamil suggest that "about-task" and "off-task" discourse episodes (i.e., conversations) may encourage writers to feel more comfortable soliciting peer feedback in the writing center (492). Hyland notes that the Chinese students in her writing workshop were "generally more formal and serious in their approach," making suggested revisions efficiently, quietly, and intensely but without realizing that two-way dialogues about their papers could help them improve as writers (290). One ELL writer "[prefers] small talk so [the tutor will] get to know [her] better personally" and be able to catch undesirable stylistic habits, such as using "a lot of colloquial words in writing, [using] simple expressions, [or if the writer quotes] something that's not [her] style [without] the quotation there, [the tutor can] point it out" (Zhu, 28 Sept.). If ELL writers are encouraged to talk about themselves, a topic they may feel knowledgeable and comfortable speaking about, they may speak up when they have things to say about the consultation itself.

Tutors should also keep in mind that some ELL writers need time to respond to questions because they must translate what tutors said into their native languages, think of an answer in their native languages, and then translate any responses into English. A tutor should therefore wait two extra beats for the writer to ruminate, and instead of immediately rephrasing following a pause, she should ask if the writer wants the tutor to rephrase or to give her more time. Tutors can even ask "permission to move on" by asking writers, "Are you ready to continue? Was there anything you did not understand that we should return to?" (Wong and Waring 200).

Evaluate

During the consultation, a tutor must evaluate the ELL writer's comprehension and ensure she understands the suggestions by asking the writer to demonstrate understanding. For example, a tutor can ask a writer to note-take—if that is how the individual learns best—and keep an eye on whether the notes mirror the tutor's suggestions, or ask the writer to repeat tasks back that are in her own words, or simply ask for the writer's input regarding the revisions. Likewise, a tutor can problematize a correct answer by asking, "Are you sure?" or "Why did you write it like this?" (Goldman, 29 Sept.). Alternatively, tutors can ask "pursuit questions," such as, "Why do you say that? How did you arrive at that? Can you explain so that I can be sure you understand?",) while always remembering to justify their evaluative questions (Wong and Waring 200). By evaluating whether the writer understands given suggestions, a tutor can avoid merely talking *at* the writer. Solicitation of writer input should occur throughout the semester to ensure that the writer comprehends the tutor's suggestions for revision. Further, in order to better evaluate whether or not their consultations are helpful, tutors can follow up in some form, such as revisiting graded final drafts with the professors' comments.

CONCLUSION

From the beginning of their writing partnership, it is essential that both tutors and their writers know what to expect. On the tutor side, being aware of ELL writers' pre-collegiate writing backgrounds can help tutors remember solutions for additional concerns apart from a general focus on the U.S. mode of writing, with its emphasis on higher order concerns, a linear structure, and argumentation. Tutors must be explicit with the ELL writer about the plan of action for the semester—that they will focus more on higher order concerns, such as structure and style, before tackling lower order issues such as spelling or grammar, and that improvement may not come immediately. A tutor should also use the first meeting as an opportunity to establish rapport with and trust in his or her ability and authority with the writer, to find out what the writer's goals for the writing partnership are, and understand the writer's background with writing. On the writer's side, the first meeting is important for ensuring he or she is aware of several things. She must know that she has the power to direct consultations and that improvement will not magically come about, but that the tutor is willing to put in a certain amount of time.

The implications of this piece depend on a writing center's institutional context. Whether a writing center is the sole form of support for ELL students on campus affects whether tutors must also choose to pay attention to grammar or proofreading, in addition to higher order concerns. But for the many writing centers that serve as the primary resource for ELL students, implementing a system of writing partnerships can help serve these writers better. Training tutors about the meta-issues surrounding consultations with ELL writers can be the first step toward awareness and understanding. For instance, if new writing tutors all take a pedagogy and theory course or have mandatory staff meetings, reading this article might be a first step in addressing these issues. By beginning where the writer is beginning and by conducting writing partnership appointments in a direct, transparent, evaluative, and self-aware manner, the tutor can eventually reach an equilibrium point that will enable writers to drive the consultation as well. Through mutual understanding and engagement, both writer and tutor can help the former to improve throughout the semester.

ACKNOWLEDGEMENTS

Many thanks to the tutors, Alex Goldman and Neil Demski, and writers, Shiwei Zhang and Ruiyi Zhu, who explicitly granted me permission to interview them and use their quotes. (One of their names has been changed in the text.) I am even more grateful to my advisor, Professor Pam Bromley, who gave invaluable, patient feedback and encouragement on numerous drafts of this article.

NOTE

1. Since the original publication of this essay, the cited study has been published. [Editors' Note]

WORKS CITED

Baker, Wendy, and Rachel Hansen Bricker. "The Effects of Direct and Indirect Speech Acts on Native English and ESL Speakers' Perception of Teacher Written Feedback." *System* 38.1 (2010): 75–84. *Science Direct Subject Collations.* Web. 27 May 2010.

Belhiah, Hassan. "Tutoring as an Embodied Activity: How Speech, Gaze and Body Orientation Are Coordinated to Conduct ESL Tutorial Business." *Journal of Pragmatics* 41 (2009): 829–41. Web. 27 May 2010.

Bromley, Pam, Kara Northway, and Eliana Schonberg. "How Important Is the Local, Really?: Cross-Institutional Quantitative Assessment of Typical Writing Center Exist Surveys." *The Writing Center Journal* 33.1 (2013): 13–37.

Bruce, Shanti. "Listening to and Learning from ESL Writers." Bruce and Rafoth 216–29.

Bruce, Shanti, and Ben Rafoth, eds. *ESL Writers: A Guide for Writing Center Tutors.* 2nd ed. Portsmouth, NH: Boynton/Cook, 2009. Print.

De Guerrero, Maria C.M., and Olga S. Villamil. "Social-Cognitive Dimensions of Interaction in L2 Peer Revision." *Modern Language Journal* 78.4 (1994): 484–96. Web. 22 May 2012.

Demski, Neil. Personal Interview. 2 Dec. 2010.

Educational Testing Service. "Sample Writing Topics." *TOEFL PBT Test Preparation.* Web. 26 March 2012.

Goldman, Alex. Personal Interview. 29 Sept. 2010.

———. Personal Interview. 30 Nov. 2010.

Goldstein, Lynn M., and Susan M. Conrad. "Student Input and Negotiation of Meaning in ESL Writing Conferences." *TESOL Quarterly* 24.3 (1990): 443–60. Web. 27 May 2010.

Griffin, Jo Ann, Daniel Keller, Iswari Pandey, Anne-Marie Pedersen, and Carolyn Skinner. "Local Practices, Institutional Positions: Results from the 2003–2004 WCRP National Survey of Writing Centers." *Writing Center Research Project,* U of Louisville, 2005. Web. 25 Nov. 2011.

Han, Ai Guo. "A Qualitative Study of ESL Student Perceptions of Student-Teacher Writing Conferences." Diss. Indiana U of Pennsylvania, 1996. *ProQuest Dissertations and Theses.* Web. 14 June 2010.

Hyland, Fiona. "Teacher Management of Writing Workshops: Two Case Studies." *Canadian Modern Language Review* Vol. 57, No. 2 (2000): 272–94. Web. 27 May 2010.

Institute of International Education. "International Students by Academic Level and Place of Origin, 2010/11." *Open Doors Report on International Educational Exchange.* Web. 25 Nov. 2011.

Minett, Amy Jo. "'Earth Aches by Midnight': Helping ESL Writers Clarify Their Intended Meaning." Bruce and Rafoth 66–77.

Myers, Sharon A. "Reassessing the 'Proofreading Trap': ESL Tutoring and Writing Instruction." *The St. Martin's Sourcebook for Writing Tutors.* 4th ed. Ed. Christina Murphy and Steven Sherwood. Boston: Bedford/St. Martin's, 2011. 284–302. Print.

Scordaras, Maria. "English Language Learners' Revision Process in an Intensive College Composition Class." Diss. New York U., 2003. Web. *ProQuest Dissertations and Theses.* 14 June 2010.

Wong, Jean, and Hansun Zhang Waring. "'Very Good' as a Teacher Response." *ELT Journal* 63.3 (2009): 195–203. Web. 27 May 2010.

Zhang, Shiwei. Personal Interview. 5 Oct. 2010.

———. Personal Interview. 4 Dec. 2010.

Zhu, Ruiyi. Personal Interview. 28 Sept. 2010.

———. "The Article on Difference of English & Chinese." Message to the author. 4 Oct. 2010. E-mail.

英汉表达差异——英语写作中的拦路虎. Differences between English-Chinese modes of Expression/Communication—Shortcuts in English Language Composition]." 4Ewriting.com, 26 May 2003. Web. 6 Oct. 2010.

Got Guilt? Consultant Guilt
in the Writing Center Community

Jennifer Nicklay

Jennifer Nicklay was an undergraduate at the University of Minnesota–Twin Cities when she wrote this article. It originally appeared in *The Writing Center Journal*.

Staff meetings, classrooms, newsletter, and journals are filled with tales of individual and collective actualization, celebrating one-to-one teaching as deeply social, collaborative, and empowering.—Harry Denny (39)

In my experience as a writing consultant, the writing center atmosphere Denny describes, and the collaboration it cultivates, results in a close community of consultants, staff, and students. Within this community, consultants and students alike collaborate and share their diverse knowledge, personalities, and words with each other, yet each individual student is looking for something a little different when she comes to us, and each has a different way of learning. This belief in the power of individuals and one-on-one learning suggests the importance of flexibility within collaboration. With a student re-organizing her paper, I might have her draw me a flow chart to visualize her ideas, or I might demonstrate how to do a reverse outline. During brainstorming sessions, I might write down the student's stream of consciousness responses to my questions, or we might search for YouTube videos related to her topic. We can read aloud, or I can watch as a student writes. The strategies are endless, and my ability to adjust to the needs of individual students—as well as our collective needs during the session—is one of the most important aspects of my job as a consultant.

While I relished my flexibility during consultations, I discovered during my consultant training course that it can also complicate consultations—that, as Denny found, flexibility and collaboration are complicated by outside forces. During our class discussions, my fellow consultants would often lament consultations that could have gone better if they had only known the "rules" of how to handle the situation. They perceived that there were acceptable and unacceptable ways to approach certain situations, rather than a range of flexible choices. I began to wonder, then, what are these "rules" that infiltrated what I saw as the flexibility and collaborative spirit of the writing center?

Following this inquiry, I explored the current discourse in writing center literature about flexibility and collaboration, with particular focus on two foundational texts—"The Idea of a Writing Center" by Stephen North and "Minimalist Tutoring: Making the Student Do All the Work" by Jeff Brooks—and critiques of them as well. I then questioned my fellow consultants about when and why they felt guilt following consultations. The pattern I discovered, within a small sample of eleven consultants, revealed that guilt originates in how the writing center community is situated within the larger university and how an individual writing center community is structured. These findings, while disconcerting, help highlight areas in which writing centers can better support their consultants through training and conversations to encourage flexibility, cultivate collaboration, and maintain the health of the writing center community.

LITERATURE REVIEW

I started by first exploring the literature of my own writing center community at a large research university; what are the "guidelines" or "rules" in this center? Before consultants receive any training, before any theory is read, the consultants interact with the center itself, where the guiding philosophy is that the writing center "helps you become a better writer. Through collaboration between the student and the consultant, we help you develop confidence and good writing habits. . . . [and] what you learn applies to all of your writing" (Student). According to this statement, consultants have a flexible framework in which to develop their own consulting style, principles, and methods. No limits are set, so it follows that consultants should not feel guilt for choosing the strategies they see fit in a consultation.

With this in mind, I looked beyond the flexible framework articulated in my own center's promotional materials to the discourse in the wider writing center community for "rules" which might stymie flexibility and collaboration. Susan Blau and John Hall note that although "flexibility has always been the hallmark of writing center work . . . it seems that certain 'guidelines' have become 'rules'" (43). As a result of hardening expectations, Blau and Hall found consultants in their center felt guilty for stepping outside the "rules," perceiving that they crossed from acceptable to unacceptable during consultations. To better understand what expectations might form, I turned my attention to two seminal texts about writing center methods discussed at length in our class: North's "The Idea of a Writing Center" and Brooks's "Minimalist Tutoring: Making the Student Do All the Work."

North's "Idea" is so prevalent in writing center scholarship that Elizabeth Boquet and Neal Lerner highlight "the ways in which one scholar—or, perhaps more to the point, one article or even one line—can come to define a field" ("Reconsiderations" 172). They reached this conclusion by analyzing citations in the 195 articles printed in *The Writing Center Journal* between 1985 and 2008. Boquet and Lerner found that North's "Idea" was cited in sixty-four articles, fifty of which cited North's statement that "in a writing center the object is to make sure that writers, and not necessarily their texts, are what get changed by instruction" ("Reconsiderations" 177; North 38). This idea of focusing on writers, rather than their work, has permeated nearly every theory, ideology, strategy, or technique introduced and discussed within the writing center community, and, as a result, impacted individual writing centers.

As with my own writing center's promotional materials, however, North proposes a broad framework—no particular methods are indicated as preferable. Indeed, North strongly advocates for consulting to consist of "talk in all its forms" in order to best fit the writer and her needs:

> We can question, praise, cajole, criticize, acknowledge, badger, plead—even cry. We can read: silently, aloud, together, separately. We can play with options. We can both write . . . and compare opening strategies. We can poke around in resources. . . . We can ask writers to compose aloud while we listen, or we can compose aloud, and the writer can watch and listen. (43)

North clearly argues for flexibility in collaboration, thus avoiding the establishment of "rules." Despite this, though, his one assertion that the writer (and not necessarily the writing itself) should be changed has come to be associated with minimalist tutoring in much of the literature—which does proscribe "rules" for consultants. Arguably, this association came to be because North's "Idea" is often read through the lens of Brooks' minimalist consulting method.

Brooks' articulation of strategies that enact North's oft-cited focus on the writer struck a "proverbial chord" in writing centers because it seemed to provide a practical way to implement North's lofty goals (Lerner and Boquet 4). However, when North's philosophy is read from the perspective of Brooks' minimalism, the realm of acceptable strategies is narrowed significantly. Suddenly, as a consultant, I am faced with reconciling the very open philosophy North espouses, in which I can choose many strategies, with the four, much more limited, steps Brooks advocates, which include sitting beside the student, having the student closer to the paper, not writing on the paper, and having the student read the paper aloud. Brooks argues that "if you follow these four steps, even if you do nothing else, you will have served the student better than you would if you 'edited' his paper" (171). Thus, consultants are given concrete ways to enact North's goal to change the writer. Minimalist methods also fit well within the writing center's focus on collaboration because, as Blau and Hall elaborate, they are "grounded in collaborative learning theory, assuming that in an ideal collaborative session, the tutor and client build knowledge together, sharing power and insight" (32). As a result, a consultant stepping outside of these strategies could be perceived as straying from North's goal as well as the principles of collaboration. We can now see how minimalist guidelines can become "rules" of engagement in a consulting session.

Adopting "rules" of using minimalist strategies into one's consulting practice, though, is complicated because the "ideal collaborative session" (Blau and Hall 32), upon which the connection between minimalism and collaboration depends, only rarely occurs. Often, the "ideal" session is undermined because power between consultants and students is not equal, whether this is because of differing education levels, backgrounds, disciplines, or all the other factors that can impact our consulting practice. Minimalism attempts to empower students in this situation by guiding them to discover the answer themselves, which is often an invaluable learning strategy. But in a situation where power is not shared equally, it is possible that using minimalist methods to communicate writing conventions and discourse could instead reinforce the idea that, in the words of Boquet, "there is a body of knowledge 'out there' that some people (like me) have access to and other people (like them) do not" (119). This perception may or may not be true in actuality; a consultant's use of minimalism does not necessarily indicate that she possesses such knowledge or, if she does, that she is withholding it from the student. However, if the student perceives that the consultant is withholding knowledge in her use of minimalism, collaborative goals can be undermined.

The options to address this student perception are limited if minimalism has been adopted as a set of "rules" in one's consulting practice because, as Linda Shamoon and Deborah Burns argue, an adherence to minimalism can limit consultants' scope of imagination regarding writing center consulting strategies (174–75). For example, when power is not shared equally, directive methods may serve the students better because the work of both the consultant and the student would be placed on the table in an effort to, in North's words, "begin from where the student is, and move where the student moves" (39). In this environment of sharing and demonstrating, Shamoon and Burns argue, "The social nature of directive and emulative tutoring serves to endorse the student's worth as an emerging professional" as she gains the skills necessary to communicate her ideas effectively (184). Which kind of authority the consultant adopts in this situation—using minimalist, directive, or a combination of both strategies—should depend on the needs of the individual student, not on adoption of one strategy or another as a "rule."

As consultants try to support writers, then, it is clear from the discussion of North, Shamoon and Burns, and Boquet that both directive and minimalist methods will be an integral part of our repertoire, depending upon the situation and student. Even without this deeper reading of writing center literature, this need for flexible methods is communicated in recent consulting handbooks. For example, the consultant training course I took used *The St. Martin's Sourcebook for Writing Tutors,* in which Murphy and Sherwood encourage an expansive consulting repertoire when they write, "If there is any one truth about tutoring, it is that no single method of tutoring, no one approach, will work effectively with every student in every situation" (1).

Frameworks that encourage flexibility in collaboration are, therefore, clearly present in writing center literature. In light of this, in the rest of this article, I explore how flexibility in scholarship becomes "rules" and guilt in actuality. What is at the root of consultant guilt? How do individual tutoring principles and methods interact with feelings of guilt? And, perhaps most importantly, how does this guilt relate to other consultants, students, and the writing center itself?

METHODS

In order to elicit information about what prompts consultants to feel guilt, I distributed a survey to fifty writing consultants, including faculty and graduate and undergraduate students. Participants were provided with a consent form, and responses were immediately de-identified. The survey consisted of six demographic and three short answer questions. The goal of the short answer questions (Figure 1) was to elicit how consultants perceived the theory and principles that they utilized to structure

1) What are some important principles and/or theories which guide your consulting practices within the subject of writing?
2) Consulting Methods:
   a. What are some writing consulting methods you use as a result of these principles? Some questions for thought, though you are not limited to answering these, include:

   How do you start a session? How do you choose what to focus on? How do you communicate with the student? Where do you place yourself in relation to the student? Where is the paper in relation to you and the student, and who writes on it?

   b. Do you utilize minimalist and/or non-directive tutoring methods (i.e., using Socratic questioning, writing on the paper very little, etc.)? In which situations have you found minimalist tutoring to be most effective?
   c. Do you utilize directive tutoring methods (i.e., providing wording, grammar, examples, ideas, etc.)? In which situations have you found directive tutoring to be most effective?
3) Have you ever used methods which you feel do not represent your principles? Have you ever felt guilt as a result of doing so? What factors led to this decision, and why did you feel guilt?

Figure 1 Consultant Guilt Survey Short Answer Questions.

sessions, methods used as a result, and when the consultants felt guilt. For the purpose of the survey, several definitions were provided to respondents:

- "Theory": principles and methods supported by writing center literature
- "Principles": tenants upon which consultants based their consulting decisions
- "Methods": how consultants enacted their theories and principles in individual sessions

This structure for analyzing consultant approaches to sessions was based upon the methods developed by Jenna Krause, a former writing center consultant at the University of Minnesota–Twin Cities (3). During analysis, principles, theories, and methods used were compared to the situations in which consultants felt guilty to highlight correlations, contradictions, and trends in answers among consultants.

RESULTS

Eleven consultants from the writing center responded to the distributed survey. Within this sample, there was a great deal of similarity in the principles that guided individual consultants (see question 1, above). Many consultants referenced several principles in their answers, though only consultant eight directly stated that "one single theory wouldn't be able to provide a useful set of guidelines for every consultation." Five consultants specifically cited collaboration as a main principle that structured their sessions (unsurprising given its prominent role in our writing center's philosophy). Each consultant, though, had a slightly different perspective on why collaboration was important, with responses specifying that it created a positive dialogue, placed the student as the expert on his writing, promoted student ownership of the writing, and cultivated the relationship between consultant and student as fellow writers. With collaboration as a guiding principle, nine consultants indicated a session was structured around both the goals the student presented at the beginning of the session and their concerns as consultants (question 2a). This process was best characterized by Consultant 3: "After the student has identified his/her concerns, I read through the paper and mentally keep track of my own concerns. For the rest of the session, we discuss our concerns together."

Within this framework, the consultants also explained their use of minimalist and directive methods (questions 2b and 2c). The most important trend was that all consultants felt there were situations in which minimalist methods could be utilized well (such as in brainstorming sessions, addressing focus, and thesis statement discussions) and, likewise, there were situations in which directive methods were more appropriate (such as during later stages of the paper, when modeling outlining and grammar). It was this inquiry into minimalism and directivity that revealed the most acute feelings of guilt.

In response to why and when consultants felt guilt (question 3), ten of the eleven respondents discussed directive methods. In fact, while the final question itself did not mention directive methods, five of the respondents answered the question as if it had asked, "Do you feel guilt for being directive?" For example, Consultant 5 (the only faculty respondent) stated that "I think being directive is warranted in some situations, so I do not feel guilty about it. . . . To withhold information would not be fair . . . where else can they go to get this information?" The other nine respondents all indicated that being overly directive, particularly in grammar-focused sessions, was the main cause of their feelings of guilt. Of those who valued collaboration as their main principle, three felt guilt as a result of being overly directive and three as a result of giving too many answers—or, in the words of Consultant 11, "I worry . . . I spoon-fed them excessively."

Within the responses addressing guilt and directivity, there were three particularly surprising answers from undergraduate consultants. Consultant 1 wrote, "Sometimes I let my mouth run off and a few minutes go by before I realize I've been exclusively running the session. This makes me very self-conscious and I immediately wonder whether my colleagues were able to hear me enjoying the sound of my own voice." This consultant expressed the fear of being judged by other consultants but diffused this worry with humor. The two other responses, however, revealed no such relief for the anxiety experienced. Consultant 8 articulated that, "I feel especially guilty when those methods were directive and go against writing center dogma"—a statement made all the more intriguing because this same consultant espoused that she followed "no single theory." The sentiment of her statement was echoed by Consultant 10: "I felt guilty, largely because I feel I broke some sort of 'code' and my co-workers would be ashamed of me." In these final two responses, it is notable that both refer to writing center "rules" and "dogma" as reasons why they experienced feelings of shame and guilt.

DISCUSSION

Consultants indicated that they most often felt guilt for being directive in sessions focused upon lower order concerns, but all also indicated, when queried about their methods, that directivity was an appropriate method to use in those very same sessions. In other words, consultants felt guilt for using a method they realized was appropriate. One reason for this might be that those consultants who felt guilt for being directive were also those who valued collaboration. These individuals likely view collaboration as a meeting of equals, of peers, to work together in order to improve the writer and the writing; this was indicated by the prevalence of responses which indicated consultants viewed themselves as allies and fellow writers and worked to establish a relaxed, peer dynamic. With this interpretation of collaboration, a feeling of guilt is understandable; if a directive method is utilized, it suggests that the consultant is taking the role of an expert, which in turn can undermine the collaboration.

This view of collaboration, as previously discussed, is a very limited view. It is a view predicated on Brooks' contention that, "the student, not the tutor, should 'own' the paper and take full responsibility for it" (169), which, as illustrated earlier by Shamoon and Burns, limits our imagination concerning what collaboration can be. To understand this phenomenon, though, we need to look beyond minimalism in our practice to the position of the writing center within the educational institution—and particularly at the academic definition of ownership.

In academia, individual ownership of ideas and writing is considered of utmost importance (Lunsford 52), and it is a norm which is embodied in Brooks' view of student ownership. As Clark and Healy argue, "Such a philosophy [of minimalist tutoring] perpetuates a limited and limiting understanding of authorship in the academy. By privileging individual responsibility and accountability and by valorizing the individual writer's authentic 'voice,' the writing center has left unchallenged notions of intellectual property" (36). Nancy Grimm builds on this idea, arguing that perpetuation of minimalist collaboration serves only to protect the privileged place of consultants within the educational system, as the consultants have obviously succeeded within academia by conforming to the established ideas of ownership and individual authorship (114–15). If knowledge is viewed as individually held and obtained, it is very difficult to be open to the idea of knowledge gained within the social interaction of consultant–student sessions (Lunsford 48). In using directive strategies, therefore, it is understandable that consultants would feel guilt because they are stepping outside the expectations of the academic institution. In doing so, consultants may be attempting (even unconsciously) to help students gain membership in the academic institution, but they are violating the very norms upon which their own success in academia was predicated.

To a certain extent, this form of guilt, stemming from ideals of authorship and ownership that are engrained in our academic lives, is very difficult to overcome. Nonetheless, it is my belief that it is possible for individual writing centers to enact collaboration if our community, both as a profession and in individual centers, is strong. Nurturing such a community will involve close attention to how writing center philosophies are communicated, how interpersonal relationships in individual centers are developed, and how guilt is processed by consultants individually and in group settings.

In explaining when they experienced feelings of guilt, two consultants specifically referenced transgressions of writing center philosophy by using directive methods. Using the terms "dogma" and "code," these consultants articulated that they felt that using directive methods went against the philosophies espoused by the writing center profession. Perhaps, as Joan Hawthorne suggests, part of the reason for this view of directive methods is that consulting manuals often emphasize minimalist methods (3). More broadly, Tom Truesdell found this emphasis on minimalism as he explored literature about writing center theory and practice: "Many of the articles I was reading seemed to endorse a purely non-directive approach to writing sessions, and I felt that any use of directive tutoring was a transgression against writing center orthodoxy" (8). In Truesdell's view of directive tutoring as a "transgression," we can see a mirror of the consultants in this study who felt shame, self-consciousness, and guilt for using directive strategies. However, as demonstrated in the literature review, there is also significant writing center scholarship devoted to complicating our focus on minimalism and promoting more imagination and incorporation of other strategies into our practice. Thus, in recognizing that the full breadth of the existing literature may not be grasped by consultants, we must ask ourselves how the full acceptance of multiple consulting strategies can be better communicated with consultants.

Two strategies to improve the effectiveness of this communication in individual writing centers have been proposed. First, as Hawthorne enacted in her writing center, a deeper exploration of the literature can be initiated (2). This, however, assumes a certain kind of tutor education that may not be in place at every writing center. However, even without engaging more deeply in the scholarship, writing center philosophies can be more effectively communicated with newer consultants through discussion with more experienced consultants. These more experienced consultants are often more comfortable with flexibility in consultations—particularly with directive methods, as evidenced in my survey by the faculty respondent's defense of directive methods. Whether this comfort was gained through delving into writing center scholarship or because of more consulting experience (or both), experienced consultants can help newer consultants as they wrestle with applying writing center philosophies in their sessions. Hawthorne also successfully used this strategy at the University of North Dakota Writing Center to re-establish a firm, less guilt-plagued community; after discussing directive methods as a group, the writing center members came to the conclusion that "When we conduct directive sessions, we've learned to think about it but not to feel bad about it" (6).

I would propose that the success of Hawthorne's discussions was also predicated on the culture she helped create in her writing center, particularly evidenced in her statement that "I promised them they wouldn't have to find their way through this thicket [navigating writing center taboos] by themselves" (5). In my own writing center, a similar culture of care, respect, and protection of your fellow consultants is palpable. Renata Solum, a former consultant in our center, articulated this when she praised our staff blog as a conduit of communication and relationship building, expressing gratitude that "there is a center full of allies to back us up even while things are going down" (12).

In light of this strong community within our own writing center, it was distressing to me when the surveys revealed that individual consultants felt guilty for betraying the perceived expectations of our center and fellow consultants. The three consultants who worried other consultants judged them for violating writing center "dogma" or "code" were clearly distressed within this community and did not feel they could count on the protection of a "center full of allies." The thought that other consultants would worry I would judge them—that I would be ashamed of them—was truly terrifying because it indicated that our community was not as strong as I perceived. Thus, for me, the most important finding in the survey was the importance of focusing on cultivating interpersonal relationships and a writing center culture, as a whole, that values care and respect. By creating this environment, we can more effectively support each other as we navigate our very complex job as writing consultants.

In addressing consultant guilt in the writing center, it is important that flexibility and a deeper analysis of collaboration are integrated not just into our center philosophies but also into our personal and professional conversations of consulting strategies, training, and research. Further research could help these conversations occur. A better understanding of how consultants interpret and enact collaboration would help clarify why consultants may feel guilt when using directive methods. On a wider scale, analyzing how community forms in individual writing centers would help ascertain how perceived expectations are disseminated, and then further inquiry into when "guidelines" become "rules" could be explored. If such steps are taken, I feel we can build an even stronger, closer, and more productive writing center community.

WORKS CITED

Blau, Susan, and John Hall. "Guilt-Free Tutoring: Rethinking How We Tutor Non-Native-English-Speaking Students." *The Writing Center Journal* 23.1 (2002): 23–44. Web. 5 Sept. 2010.

Boquet, Elizabeth H. "Intellectual Tug-of-War: Snapshots of Life in the Center." Murphy and Sherwood 116–29.

Boquet, Elizabeth H., and Neal Lerner. "Reconsiderations: After 'The Idea of a Writing Center.'" *College English* 71.2 (2008): 170–89. Web. 11 Oct. 2010.

Brooks, Jeff. "Minimalist Tutoring: Making the Student Do All the Work." Murphy and Sherwood 168–73.

Clark, Irene L., and Dave Healy. "Are Writing Centers Ethical?" *WPA: Writing Program Administration* 20.1/2 (1996): 32–48. Web. 11 Oct. 2010.

Denny, Harry. "Queering the Writing Center." *The Writing Center Journal* 25.2 (2005): 39–62. Web. 5 Dec. 2011.

Grimm, Nancy Maloney. *Good Intentions: Writing Center Work for Postmodern Times.* Portsmouth, NH: Boynton/Cook, 1999. Print.

Hawthorne, Joan. "'We Don't Proofread Here': Re-visioning the Writing Center to Better Meet Student Needs." *The Writing Lab Newsletter* 23.8 (1999): 1–7. Print.

Krause, Jenna. "The Place where Theory and Practice Meet: Flexibility within a Writing Consultant." 20 Nov. 2007. Kirsten Jamsen's WRIT 3751W Archive, University of Minnesota–Twin Cities Center for Writing. Print.

Lerner, Neal, and Elizabeth H. Boquet. "Whatever Happened to . . . Jeff Brooks?" *The Writing Center Journal* 25.2 (2005): 4–5. Web. 28 Nov. 2010.

Lunsford, Andrea. "Collaboration, Control, and the Idea of a Writing Center." Murphy and Sherwood 47–53.

Murphy, Christina, and Steve Sherwood, eds. *The St. Martin's Sourcebook for Writing Tutors.* 3rd ed. Boston, MA: Bedford/St. Martin's, 2007.

North, Stephen M. "The Idea of a Writing Center." Murphy and Sherwood 32–46.

Shamoon, Linda K. and Deborah H. Burns. "A Critique of Pure Tutoring." Murphy and Sherwood 173–88. Print.

Solum, Renata. "Informal Observation: Remembering This is a Job." 20 Nov. 2008. Kirsten Jamsen's WRIT 3751W Archive, University of Minnesota–Twin Cities Center for Writing. Web. 4 Sept. 2010.

Student Writing Support. *Getting the Most from Student Writing Support.* University of Minnesota–Twin Cities. Web. 29 April, 2012.

Truesdell, Tom. "Not Choosing Sides: Using Directive AND Non-Directive Methodology in a Writing Session." *The Writing Lab Newsletter* 31.6 (2007): 7–11. Print.

It's Not What You Say, But How You Say It (and to Whom): Accommodating Gender in the Writing Conference

Claire Elizabeth O'Leary

Claire Elizabeth O'Leary was an undergraduate at the University of Wisconsin–Madison at the time she wrote this article. It originally appeared in the journal *Young Scholars in Writing.*

A central mission of writing centers is to help writers in all disciplines, at all levels of proficiency, learn how to improve their writing skills. The primary tool for achieving this goal is the writing conference, in which a writer receives personal attention from a trained tutor who works with the writer on a specific piece of writing. Conferences, as Kenneth Bruffee suggested in his seminal essay on collaborative learning, have the potential to generate new ideas via conversation—a conversation in this case between a writing tutor and a student (645). In a writing conference, the tutor is challenged to facilitate conversation with a diverse and changing writer population which, in a successful conference, acts as a vehicle for the collaborative creation of new thoughts. Thus, conferencing and conversation are intimately linked, as the productivity of the conference depends on the quality of conversation in which the writing tutor and student engage. A tutor's ability to hold a productive dialogue with the student is the difference between a successful conference, after which the student writer feels ready to tackle revisions with new ideas, and an unsuccessful conference, which may leave both the tutor and the student feeling frustrated by a lack of communication, and, consequently, progress. For the tutor, facilitating productive conversation about an unfamiliar piece of writing requires careful attention to the back-and-forth of the dialogue and the ability to respond and adapt immediately to conversational cues from the student. A tutor's spontaneous conversational responses are influenced by more than the content of the conversation. Although "content" factors, such as the paper topic, the genre of writing, and the current state of the draft play a key role in determining what ideas will emerge in the conference conversation, the flow and development of the conversation are also affected by how the tutor and student enact and respond to each other's social identities.[1]

In a writing conference conversation, particularly if it is between strangers, the social identities that could affect conversation often correspond to physically apparent characteristics that identify different persons as belonging to different social groups. Such outwardly visible characteristics lead others to make conclusions, correct or not, about an individual's status "at first glance." Social group identifiers, which affect both how a conversational partner thinks of him- or herself and how he or she is viewed by other conversation participants, include race, age, and gender. Feminist scholar Evelyn Ashton-Jones identified gender as a feature of conversation participants that can profoundly impact conversational behaviors, proposing that the "ideology of gender" (the social expectations associated with one or the other gender) is reproduced in conversation (7). Thus, in a conference, tutors and tutees may reproduce social gender norms in their conversational interactions. Bringing together discourse analysis studies of gender and language and studies that examine the role of student and teacher or tutor gender on conference conversation, this paper investigates how student gender influences the conference style of undergraduate peer writing tutors (specifically, tutors from the Writing Fellows Program at the University of Wisconsin–Madison). I explore in a small case study how a student and a writing fellow may interact in gender roles in such a way as to affect the tutor's conversational style. In doing so, I address and draw attention to a conversation dynamic—that created between a peer writing tutor and student—that has yet to be thoroughly examined from a linguistic point of view in the literature on conference conversation. I suggest that, in keeping with the role of a tutor as a facilitator of conversation, writing fellows make what I call "conversational accommodations" for student gender behaviors. I propose that the changes in a peer writing tutor's conversational patterns with students of different genders are the manifestations of this accommodation.

Before examining how a peer tutor may accommodate student gender, it is necessary to identify what gender norms are stereotypically associated with each gender, and how this creates gender-based roles for conversation participants. In looking at gender performance in the writing conference context, I have based my definition of stereotypical masculine and feminine roles on the tutoring-style identifiers tabulated in a study by Kathleen Hunzer on students who visited a university writing center and worked with both a male and a female tutor. Students surveyed consistently described their tutors' styles in ways that identified male and female tutors as performing stereotypical gender roles, both in positive and negative ways.[2] Students described female tutors as demonstrating stereotypically female qualities: they were deferential, nonassertive, sensitive, caring, emotionally involved, and good listeners. Male tutors, in contrast, were seen as frank, self-assertive, objective, analytic, less skilled at listening, and more skilled at focusing on the task at hand (6). Hunzer noted that the identification of tutor conference styles in a way that corresponds to common gender stereotypes suggests that tutors and students interact in gender roles during the writing conference (par. 5). Similarly, in her discourse analyses of conference conversation, Laurel Johnson Black found that students and tutors interacted in gender roles, as males and females in mixed or same-sex dyads (81). Since conversation is the primary mode of interaction in the writing conference, the manifestation of these gender roles is in the conversational behaviors of the participants, in both their listener and speaker roles.

Discourse analyses of conversations between participants of the same and opposite sex in a variety of conversational contexts have shed some light on how gender performance emerges in linguistic behaviors. Critical reviews of language and gender research by Deborah James with Sandra Clarke and Janice Drakich, as well as primary research conducted by Amy Sheldon, suggest, overwhelmingly, that the linguistic behavior of an individual is highly dependent on the characteristics of other participants as well as on the nature of the conversational interaction.[3] Though specific linguistic behaviors cannot be associated definitively with one or the other gender, these studies found that some general characteristics of discourse do correlate to gender in various conversational situations. The feminine discourse style, for example, is generally described as "affiliative" because women mitigate statements and use collaborative strategies more often than men; the masculine style, on the other hand, is more adversarial, employing discourse control strategies (Sheldon 87). In addition to being affiliative and collaborative, the discourse among all-female speakers in less formal situations often evolves into the "high-involvement style" characterized by supportive interruptions, rapid flow of speech, and more laughter than typically occurs in all-male or mixed-sex conversations (James and Clarke 259). Within these general gender-specific trends, however, actual participant linguistic behavior varies most strongly based on whether the conversation is informal or formal, task-oriented or not, and if a preconceived status difference exists between participants.

In considering conversation in the writing conference context (typically between a teacher or adult tutor and a student, often in a classroom or writing center), discourse analysis suggests that writing conference interactions are task-oriented, formal, and involve status difference. In a task-oriented conversation, participants (the tutor and student) are focused on one issue (the student's paper) and together work toward a goal (improving the paper). The institutional aspect of the teacher's or tutor's relationship to the student makes the conversation more formal than informal and creates a status difference between the participants, with the teacher or tutor traditionally accorded higher status than the student because of association with institutionally granted authority. In reviewing studies on gender and interruption, James and Clarke concluded that status differences are important determinants in formal, task-oriented conversations like those in a writing conference: an individual's perception of who holds more power or a participant with a high-dominance personality will affect conversational behaviors more than performance of gender roles (249, 262).

In the studies cited above, formality emerged as one of the primary factors determining the linguistic behaviors of conversation participants. Notably, when the interaction is less formal, conversational roles taken by male and female participants often relate more directly to stereotypical gender roles. In mixed-sex informal conversation, the amount of time women talk is equal to or exceeds the talk time of male peers (James and Drakich 297). In contrast, in this same review of the literature on gender and amount of talk, James and Drakich found that in formal task-oriented situations men and women initiated the same number of vocal acts but men spent more time talking (291). They propose that this difference between informal and formal interactions, particularly those involving only a few participants, exists because women use facilitative speech to fill silences, which occur more frequently in less formally structured interactions. It seems that women often talk more in a mixed-sex group, then, because other conversation participants expect that female participants will fill silences by contributing facilitative comments (299). The types and frequencies of interruptive speech acts also correspond to whether or not a formal structure exists: the frequency of interruptions with dominating intent decreases in more informal interactions; overlap, on the other hand, increases as speakers observe the formal "one speaker at a time" rule less strictly (James and Clarke 241).

Conversation structure and context alone do not determine linguistic behaviors, as both formal and informal conversations are affected by how well the participants know each other. In many writing conferences, the student and tutor don't know each other well or have never met before; such a lack of familiarity has been shown to affect linguistic behaviors. Nervous or highly engaged participants who don't know each other well have more mistiming errors that cause unintentional overlap in both informal and formal situations (James and Clarke 257). The awkwardness of informal conversation among strangers can cause conflict, which may lead to more interruptions made with dominating intent as well as intentional topic-switching, which, according to James and Clarke (248), may minimize the value of the previous speaker's comment. Strangers are also more likely to determine self-other performance expectations based on outwardly visible status characteristics. In the formal situation, this characteristic is the position of authority one participant has relative to the other; in the informal situation, gender is one of the first status characteristics participants use as they negotiate their relationship within the conversation (Ashton-Jones 5).

Looking more specifically at conversational behaviors of participants in writing conferences, discourse analyses of conferences conducted by Terese Thonus and Laurel Johnson Black confirm the power an individual's status has on conversation. Both found that high-status individuals (the graduate student tutor or teacher) talked more, regardless of the gender of participants (Thonus 242; Black 69). Thus, institutional authority makes male and female teachers or tutors more similar than different—both genders perceive themselves as high-status individuals in comparison to students, and therefore exhibit similar conversational behaviors. According to Black, this similarity stems from the fact that "[c]onferencing so closely resembles teaching, not conversation . . . that the roles of teacher and student seem to dominate while gender roles complicate" (69). Expanding on this logic, it seems that Black is implying that, if the writing conference dialogue more closely approximated conversation between peers (were more informal), gender roles might be more of a dominating factor in determining linguistic behaviors of the participants.

If research indicates that male and female teachers and graduate student tutors exhibit conversational behaviors that are more similar than different, what in the writing conference would lead to gender-stereotypical descriptions of tutor styles, like those given by Hunzer's students? If the student, rather than the teacher or tutor, participates in the conversation in a gender-based role, the tutor may respond to the student's gendered conversational cues and accommodate student gender role performance in order to facilitate a fruitful conversation. The idea of teachers responding differently to male and female student gender performance is supported by Black's conference conversation analyses. Black found that teachers did adjust their conferencing styles according to student responsiveness and conversational behavior, and that the degree of responsiveness and types of conversational behaviors related directly to student gender. Female students actively facilitated the teacher's talk and were more likely to deny their own knowledge, thereby taking a subordinate conversational role (65). Both female and male teachers responded similarly to this gender role performance—female students, on average, received more praise, more suggestions, and were given definitions, rules, and explanations of writing conventions (77). Male students, on the other hand, did not take a subordinate role; they were more resistant to advice and suggestions, and more likely to defend their work than to offer revision strategies (70). These student behaviors relate directly to the roles males and females are conditioned to assume in similar conversational situations with peers. In a task-oriented formal interaction among peers, expectations of a high-status individual would be assigned equally to male participants; in contrast, female students in the same situation take the role of what James and Drakich (298) called "facilitators," participants who voluntarily take a low-status position by encouraging others to speak. The teacher is institutionally empowered and does not share status with the student regardless of the student's gender. In a conference, then, the female student's role identifications converge while the male student's diverge. In the conferences Black analyzed, female students, habituated to accept the low-status position in interactions among peers, interact with the teacher in a similar facilitative, low-status participant role. Male students, on the other hand, are habituated to assume a high-status position; the conversational behaviors Black identified, particularly between a male student and female teacher, show that male students engaged in a power struggle with the teacher over who would take the high-status conversational role. Black's study confirms, then, that a main determinant of linguistic behavior in formal conversation (like that of a writing conference) is how participants perceive their status relative to one another.

This research identifies writing conferences as formal interactions in which status, not gender, is the primary determinant of conversational behaviors—which led me to ask the question, In a less formal conference, will gender, rather than status, be a larger determinant of linguistic behaviors? Discourse analyses of writing conferences have not fully investigated conferences between a peer tutor and a student writer in which conversation is, according to Thom Hawkins (66), less restricted because the tutor is more accessible to the student as an equal. In what follows, I attempt to address how, in a peer–peer interaction conducted in a neutral setting (not a writing center or classroom setting, which might add to the peer tutor's status by association with instruction), an undergraduate peer tutor (writing fellow) actively accommodates student gender performance by changing conversational behaviors. In examining the conference conversation of the female writing fellows, my premise is that as these conferences will be more informal than those facilitated by teachers/graduate student tutors, students and fellows will rely more on stereotypical gender roles during the conference, performing these roles in a way that is apparent in their dialogue.[4] Though limited to a small case study, in addition to identifying possible gender accommodation I also hope to identify the peer tutor–student conversation dynamic itself, little studied from a linguistic point of view, as an intriguing subject for gender and language studies.

My case study consisted of two female undergraduate tutors in conference with one male and one female student each.[5] These tutors are in the Writing Fellows Program, run through the University of Wisconsin–Madison Writing Center, which trains undergraduate tutors to work with fellow undergraduates. I tape-recorded the four conferences between 9 November and 13 November 2007; after each conference the fellows responded to a questionnaire. After careful review of the methodologies used in the previously cited studies, I chose five aspects of conversation on which to focus my examination of the conference transcripts: time at talk, type of talk, conference tone, participants' statuses, and performance of stereotypical gender roles. I coded the transcriptions for talk time (participant conversational turns) and the following type of talk subcategories: self-correction, backpedaling, and second-guessing; praising; overlap and interruption; topic-raising; and suggestion. This coding and the fellows' post-conference responses informed my assessments of overall tone as well as each participant's status and gender performance. The results of one fellow with both students are presented first, with the analysis of the second fellow's conferences following.[6] This highlights not how the writing fellows differed from each other but rather how their individual styles did or did not change in a way that can be correlated to student gender.

The first writing fellow, "Anna," was assigned to a women's studies and literature course and worked with "Rich" and "Jillian." The writing assignment involved close reading of class texts and integration of secondary research. In both post-conference responses, Anna expressed that these students were among the more skilled writers with whom she had met. Both came to the conference with questions to discuss. Anna described the students as "proactive" writers with whom she was able to go beyond discussion of writing "basics." She felt she and the students related in the conference as fellow student writers, describing both conferences as "equal exchanges" of ideas. Based only on Anna's descriptions of the two students in her post-conference responses, one might expect these conferences to be more similar than different. My analysis, however, shows that this is not the case.

The first aspect I addressed was how Anna's two conferences compared in terms of talk time. In Anna's conference with Jillian, Anna talked more overall, held the floor for extended periods during which the student contributed only back-channel responses (affirmative signs of active listenership), and took more conversational turns than the student. Rich was more of a verbal presence than Jillian was in her conference, and talk time was more equally shared between the fellow and student in his conference. During the first few minutes of his conference, Rich talked Anna through an outline he had brought. After discussing the outline, however, he continued to take longer turns than Jillian did throughout the conversation. Consequently, Anna took shorter turns in her conference with Rich than she did in Jillian's conference.

When type of talk is analyzed, the two conferences diverge even more, with Jillian and Rich displaying different conversational behavior patterns. In her conference,

Jillian had a high incidence of self-correcting statements (indicating an unwillingness to assert her knowledge or a lack of confidence in her abilities). In Rich's conference, neither he nor Anna expressed a lack of confidence; both participants used a minimal amount of self-correction, hedging, and devaluing comments. Though the incidence was low, Anna did exhibit more of these behaviors than Rich; however, these instances were confined to mitigating phrases accompanying suggestions. Interestingly, in Rich's conference praise was used more frequently than in Jillian's conference; Anna praised Rich's revision strategies and Rich praised Anna's abilities and helpfulness.

In terms of interruption, Anna interrupted both students with a fairly high frequency—a pattern that she acknowledged as a flaw in her conferencing style in her post-conference response. In her conference, Jillian attempted interruptions, but not as often as Anna did, and with much less success than Anna. Anna was never unsuccessful in her interruption attempts while Jillian was unsuccessful more often than not. Some of Anna's interruptions of Jillian were disruptive or negated Jillian's previous statements, whereas Jillian attempted only supporting or neutral interruptions. The use of back-channel responses, generally assumed to be supportive and often not recognized as overlap, is particularly noteworthy in Jillian's conference. Jillian used back-channel responses often, to affirm and encourage Anna's conversational contributions; Anna, however, did not use such responses to an equal degree when the student had the floor. In Rich's conference, on the other hand, the use of interruption and overlap (including back-channel responses) was mutual, with Rich actually interrupting Anna more. Although a good portion of Rich's interruptions or longer overlaps were supportive or neutral, many overlaps involved completing Anna's sentences—completing her sentences seems to have been a demonstration of his understanding and a way to indicate that there was no need for Anna to explain further. He did seize the floor several times, occasionally denied Anna's suggestions, and clearly defended his point of view—behaviors the female student never exhibited.

Topic-raising was often done in the form of a suggestion, but despite the convergence of these two categories the use of topic-raising and suggestion was not uniform: the students brought most of the topics to the conversation while the fellow gave frequent suggestions. The fact that topic-raising was the only linguistic behavior that both students performed to a greater degree than the writing fellow likely relates to the fact that the students had brought questions to discuss based on the comments Anna had written on their drafts. Though she raised topics in the form of suggestion in her conference, Jillian still had a very low incidence of suggestion in comparison to Anna. Jillian used interrogative or specific modal suggestions, primarily to propose revision strategies, solicit information on topics related to writing and revision, and affirm the writing fellow's suggestions. In contrast, Anna rarely used interrogative suggestions, and instead made indirect and modal (both vague and specific) suggestions that were almost always accompanied by a mitigating phrase, tone, or sentence structure. Anna's use of indirect and mitigated suggestions in the conference implies that she sought student affirmation for her statements. Although Anna made more suggestions in both conferences (unsurprising given her role as a writing fellow), Rich almost equaled Anna in frequency of suggestion. Rich, like Jillian, took it upon himself to raise topics, but he ensured few silences by continually offering revision strategies. This contributed to Rich's high incidence of suggestions. He, like Jillian, was much more likely to use interrogative suggestions. As the conference with Rich progressed and the two got into more specific aspects of the draft at hand, Anna began to rely exclusively on specific modal suggestions. At no time did Anna offer an imperative suggestion to Rich, although she did use this type of suggestion with Jillian.

As different as these conferences were, it seems that in both cases the student and fellow interacted to create a positive conversational tone. Anna verbally dominated the conference with Jillian, but this did not seem to cause a disagreeable tone in the interaction, which Anna described as "positive and supportive," but also serious and intellectually "stimulating." The high-involvement style described previously as characteristic of all-female talk appeared only occasionally, when the participants moved off topic, although both participants seemed highly engaged throughout the conference. The high-involvement style, which my research indicated as exclusive to female discourse patterns, appeared to be less gender-specific than I expected. The conversation between Rich and Anna actually included more typical elements of the high-involvement all-female style, such as a greater supportive overlap and use of back-channel responses. Rich and Anna did stay on task even during their high-involvement exchanges, and the conversational tone was focused on the paper, with both participants highly engaged.

My analysis indicates that, although both conferences showed characteristics of informal conversation, in one conference the participants took different status roles. This occurred in Anna's conference with Jillian, in which Jillian seems to have cued Anna to take the high-status role while Jillian assumed a low-status, facilitative role. This is somewhat surprising since Anna described Jillian as "a rock star" in her conference response. At the end of the conference, Jillian did mention, in an off-topic exchange, that she felt comfortable with the material and her writing. This break from her pattern of using hedged comments and interrogative suggestions implies that she devalued her writing in order to facilitate conversation. Both participants contributed to the conversational asymmetry—although Anna acknowledged that she has the habit of interrupting, Jillian allowed these interruptions to be successful and rarely attempted to speak out of turn. In contrast, as indicated by the amount of student participation and high incidence of interruption and overlap, neither Rich nor Anna took the role of the high-status participant in their conference.

This status determination informed my assessment of participant performance of gender as it relates to the previously described stereotypically male and female conversation roles. Jillian seemed to actively perform stereotypical aspects of the female gender by voluntarily taking the low-status conversational role. Anna's conferencing style accommodated the conversational role that Jillian selected; as a response to Jillian's gender performance, Anna's conversation was more self-assertive, dominating, and could be described as more masculine. The conversation between Anna and Jillian resembled the interactions between teachers and female students described by Black (64): the student raised topics but spoke minimally, and the teacher responded to the student's performance of the stereotypical female gender role by taking a conversationally dominant position. Both students guided the conference by raising topics, but Rich's control of the conversational flow was more blatant. Although Rich and Anna's conversation approximated what characterizes the all-female "high-involvement" style, Rich seemed to take a stereotypically masculine role by verbally contributing more and not mitigating or hedging his statements. Black's study again sheds light on the student's gender performance. Male students in her study also had a high degree of cooperative overlap with the tutor, but used this overlap to demonstrate knowledge and understanding (70). It is, then, not surprising that, in her conference with Rich, Anna's conference style comes across linguistically as more feminine. Although Anna considered the two students to be of a similar writing caliber, because the students participated conversationally in different ways that correlate with gender performance, the conference between Anna and the male student seemed more like a conversation between two equal-status individuals while the conversation between Anna and the female student was more like a conversation between a tutor and a student.

"Jane's" conferences with freshmen students "Alexis" and "Benjamin," working on papers for an introductory philosophy class, present a contrast to the informality of Anna's conferences. These conferences were more formal and writing fellow-directed than were Anna's conferences. As with Anna, Jane's description of the conferences leads one to believe that the conferences were more similar than different, but again this is not the case. However, unlike Anna's conferences, in which both students came equally prepared, the differences observed between Jane's conferences could have been due, at least in part, to the fact that Alexis was more prepared for a conference than Benjamin was. Jane also acted as a scribe for her students, which decreased her verbal signs of listenership and added to the impression of a formally structured, turn-by-turn conversation. Furthermore, Jane initiated a set, and therefore more formal, conference structure: she organized both conferences around the "formula" of reverse outlining the students' drafts and then reviewing this outline to address problems. Much of what I observed in the conferences relates directly to this formal structure, Jane's intent to follow it, and how the students responded.

The reverse outline structure played a primary role in shaping talk time and turn-taking in Jane's conferences, particularly in Alexis's conference. With Alexis, talk time was fairly balanced between the student and the fellow. However, although Alexis held the floor for longer periods than Jane did, the initiation of these long turns was at Jane's behest. Jane initially suggested a reverse outline, and then steered Alexis through her paper paragraph by paragraph, encouraging Alexis's participation with consistent, qualified praise. Benjamin, on the other hand, seemed uninterested in talking about his current draft or working on new writing. It is difficult to determine, however, whether this would have been the case if Benjamin had turned in a more complete draft or come to the conference prepared to work on major revisions. As a consequence of this unresponsiveness, Jane talked more than Benjamin, despite using the same strategies that were successful in facilitating Alexis's participation. At one point, his continued unresponsiveness led her to praise him for an idea she had, in fact, proposed and repeated several times. This seemed to be an attempt to end the conference on a positive note.

Consistent with the turn-by-turn formal conversation structure followed in both conferences, the participants overlapped and interrupted each other minimally. The most significant aspect of interruption in Jane's conference with Alexis was that Alexis was unsuccessful in all of her interruption attempts. Jane did not cede the floor to Alexis, and Alexis chose to avoid extensive overlap, an indication that Alexis perceived formality in the interaction. Overlap from back-channel responses showed an interesting trend—Alexis used back-channel responses supportively during Jane's turns, but Jane rarely verbalized during Alexis's turns. However, this may have been because Jane was writing while Alexis talked. In Jane's conference with Benjamin, the interruptions that occurred were often disruptive: both Jane and Benjamin interrupted in order to seize the floor, although Jane was more successful. Jane also had a low frequency of back-channel responses in comparison to the student during Benjamin's conference, but Benjamin used fewer back-channel responses during Jane's turns than Alexis did. Furthermore, although the research previously cited identifies back-channel responses as supportive signs of active listenership, Benjamin's vocal inflections made it seem that he used these responses to push Jane toward finishing thoughts by indicating that he understood and no longer wanted to talk about a particular topic.

In both conferences, Jane did the majority of topic-raising: Alexis accepted these topics while Benjamin did not. As in Anna's conferences, topic-raising and suggestion were linked, and Jane's involvement as the primary topic-raiser contributed to her domination of suggestion use. When Jane proposed doing a reverse outline to both students, she presented it as a suggestion, and, in moving through the paper, Jane raised the "topic" of each paragraph. Of the four conferences analyzed, imperative suggestions were used with the highest frequency by Jane with Benjamin. This is not surprising given the tense tone Benjamin created by consistently denying Jane's suggestions. Although Jane suggested reverse outlining four times, Benjamin refused to go beyond the second paragraph.

The linguistic behaviors used most frequently in Jane's conferences coincide with those used in conversations with a formal tone. Despite Jane's attempts to add some levity, the turn-by-turn structure necessitated by the initial decision to organize the conference around reverse outlining restricted progression toward informality. Overall, Jane's conference with Alexis had a cooperative and supportive tone, but no real rapport was created and formality was maintained. Benjamin's conference was also formal; however, the tone seemed to be more conflictive. Both participants recognized that there was not a lot to build on, and although Jane was willing to help Benjamin move beyond this, Benjamin continually denied his ability to do so. There was a struggle for control of the conversation as Jane attempted to get Benjamin to do a reverse outline—he essentially refused to do this and, rather than taking the other options that Jane gave for continuing, made conversational plays to end the conference.

Talk time and type of talk were less useful in making an informed status assessment in Jane's conferences than they were in Anna's, so I relied on speaker intent and verbal inflections. In Jane's conference with Alexis, although turn duration indicated that Alexis was linguistically dominant, the conversation trajectory was determined primarily by Jane. Jane was the participant who kept things moving, and her leadership showed that she had the dominant role. The conversational asymmetry that favored Alexis's participation was created by Jane, and, although Jane left Alexis the opportunity to participate in a high-status position, Alexis continually deferred to Jane by following and affirming Jane's suggestions. Similarly, in Jane's conversation with Benjamin, an attempt to base status assessment on type of talk alone does not adequately represent the intent behind each participant's conversational moves. If we look only at the analysis of discourse, Jane emerges as the high-status participant and the substantial control that Benjamin asserted over this conversation is masked. Benjamin denied his knowledge of the subject, but not his status in the conversation: by denying Jane her set formula and ending the conference on his terms, he effectively controlled the conversation. Benjamin seemed uncomfortable with his draft, which may have made him feel incapable of claiming expert status in regard to the subject matter. He had no grounds upon which to defend his work, and would have had to defer to Jane's knowledge of the writing process—thereby assuming a low-status conversational role. Instead, he chose not to talk at all.

In these formal (and, with Benjamin, conflicted) conferences, what can be said about student performance of gender? Alexis assumed a low-status role even though Jane worked to get her to take a more active part. Alexis did the conversational work stereotypically expected of female conversation participants—she followed Jane's cues on when she should speak, actively encouraged Jane to speak by attempting supportive overlap, and agreed with Jane's suggestions and criticisms. Alexis, by ceding the control of the conversation to Jane, did not force Jane to act in a gendered way. Benjamin, while reluctant to take the low-status role, was unable to take a high-status role. This is similar to what Black observed in the behavior of male students with a teacher: male students resisted the teacher's suggestions but did not offer their own or accept a female teacher's revision strategies (73). Benjamin's unresponsiveness moved Jane to fill silences, be facilitative, and actively encourage his participation. Jane ended up doing the conversational work for both of them, exhibiting stereotypical female behaviors less present in Jane's dialogue with Alexis.

From my analysis of these four conferences, I conclude that the writing fellows in this study did make accommodations for the roles performed by the students that altered conference style in a way that correlated to student gender. The data of this case study suggests that gender plays a greater role in determining conversational style in more informal conferences, between peers, than in more formal conferences, such as those between a student and a tutor or teacher, which scholars have researched more fully. This indicates that the informal style allowed for a greater degree of accommodation, by the writing fellow, of a student's performance of gender. Furthermore, within peer-mediated conferences, gender affected conference style more when the writing fellow followed a looser structure, again because a less set structure allowed greater accommodation of student gender performance.

In the more informal conferences, mediated by Anna, gender more clearly affected the writing fellow's style. Anna's female student, Jillian, established herself as a low-status participant and exhibited several stereotypically female conversational traits that related directly to what Hunzer (6) identifies as commonly held gender stereotypes that can define conversational roles. Jillian deferred to Anna's

knowledge, agreed with her suggestions, rarely interrupted, and was an active listener. Although Jillian did raise topics, she did so in a nonassertive way. Anna took
Jillian's cues and assumed the high-status role by talking more, asking fewer questions, and soliciting agreement. With Rich, on the other hand, Anna did not receive
any cues to take a high-status conversational role, nor did she give any to Rich. Rich
seemed to perform traits typical of both the male and female gender. In stereotypically male fashion, he was assertive, directive, task-oriented, and likely to interrupt.
He also exhibited typically female traits, however, in his verbal signs of active listenership, his eagerness to support and affirm Anna's comments, and his suggestions of
revision strategies. In Rich's conference the typically all-female high-involvement
style was most prevalent. Anna accommodated this mixed-gender performance by
taking a more feminine role than she did with Jillian and allowing Rich to be successful in his interruptions.

Jane's style was less changed by the gender performance of her students, which
I relate to the formal structure of her conferences. In her conference, Alexis, behaving
much as Jillian did with Anna, assumed a low-status conversation role and performed a female gender role: she was deferent and amenably followed Jane's structure. Benjamin did not choose a clear conversational role, but did exhibit masculine
discourse tendencies that elicited some alterations in Jane's conference style—she
used more imperatives, talked more, and discussed content in her attempts to get
Benjamin to participate in the conference. It is difficult to know whether these changes
in Jane's conference style were primarily because Jane accommodated Benjamin's
gender performance or because she had to make accommodations for the fact that
Benjamin was in an earlier stage of the drafting process.

The results of my qualitative analysis suggest that gender performance by students significantly affects a writing fellow's conferencing style, particularly if the
conference is less formally structured. Given the small scope of this study, however,
it is impossible to make definitive conclusions about the nature of peer tutors' responses to student performance of gender. Several variables could cause similar stylistic accommodations by fellows to different students, including the tutor's preferred
conference structure, student age and writing ability, quality of the student draft,
student willingness to conference, personality types, and whether a student sees the
writing fellow as institutionally empowered. I propose, however, that accommodation of any and all of these factors would be complicated by gender.

The trends identified in these results indicate the need for further research. An
investigation into whether male and female writing fellow conferencing styles, like
those of graduate student tutors and teachers, are more similar than different would
prove illuminating. Discourse studies on a larger scale could determine if both male
and female peer tutors accommodate gender by altering conferencing style, and how
accommodation of student gender may differ for male and female peer tutors. It
would be equally interesting to investigate whether students working with writing
fellows, like the students working with tutors in Hunzer's writing center, identify male
and female writing fellows' conferencing styles in a gender-segregated way according
to gender stereotypes.

My investigation and the prospect of further studies are not only interesting for studying gender and language in the context of a university but might have practical value for peer tutors. Raising awareness of how gender may be performed by students and tutors during a writing conference may lead to an examination of what tutoring techniques can be used to effectively accommodate gender sameness or difference without actively encouraging gendered conversational behaviors that reinforce gender norms. Furthermore, self-discourse analysis is potentially a valuable tool for helping peer tutors, in all disciplines, identify which linguistic behaviors are frequently used to accommodate student gender performance, and how this may alter the conference experience for students of different genders. Particularly for peer writing tutor programs in which the tutors are predominantly female, as is the case with the Writing Fellows Program at the University of Wisconsin–Madison, it is crucial that tutors be especially aware of enacting stereotypically female behaviors in response to student gender performance. The overall perception may be that femininity in some way lends itself to successful tutoring while maleness does not, a perception that may discourage male students from participating in such peer tutoring programs.

Peer writing tutors have long been recognized as effective in teaching revision to students, because, as Hawkins has described (67), the unrestricted conversation allows for experimentation—talking through the revision process with someone who has had success in the system but will not judge the student against others. A peer tutor is in a unique situation in a conference with a student in that the tutor not only tailors the conference to the student's needs but is also capable, as a peer, of guiding the student toward becoming a more active participant in the discourse of his or her discipline. The reciprocity of the student–peer tutor relationship can operate either to maintain the gender status quo or to cause a shift in perceptions: on the one hand it can contribute to reinforcement of gender norms, but on the other hand it might allow for a peer tutor who chooses not to accommodate a student's gender performance to have an effect on how that uses gender as a self-identifier in future conversations, in the academic context and beyond. We, as peer tutors and educators, have the ability to end propagation of gender stereotypes by recognizing and actively changing gender-related conversational behaviors. The possibility that gendered behaviors could be identified and addressed within the context of a peer-mediated writing conference opens yet another avenue for discouraging institutionally accepted and reproduced gender behaviors that can contribute to perpetuating gender bias at the institutional level.

My heartfelt thanks go to Emily Hall, my wonderful faculty mentor, for spending so much time revising this piece with me, and to Susan Thomas, my faculty reviewer, who has extended my *YSW* experience beyond this work.

NOTES

1. I define "social identity" as a how an individual locates him- or herself within a particular context. This identity represents the confluence of many factors that either raise or

lower one's social status in different situations and when interacting with different individuals.

2. One variable that Hunzer does not address in her study is whether or not the students visiting the writing center at her university met with tutors who were undergraduates, graduates, or both. Since the students are all undergraduates, the status relationship might be different if undergraduate tutors were seen as peers while graduates were seen as authorities. Status determination plays a large role in how gender affects speaking style, as will be discussed.

3. These three papers are compiled in *Gender and Conversational Interaction* (1993), edited by Deborah Tannen. James and Drakich examined literature on gender and talk time (281–312); James and Clarke reviewed studies on gender and interruption (231–80); Sheldon analyzed gender effects on preschooler conversation (83–109).

4. For practical purposes, I have assumed that sex correlates to gender in selecting my subjects for analysis. However, in determining whether the conferences were affected by gender, I have attempted to avoid assuming sex–gender correlation by making assessments based on gender performance. The relativity of gender and expected performance is alluded to in many studies of gender and language—see James and Clarke; Black; and James and Drakich. Black briefly mentions this in her discussion of teachers and students interacting during writing conferences, saying that they are "socializing in gender roles as well as in institutional roles" and that students generally "perform submissiveness" but may attempt to "perform dominance" in a way that challenges teacher-performed dominance (81).

5. The number of conferences taped for transcription had to be small due to time constraints. I elected to examine two female fellows' conferences to address how tutor style changes with the gender of the student, not how tutors of different sexes may have gendered styles—I believe the pertinent factor affecting the tutor's speech is not self-gender identification but the tutor's accommodation of the student's self-gender identification. It should be noted that the fellows had previously commented on the students' drafts and that this was the second time during the semester that the students had met with the fellows about an assignment.

6. Given the small size of this case study, I believe it would be inappropriate to attempt to homogenize the interactions by using a coding system that would classify certain behaviors as necessarily dominant and remove aspects of the fellows' individual conversational styles. I have also chosen to present my results as relative comparisons, as this highlights the differences and similarities in participant conversational behavior.

WORKS CITED

Ashton-Jones, Evelyn. "Collaboration, Conversation, and the Politics of Gender." *Feminist Principles and Women's Experience in American Composition and Rhetoric*. Ed. L. W. Phelps and J. Emig. Pittsburgh: U of Pittsburgh P, 1995. 5–26. Print.

Black, Laurel Johnson. *Between Talk and Teaching: Reconsidering the Writing Conference*. Logan: Utah State UP, 1998. Print.

Bruffee, Kenneth. "Collaborative Learning and the 'Conversation of Mankind.'" *College English* 46.7 (1984): 635–52. Print.

Hawkins, Thom. "Intimacy and Audience: The Relationship between Revision and the Social Dimension of Peer Tutoring." *College English* 42.1 (1980): 64–68. Print.

Hunzer, Kathleen M. "Misperceptions of Gender in the Writing Center: Stereotyping and the Facilitative Tutor." *The Writing Lab Newsletter* 22.2 (1997): 6–11. Web. 30 Oct. 2007.

James, Deborah, and Sandra Clarke. "Women, Men and Interruptions: A Critical Review." *Gender and Conversational Interaction.* Ed. Deborah Tannen. New York: Oxford UP, 1993. 231–80. Print.

James, Deborah, and Janice Drakich. "Understanding Gender Differences in Amount of Talk: A Critical Review of Research." *Gender and Conversational Interaction.* Ed. Deborah Tannen. New York: Oxford UP, 1993. 281–312. Print.

Sheldon, Amy. "Pickle Fights: Gendered Talk in Preschool Disputes." *Gender and Conversational Interaction.* Ed. Deborah Tannen. New York: Oxford UP, 1993. 83–109. Print.

Thonus, Terese. "Dominance in Academic Writing Tutorials: Gender, Language Proficiency, and the Offering of Suggestions." *Discourse & Society* 10.2 (1999): 225–48. Print.

Postcolonialism, Acculturation, and the Writing Center

Jeff Reger

Jeff Reger was an undergraduate at Georgetown University at the time he wrote this article. It originally appeared in the journal *Young Scholars in Writing*.

Peer tutoring in the university writing center exists to help students become better writers, especially students without a strong background in academic writing. When viewed through the lens of postcolonial theory, however, tensions arise between postcolonialism's focus on preserving a student's identity and the writing center's pedagogical imperative to change the writer—ostensibly for the better. Tutors can inadvertently urge students to acculturate themselves into academic discourse—permanently altering the way students think and write. But how could we, as writing center peer tutors, not help students become better writers because we fear their assimilation into the dominant culture? At the same time, how can we help students adapt to academic discourse without destroying their identities?

In this essay, I use two case studies from my experience as a writing center tutor at Georgetown University in an attempt to address these difficult questions. The two selected cases illuminate two important concepts explored in this paper: first, postcolonial thought and its implications for writing center pedagogy; second, the implications of implementing this pedagogy and its accompanying tutoring practices. The students in the case studies have extensive problems with writing mechanics, along with other associated problems—a lack of confidence in or frustration with their writing, a pattern of incomprehensible sentences, and, most significantly, an inability to recognize problems with their writing. These are challenging obstacles to overcome, and my experiences illustrate the difficulties encountered when trying to help these clients. As I will demonstrate, my approach occasionally—and unconsciously—integrated elements of postcolonial theory, which I had been studying in class at that time. My failure to do so consistently, however, shows the need for a systematic postcolonial tutoring approach.

A CENTER FOR IMPROVING WRITERS, OR A CENTER FOR ACCULTURATION?

Kenneth Bruffee believes the purpose of education is to "reacculturate" basic writers, that tutors and teachers should help students "gain membership in another . . . [knowledge or discourse] community" by teaching its "language, mores, and values" (8). Acculturation requires the student to learn "a new discourse," which has an undeniable "effect on the re-forming of individual consciousness" (Lu, "Conflict and Struggle" 889). Students often initiate themselves into the academic discourse through acculturation—with little choice to do otherwise, as Bronwyn Williams also claims. Examples of students acculturating themselves are indicative of the incredible difficulties of the process. Williams recalls a common justification, that the "students' long-term interests" are best served by acculturation into American thought, if the students want to succeed in Western fields. This is accomplished when the teacher "takes on a civilizing role not unlike the colonial authority's," ensuring that students acculturate themselves "to the norms of the dominant culture" (590).

Anis Bawarshi and Stephanie Pelkowski argue that students in general, and underprepared students especially, learn the standards of academic writing in a haphazard way, without explanation for the existence of the standards. Students are then inclined "to treat writing as a code they must somehow crack—a guessing game—instead of something that they must participate in creating" (55). Belief in the existence of a naturalized code of academic writing manifests itself in the writing of underprepared students in various ways. In this context, where acculturation ostensibly occurs for a student's best interest, acculturation is believed to be a necessity in educating the underprepared—a sentiment that sometimes exists in the writing center.

In my experiences as a writing center tutor, the most common problem for underprepared students is a kind of hypercorrection, where students were told a rule (or are perhaps misremembering one) and misapply it, creating awkward or even unintelligible prose. No wonder "academic discourses appear as stagnant, artificial, and arbitrary formulas"; writing is then reduced to "a guessing game," where the student feels she must absorb the code of academic writing, wherever it is found, and acculturate herself (Bawarshi and Pelkowski 55).

But in reality, Bruffee's seemingly harmless call for acculturation is simply the end result of the unquestioned assumptions underlying the pedagogical ideas of Stephen M. North in his article "The Idea of a Writing Center." In defining an axiom for the writing center, North emphasizes that its job is "to produce better writers, not better writing" (237).

POSTCOLONIALISM AND WRITING CENTERS: MOVING TOWARD CRITICAL CONSCIOUSNESS

Bawarshi and Pelkowski outline the dangers of North's approach to writing center pedagogy: with the emphasis on the process of writing rather than the product, on the writer rather than the text, "in a writing center . . . the writers . . . are what get changed by instruction" (North 237). North's implicit assumption is that change is an improvement, just like the examples provided by Williams, where change is "for the students' 'own good,' so they can more successfully work within the framework of the dominant culture" (Williams 590). Bawarshi and Pelkowski characterize the language used by North as imperialist, relying on essentialist appeals such as

"The whole enterprise seems to me most natural," which allows interference with not only the text but also the writer (North 239).

The writing center undoubtedly helps students; however, the prospect of changing underprepared writers should not remain unquestioned. Postmodern and postcolonial consideration of discourses necessitates the questioning of "essentialist notions of writing as somehow ideologically innocent or even empowering," which is an incredibly dangerous aspect of North's unquestioned assumptions (Bawarshi and Pelkowski 46). Changes are intended to make the student's work acceptable at the college level, which means that the writing center is "generally unconcerned with critiquing academic standards, only with facilitating students' participation within them" (47). One of the unfortunate consequences of this uncritical perspective toward a monolithic academic discourse is a general discomfort with ambiguity and contradictions within writing styles, which are manifestations of the inherent contradictions within a person's identity.

In my view, Bawarshi and Pelkowski's essential notion of critical consciousness should underpin writing center tutoring in all forms. They characterize critical consciousness, a term taken from Edward Said, as a "critical and self-reflective form of acculturation" (42). Critical consciousness allows students to understand "why and how certain features of academic discourse come to be features in the first place," removing the condescending essentialism and allowing underprepared students to understand the standards of academic writing on their own terms (54). The related ability to allow for contradictions and ambiguity within the individual's identity has been called "new mestiza consciousness" by Gloria Anzaldúa in her book *Borderlands/ La Frontera: The New Mestiza* (80). Without the framework of mestiza consciousness, underprepared students may be inclined to see the difficult contradictions in their writing—the blend of academic writing conventions with standards rooted in the writer's background—as a personal failure. Lu has demonstrated that students sometimes see these contradictions as signals, indicating "their failure to 'enter' the academy, since they have been led to view the academy as a place free of contradictions" ("Conflict and Struggle" 897). Due to what Bawarshi and Pelkowski call "its physically and politically peripheral place—marginalized from and yet part of the university," the writing center is an ideal location for the practice of critical and mestiza consciousness, marking it as a contact zone for different discourses (42).

Mary Louise Pratt defines the contact zone as a space where "disparate cultures meet, clash, and grapple with each other, often in contexts of highly asymmetrical relations of power" (34). The concept of the contact zone is thus incredibly relevant to the contemporary writing center, which is situated in the postcolonial world. Mina Shaughnessy points out students' awareness of the contact zone, manifested in underprepared students' ambivalence toward acculturation, complicated by their anxiety to emulate the academic discourse (194). As Lu explains in her article "Conflict and Struggle," Shaughnessy is seeking to help students dissolve, not maintain, this ambivalence (904–06). Lu emphasizes the impetus to maintain the underprepared student's feelings of contradiction: "Because this ambivalence arises from sources well beyond the classroom—coming from the unequal power relationships pervading the history, culture, and society my students live in—not all students can or even want to get rid of all types of ambivalence" ("Professing Multiculturalism" 448). Envisioning the writing center as a contact zone can help maintain an ambivalence toward acculturation, effecting the creation of critical, mestiza consciousness in both tutors and clients.

While Bawarshi and Pelkowski stress the need for "helping marginalized students function within academic discourses," they are much more interested in discussing how discourses affect individuals and how the individual can achieve "critical consciousness." Bawarshi and Pelkowski emphasize that underprepared students should be instilled with an awareness "of how the mastery of academic discourses affects their home discourses" (53); but beyond implementing the concept of critical consciousness as a pedagogical guide, how can tutors in the writing center help underprepared clients? In terms of the postcolonial framework, the writing center is an exchange where dominance takes the form of a service, described as good writing: "in accepting the service . . . the oppressed consent to their own domination" (Bawarshi and Pelkowski 51). This leads tutors and other writing teachers to confront a false dilemma: acculturation or a rejection of this exchange? Following Anzaldúa, the goal of the postcolonial writing center is to implement the third option, helping writers achieve mestiza consciousness, defined by Bawarshi and Pelkowski as "a consciousness marked by the ability to negotiate multiple, even contradictory, subject positions while rooted in dominant discourse" (52). Teaching and exploring the idea of mestiza consciousness enables instruction to move beyond a criticism of the dominant ideology, allowing the student to engage with both academic and her own discourse, and thus maintaining ambivalence toward acculturation.

Treating the writing center as a contact zone allows student such as Alison or Emma (in the following case studies) to assess "what happens to their experiences—what happens to them—when they begin to master academic discourses" (Bawarshi and Pelkowski 52). Tutors in the writing center should teach underprepared students how to awaken their mestiza consciousness, to shift between different discourses, not just "encourage marginalized students to resist academic discourses or . . . have them privilege one discourse over another" (53). The postcolonial writing center can accomplish this by helping underprepared students understand the standards of academic writing, without relying on essentialist explanations; students should be taught how to analyze writing conventions themselves, so they have the ability to understand any discourse. The client is then no longer forced to guess what someone else wants, allowing underprepared students like Emma to understand "how writing constitutes [her] into a discourse community's social pattern of action . . . potentially preclud[ing] any threat to [her] home discourse" (55). In this instance, understanding the importance and uses of academic discourse allows the underprepared student to choose how and when to use the conventions of academic writing, enabling the student's mestiza consciousness.

Creating a postcolonial writing center is an invitation to challenges of contradiction and dynamic tension between discourses and conventions of writing. Lu cautions that some concerns are inherently irresolvable, since they remain part of the discussion between tutors and underprepared students when confronting contradictory discourses: "How to voice and talk to rather than speaking for or about the voices of the 'other' within and among cultures is thus not a question which can be resolved . . . outside of the process of negotiation. Rather, it must . . . [guide] our action as we take part in it" ("Professing Multiculturalism" 456). There are many real concerns, such as those encountered by Jay Sloan, a writing center director at Kent State University, who attempted to redefine the writing center as a contact zone. The response from his tutors was mixed, as evidenced by the reflection of one particularly skeptical tutor:

> I recognize what you are trying to do . . ., but it is very challenging to attempt to do it here in the Writing Center. It's very hard to politely challenge one's person-ally held views regarding a controversial thing like race. My problem is that I want the writer's paper to remain their property, under their control. . . . I don't want to influence them too much, but on the other hand, I recognize that they may need . . . someone to help them see a different point of view.

In contrast, Lu's experiences suggest that students will retain control over their texts; in fact, the greater worry is whether students would still desire to learn the standards of academic writing if given a choice of perspective. Lu quells this worry, however, explaining that "the unequal sociopolitical power of diverse discourses exerts real pressures on students' stylistic choices" ("Professing Multiculturalism" 457). Students have chosen to go to college and want to succeed, which means they must engage with the dominant academic discourse. As Bawarshi and Pelkowski have con-tinually emphasized, however, "the point is not to discourage marginalized 'Basic Writers' from functioning within academic discourses, but rather to teach them how to preserve their multiple, even conflicting social roles while doing so" (54).

Implementing ideas about the contact zone and mestiza consciousness can help students to engage with the conventions of academic writing without submitting themselves entirely to the process of acculturation. The haphazard tutoring ap-proaches I followed with Emma and Alison illustrate the need for writing center tutors to fully understand the consequences of their actions when dealing with un-derprepared students, and to best serve their particular needs by helping underpre-pared students function within the academic discourse while still maintaining their distinctive identities.

ALISON: DIFFICULTIES IN PRACTICE

When I first met Alison, I was unsure how to approach the numerous difficulties in her paper, and it became increasingly apparent throughout the session that she lacked a background in academic writing. I was profoundly uncomfortable with the contra-dictions in Alison's writing style, which seemed at first to be incomprehensible. My initial assessment of the session reveals this confusion and frustration:

> The client seems to have significant difficulties with writing. The paper has far too many issues to address in one short session at the end of my shift. Most prominent was her misuse of many verbs and nouns, and also nonstandard sentence structure. These two issues render many sentences incomprehensible

without extremely close rereading and thinking about what she means to say rather than how the sentence reads.

However, as I later discovered, Alison's writing can be understood as a version of the academic discourse, its conventions blended with her own.

In *Lives on the Boundary,* Mike Rose recalls tutoring a similar client who "had an idea about how college writing should sound, and [who] was trying to approximate her assumptions" (171). My own experience from the session with Alison seems to echo Rose's experiences; many of my client's errors had similar sources, such as misapplied rules. The misused words and inflated vocabulary mark her errors as attempts to appropriate the foreign academic discourse.

In the tutoring session with Alison, I began by assessing her organization, and then I tried to focus the paper by addressing the assignment more explicitly, guiding the client in rewriting her topic sentences. Much of the paper consisted of summary rather than her analysis, so I worked with her to explicate points critical to fulfilling the assignment. It often seemed that her ideas and assessments were buried under her confused language, and simply needed to be drawn out. Interestingly, I inadvertently followed the guidance of Bawarshi and Pelkowski, by focusing on the text and looking closely at grammar. They cite this kind of surface change "as a springboard to discussing other types of academic standards." Such a discussion could have lent insight to the client regarding the standards of academic writing, helping Alison understand how her "subjectivity" is affected by the academic discourse (55). With my limited time, however, I focused my attention solely on correcting one sentence, hoping the student could follow the approach and make similar corrections to other sentences.

The most critically flawed sentence was Alison's thesis; it was extremely opaque, making it hard for the reader to understand the objectives of the paper. I recorded my approach to correcting her thesis in my session reflections:

> When we discussed her thesis, she was clear in what she wanted to express; however, she was unable to write down what she said, and spent over five minutes rephrasing the sentence without adding further explanation or content. I tried to intervene numerous times, but I eventually had to resort to giving her ideas rather than have her work for them.

I intervened by rephrasing my previous question about her thesis, but she was simply unable to write her thoughts on paper; she struggled for minutes on each word, only to end up with another unintelligible version of her original sentence. She seemed to focus for so long on each individual word that she forgot what she was writing the sentence about, necessitating more time to recollect her thoughts, only to repeat the struggle again with the next word. Out of desperation, I repeated what I remembered her saying previously, although the result was undoubtedly distorted— less Alison's own sentence than one influenced by my ideas of good writing.

My actions in the tutoring session reflect my failure to adopt a perspective of "critical consciousness," which I could then pass on to the client for future interactions with academic discourse. With Alison, the burden of acting as a translator in the contact zone was overwhelming in conjunction with my role as a tutor, to improve her as a writer working within the academic discourse. Her difficulty in translating what she said into the style of academic discourse is indicative of a failure to maintain mestiza consciousness, an unfamiliar concept that I could have introduced to her. I should have explained to her that she need not acculturate herself, that she should maintain her ambiguous identity—as an underprepared student attempting to understand and appropriate academic discourse—instead of altering her writing to fit its precepts. Rather than explain these things to her, however, I corrected her approximation of academic discourse without explaining that academic discourse is just one standard—a style that can be maintained separately and independently—that does not have to dominate her identity.

EMMA: UNINTENTIONAL, UNCONSCIOUS SUCCESS

Prior to my interaction with Alison, Emma came into the university writing center with an essay on African American poetry for a gateway class. Her professor had already graded the paper; Emma was seeking to revise her paper and turn it in again. Emma had great ideas, but the paper had significant sentence-level issues. As a peer tutor, I went line-by-line with my client, asking her to examine carefully sentences or words marked by her professor and to explain why the professor thought they were wrong. Emma did not recognize many of the sentence-level problems from reading aloud; she continued to read unless I stopped her and pointed out very specific issues that impeded comprehension. Whenever I asked her to explain something, she was very eloquent; I then asked her to write down what she had just said, which she later incorporated into the paper. For example, Emma rewrote the sentence "Although in a time where one's true self is fogged by society, it is however possible to overcome" as "It is however possible to overcome society's judgment of oneself." Occasionally, Emma was unable to offer a reason why her professor thought something was an error, and I would be forced to suggest a way to fix it so the session could continue. With my pointed suggestions, Emma's sentence "Son of a crossed breed, intermingle of white and black, uncertain of where death will claim him is left at a crossroad" became "As a son of an intermingling of white and black, he is left at a crossroad uncertain of where death will claim him." Throughout the session, Emma was extremely receptive to my suggestions, though it was disheartening that she did not understand many of her mistakes. I tried to take as much time as the session allowed to explain them, but I was unsure the results would last. I worked with her for about an hour, until my next scheduled client came; we finished without looking over her final paragraph, which I found unchanged when she sent me a copy of the revised draft she had handed in to her professor.

Emma's background presents an opportunity to understand how tutors can unintentionally acculturate underprepared students into academic discourse. Her first language is Creole, though this fact would not have been apparent without her self-disclosure in a later email. After she told me, the Haitian roots of the writing style became evident to me; however, when I first read her paper, the style simply seemed deficient. Emma said her teachers in high school focused on literary language and conventions like imagery and metaphors, but "here [at Georgetown], [literary analysis] is deeper and more profound: you have to read in between the lines and read passed [*sic*] the obvious and make an interpretation that others may not see right away" (Emma).

Her statement lends intriguing insight into the classification of writers. David Bartholomae believes better writers are distinguished by a key gesture: "the writer works against a conventional point of view" (152). Accordingly, Bartholomae could not classify Emma as a "basic writer," since she has incorporated this approach into her writing style. This is a striking example of how underprepared students can do exactly what professors ask, become acculturated of their own volition, yet still have underdeveloped skills. Using his definition of a basic writer, Bruffee would suggest that Emma is not actually acculturated, since it is the lack of acculturation that defines a basic writer. Min-Zhan Lu characterizes Bruffee's alternate approach by setting "the goal of Basic Writing in terms of the students' acculturation into a new community" ("Conflict and Struggle" 894). Emma would fall under this definition of a basic writer because she has been underprepared for the academic discourse of college; however, like other underprepared students, she admirably confronts the challenge in her own way. Regardless of grammatical, structural, and other surface or superficial errors, the sophistication of her analysis is undeniably evident in her writing.

Her justification in our email conversation for the higher level of difficulty she experienced illuminates a common problem confronting underprepared students: it is much harder without pointed academic instruction to understand what to include in an essay. According to Emma, "being in college it is understandable that writing is more difficult because different professors ask for different things and always you have to try to write in the way they want it and write what they want to hear, and that in itself is hard too." Emma's difficulties with writing reflect reality, where instructions are not often explicit.

Yet even when her professor gave explicit instructions on what to revise, she did not fully understand her errors, nor how best to correct them. I was only partially successful in my role as a tutor, explaining errors and the necessary corrections to her. For the most part, I was able to question her and hear Emma explain her perspective, and then work through her own corrections by speaking aloud. Occasionally, she would be at a loss to explain her error, and rather than skip the issue out of concern for time, I dictated the correction if Emma was unable to come up with one herself. Though I had studied postcolonialism, I had not yet made the connection between it and my work in the writing center. I did not approach the session intending to implement an approach informed by critical or mestiza consciousness, but I never told her that her mistakes were "wrong," simply that they did not conform to the expectations of academic writing dictated by her professor. In this way, I allowed Emma to work within academic discourse by understanding it as just one standard out of many, meaning she was not necessarily deficient because of her background as an underprepared student. With this understanding, Emma can maintain her ambiguous identity—achieving mestiza consciousness. I unconsciously acted as a kind of translator for underprepared students like Emma in their initial contact with academic writing styles.

THE FUTURE OF POSTCOLONIAL THOUGHT
IN THE WRITING CENTER

Underprepared students like Emma and Alison can sustain the contradictions that comprise their identities—and thus manifest themselves in their writing—by viewing their personal ambiguity through this framework of the mestiza consciousness. For both Emma and Alison, critical consciousness—a "critical and self-reflective form of acculturation"—would allow them to understand the standards of academic writing on their own terms (Bawarshi and Pelkowski 42).

It is difficult to give a prescriptive method for incorporating postcolonial thought into tutoring while still allowing flexibility based on context and the individual; however, it is indefensible, even unethical, not to provide tutors with training in a postcolonial approach to peer tutoring. To that end, tutor training should incorporate a number of practical strategies, with an aim toward explaining academic discourse and its expectations—and allowing ambivalence about acculturation rather than unquestioning acceptance. In practice, this means changing how tutors explain errors, as well as academic discourse itself, when responding to the writing of underprepared students. Avoid absolute "wrong" or "right" judgments—identify errors always as what is expected by professors in academic discourse. Emphasize that academic discourse is not necessarily the best or the ideal, but what is expected in the context of the American university. Couch explanations in terms of better understanding academic discourse and how to write within it. Through these methods, the writing center tutor can aid underprepared students by explaining academic discourse and improving their writing within that context—and thus help underprepared students maintain their unique identities by switching between discourses, rather than forcing a permanent choice.

Tutors can take advantage of the writing center's location as a contact zone to help underprepared writers understand that acculturation is not the only option; the tutor should help the underprepared student to understand academic discourse and explain that it is only one standard, that other discourses are not "wrong" in absolute terms. Underprepared students face numerous challenges when they enter college. An approach—marked by postcolonial thought, consciously and consistently applied by tutors in the writing center—to help underprepared students gain critical and mestiza consciousness can alleviate some of this burden, helping these students develop an ability to communicate using academic discourse without unintentionally forcing the students to acculturate themselves or reconsider their personal identities and perspectives.

My deepest thanks to Professor Maggie Debelius for her consistent encouragement, for inspiring me to do something with this essay—and for giving me the opportunity to work as a writing tutor in the first place, a job that is truly its own reward.

WORKS CITED

Anzaldúa, Gloria. *Borderlands/La Frontera: The New Mestiza*. San Francisco: Aunt Lute, 1987. Print.

Bartholomae, David. "Inventing the University." *When a Writer Can't Write*. Ed. Mike Rose. New York: Guilford, 1985. 134–65. Print.

Bawarshi, Anis, and Stephanie Pelkowski. "Postcolonialism and the Idea of a Writing Center." *The Writing Center Journal* 19.2 (1999): 41–58.

Bruffee, Kenneth A. "On Not Listening in Order to Hear: Collaborative Learning and the Rewards of Classroom Research." *Journal of Basic Writing* 7.1 (1988): 3–12. Print.

Emma. "Writing Center Project Questions." Message to the author. 9 Dec. 2007. E-mail.

Lu, Min-Zhan. "Conflict and Struggle: The Enemies or Preconditions of Basic Writing?" *College English* 54 (1992): 887–913. Print.

———. "Professing Multiculturalism: The Politics of Style in the Contact Zone." *College Composition and Communication* 45.4 (1994): 442–58. Print.

North, Stephen M. "The Idea of a Writing Center." *Rhetoric and Composition: A Sourcebook for Teachers and Writers*. 3rd ed. Ed. Richard L. Graves. Portsmouth, NH: Boynton/Cook, 1990. 232–46. Print.

Pratt, Mary Louise. "Arts of the Contact Zone." *Profession* 91 (1991): 33–40. Print.

Rose, Mike. *Lives on the Boundary*. New York: Penguin, 1989. Print.

Shaughnessy, Mina. *Errors and Expectations: A Guide for the Teacher of Basic Writing*. New York: Oxford UP, 1977. Print.

Sloan, Jay D. "Collaborating in the Contact Zone: A Writing Center Struggles with Multiculturalism." *Praxis: A Writing Center Journal* 1.2 (2004). Web. 9 Dec. 2007

Williams, Bronwyn T. "Speak for Yourself? Power and Hybridity in the Cross-Cultural Classroom." *College Composition and Communication* 54.4 (2003): 586–609. Print.

Addressing the Everyday Language of Oppression in the Writing Center

Mandy Suhr-Sytsma and Shan-Estelle Brown

Mandy Suhr-Sytsma and Shan-Estelle Brown were graduate students at the University of Connecticut at the time they wrote this article. It originally appeared in *The Writing Center Journal*.

INTRODUCTION

In 1998, Catherine Prendergast observed that, although composition scholars sometimes identify a subject by race or ethnicity, "the legacy of racism in this country which participates in sculpting all identities—white included—is more often than not absent from the analysis of that writer's linguistic capabilities or strategies" (36). Since then, more composition and writing center scholars have tackled racism and related issues of marginalization, inequality, and oppression in their work. Scholars have still given very little attention, though, to ways that racist and otherwise oppressive systems shape the everyday language of writers. Our own research stems from a single but far from simple question: how can tutors better identify and challenge the everyday, often subtle, language of oppression in their own discourse and in that of other tutors and writers in writing centers? In what follows, we share our story of beginning to address this question where our fellow tutors tend to start: firsthand experiences of writing and working with writers. In this essay, we first review other approaches to addressing oppression in writing centers and explain why we decided to begin with everyday language, student writing, and tutoring practice. We then discuss our process of forming the two-list heuristic that comprises the focus of our essay and reproduce the heuristic as the primary document readers can take away from this piece. The first list, "How Language Can Perpetuate Oppression," identifies some common ways in which the language of tutors and writers can reflect as well as support oppressive systems. We've titled this list "How Language Can Perpetuate Oppression" rather than "How Tutors and Writers Perpetuate Oppression" not to downplay tutors' and writers' complicity in sustaining oppressive systems but rather because we want to emphasize that an individual's uses of oppressive language are often both unintentional and inseparable from broader discourses that reinforce oppression. The second list, "How Tutors and Writers Can Challenge Oppression through Attention to Language," outlines several practices for identifying and addressing oppressive language in writing centers. We have made tutors and writers, rather than language, the actors in this second list in order to emphasize that these individuals can be empowered to challenge oppression through specific attention to language even when that language is unintentional, subtle, and complexly intertwined with oppressive systems. After we introduce the two-list heuristic and explain its genesis, we discuss each item on the lists in turn. Finally, in our concluding section, we demonstrate how the heuristic has sparked provocative reflection and strengthened tutoring practices in our center.

In this essay, then, we argue that other writing centers can also use these lists as a heuristic for fostering productive dialogue about language, oppression, and resistance. The lists developed organically from the experiences of tutors in our writing center and are thus specific to this location. Whereas others might see the locally bound nature of the lists as a limitation, we see it as a strength. The lists are not meant to function as authoritative universals. Rather, as a heuristic, the lists might prompt tutors at other institutions to follow the process we will describe to make their own lists from scratch. Alternately, tutors might begin with a discussion of our two-list heuristic, but then revise and adapt it, making it their own source for knowledge-creation based on their experiences. Ultimately, we hope that the lists will foster dialogue across as well as within institutions, thereby building on the anti-oppression work already occurring in individual writing centers and in regional and international networks of writing center practitioners.

What is the "everyday language of oppression"? How do we define it, and why have we taken it as our focus? By "oppression" we refer to systemic inequalities and discrimination based on sites of difference such as race, ethnicity, religion, class, gender, sexuality, and/or (dis)-ability. We define "everyday language" not as informal language but rather as common language, the sort of speech and text that we see every day on college and high school campuses. The "everyday language of oppression" is subtle as well as ubiquitous. Therefore, it often goes unnoticed, not being recognized as oppressive at all and/or not receiving as much attention as more extreme forms of oppressive language such as threats or hate speech do. We focus on the everyday language of oppression in writing centers because, like the authors of *The Everyday Writing Center*, we want to root our research in the common experiences of tutors and writers. We thus analyze the language that tutors and writers commonly use in their conversations and their writing. While students' academic language may differ from their everyday speech, we still classify the language of student papers as "everyday" when it is language that commonly occurs in student writing and that would not generally be seen as expressing an extraordinary or extreme view. Our observations and research demonstrate that individual instances of everyday oppressive language are inseparable from larger oppressive systems. Whether or not individuals consciously adhere to the values of oppressive systems, the language of these systems inevitably influences the language they use, and individuals who work in writing centers, whether as directors, tutors, and/or writers, are no exception. In *Facing the Center*, Harry Denny observes that "In writing centers, [he] came to see everyday oppression, natural and exercised without effort" (21). Denny heard oppression in the rhetoric of faculty, tutors, and students whose voices made their way into the writing center (21). If writing center practitioners listen, we are confident that they too will hear the everyday language of oppression in their centers. As we further define and discuss the everyday language of oppression throughout this essay, we aim to better equip our readers to identify and challenge it.

As a tool that enables careful attention to the everyday language of oppression, our two-list heuristic uniquely contributes to the approaches of a growing number of writing center scholars and practitioners committed to anti-oppression work. Writing center scholars have taken three major approaches when addressing oppression. First, with Nancy Grimm leading the way, some scholars call for the recruitment of diverse staffs to improve tutoring quality while also combating the systematic inequalities that have caused many writing center staffs to look uniform and/or to fail to reflect the populations of students they serve (Denny; Grimm, *Good Intentions*; Grimm, "New Conceptual Frameworks"; Kilborn; Weaver). Some scholars—including undergraduate tutors—also stress the need for writing centers to support the diverse tutors they recruit, especially when those tutors experience discrimination from other staff members or from writers who, having been influenced by systems of discrimination, are sometimes skeptical about the abilities of African-American, Hispanic, multilingual, female, or other demographics of tutors (Grimm, *Good Intentions*; Harris; White et al.). The second approach writing center scholars advocate—often in combination with the recruitment of diverse staffs—focuses on staff training that guides tutors into a greater awareness about systematic oppression. Within this approach, writing center directors, teams of tutors, or staff from partner institutions, such as multicultural centers, lead tutors to do one or more of the following: engage with scholarship on systematic racism and other forms of oppression; analyze cultural and institutional artifacts as markers of systematic oppression; or reflect, via surveys, personal stories, or other tools, on their own complicity in oppressive systems, intercultural competence (and room for growth), and positions of privilege as well as marginalization within dominant societies, institutions, and discourses (Barron and Grimm; Condon; Dees, Godbee, and Ozias; Denny; Fremo; Geller et al.; Kilborn; Kynard; McDonald; White et al.). Like the second approach to addressing oppression in writing centers, the third stresses the systematic—not just personal— nature of oppression and calls for greater awareness and reflection by writing center staffs. However, it more specifically pushes for increased reflection about privileged discourses, power dynamics, and forms of oppression at play in tutors' and writers' experiences in the writing center itself (Barron and Grimm; Bokser; Davila; Dees; Denny; DiPardo; Godbee, and Ozias; Innes; Johnson; Rihn; Town).

The work we discuss in this essay builds most directly on this third approach to addressing oppression since it emerges from attention to tutors' firsthand experiences in the writing center and their reflections on those experiences. Yet our approach diverges from others in that it models how tutors' experiences and reflections can become the basis for a staff development tool, the two-list heuristic. Tutors may feel more ownership of this type of a locally produced text than they would of scholarly texts or other outside texts dealing with oppression. At the same time, as a heuristic, and especially when paired with scholarship and other resources, the tutor-generated text might prompt richer reflection than simple sharing and discussion of experiences would. By advocating increasing levels of reflection through the heuristic and multiple occasions for dialogue with other tutors, our approach seeks to simultane-ously empower and challenge tutors so they might expand their awareness about oppression as well as their strategies for resisting it in their own writing and in their conversations with other writers.

In addition to creating a heuristic by drawing on tutors' experiences and reflec-tions, our approach is also set apart by its specific focus on the language of tutors and writers. Even the most subtle instances of oppressive language emerge from and con-tribute to oppressive systems. Therefore, our attention to the particular language of tutors and writers compliments rather than opposes strategies proposed by the writ-ing center scholars who charge writing centers to expose and confront systematic oppression. Geller et al. aptly critique tutoring textbooks that discuss racism by "addressing simply language" and fail to consider racism as anything other than "individual prejudice" (97). However, we propose that we can address "simply lan-guage" without addressing language simply. Victor Villanueva observes in "Blind: Talking about the New Racism" that "'figures of speech' are 'figures of ideology' are 'figures of thought' and 'figures of often unintentional censorship'" (6). As Villanueva demonstrates, everyday figures of speech are inextricably related to the ideologies of oppressive systems, which affect one's thoughts, censorship (intentional and unin-tentional decisions that privilege certain voices while discriminating against others), and actions. Harry Denny argues, "To combat oppression is just as local and indi-vidual as it is global and collective" (26). It will take local as well as large-scale efforts to challenge systematic oppression. By exposing and addressing the figures of speech that comprise the everyday language of oppression in writing centers, tutors can con-front their own complicity in oppressive systems, challenge discourses that support oppression, and work toward more just and equitable relations within and beyond their centers. Tutors can indeed productively address structural oppression by care-fully attending to the actual words of individuals in their writing centers.

Some writing center directors may object that they do not have time to tackle oppression with their tutoring staff at all, let alone to collaboratively create or revise a heuristic for addressing oppressive language. However, our conversations with tutors from our own staff as well as tutors working in other writing centers demon-strate the need for explicit training and the value of collaboration if tutors are to improve their ability to identify and address the oppressive language from which no writing center can escape. These tutors acknowledge that experience and education enable them to recognize only some forms of oppressive language while they inevita-bly fail to notice others. We conclude that all tutors can increase their awareness of oppression's various influences over language, but only through intentional efforts. Our interactions with these tutors, moreover, attest to the benefits of approaching these efforts collaboratively with other tutors since many of these tutors have become better able to see, scrutinize, and expand their own perspectives through dialogue with one another. At the close of *Facing the Center* Denny asserts that "the writing center exists" for people and for language, for "the faces that come to the center," and "the conversations we reward and make time for" (167). When writing centers do not make time to address oppression, they miss an opportunity to enrich the people as well as the discourses that occupy their spaces.

METHODS AND HEURISTIC: FOCUSING ON TUTORS' EXPERIENCES TO BUILD COLLECTIVE KNOWLEDGE

In developing our intentional, collaborative approach for addressing oppression in our center, we decided to begin with our staff's firsthand experiences as writers and tutors. We agree with Geller et al. that writing center practitioners sometimes "rely too heavily" on manuals and "mock" situations and that the most powerful type of learning happens by way of "reflection-in-action" (21–22). We therefore focused on tutors' own writing as well as that of students with whom they had worked in actual tutoring sessions. While we certainly support bringing scholarly discussions of oppression into the writing center, we also believe that tutors can build knowledge through attention to their own practice, which they can in turn improve through that knowledge. Beginning with attention to tutors' and writers' practices not only yields valuable knowledge but also enables tutors to bring a positive sense of authority and ownership to discussions about oppression. Our conversations with tutors have not always been comfortable (conversations about oppression rarely are), but tutors have been eager to engage because they want to reflect on their practice.

Context

Even as we hope that many writing centers will benefit from practice-based discussions about oppression that draw on the two-list heuristic we have developed, we also recognize that our data will be unique to our setting. We therefore turn briefly to a description of our center. At the University of Connecticut Writing Center in Storrs, Connecticut, two faculty directors lead a staff of approximately eight graduate and twenty-five undergraduate tutors representing more than fifteen fields of study. In our roles as graduate student assistants, we serve as liaisons to our home departments (Mandy to English and Shan-Estelle to Anthropology), develop writing center programs, and tutor alongside undergraduate colleagues. In addition to fostering a team-of-peers identity for our joint graduate and undergraduate staff, our center encourages tutors to see themselves as peers to the writers they tutor. Our staff strives to learn from the writers they tutor and also seek tutoring themselves. In terms of demographics, the staff represents a variety of national, racial, class, gender, sexual orientation, religious, and other identities. The staff has become more racially, ethnically, and linguistically diverse over the last few years as the directors follow the lead of writing center scholars such as Nancy Grimm in recognizing the value of multiple literacies and recruiting intentionally.

We acknowledge the real force of demographics resulting from power structures that privilege certain populations over others. At the same time, we want to complicate reductive readings of demographics. Mandy is a white Protestant with working class roots in the rural Midwest. Shan-Estelle is a black woman from Connecticut and Virginia who grew up in a working class family and is Ivy-League educated. While working on this project, we have discovered ways in which these positions influence our perspectives on oppression, but we have also learned, from each other and other colleagues, to question our assumptions about demographics. We hope that our research will prompt critical approaches to all matters, including demographics.

From Focus Groups to Our Two-List Heuristic

To study ways that tutors grapple with the everyday language of oppression in their own writing and when working with other writers, we conducted two focus groups of tutors from our center in fall 2008 and two additional focus groups in fall 2010. Conducting interviews with individual tutors, we believed, would have been less effective, as focus groups could facilitate the sort of collaborative thinking that the tutors had already honed well in a practicum group for new tutors and during all-staff training sessions. To form the 2008 focus groups, we used systematic random sampling, selecting every fourth tutor and inviting him or her to participate. Two undergraduate tutors participated in the first focus group, and an additional two undergraduate tutors and one graduate student tutor took part in the second group. Even with our admittedly small initial sample size, these groups reflected well the varying disciplines and backgrounds of our staff at the time. The tutors also varied in the amount of time that they had worked at the writing center, with some tutors having joined the staff just a few weeks prior to our focus group meetings and others having worked in the center for years.

At the start of each focus group, we announced our interest in the everyday language of oppression and received tutors' consent to participate in the group and audio record the session. We then prompted a brief conversation about aspects of the tutors' identities, cultures, or experiences that influence their perspectives. In each of the focus groups, tutors shared where they were from as well as their social class positions, racial affiliations, personalities, and family make-ups. They considered how these factors affect their interests and values as well as what they notice or fail to notice in regard to oppression. We followed by asking tutors to think together about what might influence the perspectives of other students at the university. As the tutors in each group discussed perspectives of other students, they commented—and sometimes disagreed—on the racial, regional, class, and political perspectives that seem more and less dominant on campus. Tutors who saw themselves as part of a particular minority noted that their perspectives from that position were underrepresented and, at times, discriminated against. One tutor from the American South, for instance, described her frequent encounters on campus with offensive and inaccurate stereotypes about the region, which generally went unchallenged by other students and instructors. We hoped that this initial conversation about perspectives would position the subsequent dialogue about oppressive language in the writing center within a larger context and would encourage tutors to think in a peer mindset.

For the majority of the focus group sessions, we prompted tutors to share times when they became aware of ways in which their own language and that of students they tutored were influenced by oppressive systems. We also asked tutors to describe their responses when addressing such language. By analyzing the focus group transcripts and generalizing the tutors' observations, we generated our two lists, now titled "How Language Can Perpetuate Oppression" and "How Tutors and Writers Can Challenge Oppression through Attention to Language." The focus group participants affirmed our interpretations of their discussion as represented by the lists and helped us to use the lists as a heuristic with our staff.

A Two-List Heuristic for Addressing the Everyday Language of Oppression

How Language Can Perpetuate Oppression

1. Avoids discussing difference
2. Erases differences
3. Assumes uniform readership
4. Minimizes significance of discrimination
5. Speaks of oppression as only in the past
6. Exoticizes
7. Presents stereotypes as evidence
8. Disrespects sources from "other" perspectives
9. Fails to distinguish sources' views from writers' own
10. Misunderstands or misrelates sources' views

How Tutors and Writers Can Challenge Oppression through Attention to Language

1. Clarify meanings together
2. Express understanding of one another's meanings
3. Discuss meaning and use of sources
4. Pose counterarguments
5. Maintain a non-combative tone
6. Address language without accusations of intentional oppression
7. Name the "elephant in the room"
8. Learn to better identify and address language that perpetuates oppression

The above heuristic appears in the form we presented to our own 2008 staff following our initial creation of the lists, though our staff has since suggested revisions. In the discussions of the two lists that follow, we similarly reference only material from the 2008 focus groups and from interactions with our staff during the 2008–2009 academic year when we were initially developing the heuristic and the staff was just beginning to engage with it. We chose to represent and discuss the lists in this way in order to represent the lists' formation and their nascent heuristic function in our local writing center context. After our discussion of the original lists, this essay's conclusion draws on findings from our 2010 focus groups and more recent staff development to demonstrate how the two lists have developed into a more robust heuristic in our center. Our conclusion also offers guidance for other centers interested in using the lists.

DISCUSSION OF LIST 1: HOW LANGUAGE CAN PERPETUATE OPPRESSION

To form and annotate the "How Language Can Perpetuate Oppression" list, we drew mainly on the transcripts of the 2008 focus groups, along with other conversations with tutors and our own experiences. The list is not meant to be exhaustive but to isolate common patterns, to provoke discussion, and to prompt the identification of additional patterns. Some of these moves, such as "Misunderstands or misrelates sources' views," are ones that writers often make even when they are not evoking oppressive attitudes. Many writers, teachers, and tutors will readily recognize these tendencies and will have discussed them before. We highlight them here because we see them as especially common in writing that includes the everyday language of oppression and because we feel writing center practitioners can better understand oppressive language as well as these common moves by studying them in tandem.

1. Avoids Discussing Difference

During the 2008 focus groups, tutors discussed their own and other writers' hesitancy to speak at all about demographic differences. The tutors explained that they and their fellow students want to be polite and politically correct, and they sometimes fear that simply bringing up any differences of, say, race or gender would make them come across as racist or sexist (even if they approached the matter sensitively and recognized the socially constructed and in other ways problematic nature of these categories). Sociologists Eduardo Bonilla-Silva and David Embrick identify the "minimization of racism" as one manifestation of "color-blind racism" (7–8). They explain that Whites who see race as a matter of the past often accuse those who discuss race of "playing the race card" and thus being themselves racist in a "reverse discrimination" sense (7–8). The tutors in our focus groups and the writers they describe seem to similarly fear accusations of "playing" race, gender, or other demographic "cards" and thus skirt these subjects.

As previously noted, like most people, we sometimes misread the significance of demographics, but simply avoiding all discussion of difference is certainly not the answer to this problem. How can tutors and writers critically engage the socially constructed and value-laden categories that influence their perspectives if they do not name them at all? During the focus groups, tutors shared stories of working with writers who so feared offending others that they avoided discussions of difference even when their writing situations clearly called for them. For example, one tutor described a session in which a writer avoided identifying the gender of an author about whom he was writing even though, the tutor said, "it was really important to know that [the author] was a woman . . . it was the only way [the writer's] sentence could make any sense." Since the subject of this student's paper emphasized her perspective as a woman, the student could not write coherently without acknowledging the subject's gender. In the tutor's reading of this scenario, the writer felt so pressured to avoid topics like gender that he "skirt[ed] an issue" central to his paper, practicing obfuscation rather than the respectful discussion of difference called for by the situation.

Another tutor observed that she becomes even more hesitant in addressing race and other differences when the writer with whom she is working acts "uncomfortable" and is unwilling to talk about the issue. She argued that tutors need to not only overcome their hesitancy but also learn "how to model" productive discussions of differences. "If we don't set the tone," she explained, writers will continue their strategies of avoidance. The "How Tutors and Writers Can Challenge Oppression through Attention to Language" list provides strategies that can help all tutors and writers discuss differences themselves and model such discussion for others.

2. Erases Differences

Some tutors in the focus groups observed that writers not only erase differences by avoiding discussions of difference altogether but also by ignoring some significant differences while attending to others. For instance, tutors described writing (by themselves as well as by others) that presented "Asian" or "female" identity as importantly distinct from "non-Asian" or "male" identity but that completely ignored important differences among broadly defined categories of "Asians" and "women." Mandy herself has been called out by fellow tutors and writers when she made assumptions about their interests based on their race or ethnicity while ignoring other important aspects of their identities such as political commitments and family relationships.

One's language can also at times erase differences between the human categories one names. For example, Mandy once tutored a writer who compared attitudes about education in the experiences of Richard Rodriguez, Alice Walker, and the writer's own Italian immigrant grandfather. The writer read Rodriguez as obsessed with education, Walker as negligent of education, and his grandfather as inhabiting a perfect middle ground; he drew on his grandfather's business success as evidence. The student oversimplified and at times misread Rodriguez and Walker. Moreover, he failed to consider how or why his grandfather's experience differed in crucial ways from that of Rodriguez, a Mexican American man, or Walker, an African American woman. His line of argument called for questions like, "Why would Rodriguez need to act differently to achieve success in the academy than the writer's grandfather acted to secure business success?" and "How might the very definitions of education offered by Walker and the grandfather differ because of gender, race, culture, or other factors?" By oversimplifying the experiences of Rodriguez, Walker, and his grandfather, the writer disregarded significant differences among them. He not only put forth an underdeveloped argument but also participated (albeit most likely unconsciously) in social structures that perpetuate inequalities by marking some differences as worthy of attention and others as not.

3. Assumes Uniform Readership

In both focus groups, tutors noted that they and other writers often give little, if any, thought to the audiences of their papers, perhaps because the assignments instructors give often fail to clarify these audience(s). Tutors also noted their own and other writers' tendency to assume that theirs is an audience from the same demographic and/or ideology as themselves or to assume that their audience will hold perspectives viewed by the writers as dominant. As an anthropology instructor, Shan-Estelle routinely comes across students who write about "our culture" when comparing a behavior or belief of another culture to their own. Her students also signal their assumption that readers will be from "their culture" when they use pronouns like "we," "us," and "our." Even as she consciously tries to acknowledge diverse perspectives, Mandy has also been challenged at times by her graduate instructors for using similar pronouns in course papers and class discussion about minority-authored literature. Harry Denny observes a similar trend among writing center administrators who often speak about how "we" administrators and tutors—assumed to be white, middle/upper class, and native English speaking—can learn from "them," minority writers (5). During a staff meeting stemming from the focus groups, one tutor from our center observed that "Pronouns say a lot!" They do, and the habit of using them in ways that exclude certain readers is hard to break.

Pronouns are not the only means through which writers demonstrate assumptions about readers. For instance, Mandy tutored someone whose assumptions rested in an adjective. The writer was working on a personal statement for a physical therapy program. In the prompt for the statement, the program made clear its valuing of diversity and asked applicants to reflect on their experiences with diversity. The writer had appropriately chosen to write about an experience in an actual physical therapy setting where she had worked. In the draft she discussed with Mandy, she reflected on her handling of socioeconomic class diversity in that setting. She keenly analyzed the setting's location and the major populations it served: relatively wealthy clients affiliated with a local university and rural working class clients. She focused on a female truck driver with whom she worked several times and whom she vividly described. Throughout her statement, however, she referred to the truck driver's language and behavior as "inappropriate." Without qualifying her terminology, she seemed to assume that the admissions committee reading her statement would view the woman in the same way. But a committee from a program that strongly promotes diversity would likely challenge the writer's simple categorization of working class behavior as "inappropriate" in physical therapy clinics.

4. Minimizes Significance of Discrimination

Writers may at times minimize the weight of discrimination when they avoid discussing difference, erase differences, or assume they can speak of their readers as a single unified group. One of Mandy's former academic writing students minimized discrimination through all of these means in an essay comparing his experience as a white child getting briefly separated from his parents in a big box store to James Baldwin's account in "Stranger in the Village" of his experience being "lost" in an all-white Swiss village (a town wherein he was referred to as the devil because of his black skin). This student minimized the racism Baldwin experienced by equating it with his own relatively minor experience of distress. Whereas this student implicitly minimized the scale of racial discrimination that Baldwin experienced, others might minimize the significance of discrimination by explicitly accusing marginalized subjects of exaggerating their experiences of discrimination. For instance, in their discussion of the minimization of racism, Bonilla-Silva and Embrick describe Whites who claim that non-Whites blow racial discrimination out of proportion. These Whites figure their contenders as dwelling in the past and reading race into situations where it is irrelevant; they figure themselves, in turn, as more enlightened since they have overcome discrimination and discussions of it (7–8).

Unlike those who sidestep important differences, thereby downplaying the significance of discrimination, writers sometimes minimize discrimination while strongly emphasizing differences. For example, one of the tutors in our focus groups shared about working with writers (and teachers, by way of their assignments) who minimized discrimination in debates surrounding homosexuality. Because their assignments asked them to, the writers emphasized "sides" of various debates—about marriage laws, military policy, etc.—while wholly ignoring concerns about discrimination. Having personally experienced severe discrimination because of her sexual orientation, the tutor felt frustrated by such assignments. Prior to the focus group, however, she did not feel comfortable getting into discussions about discrimination with students during tutoring sessions, so she stuck to other issues, such as their use of sources.

5. Speaks of Oppression as Only in the Past

Previous scholarship—by Grimm, Barron, Denny, Villanueva, and Geller et al.—has effectively made the case that oppression still exists and that writing centers have a responsibility to address it. Like Bonilla-Silva and Embrick, we argue that minimizing racism—and we would add other forms of oppression—by viewing it solely as a past problem perpetuates injustice and even threatens to undo civil rights accomplishments. Hence, we include "Speaks of oppression only in the past" as a problem. During our focus groups, tutors nodded in recognition when Mandy recounted how a former student started a paper: "Spike Lee made this movie back in 1989 when racism was still a problem in the United States." Whatever the dates referenced—whether 1989 or the nineteenth century—tutors report that writers frequently speak of oppression as occurring only in the past. Perhaps writers feel they can speak with more academic authority on a subject if they position themselves as removed from it. We do not have the space here to fully explore reasons why writers figure oppression as taking place only in the past. We can say, though, that this is one of the most common enactments of the everyday language of oppression on our campus.

Tutors in the focus groups shared not only about other writers but also about their own tendency to speak of certain forms of oppression as matters of history. One tutor provocatively described his shifting attitude towards sexism. He used to think that there was "no such thing" as sexism, that "sexism has been fixed." He credited a sociology class with helping him to realize that sexism is "alive and well" and spoke of his ongoing attempts to recognize sexist attitudes among women as well as men. His candid story demonstrates how broader discussions of oppression can naturally emerge when tutors share about their practices as writers and tutors.

6. Exoticizes

Shan-Estelle's anthropology students frequently exoticize other cultures, not unlike professional anthropologists who for decades primarily studied cultures they characterized as "primitive." When Shan-Estelle's students exoticize, they tend to focus only on what they see as extreme differences between themselves and the "others" about whom they write. They also pass value judgments on these "others" and their cultural practices, often with labels like "weird," "strange," "abnormal," and "extreme." The students' exoticization inhibits their ability to relate to cultural "others" as well as their ability to engage differences with accuracy and nuance.

During the focus groups, the tutor who described writers addressing homosexuality debates also suggested that these writers' assignments promote exoticization.

Writers are meant to engage the debates objectively, considering how they apply to a group of removed gay "others." This tutor suggested that such assignments frame homosexuals as a strange and separate part of the population in much the same way that some of the anthropology papers Shan-Estelle has seen describe "other" cultures as "strange" or "abnormal."

Recall also Mandy's experience with the student who described a truck driver's behavior as "inappropriate" in her application to a physical therapy program. This case highlights the way in which one's language might normalize one's own experience when exoticizing the experience of perceived "others." As the writer described working in a physical therapy setting with a patient whose loud speech and cursing the writer labeled "inappropriate," the writer never labeled, let alone scrutinized, the physical therapy setting as the middle class or white collar space she implied it to be. Her normalization of the physical therapy setting's middle class culture served to further exoticize the truck driver's working class behavior.

7. Presents Stereotypes as Evidence

No writer can fully escape the powerful influence that stereotypes play in every society. In a 2007 entry on the Northeast Writing Centers Association's blog, Kevin Lamkins discusses an experience tutoring a writer whose language seemed to reference the stereotype of "African Americans . . . as entertainment for whites" as evidence for her argument in praise of a particular dance production. Shan-Estelle once tutored a writer who similarly relied on stereotypes for evidence and produced a shallow argument as a result. The writer had begun her project with a provocative research question asking how gender influences men's and women's expectations about marriage. As she pursued the question, though, the writer relied on the stereotype of men as breadwinners and women as housewives. Instead of exploring the reasons why these ideas are stereotypes and questioning the ways that men and women adhere to or reject these socially constructed roles, her paper presented them as facts. She described this household configuration as "traditional" but did not consider the origins of this "tradition" or articulate its role in her analysis. Both Lamkins's and Shan-Estelle's experiences are ones in which writers seem unaware of their reliance on stereotypes and thus unable to consider possibilities beyond the stereotypes or, equally important, to analyze the origins or significances of the stereotypes themselves.

Like anyone else, tutors on our writing center staff cannot escape the pervasive power of stereotypes and rely on one another to identify and confront them. During the focus groups, even as one tutor was in the midst of acknowledging his limits in recognizing certain types of oppression, it took another tutor to call him out for the sexist stereotype present in his continual references to scientists as male. At our staff training session after the focus groups, some tutors challenged others to scrutinize their own stereotypes of the international students whose stereotypes and "culturally-based prejudices" they were describing. Another tutor who had overheard one of Mandy's tutoring sessions pointed out that Mandy had failed to notice and may have been complicit in stereotypes of sexual assault victims coming across in the paper discussed in that session.

8. Disrespects Sources from "Other" Perspectives

One of our focus groups discussed the tendency among many writers to refer to published women writers by their first names, and some members of the group read this practice as discriminatory. They observed that, as writers new to academic discourse learn the convention of referring to authors by their last name, they "slip up" more often when referring to women than men. These tutors see slip-ups as significant, even if they are unintentional. Mandy's experience anecdotally supports their observations. For instance, in the previously discussed paper that erased differences between Richard Rodriguez, Alice Walker, and the writer's grandfather, the writer consistently referred to both of the men (including his own grandfather) by their last names but always used "Alice" for Alice Walker, the paper's lone female subject. More recently, Mandy taught a writing course wherein several students referred to male writers by their last names while writing "Barbara" in reference to Barbara Ehrenreich.

In a 2009 academic conference presentation, writing instructor Katie Silbereis demonstrated how extensively one's language can disrespect sources from perspectives perceived as "other." Silbereis described her composition students' response to an assignment that asked them to engage Joseph Conrad's novel *Heart of Darkness* and Chinua Achebe's essay "An Image of Africa: Racism in Conrad's *Heart of Darkness.*" Silbereis had encouraged her students—the majority of whom were white and male—to approach both texts critically and was surprised when nearly all of the students wrote of Achebe's position in belittling tones while praising Conrad's literary genius. Notably, most of these students also failed to analyze specific material from either text even though the assignment asked for such engagement. Instead, the students cast both authors into simple type: Conrad, the white canonical author of unquestionable merit; and Achebe, the whining African making too big a fuss over racism of the past.

In this case, as in the cases of writers referencing women authors by their first names, the disrespected perspectives are often but not always perceived as "other" than the writer's own. Some of the students who referred to Barbara Ehrenreich by her first name in Mandy's class were women, and while the majority of Silbereis's students were white, tutors in our center have sometimes observed students of color writing dismissively of authors from their own racial and ethnic demographics. Whether or not writers consider perspectives like "female," "African," "gay," or "disabled" as other than their own, they do often figure them as "other" than a perceived dominant or "normal" perspective and attend to them with less respect as a result.

9. Fails to Distinguish Sources' Views from Writers' Own

As we pointed out when introducing this list, some of the moves it describes are not limited to situations involving oppression but are generally commonplace. Failing to distinguish sources' views from one's own is an especially common pitfall for novice academic writers who often feel that they should share material only from other, more authoritative sources rather than clearly contributing their own voices to issues. Readers can feel offended or even oppressed, though, as well as just confused, when writers fail to distinguish their own views from the views of sources that rely on oppressive perspectives. Take, for instance, some of the papers from Silbereis's class wherein students described Africans as "savages" without clarifying that this was actually Conrad's descriptor. Whether or not they found Conrad's depiction problematic, many students likely did not mean to claim the term "savages" as their own or come across as sharing Conrad's views. However, when they failed to properly attribute terminology to Conrad or to analyze the terminology in their own voices, their positions remained unclear. They also missed out on an opportunity to expose and confront oppressive language, a practice that might have led them to a greater awareness of their own positions in relation to oppressive systems.

Several tutors who participated in our focus groups made similar observations about a group of writers they had recently tutored from First Year Experience classes who had attended a lecture on hip-hop music and the links between hip-hop musicians and political activism. The tutors frequently saw drafts of reflection papers about this lecture that included descriptions of hip-hop as "violent," "dangerous," or "crude." At first, the tutors assumed the writers held this position, but then they realized through further discussion with the writers that they were trying to summarize a common white middle class American view of hip-hop described in the lecture. In the words of one tutor, "instead of saying 'Hip-hop was seen as dangerous,' he [a writer] just wrote, 'Hip-hop is dangerous.'" This same tutor, along with others, explained that some writers also clearly stated or implied that they personally believed hip-hop to be "dangerous" or "vulgar." Whether they wanted to align or distance themselves from the position described in the lecture, had they attempted to better articulate distinctions between their own ideas and ideas belonging to specific sources, all of these writers could have more critically examined race-based assumptions and values.

10. Misunderstands or Misrelates Sources' Views

In addition to not distinguishing their own thoughts from those of their sources, the writers responding to the hip-hop lecture frequently misunderstood and/or misrelated the views of the lecturer. Shan-Estelle tutored one of these writers. When she asked where the "hip-hop is dangerous" idea came from, the writer defensively replied, "Well, that's what the lecturer said." Several tutors in the focus group saw similar responses. They also reported that most writers could not initially answer their questions about why the lecturer would say "hip-hop is dangerous" or whether or not this was the lecturer's own belief. After much more conversation with the writers, the tutors deduced that the lecturer had been describing the beliefs of many white middle class Americans and that these beliefs differed drastically from his own. The examples from the hip-hop lecture papers aptly demonstrate the way in which writers commonly 1) fail to recognize or identify a source's own views, and 2) fail to clearly reference the intermediate sources referenced by their primary sources. Some of the First Year Experience students seemed to genuinely believe that the lecturer thought hip-hop was dangerous, asserting "that's what the lecturer said." Others sensed a disparity between the lecturer's view and the views he referenced but did not know how to sort out these differing views in their own prose. The case of these writers also demonstrates the way in which the last two items on this list often merge together. Writers who completely omitted the voice of the lecturer as an identified source consequently had no means by which to consider the various sources at play in the lecturer's discussion of hip-hop. Learning to examine more of the sources (direct and indirect) at play in their own language can help tutors and writers alike to not only make their views more clearly understood but also expose and address the complex networks of influences that generate oppressive language.

DISCUSSION OF LIST 2: HOW TUTORS AND WRITERS CAN CHALLENGE OPPRESSION THROUGH ATTENTION TO LANGUAGE

Tutors in the 2008 focus groups shared their strategies for addressing the everyday language of oppression when we explicitly asked them to, but, more often, they organically wove discussions (and sometimes heated debates!) about tutoring strategy into their conversations about the oppressive language they see in their own and others' writing. We have compiled a list of strategies primarily by drawing on the 2008 focus group materials and our own experiences. As with the list of language patterns, many of these strategies are ones that tutors already use in contexts that do not involve oppressive language. Tutors in our center have found it helpful to consider how tried-and-true strategies can play out in contexts involving oppressive language. All writing center tutors likely need training in how to better recognize manifestations of the everyday language of oppression, like those discussed in the previous section, so that they can apply effective tutoring strategies (with which they may well be familiar) in those situations.

1. Clarify Meanings Together

Tutors in the focus groups reported that they often ask fellow tutors and writers to clarify their meanings when they sense oppressive language at play. They ask, "What do you mean?" "What are you trying to say here?" or "Why do you say this?" Tutors see this strategy as crucial since it enables them to maintain an open, non-accusatory stance and enables writers to take charge of their own reflection about their writing. When writers address questions about meaning, they also begin to address issues of oppression embedded in their lack of clarity. As discussion of the previous list demonstrates, tutors frequently see the language of everyday oppression when writers are unclear and vague about their own or their sources' perspectives, the subjects about whom they write, or their intended audiences. In many cases discussed in the focus groups, tutors found that their own and others' language came across as unclear because the writers themselves were actually still unclear about their ideas. In those cases, asking "What do you mean?" does not prompt definitive one-sentence answers but rather sparks conversations and more questions that can provide writers with scaffolding for developing, and sometimes challenging, their ideas and positions as well as their prose.

2. Express Understanding of One Another's Meaning

Our center encourages tutors to see themselves as readers, a test audience for writers. Therefore, some tutors in the focus groups had shared their interpretations of student writing with the writers, a somewhat more personal—and perhaps more directive— way to clarify meaning than open "What do you mean?" questions. For instance, when working with the writer applying to a physical therapy program, Mandy let the writer know that when she read her lines about the truck driver's "inappropriate" behavior, she sensed, from the writing, that the writer judged the woman's behavior as inappropriate by some authoritative outside standard and thought that it would be inappropriate in any setting (since the writer did not say that the behavior was inappropriate just for the particular physical therapy setting she described). After expressing her understanding of the text and indicating that she knew this conveyed meaning may not have been intentional, Mandy asked the writer, "Is that what you meant to say?" This question led to a conversation about the writer's physical therapy setting, what this setting valued and why, and other settings where the truck driver's behavior might have been completely appropriate.

During this session, the writer and Mandy both identified subtle forms of class discrimination they had not thought about before and questioned their own complicity in that discrimination. Tutors in the focus groups observed that interactions are more difficult when writers actually hold and want to express the oppressive stances coming across in their writing. One tutor noted, "I think that if a tutor sees a prejudice then it's not our place to tell [writers] that their prejudice is wrong because . . . it's their belief system. But if [writers] are saying something that is prejudiced that they don't know is coming off as prejudiced, then we do have a responsibility to tell them." Other tutors felt ethically obligated to challenge oppressive views in addition to clarifying them with writers, and they used some of the strategies discussed below.

3. Discuss Meaning and Use of Sources

Just as the tutors in our center are trained to see themselves as readers of writers' work, they are also trained to see reading skills as inseparable from writing skills. We were not surprised, then, when tutors in the focus groups frequently described discussions with writers about the texts writers engaged and the strategies tutors suggested for reading those texts. When writers fail to distinguish their own perspectives from those of their sources or write about sources in a confusing manner, tutors generally ask writers to "step back" and orally describe the content of their sources. In a similar vein, when writers are confused about the meaning of sources, tutors sometimes ask writers to review their notes on sources or the original sources themselves. Such strategies, we believe, help writers improve their reading comprehension. Once writers begin to better understand the meaning of their sources in this manner, tutors work with them to clarify their use of sources with questions such as, "Which source says this?" "Do you agree with this writer?" and "How do you react to that perspective?" When working with the First Year Experience students who wrote about the hip-hop lecture, for example, tutors prompted writers to distinguish their views from the lecturer's and also asked questions such as, "Is that what the lecturer believes, or is he referencing others?" While all of the tutors in the focus groups had engaged writers in conversations about their sources, one tutor in particular viewed such conversations as essential. She explained that she always asks, "What's your source?" as a way to get writers to clarify their use of sources but also to see the need for more evidence to support their positions (and, possibly, to see flaws in their positions). Beginning with questions about sources, she said, also enables her to keep some personal distance when writers express oppressive views and/or views with which she disagrees. She seeks to avoid directly critiquing writers' arguments, but she finds that talking about sources can function as an equally effective (and, for her, more comfortable) way to get writers to clarify their sources and question their positions.

4. Pose Counterarguments

This tutor, along with some others in the focus groups, did not feel comfortable posing counterarguments with writers, but others saw this strategy as one of the most effective ways to encourage writers to think critically about their ideas and consider more diverse perspectives. When commenting on an earlier draft of this article, a colleague asked, "Isn't [posing counterarguments] a common tutorial and peda-gogical strategy in general, as old as Socrates, and generally valid?" We reply, "Yes!" We have already noted that many of the strategies we discuss are not new and apply to tutoring in general even as they also serve additional roles in addressing oppres-sion. We also imagine, though, that some writing center practitioners will feel un-comfortable with this strategy (despite its tie to Socrates) since they may view it as overly directive for peer tutoring or, like the tutor discussed above, as just too per-sonal. Posing counterarguments—like any other strategy—can become too directive; tutors, for instance, might tell writers which counterarguments to include in a paper and give a detailed outline of how to respond to those counterarguments. However, posing counterarguments does not need to be overly directive. Along with most of the tutors in our focus groups, we see posing counterarguments, in the spirit of a peer reader, as an effective strategy and, in some cases, the best strategy for address-ing the everyday language of oppression.

One tutor observed in her focus group that tutors may best tackle oppressive strains in a writer's argument by "just bringing up the multiple ways that people could argue and those [counter] arguments could be valid." Other tutors in this focus group also spoke in general terms about the effectiveness of raising "other perspectives"—posing "counter audiences," if you will—who might take offense at a writer's argument. During informal conversations around our center, several tutors have recounted tu-torials wherein they drew on their own subject positions as readers to pose specific counterarguments. For instance, one tutor explained to a writer how she would find fault with part of his argument "as a woman." Many tutors on our staff seem comfort-able speaking personally and somewhat confrontationally, but tutors do not always rely on direct personal experience to raise counterarguments. One tutor, for example, recalled raising a counterargument that an atheist might make to a writer who as-sumed a uniformly religious readership even though that tutor is not an atheist. In her tutoring, Mandy has also encouraged writers to draw on their own and others' experiences to pose counterarguments to sources, including sources that discriminated against groups with which the writers identified.

5. Maintain a Non-Combative Tone

Tutors who are comfortable with counterarguments and confrontation still seek to maintain a positive, collaborative tone. The focus groups recognized that hostility can quickly render a session unproductive as well as uncomfortable. Even the tutor most vocal about his commitment to "say[ing] what [he] think[s]" noted that he does not tell writers, "I think you're wrong," but instead readily shares his opinions and asks questions like "Why do you say this?" In "Centering Difference," Jay Sloan describes himself as a nonjudgmental reader and someone who "posed no threat" to a writer (65). Tutors in our focus groups similarly recognized the importance of maintaining an open-minded and non-threatening posture with writers as they pose counterarguments and deploy other strategies for addressing oppressive language.

6. Address Language without Accusations of Intentional Oppression

Accusing writers of being oppressive, for example by making statements such as, "you're being very sexist here," will clearly counteract the tutoring goal of maintaining a non-combative tone. Tutors also want to avoid accusations since, as we discussed in the opening of this article, writers often do not intend to express the oppressive stances that their language conveys. Moreover, some tutors in the focus groups felt that offending writers or putting them in a defensive position would compromise the tutoring relationship and the writers' receptivity to their feedback. As we have talked with tutors in the focus groups and informally, we find ourselves frequently returning to the importance of rapport building. The experience of tutors in our center suggests that asking students about their lives beyond their writing and creating a non-judgmental atmosphere of trust, while always important for peer tutoring, is especially key in fostering productive conversations about oppressive language. Because tutors in our 2010 focus groups and recent all-staff discussions have significantly developed our consideration of tone and rapport, we save further attention to these issues for our conclusion.

7. Name the "Elephant in the Room"

We take the name of this strategy directly from the focus group transcripts. As tutors in one of the focus groups discussed writers' and tutors' tendency to avoid discussions of difference—often out of fear of coming across as discriminatory or non-politically correct—one tutor observed, "It's like, there's an elephant in the room here, and it's called race." This same tutor acknowledged that tutors "have to know how to model" respectful talk about race and other sites of difference. Writing center practitioners can begin this modeling through some simple naming. One tutor worked with a student who was "so afraid of talking about [race]" that he "didn't talk about it at all" in his paper even though the assignment asked him to summarize and analyze a lecture entirely about race relations. During the tutoring session, the tutor identified the subject of race as well as the student's hesitancy in addressing it. As a result, the tutor and writer had a productive dialogue, attending to what the speaker actually said about race and why, along with the student's response. Our writing center staff has come to see again and again the importance of tutors' willingness to openly discuss sites of difference and oppression with one another as well as other writers if they are to increase their collective awareness, understanding, and ability to confront oppressive language.

Sometimes tutors' demographic markers are the elephants that need naming. In the focus groups, some tutors came to see their limits in failing to recognize class discrimination only after they came to name themselves as middle-upper class. Another tutor realized that he is unlikely to notice assumptions rooted in identities that he shares, such as "male," "Catholic," and "Irish American." These tutors demonstrate that naming one's perspectives can play a significant role in identifying certain forms of oppression as well as the gaps in one's viewpoints.

8. Learn to Better Identify and Address Language That Perpetuates Oppression

Even as they identified patterns of oppressive language in writing and shared methods for addressing such language, the focus groups also repeatedly referenced tutors' limits in identifying oppressive language as well as their desire to improve their strategies. Everyone who participated in the focus groups co-created knowledge that immediately influenced their practices as writers and tutors, but they all left knowing that they had much more to learn. As we have emphasized throughout this article, our lists are meant to serve as a springboard to further knowledge, reflection, and resistance to oppression.

GOING FORWARD: THE LISTS AS A HEURISTIC IN OUR OWN CENTER AND BEYOND

While the 2008 focus groups revealed forms of oppressive language that tutors were already observing and responding to, the groups also generated new knowledge, new strategies, and new language for identifying and addressing effects of oppressive systems on language. Our staff continues to develop their knowledge of oppression and strategies for resisting it. In fall 2010, two years after our initial round of focus groups and staff training around the everyday language of oppression, our staff revisited the two lists during a staff training session and subsequent online discussion. We were taken aback by the tutors' insights as they, more than ever before, embraced the work of challenging oppressive language as their own. Since we were, by this time, shaping our work to share with audiences beyond our own center, we also gained Institutional Review Board approval for an additional round of focus groups with tutors, which we conducted shortly after the fall 2010 all-staff training session. We again used systematic random sampling to select participants for two focus groups. One focus group consisted of four undergraduate tutors and one graduate tutor; three undergraduate tutors participated in the second focus group. Whereas the information tutors shared during the 2008 focus groups enabled us to create our two-list heuristic, tutors in the 2010 focus groups drew on their experiences as writers and tutors to elaborate on the staff's engagement with the heuristic and to identify questions, concerns, and goals for our staff going forward.

As other writing centers similarly work to better identify and address the everyday language of oppression, they can use our two lists as a valuable heuristic for sparking new knowledge and strategies. We have created a blog with the same title as this essay to compliment the *Antiracist Writing Centers* blog and serve as a forum where writing center practitioners can share insights they generate as they use and adapt the lists. When we first presented the lists at a 2008 staff training session, tutors annotated them with their own experiences. They also debated what challenging oppression as a writing center could look like and how involved (or not) they wanted to be in such work. While the lists certainly became a knowledge-generating heuristic for our 2008 staff, our 2010 staff offers a better model for other institutions since most of them (like tutors at other writing centers) were not involved in the lists' initial creation; by fall 2010, most of our 2008–2009 staff had graduated. The tutors still on board had worked with the directors to build a staff community that is more diverse and tightly knit than ever. As they worked with the lists, the 2010 staff emphasized the following: the value of addressing oppression through deep attention to language; the roles of education, rapport, and receptivity when discussing oppressive language; and whether the terminology of "oppression" provides the best frame for the kind of work we have been discussing throughout this article.

Unlike the 2008 staff, which was very concerned with differentiating intentionally and unintentionally oppressive language, most tutors on the 2010 staff emphasized the effects of oppressive language regardless of writers' intentions. Many of these tutors therefore challenged one another to avoid just making language "sound nicer" without addressing the underlying assumptions that make it oppressive (whether those assumptions are the writer's own or not). One tutor in the 2010 focus groups said that she, on the one hand, thought it was "not at all useful" to show a writer how to be politically correct and described a tutoring experience that confirmed for her that she "couldn't care less about fixing student language" unless she and the writers were "actually talking about the issues." On the other hand, she saw oppression and language as intricately related and was incredibly frustrated when she voiced her "very real feelings" of being oppressed by language only to have friends respond by dismissing her as being too worried about political correctness. She gave the example of a roommate's frequently using words like "gay" and "homo" in a derogatory way. As a bisexual woman, the tutor felt "uncomfortable" around this roommate; she altered some of her behaviors and was constantly worried about how she would be treated if the roommate discovered her sexuality. Now the tutor does not think the roommate was "intending to oppress" her, but, she says, the language the roommate used did oppress her. "Language is powerful," the tutor said, and she wants tutors and writers to recognize that power.

This tutor and others articulate the value of focusing on a writer's language as a unique, effective way to address oppression. They find that focusing on writers' own words makes them "much more receptive" and "less defensive." As one tutor, a self-identified "social advocate," said in her focus group, "you can't make a closed-minded person open-minded in forty-five minutes," but, by focusing on their language, you can show writers "opposing views" and "alternative paths" so they have more approaches to choose from. As our staff considers just what tutors can do in their forty-five minute sessions with writers, they are also considering how our center's work of attending to writers' specific language differs from other types of diversity and anti-oppression programming on campus. Tutors cannot, in a single tutoring session, delve into all of the ways oppressive systems impact our society. They can, however, foster peer dialogue about very particular, personal, and often subtle expressions of oppression, thereby contributing uniquely to larger anti-oppression work.

Based on our 2010 staff's insights, the next time our staff works with the lists in our center, they will need to add at least two items to the "How Tutors and Writers Can Challenge Oppression through Attention to Language" list: 1) Be willing to teach and learn from one another, and 2) Leverage respect, sensitivity, and understanding to open conversations about difference. Many tutors have observed that their role as peers should not preclude them from drawing on their own experiences and education to teach others, just as they ought to be open to learning from the writers with whom they work. In our 2010 focus groups and online discussion, several tutors shared experiences of working with writers who were very receptive to learning. In the online discussion, one tutor summarized a conversation she had had with other tutors during the staff training session. In these tutors' experiences, she said, "ignorance and unawareness" were more often to blame for oppressive language in writers' work than "intolerance and animosity." "However," she noted, "on the list there was nothing about educating the student about the issue at hand." She continued, "Sometimes it's difficult to change your writing . . . especially if no one challenges your beliefs or word choice." Another tutor wrote, "Allowances must also be made for those who WANT to write without prejudice, but don't know HOW." The majority of writers and tutors in our center are receptive to learning from one another so as to more critically engage their own language and ideas. Some tutors, though, express frustration with fellow staff members and visiting writers alike who, as one tutor put it, don't seem interested in "listening at all."

Though their approach will not solve all questions about receptivity, tutors in the 2010 focus groups argued that a tone of respect, sensitivity, and understanding can increase receptivity and bolster an atmosphere of peer learning. Rather than just maintaining a non-combative tone, as suggested by our initial "How Tutors and Writers Can Challenge Oppression through Attention to Language" list, these tutors use supportive comments, shared experiences, and humor to build rapport, often leading to productive dialogue. Shan-Estelle and one of the tutors in our 2010 focus groups even reported telling writers that they sounded "like a jerk" (both used the same phrase on different occasions), a move that on the surface seems to conflict with the strategy of using a non-combative tone. However, in the context of tutorials in which they had built relationships with writers by engaging them openly and humorously, these tutors in fact showed a great deal of respectful camaraderie as they addressed oppressive language. They helpfully remind other writing center practitioners that they do not need to always take themselves so seriously as they engage in this seriously important work.

As they strategize toward building respectful rapport with writers, tutors on our 2010 staff frequently raise questions about linguistic ownership. Tutors respect writers and want writers to respect themselves as owners of their own words. At the same time, tutors understand that many voices influence the production of any individual's writing. For instance, one tutor in the focus groups described working with a writer who framed her paper as an analysis of Latin American governments' relative "success" in "dealing with" indigenous peoples. Through respectful dialogue, the tutor and writer exposed dominant perspectives at work in the writer's approach. Afterward, the tutor recalled wondering, "Why did she state it that way? Is it what was being taught in her class? Is it something from her high school education? Or is it something she learned at home?" Others in this group further explored the influence of teachers, observing that "a lot of people write what the teacher wants" or "what they think their professors think."

Some tutors felt that instructors sometimes perpetuated oppressive language in student writing, particularly when they actually insisted on or were perceived by their students to be insisting on shallow political correctness, "colorblind" ideology, or restrictive adherence to dominant discourses. A few tutors spoke of personal experiences with such instructors. Resonating with scholars like Carmen Kynard, Nancy Barron, Bethany Davila, Andrew Rihn, and Donna LeCourt, who envision writing tutors and instructors as challenging, not just serving, privileged discourses, one tutor argued, "Sometimes the authority figure isn't necessarily right, and it's likely important to get across to our tutees that it's okay to deviate from authority because new ideas aren't going to come up out of nowhere." This tutor also spoke to the ownership issue, suggesting that learning to own one's ideas, rather than just parroting others, is essential to college writing. When writers claim that their work repeats their teachers' or another source's ideas, Shan-Estelle sometimes replies, "But you wrote that; it's yours. Now let's talk about what you actually think." As writers find more agency, they come to see more clearly where their words entwine with oppressive discourses and can begin to identify possibilities for resistance.

As tutors address oppressive language, what are they doing exactly? Resisting oppression? Combatting discrimination? Working towards social justice? Since our project so robustly recognizes the significance of language, it makes sense that our staff continues to debate the best terminology for characterizing this work. We have been convinced by other scholars in the field—notably Frankie Condon—that "oppression" rather than "prejudice" (a term we had used in earlier stages of this project) is the right word for describing the effects of the language we are studying since these effects are systemic, ideological, and tied to many more histories than the term "prejudice" (often used to express personal bias) is able to convey. Many on our staff agree, and as they dialogue with tutors who do not see oppression as the best descriptor for this work, we see their debate about terminology as inseparable from their debate about practice (for instance, their exchange over whether or not tutors should help writers sound more politically correct). Some tutors at our writing center join other tutors we have met in seeking positive terminology—and thus positive mindsets and practices—for this work that represents tutors and writers as not just resisting, combatting, or working against something bad but also (or instead) working toward something good, such as social justice or equality. Some tutors on our 2010 staff suggested that we talk more about "raising awareness," a positive phrase that resonates with the staff's newly articulated commitment to teaching and learning from one another and other writers.

Our staff's emphasis on education and awareness confirms our sense that we should now pair our two-list heuristic with published scholarship. Geller et al. recommend having tutors read scholarship that prompts discussions of race, systematic racism, whiteness, and white privilege (97). By referencing their suggested reading list and other sources, tutors in our center can select texts to read as a staff that will enable us to complement our practice-based approach. Tutor-selected readings in critical pedagogy could especially further writing center practitioners' understanding of a tutorial's ability to expose ideology and power dynamics at play in discourse. In addition, one of our directors suggested Thomas Recchio's article on Bakhtinian "heteroglossia" in student papers, a piece that may especially appeal to tutors now as they discuss writers' agency in relation to the many voices that influence an individual's words. Jay Sloan's article "Centering Difference: Student Agency and the Limits of 'Comfortable' Collaboration" may likewise have special relevance for our staff as they consider issues of receptivity and rapport. As our fellow tutors express a renewed sense of themselves as peer educators and learners, our staff might also add to their development some activities suggested by Condon, Fremo, Geller et al., and Cynthia White et al. that can increase awareness of their own complicity—as individuals and writing centers—in systems of oppression and help keep them from slipping from peer to expert mode. Through sustained analysis of systematic oppression, writing center practitioners can increase their awareness that they are never completely outside of oppressive systems even as they seek to be more reflective, critical, and resistant from within.

Wherever we go from here, we will strive to keep tutors in the driver's seat. Barron and Grimm argue that training around race—and we would add other sites of oppression—is more likely to succeed when tutors are invited "as designers rather than as recipients of an imposed diversity experience" (72). Tutors drew on their experiences to create the knowledge that led to our heuristic. We are excited to see our current staff taking ownership of this work, and we will encourage them to collectively design ongoing training, programs, and actions. Thus far, the most fruitful dialogue in our center happens when our staff revisits, revises, and recreates our two-list heuristic. We are eager to hear about the critical conversations the lists will provoke at other writing centers.

WORKS CITED

Antiracist Writing Centers. Weblog. 5 Nov. 2008. Web. 17 May 2011.

Barron, Nancy, and Nancy Grimm. "Addressing Racial Diversity in a Writing Center: Stories and Lessons from Two Beginners." *The Writing Center Journal* 22.2 (2002): 55–83. Web. 15 Nov. 2008.

Bonilla-Silva, Eduardo, and David. G. Embrick. "The (White) Color of Color Blindness in Twenty-First Century Amerika." *Race and Antiracism in Education.* Ed. E. Wayne Ross. Westport, CT: Praeger, 2006. 3–24. Print.

Bokser, Julie. "Pedagogies of Belonging: Listening to Students and Peers." *The Writing Center Journal* 25:1 (2005): 43–60. Web. 17 May 2011.

Brown, Shan-Estelle, and Mandy Suhr-Sytsma. *Addressing the Everyday Language of Oppression in the Writing Center.* Weblog. 21 Oct. 2008. Web. 25 May 2011.

Condon, Frankie. "Beyond the Known: Writing Centers and the Work of Anti-Racism." *The Writing Center Journal* 27:2 (2007): 19–38. Web. 16 Nov. 2009.

Davila, Bethany. "Rewriting Race in the Writing Center." *The Writing Lab Newsletter* 31.3 (2006): 1–5. Web. 22 Jan. 2009.

Denny, Harry. *Facing the Center: Toward an Identity Politics of One-to-One Mentoring.* Logan, UT: Utah State UP, 2010. Print.

Dees, Sarah, Beth Godbee, and Moira Ozias. "Navigating Conversational Turns: Grounding Difficult Discussions on Racism." *Praxis: A Writing Center Journal* 5.1 (2007): n. pag. Web. 17 May 2011.

DiPardo, Anne. "'Whispers of Coming and Going': Lessons from Fannie." *The Writing Center Journal* 12: 125–44 (1992). Web. 17 May 2011.

Fremo, Rebecca Taylor. "Unlearning 'Habits, Customs, and Characters': Changing the Ethos of our Writing Center." *The Writing Lab Newsletter* 34.8 (2010): 1–6. Web. 17 May 2011.

Geller, Anne Ellen, Michele Eodice, Frankie Condon, Meg Carroll, and Elizabeth H. Boquet. *The Everyday Writing Center: A Community of Practice.* Logan, UT: Utah State UP, 2007. Print.

Grimm, Nancy Maloney. *Good Intentions: Writing Center Work for Postmodern Times.* Portsmouth, NH: Boynton/Cook, 1999. Print.

——. "New Conceptual Frameworks for Writing Center Work." *The Writing Center Journal* 29.2 (2009): 11–27.

Harris, Vincent. "The Journey Continues." *When Tutor Meets Student.* 2nd Ed. Ed. Martha Maxwell. Ann Arbor: U of Michigan P, 1994. 121–25. Print.

Innes, Sarah. "Literacy Myths, Literacy Identities: The Writing Center Regulates Institutional Constructions of Racial Identity." *Social Change in Diverse Teaching Contexts: Touchy Subjects and Routine Practices.* Eds. Nancy Barron, Nancy Grimm, and Sibylle Gruber. New York: Peter Lang, 2006. 183–200.

Johnson, Mariah. "Different Words, Different Worlds." *The Writing Lab Newsletter* 24.5 (2000). 14–16. Web. 17 May 2011.

Kilborn, Judith. "Cultural Diversity in the Writing Center: Defining Ourselves and Our Challenges." *The Allyn and Bacon Guide to Writing Center Theory and Practice.* Eds. Robert W. Barnett and Jacob S. Blumner. Boston: Allyn and Bacon, 2001. 391–400. Print.

Kynard, Carmen. "Writing While Black: The Colour Line, Black Discourses and Assessment in the Institutionalization of Writing Instruction." *English Teaching: Practice and Critique* 7.2 (2008): 4–34. *EBSCOhost.* Web. 18 Sep. 2010.

Lamkins, Kevin. "The Challenging Tutee-Racially Sensitive Writing." *NEWCA's Weblog: The Online Forum of the North East Writing Center Association.* North East Writing Center Association, 24 Sept. 2007. Web. 2 Oct. 2009.

LeCourt, Donna. "WAC as Critical Pedagogy: The Third Stage?" *JAC: A Journal of Composition Theory* 16.3 (1996): 388–405. *EBSCOhost*. Web. 20 Sep. 2010.

McDonald, James C. "Dealing with Diversity: A Review Essay of Recent Tutor-Training Books." *The Writing Center Journal* 25.2 (2005): 63–72. Web. 17 May 2011.

Prendergast, Catherine. "Race: The Absent Presence in Composition Studies." *College Composition and Communication* 50.1 (1998): 36–53. Print.

Recchio, Thomas E. "A Bakhtinian Reading of Student Writing." *College Composition and Communication* 42.4 (1991): 446–54. Print.

Rihn, Andrew. "Not Playing it Safe: Tutoring an Ethic of Diversity in a Non-Diverse Environment." *Praxis: A Writing Center Journal* 5.1 (2007): n. pag. Web. 4 Jun. 2009.

Silbereis, Katie. "Writing Between Drafts: Coming to Terms with Racism in Conrad's *Heart of Darkness* through Personal Narrative." *University of Connecticut Freshman English Conference on the Teaching of Writing*. U of Connecticut, Storrs, CT. 27 March 2009. Conference Presentation.

Sloan, Jay. "Centering Difference: Student Agency and the Limits of 'Comfortable' Collaboration." *Dialogue: A Journal for Writing Specialists* 8.2 (2003): 63–74. *EBSCOhost*. Web. 4 Jun. 2009.

Town, Jessamy. "Langston Hughes Takes on Tutoring." *When Tutor Meets Student*. 2nd ed. Ed. Martha Maxwell. Ann Arbor: U or Michigan P, 1994. 128–31. Print.

Villanueva, Victor. "Blind: Talking about the New Racism." *The Writing Center Journal* 26.1 (2006): 3–19. Web. 3 Oct. 2008.

Weaver, Margaret. "A Call for Racial Diversity in the Writing Center." *The Writing Center Director's Resource Book*. Eds. Christina Murphy and Byron Stay. Mahwah, NJ: Erlbaum, 2006. 79–92. Print.

White, Cynthia, Priscilla Lizasuian, Ashvin Kini, Kimberly Norris, Vicky Lim, Salvatore De Sando, and Somaiyya Ahmad. "Anti-racism and Peer Tutoring Praxis." *International Writing Centers Association Conference*. Alexis Park Resort Hotel, Las Vegas, NV. 31 Oct. 2008. Conference Presentation.

A Quest for Student Engagement: A Linguistic Analysis of Writing Conference Discourse

Molly Wilder

Molly Wilder was an undergraduate at Swarthmore College at the time this article was written. It originally appeared in *Young Scholars in Writing*.

Writing centers have a culture all their own. They have both individual cultures peculiar to their schools and histories and a common intellectual culture that has evolved over the past century. I entered this culture as a newly hired writing associate for Swarthmore College's Writing Associates Program. In the culture of our program, as well in the larger culture, a major topic of conversation and debate is directive and nondirective tutoring styles. The lore of our program and of the wider community has tended to encourage, if not expect, a nondirective style. The focus on peer collaboration, embodied by nondirective tutoring, as opposed to classroom hierarchy, embodied by directive tutoring, has been a backbone of writing centers' philosophy and existential justification (Boquet). But the expectation of nondirective tutoring is questioned both at Swarthmore and by recent empirical research (Thompson).

The conversation about directive/nondirective tutoring gets to the heart of what we care about in writing tutoring: First, what characterizes successful tutoring? Second, how do we achieve successful tutoring once we know what it is? Research studies often look for answers to these questions by asking tutors and students to evaluate their own conferences and methods. As a linguistics major, however, I was interested in a different approach for this study. I sought to identify categorizable linguistic units that were associated with tutoring success, look at how they functioned in actual conferences, and evaluate how well they worked as indicators of success from a third-person perspective. Because I did not want to lock myself into the directive/nondirective framework, I defined tutoring success in the more general terms of student engagement.

Defining student engagement can, however, be challenging. Although tutors generally have an intuitive understanding of what student engagement is and how to identify it (when the student pays attention, contributes agenda items, listens closely), there are many situations where it is unclear whether a student is engaged, or whether he/she could be more productively engaged. Even when a tutor does find that a student

533

is engaged, he/she may not know how or why it happened, and therefore will not necessarily be able to repeat what he/she did right in the future. This study is based on the conviction that tutors will better be able to elicit student engagement if they have more linguistic information about how student engagement manifests and how tutors elicit it. My intent was to analyze how a linguistic conception of student engagement might complicate the dichotomy of directive/nondirective tutoring.

DATA COLLECTION

In spring 2008, I solicited volunteers to participate in this study by e-mailing about thirty writing tutors to ask if I could videotape their writing conferences. The tutors I contacted constituted a diverse sample that included men and women from various academic majors and with different levels of tutoring experience. About half of those tutors I contacted were willing to participate. In total, I videotaped fourteen writing conferences, three of which are featured in this article. All participants were told that the project was intended to study writing tutor discourse, and they all consented in writing to participate with the understanding that they would be identified by pseudonyms.

Coding Development and System

The goal in using a linguistic frame to analyze student engagement was to build the frame from the data itself, thereby avoiding confusing or narrow predetermined conceptions of student engagement. Coded conversational analysis of writing conferences gave me a way to look for structural regularities in discourse related to student engagement and thus to analyze student engagement from the bottom up. The basic unit of my analysis is the conversational *move*. A conversational move is an utterance or set of utterances performed with a particular intent within the conversation, bounded either by a course-changing move by the other interlocutor or by a change in conversational direction by the speaker him- or herself, as I will show in examples at the end of this section.

The work of Ross MacDonald, who has a similar focus on conversational moves as the key unit in writing conference analysis, provided the foundation from which I constructed my coding system. MacDonald begins with a model common in classroom discourse (e.g., Mehan; Cazden) consisting of three basic conversational moves: initiation, reply, and evaluation (IRE). He expands this model to the MacDonald Tutoring Interaction Codes (MTIC), which adds two moves, marker and addition. Their definitions are, in his own words:

> An initiation is an utterance which intends to elicit a verbal or nonverbal response from another interactant. A reply is an utterance which is directly occasioned by a previously occurring initiation. An evaluation is an utterance which by inflection, tone, or word rates as positive or negative the accuracy or utility of a previous reply. . . . An addition move is an utterance, which has not been initiated, which clarifies, illustrates, extends, or elaborates the current topic. A marker is a one or two-word utterance ("um hum," "OK," "right") which indicates one's on-going attention to utterances of the other or indicates a boundary between topics. (4)

These definitions provided the basis for my own coding system. Although my system has some significant differences from MacDonald's, the core is the same, which gives me the benefit of retaining his conclusion that student-dominated addition-marker sequences are indicative of successful student engagement.

My framework for analysis was also influenced strongly by several other sources. First, the particular attention I pay to initiations was sparked by the work of Joann B. Johnson and informed by later work in a similar vein (Blau, Hall, and Strauss). Johnson brings together literature challenging the use of questions in educational contexts and invites further investigation of initiations in the form of, for example, statements or commands, specifically in writing tutoring. Her work encouraged me to look at initiations as key places to evaluate student engagement and, in particular, student structuring of the conference. Blau, Hall, and Strauss provided me with guiding questions for question analysis: Who asks the question, student or tutor? What type of question is it—open-ended, closed, rhetorical? What is its purpose? To move the conference forward? Get information? Elicit student participation? Couch a statement in question form? Though these are specifically about questions, modified versions of this list generally guide me in my analysis of all initiations.

Based on the above considerations, I developed the following coding system by coding and recoding the transcripts by hand and modifying the categories until they best fit the data:

> *Initiation (I):* a move that directly solicits a response or overtly changes the direction of the conversation
>
> Subcategories: request evaluation (req-eval), clarification (clar), suggestion (sug)
>
> Syntax tags: question (ques), statement (stat)
>
> *Reply (R):* a direct response to an initiation
>
> *Marker (M):* a short utterance or gesture signaling continued attention, encouragement, or a boundary between conversational moves
>
> *Addition (A):* an uninitiated move that may clarify, extend, or evaluate a previous move

I added subcategories to *initiation* for the purpose of being able to more specifically identify what kinds of initiations set up different types of exchanges, particularly those associated with student structuring of the conference. I could have added similar subcategories to the other categories (e.g., *evaluation, clarification,* and *related point* for *addition*), but these subcategories are not critical to my analysis, and therefore I have considered them encompassed by the definitions of the larger categories. I could also have added more subcategories to *initiation,* but these three alone captured almost all of the data, and so I decided to keep my subcategories as simple as possible.

Notice my removal of *evaluation* from the list of MTIC moves. *Evaluation* in MTIC and in IRE is a move directly following a reply that evaluates in some manner that reply. In my data, this very rarely happened. I decided instead to consider *evaluation* as an aspect that could manifest in several types of moves (e.g., *initiation, reply, addition*) rather than as a crucial element to my analysis.

The boundaries between additions and markers were difficult to decide some-times, but that distinction is not terribly important to my analysis; it is the boundar-ies between initiations and addition-marker sequences that matter, and those are relatively easy to pinpoint. When I made that boundary, I asked myself these ques-tions: Is this a new point? Could the speaker have stopped here?

To illustrate my coding process, here are several examples with explanation:

> HEIDI: I just kinda like wanted your comments mostly on, on like the argument and like if there's anything that you went, "Wow, that's problematic." (SI-ques:req-eval)

This is a student (S) initiation (I). Syntactically it is a question, and because the student is looking for an evaluative response, whether her argument is good or bad, it is a request for evaluation.

> DEREK: Um, so I think it might work best if we just go through the paper. (TI-stat:sug)

This is also an initiation, as it changes the direction of the conversation, but it is a statement (stat) by a tutor (T) and as it gives possible options for how to structure the conference, it is a suggestion (sug).

> LIDIA: So in this paragraph where you're talking about like the one Darly study and you're also talking about like the Lyson and Darly like sort of conceptual. (TI-ques:clar)
>
> MARSHA: Mhmm. (SM)
>
> LIDIA (*nodding*): Steps, right? (cont. prev. move)

This is the last kind of initiation, clarification (clar). It is the kind of initiation that asks for more information on the same topic or, as in this example, repeats back some information to check that the information was understood as intended.

> MARSHA: Yeah, it definitely does (SA) and um, also, I just don't know if like the kind of you know. (SA)
>
> *LIDIA NODS.* (TM)
>
> MARSHA: I thought I had you know. (cont. prev. move)
>
> *LIDIA NODS.* (TM)

Sometimes moves are punctuated by, but not ended by, other moves. I represent this by a tag (cont. prev. move), meaning that the move is a continuation of the previ-ous move by that speaker.

This coding guided my analysis of the conferences in my working model of how student engagement manifests linguistically: I looked for the addition-marker sequences favored by MacDonald as indicative of engaged tutoring interaction, and I focused on different kinds of initiations, particularly initiations representative of student agenda-setting. In the discussion below, I analyze three conferences that illustrate different manifestations of student engagement.

DISCUSSION

Conference 1

This first conference, a drop-in writing center conference, took place between two senior writing tutors and lasted thirty-one minutes. My expectation going into the analysis of this conference was that it would show a particularly high level of student engagement and student structuring of the conference, considering the strong emphasis on those qualities in the writing program and the experience level of the participants both as students and writing tutors. After explaining what the paper was for, a women's studies class, Heidi, the student, makes the first initiation, a request for evaluation in statement form:

> HEIDI: I just kinda like wanted your comments mostly on, on like the argument and like if there's anything that you went, "Wow, that's problematic." (SI-ques:req-eval)

Derek, the tutor, continues in a manner that encourages Heidi to keep control of the conference's agenda:

> DEREK (*nodding*): Okay. (TM)
> HEIDI: Yeah. (SM)
> DEREK: Um, well, do you want to talk about like where you're kind of like at and like your concerns or do you just want to go through the paper and see kind of how it's going? (TI-ques:sug)
> HEIDI: Um, okay, um, let's start with my concerns. (SR)

He gives her time and encouragement to continue that first marker, and then, when Heidi doesn't seem to know where to go next, he gives her two options for how to start the agenda of the conference. Notice that Heidi picks the option that will require her to direct the conference more, as opposed to following the paper.

For the next five and a half minutes, neither participant makes an initiation that changes this initial agenda. Heidi initiates one request for evaluation. Derek asks one clarifying question, but after answering, Heidi immediately continues with her concerns, with which they spend about seven minutes. Then, at a natural pause, Derek directs the conference towards the other option he initially offered:

> DEREK: Um, so I think it might work best if we just go through the paper. (TI-stat:sug)
> HEIDI (*nodding*): Let's do that. (SR)

Derek follows with a fairly indirect initiation:

> DEREK: Um, so the first thing: terminology. I really like it when people like define their terms. Um, it struck me, though, that you didn't define gender. (TI-stat:sug)
> HEIDI: Oh, right. Good point. (SM)

Both of these initiations are statements, and the second is a particularly good example of how a statement can be a more inviting initiation than a question. One could imagine Derek, with the best of intentions, asking at this point, "I was wondering, why didn't you define gender?" In the form of a question, this initiation might have several negative effects: (1) Heidi feels pressed to respond directly to the question, without understanding it better. (2) Feeling pressed, Heidi may try to construct an answer defensively such that it may be harder to convince her to consider the suggestion. (3) There is a sense of judgment and negativity—Heidi feels she missed something that is obviously important. (4) Heidi doesn't get the benefit of working out for herself why she didn't define gender and what she should change. In the conference as it unfolded, though, Derek continues to explain he had expected such a definition until Heidi offers a proposition for what her definition might be, and then herself decides to revise that definition.

The conference continues with exchanges of a general form, Heidi explaining her arguments and requesting evaluation on certain points, and Derek mostly asking questions to help her clarify her position and offering suggestions on structure. Every time one participant loses steam, the other picks up the conversation, each adding and explaining without prompting. The conference ends on a final request for evaluation and a transition into friendly chat.

In this conference, there were two major structuring moves with respect to the agenda. From the options Derek offers, Heidi first chooses to start with her concerns. The following conversation consists almost entirely of Heidi explaining her concerns, and Derek encouraging her to talk them out. This part lasts for seven minutes, so about a fourth of the entire conference. When Heidi ends with a request for evaluation, Derek suggests going through the paper as a way to structure the agenda. From that point on, topics of conversation are pulled either from Derek's written comments on the paper or the text itself. But it is important to note that when there was a lull in conversation, it was not always Derek who brought the conference back to the agenda. Once they settled on going through the paper, I counted twelve distinct topics of conversation. Five were initiated by Heidi and seven by Derek, so the structuring in this conference seems to be fairly equally distributed to both participants, although still slightly in favor of the tutor. The domination of addition-marker sequences was also fairly equal; sometimes Derek would explain his perspective and sometimes Heidi would talk out their ideas. Each encouraged the other to continue regularly, and each immediately picked up the thread of conversation when the other lagged. This conference seemed exemplary of a nondirective conference, where student and tutor interact as peers having a conversation as writer and reader. However, considering the unusual qualifications of the participants, this is probably not the most typical model for a Swarthmore conference.

Conference 2

This conference lasted only five and a half minutes—significantly shorter than other conferences in this sample. It also took place in the drop-in writing center. The participants were two sophomores: Lily, the writing tutor, and Wally, who had brought in an economics paper. In a move that seems like it could set up the kind of student agenda-setting seen in Conference 1, Lily begins with a solicitation of Wally's input on the agenda:

LILY: Um, is there anything in particular you wanted to start off with talking about, about this paper? (TI-ques:req-eval)

Wally explains vaguely that he is confused, ending with a general question for Lily:

WALLY: I guess a lot of it is just kind of like, does it sort of make sense? (SI-ques:reqeval)
LILY NODS. (TM)
WALLY: And flow? And like . . . I don't know. (cont. prev. move)

Lily responds with fairly general but very positive feedback:

LILY (*nodding*): Okay, sure, um, I mean, I thought it was actually really well written. (TA)
WALLY NODS. (SM)
LILY: And I thought it flowed and your organization was really good. (TR)
WALLY NODS. (SM)
LILY: To be honest, I really didn't have much to say about it, cuz I just thought it was so well written as it was. (TA)

Already, thirty seconds into the conference, it seems clear that it is going to be a short conference—very different from Conference 1. Wally, though he doesn't seem terribly confident about his paper, does not volunteer any specific issues to work on, and Lily has minimal criticism. She does give him one substantive criticism:

LILY: Um, so you have a very coherent argument, but you don't have a thesis. (TA)

The next move of Lily's framing is particularly interesting, though:

LILY: Um, but to be honest, reading it, it didn't seem like it would, um, be . . . (TI-stat:sug)
WALLY NODS. (SM)
LILY: . . . like, I mean, like it seems like maybe just kind of, you know, reread it for yourself . . . (cont. prev. move)
WALLY NODS. (SM)
LILY: . . . and then . . . (cont. prev. move)
WALLY (*NODDING*): Mhmm. (SM)
LILY: . . . just summarize in a couple sentences. (cont. prev. move)
WALLY NODS. (SM)
LILY: Um, I don't know, to be honest, I thought it was a really good paper. (TA)
WALLY NODS. (SM)
LILY: So I don't really have all that much to say about it, I'm afraid, um. (cont. prev. move)

Unlike Derek, Lily does not engage the student in talking through her criticism, either by soliciting his opinion or by trying to get him to come up with a solution, but rather just expresses confidence that he will be able to fix it on his own. Notice, also, that she gives one very specific suggestion; she does not enlist the student's help in identifying or understanding the problem. Lily then reiterates that she doesn't have much to say. Wally now expresses some confidence:

WALLY: Well, no, that's fine, I felt, I actually felt pretty good about it. (SA)

He talks through what his writing process was for a while, and then Lily raises another concern, a lower-level concern about citations and sources. Wally ends up deciding that he needs to talk to his professor about this issue and the conference, with respect to talking about writing, ends. Lily summarizes the content of the conference and then apologizes for how short the conference was and repeats that she didn't have much to say.

This conference shows very little student engagement. Wally does not come to the conference with any specific agenda. Lily comes with a very limited agenda, does not elicit any further agenda items from Wally, and does not engage him in addition-marker sequences of any length. Thus, neither of the two factors of student engagement I was looking for appeared in this conference.

Conference 3

This conference involved Lidia, a senior writing tutor who worked as the writing associate in the psychology course in which Marsha, a sophomore, was enrolled. The conference lasted thirty-one minutes. After some clarification about which parts of the paper to address, Lidia begins the conference by asking Marsha how she feels about the paper. Marsha responds at length:

MARSHA: Um, mhmm, let's see, I don't . . . it's hard because I've read plenty of like articles, you know, journal articles. (SR)

LIDIA NODS.

MARSHA: I've just never written one. (cont. prev. move)

LIDIA: Yeah, yeah. (TM)

MARSHA: So I thought it was a weird thing to write, I don't know. (cont. prev. move) I'm, I guess also, one, I'm not sure if I did enough in my results section. (SA)

LIDIA (*nodding*): Mhmm. (TM)

MARSHA: Or if I reported it correctly (cont. prev. move), cuz I like had like intro stat but . . . (SA)

LIDIA: (*nodding*): Yeah. (TM)

MARSHA: . . . but, you know, it kinda starts to . . . (cont. prev. move)

LIDIA: Well, it helps a lot. (TA)

MARSHA: Yeah, it definitely does (SA) and um, also, I just don't know if like the kind of you know. (SA)

LIDIA NODS. (TM)

MARSHA: I thought I had you know. (cont. prev. move)

LIDIA NODS. (TM)

MARSHA: I was kind of going on the, with my lit review, kind of like the right direction, but I just wasn't sure. (cont. prev. move)

LIDIA (*nodding*): Yeah. (TM)

MARSHA: So yeah, I don't know. (cont. prev. move)

LIDIA: Okay. (TM)

MARSHA: I mean, I also definitely like stylistically I have a lot of like, like where I am, mhmm, I have to go back . . . (SA)

LIDIA NODS. (TM)

MARSHA: . . . and like make this sound better. (cont. prev. move)

LIDIA LAUGHS. (TM)

MARSHA: But I'm like okay, this is like mainly like . . . (cont. prev. move)

LIDIA NODS. (TM)

MARSHA: . . . put my ideas out there . . . (cont. prev. move)

LIDIA (*nodding*): Yeah. (TM)

MARSHA: . . . and then have time to go back . . . (cont. prev. move)

LIDIA (*nodding*): Yeah, totally. (TM)

MARSHA: . . . make it stylistically better. (cont. prev. move)

LIDIA: Yeah, so are those the things that you're kind of like most interested in fixing?

Like, or like looking at? Like making sure that the lit review flows and like? (TI-ques:req-eval)

MARSHA: Yeah. (SM)

LIDIA: And that the results are right, that kind of stuff? (cont. prev. move)

This exchange is the first of several that reveal Lidia's tutoring style relies on encouraging markers and repeating the student's words back to her. The exchange contains several examples of places that Lidia could have jumped in, but instead used markers to encourage Marsha to continue. Many tutors might feel compelled to reply with feedback after statements such as "I'm not sure if I did enough in my results section," "I thought . . . I was kind of going on the, with my lit review, kind of like the right direction, but I just wasn't sure," and "So yeah, I don't know." One could imagine Lidia jumping in with an evaluation of Marsha's results section, her literature review, or just starting in on the concerns Lidia herself wants to address at any of these points. Lidia, however, does not reply, except with encouraging markers, to any of these, and Marsha comes up with another substantive concern, about the stylistic elements of her paper. At the end of the exchange, Lidia both repeats back specific concerns she heard, "making sure that the lit review flows," "that the results are right," and verifies with Marsha that these are the concerns she wants to address, "are those the things you're kind of like most interested in fixing?"

Next, they turn to the paper, and Lidia starts with what Marsha does well:

LIDIA: Um, so, just as like an overview, like basically like, um, I thought like you obviously like had a lot of really good studies that you'd found, and like I think you talk about those really well. (TA)

MARSHA: Okay. (SM)

LIDIA (*NODDING*): So like that's like, that's really great, yeah. (TA)

MARSHA: I wasn't sure, because I just, I had the model . . .

LIDIA NODS. (TM)

MARSHA: . . . I wanted to work off relying on Darly . . . (SA)

LIDIA (*NODDING*): Mhmm. (TM)

MARSHA: . . . and I'm like, okay, like they talk about this in my social psych textbook . . . (SA)

LIDIA: Yeah. (TM)

MARSHA: . . . and I don't just want to be like, you know . . . (SA)

LIDIA NODS. (TM)

MARSHA: . . . it is the studies that are supporting the concepts . . .

LIDIA (*NODDING*): Yeah. (TM) (cont. prev. move)

MARSHA: . . . but I don't want to just like reiterate what they say. (cont. prev. move)

LIDIA (*NODDING*): Yeah. (TM)

MARSHA: I want to like, you know, so, I . . . (SA)

LIDIA: Yeah, definitely. (TM)

MARSHA: I had to rewrite that a couple times. (cont. prev. move)

LIDIA (*NODDING*): Uh huh, yeah, so I think like, maybe like the direction you could go in then is like moving from the studies towards explaining your study . . . (TI-stat:sug)

MARSHA (*NODDING*): Okay. (SM)

LIDIA: . . . which is something that you like, you sort of like, you do like talk about in the introduction. (TA)

Lidia begins with positive feedback, but Marsha interrupts with a concern. Again, there are several places where Lidia could reply with feedback, but chooses not to, such as "I wasn't sure, because I just, I had the model I wanted to work off relying on Darly," and "I don't just want to be like, you know, it is the studies that are supporting the concepts, but I don't want to just like reiterate what they say." Like several examples above, these are all expressions of the student's uncertainty, which often prompts some kind of (usually positive or encouraging) feedback from the tutor. Lidia, however, encourages Marsha to continue explaining her concern with markers. When Marsha loses steam, Lidia does give her a suggestion, but in doing so, she points to a specific place where Marsha is already going in the right direction: "which is something that you like, you sort of like, you do like talk about in the introduction." By giving this kind of specific, relevant positive feedback, Lidia accomplishes several things: First, she gets the general benefits of giving positive feedback, such as improving the student's self-confidence, morale, and general goodwill towards the tutor and the conference. Second, she is able to give a concrete example of what she is talking about, one that the student understands. Finally, she frames her suggestion in a way that implies that the student already can and has done to some extent the suggested task, that it isn't a radical change or a completely new idea, but rather builds on what the student already knew to do.

Just as in the first exchange above, in which Lidia repeated back to Marsha what she heard Marsha say, Lidia explains her concern by repeating what Marsha does in her paper:

LIDIA: So you're sort of going through like the different things that can get in the way of helping, um, and then you start saying, like um, that you might, like here are like other things that could be risks . . . (TA)

MARSHA: Mhmm.

LIDIA: . . . and then you say like in this situation the researchers hypothesize (TA) and then all of a sudden like I think you're talking about your study, right? (TI-ques:req-eval)

MARSHA: Uh huh.

LIDIA: Did I interpret that correctly? (TI-ques:req-eval)

MARSHA: Yeah, yeah.

LIDIA: Okay, yeah, so like, so I'm reading this and I'm like, oh wait a minute, like, now you're not just talking about like general principles, all of a sudden you're talking about like your study . . . (TA)

MARSHA: Yeah.

LIDIA: . . . and it, I was just, it just took me a second to like process like, oh wait a minute. (TA)

MARSHA (*NODDING*): Okay. (SM)

LIDIA: Like that's where you are now. (cont. prev. move)

MARSHA (*NODDING*): Mhmm. (SM)

LIDIA: Um, so maybe like, there might be some way to like structure it so that it's making it clearer that that's what you're moving toward. (TI-stat:sug)

MARSHA: Mhmm. (SM)

LIDIA: Um, so that might be something like here's the literature I've summarized so far, but here's a gap in that literature . . . (TA)

MARSHA: Okay. (SM)

LIDIA: . . . and, which is, which is like kind of . . .

MARSHA: Yeah. (SM)

LIDIA: . . . which is the sort of thing you're saying here.

Lidia starts by giving a summary of what Marsha did: "So you're sort of going through like the different things that can get in the way of helping . . . and then you start saying, . . . here are like other things that could be risks, and then you say like in this situation the researchers hypothesize and then all of a sudden like I think you're talking about your study." Next, she verifies that this is what Marsha thought she said in the paper as well: "Did I interpret that correctly?" Then Lidia explains the issue by giving her personal reaction to the structure: "so I'm reading this and I'm like, oh wait a minute like, now you're not just talking about like general principles, all of a sudden you're talking about like your study." By giving her personal reaction, rather than just a direct suggestion, she invites Marsha to see her writing through the eyes of her audience (the specific audience of Lidia) and thereby see the problem for herself. This, assuming it is successful, helps Marsha understand the suggestion and give it more credibility. Again, then, when Lidia gives her suggestion, she points out that some of what Marsha has written already emulates Lidia's suggestion when she says, "which is the sort of thing you're saying here." This again implies that Marsha is already partially on the right track, and that she just needs to continue in that direction.

In terms of initiations, this looked like a very tutor-directed conference; Lidia had almost all the initiations (thirty-three for Lidia, only two for Marsha). This looks very different from the nondirective conference between Derek and Heidi. However, the kind of initiations Lidia used, usually clarifying questions and statements of her reaction to the writing, tended to set up long addition-marker sequences of the kind above, which involved Marsha working out her ideas in a very engaged way. Thus this style shows a way to evoke student engagement even within the framework of a tutor-directed and tutor-structured conference. One potential advantage of the control Lidia maintains in this conference is that she retains her agenda and is able to prioritize issues; although they do address the concerns Marsha brings up in the beginning (her literature review and results sections), the majority of the conference is spent discussing the introduction, which Lidia raises as her first concern. Thus, as a tutor, Lidia neither completely leaves the direction of the conference to the student, nor does she steamroll the student's concerns. Instead, she maintains the prioritization of her agenda in the conference, but integrates the student's concerns. This approach is also less dependent on having a proactive student, which probably contributed to Derek's ability to be nondirective in Conference 1.

Marsha also volunteered a significant amount of positive feedback. First, after they finish talking about the introduction:

> LIDIA: Okay, um, let's see, yeah, okay, alright, um, was there anything else from the introduction that you'd had a question about or . . .? (TI-ques:req-eval)
> MARSHA: No, I think you did a really good job. (SR)

Then again at the end of the conference:

> MARSHA: Thank you so much for your help. (SA)
> LIDIA: Sure, no problem, great. (TA)
> MARSHA: It was really, you really went through well . . . (SA)
> LIDIA NODS. (TM)
> MARSHA: . . . the issues that I had questions about. (cont. prev. move)

Of course, giving positive feedback may just be Marsha's personality, but it may also reflect that the conference was genuinely successful from her point of view, which is significant if the ideal tutoring style is intended to evoke student satisfaction and empowerment. If this conference was a genuine success from Marsha's point of view, it corroborates Thompson et al.'s findings in that Lidia both addressed Marsha's concerns and incorporated a lot of positive feedback into the conference.

SUMMARY OF RESULTS AND CONCLUSIONS

In Conference 1 Derek's nondirective style and Heidi's active participation style made for a conference in many ways exemplary of student engagement, such as Heidi's control of the agenda, frequent initiations, and addition-marker sequences. Conference 2 was an example of a conference that did not show much student engagement. Wally's lack of specific concerns and Lily's insistence that she did not have much to talk about quickly ended the conference, leaving little room for student engagement. In Conference 3, Lidia took a much more directive approach than Derek had done in Conference 1, but she evoked student engagement in a different way. Her style included summarizing Marsha's writing, offering her own reactions, and then rephrasing and focusing Marsha's spoken ideas. This approach did not allow for or elicit as much student-directed agenda-setting as the nondirective style of Conference 1, but it did regularly elicit addition-marker sequences in which Marsha talked her ideas out.

The vision of student engagement that emerges from these results is a bit different from the idea I started out with. Initially, I had a fairly nondirective expectation of what student engagement should look like; the goal is to get the student to set the agenda and talk through his/her concerns, a vision reflected in the two linguistic patterns I was looking for: student agenda-setting manifested in initiations and student-dominated addition-marker sequences. I still think those patterns are a good place to start when looking for engagement, but the concept is more complicated. Student agenda-setting as a model of student engagement probably works only with the kind of students who are able and willing to set the agenda and with tutors who are comfortable with that style. When considering addition-marker sequences, it matters not only who dominates them, but also what the content is and how much those sequences actually reflect student investment and understanding.

While Conference 1 is a model of how nondirection can elicit student engagement, Conference 2 shows how nondirective student engagement can fall flat if the student does not bring his own concerns to the table and the tutor is not able to otherwise draw the student into conversation. Conference 3 shows how a more classically directive style of conferencing can also be very effective in eliciting student engagement, and particularly how certain kinds of addition-marker sequences allow students to very constructively talk their thoughts out. These observations point towards a philosophy aimed not only at encouraging student engagement overall, but at considering the different ways student engagement can manifest and ways conferencing styles need to be individualized for particular students as well as take into account the strengths of particular tutors.

DIRECTIONS FOR FURTHER RESEARCH

As a sole researcher, I was limited in what I could do in this study, and I hope to see larger-scale research take these questions in several directions. First, it would be useful to be able to combine breadth of kinds of conferences and tutors with breadth of detailed analysis. Ideally, a future project would have the time and resources to analyze in detail a large body of data for more general trends and conclusions. Examples of specific and significant factors I was unable to incorporate include intonation, laughter, interruptions, pauses, and a more detailed analysis of nonverbal communication. My conclusions further suggest that it will be important to study not only what tutors do, but how students differ in the way they react to tutoring and how tutors see their own tutoring. It is quite unlikely that there is some kind of blanket method of tutoring that always successfully elicits student engagement. Rather, the success of the approach depends on how well it matches the style of both the tutor and the student. My hope is that others will continue to take the conception of student engagement beyond the directive/nondirective debate and look instead at how the particular context of each conference can give rise to particularized manifestations of student engagement.

NOTE

1. This study, with full IRB approval, was done for my senior thesis in linguistics at Swarthmore College.

WORKS CITED

Blau, Susan R., John Hall, and Tracy Strauss. "Exploring the Tutor/Client Conversation: A Linguistic Analysis." *The Writing Center Journal* 19.1 (1998): 19–48. Print.

Boquet, Elizabeth H. "'Our Little Secret': A History of Writing Centers, Pre—to Post-Open Admissions." *College Composition and Communication* 50.3 (1999): 463–82. Print.

Cazden, Courtney B. "Classroom Discourse." *Handbook of Research on Teaching*. 3rd ed. Ed. Merle C. Wittrock. New York: Macmillan, 1986. 432–63. Print.

Johnson, Joann B. "Reevaluation of the Question as a Teaching Tool." *Dynamics of the Writing Conference*. Ed. Thomas Flynn and Mary King. Urbana: NCTE, 1993. 34–50. Print.

MacDonald, Ross B. "An Analysis of Verbal Interaction in College Tutorials." *Journal of Developmental Education* 15 (1991): 2+. Print.

Mehan, Hugh. *Learning Lessons: Social Organization in the Classroom*. Cambridge: Harvard UP, 1979. Print.

Thompson, Isabelle, et al. "Examining Our Lore: A Survey of Students' and Tutors' Satisfaction with Writing Center Conferences." *The Writing Center Journal* 29.1 (2009): 75–105. Print.

Works Cited

Adelman, Clem, David Jenkins, and Stephen Kemmis. "Rethinking Case Study: Notes from the Second Cambridge Conference." *Cambridge Journal of Education* 6.3 (1976): 139–50. Print.

Adler-Kassner, Linda. "Ownership Revisited: An Exploration in Progressive Era and Expressivist Composition Scholarship." *College Composition and Communication* 49.2 (1998): 208–33. Print.

Alley, Michael. *The Craft of Scientific Presentations: Critical Steps to Succeed and Critical Errors to Avoid.* 2nd ed. New York: Springer Science+Business Media, 2013. Print.

Anderson, Paul V. "Simple Gifts: Ethical Issues in the Conduct of Person-Based Composition Research." *College Composition and Communication* 49.1 (1998): 63–89. Print.

Ashton-Jones, Evelyn. "Collaboration, Conversation, and the Politics of Gender." *Feminist Principles and Women's Experience in American Composition and Rhetoric.* Ed. Louise Wetherbee Phelps and Janet A. Emig. Pittsburgh: U of Pittsburgh P, 1995. 5–26. Print.

Babcock, Rebecca Day. "Interpreted Writing Center Tutorials with College-Level Deaf Students." *Linguistics and Education* 22.2 (2011): 95–117. Print.

———. *Tell Me How It Reads: Tutoring Deaf and Hearing Students in the Writing Center.* Washington DC: Gallaudet UP, 2012. Print.

———. "When Something Is Not Quite Right: Pragmatic Impairment and Compensation in the College Writing Tutorial." *The Writing Lab Newsletter* 35.5–6 (2011): 6–10. Print. Rpt. in this book.

Babcock, Rebecca Day, Kelleye Manning, and Travis Rogers with Courtney Goff and Amanda McCain. *A Synthesis of Qualitative Studies of Writing Center Tutoring, 1983–2006.* New York: Peter Lang, 2012. Print.

Babcock, Rebecca Day, and Terese Thonus. *Researching the Writing Center: Towards an Evidence-Based Practice.* New York: Peter Lang, 2012. Print.

Bailey, Steven K. "Writing Center Handbooks and Travel Guidebooks: Redesigning Instructional Texts for Multicultural, Multilingual, and Multinational Contexts." Diss. Michigan Technological U, 2010. Print.

Balester, Valerie, and James MacDonald. "A View of Status and Working Conditions: Relations Between Writing Program and Writing Center Directors." *WPA: Writing Program Administration* 24.3 (2001): 59–82. Web. 3 October 2013.

Baker, Brooke. "Safe Houses and Contact Zones: Reconsidering the Basic Writing Tutorial." *Young Scholars in Writing: Undergraduate Research in Writing and Rhetoric* 4 (2006): 64–72. Web. 6 June 2014. Rpt. in this book.

Barajas-Román, Maria E. "Writing Beyond the Words: Language Minority Students and School Discourse." Podis and Podis 301–10.

Barron, Nancy, and Nancy Grimm. "Addressing Racial Diversity in a Writing Center: Stories and Lessons from Two Beginners." *The Writing Center Journal* 22.2 (2002): 550–83. Print.

Bawarshi, Anis, and Stephanie Pelkowski. "Postcolonialism and the Idea of a Writing Center." *The Writing Center Journal* 19.2 (1999): 41–58. Print.

Bastian, Heather, and Lindsey Harkness. "When Peer Tutors Write about Writing: Literacy Narratives and Self Reflection." *Young Scholars in Writing: Undergraduate Research in Writing and Rhetoric* 1 (2003): 101–24. Web. 8 Jan. 2013.

Bazerman, Charles, Joseph Little, Lisa Bethel, Teri Chavkin, Danielle Fouquette, and Janet Garufis. *Reference Guide to Writing Across the Curriculum.* West Lafayette, IN: Parlor. The WAC Clearinghouse, 2005. Web. 6 June 2014.

Bean, Janet. "Feminine Discourse in the University: The Writing Center as a Site of Linguistic Resistance." *Feminism and Empirical Writing Research: Emerging Perspectives.* Ed. Joanne Addison and Sharon McGee. Portsmouth, NH: Heinemann, 1999. 127–44. Print.

Bean, John C. *Engaging Ideas: The Professor's Guide to Integrating Writing, Critical Thinking, and Active Learning in the Classroom.* 2nd ed. San Francisco: Jossey-Bass, 2011. Print.

Beck, Paula, Thom Hawkins, Marcia Silver, Kenneth A. Bruffee, Judy Fishman, and Judith T. Matsunobu. "Training and Using Peer Tutors." *College English* 40.4 (1978): 432–49. Web. 3 Feb 2014.

Bell, Diana Calhoun, Holly Arnold, and Rebecca Haddock. "Linguistic Politeness and Peer Tutoring." *Learning Assistance Review* 14.1 (2009): 37–54. Print.

Belmont Report: Ethical Principles and Guidelines for the Protection of Human Subjects of Research. Department of Health and Human Services, 1979 Web. 3 June 2014.

Berlin, James. *Rhetoric and Reality: Writing Instruction in American Colleges, 1900–1985.* Carbondale, IL: Southern Illinois UP, 1987. Print.

Bielski Boris, Monica. "My Hidden Class Consciousness and the Impact of Socioeconomic Class in Academia." Podis and Podis 327–34.

Bitzer, Lloyd F. "The Rhetorical Situation." *Philosophy and Rhetoric* 1.1 (1968): 1–14. Print.

Bloch, Benjy. "Portrait of a Writer." Unpublished Manuscript. Yeshiva U. 21 Feb. 2012.

Bokser, Julie. "Peer Tutoring and the Gorgias: Acknowledging Aggression in the Writing Center." *The Writing Center Journal* 21.2 (2001): 21–34. Print.

Boquet, Elizabeth H. "'Our Little Secret': A History of Writing Centers, Pre- to Post-Open Admissions." *College Composition and Communication* 50.3 (1999): 463–82. Print.

———. *Noise from the Writing Center.* Logan, UT: Utah State UP, 2002. Print.

Bouman, Kurt. "Raising Questions about Plagiarism." Bruce and Rafoth 161–75.

Boyer, Ernest. *Scholarship Reconsidered: Priorities of the Professoriate.* New York: Jossey-Bass, 1997. Print.

Braddock, Richard, Richard Lloyd-Jones, and Lowell Schoer. *Research in Written Composition.* Urbana, IL: NCTE, 1963. Print.

Brazeau, Alicia. "Groupies and Singletons: Student Preferences in Classroom-Based Writing Consulting." *Young Scholars in Writing: Undergraduate Research in Writing and Rhetoric* 2 (2004): 46–55. Web. 6 June 2014. Rpt. in this book.

Brecht, Mara. "Basic Literacy: Mediating between Power Constructs." *Young Scholars in Writing: Undergraduate Research in Writing and Rhetoric* 1 (2003): 61–79. Web. 6 June 2014. Rpt. in this book.

Brereton, John C. *The Origins of Composition Study in the American College, 1875–1925.* Pittsburgh: U of Pittsburgh P, 1995. Print.

Bromley, Pam, Kara Northway, and Eliana Schonberg. "How Important is the Local, Really? A Cross-Institutional Quantitative Assessment of Frequently Asked Questions in Writing Center Exit Surveys." *The Writing Center Journal* 33.1 (2013): 13–37. Print.

Brooks, Jeff. "Minimalist Tutoring: Making Students Do All the Work." *The Writing Lab Newsletter* 15.6 (1991): 1–4. Print.

Brown, Robert. "Representing Audiences in Writing Center Consultation: A Discourse Analysis." *The Writing Center Journal* 30.2 (2010): 72–97. Print.

Brown, Renee, Brian Fallon, Jessica Lott, Elizabeth Matthews, and Elizabeth Mintie. "Taking on Turnitin: Tutors Advocating Change." *The Writing Center Journal* 27.1 (2007): 7–28. Print. Rpt. in this book.

Bruce, Shanti, and Ben Rafoth, eds. *ESL Writers: A Guide for Writing Center Tutors* 2nd ed. Portsmouth, NH: Boynton/Cook Heinemann, 2009. Print.

Bruffee, Kenneth A. "Peer Tutoring and the 'Conversation of Mankind'." *Writing Centers: Theory and Administration.* Ed. Gary A. Olson. Urbana, IL: National Council of Teachers of English, 1984. 3–15. Print. Rpt. in this book.

Bunn, Michael. "Motivation and Connection: Teaching Reading (and Writing) in the Composition Classroom." *College Composition and Communication* 64.3 (2013): 496–516. Print.

Burke, Seán. "Changing Conceptions of Authorship." *Authorship: From Plato to the Postmodern.* Ed. Sean Burke. Edinburgh: Edinburgh UP, 1995. 3–11. Print.

Bushman, Don. "Theorizing a 'Social Expressivist' Writing Center." *The Writing Lab Newsletter* 22.7 (1998): 6–11. Print.

Caposella, Toni-Lee. *The Harcourt Brace Guide to Peer Tutoring.* Orlando, FL: 1998. Print.

Carino, Peter. "Computers in the Writing Center: A Cautionary History." *Wiring the Writing Center.* Ed. Eric H. Hobson. Logan, UT: Utah State UP, 1998. 171–93. Print.

———. "Early Writing Centers: Toward a History." *The Writing Center Journal* 15.2 (1995): 103–15. Print.

———. "Open Admissions and the Construction of Writing Center History: A Tale of Three Models." *The Writing Center Journal* 17.1 (1996): 30–48. Web. 4 April 2013.

Carpenter, Russell, and Shawn Apostel. "Communicating Center Ethos: Remediating Space, Encouraging Collaboration." *Communication Centers and Oral Communications Programs in Higher Education: Advantages, Challenges, and New Directions.* Ed. Eunkyong L. Yook and Wendy Atkins-Sayre. New York: Lexington, 2012. 163–74. Print.

Charlton, Jonikka, and Shirley K Rose. "Twenty More Years in the WPAs Progress." *WPA: Writing Program Administration* 33.1–2 (2009): 114–45. Web. 10 Oct. 2012.

Chewning, Bill. "The Expanding Center: Creating an Online Presence for the UMBC Writing Center." *Young Scholars in Writing: Undergraduate Research in Writing and Rhetoric* 5 (2007): 50–62. Web. 7 June 2014.

Clair, Efrayim. Message to Lauren Fitzgerald. 7 Aug. 2013. Email.

Clark, Irene. "Addressing Genre in the Writing Center." *The Writing Center Journal* 20.1 (1999): 7–32. Print.

Clark, Irene L., with Julie Neff Lippman, Deborah Burns, John Edlund, Kathryn Nielson-Dube, and Ilene Rubenstein. *Writing in the Center: Teaching in a Writing Center Setting.* 4th ed. Dubuque, IA: Kendall/Hunt. 2008. Print.

Cogie, Jane, Kim Strain, and Sharon Lorinskas. "Avoiding the Proofreading Trap: The Value of the Error Correction Process." *The Writing Center Journal* 19.2 (1999): 7–31. Print.

Condon, Frankie. "Beyond the Known: Writing Centers and the Work of Anti-Racism." *The Writing Center Journal* 27.2 (2007): 19–38. Print.

Conference on College Composition and Communication. *Guidelines for the Ethical Conduct of Research in Composition Studies.* November 2003. Web. 5 June 2014.

Connors, Robert J. *Composition-Rhetoric: Backgrounds, Theory, Pedagogy.* Pittsburgh: U of Pittsburgh P, 1997. Print.

——. "Dreams and Play: Historical Method and Methodology." *Methods and Methodology in Composition Research.* Ed. Gesa Kirsch and Patricia A. Sullivan. Carbondale: Southern Illinois UP, 1992. 15–36. Print.

Corbin, Juliet M., and Anselm C. Strauss. *Basics of Qualitative Research: Techniques and Procedures for Developing Grounded Theory.* Thousand Oaks, CA: Sage, 2008. Print.

Cuperfain, Ari. "Can I Help You with That?: Directive Tutoring and the Status of Contextual Information in the Writing Center." *The Writing Lab Newsletter* 37.7–8 (2013): 14–15. Print.

DeCheck, Natalie. "The Power of Common Interest for Motivating Writers: A Case Study." *The Writing Center Journal* 32.1 (2012): 28–38. Print. Rpt. in this book.

Denny, Harry. *Facing the Center: Toward an Identity Politics of One-to-One Tutoring.* Logan, UT: Utah State UP, 2010. Print.

——. "Queering the Writing Center." *The Writing Center Journal* 25.2 (2005): 39–62. Print.

Diab, Rasha, Beth Godbee, Thomas Ferrel, and Neil Simpkins. "A Multi-Dimensional Pedagogy for Racial Justice in Writing Centers." *Praxis: A Writing Center Journal* 10.1 (2012). Web. 7 June 2014.

Dinitz, Sue, and Susanmarie Harrington. "The Role of Disciplinary Expertise in Shaping Writing Tutorials." *The Writing Center Journal* 33.2 (2014): 73–98. Print.

Dinitz, Sue, and Jean Kiedaisch. "Tutoring Writing as Career Development." *The Writing Lab Newsletter* 34:3 (2009): 1–4. Print.

DiPardo, Annie. "'Whispers of Coming and Going': Lessons from Fannie." *The Writing Center Journal* 12.2 (1992): 125–44. Print.

Dirk, Kerry. "Navigating Genres." *Writing Spaces: Readings on Writing.* Ed. Charles Lowe and Pavel Zemliansky. Vol. 1. Anderson, SC: Parlor P, 2010. 249–62. Web. 7 June 2014.

Donahue, Christiane. "'Internationalization' and Composition Studies: Reorienting the Discourse." *College Composition and Communication* 61.2 (2009): 212–43. Print.

Donesch-Jezo, Ewa. "Comparison of Generic Organization of the Research Paper in English and Polish: Cross-Cultural Variation and Pedagogical Implications." *Journalism and Mass Communication* 1.3 (2001): 185–200. Print.

Downs, Douglas, and Elizabeth Wardle. "Teaching about Writing, Righting Misconceptions: (Re)Envisioning First-Year Writing as 'Introduction to Writing Studies'." *College Composition and Communication* 58.4 (2007): 552–84. Web. 3 June 2014.

Doucette, Jonathan. "Composing Queers: The Subversive Potential of the Writing Center." *Young Scholars in Writing: Undergraduate Research in Writing and Rhetoric* 8 (2010): 5–15. Web. 6 June 2014. Rpt. in this book.

Driscoll, Dana Lynn, and Sherry Wynn Purdue. "Theory, Lore and More: An Analysis of RAD Research in *The Writing Center Journal*, 1980–2009." *The Writing Center Journal* 32.2 (2012): 11–39. Print.

Ede, Lisa. "Writing as a Social Process: A Theoretical Foundation for Writing Centers." *The Writing Center Journal* 9.2 (1989): 3–13. Print.

Elbow, Peter. *Writing Without Teachers.* New York: Oxford UP, 1998. Print.

Fallon, Brian. "The Perceived, Conceived, and Lived Experiences of 21st-Century Peer Writing Tutors." Diss., Indiana U of Pennsylvania, 2010. Print.

———. "Why My Best Teachers Are Peer Tutors." National Conference on Peer Tutoring in Writing. Florida International University–Biscayne Bay, Miami. 4 Nov. 2011. Keynote Address. Edited version in this book.

Fishman, Teddi. "When It Isn't Even on the Page: Peer Consulting in Multimedia Environments." *Multiliteracy Centers: Writing Center Work, New Media, and Multimodal Rhetoric.* Ed. David M. Sheridan and James A. Inman. Cresskill, NJ: Hampton, 2010. 59–73. Print.

Flower, Linda. "Writer-Based Prose: A Cognitive Basis for Problems in Writing." *College English* 41 (1979): 19–37. Print.

Flower, Linda, and John R. Hayes, "The Cognition of Discovery: Defining a Rhetorical Problem." *College Composition and Communication* 31.1 (1980): 21–32. Print.

Friere, Paulo. *Pedagogy of the Oppressed.* New York: Continuum, 1993. Print.

Gaillet, Lynée Lewis. "Archival Survival: Navigating Historical Research." *Working in the Archives: Practical Research Methods for Rhetoric and Composition.* Ed. Alexis E. Ramsey, Wendy B. Sharer, Barbara L'Eplattenier, and Lisa S. Mastrangelo. Carbondale: Southern Illinois UP, 2010. 28–39. Print.

Gaines, Robert. "Phronēsis." *Encyclopedia of Rhetoric.* New York: Oxford UP, 2001. 601–03. Print.

Gaonkar, Dilip P. "The Idea of Rhetoric in the Rhetoric of Science." *Rhetorical Hermeneutics: Invention and Interpretation in the Age of Science.* Ed. Alan Gross and William M. Keith. Albany: State U of New York P, 1997. 25–88. Print.

Geller, Anne Ellen, Michelle Eodice, Frankie Condon, Meg Carroll, and Elizabeth H. Boquet. *The Everyday Writing Center: A Community of Practice.* Logan, UT: Utah State UP, 2007. Print.

Genung, John Franklin. "English at Amherst." Brereton 172–77.

Gilewicz, Magdalena, and Terese Thonus. "Close Vertical Transcription in Writing Center Training and Research." *The Writing Center Journal* 24.1 (2003): 25–50. Print.

Gillam, Alice, Susan Callaway, and Katherine Hennessy Wikoff. "The Role of Authority and the Authority of Roles in Peer Writing Tutorials." *Journal of Teaching Writing* 12.2 (1994): 161–98. Web. 5 June 2014.

Gillespie, Paula, and Neal Lerner. *The Longman Guide to Peer Tutoring.* New York: Pearson Longman, 2008. Print.

Gilligan, Carol. *In a Different Voice: Psychological Theory and Women's Development.* Cambridge: Harvard UP, 1998. Print.

Gladstein, Jill. "Conducting Research in the Gray Space: How Writing Associates Negotiate between WAC and WID in an Introductory Biology Course." *Across the Disciplines 5* (March 29, 2008). Web. 7 June 2014.

Gladstein, Jill M., and Dara Rossman Regaignon. *Writing Program Administration at Small Liberal Arts Colleges.* Clemson, SC: Parlor, 2012. Print.

Glaser, Barney, and Anselm C. Strauss. *The Discovery of Grounded Theory: Strategies for Qualitative Research.* New Brunswick, NH: Aldine Transaction, 1999. Print.

Glover, Carl. "Kairos and the Writing Center: Modern Perspectives on an Ancient Idea." *The Writing Center Director's Resource Book.* Ed. Christina Murphy and Byron L Stay. Mahwah, NJ: Erlbaum, 2006. 13–20. Print.

Goldsby, Jackie. *Peer Tutoring in Basic Writing: A Tutor's Journal.* Berkeley: Bay Area Writing Projects, 1981.

Graff, Gerald. *Professing Literature: An Institutional History.* 20th Anniversary Edition. Chicago: U of Chicago P, 2007. Print.

Grant-Davie, Keith. "Rhetorical Situations and Their Constituents." *Rhetoric Review* 15.2 (1997): 264–79. Print.

Greenfield, Laura, and Karen Rowan, eds. *Writing Centers and the New Racism: A Call for Sustainable Dialogue and Change.* Logan, UT: Utah State UP, 2011. Print.

Griffin, Jo Ann, Daniel Keller, Iswari P. Pandey, Anne-Marie Pedersen, and Carolyn Skinner. "Local Practices, National Consequences: Surveying and (Re)constructing Writing Center Identities." *The Writing Center Journal* 26.2 (2006): 3–21. Print.

Grimm, Nancy Maloney. *Good Intentions: Writing Center Work for Postmodern Times.* Portsmouth, NH: Boyton/Cook, 1999. Print.

———. "New Conceptual Frameworks for Writing Center Work." *The Writing Center Journal* 29.2 (2009): 11–27. Print.

———. "Retheorizing Writing Center Work to Transform a System of Advantage Based on Race." Greenfield and Rowan 75–100.

Grobman, Laurie. "The Student Scholar: (Re)Negotiating Authorship and Authority." *College Composition and Communication* 61.1 (2009): W175–96. Web. 8 Jan. 2013.

Grutsch McKinney, Jackie. "New Media Matters: Tutoring in the Late Age of Print." *The Writing Center Journal* 29.2 (2009): 28–51. Rpt. in this book.

Guest, Greg, Emily E. Namey, and Marilyn Z. Mitchell. *Collecting Field Data: A Manual for Applied Research.* Thousand Oaks, CA: Sage, 2013. Print.

Habermas, Jürgen. *The Structural Transformation of the Public Sphere: An Inquiry into a Category of Bourgeois Society.* Cambridge: MIT P, 1989. Print.

Hall, Emily, and Bradley Hughes. "Preparing Faculty, Professionalizing Fellows: Keys to Success with Undergraduate Writing Fellows in WAC." *The WAC Journal* 22 (2011): 21–40. Web. 7 June 2014.

Hall, R. Mark. "Using Dialogic Reflection to Develop a Writing Center Community of Practice." *The Writing Center Journal* 31.1 (2011): 82–105. Print.

Haring-Smith, Tori. "Changing Students' Attitudes: Writing Fellows Programs." *Writing Across the Curriculum: A Guide to Developing Programs.* Ed. Susan McLeod and Margot Soven. Newbury Park, CA: Sage, 1992. 123–31. Print.

Harris, Joseph. "After Dartmouth: Growth and Conflict in English." *College English* 53.6 (1991): 631–46. Print.

———. "From the Editor: The Work of Others." *College Composition and Communication* 45.4 (1994): 439–41. Print.

Harris, Muriel. "Talking in the Middle: Why Writers Need Writing Tutors." *College English* 57.1 (1995): 27–47. Print.

Harris, Vincent. "The Journey Continues." Maxwell 121–25.

Hartwell, Patrick. "Grammar, Grammars and the Teaching of Grammar." *College English* 47.2 (1985): 105–27. Web. 7 June 2014.

Haswell, Janis, and Richard Haswell. *Authoring: An Essay for the English Profession on Potentiality and Singularity.* Logan: Utah State UP, 2010. Print.

Hesse, Douglas. "Teachers as Students, Reflecting Resistance." *College Composition and Communication* 44.2 (1993): 224–31. Print.

Hewitt, Beth L. *The Online Writing Conference: A Guide for Teachers and Tutors.* Portsmouth, NH: Boynton/Cook Heinemann, 2010. Print.

Hill, A. S. "A Cry for More English." *The Origins of Composition Studies in the American College, 1857-1925: A Documentary History.* Ed. John C. Brereton. Pittsburgh: U of Pittsburgh P, 1995. 45–57. Print.

Hitt, Allison. "Access for All: The Role of Dis/Ability in Multiliteracy Centers." *Praxis: A Writing Center Journal* 9.2 (2012): 1–7. Web. 6 June 2014. Rpt. in this book.

Hobson, Eric. "Writing Center Practice Often Counters Its Own Theory: So What?" *Intersections: Theory-Practice in the Writing Center.* Urbana, IL: NCTE, 1994. 1–10. Print.

Howard, Rebecca Moore. "Sexuality, Textuality: The Cultural Work of Plagiarism." *College English* 62 (2000): 473–91. Print.

Hughes, Bradley, Paula Gillespie, and Harvey Kail. "What They Take with Them: Findings from the Peer Writing Tutor Alumni Research Project." *The Writing Center Journal* 30.2 (2010): 12–46. Print.

Hunzer, Kathleen M. "Gender Expectations and Relationships in the Writing Center." *The Writing Lab Newsletter* 22.2 (1997): 6–11. Web. 5 Feb. 2014.

Ingalls, Rebecca. "Writing 'Eyeball to Eyeball': Building a Successful Collaboration." *Writing Spaces: Readings on Writing,* Vol. 2. Eds. Charles Lowe and Pavel Zemliansky. Anderson, SC: Parlor, 2011. 122–40. Web. 7 June 2014.

International Writing Centers Association. *Position Statement on Disability and Writing Centers.* 2006. Web. 7 June 2014.

Jarratt, Susan. "Feminism and Composition: The Case for Conflict." *Contending with Words: Composition and Rhetoric in a Postmodern Age.* Ed. Patricia Harkin and John Schilb. New York: MLA, 1991. 105–23. Print.

Johanek, Cindy. *Composing Research: A Contextualist Research Paradigm for Rhetoric and Composition.* Logan, UT: Utah State UP, 2000. Print.

Johnson, Ruth, Beth Clark, and Mario Burton. "Finding Harmony in Disharmony: Engineering and English Studies" *Young Scholars in Writing: Undergraduate Research in Writing and Rhetoric* 5 (2007): 63–73. Web. 6 June 2014. Rpt. in this book.

Jolliffe, David A. *Inquiry and Genre: Writing to Learn in College.* Boston: Allyn and Bacon, 1999. Print.

Kavadlo, Jesse. "The Message Is the Medium: Electronically Helping Writing Tutors Help Electronically." *Praxis: A Writing Center Journal* 10.2 (2013). Web. 7 June 2014.

Kennedy, Mick. "Expressionism and Social Construction in the Writing Center: How Do They Benefit Students?" *The Writing Lab Newsletter* 22.3 (1997): 5–8. Print.

Kerschbaum, Stephanie L. "Avoiding the Difference Fixation: Identity Categories, Markers of Difference, and the Teaching of Writing." *College Composition and Communication* 63.4 (2012): 616–44. Web. 7 June 2014.

Kiedaisch, Jean, and Sue Dinitz. "Changing Notions of Difference in the Writing Center: The Possibilities of Universal Design." *The Writing Center Journal* 27.2 (2007): 39–59. Print.

———. "Look Back and Say 'So What': The Limitations of the Generalist Tutor." *The Writing Center Journal* 14.1 (1993): 63–75. Print.

Kinkead, Joyce. "The National Writing Centers Association as Mooring: A Personal History of the First Decade." *The Writing Center Journal* 16.2 (1996): 131–43. Print.

Konicki, Skyler. "De-Centering Peer Tutors: Research Applications for Undergraduates in the Writing Program." *Young Scholars in Writing: Undergraduate Research in Writing and Rhetoric* 9 (Fall 2010): 77–86. Web. 7 June 2014.

Lauer, Janice M., and J. William Asher. *Composition Research: Empirical Designs.* New York: Oxford UP, 1988. Print.

Leahy, Richard. "What the College Writing Center Is — And Isn't." *College Teaching* 38.2 (1990): 43–48. Print.

Lebduska, Lisa. "Classical Rhetoric and the Professional Peer Tutor." *The Writing Lab Newsletter* 30.8 (2006): 6–9. Print.

Lee, Sohui, and Russell Carpenter. "Introduction: Navigating Literacies in Multimodal Spaces." *The Routledge Reader on Writing Centers and New Media.* Ed. Lee and Carpenter. New York: Routledge, 2014. xiv–xxvi. Print.

Leit, Lisa, James Riddlesperger, Ashley Squires, Kanaka Sathasivan, and Justin Smith. "A Room of One's Own in the Academy: The Writing Center as Feminized Space." *Praxis: A Writing Center Journal* 5.1 (2007). Web. 11 June 2012.

Leki, Ilona. "Before the Conversation: A Sketch of Some Possible Backgrounds, Experiences, and Attitudes Among ESL Students Visiting a Writing Center." Bruce and Rafoth 1–17.

Lerner, Neal. "Archival Research as a Social Process." Ramsey et al. 195–205.

———. "Choosing Beans Wisely." *The Writing Lab Newsletter* 26.1 (2001): 1–5. Print.

———. "Chronology of Published Descriptions of Writing Laboratories/Clinics, 1894–1977." WPA-CompPile Research Bibliographies, No. 9. *CompPile.* Web. 7 August 2013.

———. "Counting Beans and Making Beans Count." *The Writing Lab Newsletter* 22.1 (1997): 1–4. Print.

———. *The Idea of a Writing Laboratory.* Carbondale: Southern Illinois UP, 2009. Print.

———. "Introduction to a List of Dissertations and Theses on Writing Centers, 1924–2008." *The Writing Lab Newsletter* 33.7 (2009): 6–9. Print.

———. "Searching for Robert Moore." *The Writing Center Journal* 22.1 (2001): 9–32. Print. Rpt. in this book.

Liggett, Sarah, Kerri Jordan, and Steve Price. "Makers of Knowledge in Writing Centers: Practitioners, Scholars, and Researchers." *The Changing of Knowledge in Composition: Contemporary Perspectives.* Ed. Lance Massey and Richard Gebhardt, eds. Logan, UT: Utah State UP, 2011. 102–20. Print.

———. "Mapping Knowledge-Making in Writing Center Research: A Taxonomy of Methodologies." *The Writing Center Journal* 31.2 (2011): 50–88. Print.

Linville, Cynthia. "Editing Line by Line." Bruce and Rafoth 116–31.

Lu, Min-Zhan. "Professing Multiculturalism: The Politics of Style in the Contact Zone." *College Composition and Communication* 45.4 (1994): 442–58. Print.

Lunsford. Andrea. "Collaboration, Control, and the Idea of a Writing Center." *The Writing Center Journal* 12.1 (1991): 3–11. Print.

Lunsford, Andrea, and Lisa Ede. "Reflections on Contemporary Currents in Writing Center Work." *The Writing Center Journal* 31.1 (2011): 11–24. Print.

Lutes, Jean Marie. "Why Feminists Make Better Tutors: Gender and Disciplinary Expertise in a Curriculum-Based Tutoring Program." *Writing Center Research: Extending the Conversation.* Ed. Paula Gillespie, Alice Gillam, Lady Falls Brown, and Byron Stay. Mahwah, NJ: Erlbaum, 2002. 235–57. Print.

Lyotard, Jean-François. *The Postmodern Condition.* Minneapolis: U of Minnesota P, 1984. Print.

Mackiewicz, Jo, and Isabelle Thompson. "Motivational Scaffolding, Politeness, and Writing Center Tutoring." *The Writing Center Journal* 33.1 (2013): 38–73. Print. Rpt. in this book.

Malenczyk, Rita. "'I Thought I'd Put that in to Amuse You': Tutor Reports as Organizational Narrative." *The Writing Center Journal* 33.1 (2013): 74–95. Print.

Matsuda, Paul Kei, and Michelle Cox. "Reading and ESL Writer's Text." Bruce and Rafoth 42–50.

Maxwell, Martha, ed. *When Tutor Meets Student.* 2nd ed. Ann Arbor: U of Michigan P, 1994. Print.

McAndrew, Donald A., and Thomas J. Reigstad. *Tutoring Writing: A Practical Guide for Conferences.* Portsmouth, NH: Boynton/Cook 2001. Print.

McCloskey, Deidre. "Big Rhetoric, Little Rhetoric: Gaonkar on the Rhetoric of Science." *Rhetorical Hermeneutics: Invention and Interpretation in the Age of Science.* Ed. Alan G. Gross and William M. Keith. New York: SUNY P, 1997. 101–12. Print.

McLaughlin, Becky, and Bob Colemen, eds. *Everyday Theory: A Contemporary Reader.* New York: Pearson/Longman, 2005. Print.

Mendelsohn, Susan Elizabeth. "Rhetorical Possibilities: Reimagining Multiliteracy Work in Writing Centers." Diss. U of Texas at Austin, 2012. Print.

Miller, Thomas P. *The Formation of College English: Rhetoric and Belles Lettres in the British Cultural Provinces.* Pittsburgh: U of Pittsburgh P, 1997. Print.

Minett, Amy Jo. "'Earth Aches by Midnight': Helping ESL Writers Clarify Their Intended Meaning." Bruce and Rafoth 66–77.

"Mission and History." *European Writing Centers Association.* n.d. Web. 28 March 2013.

Moore, Julie L., Erin SanGregory, Sarah Matney, and Julie Morris. "Designing Tutor Guides to Enhance Effectiveness across Disciplines and with Special Demographics." *The Writing Lab Newsletter* 34.4–5 (2009/2010): 1–5. Print.

Moreau, Michelle A., and A. Paige Normand. "Technology Tutoring: Communication Centers Take the Lead." *Communication Centers and Oral Communications Programs in Higher Education: Advantages, Challenges, and New Directions.* Ed. Eunkyong L. Yook and Wendy Atkins-Sayre. New York: Lexington, 2012. 223–48. Print.

Mozafari, Cameron. "Creating Third Space: ESL Tutoring as Cultural Mediation." *Young Scholars in Writing: Undergraduate Research in Writing and Rhetoric* 7 (2009): 47–59. Web. 6 June 2014. Rpt. in this book.

Mueller, Susan. "Documentation Styles and Discipline-Specific Values." *The Writing Lab Newsletter* 29.6 (2005): 6–9. Print.

———. Rev. *The Publication Manual of the American Psychological Association*. 6th ed. *The Writing Lab Newsletter* 34.3 (2009): 10–12. Print.

Mullin, Joan, Susan Schorn, Tim Turner, Rachel Hertz, Derek Davidson, and Amanda Baca. "Challenging our Practices, Supporting our Theories: Writing Mentors as Change Agents across Discourse Communities." *Across the Disciplines* 5 (2008). Web. 7 June 2014.

Muñoz, Eduardo. "A Minority Writing Tutor at the Golden Bear." Maxwell 144–49.

Murray, Donald. "Teach Writing as a Process, Not Product." *The Leaflet* Nov. (1972): 11–14. Rpt. in *Cross-Talk in Comp Theory: A Reader*. Ed. Victor Villanueva. 2nd ed. Urbana, IL: NCTE, 3–6. Print.

Nan, Frances. "Bridging the Gap: Essential Issues to Address in Recurring Writing Center Appointments with Chinese ELL Students." *The Writing Center Journal* 32.1 (2012): 50–63. Print. Rpt. in this book.

New London Group. "A Pedagogy of Multiliteracies: Designing Social Futures." *Harvard Educational Review* 66.1 (1996): 60–92. Print.

Nicklay, Jennifer. "Got Guilt? Consultant Guilt in the Writing Center Community." *The Writing Center Journal* 32.1 (2012): 14–27. Print. Rpt. in this book.

Nicolas, Melissa. "Retelling the Story: An Exploration of the Feminization of the Writing Center." Diss. Columbus, OH: Ohio State U, 2002. Print.

North, Stephen. "The Idea of a Writing Center." *College English* 46.5 (1984): 433–46. Print.

———. *The Making of Knowledge in Composition: Portrait of an Emerging Field*. Portsmouth, NH: Boynton/Cook, 1986. Print.

Nunan, David. *Research Methods in Language Learning*. Cambridge UP, 1992. Print.

"Octalog: The Politics of Historiography." *Rhetoric Review* 7.1 (Fall 1988): 5–49. Web. 7 June 2014.

O'Leary, Claire Elizabeth. "It's Not What You Say, but How You Say It (and to Whom): Accommodating Gender in the Writing Conference." *Young Scholars in Writing: Undergraduate Research in Writing and Rhetoric* 7 (2009): 60–72. Web. 6 June 2014. Rpt. in this book.

Olson, Gary, and Evelyn Ashton-Jones. "Writing Center Directors: The Search for Professional Status." *WPA: Writing Program Administration* 12.1–2 (1998): 19–28. Web. 7 July 2013.

Ostrom, Hans. "Tutoring Creative Writers: Working One-on-One on Prose and Poetry." *Creative Approaches to Writing Center Work*. Ed. Kevin Dvorak and Shanti Bruce. Cresskill, NJ: Hampton, 2008. 147–58. Print.

Pemberton, Michael. Foreword. *The Online Writing Conference: A Guide for Teachers and Tutors*. By Beth Hewett. Portsmouth, NH: Boynton/Cook Heinemann, 2010. ix–xii. Print.

———. "Planning for Hypertexts in the Writing Center . . . Or Not." *The Writing Center Journal* 24.1 (2003): 9–24. Print.

———. "*The Writing Lab Newsletter* as History: Tracing the Growth of a Scholarly Community." *The Center Will Hold: Critical Perspectives on Writing Center Scholarship*. Ed. Michael A. Pemberton and Joyce Kinkead. Logan, UT: Utah State UP, 2003. 21–40. Print.

Perkes, Rachael. "How Old is Your Writing Center? (A Preliminary Look at Writing Center Development)." *The Writing Lab Newsletter* 26.4 (December 2001): 15. Web. 8 Aug. 2013.

Perl, Sondra. "The Composing Processes of Unskilled College Writers." *Research in the Teaching of English* 13.4 (1979): 317–36. Print.

———. "Understanding Composing." *College Composition and Communication* 31 (1980): 363–69. Print.

Plato. "Pericles' Funeral Oration from Plato's *Menexenus*." *Available Means: An Anthology of Women's Rhetorics*. Ed. Joy Ritchie and Kate Ronald. Pittsburgh: U of Pittsburgh P, 2001. 2–8. Print.

Podis, Leonard A., and JoAnne M. Podis, eds. *Working with Student Writers: Essays on Tutoring and Teaching*. 2nd ed. New York: Peter Lang, 2010. Print.

Pratt, Mary Louise. "Arts of the Contact Zone." *Profession* 91 (1991): 33–40. Web. 7 June 2014.

Pryor, Virginia. "Writing in Academia: The Politics of 'Style.'" Podis and Podis 335–51.

Rafoth, Ben. "Responding Online." Bruce and Rafoth 149–60.

Ramsey, Alexis E, Wendy B. Sharer, Barbara L'Eplattenier, and Lisa S. Mastrangelo, eds. *Working in the Archives: Practical Research Methods for Rhetoric and Composition*. Carbondale: Southern Illinois UP, 2010. Print.

Reger, Jeff. "Postcolonialism, Acculturation, and the Writing Center." *Young Scholars in Writing: Undergraduate Research in Writing and Rhetoric* 7 (2009): 39–46. Web. 6 June 2014. Rpt. in this book.

Rich, Laura. "When Theologies Conflict: Reflections on Role Issues in a Christian Writing Center." *The Writing Lab Newsletter* 28.4 (2003): 10–11. Print.

Riley, Terrance. "The Unpromising Future of Writing Centers." *The Writing Center Journal* 15.1 (1994): 20–34. Print.

Robertson, Wayne, dir. *Writing Across Borders*. Corvallis, OR: Oregon State U, 2005. DVD.

Robinson, Heather. M. "Writing Center Philosophy and the End of Basic Writing: Motivation at the Site of Remediation and Discovery." *Journal of Basic Writing* 28.2 (2009): 70–92. Print.

Ronesi, Lynne. "Multilingual Tutors Supporting Multilingual Peers: A Peer-Tutor Training Course in the Arabian Gulf." *The Writing Center Journal* 29.2 (2009): 75–94. Print.

Rose, Mark. *Authors and Owners: The Invention of Copyright*. Cambridge, MA and London: Harvard UP, 1993. Print.

Rose, Mike. "Rigid Rules, Inflexible Plans, and the Stifling of Language: A Cognitivist Analysis of Writer's Block." *College Composition and Communication* 31.4 (1980): 389–401. Print.

Rowan, Karen. "All the Best Intentions: Graduate Student Administrative Professional Development in Practice." *The Writing Center Journal* 29.1 (2009): 11–48. Print.

Russell, David R. "Activity Theory and Its Implications for Writing Instruction." *Reconceiving Writing, Rethinking Writing Instruction*. Ed. Joseph Petraglia. Hillsdale, NJ: Erlbaum, 1995. 51–78. Print.

Ryan, Emily. "Attention Deficit Hyperactivity Disorder and the Writing Process." Podis and Podis 289–300.

Ryan, Leigh, and Lisa Zimmerelli. *The Bedford Guide for Writing Tutors*. 5th ed. Boston/ New York: Bedford/St. Martin's, 2010. Print.

Savini, Catherine. "An Alternative Approach to Bridging Disciplinary Divides." *The Writing Lab Newsletter* 35.7–8 (2011): 1–5. Print.

Schendel, Ellen. "We Don't Proofread, So What Do We Do: A Report on Survey Results." *The Writing Lab Newsletter* 37.3–4 (2012): 1–6. Web. 2 June 2013.

Schiappa, Edward. "Second Thoughts on Critiques of Big Rhetoric." *Philosophy and Rhetoric* 34.3 (2001): 260–74. Web. 7 June 2014.

Schön, Donald A. *Educating the Reflective Practitioner*. New York: Basic, 1983. Print.

Scott, Joan. *Gender and the Politics of History*. New York: Columbia UP, 1988. Print.

Scott, Marc. "The Right Time and Proper Measure: Assessing in Writing Centers and James Kinneavy's 'Kairos: A Neglected Concept in Classical Rhetoric.'" *Praxis: A Writing Center Journal* 11.1 (2013). Web. 4 March 2014.

Severino, Carol, and Elizabeth Deifell, "Empowering L2 Tutoring: A Case Study of a Second Language Writer's Vocabulary Learning." *The Writing Center Journal* 31.1 (2011): 25–54. Print.

Severino, Carol, and Megan Knight. "Exporting Writing Center Pedagogy: Writing Fellows Programs as Ambassadors for the Writing Center." *Marginal Words, Marginal Work? Tutoring the Academy in the Work of Writing Centers*. Ed. William J. Macauley, Jr. and Nicholas Mauriello. Cresskill, NJ: Hampton, 2007. 19–34. Print.

Severino, Carol, Jeffrey Swenson, and Jia Zhu. "A Comparison of Online Feedback Requests by Non-Native English-Speaking and Native English-Speaking Writers." *The Writing Center Journal* 29.1 (2009): 106–29. Print.

Severino, Carol, and Mary Traschel. "Theories of Specialized Discourses and Writing Fellows Programs." *Across the Disciplines* 5 (2008). Web. 7 June 2014.

Shamoon, Linda, and Deborah H. Burns. "Plagiarism, Rhetorical Theory and the Writing Center: New Approaches, New Locations." *Perspectives on Plagiarism and Intellectual Property in a Postmodern World*. Ed. Lise Buranen and Alice M. Roy. New York: State U of New York P, 1999. 183–92. Print.

Shaughnessy, Mina. *Errors and Expectations*. New York: Oxford UP, 1977. Print.

Sheridan, David M. "All Things to All People: Multiliteracy Consulting and the Materiality of Rhetoric." *Multiliteracy Centers: Writing Center Work, New Media and Multimodal Rhetoric*. Ed. Sheridan and James A. Inman. Cresskill, NJ: Hampton, 2010. 75–107. Print.

———. "Introduction: Writing Centers and the Multimodal Turn." *Multiliteracy Centers: Writing Center Work, New Media and Multimodal Rhetoric*. Ed. Sheridan and James. A Inman. Cresskill, NJ: Hampton, 2010. 1–16. Print.

———. "Words, Images, Sounds: Writing Centers as Multiliteracy Centers." *The Writing Center Directors' Resource Book*. Ed. Christina Murphy and Byron L. Stay. Mahwah, NJ: Erlbaum, 2006. 339–50. Print.

Siepmann, Dirk. "Academic Writing and Culture: An Overview of Differences between English, French and German." *Meta: Translators' Journal* 51.1 (2006): 131–50. Web. 7 June 2014.

Simpson, Jeanne, Steve Braye, and Beth Boquet. "War, Peace, and Writing Center Administration." *Composition Studies/Freshmen English News* 22.1 (1994): 65–95. Print.

Smith, Jeanne, and Jay D. Sloan. "Sustaining Community and Technological Ecologies: What Writing Centers Can Teach Us." *Technological Ecologies and Sustainability.* Ed. Dànielle Nicole DeVoss, Heidi A. McKee, and Richard (Dickie) Selfe. Logan, UT: Computers and Composition Digital/Utah State UP, 2009. Web. 7 June 2014.

Soliday, Mary. "General Readers and Classroom Tutors across the Curriculum." *On Location: Theory and Practice in Classroom-Based Writing Tutoring.* Ed. Candace Spigelman and Laurie Grobman. Logan, Utah: Utah State UP, 2005. 31–43. Print.

Sommers, Nancy. "Responding to Student Writing." *College Composition and Communication* 33.2 (1988): 148–56. Print.

———. "Revision Strategies of Student Writers and Experienced Adult Writers." *College Composition and Communication* 31.4 (1980): 378–88. Print.

Soven, Margot Iris. *What the Writing Tutor Needs to Know.* Boston: Thomson Wadsworth, 2006.

Staben, Jennifer E., and Kathryn Dempsey Nordhaus. "Looking at the Whole Text." Bruce and Rafoth 78–90.

Suhr-Sytsma, Mandy, and Shan-Estelle Brown. "Addressing the Everyday Language of Oppression in the Writing Center." *The Writing Center Journal* 31.2 (2011): 13–49. Print. Rpt. in this book.

Summerfield, Judith. "Writing Centers: A Long View." *The Writing Center Journal* 8.2 (1988): 3–9. Print.

Thompson, Isabelle. "Scaffolding in the Writing Center: A Microanalysis of an Experienced Tutor's Verbal and Nonverbal Tutoring Strategies." *Written Communication* 26.4 (2009): 417–53. Print.

Thompson, Isabelle, and Jo Mackiewicz. "Questioning in Writing Center Conferences." *The Writing Center Journal* 33.2 (2014): 37–70. Print.

Thompson, Isabelle, Alyson Whyte, David Shannon, Amanda Muse, Kristen Miller, Milla Chappell, and Abby Whigham. "Examining Our Lore: A Survey of Students' and Tutors' Satisfaction with Writing Center Conferences." *The Writing Center Journal* 29.1 (2009): 78–105. Print.

Thonus, Terese. "Acquaintanceship, Familiarity, and Coordinated Laughter in Writing Center Tutorials." *Linguistics and Education* 19.4 (2008): 333–50. Web. 7 June 2014.

Tierney, Robert J., and P. David Pearson. "Toward a Composing Model of Reading." *Language Arts* 60.5 (1983): 568–80. Print.

Tipper, Margaret O. "Real Men Don't Do Writing Centers." *The Writing Center Journal.* 19.2 (1999): 33–40.

Town, Jessamy. "Langston Hughes Takes on Tutoring." Maxwell 128–31.

Trachsel, Mary. "Nurturant Ethics and Academic Ideals: Convergence in the Writing Center." *The Writing Center Journal* 16.1 (1995): 24–45. Print.

Trimbur, John. "Multiliteracies, Social Futures, and Writing Centers." *The Writing Center Journal* 20.2 (2000): 29–31. Print.

Varma, Anita. "Politics of Difference in the Writing Center." *Young Scholars in Writing: Undergraduate Research in Writing and Rhetoric* 7 (2009): 30–38. Web. 7 June 2014.

Villanueva, Victor. "Blind: Talking about the New Racism." *The Writing Center Journal* 26.1 (2006): 3–19. Print.

Wardle, Elizabeth, and Doug Downs. *Writing about Writing: A College Reader.* 2nd ed. Boston: Bedford/St. Martin's, 2014. Print.

Waring, H. Z. "Peer Tutoring in a Graduate Writing Centre: Identity, Expertise, and Advice Resisting." *Applied Linguistics* 26.2 (2005): 141–68. Web. 7 June 2014.

Weaver, Richard. "Language is Sermonic." *Language is Sermonic: Richard M. Weaver on the Nature of Rhetoric.* Ed. Richard L. Johannesen, Rennard Strickland, and Ralph T. Eubanks. Baton Rouge: Louisiana State UP, 1970. 201–25. Print.

Wegner, Etienne. *Communities of Practice: Learning, Meaning, and Identity.* Cambridge: Cambridge UP, 1998. Print.

Welch, Nancy. "Playing with Reality: Writing Centers After the Mirror Stage." *College Composition and Communication* 51.1 (1999): 51–69. Print.

Wewers, Jennifer. "Writing Tutors and Dyslexic Tutees: Is There Something Special We Should Know?" Podis and Podis 229–37.

White, Hayden. *Tropics of Discourse: Essays in Cultural Criticism.* Baltimore: Johns Hopkins UP, 1978. Print.

Wilder, Molly. "A Quest for Student Engagement: A Linguistic Analysis of Writing Conference Discourse." *Young Scholars in Writing: Undergraduate Research in Writing and Rhetoric* 7 (2009): 94–105. Web. 6 June 2014. Rpt. in this book.

Wolfe, Joanna. *Team Writing: A Guide to Working in Groups.* Boston and New York: Bedford/ St. Martin's. 2010. Print.

Woolbright, Meg. "The Politics of Tutoring: Feminism Within the Patriarchy." *The Writing Center Journal* 13.1 (1992): 16–30. Print.

"The Writing Centers Research Project." *Writing Center Research Project.* International Writing Centers Association, 1 Jan. 2011. Web. 1 Sept. 2014.

Yahner, William, and William Murdick. "The Evolution of a Writing Center: 1972–1990." *The Writing Center Journal* 11.2 (1991): 14–26. Print.

Yancey, Kathleen Blake. "Looking Back as We Look Forward: Historicizing Writing Assessment." *College Composition and Communication* 50.3 (1999): 483–503. Web. 7 June 2014.

———. "Seeing Practice Through Their Eyes: Reflection as Teacher." *Writing Center Research: Extending the Conversation.* Ed. Paula Gillespie, Alice Gillam, Lady Falls Brown, and Byron Stay. Mahwah, NJ: Erlbaum, 2002. 189–202. Print.

Zawacki, Terry Myers. "Writing Fellows as WAC Change Agents: Changing What? Changing Whom? Changing How?" *Across the Disciplines* 5 (2008). Web. 6 June 2014.

Credits

Page 267 from Babcock, Rebecca Day. "When Something Is Not Quite Right: Pragmatic Impairment and Compensation in the College Writing Tutorial" from *The Writing Lab Newsletter*, 35:5–6 (2011). Copyright © 2011. Reprinted by permission.

Page 275 from Baker, Brooke. "Safe Houses and Contact Zones: Reconsidering the Basic Writing Tutorial" from *Young Scholars in Writing*, vol. 4 (2006). Copyright © 2006. Reprinted by permission.

Page 284 from Brazeau, Alicia. "Groupies and Singletons: Student Preferences in Classroom-Based Writing Consulting" from *Young Scholars in Writing*, vol. 2 (2004). Copyright © 2004. Reprinted by permission.

Page 296 from Brecht, Mara. "Basic Literacy: Mediating Between Power Constructs" from *Young Scholars in Writing*, vol. 1 (2003). Copyright © 2003. Reprinted by permission.

Page 307 from Brown, Renee, Brian Fallon, Jessica Lott, Elizabeth Matthews, and Elizabeth Mintie. "Taking on Turnitin: Tutors Advocating Change" from *The Writing Center Journal*, 27.1 (2007). Copyright © 2007. Reprinted by permission.

Page 325 from Bruffee, Kenneth. "Peer Tutoring and the 'Conversation of Mankind'" from *Writing Centers: Theory and Administration*. Copyright © 1984 by the National Council of Teachers of English. Reprinted by permission.

Page 336 from DeCheck, Natalie. "The Power of Common Interest for Motivating Writers: A Case Study" from *The Writing Center Journal*, 32.1 (2012). Copyright © 2012. Reprinted by permission.

Page 343 from Doucette, Jonathan. "Composing Queers: The Subversive Potential of the Writing Center" from *Young Scholars in Writing*, vol. 8 (2010). Copyright © 2010. Reprinted by permission.

Page 356 from Fallon, Brian. "Why My Best Teachers Are Peer Tutors." Copyright © 2011. Reprinted by permission.

Page 365 from Grutsch McKinney, Jackie. "New Media Matters: Tutoring in the Late Age of Print" from *The Writing Center Journal*, 29.2 (2009). Copyright © 2009. Reprinted by permission.

Page 377 from Clarion University, "Criminal Justice Poster." Used by permission.

Page 382 from Hitt, Allison. "Access for All: The Role of Dis/ability in Multiliteracy Centers" from *Praxis: A Writing Center Journal*, 9.2 (2012). Copyright © 2012. Reprinted by permission.

Page 391 from Johnson, Ruth, Beth Clark, and Mario Burton. "Finding Harmony in Disharmony: Engineering and English Studies" from *Young Scholars in Writing*, vol. 5 (2007). Copyright © 2007. Reprinted by permission.

Page 404 from Lerner, Neal. "Searching for Robert Moore" from *The Writing Center Journal*, 22.1 (2001). Copyright © 2001. Reprinted by permission.

Page 422 from Mackiewicz, Jo, and Isabelle Thompson. "Motivational Scaffolding, Politeness, and Writing Center Tutoring" from *The Writing Center Journal*, 33.1 (2013). Copyright © 2013. Reprinted by permission.

Page 449 from Mozafari, Cameron. "Creating Third Space: ESL Tutoring as Cultural Mediation" from *Young Scholars in Writing*, vol. 6 (2008). Copyright © 2008. Reprinted by permission.

Page 464 from Nan, Frances. "Bridging the Gap: Essential Issues to Address in Recurring Writing Center Appointments with Chinese ELL Students" from *The Writing Center Journal*, 32.1 (2012). Copyright © 2012. Reprinted by permission.

Page 473 from Nicklay, Jennifer. "Got Guilt? Consultant Guilt in the Writing Center Community" from *The Writing Center Journal*, 32.1 (2012). Copyright © 2012. Reprinted by permission.

Page 483 from O'Leary, Claire Elizabeth. "It's Not What You Say, But How You Say It (and to Whom): Accommodating Gender in the Writing Conference" from *Young Scholars in Writing*, vol. 6 (2008). Copyright © 2008. Reprinted by permission.

Page 498 from Reger, Jeff. "Postcolonialism, Acculturation, and the Writing Center" from *Young Scholars in Writing*, vol. 6 (2008). Copyright © 2008. Reprinted by permission.

Page 508 from Suhr-Sytsma, Mandy, and Shan-Estelle Brown. "Addressing the Everyday Language of Oppression in the Writing Center" from *The Writing Center Journal*, 31.2 (2011). Copyright © 2011. Reprinted by permission.

Page 533 from Wilder, Molly. "A Quest for Student Engagement: A Linguistic Analysis of Writing Conference Discourse" from *Young Scholars in Writing*, vol. 2 (2004). Copyright © 2004. Reprinted by permission.

Name Index

Subject Index